Man, Location, and Behavior: An Introduction to Human Geography

Man, Location, and Behavior: An Introduction to Human Geography

KEVIN R. COX

Department of Geography
The Ohio State University

John Wiley & Sons, Inc.
New York · London · Sydney · Toronto

Library of Congress Cataloging in Publication Data:

Cox, Kevin R   1939–
  Man, location, and behavior.

  1. Anthropo-geography.   I. Title.

GF41.C6   301.2'09   72-4790
ISBN 0-471-18150-1

Printed in the United States of America.

10 9 8 7 6 5 4 3 2 1

Preface

〰〰〰

As a graduate student and teacher in geography during the past decade I have been impressed with the profound changes that have overtaken the discipline and the relevance of those changes for undergraduate teaching. And yet, as a teacher I found it increasingly difficult to locate textual materials that adequately reflected that revolution in terms readily understandable to the beginning undergraduate student in geography. This textbook is the offspring of my necessity and, hopefully, of the necessity of others.

The book simplifies the essential ingredients of an explicitly scientific human geography to the point at which they can be readily understood by the beginning student. It reflects, therefore, the conceptual rather than the technical advances of the past ten to fifteen years; the revolution in geography has, after all, been as much one of concept as it has been one of quantitative technique. Since these conceptual advances have included generality in description, the book stresses the general concept of spatial pattern or locational predictability. More recently, geographers have become aware of the need to examine pattern in terms of its dynamics. This is a view to which I subscribe, and it is apparent in my concern in this book with the spatial dynamics of migration fields, communication networks, land-use patterns, and the like.

In an explanatory mode, geographers have emphasized, more and more, the roles of movement and human decision. The large body of work dealing with spatial interaction has consequently been drawn upon; also I have used the more recent but rapidly expanding body of work in so-called behavioral geography. Concepts such as "information flow" and "mental map" have the capability of remedying much of the inadequacy apparent in many explanations provided by introductory human geography textbooks. The emphasis on the role of human behavior in producing spatial patterns is evident in the title of this book.

In addition to developing geography as an abstract field of study by the formulation of general laws of location, it is also important that geographers apply this expanding body of knowledge to an understanding of the human problems that are too readily apparent in the world around us. Problems of economic development and of the contemporary city have a locational dimension that is useful not only in characterization but also in explanation. This spatial interpretation of real-world human problems is made evident in separate chapters of this book dealing with the urban crisis, economic development, and the quality of the environment.

With respect to the use of this book, two prefatory comments seem warranted. First, the reader will find very few citations to the literature in the body of the textbook.

Given the stated aim of providing a textbook for beginning undergraduate students in geography, such citations to articles (which are often technical in character) seemed superfluous. However, it is certainly hoped that students will be motivated to pursue the broader points presented. Toward this end, a select bibliography has been provided at the end of the book. It is selective with respect to both the philosophy of this writer and the intellectual limitations of the beginning student.

Second, no student should read any book attempting to introduce the broad field of human geography without a good atlas at hand. While numerous illustrative maps are provided in this book, the inclusion of maps showing the locational relationships of every place referred to would have resulted in a multi-volume work. A number of good atlases are available; this author has found the paperback Rand McNally *Regional Atlas,* edited by Edward B. Espenshade, Jr., to be both reasonable in price and adequate to the student's purpose when reading this book. It is an abridged edition of Good's *World Atlas,* which more affluent students may wish to purchase.

Many individuals provided inspiration for this volume. More particularly, however, I thank Ned Taaffe not only for his active and generous encouragement but also for the provision of a high-quality intellectual environment in the form of the Geography Department at The Ohio State University. Within that environment, I especially thank Larry Brown and Reg Golledge for their continual encouragement and inspiration. In addition, Bill Clark of UCLA, Bob Colenutt and Tom Wilbanks of Syracuse, and Jack Jakle of the University of Illinois provided very useful comments on the manuscript at varying stages of its preparation. First-year cartography students at Ohio University working under the direction of Gerry Zeck, presently at Syracuse University, admirably performed the cartographic chores. Andy Bodman of Ohio State assisted me in the arduous task of indexing. I also appreciate the assistance of many typists who played a large part in the production of the manuscript, particularly Debbie Corotis and Cheryl Boehm. Finally, I thank my wife Marjorie for her continual encouragement.

Kevin R. Cox

Contents

Man, Location, and Behavior: An Introduction to Human Geography

CHAPTER ONE

The Content of Human Geography: An Overview

INTRODUCTION

What is human geography? What are some of the basic concepts which human geographers employ in looking at the world around them? How do these concerns relate to the structure of this book? These are the three major questions to which we address ourselves in this chapter. Toward these ends the first section of the chapter discusses the foci of human geography from the viewpoint of both the problems that interest human geographers and the more abstract definitions of their objectives. The second section of the chapter attempts, by describing two case studies, to identify some of the basic concepts of description, explanation, and application that are employed by the geographer. Finally, we shall look at the problem of how this definition of objectives and these concepts relate to the remainder of the book.

THE FOCI OF GEOGRAPHY

GEOGRAPHICAL PROBLEMS

The idea of *location* has always been central to the subject of geography. In the ancient world, for example, it was the task of the geographers to fix the boundaries of land divisions and to draw maps of emerging empires. In the late Middle Ages and beyond, exploration—that is, the discovery of locations and the recording of their characteristics—was regarded as a major function of the geographer. This type of geography, although concerned with location, was very descriptive: simply the recording of the locations of places in terms of longitude and latitude and some of the characteristics of the place in terms of, for example, population size. Some of the Victorian geography textbooks, in fact, were little more than detailed gazetteers listing the major towns of Britain, the rivers on which they were situated, their populations and major manufactures, and the railroads running through them.

Just as history was a list of dates, so geography was a list of places or locations. As society's problem of adapting to the physical and social environment became more complex, however, it was realized that each of the subjects of the standard educational curriculum could be addressed to a set of real world problems; and if it decided to respond to the challenge, a subject could develop analytically so that it would be capable of solving problems. Geography has recently decided to respond with vigor to this challenge.

In brief, geography is interested in the locations of different items at different places on the earth's surface and in *explaining* why things are located where they are. More specifically, the human geographer is interested in the locations of items which have been placed by human agency whether it is humanity itself or the acts of humanity such as railroads, towns, stores, offices, factories, fields, and fences. What type of concrete question, therefore, interests the modern analytical geographer? As a backdrop for the discussion of this chapter, let us list and exemplify four questions of critical concern to the geographer; often the questions refer to locational problems experienced so frequently that we fail to see the interesting questions which they prompt.

1. *Why are shops and offices located where they are in cities?* If we are on a long automobile trip and wish to purchase a clean shirt, we choose a city and are almost instinctively drawn into the center of the town in our search for the relevant store. We seem to have some sort of imaginary map of cities which tells us what stores tend to be found in the center of town. Yet we rarely stop to ask ourselves just why they should be located in the center of town, or why we would be more likely to find an item in the downtown department store than in the department store which we saw in the suburban shopping center on our way downtown.

2. *Why do the shopping trips which we undertake for various purposes vary so much in length and in such a systematic manner?* Why is it, for instance, that we usually have to travel further in order to buy a Cadillac than a Chevrolet? Similarly, for most of us, trips to smaller towns for shopping trip purposes tend to be shorter than trips to large towns. Why? Such trips are not only locational phenomena (that is, they have a location in space) they are also useful in explaining other locational phenomena—such as the location of Cadillac dealers!

3. *Why are certain places losing population while others are gaining it?* Some areas of the United States such as the Great Plains states of the Dakotas, Montana, and Nebraska, and Southern states such as Mississippi, Arkansas, and Alabama are either losing population as a result of net out-migration or stagnating in terms of population growth. Other states, on the other hand, such as California, Florida, Arizona, Washington, and Colorado show considerable net gain. Identifying the precise reasons for this state of affairs is important for those who would care to reverse it, whether they are harassed governors of Southern states or harassed mayors of Northern cities dealing with bulging welfare rolls!

4. *Why is there greater migration between some pairs of places than between other pairs of places?* The locational pattern of population decline and population growth is to a large extent a reflection of the locational pattern of migration. Migration streams have a location in terms of origin and destination locations and are grist for the geographer's mill. Why is it, for example, that Negro out-migrants from some Southern counties are destined largely for Chicago while those from neighboring counties are going largely to Detroit? Why is it that when people move within a metropolitan area they tend to move to a vacant house within, for instance, a two-mile radius of their previous residence? At such distances it is hardly a question of exorbitant moving expenses.

Such problems as are indicated by this brief sample are interesting and stimulate curiosity; for these reasons alone they are worth our attention. They are also typical of the questions which the human geographer is interested in asking of the world around him.

A WORKING DEFINITION OF GEOGRAPHY

Given these examples of the type of problem which interests the geographer, can we arrive at a working definition of the field? Three considerations seem to be important here. First, we know that geographers are interested in both *describing* and *explaining.* We also know that the idea of *location* is central to all the problems with which they are concerned. A final consideration is that the geographer has tended to focus upon the location of a rather wide diversity of things. People, highways, stores, airline routes, ethnic groups, political boundaries, towns, movements of migrants, movements of goods, etc., are but a few of the items with which the geographer is likely to be concerned from the locational viewpoint. Further, he is interested in both *moving items,* such as commodity flows and migration or tourist flows, and in more *static items,* such as towns or highway networks.

Therefore given these three basic considerations—description and analysis, the central idea of location, and the diversity of phenomena—the following will be employed as a working definition of geography in this textbook:

▶ *Geography is concerned with the description and explanation of locational patterns of static or moving phenomena on the surface of the earth. Human geography, therefore, is concerned with the description and analysis of locational patterns of static or moving phenomena of human origin on the surface of the earth.*

SOME BASIC CONCEPTS

Given such a broad and necessarily general definition and a range of problems regarded as geographic, what specifically do geographical studies consist of? Descriptively, what is meant by the idea of *locational pattern* or of *spatial structure?* Analytically, what factors are regarded by geographers as important in explaining the characteristics of locational patterns? Furthermore, what are the implications of these concepts for the application of human geography to solving human problems?

In this section we intend to provide some answers to these questions by working from the specific to the general. Initially we shall proceed by example, giving two small geographical studies in order to clarify the nature and scope of the geographer's task. The first example concerns the problem of locational change within the Western city; the second example examines metropolitan-oriented migration patterns within the United States. The chapter then takes a slightly more abstract look at pattern, explanation, and application in geography so that we can extend these ideas fluently and easily to other types of geographic problems.

CASE STUDY: LOCATIONAL CHANGE WITHIN THE WESTERN CITY

During the past half-decade or so, the Western city has experienced rather drastic changes in its geographic form; it is the intent of this section to examine these changes, to attempt to explain them, and to identify some of the implications of these ideas for public policy.

At the end of the 19th century the prevalent urban *shape,* as revealed by maps of built-up areas, was the star. The center of the city corresponded to the center of the star and each limb of the star represented a clustering of housing around a railroad line or streetcar line. Further out, beyond the tips of the limbs there might be small "beads" of housing around suburban stations on the railroad lines. In between the limbs of the star,

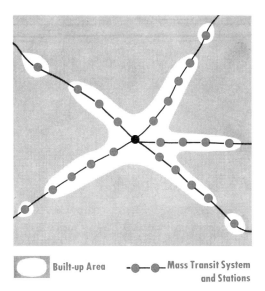

Built-up Area   Mass Transit System and Stations

FIGURE 1-1.   A schematic view of the star-shaped city.

however, land would still be largely devoted to agricultural purposes (see Figure 1-1).

The extreme *centralization* of transportation systems on the city center was matched by a centralization of employment opportunities. Employment in factories as well as in retailing, offices, and other services tended to be concentrated at that point most accessible to the railroad network and to the mass transit system where the latter differed from the railroad network. All amenities such as hotels and theaters exhibited a similar concentration. The close geographical correspondence between the pattern of transportation and that of employment opportunities suggests a symbiotic relationship between the two such that the population would try to locate itself as close to the city as possible; that is, on a railroad or a streetcar line, where the individual was not within walking distance of the city center, and indeed this does appear to have been so.

Over the past half-century, however, this schematic locational pattern has changed rather dramatically. The inter-

stices of the star have been filled in by residential development, for example, and the city has expanded around its edge to produce a much more compact shape. Concomitant with this change in shape has been decentralization of the route system. In particular, the highway network has expanded into the interstices and linked one limb with another. The general effect of this has been to reduce the relative accessibility advantages enjoyed by the central city.

Along with the decentralization of the metropolitan transportation network there has been a dispersion of employment opportunities away from the central city and into more peripheral, more suburban locations; this has been particularly true of the retailing and manufacturing sectors of the local economy and less true of office employment. Service industries such as cinemas, taverns, restaurants, and hotels have undergone a similar decentralization.

And finally, one finds that people no longer cluster around the central business district or around the mass transit system leading to it.

So far we have described the changing locational pattern of the Western city. We have described the *centralization* of the mass transit system, the *concentration* of employment opportunities and their subsequent *dispersion,* and the changing *shape* of the city. What factors, however, can we call upon for an adequate explanation of these locational changes? At least two factors appear to be important: (1) the increased accessibility of suburban locations relative to the central city and (2) the increased demands for space.

The *accessibility* factor is critical. In assembling raw materials for an industrial process, for example, the cost of the finished product can soar to a noncompetitive level if movement costs are too expensive as a result of relatively inaccessible raw materials. Likewise, for the department store, accessibility to the market is a major consideration in selling the goods. Indeed, many of our *locational decisions* are guided by a strong desire to minimize movement effort or cost in time or money. Consequently, we try to be as accessible to the items that we want as we possibly can be. Just as the store tries to get close to its market and the factory tries to minimize distance from its raw materials, so the individual tries to get close to his children's school and to his place of work.

In 1900 in the Western city the central business district was by far the most accessible place in the city. It was the point at which the costs of assembling everybody were at a minimum, and this was a result of the centralized mass transit system.

Since 1900 there have been drastic changes in the relative accessibility of places within the metropolitan area. In particular, as we described above, the *decentralization* of transportation networks has contributed to a vastly increased relative accessibility of the more suburban locations. In some cases the decentralization has been accompanied by a decentralization of routes followed by the mass transit system. More important, however, has been the combination of the private automobile and the development of highways in the interstices, which have opened them up for residential development.

Other considerations have also been important. Firstly, the automobile has had negative effects upon the accessibility of the central city as well as positive effects upon the accessibility of the suburbs; these negative effects have been particularly evident in the traffic congestion of downtown areas and the resultant high prices of automobile parking.

A second consideration is the effect of the internal combustion engine upon the accessibility of different sites within the metropolitan area for manufacturing industry. Before the widespread use of the truck, the factory was usually oriented to the downtown goods yard of the railroad companies for its supply of raw materials. The long-distance truck, however, has made the manufacturer, particularly the light manufacturer, independent of the railroad. For many manufacturers the suburb is absolutely the most accessible location for their particular purposes. The entrepreneur has also benefited from the use of the automobile among his work force. This has made him less dependent upon a position at the most accessible point of the 19th-century labor market — the *central business district*.

In summary, suburban locations have increased in *accessibility to the metropolitan area as a whole* relative to the accessibility of the downtown area to that same metropolitan zone. Suburban locations, therefore, have proven very attractive for such land uses as retailing, cinemas, restaurants, and auto distribution. The post-1945 efflorescence of suburban shopping centers in the United States is a striking example of this. In addition, however, suburban locations have increased their accessibility to extra-metropolitan areas relative to the accessibility of the downtown area to those same extra-metropolitan areas; the possibilities of long-distance truck transportation in the suburban context have proven attractive to manufacturing employment.

The second major factor in the explanation of the changing locational pattern of the Western city is that of *demand for space*. For a variety of reasons, industrialists, private house owners, and shopping facilities all require more space. A particularly important reason, of course, is that all land-use functions which assemble people in the age of the internal combustion engine need space for car parking; this is true of the factory as it is of the suburban cinema and the suburban shopping center with its vast acres of free parking.

The second reason applies particularly to factories. Factories in the 19th century developed vertically and were often four, five, or six stories high—and for good technical reasons. In particular, the internal transmission of power from a steam engine demanded a set of belts to transmit the power; these provided much less of an impediment to movements within a factory if they were organized vertically rather than horizontally. Electricity altered all of that, and we now have the much lower, horizontal, and aesthetically pleasing designs so common today—but designs which require much more space than the old vertical structures.

Finally there is the question of public taste in the matter of space consumption. This has been particularly significant in the spread of residential land uses within the city although the existence of this change in public taste is more conjectural than verified. It is conjectured because up until the end of the Second World War decentralization of residential housing and increased lot sizes had been on a very modest scale, despite the fact that most families had the automobile at that time. Only after 1945 was there a marked increase in the demand for larger residential lots.

How, you may ask, does this relate to the suburbanization of activities within the metropolitan area? Space demands are an important factor in location because land is much cheaper in some parts of the metropolitan area than it is in other parts. In particular, land is still considerably cheaper in suburban locations as opposed to locations in the central city. Space consumption on the scale now demanded by factory owners or by

cinemas with their attendant parking space would be prohibitively expensive in the downtown locations—hence the attraction and positive evaluation of the suburb where an acre of land is so much cheaper.

Such changes in locational pattern, however, are not without important implications for the human condition and therefore for public policy goals. A knowledge of the mechanisms producing change in locational pattern provides an important basis for such public policy. Thus the suburbanization of residences in the U.S.A. has not been enjoyed by all social and racial groups to the same degree. In particular, forces of racial discrimination and income distribution have hindered the suburbanization of Negro populations. At the same time suburbanization of employment opportunities has proceeded apace, thus making jobs more and more inaccessible to the Negro population and increasing ghetto social problems. Clearly policies aimed at alleviating ghetto poverty should focus partly upon the increasing geographical mismatch between jobs and residences for the Negro population.

To summarize: the Western city has undergone dramatic changes in geographical form over the last 60 years or so. The shape of the city has changed from a *stellar* form to a more *compact form* in which the interstices of the star have been filled in by residential land uses. The transportation system has undergone a marked decentralization as have the locations of such activities as manufacturing and retailing. Two factors have been adduced to account for this: accessibility changes, which have closed the accessibility difference between central city and suburbs, and changes in the space requirements of many land users, which have made the cheaper land of the peripheral location much more attractive. Such, moreover, contain the seeds of serious social problems; ghetto unemployment is a case in point.

We now turn to consider a second geographical pattern on a much larger scale—that of metropolitan-oriented migration in the United States.

CASE STUDY: METROPOLITAN-ORIENTED MIGRATION IN THE U.S.A.

The focus of the second geographical study is the map shown in Figure 1-2. The map presents *regions of migrant origin* or *in-migration fields* for the 24 largest cities of the United States. The map has been constructed by taking out-migration figures for each of the 509 State Economic Areas and asking: for this State Economic Area which metropolitan area did it send most migrants to? If a State Economic Area in New Mexico sent more of its migrants to Los Angeles, we would say that Los Angeles *"dominates"* that particular State Economic Area in New

Mexico. Given this necessary background, what can we say about the pattern of migration flows on the basis of this map? In fact, three generalizations seem feasible.

The first point that we can make on the basis of the map is that *cities tend to draw their migrants from closer places rather than from more distant places.* Kansas City dominates places in east Kansas, western Missouri, and northern Arkansas but nowhere else; Atlanta dominates Georgia and adjacent parts of eastern Alabama and North Carolina but nowhere else; Milwaukee's in-migration field is confined to Wisconsin and the Upper Peninsula of Michigan, while Portland's is coextensive with the local state of Oregon.

Parenthetically, however, note that there are some exceptions. The in-migration field of Los Angeles, for example, penetrates into the eastern Midwest jumping over the in-migration fields of

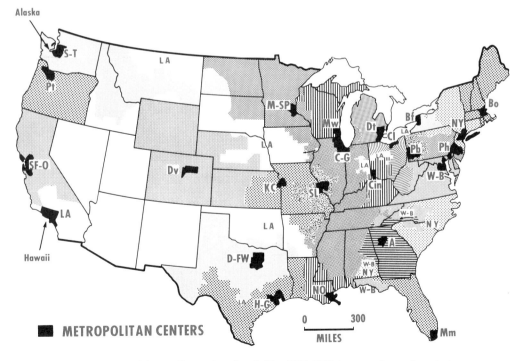

FIGURE 1-2. Metropolitan migration fields, 1955–1960 (see text for explanation).

cities like St. Louis and Chicago. Note particularly that Erie, Pennsylvania sends more of its migrants to Los Angeles than to any other city—including much closer cities like New York, Philadelphia, Pittsburgh, and Cleveland. The in-migration field of New York City also extends a rather long distance into the South jumping over the migration fields of such cities as Atlanta and Washington–Baltimore. We will return to this particular problem in Chapter Five.

A second facet of the locational problem which requires explanation is *that some cities have larger in-migration fields than others.* The in-migration fields of Los Angeles, Denver, and Seattle–Tacoma, for instance, are particularly large. The in-migration fields of cities like Buffalo or New Orleans or Cincinnati or even Boston, on the other hand, seem rather small—despite the fact that one would think the latter cities would be at least as attractive to migrants as Denver or Seattle–Tacoma.

Third and finally, there is the fact that *some cities are excentrically located relative to their in-migration fields.* Minneapolis–St. Paul, for example, is displaced eastwards from the center of its source region while Washington–Baltimore is displaced northwards and Dallas–Fort Worth is displaced eastwards. A comprehensive theory of the geography of migration must be capable of explaining these three locational phenomena: the nearness component, the area component, and the excentricity component.

What factors can be adduced, therefore, to explain this pattern? Migration is a highly complex process responding in its intensity, distance, and direction to a variety of phenomena which we will examine in greater detail later in the book. Here we confine ourselves to a consideration of two factors only: *the role of the information* that is available to the

potential migrant, and *the costs that he is attempting to minimize in his migration.*

What type of information is vital to the migrant? First and foremost, information regarding job opportunities. While a given city may be highly desirable from the point of view of living expenses, cultural amenities, and recreation, these serve little purpose if the migrant cannot obtain a job. Particularly important, therefore, are the media through which information about jobs is circulated; in the United States this takes the form of the regional press. The regional press has a highly localized circulation: the *Cleveland Plain Dealer* circulates largely in northern Ohio; the *Kansas City Star* in western Missouri and eastern Kansas, and so on. Hence the person living in Akron, Ohio is much more likely to hear about a job-opening in Cleveland than in Philadelphia simply because he reads the *Plain Dealer* rather than the *Philadelphia Bulletin.*

Such localized information flows about jobs in different cities tend to be intensified by informal links with relatives and friends who have migrated to the city sometime before. The closer the city is to the potential migrant the more likely he is to keep in touch with old friends and relatives and receive information regarding job openings and, ultimately, housing possibilities.

If job opportunities are equivalent in two cities, however, which will the potential migrant choose as his destination? In brief, *people tend to move to the nearest opportunity* and they do this in order to minimize effort. This is not so much the effort in moving a longer distance compared with a shorter distance; rather it is the post-migration effort of keeping in contact with kinfolk and friends in the place from which the migrant hails. He will need to consider the possibility of weekend trips back home or possibly an annual vacation.

Thus this least-effort criterion is of some assistance in explaining the fact that places tend to attract migrants from nearby locations rather than from places further away. In this sense it merely adds reinforcement to the information-flow argument presented above. Beyond this, however, the criterion adds additional clarification to migrant patterns. One interesting facet of the migration fields, for example, was the frequent excentricity of the metropolitan center relative to its in-migration field. In this context consider cities arranged on a line as in Figure 1-3a. According to the least-effort criterion migrants should move to the nearest city. In-migration zones are mapped in Figure 1-3b providing excentricities in the case of cities located close together. Thus A and B might be equivalent to the adjacent cities of Chicago and Milwaukee *or* Boston and New York. On the other hand, C is represented by the in-migration fields of cities that stand in fairly lofty isolation from other cities: Denver and Kansas City are cases in point.

This argument also allows us to clarify the phenomenon of the variability of the areas of the different in-migration fields. If migrants tend to move to the nearest metropolitan center, then where cities are closer together their in-migration fields will be smaller; where cities are further apart, however, in-migration areas will be correspondingly larger. This idea may be illustrated again with

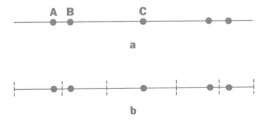

FIGURE 1-3 (*a*) Cities located on a line. (*b*) Cities and corresponding migration fields located on a line.

FIGURE 1-4. Cities on a line and corresponding in-migration fields located on a line. Note the relationship between town density and field area.

points on a line standing for cities (Figure 1-4). The boundaries of in-migration fields have been drawn in to show the way in which the extent of the field will vary according to the closeness of adjacent cities. Clearly, on this diagram the points on the left of the line are analogues of cities in the western part of the United States where cities are separated by long distances; the points on the right-hand side of the line are more like the cities in the northeastern United States in terms of their density.

A knowledge of the geography of migration fields is also important from a public policy viewpoint. A major problem in northern cities such as Chicago and New York is the very heavy welfare payment burden which they are carrying. Much of this is due to the in-migration of undereducated and barely employable Blacks and poor Whites from the rural South. Our analysis has suggested the role of information flows in sustaining migratory movements; the implications of this for controlling such movements should be apparent.

In conclusion, therefore, we have examined the in-migration fields of metropolitan places in the United States and found them to be: (1) located in the vicinity of the destination city rather than further away; (2) to be sometimes located excentrically relative to the destination city; and (3) to be sometimes geographically large and at other times small. Explanation was provided in terms of two factors: an information-flow factor, by which the potential migrant finds out more about jobs in closer cities than in cities further away, and a least-effort factor, according to which the migrant tends to move to that opportunity closest to him in space. Because migration can be a source of serious social problems, knowledge of the factors accounting for the geography of migration are of clear significance in formulating mitigating policies.

LOCATIONAL PATTERN

In the descriptive sections of the two case studies reported above, we used a number of locational or spatial concepts to describe the geographical distributions with which we were dealing. These included such ideas as *density, excentricity, dispersion, concentration, focus, shape, compactness, expansion, accessibility, closeness,* and *distance.* The meaning of these terms is probably intuitively obvious to all readers of this book. However, the fact that they are all descriptive of locational patterns is probably not so obvious. Yet definition of each of these words requires that we use the concept of location: the meaning of these descriptions of locational patterns cannot be executed in an unambiguous manner without reference to the concept of location.

Concepts of locational pattern have not only a locational component, however. The word "pattern" is also rich in its implications signifying a certain *predictability* in the occurrence of phenomena; in the current context, the predictability is one of locational occurrence. Thus concepts of locational pattern such as *density* or *concentration* or *centralization* are predictive of the occurrence of events at different locations. The concept of *concentration,* for example, signifies that locations close to one another are likely to be highly similar with respect to the event occurring over space, while locations distant from one another are likely to be highly dissimilar. In like manner, the concept of *centralization* indicates that the communication links of a location are

likely to be focused on a small number of all possible locations rather than on a large number of all possible locations with equal likelihood. When a concept of locational pattern is discussed, therefore, *locational or spatial predictability* is at the heart of the concept. But how to explain such predictability?

EXPLANATION IN GEOGRAPHY

Explanation in geography can be viewed on at least two levels of abstraction: (1) At the first level, locational patterns are seen as a product of *human decisions*—decisions to migrate, decisions to locate a store here rather than elsewhere, etc. (2) At a second level, locational patterns are seen as a product of *locational processes* involving movements of messages, people, commodities, etc., between locations on the earth's surface. In another sense, of course, the processes that we use to explain the locational pattern may, in turn, be viewed as a pattern to be explained either by another set of processes and/or by human decision making. Migration, for instance, has a locational pattern which can be explained in terms of locational processes, such as the movement of information, or more explicitly in terms of the choice mechanism of the migrant.

A second examination of the broad explanatory problem, however, suggests that the two approaches are in fact complementary. On the one hand, while movements may produce patterns, they are, in turn, a result of decisions (decisions to migrate, etc.). On the other hand, patterns of movement provide part of the locational context affecting other decisions; thus movements of shoppers to shopping centers provide part of the locational context in which the locational decisions of retailers are made; movements of commodities provide part of the locational context in which marketing decisions are made. These ideas are summarized in the following diagram.

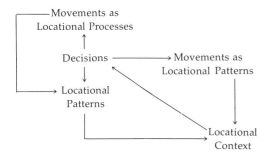

Clearly, at a broader level, the *locational context, that is, the environment of places, their locational relationships, and their characteristics,* is of critical significance. It affects the movement decisions which ultimately produce a variety of locational patterns. The migrant's decision, as we saw in the case study above, is affected by his *accessibility* to various urban centers and by *linkages* to sources of information about various urban centers. Our shopping trip movement decisions are also made in a locational context of shopping opportunities of varying attractiveness and accessibility, and that locational context importantly affects our shopping trip decisions; ''how far away is it compared with other stores?'' is a critical question that we ask when deciding whether or not to patronize a store.

On the other hand, the decisions which produce locational patterns may produce them directly without intervening movement over space. In this case, also, the locational context assumes significance. In the case study of urban change, for instance, the changing pattern of accessibility — and therefore of movement costs — was seen as having very important implications for the locational decisions of retailers, industrialists, and residential developers.

The decisions which produce loca-

tional patterns, however, cannot be explained purely in terms of a locational context in which the decision maker finds himself and about which he has a varying degree of knowledge. The decision maker also brings *a set of preferences* to the locational stage and these have important effects on resultant decisions. Thus we suggested in the first case study that residential suburbanization was partly the result of changing preferences; in that case, preferences were for larger lot sizes. Similarly, increasing metropolitan-oriented migration may be a result of changing preferences in favor of the bright city lights as opposed to the bucolic charm of the small country town. If this change in preference has proceeded further in one part of the nation than in another, then presumably this will be reflected in the rate of migration towards metropolitan centers. Such preferences also change over time, of course; thus we shall see that the migration geography of older retired people is quite different from that of younger people, the latter preferring job and income opportunities to physical amenities, while the former — quite logically — prefer physical amenities.

When we talk about the *locational context* in which decisions are made an important distinction found in the geographic literature is that made between *site factors* and *situation factors.*

Situation factors refer to the location of a place relative to some other place: its accessibility or its distance or direction from some other place or places. Every place has a situation and such situational factors are important criteria in geographical choice situations. They are important, moreover, because in deciding where to locate, men try to choose a location that is *optimally* situated for satisfying their needs. When looking for a house, we evaluate the situations of houses in terms of such criteria as: How far will it be to drive to work? How far will the children have to walk to school? Will they have to cross a busy highway on the way? How far is it from the shops, etc.? In the 19th century, apparently, the major criterion was how accessible a house was to the mass transit system, resulting in the stellar city form which we have already discussed. *Situational factors, therefore, are frequently a substitute for the behaviorally more relevant movement costs.* We consider situation but only to the extent that it will affect the cost of obtaining those goods and services which we require.

Site characteristics refer to those variable attributes of places that are not situational in character. In explaining migration, for example, we have to consider such site factors as the job opportunities available in a place or the scenic amenities. These are clearly characteristics of places which do vary a great deal in their geographical incidence bestowing some areas with a bounteous endowment and other areas with the paltriest of dowries. Many of these site characteristics are often described by a summary factor such as attractiveness. Thus states which are scenic or have a wide diversity of job opportunities are "attractive"; states which have a depressing or monotonous aesthetic legacy and/or a cramped employment structure tend to be "unattractive." Such attractiveness is something which frequently has to be traded off against situational disadvantages of the same location: we are willing to travel further to a more attractive town for shopping purposes than we are to a less attractive town.

It should be stressed, however, that we cannot expect the objective site and situation characteristics of places to be perfect predictors of man's locational decisions. We must recognize, for example, that the decision maker's knowledge of

the range of locational choice open to him is usually only partial; thus when relocating within a city we are rarely aware of all the housing vacancy options open to us. Similarly, our knowledge of the environment of locations around us is hardly objective in a scientific sense; our knowledge of places is often inaccurate and colored with value judgements. Places have reputations which may be more or less accurate but which nevertheless influence our migration decisions. Clearly our decisions are made not with reference to the locational context as it actually is and as it is scientifically verifiable, but as we see it through our not all-encompassing and often rose-colored spectacles. These arguments will be introduced in greater detail later in the book. Initially we make some simplified assumptions regarding, for example, the knowledge which decision makers have of movement costs and of movement opportunities and later show how our predictions can be strengthened by taking into account the variable amounts of information which decision makers have.

Such considerations as these are important to us because they provide the basis of the *geographical theory* that we call upon to *explain locational pattern* in an accurate and economical manner. This has ramifications for the *predictive capability of geography* and its ability to interfere fruitfully in the geographical allocation of human and physical resources. Only on the basis of valid theory can truly reliable predictions be made. This, therefore, brings us to a consideration of the role of modern geography in public policy formulation.

THE APPLICATION OF GEOGRAPHIC KNOWLEDGE

Locational knowledge (whether it is of a descriptive character or of a more analytical nature), by which one gains insights into the origins of locational patterns, has important implications for the policy makers of society. Industrial executives have to locate factories and plan flows of commodities. Government departments have to locate offices, hospitals, highways, and all manner of items which usually go under the heading of "national infrastructure." These latter considerations are especially important when one pauses and considers the increasing role which government plays in society as a whole. It seems no accident, moreover, that as that role has increased in significance, there has been a rapid blossoming of interest in *urban* and *regional planning*—precisely that type of planning to which the geographers can make an important contribution. That contribution is of both a descriptive and an analytical character.

Descriptively, a knowledge of *locational trends* providing predictions of the future locations of people, factories, and retail facilities provides the basis for a rational and efficient allocation of government monies to such purposes as the construction of highways, public housing, and hospitals. If the taxpayer is to receive a maximum payoff from his taxes it is important that government expenditures be allocated to places where there is a demand for it, that is, that hospital beds be added where population is likely to grow most rapidly and that upgraded highway facilities be provided between adjacent urban places for which high rates of population growth are forecast.

Beyond such locational knowledge of a *descriptive* character, however, there is also *analytical* knowledge which can be of great assistance in allowing policy makers to achieve social goals. Thus knowledge of the *reasons for certain locational trends* can be of considerable importance in altering locational trends so as to maximize some item—such as social welfare—which policy makers are

interested in maximizing. A locational trend that has given considerable alarm to government policy makers in Britain, for example, is the increasing concentration of new industries in the southeastern part of the country to the detriment of areas elsewhere. It is a perturbing trend because it brings in its wake certain social problems: increased susceptibility to unemployment in areas outside southeastern England, for example, and increasing congestion in that area. The precise sort of medicine to be administered in this case depends very much on the reasons for such *locational concentration*. It is possible, for example, that southeastern England represents a *minimum movement cost location* for factory industry, that is, the cost of assembling the raw materials and distributing the finished product to market could be lower in southeastern England than anywhere else. If this were the case, appropriate medicine might take the form of transportation subsidies to firms locating *outside* of the southeastern zone.

On the other hand, it is perfectly conceivable that movement costs are so negligible within an area as small as that of Britain that the reasons for the trend must be found elsewhere. Certainly southeastern England has advantages other than those accruing from low movement costs. It is, for example, a relatively pleasant area in which to live. It is close to the shopping and cultural amenities of London, it is close to the largest airport in Europe just west of London, and it is not aesthetically unattractive. The latter consideration seems a particularly telling one when one compares the southeastern area with the slagheap scarred, grimy, despoiled urban landscape that is the heritage of the Industrial Revolution in such areas as Lancashire, South Wales, and northeastern England. These, of course, are the areas which suffer from concentration in southeastern

England. It could be, therefore, that there is an *amenity factor* accounting for this locational trend: entrepreneurs locate in southeastern England because they themselves like it there; and they do not like what they have seen or heard about central Scotland or northeastern England or any of the other wastelands crying out for new industry. If the amenity factor is critical, then the appropriate medicine will not be a transportation subsidy; rather it may more effectively take the form of subsidy to management salaries in order to offset the deprivation, in terms of amenity, to which they will be exposed. Such a policy would be analogous to one that the Soviet Union employs in order to attract management personnel and even less-skilled elements of the labor force to the environmentally unattractive areas of Siberia and the Soviet Far East.

Given that locational knowledge is important for rational decision making by the policy makers of society, however, we must remember that those policy makers are responsible to others on whose behalf they are making their locational decisions. The private company, for example, is accountable to its shareholders; the government is ultimately responsible to the people as a whole. Indeed as members of society and its numerous institutions, we, as citizens or shareholders, need to evaluate the *locational policies* of those to whom we have consigned the task of locational policy making. Evaluation needs to be carried out not only in terms of the benefits and costs to us of particular *locational decisions* but also in terms of the well-being of society as a whole.

For example, we need to evaluate the benefits and costs that accrue to society as a whole from an industrial location policy which subsidizes industry in certain areas of high unemployment and impedes location in areas where there is pressure on available labor resources. In brief, should jobs move to labor or should labor move to jobs? Which solution is likely to be most beneficial for national economic growth? In underdeveloped countries it would appear that such devolution is likely to be highly inefficient and result in a loss of that national income from which, ultimately, all citizens benefit. In more developed societies, on the other hand, it seems likely that such decentralization measures are less inefficient, though the issue needs to be looked into much more carefully than hitherto. If geographers are to have an effect upon the locational decisions of the society to which they belong, it is clear that they must have an accurate indication of the welfare — and illfare — implications of various alternative policies.

THE STRUCTURE OF THIS BOOK

The structure of the remainder of this book can be understood in terms of the context provided by this chapter. Obviously there are no clear distinctions among pattern, process, and decision making. One can view a process, such as migration, as a pattern to be explained, just as one can take a map of decisions as a pattern to be explained. It is also apparent that everything is related to everything else, and it is therefore very difficult to discuss patterns without discussing the processes underlying these patterns. It is also difficult to discuss decisions and resultant processes without knowing something of the locational patterns which constrain such decision making; and, similarly, understanding how such knowledge can be applied to solving society's problems requires that we have some idea of the locational patterns and locational decisions that create such problems and that have to be altered if the hardships resulting from such problems are to be mitigated.

It is for these reasons that this book is not structured into clear compartments of pattern, explanation, and application. This is not to say that there is no internal logic; in general we do proceed from considerations of explanation in the earlier chapters, through chapters more explicitly devoted to pattern, to the final three chapters dealing with applications. Nevertheless, the pattern chapters have large ingredients of explanation, the chapters dealing with explanation obviously have to be represented in terms of something to explain, and the applications chapters are also heavily involved in explanation and pattern.

The book is divided into six sections. The first section deals with the important topic of movement—important because we examine movements both as patterns to be explained and as explanations of other patterns. While Chapter Two is relatively descriptive and provides some pattern grist for our explanatory mill, Chapters Three and Four are emphatically analytic relating these patterns and others to a simple theory of movement decisions in a locational context. Such an explanation of decisions is later found to have broader applicability in terms of the component concepts of movement cost, attractiveness, etc. It is, for instance, a theory which can be used to a certain extent in explaining industrial location patterns.

The model of locational decision making employed in the first section of the book, however, is a relatively simple one, and a conclusion of the section is that assumptions as to the availability of complete and accurate information by all decision makers are not warranted. This sets the stage for the second section where a more sophisticated model of decision making is employed in reexamining migration and in taking a look at the decisions underlying the progressive spread of items across space. In this section we make considerable use of two ideas: (1) information availability, and (2) the accuracy and subjective interpretation of the information upon which decisions are based and the consequent idea of perceptions of locations.

The third, fourth, and fifth sections of the book are much more pattern oriented: the third section deals with the patterns created by lines—communication channels and boundaries, for instance; the fourth section deals with patterns which can be represented abstractly as points, while the fifth section is more concerned with patterns in the use of areas—agricultural land use and land use within cities, for example. In all three sections, however, pattern is explained in terms of the decisions of locators, and the pattern itself is also interpreted as an important component of the locational context within which locational decisions are made.

The sixth and final section considers the application of the type of knowledge presented in the earlier sections of the book to three of the most pressing problems faced by society at different geographic scales. At the scale of North America we consider the crisis of the city, its geographical bases and the types of mitigating policy—locational or otherwise—that have been proposed. At the scale of industrial society as a whole we consider the pressing problem of environmental quality; while at the global scale the issues posed by underdevelopment receive our geographic attention.

CONCLUDING COMMENTS AND SUMMARY

In this opening chapter three objectives have been followed: (1) to explain what human geography is about; (2) to identify and give some initial interpretation to some of the basic concepts that geographers use in looking at the world around them; and (3) to relate these concerns to the structure of the book.

The idea of *location* is central to the geographer's task. Geography is concerned with *describing the locations of different items at different places on the earth's surface and explaining why things are located where they are.* Human geographers confine their attention to the locational expression of humanity and of the works of humanity. In addition to *description* and *explanation* geographers have also found themselves increasingly involved in *application,* that is, applying their ideas to the solution of society's problems.

In order to provide an initial interpretation of basic concepts of description, explanation, and application, we proceeded via two geographic case studies: locational change within the Western city and metropolitan in-migration fields in the United States. These led to the application of concepts of *locational pattern* such as *centralization* and *excentricity* and also allowed us to demonstrate the type of explanatory strategy employed by the human geographer.

Concepts of *locational pattern* have two components: a *locational component,* such that a concept of locational pattern cannot be defined without reference to relative location, and a *pattern component* signifying a *predictability* in the occurrence of items across a set of locations.

In seeking *explanations* for locational patterns, the human geographer must ultimately go to the *decisions* that men make about their movements, about their residential sites, etc. At a lower level of abstraction many patterns can be interpreted in terms of *locational processes* of interlocational transaction: processes of message flow, migration, trade, etc. Such processes, however, can also be viewed as patterns and as such form an important ingredient of the *locational context* with reference to which *locational decisions* are made. The locational context is the environment of places, their characteristics and their locational relations, which affect man's locational decisions.

Important concepts employed by human geographers to describe the locational context include *site* and *situation. Situation* refers to the relative location of a place; particularly critical here are the costs of moving from one place to another. *Site* refers to nonlocational attributes of places such as their *attractiveness.*

Decisions, however, are based on *information* about the *locational context* and such information is variable with respect to amount, accuracy, and evaluative connotation. More profoundly, decisions are the result of human *preferences* for various goods, services, and benefits, and the locations at which they can be secured in a more or less efficient manner.

In addition to description and explanation in human geography we have also considered the *application* of such knowledge to the solution of social problems. In such application, however, locational decision makers are responsible to others and there is, therefore, a clear need for an accurate accounting of the *welfare and illfare implications* of alternative policies.

Finally, we have briefly outlined the content of the remainder of the book demonstrating how it relates to the ideas of pattern, explanation, and application reviewed in this chapter. The next three chapters, therefore, deal with the important topic of movement: Chapter Two describes some recurrent patterns of movement; Chapters Three and Four elaborate upon a schema for explaining such patterns, and the identification and application of such theory is the major aim of this section of the book.

CHAPTER TWO

Patterns of Movement

INTRODUCTION

In considering migration in the United States and locational change within the city in Chapter One we emphasized the role that movement costs play in man's locational decisions: for example, accessibility to city centers, accessibility to cities as places to which to migrate, etc. It seems, therefore, that movement costs may be a very fundamental factor in understanding locational patterns. We also observed that movements themselves create a pattern linking one location with another and creating regularities deserving explanation. Indeed, there is an interesting complementarity between movement as pattern and movement as explanation, for while locations are often selected on the basis of their lower movement costs, the choice of location in itself feeds back to affect the pattern of movement. Thus a store owner may select a particular site on the basis of its accessibility to shoppers; the store itself, however, will likely exert an effect on the aggregate pattern of movement as a result of, for example, the generation of traffic intrinsic to itself. A consideration of patterns of movement over the earth's surface and of the factors affecting such patterns of movement, therefore, should be of fundamental importance not only for its own sake but also for understanding a diversity of locational patterns—cities, land uses, factories, political affiliations, and the like.

Movements over the earth's surface take a large diversity of forms. We can consider, for example, movements of people, which include not only migration but also commuting or the journey to work, movements of children to school, and movements of housewives to retail outlets.

Not only are there human tangibles but there are also material tangibles, such as the commodity flows that move by rail, road, air, and water to provide us with that succor without which we would be useless. There are also less tangible movements which we will need to refer to, such as the flow of information that takes place by letters or telephone calls or face-to-face conversations.

Indeed the diversity of movements of various kinds over the earth's surface is such as to induce a little scepticism. We wonder whether such different types of movement as telephone calls, migration, and transport of wheat have similar locational patterns that will enable us to discuss the factors affecting movement with economy and simplicity. Is it possible to explain the locational pattern of telephone calls by using the same set of factors (that is, theory) we use to explain movements of wheat? In brief, it is possible. In this chapter we shall examine the high degree of geographical regularity that exists in the locational patterns of a wide diversity of movements; in the next chapter we will explore the reasons for this high level of regularity.

LOCATIONAL REGULARITY IN MOVEMENT PATTERNS

Movements are often mapped as lines connecting places between which the movements are taking place; the thickness of the lines is proportional to the intensity of the flow. Thus if there is a large number of telephone calls moving between two places in a 24-hour period the line representing these calls will be much thicker than if there is only a small number moving between the two locations. Figure 2-1 presents such a flow map; the map is hypothetical, however, and is devised to illustrate certain ideas that can be extracted from actual flow maps. The thickness of any line is proportional to the *number of telephone calls* passing between the two places joined by the line; these telephone calls can be moving in either direction along the line.

If we examine the map carefully, a certain geometrical regularity will become clear: there are, in fact, certain *relationships or associations* between location and intensity of flow. First, there is a relationship between the *distance between two locations* and the *intensity of movement*. The thicker lines are in general the shorter lines, while the longer lines tend to be rather thin, indicating low levels of telephone communication. Where such a relationship exists in a movement pattern we say that the movement pattern is *distance biased.*

▶ *Distance-biased movements are movements in which the intensity of movement is an inverse function of distance; short-distance movements tend to be relatively more intense than long-distance movements.*

Such distance-biased movements are extremely frequent in the real world. Some actual examples are presented below.

The second facet of the map is that the movements also seem to be biased as to direction. All movements seem to be towards or away from the two locations identified as X and Y; X and Y are points of *convergence* or *divergence* in telephone-call flows. There is a correlation

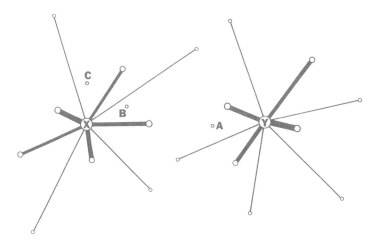

FIGURE 2-1. A hypothetical flow map of telephone call intensity.

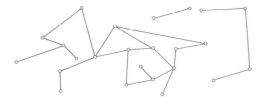

FIGURE 2-2. A hypothetical flow map without directional bias.

between direction and movement such that movements are restricted to a small number of all possible orientations. This type of *direction bias* contrasts with the unbiased situation where there is no relationship between direction and movement, that is, where movements tend to be in a wide diversity or an almost random set of directions. This situation is illustrated in Figure 2-2.

In other movement patterns, the *direction* or *orientation* bias takes the form not simply of a correlation between direction and whether or not there is a movement at all, but between direction and the intensity of movement. In Figure 2-3, for example, movements take place in all directions but there is a clear tendency for the more intense movements to be along an east–west axis. This type of pattern corresponds to that in the United States and Canada, where commodity flows are dominated by the eastward movement of foodstuffs and raw materials and the westward shipment of manufactured goods. In France, on the other hand, flow is dominated by movements in the direction of Paris: movements of

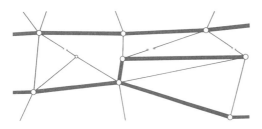

FIGURE 2-3. A hypothetical flow map with directional bias.

migrants, foodstuffs, mail, telephone calls, and capital are all more intense in the direction of Paris than in the direction of any other city in France.

▶   *Direction-biased movements are movements in which movement or the intensity of movement is related to direction. All movements or the more intense movements are restricted to a few of all possible directions. In nondirection-biased movement patterns, flows tend to take place in all possible directions.*

Finally, a third consideration arising from study of Figure 2-1 is that flows do not take place between all pairs of places. Thus even though place A is close to Y there is no telephone communication; similarly, B and C are not far distant from X but they have no telephone communication with X. A conceivable common-sense reason for this would be that place A is not linked by telephone lines to place Y, and places B and C are not linked by telephone lines to place X. In other words, in addition to *distance bias* and *direction bias* we must also recognize that movements tend to flow along channels. If such *channels* or *connections* do not exist, then there will be no movement. If the channel is constricted, movement will be reduced to an intensity inferior to what it might be if the channel were not constricted.

An obvious example of the effect of connection upon movement is the way in which a new bridge transforms locational relationships by providing connection between places that were not connected before. If the bridge is destroyed, then movement patterns will revert to what they were before. An interesting instance of this effect was provided in the interwar period when a bridge across the Mississippi between Iowa and Wisconsin was destroyed in a flood (see Figure 2-4). The bridge had af-

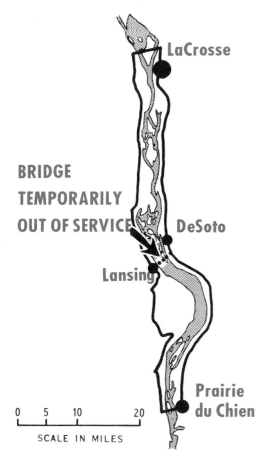

FIGURE 2-4. The effect of a bridge on space relationships: note how the accessibility of Lansing and DeSoto was drastically altered when the bridge was swept away.

forded an easy means of access between communities on either side of the Mississippi, and a number of marriages of people from the two towns occurred. Destruction of the bridge led to a drastic deterioration of communication between the two towns since the nearest alternative bridge was 27 miles to the south. The impact of this reduced communication on love and marriage between people from the two towns can be imagined!

▶ *Connection-biased movements are movements in which the presence or absence of movement or the intensity of move-*

ment is related to the presence or absence of a connecting channel or to the capacity of that connecting channel.

We shall now examine each of the locational biases in greater detail.

DISTANCE–BIASED MOVEMENTS

For a variety of reasons shorter-distance movements tend to be more intense than longer-distance flows. Longer movements tend to be more costly, for example; this is important given the tendency for people to minimize the effort involved in achieving any goal. If we go shopping for groceries we try not to take too long about it. Consequently, shopping trips tend to be short rather than long.

Such a distance bias in movement is exceedingly common. Figure 2-5 demon-

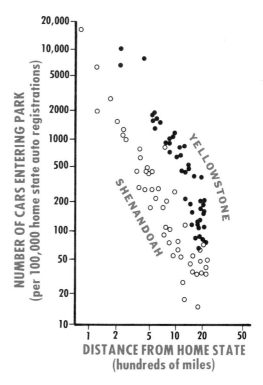

FIGURE 2-5. Automobile visitation rates at Yellowstone and Shenandoah National Parks, 1968; note the *negative exponential* relationships.

strates the phenomenon for the case of the patronization of national parks. These figures provide very eloquent testimony to the regular falloff of such movements with increasing distance; such distance decay is also evident in other interactions such as migration. Thus Figure 2-6 depicts the relationship between the intensity of migration to Ohio and distance from Ohio.

An interesting feature of *distance-bias* or *distance decay* phenomena, however, is that the intensity of movement does not fall off in a regularly decreasing manner with increasing distance. Rather, it tends to decrease at a decreasing rate (see Figure 2-7). Such a relationship is called a *negative exponential relationship*. This relationship implies that movements do not suddenly cease beyond a certain distance. Rather, there will always be a very gradual attenuation of movement with distance. Thus most telephone calls from Columbus, Ohio are

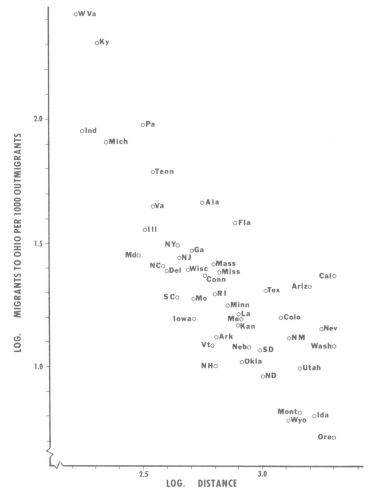

FIGURE 2-6.   Intensity of migration to Ohio and distance from Ohio: states close to Ohio send much greater proportions of their out-migrants to Ohio than do more distant states. Note the negative exponential character of the relationship as indicated by the linear relationship resulting from the plotting of logarithms.

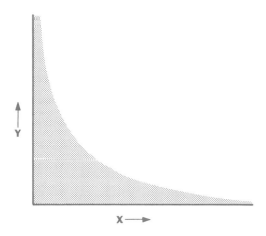

FIGURE 2-7. A negative exponential relationship; as one variable *increases* in value so the value of the other variable *decreases* at a *decreasing rate.*

greater than the reduction in magnitude of a small arithmetic number. Thus the logarithm of 10 is 1.0 while the logarithm of 20 is 1.30. The consequent greater reduction of extreme values of, for example, movements or miles on a negative exponential graph, such as that shown in Figure 2-7, tends to linearize the relationship.

▶ *If we plot a negative exponential relationship on a scatter diagram with axes marked off as logarithms the relationship will appear as a straight line.*

DIRECTION–BIASED MOVEMENTS

While movements diminish as distance increases, they also have an orientation or a direction from the point of origin. However, why are some directions more favored than others? In brief, direction bias occurs because of the greater attractiveness of certain places and their ability to satisfy the needs of the individual instigating the movement. We may go to a large town rather than a small town to see a movie simply because the larger town has a larger selection of movies.

In classifying the variety of patterns created by the directional orientation of movements we have employed two criteria. The first is the geometrical character of the location towards or away from which movement is proceeding—this can be a point or a line. The second is the attractiveness or unattractiveness of the location. These two criteria define four types of direction-biased movement as shown in Table 2-1. Each of these types of movement can be illustrated quite easily.

Converging movements are directed towards some attractive point. Examples include the gold rush to California, the movement of Bedouin Arabs towards oases, and the movement of sports spec-

concentrated within a ten-mile radius of the city center but there are people who make occasional long-distance phone calls to Australia or New Zealand.

▶ *In a negative exponential relationship an item* y *decreases in magnitude at a decreasing rate with increases in magnitude of a second item* x. *In the current context* y *would refer to the intensity of flow while* x *would refer to the distance over which that flow is taking place.*

The question may be raised at this point that if the relationships we have been discussing so far are negative exponential relationships, why do they form such neat linear arrays on scatter diagrams? Why, for example, does tourist patronage appear to fall off at a constant rate with increasing distance in Figure 2-5? If one looks carefully at that particular scatter diagram, the answer will be clear: the axes of the scatter diagram are marked off in logarithms and *not* arithmetically. Logarithms are always smaller than the arithmetic numbers which they represent. The reduction in magnitude for a large arithmetic number, however, is proportionally

TABLE 2-1. Types of Direction-Biased Movement.

Spatial Situation:	Location is: Attractive	Location is: Unattractive
Point	Converging Movements	Diverging Movements
Line	Advancing Frontier Movements	Retreating Frontier Movements

tators to a sports stadium. *Diverging movements*, on the other hand, are directed away from less attractive points to relatively more attractive surrounding points. The evacuation of Londoners during World War II is a graphic example of such movement, as is the movement of farmers from the Dust Bowl in the 1930s.

Advancing frontier movements are directed towards a line that is, for some reason, attractive. The movement of day trippers to the coast on a warm Sunday in summer is an advancing frontier movement. Another example, on a vastly grander historical canvas, is the tide of humanity that swept from east to west across 19th-century America. And finally, *retreating frontier movements* are directed away from a line regarded as unattractive. Striking examples are the movement inland of coastal dwellers alerted to the imminence of a hurricane and the movement of refugees behind a retreating military front.

Naturally, diverging movements are the obverse of converging movements. Convergence on some point such as a market is frequently followed by divergence when the market closes down and therefore looses its attractiveness. Similarly, advancing frontier movements are related to retreating movements. Frequently the advance of a frontier is followed by temporary retreat because of, for example, an unusually arid period

on the colonizing agricultural frontier, followed subsequently by further advance with a change in climate or in the technology available for combating climatic hazards. To a very large extent this pattern has been the story of the settling of the Great Plains in the United States.

Converging and diverging movements will be discussed together, therefore, as they are in many senses complementary to one another. A great deal has been written about such movements and we can exemplify them at length. Less is known about frontier movements and so our subsequent treatment of these will be necessarily scantier.

CONVERGING AND DIVERGING MOVEMENTS

Many movements over the earth's surface tend to converge towards a discrete point in space in *exchange* for flows that diverge from that central point in all directions. Also, many movements are sequential, that is, they converge on an attractive point but tend to diverge and retreat with the *periodic* ebbing of that attractiveness.

Among the best examples we have of *complementary* converging and diverging movements are those which link a town or city to surrounding settlements of a smaller size. The city, for example, is the focus towards which some goods move, and in exchange other goods move to their recipients in the surrounding rural area. Similarly, the city is the focus for commuters from the surrounding rural area and in return there is a movement of purchasing power. Telephone calls to the city are exchanged for telephone calls from the city, and marketing trips by farmers are balanced by returns of livestock or cash.

There is also a *sequential* element in the convergences and divergences characterizing the city and surrounding communities. At the beginning of the day there is a movement of workers to the city, followed shortly by school children and then by shoppers; at the end of the day the workers, children, and shoppers return as the facilities which had attracted them during the day close down. In the evening there are new movements: the convergence of people in search of entertainment and their divergence in the small hours.

Hence there is a *symbiotic* relationship between the city and the surrounding area with which it has strong movement ties. The area depends on the city for a wide range of goods and services including employment, newspapers, and health services. Moreover, the city is partly dependent on the surrounding area for the profitable operation of many of its shops and services. Without the market of the surrounding area many of the stores in the city would have to close down.

In addition to the *symbiotic* nature of the relationship between city and surrounding area, however, there is also a *hierarchical* component. In many ways the city *dominates* the small communities of the surrounding rural area while that area is, conversely, *dependent* on the city. The small rural community may be dependent upon the city as a shopping center, as an entertainment center, and also for jobs; what happens in the city is, therefore, of vital and critical concern to the nearby village. The village, however, is of far less importance to the city. A reversal in the economic fortunes of the individual village, for example, will be of far less significance to the city *simply because so many other villages look to it for a range of needs*. In brief, the city *dominates* the small communities of the surrounding area due to its monopoly position in supplying their needs. The small communities do not enjoy such power since they must compete to satisfy the demands placed upon them by the city. A geographical expression of this *dominance–dependence* relationship is the city's *sphere of influence, service area,* or *urban field.*

▶   *A city's sphere of influence or field is that area surrounding the city which depends on the city for a wide range of needs including employment, retail goods and services, information (newspapers), marketing facilities, education, and banking services.*

Figures 2-8*a* to 2-8*e* provide information about the *urban field* of the English market town of Melton Mowbray. The criteria used for field definition here include (*a*) the places in which a majority of households look to Melton Mowbray for weekly shopping needs, (*b*) the places which depend on Melton for banking services and (*c*) for cinema entertainment, (*d*) places in which the newspaper, the "Melton Times," circulates, and (*e*) settlements served by retailers located in Melton.

Several characteristics are outstanding in these maps. First, there is a high degree of agreement existing between these different definitions of Melton's sphere of influence. The area that depends on Melton for cinema entertainment, for instance, is very similar to that dependent on the town for banking services. The second interesting facet of these maps is the way in which the northeastern and northwestern boundaries of the field almost coincide with the boundaries of the county—Leicestershire—in which Melton Mowbray is located. We will return to this problem of boundary effects upon movement later in this book. A third interesting feature of two of the maps is that there is some evidence *for a decay in the intensity of the urban field* with increasing distance from Melton Mowbray. Thus, in the map showing settlements served by Melton

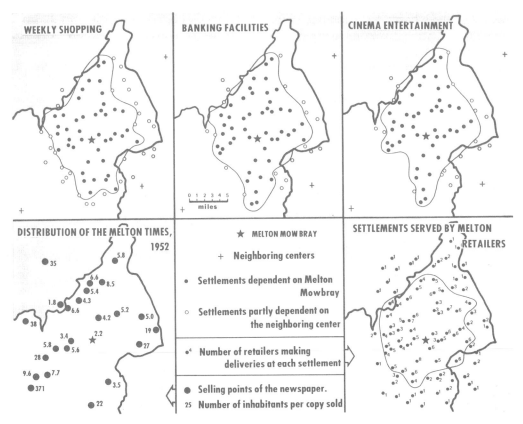

FIGURE 2-8. (*a*)–(*e*). The urban field of Melton Mowbray as defined by several criteria. The thick black line defines the boundary between Leicestershire to the south and other counties to the north. The thin lines in four of the maps provide definitions of Melton's urban field; note the relationship of these definitions to the county boundary.

retailers, far more retailers serve any one village close to Melton than serve any village further away. Also, in the map of newspaper circulation the number of inhabitants per copy sold is lowest in Melton itself and increases with increasing distance from Melton.

The city and its sphere of influence, however, are not the only examples we have of symbiotic and hierarchical relationships between a point and some surrounding area. We can envision similar relationships with associated movements on a variety of geographical scales. Within nations as a whole some *point* or small area usually serves as a dominant place in terms of decision making, the distribution of services, and the dissemi-

nation of information to the rest of the nation. In Britain this function is performed by London: not only is London the seat of national government where a large majority of the political decisions affecting Britain are made, but it is also the site for the headquarters of major corporations that make decisions affecting private economic life in Britain. It is with London that one transacts for a wide range of public and private purposes, from dealings with government ministries and departments at one end of the scale to the taking out of an insurance policy and the buying of stock at the other end of the scale. London is also the control point in the national communication system; it is from London that the vast majority of British families receive a newspaper every morning and it is in London that most radio and TV programs originate. If our hypothetical citizen reads a book, it is almost inevitable that if it is a British book it has a London publisher. In another sense, London is the vital nexus: for anyone leaving Britain to travel overseas a trip to London is *almost* mandatory, since London airport has such an overwhelming monopoly on all overseas flights leaving the United Kingdom. Overseas flights are also made from Glasgow, Manchester, and Birmingham, but these form a very slight fraction of the total—certainly much lower than one would anticipate on the basis of the population sizes of these three cities. And as a final factor in London's *dominance* consider the large number of national institutions located in London: exhibition halls, national monuments, museums, symphony orchestras, ballet, theater, and educational institutions.

Such dominance-dependence is not necessarily typical of movement relationships between the national capital and its territory, however. In the United States, for example, Washington certainly does not enjoy the preeminence which London enjoys in Britain. Not only is national decision making less centralized and more shared with the individual state capitals, but Washington also shares with New York many of the functions of a nationally dominant city. Therefore it is probably more reasonable to think in terms of a cluster of nationally dominant cities in the northeast United States rather than of a single dominant city, as in the case of Britain. New York City has a virtual monopoly of national book publishing; it also has most corporation headquarters, although this dominance is shared with other cities such as Chicago, Los Angeles, Detroit, Washington, and Boston. New York City is the site of Wall Street, fi-

nancial capital of the United States and the American equivalent of London's Thread-Needle Street. Compared with London, however, New York City has less of a monopoly on overseas airlinks and on the means of written and oral communication. Thus the *dominance* which New York City and Washington enjoy in the United States is rather less than that of London in Britain. American life is more decentralized, and movements converge and diverge not only to and from New York City and Washington but also, to a lesser degree, from such *regionally dominant* centers as Los Angeles, Chicago, and Atlanta. We will return to this idea of a *range* of dominant places shortly; we will also have more to say about why American movements are less centralized than those in Britain. Certainly the factor of geographical size is probably important, though this is unlikely to be the only consideration.

A Hierarchy of Urban Fields. Thus far the discussion has been in terms of the relationships of a single, more attractive, and dominant place with other, dependent places of similar dependence and lesser degree of attractiveness. However, while some places are more attractive than others so that movements take place from the less attractive to the more attractive places we have to reckon with the idea of a range of attractiveness. Consider for example in Figure 2-9 the place Y which is *dependent* upon X. In order to satisfy the multitudinous needs of the inhabitants of Y, X will be dependent upon some other still more attractive place Z. Thus Z may be a wholesaling

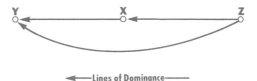

FIGURE 2-9. A hierarchy of dominance–dependence relationships in schematic form.

center from which the retailers in place X obtain the goods which they ultimately distribute to the people at Y. Z may represent a superordinate level in the administrative hierarchy so that decisions made in X have to be made within a framework established by the decision makers of Z. This may apply to both public and private sectors—to the marketing organization of a firm, for example, just as much as to the local government. Finally, Z may be a market for goods initially collected at X from producers at such places as Y. Therefore, Z may be the place in which the wheat transported by farm pickup truck from Y to X, and from Y to Z by tractor trailer, is put on the railroad for shipment outside of the region.

Even with this intermediary role, however, X may not be able to satisfy all the needs of Y, and so inhabitants of Y have to go to Z themselves in order to satisfy these needs. Thus place X may not have a symphony orchestra whereas Z does; the classical music lovers at Y therefore will have to journey to Z. Similarly, X may not have a large department store so the people from Y have to go to Z to do their Christmas shopping. And finally, the newspaper in X may be published once a week and dwell on local news and advertising; for more regular local news and for national and international news the inhabitant at Y may have to look to a newspaper published in Z.

These arguments, of course, apply just as much to the people living at X as to the people living at Y. If there is no symphony orchestra at X then they, too, will have to journey to Z, as will Christmas shoppers. And for national news and regional advertising they will have to rely on information disseminated from Z.

What we have to conceive of therefore is a *hierarchy of dominance-dependence relationships*. Some towns are *more dominant* than others and some towns are *more dependent* than others. New York City is more dominant than Chicago; Chicago is more dominant than Fort Wayne, Indiana; Fort Wayne, Indiana, is more dominant than Lebanon, Indiana; and Lebanon, Indiana, is more dependent than Chicago.

The dominance of one place over another place, however, is rarely absolute. Dependent places are usually dependent on more than one place. Thus Lebanon, Indiana, is dependent on Fort Wayne for a daily newspaper but on Chicago for a symphony orchestra, many of its wholesale needs, and possibly for the sale of hogs collected at Lebanon. It is only the more dominant places that are likely to approach the position of *absolute dominance*. London, for instance, is probably absolutely dominant within the United Kingdom while Paris is almost certainly absolutely dominant in France. Nevertheless, if we wish to expand our scale a little even London and Paris would lose this property of absolute dominance. If we look at movements between places on a world scale, for instance, London and Paris can be shown to be dependent in certain respects on New York City. Stock exchange decisions made in London and Paris are dependent upon the flow of information about decisions made on Wall Street; and cinema showings in Paris and London are dependent on the flow of movies from worldwide distributors based in New York City.

An additional consideration, however, is that some places are of similar dominance to each other. Chicago and Los Angeles for example have similar degrees of dominance. probably similar numbers of people are dependent on these two centers and people have to move to either of them in order to fulfill similar needs. Cleveland, Boston, Philadelphia, Atlanta, St. Louis, San Francisco, Dallas, and Seattle are probably at a similar level of dominance; they are less dominant than Los Angeles, Chicago, or New York City in that they have to look to one of those cities for various needs such as national news broadcasts, wholesaling functions, meetings at corporation headquarters, and active theater life. Nevertheless, similar numbers of people are probably dependent on each of these eight cities.

What becomes very strikingly apparent from this discussion is that there are more *very dependent places* than there are *very dominant places.* Precisely why this should be so will be left to Chapter Eleven, but it is a fact that we need to recognize if we are to understand movement patterns. It is a fact, moreover, that we tend to recognize intuitively. We tend to think in terms of national centers such as New York City and London; regional centers such as Birmingham, Glasgow, Los Angeles, and Chicago; subregional centers such as Dallas, San Francisco, Atlanta, Bristol, and Norwich; and local centers such as Lebanon, Indiana; Marion, Ohio; and Melton Mowbray, Leicestershire. And we know that there are more local centers than subregional centers; and more subregional centers than regional centers, and so on.

The important implication of this pattern is that if there are fewer places of a certain type—if there are fewer very dominant places for example, than less dominant places—then we expect them geographically to be spaced further apart. And this, in fact, is exactly what we do find.

This spread, in turn, affects the pattern of movement. Given that the more dominant places are more scattered than the less dominant places and given a tendency for people to move to the nearest place that can satisfy their requirements, we can expect movements to more dominant places to be, on the average, longer than movements to more dependent

places. Thus, in terms of purposes, movements for purposes that can only be satisfied at more dominant centers (for example, listening to a symphony orchestra) will be on the average longer than movements for purposes that can be satisfied at more dependent places (for example, buying groceries).

If movements to more dominant centers are in general longer, however, this means that the *spheres of influence,* the *urban fields,* of the more dominant centers are going to be much larger in geographical area than are those of the less dominant centers. Consider the case of newspaper distribution. The circulation of the *New York Times*—the only approach to a national press which the U.S.A. has—is national. The circulations of such newspapers as the *Los Angeles Times* and the *Chicago Tribune* are more regional in scope; while the circulation areas of newspapers such as the *Kansas City Star, Cleveland Plain Dealer, St. Louis Post Dispatch,* and *Philadelphia Bulletin* are even more restricted.

▶ *Thus the fact that urban fields differ in size and that more dominant places have larger urban fields entails another interesting fact: the urban fields of less dominant places tend to nest in the urban fields of more dominant places.*

The urban field of San Francisco nests in that of Los Angeles; Los Angeles' urban field nests inside that of New York City, and so on. Similarly, if we were to examine telephone calls we should find that the spheres of influence of the more dominant places are larger and include within them the spheres of influence of the less dominant places. As Figure 2-10 demonstrates, this is certainly the case for telephone communication in Denmark. The sphere of influence of the most dominant place, Copenhagen, is clearly the largest in the country and

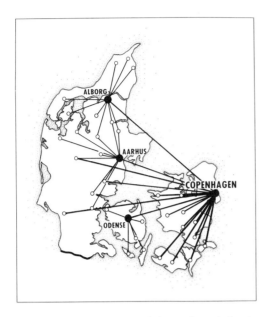

FIGURE 2-10. The nested hierarchy of dominance-dependence relationships for telephone calls in Denmark: note the dominance of the capital city of Copenhagen and the nesting of the spheres of influence of smaller cities within the sphere of influence of Copenhagen.

overlaps the smaller fields of the next three most dominant places, Aarhus, Odense, and Alborg.

FRONTIER MOVEMENTS

Much less studied than converging and diverging movements are wavelike movements over the earth's surface of colonists, missionaries, migrants, etc. Such a movement may advance towards some *attractive linear resource* such as a coastline or belt of cheap land or linear zone of pagan population; or it may retreat from some *unattractive linear resource* such as a zone of climatic hazard or of less fertile soil. One can also discriminate between frontier movements according to the dynamic properties of the linear resource towards which movement is oriented; thus some linear resources like a coastline or a highway are relatively static, while others, such as a frontier of agricultural colonization,

tend to show shifts in location from year to year. Here we will initially discuss more static frontier phenomena and then turn toward more dynamic cases.

Movements Towards Static Linear Resources. Movements towards a static linear resource can be conceptualized in the form of the schematic diagram shown in Figure 2-11. The arrows represent movements while the two oblongs represent respectively a set of unattractive places from which movement is taking place (minus signs) and a set of attractive places towards which movement is oriented (plus signs).

Examples of movement toward a static linear resource include the shipment of goods in the United States between the complementary eastern and western portions of the continent, with flows of surplus raw materials in one direction and flows of surplus manufactured goods from the Northeast to the West. A more interesting and recurrent linear resource, however, is that represented by coastlines. For a variety of reasons coastal locations are attractive to migrants from less attractive transoceanic locations. Thus, many of the world's ethnic minority problems derive from coastal settlement by some exogeneous group and the resultant displacement of, dominance of, or competition with some host population. The French colonists of Algeria, for example, concentrated along the Mediterranean coast of that country

ZONE OF REPULSION

ZONE OF ATTRACTION

FIGURE 2-11. Movement and a static linear resource.

as did the Italians on the Adriatic coast of Yugoslavia during the period of Venetian dominance. Many of the minority problems of Latin America derive from a coastal settlement by Spanish and Portuguese colonists while the native Indians were progressively confined to interior locations away from the coast.

Why the coastline is such an attractive linear resource is an issue which will become clearer as we continue into Chapter Three. Here, however, it should be pointed out that much of the attraction derives from the historically superior means of transportation afforded by boat and barge. Many of the coastal colonists have been involved in trade with other coastal locations or with the mother country. Witness the activities of the Hanseatic League in the Baltic for example, or of the Arabs along the east coast of Africa.

Movements Towards Dynamic Linear Resources. Other linear resources towards which movement is oriented, however, can be regarded as themselves shifting over space. This is shown schematically in Figure 2-12 which relates the changing attractiveness of the line to different points in time. Of what sort of movement might this be an accurate representation, however? Particularly important in this regard are frontiers of colonization. Examination of the history of colonization movements suggests that at least two features of the frontier environment have been especially attractive to the colonists: (1) the availability of cheap virgin land capable of high yields for a few years with only small investments of capital and labor, and (2) the political environment of the frontier characterized by the absence of a highly structured legal and political framework. These features have proven particularly attractive to nonconforming religious groups like the Amish and the Mennonites who have desired a high degree

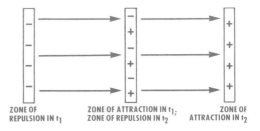

FIGURE 2-12. Movement and a dynamic linear resource.

of collective autonomy in the conduct of their lives with a minimum of state interference with regard to such public services as education or health. These characteristics at least seem to have been important in the expansion of agricultural colonization in the United States and to a less extent in 19th-century Russia and Australia.

The frontier of agricultural colonization, however, has an internal dynamic of its own, which, *given the possibility of expansion,* promotes renewed waves of frontier colonization. For a start, after a few seasons of agricultural exploitation, the soil begins to show signs of depletion, yields fall, and without increased applications of labor and/or capital, income decreases and the erstwhile frontier becomes a less attractive location for the colonist. Such stimuli to renewed movement have been particularly critical in countries such as Brazil where frontier colonizations have been especially exploitative, leaving behind a worked-over area of exhausted soil—the so-called "hollow frontier." Second, the increasing settlement of the frontier provides an impetus towards the introduction of formal governmental institutions and a deterioration in the attractiveness of the zone for minority religious and ethnic groups desirous of a minimum of government constraint. This situation stimulates renewed waves of colonizing movement, given that there are areas available for colonization. An interesting example of this pattern seems to have been the frontier movements of Mennonites. In the United States, at least, they often seem to have been in the vanguard of colonization, often jumping ahead of the frontier to attain the maximum freedom they cherished.

NETWORK BIAS

We started this chapter by discussing the types of geographical bias to which a variety of movements are subject. We have now discussed two of those biases in some depth: distance bias and direction bias. All that remains is the discussion of network bias. This discussion will be brief since we shall deal at greater length with the topic in Chapters Eight and Nine.

Movements require channels. Even though people may want to move to the nearest attractive point, there may be an inadequate network of channels to allow them to do this. Every movement presupposes a network of information channels by which the instigator of movement learns of the opportunities open to him at different locations. These information channels are in the form of the newspapers he reads or the letters he receives from his friends, for example. There must also be a network of transportation routes for movement of commuters or migrants or goods. Clearly, if places belong to the same *network,* they are more likely to interact than if they belong to different networks.

Consider the case of the networks of information channels from which the individual learns of the different opportunities open to him at different places. In Chapter One we described the role of newspapers in spreading information about employment opportunities in different places and encouraging migration to such places. One of the examples we gave was the likelihood of a northern

Ohioan migrating to Cleveland on the basis of job information acquired from the *Cleveland Plain Dealer.* If the potential migrant was not connected to that particular channel, however, he would be less likely to migrate to Cleveland. It is for such network-bias reasons that migration tends to run in families — migration from a particular small town into a larger city may be dominated by one kinship group alone, simply because relatives tend to write to each other! In Algeria, for example, a village will send migrants to one town in France and to one town alone.

Given that the potential migrant, commuter, trader, etc. has information about the set of movement opportunities confronting him, movement to any one of them is obviously conditional upon the existence of routes. The role of such channels in the movement of people and of goods is brought out strikingly by an examination of changes in flow consequent to a change in the availability of channels. Thus, the construction of the Erie Canal in 1825 had immense locational implications. Not only did it link New York City up with a rich agricultural hinterland but it also ensured the preeminence of New York City over such ports as Philadelphia, Baltimore, and Boston, which lacked such links. Similarly, the completion of the first transcontinental line in the United States in 1869 was very important in welding the nation into one national market through which goods could move freely.

Less obvious examples of the effect of network bias upon movement patterns come from a superimposition of one transportation network, such as a railroad network, upon another as in the case of a river system. The replacement of river transportation by the speedier railroad in the United States, for instance, led to important reorientations of flow in the midcontinental sections.

Until the railroad emerged, the commerce of the Ohio Valley had tended to move downstream to New Orleans and hence by coastal vessel to the Northeast. After the railroad, Pittsburgh, Cincinnati, Louisville, etc. looked eastward.

CONCLUSIONS AND SUMMARY

In this chapter we have examined at some length the geographical regularities which are apparent in a wide diversity of movements over space. In brief, we have examined three types of locational bias to which movements appear subject: *distance bias, direction bias,* and *network bias.* Each bias refers to a distinctive association between the movements which take place between an origin and a destination, on the one hand, and the locational relationships of the origin and destination relative to each other, on the other hand.

Distance bias refers to that situation in which movement is either more likely or is more intense over shorter distances than over longer distances. This very common type of bias is manifest in a wide variety of movements such as those to state parks, commodity flows, information flows, and migration. In many cases of distance bias, however, the relationship between movement intensity and intervening distance is not a linear one; rather, movement intensity declines at a decreasing rate with increasing intervening distance — the so-called *negative exponential* relationship.

Directional bias, on the other hand, refers to that geographical configuration of movement in which movement appears to take place in certain preferred directions rather than in all possible directions. One basis on which such directionally biased movement patterns can be classified is that of *convergence-divergence of movement* and also that of the geometrical characteristics of the location towards which, or away from which, the movements are converging or diverging respectively; the *point* or *line* is a useful distinction here.

A very common locational pattern of movement is that which involves converging and diverging movements relating a point to a set of locations in the surrounding area. Such is the situation which exists between a city and its hinterland as a result of the complementarities existing between the two. The population of the hinterland moves towards the town for shopping, employment, and entertainment purposes; salaries, goods, and services move from the city in order to satisfy demands of the hinterland. It is useful to think of certain *symbiotic* or *mutually dependent* relations existing between a city and the surrounding area, therefore.

Nevertheless, any one hinterland location *depends* on the city more than the city depends on that location. The location may contribute a miniscule number to the city's labor force and to the demand for retail goods and services purchased in the city. For that particular location, however, the city may provide all employment and all of a particular range of retail goods and services. There exist, therefore, hierarchical relationships between the city and its hinterland, the greater *dependence* of the hinterland on the city placing the city in a more *dominant* position. What goes on in the individual location is of very limited concern to the city. The hinterland, therefore, forms the city's *sphere of influence* or *service area* or simply *urban field*.

When we examine a large set of cities, however, it is clear that there is a range of *dominance-dependence*. Some cities are more dominant than others which, in turn, are more dominant than still other cities. Not only that but there are *fewer very dominant cities* and they are *spaced further apart* than less dominant cities. Given that the *more dominant cities are more attractive for movement*, trip lengths are affected so that *the more dominant cities have larger spheres of influence*. Given these different areal sizes, it is quite logical that the spheres of influence of more dominant cities should nest within the spheres of influence of less dominant cities.

A second broad category of converging-diverging movement patterns concerns those which are oriented with reference to *linear resources* exercising *an attractive or repellent force on movement*. We can conceive, therefore, of *advancing and retreating frontier movements*. These have been much less studied than systems which converge on or diverge from a point, but they are of considerable interest. It is possible, for instance, to discriminate between movements which are related to *static linear resources* as opposed to *dynamic linear resources*. An example of the former is provided by the coastline while the latter is exemplified by the moving frontier of colonization with its cheaper, more naturally fertile land and lower degree of political control.

A third and final bias which constrains movement is that of *network* or *connection bias*. Connections between people, provided by interpersonal contacts, constrain the flow of information, for instance. The availability of routes of a given capacity constrains the movement of goods and people in a similar manner.

This chapter has been primarily descriptive, concerning itself with the identification of locational regularities in movement patterns. What, however, of the forces which produce these regularities? These are considered in the next chapter.

CHAPTER THREE

The Bases of Movement

INTRODUCTION

Thus far in our treatment of movement we have discussed the geometry of flows: the distance and direction biases, for example, which characterize a wide range of movements including migration, shopping trips, and commodity flows. These descriptive regularities raise an analytical question. Precisely why do we get these real world configurations? Is there any simple body of economical and consistent ideas that can be applied to this task of explanation? It is our belief that indeed there is, and these ideas form the focus of this chapter.

We shall start out by considering the factors which affect movement in a fairly abstract manner, and we shall show how these abstract concepts can be applied to produce the locational configurations of movement observed and described in Chapter Two. We shall then consider each of the factors in greater detail, identifying the explanatory richness of the concepts and the factors to which they themselves respond before they exert their effects on the pattern of movement. In the next chapter, we shall apply these ideas to two case studies of movement: commodity flow and migration. Taking this chapter and the next together, therefore, we shall move from more abstract considerations to more substantive ap-

plications. Close attention to this chapter will be more than amply repaid with the clarifications of real world movement patterns in the chapter to follow.

THE BASES OF MOVEMENT: AN ABSTRACT CONSIDERATION

Movement patterns are instigated by people who decide from a range of possible destinations or *movement opportunities* where to shop, where to go to school, where to work, and the like. As a first approximation, individual *movement decisions* can be seen as a function of two considerations: (1) *the attractiveness of particular destinations or movement opportunities,* and (2) *the costs of movement to these particular opportunities.* Thus in the evaluation of movement opportunities, people tend to consider both the rewards they obtain from a particular movement opportunity, such as a store, and the costs involved in getting there.

When aggregated and mapped, the movements resulting from such individual *movement decisions* provide a *movement pattern* to be explained. In explaining *movement patterns* as opposed to the *movement decisions* of individuals, an additional consideration is that the choices are carried out in an environment of movement opportunities that are singly characterized by movement costs and a level of attractiveness. Taken in toto, however, all *movement opportunities*—the *opportunity set*—have a locational structure of great significance for the pattern of movement. The *locational structure of movement opportunities* can be characterized, for example, as to its density. If movement opportunities are spread out, movements will tend to be of longer distance than if the opportunities were spaced closer together.

▶   *In summary, three factors need to be considered in explaining movement patterns: the attractiveness of each movement opportunity, the respective movement costs incurred by each movement opportunity, and the locational structure of the movement opportunities.*

Thus, in order to explain individual movement decisions, we need to consider only the attractiveness of different movement opportunities and the respective movement costs incurred. In order to explain aggregate movement patterns, however, we must also consider the locational pattern of movement opportunities. Let us consider each of these factors in rather more detail.

ATTRACTIVENESS

Movements are carried out to achieve goals of the people or organizations instigating them. A destination is chosen, therefore, because it can provide something which is needed by the instigator of the movement. The destination has an attribute which is *valued* by the instigator, and which makes the destination *attractive*. Some of the possible destinations for particular movements are more attractive than others and afford higher degrees of utility, so that it is possible to rank the movement opportunities in terms of the rewards they will provide.

Of course, in estimating the attractiveness of the destination, it is the *net reward* which we are interested in, as we have to offset the penalties of a particular place against its rewards. It is a foolish man who is attracted to Los Angeles on the grounds of its pleasant climate, and does not take into account the penalties imposed by smog, crowding, and national isolation.

Attractiveness is *functional*. What is attractive for one type of movement will differ from what is attractive for other types of movement. A place may be attractive for shopping and be included in the set of movement opportunities which we consider for shopping purposes, but it may not have the facilities which would make it attractive for entertainment-oriented trips.

MOVEMENT COSTS

Movements to attractive destinations involve costs of movement, and some movement opportunities involve higher movement costs than others do. Such costs of movement may not be merely monetary as represented by the cost of an airline ticket. When making a movement we spend time which could be devoted to other more rewarding purposes; while the university professor makes a trip to give a lecture, he is losing time which could be devoted to working on his textbook. Thus movement involves an *opportunity cost* in addition to a *monetary cost*. There may also be costs which are *incidental* to movement but which do figure as part of the cost of getting to an attractive destination—the costs of overnight stays on trips to visit relatives on the West Coast, for example. Such incidental and time costs may make it more advantageous to use speedier, though monetarily costlier, forms of transportation such as airplanes than to use slower modes of movement such as the automobile for long-distance trips.

The movement cost is incurred in obtaining something of value at the destination. That "something" may be tangible, such as a consumer good or education, or it may be intangible, such as the pleasure afforded by Las Vegas. Whatever the nature of the net reward to be obtained at the destination,

▶ *if the movement costs are judged to be too high relative to the value of the net reward, we say the net reward is nontransferable; if movement costs are judged sufficiently modest, on the other hand, the net reward is regarded as transferable.*

Thus, we may regard a bottle of shaving cream purchased from the neighboring drugstore as transferable, whereas the same good from some more distant source would probably be regarded as nontransferable. Of course, if other purposes are involved in the longer shopping trip, such as the purchase of a color TV set, the shaving cream may become transferable, since the movement cost involved in getting the cream is spread out over a greater total net reward. This is a feature of *multiple-purpose shopping trips* and *multiple-purpose movements* which we will discuss later.

The movement cost factor is often referred to in the literature as a *friction-of-distance factor* or an *intervening opportunity factor*. The term "friction-of-distance factor" describes the tendency for movement costs to show an increase with the increasing distance of movement; this increase poses a deterrent to choosing more distant movement opportunities. "Intervening opportunity factor" also describes this tendency to move to closer rather than to more distant opportunities because of the movement cost criterion. We will see shortly, however, that intervening distance is not necessarily a good guide to the costs of movement between a pair of places.

THE LOCATIONAL STRUCTURE OF MOVEMENT OPPORTUNITIES

To illustrate the utility of the concept of the locational structure of movement opportunities in explaining movement patterns, consider the case in which all movement opportunities are equally attractive, that is, characterized by the same level of net reward for a particular movement. Let us also assume that movement costs are proportional to the distance of a movement opportunity from a person instigating the movement, and that the instigators of movements are spread evenly over the area. Now let us consider a variation in the locational structure of these movement opportunities: density.

With regard to density, consider the case in which the equally attractive movement opportunities are located at the corners of rectangles with sides one mile in length (see Figure 3-1). Application of the Pythagorean theorem will show that the farthest any individual will have to move in order to obtain the reward available at the movement opportunity is 0.707 miles, assuming that movement is possible in all directions. Now let us alter the densities so that the movement opportunities are located at the corners of rectangles with sides two miles in length; that is, the density of movement opportunities per unit area has declined. In this case, the farthest an individual will have to move is 1.414 miles. For the lower-density case, therefore, we would expect movement distances to be, on the average, longer than in the case where the density is higher.

Given this explication of the three factors and to demonstrate their applicability to more concrete movement situations, let us consider a frequent movement: the shopping trip. In considering the shopping trip and confining ourselves to the shopping good represented by the phonograph record, the set of

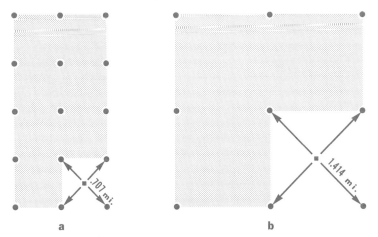

a   b

FIGURE 3-1.   The density of movement opportunities and length of movement. In the diagram on the left, movement opportunities are spaced at the corners of rectangles with sides of 1 mile in length; the furthest distance any person will have to move therefore is 0.707 miles; in the diagram on the right, on the other hand, movement opportunities are spaced further apart (2 miles along the top and side) so that the furthest a person will have to move will be 1.414 miles.

movement opportunities becomes the set of stores selling phonograph records as the whole or as part of their business. A moment's reflection will demonstrate that such opportunities can be quite easily scaled in terms of their attractiveness for the purpose of obtaining the phonograph record. At some stores there will be the reward of lower prices and possibly the penalty of impoliteness on the part of service and clientele. Other stores may have higher prices, but a wider selection of records, and the likelihood that the customer can exchange the record within a certain time period if he is not satisfied. These are some of the criteria which we employ in deciding on the relative attractiveness of stores for purchasing a phonograph record.

There is also, however, the problem of movement costs. Some stores will be farther away than others, requiring a longer trip to get to them. Patronage at some stores may necessitate paying a parking fee not required when visiting other stores. When considering in which record store to shop, we shall find ourselves unconsciously balancing or *trading off* the net rewards of a particular store against the movement costs that a visit there will incur. The record store with the widest range of choice and lowest prices may be located at a considerable distance. Is it worth patronizing that store? Will the net rewards obtainable at the store be more than offset by the costs of getting there and back?

Finally, consider the locational structure of record stores. For the buyer living in the country, the locational structure of record stores is a highly dispersed one and his record-buying trips are therefore likely to be rather lengthy. For the urbanite, however, record stores are much more accessible and buying trips are therefore likely to be shorter. An extension of the net reward–movement costs type of logic also suggests that the record-buying trips of the ruralite are more likely to be multiple in purpose than are those of the urbanite.

In sum, it appears to be quite easy and quite satisfactory to apply our conceptual scheme to a common type of movement.

You may also find it useful to introspectively apply the explanatory schema to your own movement decisions concerning choice of university, grocery shopping, or where to go for a vacation.

What seems to be a particularly important feature of the example above, however, and probably of those which you can think of yourself, is the idea of a *trade-off between attractiveness and movement costs.* For a particular purpose it seems that one can rank all places which would serve that purpose in terms of *how well* they would serve it; that is, how attractive they are in terms of cost, likely availability, crowdedness of facilities, quality of product, and service. But all those places are also characterized by movement costs, and some will incur higher movement costs than others.

Clearly those places with higher movement costs can only induce movement if they are also *more attractive* than places with lower movement costs. The degree to which they must be more attractive will depend on how large the movement costs incurred will be; if movement costs are very great, the attractiveness of the destination must be equivalently greater. In making our movement decisions, we must constantly trade off in our minds the net rewards available at particular places and the costs of getting to those places. Where movement costs are too high relative to the attractiveness of a particular place, there will be a tendency to substitute places of equivalent attractiveness or possibly lower attractiveness which involve lower movement costs. This will frequently imply the substitution of a place which is geographically closer (see Table 3-1).

THE BASES OF MOVEMENT AND LOCATIONAL PATTERNS OF MOVEMENT

The aim of the initial section of this chapter was to provide a set of concepts capable of explaining the geometrical regularities in locational patterns of movement which we identified in Chapter Two: distance bias, direction bias, spheres of influence, and so on. To what extent have we been successful in identifying the relevant mechanisms which produce such patterns of movement?

In order to answer this question, let us assume a hypothetical area with a locational structure of movement opportunities and residence of movers as given, and see what sort of patterns are produced when we allocate movers to movement opportunities on the basis of the criteria discussed in the first part of this chapter. Specifically, assume an area in which there is a small number of places which are attractive for some single purpose, such as the buying of phonograph records: this is the set of movement opportunities (see Figure 3-2). Assume also that the population of potential movers is distributed fairly uniformly across space (see Figure 3-2) and that movement costs are proportional to intervening distance such that longer distances involve higher movement costs.

Given this locational structure, we can apply our movement theory by allocating

TABLE 3-1. The substitution of movement costs and attractiveness. Movers tend to trade one off against the other; where movement costs are too high, they may opt for a less attractive opportunity which has lower movement costs attached to it.

| | | Movement Costs | |
		Low	High
Attractiveness	Low	Movement Possible	Movement Highly Unlikely
	High	Movement Highly Likely	Movement Possible

movers to movement opportunities according to the simple criterion: allocate according to lowest movement costs so that, in actuality, the mover is allocated to the nearest movement opportunity (see Figure 3-2). This simple exercise produces very clear direction biases in movement, spheres of influence for the movement opportunities, and a distance-biased movement. Note that the distance bias is of the sort where movement takes place over short distances but not over long distances; it is not of the sort where intensity of movement, varying in a continuous manner, is a function of intervening distance (see Figure 3-3). A more continuous distance bias, however, could be easily produced by assuming that the number of trips which a household makes to a movement opportunity is an inverse function of

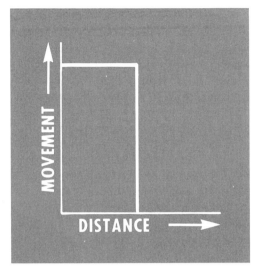

FIGURE 3-3. A discontinuous distance bias. Over shorter distances there is movement; over longer distances there is no movement. This is the type of distance bias apparent in Figure 3-2.

movement costs (see Figure 3-4). This certainly seems intuitively reasonable in that people who live farther away from a grocery store are likely to make fewer trips, but buy more groceries per trip, than the individual who has a grocery store on the corner of his block.

A second factor conducive to a more continuous distance bias in movement concerns the trade-off mechanism. Given the choice between a more attractive movement opportunity at a greater movement cost and a less attractive movement opportunity at a lower movement cost, it is likely that a majority of movers will opt for the latter. This effect is due partly to the nature of the distribution of income in a population. The marginal substitutability of the money spent on additional movement is much greater for the poorer person than for the more wealthy; that is, the poor person has demands on his resources more critical than movement to obtain a reward no greater than that received by the more wealthy individual who spends proportionally less of his resources to obtain it.

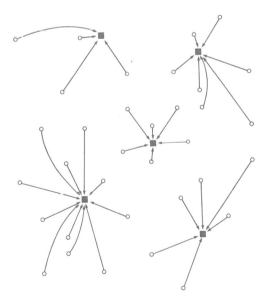

○ **MOVER LOCATION**　■ **MOVEMENT OPPORTUNITIES**

FIGURE 3-2. The allocation of movers to movement opportunities (hypothetical). Assuming that movement costs are proportional to distance, movers have been allocated to the nearest movement opportunity; note the emergence of spheres of influence, direction biases, and distance biases in movement.

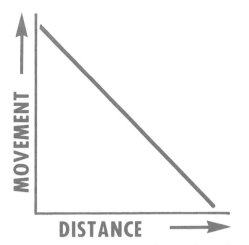

FIGURE 3-4. A continuous distance bias. Over shorter distances movement is more intense, while over longer distances it is less intense. This could result from a discontinuous distance bias if, for example, more distant shoppers shopped *less frequently.*

The idea is colloquially expressed by the common statement, "he has more money than he knows what to do with." A reinforcing factor (which we will deal with at length in Chapter Five) is that most people know about the movement opportunities close to them in space, but only a relatively small proportion know about more distant though possibly more attractive movement opportunities.

A final consideration is the manner in which the mechanism we have defined can produce *nested spheres of influence* in the hierarchical manner discussed in Chapter Two. Assume that a few of the movement opportunities where phonograph records are sold are also attractive for another purpose—say, entertainment. This application of the movement cost minimization criterion produces spheres of influence something like those shown in Figure 3-5. An interesting consideration here, however, is that the existence of a second attraction in those few movement opportunities makes their attractiveness for the purchase of phonograph records even

greater, since movement costs can be spread out over a greater number of purchases. The spheres of influence of the movement opportunities for both phonograph records and entertainment, therefore, are likely to expand geographically at the expense of the spheres of influence of the majority of movement opportunities which sell only phonograph records. A moment's reflection will show that this mechanism also will promote a continuous distance bias in movement as opposed to the stepped distance bias with which we commenced.

THE FACTORS CONSIDERED IN DETAIL

Given that the factors we have defined so far—movement costs and attractiveness of movement opportunities within a given locational structure—can produce the movement patterns discussed in Chapter Two, we now need to inquire into the meaning of these concepts in greater detail and with greater

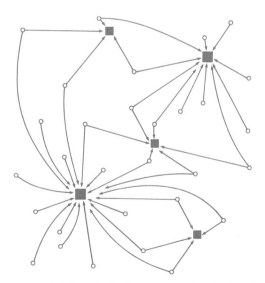

FIGURE 3-5. Production of nested spheres of influence by the allocative mechanism: smaller squares have only phonograph stores while larger squares have entertainment services in addition.

reference to the real world in order to sharpen their utility as analytical tools. Each of the three factors is considered in turn.

A number of terms have been used to describe the attractiveness property of places in a system of movements between locations. In studies of commodity flow between places, for example, a common concept of attractiveness is that of *complementarity;* while in studies of migration an analogous concept is that of *place utility.* Both of these concepts will be examined in greater detail.

Complementarity refers to an antecedent condition such that in order for a flow of a commodity to take place from location X to location Y, location X must have a supply of this specific commodity in excess of demand and location Y must have a demand for it in excess of supply.

▶   *Complementarity describes the relationships of two places when one place has a surplus of a commodity while the other place has a deficit of the same commodity. It describes one of the preconditions for movement; it does not describe an actual movement pattern.*

Examples of movement associated with such complementarity include the flow of grain from the Great Plains to the urbanized Midwest and Northeast of the United States, and the movement of ore and its products from the gold mines of South Africa to the manufacturing commercial economies of Western Europe and North America.

Other instances include the complementarities between industrialized nations of the Northern Hemisphere such as the U.S.A. and West Germany and the less-developed nations of the Southern Hemisphere, which make up the deficits of the industrial nations in such commodities as iron ore and copper and tropical foodstuffs, such as bananas, coffee, and cacao. Complementarity indicates potential gains for both deficit and surplus nations; the former are able to make good their deficit, while the latter find a market for their surplus supply.

The relationship of the idea of complementarity to the idea of attractiveness may not be immediately obvious to the reader. Consider, however, the viewpoint of the shipper of, for example, iron ore from Brazil. The attractive places, the places which he values, are those where he can get a high price for his iron ore. The higher prices for iron ore are likely to be found in areas of deficit, that is, where demand for iron ore is strong. On the other hand, prices will be weaker in areas of iron-ore surplus — where, in fact, demand is also weak. Brazil produces very little iron and steel, certainly not enough to consume a significant proportion of Brazil's iron-ore output; if all the iron ore was sold on the Brazilian market, the price would be very low indeed. The shipper of iron ore, therefore, values the deficit areas with their higher prices, such as the United States, far more than he values Brazil with its iron-ore surplus and lower prices. The United States is attractive to the Brazilian iron-ore shipper while Brazil is relatively unattractive. As iron-ore prices in Brazil and the United States approach parity, so the complementarity of the two countries in terms of iron ore will decline.

Place utility is a term coined by the geographer Julian Wolpert in his studies of migration. It refers to *the value an individual bestows on a place relative to his goals.* Thus, for a high school graduate, the place utility assigned to Harvard University will be rather different and more positive than that assigned to East Walnut Creek Tech.

While the concept of *place utility* or *locational utility* has been applied largely to the migration phenomenon, it seems also feasible to apply it to other human movements such as those of shoppers or tourists. Thus the place utility of a town for a shopper might reside in its range of shopping opportunities, while scenic and climatic amenities would provide the yardstick of place utility in decisions on recreational movements.

As a final comment on the concept of attractiveness, it is necessary to underline its functionality. Recall that we defined place utility as the value an individual bestows upon a place relative to his goals. Places are more or less attractive for specific purposes. Thus, a particularly interesting predictor of the attrac-

tiveness of places for different people is life-cycle status. What is attractive for a specific purpose for a young family man is often quite different from that which is attractive for the retired person and his wife. Especially attractive as a residential site for the younger family is the suburb, with its larger lots providing ample play space for children. Less attractive is the apartment development closer downtown, where there is little space for children and where there may actually be rules barring children from apartment complexes. The presence of so many young people in suburbia, however, makes it a much less attractive place for older people, as does the problem of a larger amount of housework and gardening for the aged. Little wonder,

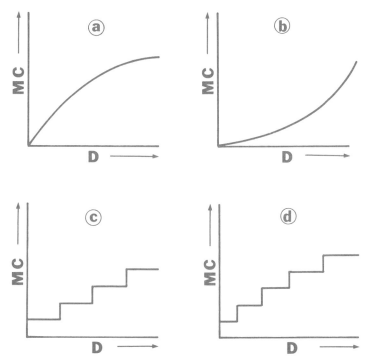

FIGURE 3-6. Possible nonlinear relationships between movement cost (MC) and distance (D). The relationship between movement cost and distance moved is not necessarily *straight-line* (i.e., linear); it may, for example, be *curvilinear* and *convex* upwards as in (a) or *curvilinear* and *concave* upwards as in (b). Alternatively, it may be stepped (c) or a combination of a *stepped* and *curvilinear* relationship (d).

therefore, that apartment developments are overwhelmingly populated with young people without families or older retired couples whose children have long since left home.

MOVEMENT COSTS

So far in our discussion we have made the assumption that movement costs tend to increase in a highly regular manner with increasing distance. While in most cases such an assumption is not too inaccurate, we must recognize certain deviations from this pattern and understand why and under what circumstances these deviations occur.

Three possible deviations should be noted in this context. First, the relationship may not necessarily be linear; it may in fact be concave or possibly convex upwards, that is, a *curvilinear relationship*. It may also be a stepped relationship, or a combination of stepped and curvilinear relationships (Figure 3-6). A second possibility is that the *form* of the relationship may differ from one situation to another; thus if the rela-

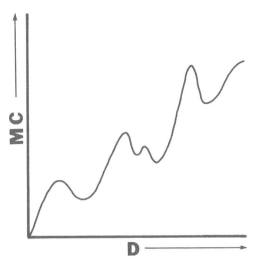

FIGURE 3-8. Nonmonotonic movement cost–distance relationships: usually it is cheaper to ship goods over shorter distances rather than over longer distances. Under certain circumstances, however, this may not be so; that is, the relationship may not be monotonic. Over some longer distances, movement costs may actually be lower than over some shorter distances.

tionship is actually linear, the angle of the slope may differ from one type of movement to another. Alternatively, if the relationship is curvilinear, the nature of the curvilinearity may differ (see Figure 3-7). And third, it is quite possible that the relationship by which movement costs increase with increasing distance is *not* monotonic; that is, there may be certain situations in which movement costs actually decline with increasing distance (see Figure 3-8). These three possibilities will be examined in turn.

The Linearity of the Relationship Between Movement Costs and Intervening Distance. When we examine the linearity or nonlinearity of the relationship between movement costs in strictly monetary terms and the distance traveled, the commonest form of relationship is one which is convex upwards as in Figure 3-6a. For most transportation media, longer movements per unit distance are cheaper than shorter movements. Thus, if we have

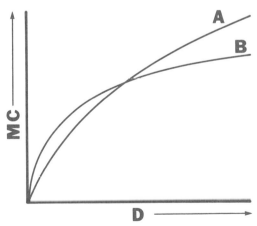

FIGURE 3-7. Changing forms of movement cost-distance relationships: the form of a relationship often differs from one circumstance to another; thus relationships *A* and *B* might represent different transportation media or the relationships existing at different points in time.

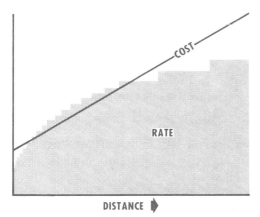

FIGURE 3-9. The typical relationship of distance of movement to transport rate and transportation cost, respectively. Note that the transportation rate line (cost to consumer of transportation services) tends to be convex upwards while the transportation cost line (cost to producer of transportation services) tends to be linear. For purposes of clear exposition, the regularity and convexity of the rate curve have been exaggerated

the price per mile for longer distances as opposed to that for shorter distances.

Frequently superimposed upon such a taper, however, and injecting another complicating element into the linearity of the relationship of movement costs and distance is a certain zonation specified in the prices set by carrier agencies, be they trucking firms or railroad companies. While movement rates in general increase with distance (though at a decreasing rate), the increase is not continuous either within a nation or between nations. Within a nation, movement rates tend to be stepped as in Figure 3-9, with the steps becoming of greater extent as the distance moved increases. This simplification of rates by the grouping of points of origin and destination into zones means that a uniform rate may apply over a considerable variation in distance. Thus in the diagram shown in Figure 3-10, it is as cheap to ship mineral water from Vichy to place Y as it is to

three points in space X, Y, Z and the mileage between X and Y is the same as that between Y and Z, the cost of moving from X to Y will be more than half the cost of movement from X to Z. This phenomenon results from the fact that certain expenses incurred by a transportation agency, such as the costs of handling at terminal points, are independent of the length of haul. It also results from the varying competitive capabilities of different movement media over different lengths of haul—a problem we shall consider shortly. For the time being, the most important point is:

▶ *For most transportation media there is a tapering off of movement costs with increasing distance moved.*

Even if the customary rate schedules do not exhibit such a taper, the tendency for special rates to be confined to longer-distance trips (charter flights, special night fares) frequently leads to a reduction in

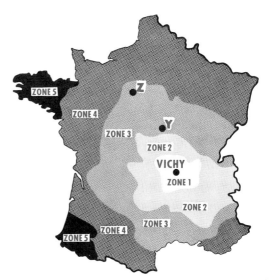

FIGURE 3-10. Movement cost zones for the shipment of Vichy water within France. Movement costs increase with distance from Vichy but are the same within a given zone; the cost of movement to Y, therefore, is the same as the cost of movement to Z.

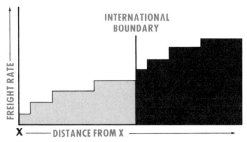

FIGURE 3-11. The impact of international boundaries on the tapering progression of freight rates with distance. Note how the progression recommences with movement across the international boundary.

place Z. Clearly these considerations apply to the case of telephone calls where long-distance rates are grouped by distance zone with the zones becoming of increasing width with distance from the origin of the call.

Between nations an analogous zonation applies, though in this case the zones are nations themselves rather than zones imposed by the transportation company. In the absence of internation agreements on freight rates, the usual structure is one in which the tapering off of freight rates with distance has to be set at zero miles again when an international border is crossed. The type of pricing situation involved is illuminated in Figure 3-11. A similar structure applies to the movement of information by telephone calls and mail and, in addition to the usual quotas and tariffs imposed on international commerce, is a considerable impediment to movement across political boundaries.

The Variable Form of the Relationship between Movement Costs and Intervening Distance. A major consideration in deciding how to consign goods or passengers to a specific destination is the fact that the tapering off of movement costs with distance discussed above varies from one transportation medium to another. In general, the taper is more

marked in those media which incur heavy handling costs at points of origin and destination. A railroad, for example, must collect the freight on a truck, transport it to the railroad, unload it onto a flatcar, move it to its railroad destination, unload it again, and then transfer it by truck to its ultimate destination. By comparison, the handling costs incurred by a trucking company are minimal.

The variations in the costs incurred by the different carrying media with increasing distance moved, as opposed to the costs eventually incurred by the customer in the form of price are shown in Figure 3-12. Clearly, over a short distance, truck transportation of commodities is cheap, and this is reflected in the prices offered to the customer. For longer distances, however, railroad transportation is cheaper per unit of distance

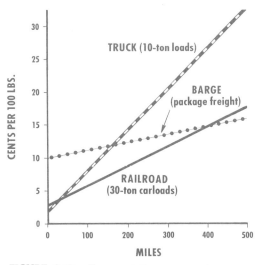

FIGURE 3-12. Transportation agency transportation costs as a function of distance for different media; these cost estimates refer to movements of commodities in the lower Mississippi Valley, 1939 to 1940. Note how truck transport has cheaper costs over shorter distances while barge transportation is cheaper over the longer distances. Note also that the costs are transportation agency costs; the line relating distance moved to the rate charged to the consumer tends to be convex upwards (see Figure 3-9) rather than linear as above.

traveled; for still longer distances water transportation comes into its own. In a sense, therefore, this cost structure preserves a certain complementarity among the different media, with the trucking companies feeding goods over short distances to railheads where they will be transferred over longer distances for possible oceanic shipment overseas or to another point in the nation (for example, from the east coast of the United States to the west coast by Panama).

An important question concerns why these *linear* relationships between *movement cost incurred by carrier* and *intervening distance* are converted into a *convex upwards taper* relating *distances of movement and the price charged to the user of transportation services*. In this context consider the competitive situations of the media: the trucker is most threatened by railroad competition at distances greater than 35 to 40 miles (see Figure 3-12). He is least threatened over the

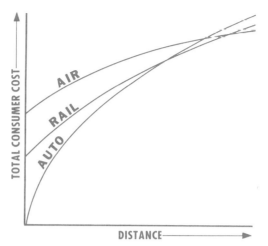

FIGURE 3-14.   Hypothetical cost–distance relationships for interurban passenger transportation; if we enlarge our concept of costs-to-consumer to include not only actual monetary cost, but also such incidentals as meals and overnight lodging plus opportunity costs, these relationships appear plausible. In Europe the cutoff point between railroad and air transportation seems to be at about 300 miles.

shorter distances. There is an incentive for the trucker therefore to charge higher prices for those short and medium distances where he will get the freight anyway and lower his prices where the railroad offers stiff competition. Similar considerations apply to the other media, and they produce the types of relationship between the different media shown in Figure 3-13. The general effect is to provide complementarities among the different commodity-carrying media.

If we now enlarge our concept of cost, we can observe similar complementarities for passenger movement both between cities and within cities. Thus, if we allow total movement cost to equal the sum of actual monetary costs, opportunity costs, incidental costs (meals and lodging), and such inconvenience costs as having to sleep on a train, the relationships for interurban passenger movement by different media shown in Figure 3-14, seem feasible.

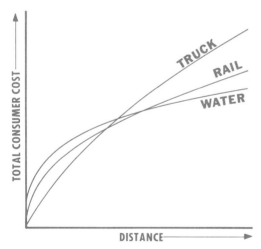

FIGURE 3-13.   The competitive relationships of commodity-carrying transportation media. For clarity, the stepping of the cost curves has been eliminated. Note that in terms of rates offered to the consumer of transportation services, truck transportation has the advantage over shorter distances with water transportation being most competitive at longer distances and rail transportation at intermediate distances.

Thus the automobile seems the cheapest method of movement over short distances, the railroad seems cheapest over longer distances, and air carriers provide least expensive transport over the longest distances. In the U.S. the distances over which railroad transportation is dominant seem to be shrinking as railroad services are withdrawn, thus increasing the opportunity costs and inconvenience costs of railroad transportation and favoring either the automobile or the airplane. In Britain, France, and Germany the large numbers of people still without cars and the relatively short distances involved in passenger movement have conspired to preserve a healthy monopoly for railroads over these intermediate distances; consequently, service is much more frequent between comparable pairs of cities than in the United States. Nevertheless, the spread of the automobile to an increasing number of families has led to an erosion of the lower bounds of economical distances for rail transportation so that many of the shorter lines have been closed down since 1945. We will return to this topic at greater length when we consider the geographical evolution of transportation networks.

Turning to the intraurban level of transportation, we find that the competition is largely between the automobile or bus and the railroad, with the railroad being confined to longer-distance movements. Thus larger cities tend to be characterized by a greater use of mass transportation facilities since such urban agglomerations cover wider areas, often involving longer journeys to work and to shopping areas. As Table 3-2 shows, it is in the more populous cities that mass transportation is important; in the American context mass transportation is largely rail service.

Thus far in our discussion of the form of the relationship between movement costs and the distance moved, we have confined ourselves to the effect of the *mode of movement.* Additional factors affecting the relationship between movement costs and the distance of movement, and hence affecting locational decisions, include the volume being moved and the direction in which commodities or passengers are being moved.

The volume moved is important because, in general, it is cheaper for the transportation company to transport large volumes of a commodity per unit distance than to transport small volumes. Handling costs per unit commodity are reduced and such cost reductions are reflected in the prices charged to the consumer. An interesting case involving

TABLE 3-2.   Urban Size in the United States and the Mode of Travel to Work: 1960. Figures are percentages; mass transit is much more common as a means of transportation in larger cities than in smaller cities.

Standard metropolitan area (population)	Private automobile or car pool*		Mass transportation	
	Central city	Suburbs	Central city	Suburbs
Over 1,000,000	48	76	39	12
500,000–1,000,000	68	78	18	6
300,000–500,000	70	80	15	4
250,000–300,000	72	76	13	4
200,000–250,000	72	75	11	3
Under 100,000	76	64	6	3

* The balance other than private automobile, car pool, and public transportation represents ''walked to work,'' ''worked at home,'' and ''other.''

volume flow over long distances concerns the California fruit farmer. Though at a disadvantage relative to the Florida fruit farmer in terms of access to the markets of the northeastern United States, the California fruit farmer is able to obtain a lower freight rate by joining a cooperative, which can offer bulk shipments to the railroads and obtain lower freight rates in return. Another example of volume economics in movement costs is the car pool. The theories expounded thus far suggest that car pools would be more common for longer trips (where the costs of single-passenger automobile transportation tend to be prohibitively expensive) than for short distances.

Directionally, movement prices of-fered by a carrier are often biased so that movement is cheaper in one direction than in another. In commodity-flow parlance, this is often referred to as a *backhauling economy;* it is a response to a frequently encountered situation in which freight or passengers are plentiful in one direction, but not in the other. It is not much more expensive to transport full trucks or cars or barges or airplanes than empty ones; hence a low movement rate may be offered as an incentive to movement in a direction in which a high degree of spare capacity exists. Apparently backhaul economics has been important in the establishment of iron and steel plants at such Great Lake locations as Duluth. Close to the iron-ore

FIGURE 3-15. Flows of coal and iron ore in the Great Lakes Region and the location of Duluth. An iron and steel industry has been established at Duluth due to the accessibility of the iron ore of upper Minnesota together with a low freight rate due to backhaul economies on coal from Pennsylvania and Kentucky moving through such lake ports as Erie. Iron and steel is very important at points where coal moving by land meets iron ore moving by water (i.e., the point of break-of-bulk or of transshipment as at Gary, Chicago, and Cleveland).

fields from which iron ore was shipped to the steel centers of Pittsburgh, Cleveland, and Detroit, Duluth was able to benefit from the empty barges returning to the iron-ore fields by obtaining a low price quotation on coal from West Virginia and Western Pennsylvania (see Figure 3-15).

The Monotonicity of the Relationship between Movement Costs and Intervening Distance. Thus far we have considered cases in which the transportation cost incurred by the consumer is greater over longer distances than over shorter distances. Such may not always be the case, however. In order to understand why movement costs may, under certain circumstances, actually decrease with increasing distance moved, consider the case of a land mass surrounded by ocean (see Figure 3-16). The figure shows two port cities X and Y and two interior cities A and B. Let there be a railroad line from X to Y via A and B and an oceanic shipping service between X and Y. Now consider the transportation of some commodity from Y to B and the transpor-

tation of some commodity from Y to X. Ordinarily we would expect the price of movement (P) from Y to X ($P_{Y \to X}$) to be greater than that for the trip from Y to B ($P_{Y \to B}$). We would also expect the price $P_{Y \to A}$ to be greater than the price $P_{Y \to B}$. However, there is a strong intermodal competitive situation involved here in that goods can be transported from Y to X by ocean as well as by land. Over longer distances water transportation is increasingly competitive with rail transportation. In order to attract traffic for the route from Y to X, therefore, the railroad company may have to lower its prices to slightly below the price for water transportation between Y and X. For the trip from Y to B, however, the railroad company is relatively sheltered from competition because it would be much more costly to transport a commodity from Y to X by water and thence to B by rail. The railroad company therefore is in a position where monopoly leads to quotation of a higher price for $P_{Y \to B}$ and where competition leads to a lower price for $P_{Y \to X}$.

An outstanding example of this type of situation prevails in the North American continent where railroad shippers of goods from the East Coast to West Coast cities, such as San Francisco, Seattle, and Vancouver, have to confront the possibility of competition of many types of freight with water transportation of those freights through the Panama Canal. The result is that railroad freight rates from, say, New York City to, for example, Reno or Phoenix or Salt Lake City are frequently higher than railroad freight rates to such cities as Seattle and Los Angeles. In Canada, similarly, it has been shown that the transportation of some types of freight from the East Coast port city of Montreal to the inland center of Calgary (2240 miles) costs one-third more than what it costs to transport the same type of freight to the West Coast

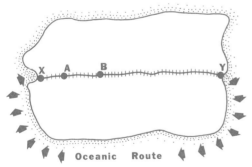

FIGURE 3-16. A possible context for freight rates that are nonmonotonic with distance: oceanic transportation between X and Y keeps the railroad freight rate down between the same two places and also between places such as A, which are accessible from Y. B, on the other hand, is not so accessible from Y, and it is therefore likely that the greater monopoly position of the railroad will allow it to charge a higher freight rate for movements from Y to B than from Y to A or from Y to X.

port city of Vancouver which is 640 miles further on!

This type of nonmonotonicity in the relationship between movement distance and movement costs is not a well-researched problem, but it raises many interesting questions. To what extent are trucking freight rates higher in areas distant from railroad competition? How does this affect the cost of transportation in underdeveloped nations which frequently have much better-developed systems of highway transportation than of railroad transportation? The locational implications of this type of nonmonotonicity are also impressive: it gives, for example, an additional impetus to that concentration of economic activity in maritime locations which is so marked around the shores of the Atlantic and Pacific Oceans.

In summary, what is clear from these notions of the factors affecting the cost of movement of commodities, people, and information is that the space in which individuals move cannot be regarded simply in terms of distance. Locations are separated by movement costs that are not necessarily proportional to distance in terms of miles. Rather, geographical spaces are distorted by movement cost considerations which are more potent determinants of locational pattern than space itself. Man's locational decisions are made not in terms of the spatial correlates of interaction—distance moved, direction in which movement occurs, etc.—but in terms of the real costs of spatial interaction.

LOCATIONAL STRUCTURES

The final consideration in explaining movement is that of the locational context—the locational pattern of the movement opportunities available to the mover for any particular purpose. We have already examined the *density of movement opportunities* as a critical con-

trol of the distances over which movements take place. Thus, shopping trips are, on the average, lengthier the further west we go in the United States because of the greater distances separating the towns at which shopping facilities are available.

The density of movement opportunities, however, is by no means the only aspect of locational structure that is important for movement patterns. There is also the problem of *sectoral biases* in the density of movement opportunities. Thus for a suburban dweller movement opportunities are concentrated in the direction of the central business district, and this concentration is reflected in the directions of movements undertaken by suburbanites.

A second consideration relevant to our discussion of the role of locational structure in controlling movement patterns is the *functionality of locational structure.* The locational structure of employment opportunities faced by the musician is very different from that faced by the semiskilled worker. For the latter, opportunities are widely distributed across the land and we would therefore expect the migration distances of semiskilled workers to be relatively short compared with those of musicians, for whom employment opportunities are concentrated in a few major metropolitan centers. Likewise, for the person who prefers big city lights to a buccolic small town existence, migration distances will tend to be relatively large in magnitude. Again life-cycle status seems to be a potent predictor of the appropriate locational structure of opportunities confronting the mover. If one considers recreational trips, for instance, a younger person is likely to be oriented towards the thickly distributed ice-cream stands and drive-in movie locations, while the older person must move farther to his theatres and restaurants.

CONCLUSIONS AND SUMMARY

This chapter has attempted to provide an explanation for a wide variety of movement patterns. Some of these—for instance, distance bias, direction bias, and spheres of influence—were identified in Chapter Two.

Explanation of such geographical patterns of movement has been in terms of three factors: the *attractiveness* of locations for a specific purpose; the *cost of moving* to those different locations; and the *locational arrangement* of those more or less attractive locations. We have termed the set of attractive locations the *movement opportunities.*

For a place to be *attractive* it must have something of *value* to the instigator of the movement. Students of different types of movement have developed their own terms for the concept of attractiveness: students of commodity movements tend to think in terms of *complementarity*, rather than attractiveness, while students of migration use the concept of *place utility.*

Movement costs are important because they can detract from the value of the item—a retail good, a pleasant vacation, or a job obtained at the attractive location. An important concept here is that of *transferability*, usually applied to commodity flows: if the cost of getting to a location to consume a net reward or transferring the net reward available at a location to your location in order to consume it is greater than the value of the net reward, then the net reward is not transferable. Also associated with this concept is that of *trade-off* between attractiveness and movement costs by which less attractive opportunities incurring lower movement costs are substituted for more attractive opportunities associated with higher costs of movement.

Movement costs may not only be *monetary*, however. We can also think in terms of such components of movement cost as *opportunity* cost—the cost of foregoing rewarding activities when moving. The concept of movement costs is frequently referred to as the *friction of distance* factor on the assumption that movement costs will be lower to closer, less distant movement opportunities. This assumption is not completely valid because the relationship between geographical distance and movement cost is rather complex. In particular, we have shown how freight rates per unit distance frequently decrease with increasing distance moved; how freight rates are often grouped into zones; how rates may differ in one direction as compared with the reverse direction; and how under certain circumstances movement costs may actually increase with increasing distance. *Men move in a movement cost space, therefore, which is not the same as the geographical space defined purely in terms of distances.*

CHAPTER FOUR

Two Case Studies of Movement: Commodity Flow and Migration

INTRODUCTION

In the last chapter we set forth a simple framework for understanding the geographical configurations of movement patterns: the application of the two criteria of attractiveness and movement costs in a locational structure of movement opportunities. It is the purpose of this chapter to apply these ideas to an interpretation of two sets of movements—commodity flows and migration. The initial section considers an important commodity movement: world ocean trade patterns in iron ore, a basic raw material. The second section takes a broad look at migration and some of the components of attractiveness and movement cost which have affected specific migrations.

IRON–ORE FLOWS

Figure 4-1 presents major oceanic movements of iron ore between nations in 1965. A cursory inspection of the map suggests two things, both of which link up with what we have been saying about the factors underlying movement: (1) there appears to be a least-effort mechanism at work, suggesting that movement costs have been important factors in producing the pattern; (2) flows occur largely from less-developed to more-developed nations, suggesting a possible concomitant of complementarity.

With regard to least-effort movement cost considerations, it is evident that the importing nations tend to obtain their iron ore from closer locations rather than from those farther away. Japan's sources, for example, are confined to Southeast Asia and to the west coast of Latin America with India and Malaysia particularly prominent; the United Kingdom has even shorter hauls for its iron-ore imports from Sweden, West Africa, and North Africa; while the United States obtains most of its foreign iron-ore needs from adjacent Labrador and Venezuela.

Complementarity is also apparent. Flows tend to be *from* nations having large iron-ore production relative to their production of iron and steel. Some underdeveloped nations like Chile, Brazil, Venezuela, and Algeria have only small domestic iron and steel industries. West Africa and Malaysia have virtually no modern iron and steel industry at all. On the other hand, flows tend to be *towards* nations that produce a large amount of iron and steel relative to their iron-ore production. For a number of years, for instance, the United States iron and steel industry has been concerned about the declining quality of the iron ores from its major domestic source, the Mesabi range of upper Minnesota. It is

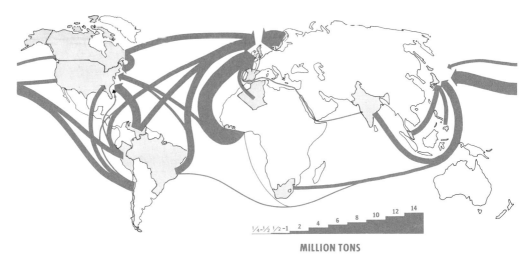

MILLION TONS

FIGURE 4-1. Oceanic movements of iron ore between nations, 1965. The movement pattern is not random—nations tend to draw their iron ore from nearer sources rather than from more distant sources; most movements are from less developed areas such as West Africa, Latin America, and Southeast Asia to more developed areas such as Japan, the United States, and Western Europe. Since 1965 there have been some important changes, notably a large increase in Japanese imports of iron ore from Australia.

not surprising, therefore, to learn that American companies have been instrumental in the development of iron-ore extraction in Venezuela and Labrador. Japan is another case in point: she has virtually no iron ore of her own but needs a large iron and steel industry to support the manufacture of her myriad metal products; Japan has recently been prominent in the development of new iron-ore reserves in North Australia. Britain and Germany also must import most of the iron ore for their large iron and steel industries.

While revealing something of the *static* or *cross-sectional* locational patterns of oceanic iron-ore movement, however, the map fails to expose the *dynamics* of those movements. Specifically it fails to show that, according to Manners, a student of these flow patterns, "in recent years . . . the average length of iron-ore haul for most iron and steel producers in the world has increased dramatically; for West Germany it is now about 3,000 miles, for Japan nearly 7,000; and some ores are today transported over 12,000

miles to their markets. Between 1950 and 1965 oceanic iron-ore traffic increased from about 64,000 to 527,000 million ton-miles." In 1950, moreover, there were no trans-Pacific flows of the sort shown on the map for 1965; the flows from West Africa were of very minor importance and there were no movements between Latin America and northwest Europe like those that exist today.

The reasons for this geographical revolution are the changing attractiveness of ore sources and the decline in movement costs per ton-mile. With reference to the former, there has been an increasing substitution of higher-grade (i.e., higher value) iron ores for the lower-grade ores; this has frequently implied the substitution of more distant ore sources for closer sources, the increased attractiveness of the new ore sources probably compensating for the necessarily increased and more costly movements of the ore carriers.

The most significant factor in the lengthening of the movements, however, has been a drastic lowering of ocean freight rates on iron ore. To take a specific instance, in 1958 it cost about $5.80 to transport iron ore from the West African port of Monrovia to the iron and steel plant at Sparrows Point near Baltimore. By 1966 this cost had fallen to about $2.00 per ton. The reasons for such a steep decline in movement costs over such a short period of time can be traced to two factors: (1) modal innovation and (2) backhauling economies.

The major modal innovation in transporting iron ore by ocean has been the advent of the giant ore carrier. The size of the ocean-going vessels which carry iron ore has increased markedly over the last 15 to 20 years. In the early part of the 1950s most iron ore was carried in small tramp steamers; their general-purpose character made them relatively inefficient in handling any one particular freight, such as iron-ore. Their small size also increased operating costs per ton of freight compared with larger vessels. In the 1960s large carriers of 50,000 to 60,000 dead weight tons specifically designed to carry iron ore appeared, resulting in considerable economies in the costs of movement. Thus, as Figure 4-2 shows, for a vessel of 5,000 dead weight tons the cost of transporting iron ore 2000 miles is about $3.00; while with a vessel of 65,000 dead weight tons the cost would be about $0.84. Over long routes the savings are even more dramatic. Such modal innovation has had similar effects in the transportation of other commodities; the introduction of bulk oil carriers, for instance, allows oil companies to transport oil from the Persian Gulf around the Cape of Good Hope more cheaply than they could transport it in a vessel small enough to pass through the Suez Canal.

Whenever possible, backhauling economies are also used to reduce movement costs. A major problem with the transportation of bulk commodities such as iron ore is that frequently the ship must

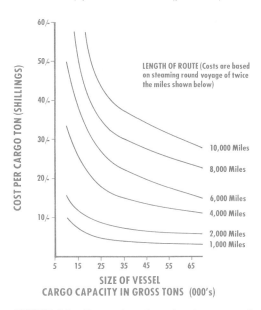

OCEAN BULK TRANSPORT COST
(by size of vessel and length of route)

LENGTH OF ROUTE (Costs are based on steaming round voyage of twice the miles shown below)

10,000 Miles
8,000 Miles
6,000 Miles
4,000 Miles
2,000 Miles
1,000 Miles

COST PER CARGO TON (SHILLINGS)

SIZE OF VESSEL
CARGO CAPACITY IN GROSS TONS (000's)

FIGURE 4-2. Economies of moving iron ore and size of cargo vessel: as vessel size increases movement cost per ton declines over a given distance. The economies realized are much greater for longer distance movements so that the giant ore carrier has allowed nations to obtain iron ore from increasingly far afield. N.B. One shilling = 13¢.

return in ballast because of the absence of suitable return cargo. There are some cases, however, in which excess capacity has been avoided; the ore vessels bringing iron ore from Venezuela to the northeast of the United States, for example, often return with a load of coal for the embryonic iron and steel industry in eastern Venezuela. There have also been triangular movements which have allowed a curtailment of excess capacity; thus ore vessels have shipped iron ore from Liberia to the northeast coast of the United States, then taken on a load of coal for western Europe, and finally shipped in ballast from western Europe to Liberia for another load of iron ore.

Nevertheless, excess capacity has been a critical problem in the shipping industry. The major source of reduced movement costs, therefore, combines modal innovation and backhauling economies by introducing more versatile vessels allowing greater use of spare capacity. For example, vessels have been constructed to carry both ore and oil and this has permitted the eradication of much spare capacity either in the form of a simple return voyage or in the form of a more complex triangular trade pattern.

MIGRATION

The object of this section is to apply our explanatory schema to an important class of human movements—migrations. An initial survey of migrations, however, suggests that this may be easier said than done. In particular, migrations differ both in their *geographical scale* and in their *permanence,* and a major problem is developing a theory that says something of generality about these diverse movements.

In terms of *geographical scale,* students of migration have tended to classify movements into three types: (1) intra-urban migrations, or those that originate and terminate within the boundaries of a given city; (2) intranational migration, or movements from one part of a nation to another part of the same nation; and (3) internation migrations, or movements between nations.

A second major dimension along which we can classify migrations is one describing their permanence. In the developed nations, most job-oriented migrations tend to be permanent: the migrants undertake them intending to stay at the destination for the foreseeable future and not to return to the point of origin. Migration within or from underdeveloped nations, however, is frequently of a more temporary sort in which the migrant plans to return home after a certain planned period of work

in the destination area. Such migrants frequently move without their families and often the temporary migrant's income is seen as a means of supplementing income from a plot of land cultivated in his absence by his wife and family. Such more or less temporary migrations include the annual movements of Mexicans into Texas and California; the movements of Turks and Portuguese into Germany and France; and the long-distance movement of Africans from their tribal territories to the mining areas of South Africa, Zambia, and the Congo.

Given such a range of different types of migration, it is clearly quite a challenge to develop a theory applicable to all types. From our schema for explaining the geographical pattern of movement, we know which factors are important, but how important are they at different geographical scales? Is it likely, for example, that movement costs weigh as significantly in intra-urban migration decisions as they do in intranational decisions?

A second problem in considering migrations is the interrelationship among the different types of movement. No migration can be regarded as purely intranational, for example. If a city is a destination, the migrant has to undergo the same problem as the intra-urban migrant of choosing a destination within the city as well as the problem of selecting one area of the nation as opposed to some other area of the nation. Migration therefore involves a hierarchy of decisions, each successive stage of the hierarchy involving a search within an area of smaller geographical scale. There are strong relationships, therefore, between migrations at different geographical scales.

It is probable that there are also relationships between migrations of differing permanence. Temporary migration, for instance, is often an antecedent of a more permanent migration. It permits a degree of assimilation into the host population and some familiarity with the area, both of which are important in easing the pain of migration. There must be many students, for example, who undertake temporary migrations between home area and university and eventually migrate permanently to the vicinity of the university city.

Clearly migration is a complex phenomenon with multiple manifestations. Our approach here is to start with our schema as a point of departure. We will take the factors of place utility, movement cost, and locational structure in turn and examine their relevance for the migration decision. We will then discuss the relative importance of the various factors for migrations at different scales and for migrations of varying permanence.

PLACE UTILITY

For a person considering migration, all possible destinations and his present location fall along a range of attractiveness. Presumably his present loca-

tion falls toward the unattractive end of that range, possibly there is a lack of job opportunities, or marriage opportunities. Of the places that can satisfy his needs, he will perceive some locations as likely to satisfy them to a greater degree than others; these locations therefore will be more attractive and hence more *valued*.

The concept of attractiveness or place utility for migrants is clearly made up of several different things. What looks attractive to one migrant may not be attractive to another. At least five components of place utility can be identified: economic opportunity, amenity, ethnic-religious composition, language, and housing. Each will be discussed in turn. We shall then turn to a consideration of the varying importance of these components according to life-cycle status and income.

Economic Opportunity. Surveys of migrants suggest that factors related to economic opportunity comprise the single most important group of factors accounting for migratory destinations. Table 4-1, for example, presents data on reasons for

TABLE 4-1.   Migrants' reasons for moving within France; note the significance of employment-related reasons.

Migrants' Statements of Reasons for Moving

	Paris Region %	Provincial France %
1. Employment considerations of which:	56	50
promotion (within firms)	12	13
better prospects	17	*
higher wages	12	*
unemployed	2	*
2. Studies and training	6	*
3. Retirement	—	6
4. Personal, family, housing	27	40
5. Psychological reasons	8	*
6. Other reasons	3	10
	—	—
	100 (1,256)	106† (1,227)

* Information not available.
† Total is over 100 due to multiple replies.

moving in France: for both the Paris region and provincial France, employment-related reasons account for at least half of all the reasons given.

Employment opportunity factors also characterize larger-scale migrations, such as those from poorer Mexico to wealthier United States, from Algeria to France, from the West Indies to Britain, and from Turkey to West Germany. It also explains some interesting facets of the contemporary geography of ethnic minorities in the United States. One of these is the marked absence of southern European and eastern European elements in the South: there are few Greeks, Italians, Poles, or Hungarians in Atlanta, New Orleans, Dallas, or Birmingham, Alabama. The reason for the overwhelmingly Anglo-Saxon composition of the Southern white population resides in the timing of migrations and the changing geography of economic opportunity in

the United States. Most of the eastern and southern European movements occurred well after the Civil War and terminated about the end of the First World War. During this period the South hit the nadir of its economic fortunes, employment stagnated, and jobs could be obtained only in the burgeoning cities of the Midwest and Northeast.

More rigorous tabulations and graphs of migration data confirm the significance of economic opportunity factors. Figure 4-3*a*, for instance, relates the net in-migration to various areas of France to the mean incomes prevailing in those areas. The Paris region is easily the area with the highest in-migration rate; it is also by far the wealthiest area. Also significant as destinations of migration are other wealthy areas of northern and eastern France such as the Rhône-Alpes region, with the city of Lyons at its heart, and the Provence region, with the busy

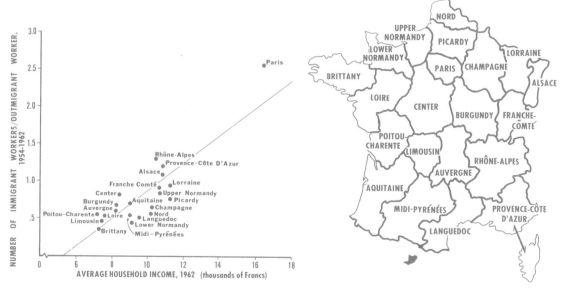

FIGURE 4-3. (*a*) Migration and regional income levels in France (see Figure 4-3*b* for locations of the areas involved); note how amenity-rich areas such as Paris, Rhône-Alpes, and Provence–Côte d'Azur attract more in-migrants relative to out-migrants than one would expect on the basis of income differences. The line indicates the average position of the points on the graph and is a "least squares" line. (*b*) The economic regions of France: these are the same regions as are indicated on the graph in Figure 4-3*a*.

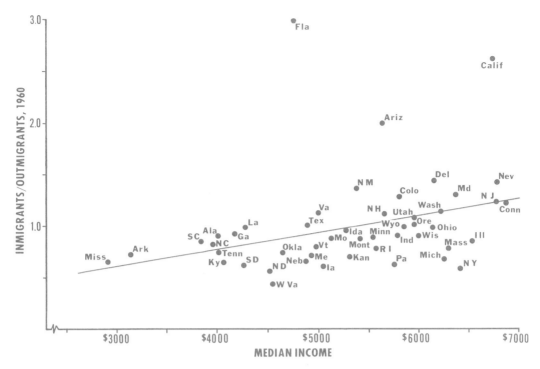

FIGURE 4-4. Migration and state median income for the United States, 1960. In general, states that are wealthier have larger numbers of in-migrants per out-migrant; there are some surprises, though, such as New York, Michigan, and Pennsylvania. Note also how amenity-rich states such as Arizona, California, and Florida have higher rates of in-migrants per out-migrant than expected on the basis of median income. The line is a "least squares" line.

port city of Marseilles and the concentrations of aristocratic wealth on the French Riviera. Poorer areas of France in the west and the southwest have tended to be net losers of population; this has been especially true of Limousin, the poorest of the French regions, and also of Brittany.

A similar though possibly less close relationship is exhibited for the states of the United States in Figure 4-4. Wealthier states such as California, Connecticut, Washington, and New Jersey show fairly high net in-migration rates; poorer states, such as those of the South and of the Great Plains, show low net rates of in-migration or even a net out-migration.

Finally, in this array of evidence on the relationship between economic opportu-

nity and migration, consider the maps shown in Figures 4-5 and 4-6. Figure 4-5 plots the distribution of average labor demand between 1951 and 1961 across various areas of the United Kingdom. Figure 4-6 plots the current locations of groups of recent in-migrants—West Indians, Indians, and Pakistanis—across those same areas. The similarities of these maps are quite striking. There seems to have been a clear tendency for the recent in-migrants to seek out those areas in London and the Midlands which have more abundant job opportunities and to neglect areas where unemployment has been relatively high—areas such as Wales, the north of England, and Scotland, in particular.

Of course one may ask whether income levels and unemployment rates can

FIGURE 4-5. Regional demand for labor in the United Kingdom, based on regional unemployment and unfilled adult vacancies tables 1955–1961. Note the relatively strong demand for labor in southern England and in the Midlands; Wales, Scotland, and northern England tend to have relatively high unemployment rates.

both be regarded as adequate measures of the same thing—employment opportunities. They both certainly seem to be a function of *economic opportunity*. Economic growth in a particular area, whether it is a state or a region, tends to put pressure on existing labor resources which forces unemployment down and wages up.

One of the consequences of such economic-opportunity-oriented migration is that it frequently fills jobs that economic growth has made unattractive to residents. Therefore much of the West Indian and Irish migration into the London area has gone into the lower-paid occupations of public transport and nursing which have been vacated by individuals moving into the growth industries of electronics and engineering with their higher rates of remuneration. In the case of the West Indians, of course, job discrimination has provided forces in the same direction.

Amenity. Closer inspection of the graphs in the last section suggests further ingredients of the concept of place utility. Figure 4-3*a*, for example, suggests that in France such areas as Rhône-Alpes and Provence have rather higher rates of in-migration than we would expect from their income levels. A line has been drawn in on the graph to define the average location of points: places above the line have higher rates of in-migration than expected on the basis of their average income characteristics, while places below the line have lower rates of in-migration; this latter condition applies to Languedoc and Champagne.

A closer scrutiny of the United States graph reveals a similar situation: some states such as California, Florida, Texas, Colorado, New Mexico, and Arizona have higher rates of in-migration than

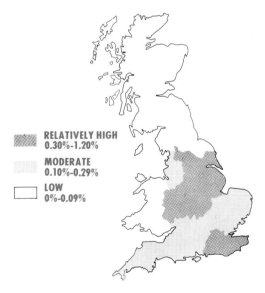

FIGURE 4-6. Percent of British population that is West Indian, Indian, or Pakistani, 1961; these ethnic groups are relatively recent immigrants and, comparing this figure with Figure 4-5, seem to have been strongly attracted towards areas of labor deficit. As a consequence, Wales, Scotland, and northern England have been relatively free of the racial conflicts that have affected such Midland towns as Wolverhampton and Smethwick.

expected while such states as North Dakota, South Dakota, Nebraska, and West Virginia have lower rates. If one considers those areas which have higher rates than expected in France and in the United States from the viewpoint of what they have in common that other areas lack, a major conclusion is that they have certain *amenity advantages.* California, Florida, Provence, Arizona, and New Mexico are all areas of relative warmth in the climatic contexts of the two nations and for this reason are pleasant to live in. Some of the areas have other amenity advantages in addition: for example, ocean in Florida, Provence, and California and mountains in Colorado and Arizona. In contradistinction, such areas as North Dakota, South Dakota, and Nebraska are not only topographically dull; in winter they are also relatively cold, and therefore not very pleasant to live in.

Clearly such natural amenities are not the only type of leisure-time amenity to which men are attracted. There are also man-made cultural amenities such as museums, art galleries, symphony orchestras, shopping facilities, educational facilities, and theaters; these tend to show a strong direct relationship to urban size. Little wonder, therefore, that population tends to be increasingly concentrated in larger cities so that the major cities take an increasingly large share of national population in both the United States, Britain, and France (see Table 4-2).

Natural amenities are attractive not only to migrants; they are also attractive to the entrepreneurs who create economic opportunities for migrants. The warm climate of Texas or California offers a low heating bill—an important consideration for industries like the aircraft industry which consume large amounts of floor space. They also offer relatively cloud-free skies significant for aerospace industries, and often the envi-

TABLE 4-2. Urban size and concentration of the urban population in France 1851–1962. Columns sum to 100%.

Urban size class	1851	1901	1954	1962
Less than 20,000 inhabitants	62.2	41.4	32.6	26.8
20,000–50,000	13.5	15.8	14.9	13.4
50,000–100,000	6.1	9.3	8.0	8.3
100,000–200,000	6.6	7.6	9.2	10.4
Over 200,000	. . .	8.8	15.0	19.3
Paris agglomeration	11.5	17.0	20.1	21.8

ronment of low humidity required by many of the newer electronics industries. The 19th-century growth industries of iron and steel would have found disadvantages in such locations because they lack raw materials, but this is not true of the mid-20th-century growth industries of aerospace and electronics.

Such arguments also apply to those locations rich in man-made amenities. Those large cities with an abundance of cultural amenities also offer big advantages for the location of industries: superior transportation facilities, access to a diverse and large labor force, access to complementary industries within the metropolitan area are but some of the advantages to industry which the large city offers.

It is possible, therefore, that for many individuals the effect of amenity is spurious. They are attracted by job opportunities and only later discover the amenity advantages. For still others, however, the causal sequence may be rather different: they are initially attracted by the bright lights of the big city or by the sun of California and move in the hope of obtaining a job there. Given the range of economic opportunity available in such environments permanent residence will ensue, but the initial stimulus to movement was the amenity factor.

Ethnic-Religious Composition. A phenomenon frequently encountered in the changing locational patterns of minority ethnic or religious groups is that their areas of initial settlement seem to grow by accretion. There is a tendency, for example, for initial areas of Pakistani settlement in Britain to be attractive to later Pakistani in-migrants. In the United States the Jewish minority is concentrated in about six major metropolitan centers and within these centers there is further concentration: Brooklyn and White Plains in New York City, Shaker Heights in Cleveland, Skokie in Chicago, etc. In Britain there is a similar concentration of the country's 500,000 Jews in the three cities of London, Manchester, and Leeds. This type of clustering phenomenon is especially prevalent where the ethnic or religious group is socially or culturally very different from the host society. It suggests that the area of initial settlement is attractive for coping with this relatively alien social or cultural environment.

For the person of minority ethnic or religious background the cluster of people of similar background performs at least three important functions: social, political, and cultural. Socially the group affords an instrument of assimilation into the host society: it offers channels by which housing and jobs can be obtained in the alien society. Frequently the co-ethnic will be in a position to refer the new migrant to his foreman for a job or to a particular lodging house that does not discriminate against the ethnic group in question. The ethnic group will also be able to provide the migrant with guidance on questions of personal conduct that will help him to move less painfully in the host society. Some sort of basic language instruction may also be available.

The second function is political. Ethnic and/or religious minorities in an alien environment frequently arouse strong political forces in opposition to them and

for self-defense the minority has to develop its own political apparatus. This serves as a defense for the migrant in what has often become a hostile environment. Every cluster of Indians in Britain, for example, has some sort of organization for coping with the political pressures of the white community or for coping politically with the nonpolitical pressures of the whites. Clustering may also provide the minority with representation in local representative groups, whereas a scattering of the group throughout a larger area would not insure a majority in any one electoral subdivision of the city.

And finally there is the cultural function of the ethnic and/or religious cluster. By clustering together a group can live much as it did in places where it was in the majority: the individual migrant will be able to marry group members and he will be able to speak his native language. Numbers also mean that group-specific institutions can be provided where they would not be economical if the size of the group was smaller—ethnic restaurants, minority churches, ethnic schools, and ethnic cinemas are cases in point. Some cinemas in highly Indian cities in Britain, for example, show Indian movies once a week or, in at least one case, all the time. Large numbers also permit easier contact with the area of origin; the ethnic cluster often runs its own travel service, for example, allowing cheap charter service trips home periodically.

Of course, as the group becomes assimilated into the host society, and as the latter becomes less of a political threat, so the virtues of concentration become less clear cut and the role of ethnic-religious composition declines as a component of place utility. Locationally this should result in a more even spread of migration destinations as attractiveness dominated by ethnic considerations gives way to one in which other considerations are important. Indeed in the United States, for most groups length of residence in the U.S. does seem to be associated with the degree of spatial concentration in metropolitan areas. The more recent arrivals, such as the Cubans, Puerto Ricans, and Greeks, show much higher levels of segregation than do groups of longer residence, such as the Swedes, Finns, and Irish. Figures 4-7 and 4-8 present similar evidence for the locational pattern of the Irish-born across the counties of Britain in 1841 and 1951, respectively. In 1841 the Irish-born population was highly concentrated in southwest Scotland and in Lancashire; many counties had almost no Irish at all. By 1951 the dominance of southwest Scotland and Lancashire had clearly declined

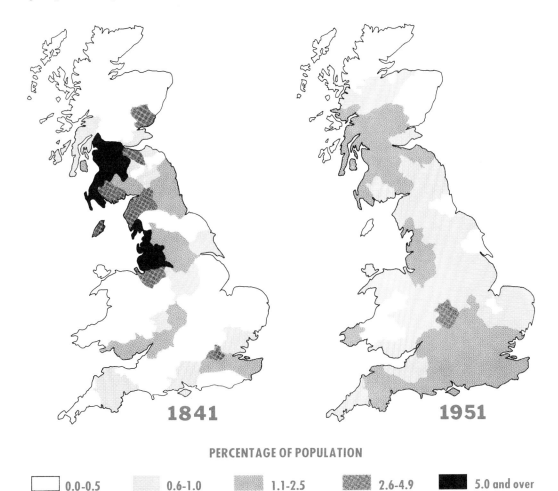

1841   1951

PERCENTAGE OF POPULATION

☐ 0.0-0.5   0.6-1.0   1.1-2.5   2.6-4.9   ■ 5.0 and over

FIGURE 4-7. The distribution of the Irish-born population in Great Britain, 1841. Note how the Irish-born population was concentrated in those economically advanced areas of Britain—Lancashire and Central Scotland, especially—closest to Ireland. Many counties at this time had almost no Irish at all; there was a good deal of geographical clustering of migrants in a limited number of areas.

FIGURE 4-8. The distribution of the Irish-born population in Great Britain, 1951. Note how the distribution had become geographically more even giving much less evidence of geographical clustering. The earlier importance of closeness to Ireland also seems to have declined.

and there were only three counties in which the Irish-born made up less than 0.3% of the total population.

The discussion so far has concentrated almost entirely upon ethnic-religious composition from the viewpoint of the ethnic migrant. Consider it now from the viewpoint of the migration behavior of the host population. The social and political tensions consequent to settlement by an ethnic minority or the antecedent prejudices of the host population frequently make areas dominated by the ethnic minorities unattractive for the majority of migrants. The ultimate example of this is the fleeing of whites from areas adjacent to a Negro ghetto—a phenomenon to be discussed in greater detail later in this book—or even from cities politically dominated by an ethnic minority such as those cities that have elected Negro mayors.

Language. The fourth consideration, one that is particularly important in explaining internation migrations, is language. For the migrant it is important that he have a facility in the language of the people among whom he is going to live if he is going to obtain employment or even the most elementary satisfaction in the host society. It is probably for this reason that Algerians tend to move to France and West Indians tend to move to Britain: French is or was taught in the schools of Algeria and English in the schools of Jamaica, Barbados, Trinidad, etc.

An especially striking example of the role of language concerns the in-migration field of Budapest as it existed just after the turn of the century (see Figure 4-9). As can be seen, the field demonstrated a fairly strong distance-decay component but with a peculiar outlier of

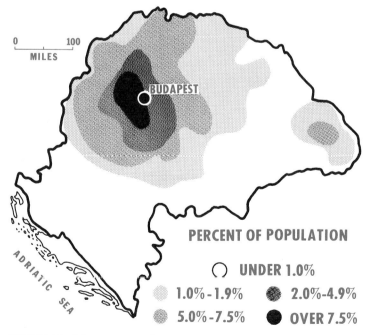

FIGURE 4-9. Migration to Budapest 1900–1910 (as a percent of the population in the area of origin); note the *distance-biased* component in the movement pattern and the curious outlier in the southeast contributing more migrants than we would have expected on the basis of distance alone.

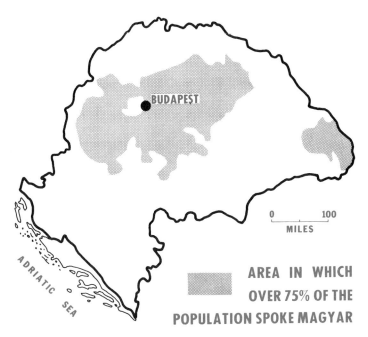

FIGURE 4-10.   The Magyar-speaking area of pre-1918 Hungary. A comparison of this map with that shown in Figure 4-9 demonstrates the potency of linguistic factors in explaining migratory movements.

migration intensity in the southeast. Clarification of this comes from an examination of the linguistic map in Figure 4-10. The outlier corresponds to an area of Magyar speech; an outlier, moreover, in a sea of Rumanian speakers. Instead of migrating to Rumanian-speaking Bucharest at an approximately similar distance as Budapest, therefore, the Magyar-speaking Szeklers of northwest Rumania oriented themselves towards the latter city. The surrounding Rumanians, however, migrated elsewhere where they could speak the language!

Such language considerations seem to apply particularly strongly to migration between nations, since nations are usually homogenous in language. In cases where such homogeneity does not exist, however, language may exert an effect on migration at the intranational level also. The French-speaking population of Quebec in Canada, for example, is relatively immobile as far as movement outside of the province into English-speaking Canada is concerned.

Housing.   The final factor which helps to make up the attractiveness of different destinations for a potential migrant is that of housing—in both quantity and quality. Housing questions seem particularly important for migration within cities since different migrants have different housing needs and housing tends to cluster as to both quantity and quality. Thus moves within a city are frequently precipitated by changes in the life-cycle status of the individual and a consequent change in his housing needs. While the young childless married couple in which both husband and wife are working may find an apartment or townhouse close to the downtown area perfectly adequate, a family would probably search for more adequate housing elsewhere.

In certain national contexts housing may even be a critical factor for migration over longer distances. In Britain

lower-income groups are relatively immobile compared with their American
counterparts because of the rigidities
of the housing market. Lower-income
housing there is dominated by the public rental market in which local government with central government assistance constructs low-cost homes for rent
at subsidized prices. This is the so-called
council housing, which is particularly attractive to lower-income groups because
of its low rents. Its constraining effect on
lower-income group migration derives
from two factors: first, alternative housing either for rent or purchase by lower-
income groups is very poorly developed
for a variety of reasons; second, and most
important, laws surrounding the allocation of council housing are bizarre, to say
the least. To acquire such subsidized
housing one has to be on the town housing authority's waiting list; but to get on
that list one has to already reside in that
town! The consequences for migration
can be easily deduced.

While place utility can be characterized in terms of the five constituent components — economic opportunity, amenity, ethnic-religious composition, language, and housing — it is clearly a functional matter. What is attractive for one
individual may not be attractive for another. Two of the best available predictors of what will be attractive are
life-cycle status and income.

Place Utility and Life-Cycle Status. What
is valued by a retired person may not be
valued by a younger person who has to
think of a place of work as well as of
leisure time and amenity. Consequently,
the migrational patterns of older people
are not the same as those of people in the
gainfully employed age groups. Partial
confirmation of this idea comes from a
study of migration maps for different age
groups in France (see Figures 4-11 and
4-12): areas of high in-migration for
younger people in France are not at all

the same as those for older people.
Judging from the types of destination in
which younger elements dominate the
migration stream, it would seem that
economic opportunity factors are particularly important (see Figure 4-11). Paris
and Rhône-Alpes, two of the wealthiest
regions, receive the highest proportions
of young people followed by other
wealthy areas such as those of Alsace,
Lorraine and Franche-Comté. Older
people, on the other hand, seem more attracted to areas of high natural amenity
such as the Riviera and Corsica (see Figure 4-12). The lower degree of variation
in the percentages for older people
suggests that some less spatially concentrated phenomenon may be exercising
an effect — possibly the attraction of re-

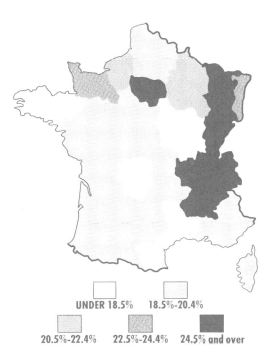

FIGURE 4-11. In-migrants aged 25–34 as a percent
of all in-migrants by region in France 1954–62; the
migration of gainfully occupied younger people is
more affected by economic opportunity factors: the
higher income areas of Paris, Lyons (Rhône-Alpes),
and Alsace-Lorraine have been especially attractive, therefore, while the economically laggard
areas of the west and south have been unattractive.

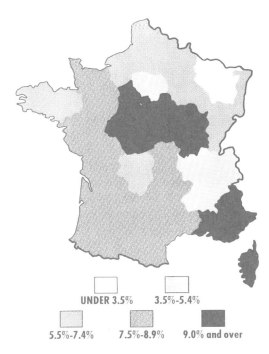

UNDER 3.5%   3.5%-5.4%

5.5%-7.4%   7.5%-8.9%   9.0% and over

FIGURE 4-12. In-migrants aged 65 and over as a percent of all in-migrants by region in France 1954–62; the migration of older, retired people is much less affected by economic opportunity factors and more affected by amenity factors. Note the great popularity of the regions of the southeast in the Mediterranean area and the general interest in the more unspoilt areas of southwest and western France.

tiring to an area where one was born and raised.

Place Utility and Income. Equally important in initiating migration decisions are income levels. Within cities, housing clusters not only by type but also by price: there are expensive single-family households in suburban locations as well as cheaper suburbs. Income is a powerful differentiator of housing choice within the metropolitan area and affords not only an explanation of migration destinations at any one time period but also over time as some individuals acquire increased levels of income and can afford higher-cost housing.

Even for intranational migration, income level and its correlates, such as education, appear to provide some explanation of migration patterns. Thus amenity factors seem considerably more important for more educated, higher-income groups than for lower-income groups. This may be something to do with the greater amount of leisure time—or the greater flexibility of leisure time—available to the higher-income element. It seems also to have something to do with the locational pattern of leisure opportunities for upper-income groups: upper-income groups have leisure pursuits which are likely to be dependent on locationally restricted phenomena—skiing, fishing, walking, climbing, boating, hunting. This is less likely to be true for lower-income, less-educated groups.

Income and life-cycle status therefore appear to be important differentiators of the type of movement opportunity attractive to different types of migrants. They represent a far from exhaustive listing of such differentiators however; occupational specialization, for example, is almost certainly an important factor in choice of migration destinations. This is represented by some striking historical examples such as the migration of Cornish tin and copper miners from England when the metal became depleted to Galena, Illinois, to work local lead and zinc mines. It is also represented by the movement of coal miners within Britain from one coal field to another though partly under the stimulus of the circulation of information by the National Coal Board. Much occupation-specific migration in fact seems to be mediated by some occupation-specific institution disseminating information about jobs elsewhere. In conclusion, however, what all this means is that discussions of place utility and attractiveness must always be couched in terms of the caveat "attractive for whom?" We now turn to examine the role of movement costs.

THE ROLE OF MOVEMENT COSTS

A great number of geographical phenomena suggest, superficially at least, that movement costs are important in explaining patterns of migration. Most significant in this respect, of course, is the distance biasing of human movement such that shorter moves tend to be more common than lengthier movements. This feature of *migration fields* seemingly applies to all geographical scales. At the level of the nation as a whole, for instance, we have already remarked upon the role of distance in the locational pattern of Budapest's migration field immediately before the First World War.

At the level of the city, migration patterns also appear to show some relationship to distances between areas of migrant origin and areas of migrant destination; Figure 4-13, for example, plots the proportion of the migrants from an area of the Australian city of Melbourne moving to other areas of that city. The percentages decline in all directions though not at the same rate. Such a distance bias in intra-urban migration is rather more apparent when information from several cities is recorded and related to intervening distance: within any one city there are frequently other factors such as ethnic concentrations which distort the simplicity of the distance-bias structure.

Finally, when one examines the internation level, short moves also seem to predominate. Consider for instance the fact that most in-migrants into the United States from Mexico are concentrated in the states closest to the Mexican boundary — Texas and California are outstanding in this regard (see Figure 4-14). Canadian in-migrants also demonstrate a distance bias, being concentrated largely in the New England states close to their areas of origin in Ontario and Quebec (see Figure 4-15).

A simple rationale for such a distance bias in migration would be the movement cost factor. The costs of moving over longer distances are greater and the costs of maintaining contact with the relatives and friends left behind are also greater the longer the move. While the argument has an appealing simplicity, one should exercise some caution in applying it as a "blanket explanation" of such distance-bias patterns. Certain other situations can also produce such a distance bias and may be more important at some geographical scales than at others.

Recall, for example, Table 3-1 in Chapter 3 where we tried to relate the likelihood of movement to variations of attractiveness and movement costs. If we examine that schematic diagram, it becomes quite evident that for the combi-

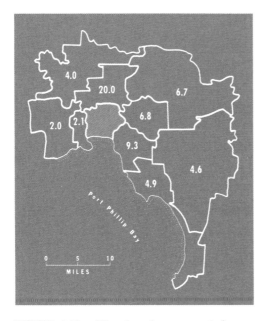

FIGURE 4-13. Migration from a central area (shaded) of Melbourne, Australia to other parts of the city: percentages are the percentage of the central area's population at one time interval now residing elsewhere at a later time interval. Note the distance decay: does this suggest that a movement cost factor is important? What other interpretations might you put on this locational pattern?

FIGURE 4-14. Mexican in-migration to the United States: shaded are all states in which over 0.5% of the total population was born in Mexico; note the clustering near the Mexican border. Figures are for 1960.

nation *low movement costs–high attractiveness,* movement is highly likely; while for the combination of *high movement cost–low attractiveness,* movement is highly unlikely. In other words, if we assume that movement costs increase with increasing distance of migration, then a *distance bias in migration could be a result of not only movement considerations but also of the locational pattern of attractiveness.* A situation in which closer places are more attractive than more distant places, therefore, would be much more likely to produce a distance-biased

FIGURE 4-15. Canadian migration to the United States: shaded are all states in which over 0.5% of the total population was born in Canada; note the clustering near the Canadian border, particularly in New England which is adjacent to the most densely populated areas of Canada. Canadians also seem to share, with their fellow North Americans, a proclivity for California and Florida! Figures are for 1960.

migration pattern than a locational arrangement of attractiveness in which the more attractive locations are more distant from the origin than the less attractive locations.

These ideas can be matched up rather easily with some real world instances. Consider the case of the Negro ghetto: the Negro ghetto expands at its edge; out-migration to blocks close to the ghetto is much more likely than to blocks further away. We know, however, that this has very little to do with movement cost considerations. Rather it is a result of the fact that blocks close to the ghetto are more attractive to the Negro city migrant than blocks further away. White hostility and Negro fear have created a situation in which the Negro would much rather locate near those of his own race than among predominantly white populations. Mexican migration destinations within the United States can be explained by an analogous locational arrangement of attractiveness. The unskilled Mexican looking for temporary work is highly attracted to the border states of Texas and California where a great deal of seasonal work requiring unskilled labor in vineyards, orchards, and truck farming is located. In other cases, of course, attractiveness does not have such a simple symmetrical arrangement relative to the place of origin. The pre-1914 migration of the Magyar Szeklers of Rumania, for instance, showed very little distance bias since a wide zone of unattractive migration destinations intervened between themselves and the more attractive Magyar-speaking Hungary.

However, quite apart from the locational arrangement of attractiveness there are still other reasons of an information-availability character which should discourage us from attributing distance-biased migration patterns wholly, or sometimes even in part, to

movement cost considerations. If we are considering a move within a city, for instance, we tend to *know* more about nearby housing vacancies than about more distant vacancies simply because we pass them on our way to work or to shop. For many people such localism in knowledge of opportunities is reinforced by information from friends and relatives who frequently live close by and also by the listings of local realtors. The intra-urban case is especially interesting in this regard for it seems highly implausible that movement cost considerations could be important in producing the distance-bias character of migration in that particular context.

Even at a larger geographical scale, however, the information we receive regarding jobs and housing may have a distinctly local bias as a result of the local bias of the newspapers purveying such information. If one lives in the sphere of influence of Birmingham, for instance, one is much more likely to read of job opportunities and housing in Birmingham than anywhere else in Britain simply because it is likely that one reads the Birmingham newspaper.

The role of movement costs, therefore, must be placed in perspective: clearly they are an important factor in explaining migration patterns, but one should be careful not to exaggerate their significance. The effects may actually be much less significant when one takes account of the relationships between intervening distance and the locational arrangement of attractiveness and of places known. In addition movement costs seem to be of variable significance for different social groups. The greater mobility of middle-class groups than of lower-class groups (see Table 4-3) is probably influenced by their greater financial ability to bear the costs of moving.

Again, however, such a movement

TABLE 4-3. Social class and migration distances for males in England and Wales (from the 1961 census); each row sums to 100% subject to rounding errors; note how lower-class groups tend to migrate, on the average, over shorter distances than middle-class groups. This may be due to the greater financial resources of the middle class or alternatively to their greater knowledge of more distant migration opportunities and lower degree of attachment to specific places.

| | Distance of Migration | | | |
Social class	Under 5 miles	5–14	15–39	40 and Over
Upper-middle class	22%	27%	17%	34%
Lower-middle class	27%	27%	17%	29%
Lower class	38%	29%	13%	21%

cost interpretation specific to different social groups may be an overly simplified view of reality. For lower-class urban dwellers, for instance, the immediate neighborhood often offers attractions of such a magnitude that the attractiveness of other possible areas of residence pales into insignificance. Such lower-class residential areas tend to be characterized by very close ties between members of an extended family with sons and daughters and their spouses, mothers, fathers, grandparents, uncles, and aunts all living in close proximity. This was found to be true, for instance, in the Bethnal Green area of east London. In the American city, the old lower-class ethnic neighborhoods have provided many of the same satisfactions of an active social life and needed support in times of emergency. For such people areas outside of the immediate residential area are often viewed as threatening rather than attractive. This is a function not only of the manifold social attractions of the lower-class residential area

but also the difficulty which the lower-class person characteristically has in coping with a strange environment.

For the middle class, on the other hand, such a localization of attractiveness is unlikely. Not only is the middle-class individual likely to have the education allowing him to manipulate the new environment to his own satisfaction and advantage, but it is unlikely that he comes from a neighborhood in which large numbers of his relatives live. In fact the middle class often seems to make a positive virtue of living away from relatives in order to be "independent."

Not only is attractiveness more localized for the lower class, however, but so are the alternative places of residence about which the individual has information. The middle class has access to all kinds of sources of information on jobs and housing over a wide geographical area to which the lower class does not have access. The British national newspaper the *Sunday Times*, for example, contains national coverage in advertisements of job openings in a wide range of professional occupations. There is also a high degree of national coverage in housing particularly by large builders operating on a national scale who advertise a geographically dispersed range of offerings. No newspaper, however, offers geographically comparable information on jobs available for lathe operators, truck drivers, and millwrights or on lower-priced housing. The more middle-class occupations such as teaching, law, medicine, and computer programming frequently have their own specialized journals with a large section on jobs available throughout the nation. Such is not the case for the capstan operator or for the assembly-line worker.

The role of movement costs in the explanation of migration patterns therefore should not be exaggerated. Undoubtedly it has an importance but it has the appearance of being of greater importance than it actually is, because of the operation of some closely related factors. For many, more adjacent locations are attractive; one is more likely to know about closer locations than about those further away; and movement costs vary in significance according to social group just as does the localization of attractiveness and of information sources. Indubitably this last factor is a major reason why the middle class is capable of adjusting so quickly to a localized change in economic conditions while the lower class often sits and lets the catastrophe of unemployment and poverty overtake it.

A final consideration underlying migration patterns, however, is that of the role played by the locational structure of movement opportunities. While middle-class people migrate further than lower-class people, to what extent is that a result of a lower density of movement opportunities for lower-class people? Such questions are treated in the next section of this chapter.

THE ROLE OF LOCATIONAL STRUCTURE

Two components of the locational structure of *movement opportunities,* or in this case, of *migration opportunities,* that appear to throw some light on geographical patterns of migration are reviewed in this section: the spacing of opportunities and the barriers interfering with access to opportunities.

In some cases opportunities are spaced further apart than in other locational contexts. If one is only interested in the opportunities and satisfactions afforded by large cities, for instance, then one would tend to be confronted by a set of opportunities spaced rather further apart than if one was interested in only medium-sized towns. That some people do, in fact, confine their migration des-

tination choices to larger cities is suggested by a large body of data that indicate that large cities attract migrants from longer distances than the more closely spaced smaller cities.

In addition, in areas of sparse population density, opportunities tend to be spaced further apart than in thickly settled areas. The effects of such density on migration distance are brought out rather strikingly by some data for ten regions of England and Wales which relate (a) the ratio of short-distance to long-distance migrations terminating in a region to (b) the density of population (see Figure 4-16). In sparsely populated areas such as Wales the ratio tends to be particularly small, testifying to the role of the widely spaced set of movement opportunities. In more densely settled

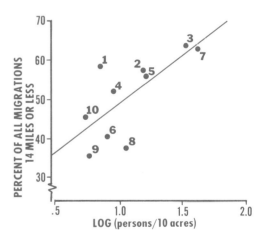

FIGURE 4-16. Density of population and migration distances, England and Wales, 1961. As population density increases, the distances of migrations terminating in the area tend to become shorter; thus the migration distances terminating in Wales tend to be much longer than those terminating in the more densely populated northwestern region. To the extent that population density is an adequate measure of the density of migration opportunities, this relationship can be understood. Key to areas: 1 = Northern; 2 = East and West Ridings of Yorkshire; 3 = Northwestern; 4 = North Midland; 5 = Midland; 6 = Eastern; 7 = London and Southeastern; 8 = Southern; 9 = Southwest; 10 = Wales.

areas such as the London and South-eastern areas, on the other hand, the ratio tends to be appreciably larger.

A second aspect of spacing is its *variability*. Movement opportunities may be close together in a certain region but some opportunities may be closer together than others. Such a spacing structure gives rise to the situation reviewed in Chapter One: it was shown that in-migration fields developed under such circumstances tend to be highly asymmetrical around the city towards which migration is proceeding. The in-migration field of Minneapolis–St. Paul, for example, has developed much further

in a westerly direction where it has little competition from alternative migration opportunities than it has in the south-easterly direction where it encounters strong competition from Chicago. This type of asymmetric development is also brought out rather effectively in the in-migration fields of Dallas–Fort Worth, on the one hand, and Houston–Galveston, on the other. As Figure 4-17 shows, there is a marked asymmetry in the in-migration field of Dallas–Fort Worth. Areas to the west at a given distance from Dallas–Fort Worth supply a far greater proportion of their migrants to that urban complex than do areas to the southeast at a

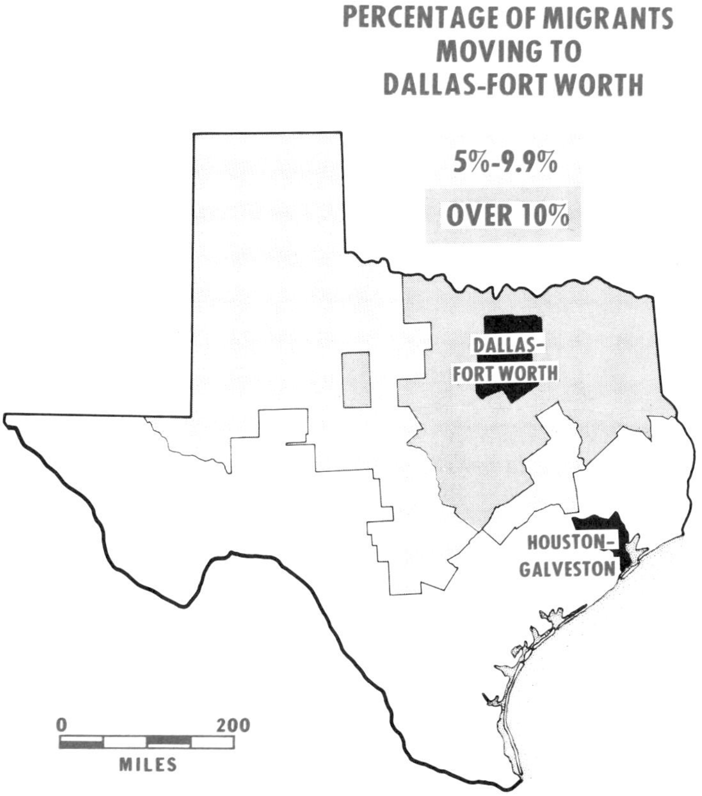

PERCENTAGE OF MIGRANTS MOVING TO DALLAS-FORT WORTH

FIGURE 4-17. The inmigration field of Dallas–Fort Worth, 1955–1960. Note how the migration field is developed much more extensively in a direction away from Houston–Galveston where competition from that migration opportunity is less severe. The gradient relating migration to distance from Dallas–Fort Worth is much less steep in a northwesterly direction than in a southeasterly direction.

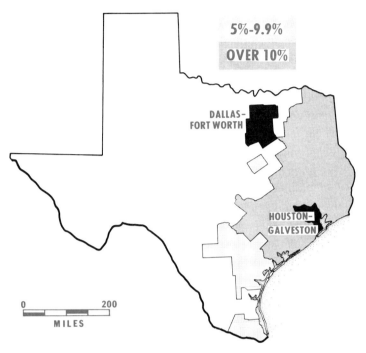

PERCENTAGE OF MIGRANTS MOVING TO HOUSTON-GALVESTON

5%-9.9%

OVER 10%

DALLAS-FORT WORTH

HOUSTON-GALVESTON

0   200
MILES

FIGURE 4-18.   The inmigration field of Houston–Galveston, 1955–1960. Note how the migration field ends abruptly on the east of Dallas–Fort Worth; only in the southwest where competition of other metropolitan areas is less severe is the gradient of the immigration field less steep.

similar distance; for the migrants from the latter areas Dallas–Fort Worth must compete with Houston–Galveston (see Figure 4-18).

The notion of the locational structure of migration opportunities can be conceptualized thus far as a set of discrete locations or movement opportunities distributed across the landscape. Superimposed upon this landscape, however, are certain barriers to movement which severely limit the geographical distribution of the opportunities a potential migrant can consider. There is little doubt today that political boundaries, and the policies that are enforced at political boundaries, exercise a very potent effect on the range of migration opportunities considered by the individual. Such

restrictions include temporary labor permits: Italian workers in Switzerland are restricted to about 30,000 at any one time and must return to Italy after two years of work. Another restriction is the system of quotas, such as those which the United Kingdom has imposed upon immigrants from the West Indies, India, and Pakistan. Restrictions also include outright bans such as the infamous white Australia policy aimed at keeping black and yellow races from the continent.

Between nations such barrier effects play an important part in structuring migration flows. Within nations, however, there are also discernible effects since the maximum feasible length of movement for a migrant will be largely determined by the area enclosed by the boundary relevant for migration. In the U.S.A., for instance, a person can migrate over 3000 miles from Maine to Southern California. In Britain, however, he can migrate barely 1000 miles before reaching the national limits. Such a spatial restrictiveness is common in Western Europe and is reflected in lower migration distances there than in North America.

Of course the effect exercised by a barrier does not emanate purely from considerations of national immigration policy. For the migrant, places within his own nation are usually more attractive for a variety of reasons such as language and familarity with customs than are areas beyond the boundary. In like manner one tends to know more about one's own nation than about places beyond the boundary.

THE GENERALITY OF THE CONCEPTS

We have established that the locational structure of movement opportunities, locational attractiveness, and movement costs are all significant for understanding geographical patterns of migration. But what about the scale issue mentioned at the beginning of this section and what of the classification of migrants according to their degree of permanence? Concerning geographical scale, it should be readily apparent that different factors apply to different scales. Within a city, for example, it is likely that the housing and ethnic-religious components of place utility play a major role in the migrant's decision. Economic opportunity and amenity factors are insignificant because of the relative ease of movement over the short distances involved within the city. Similarly, it seems highly unlikely that movement costs would be of significance in intra-urban migration; rather, any distance bias that is apparent is likely to stem from a localization of attractiveness or of information around the present residence.

Between different areas of a nation, however, economic opportunity, amenity, and movement costs are likely to be of much greater significance. Between nations they appear to be of critical importance in explaining migration patterns, though at the internation level such factors as language and the barrier effect of political boundaries should be added. Amenity factors are likely to be of reduced significance also, because of the low proportion of retired people among internation migrants. Nevertheless, large numbers of British immigrants are attracted to Australia and South Africa on amenity grounds in addition to economic opportunity grounds.

Migrants can also be classified as more or less temporary or more or less permanent. Most Italian migrants to Germany, for example, will return to Italy after a period of one or two years. Most Pakistani migrants to Britain see themselves as temporary residents who are staying only long enough to accumulate sufficient money to go back and start a business in their native Pakistan. Most West Indian migrants living in Britain, however, see themselves as permanent as do most German migrants to the United States. Nevertheless, hard and fast division between permanent and temporary migrants is difficult to sustain: many Irish migrants to Britain, for instance, regard themselves as temporary migrants but they are certainly less temporary and more permanent than migrant girls from the European continent who come for a few months on an *au pair* assignment.

For the more temporary migrants, economic opportunity considerations of place utility are of overwhelming significance. Migration of Africans from subsistence agriculture areas to industrial areas, for instance, was aimed primarily at obtaining cash to pay taxes imposed by colonial powers. Today, migration towards the industrial centers of southern and central Africa is strongly related to the magnitude of agricultural harvests and the prices of crops normally sold for cash. The importance of the economic opportunity component of place utility is further underlined by the relationship between the timing of the migration and the temporariness of the economic opportunity. Much temporary migration is related to periodically increased requirements for agricultural labor at certain times of the year. The movement of Mexicans into the United States is strongly related to the seasonal demands of the vineyard and the truck farm. In France large numbers of Belgians migrate at certain times of the year to the area northeast of Paris to assist in sugar beet operations, while in southeastern France in the Languedoc area the vineyard harvest attracts large numbers of temporary Algerian immigrants. A further consideration emphasizing the significance of economic opportunity factors are the very poor housing conditions that the temporary migrants are prepared to tolerate.

But why are temporary migrants temporary? Economic opportunity is also important for more permanent migrations, so what is different about the temporary migrant? For many, *temporary migration is income maximizing;* permanent migration would result in a net decline of migrant income. The typical African social system, for instance, is such that the women do much of the cultivation and harvest. Temporary migration by the males, therefore, adds to family income whereas permanent migration of the whole family would result in the loss of the income represented by subsistence food production.

A second set of factors are more political in character. Temporary migrants are usually low-income, unskilled workers and present a social welfare problem the host country would rather avoid because of the small addition to the tax base that the migrants provide. By restricting migration to a temporary basis a country can often solve some of its labor problems *and* avoid the welfare and public service problem. In Switzerland, for instance, Italian migrants are forbidden to bring their families with them, thus eliminating the obligation of the Swiss government for such costly services as education, post- and prenatal care and health care.

The migrant may also have his own reasons for moving to an area only temporarily. The lower-class person frequently has a stronger attachment to his home area. If he is of a different ethnic or linguistic group than the host society, he may experience difficulties of assimilation and coping with a new environment not encountered by the more skilled, middle-class migrant. These reasons refer primarily to such characteristically temporary migrants as the Mexicans in the United States and the Algerians in France; little is known about the temporary nature of migrations of native-born Americans, British, and French within their own nations. A hypothesis worth investigating, however, would be that lower-class migrants are more temporary than middle-class migrants—discounting the effects of labor direction such as that experienced by the executive shifted from one branch to another.

The lower skill of the temporary migrant, moreover, leads to vicious circles that help to guarantee that he will remain a temporary rather than a permanent migrant. Such workers need training, but an employer would not invest in the training of a worker who is likely to return home after six months. The nature of the temporary migrant discourages his accepting training which might over a period of time make him more likely to migrate permanently.

CONCLUSIONS AND SUMMARY

This chapter has attempted to illustrate the principles explained in Chapter Three with two case studies: (1) oceanic movements of iron ore and (2) human migration patterns. The first illustrates especially well the role of movement costs and the tendency for movement costs to be lower over a shorter distance. Japan, therefore, has looked to adjacent South and Southeast Asia for its iron-ore imports rather than further afield. Technological innovations such as the giant ore carrier, however, are increasing the *transferability* of iron ore. Also exemplified is the idea of *complementarity* between underdeveloped nations with iron-ore surpluses and steel-producing nations deficient in domestic iron ore, such as the U.S.A., West Germany, and the United Kingdom.

The study of migration, on the other hand, illustrates the fact that *attractiveness* or *place utility* for the migrant is made up of several components such as *amenity, economic opportunity,* and *housing.* The significance of these factors varies for *migrations at different geographical scales;* for migrations within the city, for instance, variations in housing are important but economic opportunity is not.

The migration case study is also useful from the viewpoint of illustrating an *inferential* problem often encountered in geography. In brief, it is often tempting to *argue from pattern to process:* we are inclined to attribute distance biases in migration to movement cost factors, for instance. *Several processes can produce the same geographical pattern,* however, and more subtle mechanisms may be at work in this particular case: the fact that most migrants *know* more about closer than about more distant places is a case in point.

CHAPTER FIVE

Information and Decisions
in a Locational Context

INTRODUCTION

In Chapter Three, we discussed movement decisions in terms of an evaluation by the individual of the attractiveness of different locations and the cost of getting to alternative locations within a particular locational structure of movement opportunities. Implicit in the discussion has been the idea that the decision maker has *perfect knowledge* of all movement opportunities and chooses the one which maximizes his satisfaction; it is clear, however, that not only does the *amount of information* a person has about a location or about some item vary but so does the *accuracy of that information* and the *interpretation* which the decision maker gives it. All three factors are important in explaining differences in the decisions—locational or otherwise—which men make. We shall now explore the effect of the amount of information a decision maker has (Chapter Five) and the accuracy and interpretation of that information (Chapter Six) on decisions that have implications for locational patterns: migration decisions, innovation-adoption decisions, search decisions, and so forth.

In adequately explaining at least two types of locational pattern, some geographers have found it of critical importance to take into account the information which the decision maker has prior to making his decision; these locational patterns are *migration patterns* and *patterns of the spatial diffusion of innovations* such as those of new technologies or consumer goods. Both are discussed in this chapter from the viewpoint of how the degree to which the individual has knowledge of his environment and of innovations affects migration and innovation-adoption decisions, respectively.

It is true that we have already discussed migration patterns and made some suggestions as to how they might be produced. As we shall show shortly, however, there are some aspects of those patterns that an explanation couched in terms of movement costs and variable attractiveness does not explain. The spatial diffusion of innovations, on the other hand, is a locational phenomenon that can only be explained in terms of the variable degree to which people have information about the innovation. The spatial diffusion of innovations also provides an example of a case in which, although the antecedent decision is not in itself locational (i.e. the decision to adopt), the patterns of times of adoption do exhibit a great regularity which demands an explanation.

Finally we need to consider an effect of the acquisition of information that is not adequately illustrated by a consideration of either migration processes or spatial diffusion of innovation: the slow alteration of locational policy in response to the acquisition of increased information about the environment to which the policies apply. This dynamic element of information acquisition, which takes the form of *learning* about the surrounding environment, will be considered in the final section of this chapter.

MIGRATION PATTERNS

DEVIANT LOCATIONAL PATTERNS

When a number of maps of migration patterns are compared with each other, it becomes apparent very quickly that the explanation which we have advanced so far is not completely adequate. For a start, both in-migration and out-migration fields show deviations from the regular distance decay which movement cost considerations in an environment of destinations of similar attractiveness would lead us to expect. Places of migrant origin do not necessarily cluster around the place of destination, nor is such clustering, where it occurs, devoid of any directional orientation. Similarly, for a specific locational origin of migrants, places of destination may not cluster around the place of origin but may be a long distance from the place of origin and/or consist of a small number of all possible adjacent destinations.

Examples of such patterns are common. Figure 5-1 depicts the locational origins of migrants to Paris from places in France in 1833. A strong distance decay is immediately evident: places closer to Paris clearly contributed more migrants than places further away. More striking, however, are the *deviant cases*—those places contributing more migrants than we would expect on the basis of distance from Paris. Similar cases are found in more contemporary

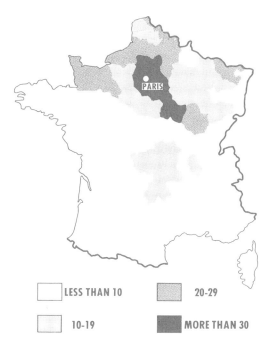

LESS THAN 10   20-29

10-19   MORE THAN 30

FIGURE 5-1. Migration to Paris 1833; figures refer to the number of migrants per 1000 inhabitants in the department of origin; note the *distance decay* component in the migration field and also the relatively high rates of migration from south-central France (Auvergne).

times. In Chapter One, for example, we remarked on the way in which the in-migration field of Los Angeles had some curious outliers, particularly in the Erie district of Pennsylvania, even though areas in the immediate vicinity of Erie were contributing more migrants to such closer places as Detroit, Cleveland, and Pittsburgh rather than to Los Angeles. Other examples can be found in Britain; the towns of Slough (west of London) and Corby in Northamptonshire both have two components in their in-migration fields: a distance-decay element, such that places in the immediate vicinity of the two towns contribute relatively large numbers of migrants to them, and a deviant component. Slough, for example, has the largest proportion of Welsh-born population of any English town and for some odd reason attracted very large numbers of Welsh people during the depression of the 1930s. Corby has a similar status as far as Scottish-born population is concerned, even though it is over 200 miles from the Scottish border.

International migration reveals similar deviations. Highly deviant from a regular distance decay in migration are the migrations of Europeans in the 19th century over very long distances to the Americas and Australasia. What is interesting, however, is that just as all *départments* in France that were a long distance from Paris did not contribute migrants to Paris in 1833, so different towns and regions in 19th-century Britain or Germany did not contribute to the overseas migration streams to the same extent. Nor does there seem to be any obvious characteristic of these places that would explain their different contributions. Often, for example, the places in Britain contributing more migrants did not seem to lack any economic opportunity that places contributing fewer migrants had in abundance. The new migrations of Indians and Pakistanis to Britain and of Algerians to France reveal similar inexplicable selectivities of origin and destination. Why, for example, should Southall have such a large fraction of its population from India and why should Bradford be the most Pakistani of British towns?

Of course, one explanation of such deviations might be in terms of the locational pattern of attractiveness. It might be, for example, that Auvergne (see Figure 5-1) was unusually unattractive compared to Paris in the 19th century, or that Southall is by far the most attractive British town for Indian immigrants and they would not be able to obtain similar satisfaction at any other British town. In some cases, place utility considerations clearly do explain the type of deviance we are discussing. For example, Hungarian Szekler migration from Rumania to Bu-

dapest can be explained in terms of the linguistic component of place utility. In many cases, however, it is just as evident that there is no such explanation and that we must look elsewhere. Thus there were many other growing towns in southeast England during the depression but one of them—Slough—attracted a disproportionately large number of Welsh immigrants for no apparent reason. To understand why, we need to probe into the nature of the individual migration decision a little more carefully.

THE MIGRATION DECISION

Conceptually it is useful to regard the migration decision as divisible into two stages: an initial stage in which one decides to move to a particular place, and a second stage of locational adaptation in which one decides whether or not to stay. Adaptation is clearly contingent upon one's continuing evaluation of the location and its associated satisfactions.

The decision to move to a particular place is based upon knowledge of the place in which one lives at present and knowledge of the places to which one might move, that is, an evaluation of place utility for all those places for which one has information. If the geographer had some knowledge of the locational pattern of the places about which the individual migrant typically has information, he might more readily understand the geometry of migration patterns.

Much of the information which the layman collects about places has a strong distance-decay component in its origin or in the places to which it refers. For a variety of reasons we tend to know more about places closer to us than about places further away. Newspapers, apart from the national press, for instance, show a bias towards the local area while our own day-to-day movements tend to reinforce this localistic bias in our information as do the locationally restricted movements of our friends and relatives. The latter sources of information are particularly important as they tend to be much more *persuasive* than the mass media; the mass media tend to alert and make a person *aware* of locational alternatives but they do not often persuade.

In addition to the distance-decay component in the individual's *information field*—that set of places about which he has knowledge—there are also connection and random components. We tend to know about places where we have friends and relatives independent of how distant they are (we might correspond or visit back and forth) and this is the connection component. There is also, however, a chance or random component which must be considered very carefully because of its power to produce apparently anomalous locational patterns. Purely fortuitously we may learn about some place; it may be an introduction at the party that we almost missed due to illness or it may be some chance contact made in the army or university.

Following migration, the decision to stay in the new place of residence is dependent upon the satisfactions obtained at the new destination, especially in terms of jobs and housing. Such satisfaction is more likely the greater the amount of information (and hence the greater the amount of choice) that one has about jobs, housing, and other needs related to one's satisfaction with a place. Here again, *friends and relatives play a very important role in the locational adaptation process.*

A THEORY

Given the nature of the migration decision as we have outlined it above, it is possible to develop a theory which explains the deviant locational patterns we have identified at the beginning of this chapter. This theory emphasizes two basic ideas: (1) the occasionally random nature of information acquisition such that would-be migrants may hear of a possible destination quite fortuitously; (2) the roles which friends and relatives play in the migration decision. Each idea is considered in turn, the first briefly and the second at greater length.

If we examine the origins of some migration streams—and it is possible to trace some of them to their beginnings—it is often surprising to find how fortuitous was the initial acquisition of knowledge about the place. The Indian Sikh community of Southall, England is an outstanding case in point. An article in the *Sunday Times* of London recently stated: "The build-up of Sikh communities in Great Britain was in many ways as random as that triggered by the Sylhetti merchant seamen who jumped ship to become the pioneers of the Pakistani migration. In Southall, for example, which now has one of Britain's most strongly rooted Indian communities, owning two cinemas and substantial property in the borough's main street, it developed out of a chance war-time contact. The personnel manager at Wolf's Rubber Factory had met members of a Sikh regiment in the Middle East. When the labor shortage in Southall became acute he knew where to turn." [*Sunday Times,* 7.13. 1969, p. 15.]

Once the migration stream between two places has commenced, however, it is likely that information supplied by friends and relatives will become very important in sustaining this stream. Not only do they supply information to the would-be migrant when making visits home but they also embody, in terms of their new-found wealth, accouterments, and style of life, the virtues of the place to which they have migrated, thus increasing the incentives to move for the potential migrant.

In addition to providing information, friends and relatives may add to the net attractions of the possible migration destination by removing the movement cost barrier. This has been particularly so where the income difference between the place of destination and the place of origin is rather large: migration from Ireland to the United States, for example, has been extensively funded by Irish already in the United States.

A third and final role which the friends and relatives may play is that of assisting in the adaptation of new migrants to the place of destination: finding housing, finding a job for the new arrival, and generally assisting him in his adaptation to a new environment. This, of course, is particularly so where the new environment is strange or alien, as in the case of the migration of an ethnic minority. We have already referred to the ethnic-specific institutions which have developed for the Sikh community of Southall. This seems to be a common pattern for migrant ethnic minorities providing them with a "home away from home" and greatly assisting locational adaptation. It is probably as a result of ethnic assistance in locating jobs that ethnic minorities at certain migrant destinations tend to be concentrated in one or in a small number of occupations. The Pakistanis in Bradford, for instance, are overwhelmingly employed in woolen textile manufacture. And many Jewish migrants to New York City have entered the ready-made clothing industry as they did in Leeds, Manchester, and London.

While some chance information frequently provides the initial source of a migration stream, the stream is maintained by the friends-and-relatives effect, which may intensify the links between a particular place of origin and a particular place of destination as new migrants arrive and start providing information to *their* friends and relatives who contemplate migration from the origin region. This phenomenon is known as *chain migration:*

▶ *Chain migration is the continual movement of people who perform the sequential functions of migrant, information provider for following migrants, and agent of locational adaptation for following migrants.*

Clearly, so long as these functions continue to be performed, the migration is likely to be strengthened rather than extinguished, though it may show fluctuations over time with the business cycle. Indeed chain migrations seem to show a high degree of sensitivity to variations in local unemployment, as news of these is relayed back to would-be migrants by friends and relatives in a far more effective manner than would be possible by the less localized media. In some cases chain migration is formalized in some sort of migrant sponsorship system; the same *Sunday Times* article we referred to above also had some general comments on Pakistani migration to Britain: "In Britain their fundamental social link is with their 'sponsor'—the man, frequently a kinsman, who helped them through the complex of difficulties in obtaining entry into this country. At all stages of emigration, money and sifarish (influence, connections) are needed. Passports can be very expensive. Suspicion of bureaucracy, endemic in the Pakistani peasant, is often carried over into a distrust of all regulation." [*Sunday Times*, 7.13. 1969, p. 15]

EVIDENCE FROM MIGRATION TO PARIS

That this theory has some validity is confirmed by a recent interview survey of migrants to Paris. This study clearly shows the role of friends and relatives in (1) supply of information, (2) assisting adaptation to the new location, and (3) providing the basis for a chain migration such as that defined above.

The survey demonstrated that 58% of

the migrants already knew someone who was capable of helping them and who was living in Paris before they migrated there. Forty-three percent had a relative there and 11% had a friend. Information supply was especially important for younger people: 68% of those less than 19 years of age knew someone already living there. It was also very important for certain areas with a long tradition of migration to Paris. Particularly interesting is the fact that 76% of those migrating from Auvergne, the major deviant source of migrants in Figure 5-1, already knew someone in Paris. Figure 5-2 shows that this particular deviant pattern has persisted into contemporary times giving rather striking evidence in favor of the idea that a friends-and-relatives mechanism explains these deviant migration patterns.

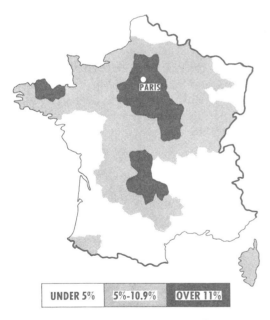

FIGURE 5-2. Rates of migration to Paris, 1954: note the *persistence* of high levels of migration from Auvergne in south-central France *in addition* to the distance decay pattern around Paris. Brittany in the northwest has also emerged as supplying more migrants than one would have expected on the basis of distance from Paris.

It is also clear that friends and relatives have frequently played a critical role in facilitating the adaptation of migrants to Paris. About 40% of the migrants found their first jobs through the intermediary of friends and relatives. This was particularly important for younger people, working-class people, and those from rural areas, that is, those not moving as a result of promotion or work guaranteed in advance of arrival. In housing, also, the helpful role of friends and relatives is obvious: 33% of the migrants stay initially with family or friends, though this role is likely to be less important in countries having a less critical housing shortage than France. And adaptation in general to life in Paris seems to have been much more widespread among those who knew someone in Paris than among those who did not. These facts radically change the romantic image of the migrant, as the author of the research report states: "We touch there, it seems, an essential aspect of migration to Paris from the provinces. Instead of the image of an individual who breaks his ties with his background and leaves his family, defined in a narrow or broad sense, in order to try something new, we find a quite different picture: that of an individual who on the contrary will go to a city where he finds friends and relatives already living there and on whom he can rely." [Guy Pourcher, ed., *Le Peuplement de Paris* (Paris: Presses Universitaires de France, 1964).]

Some of the more critical evidence relating to *chain migration* to Paris is presented in Table 5-1. An astonishing 37% of all the migrants interviewed not only knew someone in Paris before they moved there but also knew someone who migrated after them. Only 16% did not know anyone in Paris before they migrated or anyone who migrated to Paris after them. Admittedly this evidence for chain migration is circum-

TABLE 5-1.   Chain migration to Paris. At least a third of the migrants to Paris knew someone already living there before they moved and knew someone who arrived later.

| | | Migrants to Paris *after* migrating | |
		Knew someone arriving later	Didn't know someone arriving later
Migrants to Paris *before* migrating	Knew someone already there	37%	21%
	Didn't know someone already there	26%	16%

stantial rather than conclusive, but it is strengthened when we learn that the majority of the migrants had helped — with jobs or housing — migrants who followed after them, and that knowing and helping later migrants occurred more often among those who visited their homes in the French provinces more frequently.

LOCATIONAL IMPLICATIONS

The evidence for the random origin plus chain migration theory, which we are proposing to account for deviant migration patterns, seems quite striking. Its explanatory power, however, extends to other locational aspects of migration patterns which are worth referring to.

A major phenomenon of the 19th and early 20th centuries, for example, was the spatial expansion of the in-migration fields of such cities as Paris, Glasgow, London, etc. As Figures 5-1 and 5-2 show, Paris was drawing its migrants from much farther afield in 1954 than in 1833. The data on migration to the Swedish town of Västeras in the 19th and 20th centuries shown in Table 5-2 present the same picture of a city drawing most of its migrants over increasingly lengthy distances. A number of hypotheses could be adduced to explain this phenomenon. It might be suggested that this is nothing more than a manifestation of the decline

in real movement costs which has accompanied the transportation revolution of the last 150 years. An alternative explanation, however, is made in terms of chain migration. Consider Figure 5-3, in which Z represents a large city such as Glasgow while Y and X represent two possible sources of migrants with Y being the nearer of the two. In time period 1 assume that : (1) a person A moves from X to Y and (2) a person B moves from Y to Z. In time period 2 both send back information to their respective origins and are followed by other migrants in time period 3. In time period 4 information sent from Z to Y may be received by someone originally from X

TABLE 5-2.   Migration to and from Västeras in the years 1850, 1904, and 1950. Columns sum to 100% subject to rounding error.

Origin/ Destination	1850 In	1850 Out	1904 In	1904 Out	1950 In	1950 Out
0–50 km	72.8	50.0	65.3	40.6	29.6	24.3
50–100 km excluding Stockholm	8.7	14.0	12.7	12.4	13.4	14.0
90–100 km Greater Stockholm	7.9	29.0	8.2	28.4	9.7	16.7
Rest of Sweden	10.7	7.0	13.7	18.6	47.3	45.0

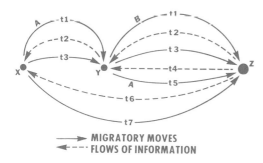

MIGRATORY MOVES
FLOWS OF INFORMATION

FIGURE 5-3. Chain migration and the spatial extension of a migration field (schematic); see text for explanation.

who then migrates to Z in time period 5. In time period 6 information is sent to X by this migrant, and in time period 7 a chain is established between X and Z.

A second widespread phenomenon of the 19th and 20th centuries has been the progressive spatial concentration of people in large cities. To an extent, we might interpret this as a result of the increasing locational advantages accruing to large cities as a result of their large markets for consumer goods and for transportation services. It is easy to envisage a process in which initial locational advantages are amplified by the consequent capital investments of those seeking to take advantage of the favored location. Chain migration processes, however, offer an additional explanation. The more people move to larger cities, presumably the greater the tendency becomes for information channeled to potential migrants to originate in the larger cities and possibly accelerate the concentration process. Hence, the greater the proportion of the English population which lives in London the greater the amount of information circulating about life, love, and labor in London relative to information about the same pursuits in remaining English cities. Of course, using this as an explanation of the increasing spatial concentration of population assumes that the information circulated is of a positive rather than of a negative character. Obviously, this need not be so, and the matter needs detailed inquiry.

A third regularity concerns the locations of migrants within the destination places to which they migrate. Particularly for those migrating to a relatively alien social environment there appears to be a tendency to locate in the city close to those coming from the same area of origin. Thus Bretons in Paris tend to cluster in Montparnasse, while Alsaciens tend to group themselves around Gare de l'Est. This is very much what one might expect if former migrants perform an adaptation function for later migrants helping them to obtain lodging and employment. Certainly one would anticipate this assistance to be more necessary where the host environment into which the individual is moving is either strange or hostile. This is brought out very strikingly in the locations of different groups of Algerians within Paris. Algerian migrants in Paris tend to arrange themselves residentially according to the area from which they came, so that the Algerian migrants in a given *quartier* of Paris will be dominated by individuals from a particular area of Algeria. Indeed, within clusters of migrants of a given regional origin there is also clustering by village. As a report on Algerian migration to France has stated: "A network of threads, invisible but powerful, is extended between Algeria and France and ties together each village to a given quartier of a French town to such and such factory or construction site." [Guy Pourcher, ed., *Le Peuplement de Paris* (Paris: Presses Universitaires de France, 1964).]

SOME QUALIFICATIONS

We have identified some deviant migrational patterns and have suggested a theory to account for them. Some evidence consistent with that theory has also been presented. In the discussion of the Parisian migrant data, however, we did point out that the evidence seemed to apply more to some social groups than to others. We have made similar comments with regard to ethnic minorities. It seems, therefore, that some qualifications to the theory are appropriate, since if current social trends continue, we may conceivably see a blurring of the deviant migration patterns identified apart from those associated with ethnic minorities.

In our discussion of migrants to Paris we found that the help of friends and relatives was particularly important for those who arrived in Paris without a job. We also suggested that the housing shortage common to France and many other nations increased the initial dependence of migrants on friends and relatives. We would like to suggest here that society is evolving in such a way as to reduce such dependence for jobs and housing.

First, occupational structures tend to evolve in such a way as to increase the proportion of occupations that are professionalized and that have widely circulated notices regarding job openings relative to the less professionalized, less-skilled occupations that do not have the same advantages in terms of access to information. One of the reasons that the nursing profession has been so mobile in Britain is because of the *Nursing Mirror* which has spread news of job openings far and wide; another reason is the institutional nurses' homes which reduce dependence on friends and relatives for lodging. It would seem that as more and more occupations are professionalized in this way, reliance on the mediating influence of friends and relatives for employment will decline.

The second point is that housing is less critical in some societies than in others. In general, wealthier societies like the United States, Canada, and

Sweden have solved their housing problem to a far greater degree than less wealthy societies like Britain or France. As the wealth per capita of the latter countries increases, so we can expect them also to reduce the housing shortage and hence dependence of migrants on friends and relatives.

In summary, it may well be that the random origin and chain migration mechanism to which we have ascribed deviant migration patterns is a function of a particular stage in economic development, a stage in which the work force is relatively unprofessionalized and in which housing is a critical consideration in movement. If so, then we can look forward to a decline in the overall geographic significance of the deviant patterns as the economy develops.

FIGURE 5-4. The spatial diffusion of lodges of the Manchester Unity Friendly Societies, 1825–1876; note the strongly divergent trend character of the diffusion with earlier establishment in the Manchester area and later establishment with increasing distance from Manchester.

THE SPATIAL DIFFUSION
OF INNOVATIONS

Man is continually innovating; he acquires new technology such as seeds or fertilizers or fluoridation at some places before other places. Different groups of people acquire new institutions such as labor unions at different times: new ideologies spread across the landscape as the sequence of places is touched by the

ideology for the first time. Languages spread across the landscape and replace older languages and their associated culture. The fact that such innovations locate or are adopted at different times so that one can draw a map of adoption times suggests that diffusion patterns may exhibit spatial regularities akin to those exhibited by other items with locations in space.

Figures 5-4 to 5-6 present several dif-

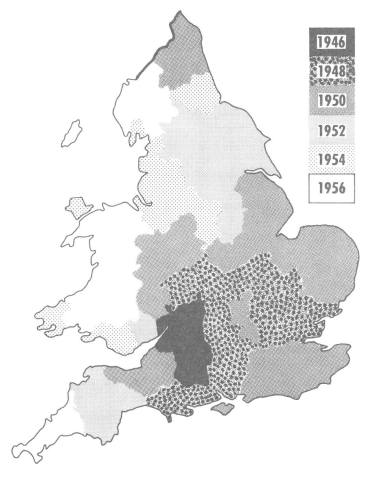

FIGURE 5-5. The spatial diffusion of combine harvesters in England and Wales: dates are the years by which each county had achieved 1 combine per 1000 acres of cereals. Note the strongly diverging trend of the diffusion with adoption being earliest in south-central England and then spreading in all directions. Adoption was particularly late in upland areas such as Wales and northwest England where arable acreages are low, and hence there is only a limited need for the combine harvester.

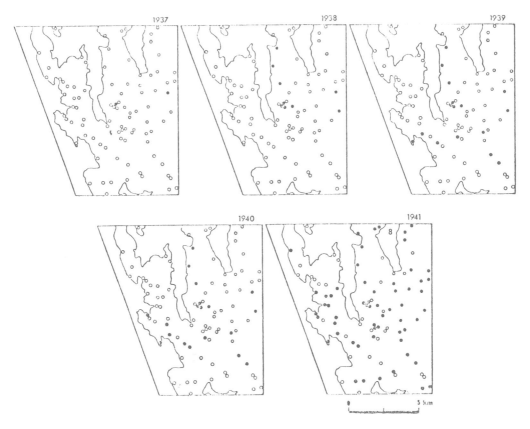

FIGURE 5-6.   The spatial diffusion of systematic control of bovine tuberculosis in an area of southern Sweden; black circles represent farms with organized control of bovine tuberculosis. Note how innovation in a given time period tends to occur close to those farms where it occurred in the previous time interval; this exemplifies Hägerstrand's "neighborhood effect."

fusion patterns for a variety of phenomena and suggest some of the spatial structures that are repetitive from one diffusional pattern to another. Figure 5-6 presents a map of the mean times of foundation of branches of a friendly society, the Manchester Unity, in the counties of England in the 19th century. In general, mean times of foundation increase with increasing distance from Manchester. Figure 5-5 presents the diffusion of a different type of innovation: that of agricultural mechanization. This information is presented by means of a map of the dates at which the different counties of England and Wales achieved agricultural mechanization to the extent

of one combine per thousand acres of cereal crops. A similar type of distance decay is evident here with combines being adopted earlier in south-central England (Figure 5-5) and spreading in all directions but with particular rapidity in an eastward direction where most cereal production in England and Wales is concentrated.

Finally, Figure 5-6 shows the spread of measures to combat bovine tuberculosis in Sweden. These phenomena are diverse but they do exhibit similarities in both their geometry and in their generating mechanisms. It is to those locational patterns and processes that we now turn.

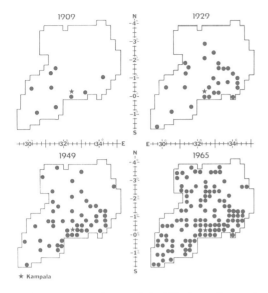

FIGURE 5-7. The spatial diffusion of postal agencies in Uganda, 1909–1965. Note the strong spatial-inversion component in the pattern.

LOCATIONAL PATTERNS

Broadly, two types of locational pattern are evident on maps of the spatial diffusion of innovations: (1) *spatial trend,* in which dates of innovation increase regularly with distance from some place or places; the diffusion of Manchester lodges in 19th-century England presents striking evidence for such trends with Manchester as the place from which the mean dates increase; (2) *spatial inversion,* in which dates of innovation do not

increase regularly with distance from a place or places at a point or line. The diffusion of post office agencies in Uganda, for example, (see Figure 5-7) does not exhibit a very clear trend component. The diffusion of control of bovine TB (Figure 5-6) shows a stronger trend component, but there is also a spatial-inversion component testifying to the fact that the initial spread of the innovation was uneven and places were left behind in the wake of the innovation wave to receive the innovation much later. Figure 5-8 schematically presents the characteristics of spatial trend and spatial inversion.

Spatial-trend types of diffusion can be further divided according to whether the spread takes place from a point or from a line. It is clear, for example, that the spread of lodges of the Manchester Unity Friendly Society is a diverging phenomenon spreading in all directions from the vicinity of Manchester. In contradistinction to such diverging trend diffusions, however, there are also frontier trend diffusions where spread takes place along an even front. This is evident in the spread of the English language in Wales with the Welsh language retreating parallel to a line running northeast to southwest. The last strongholds of the Welsh language are consequently now in the northwestern section of the country.

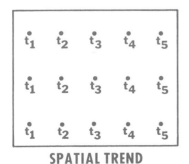

SPATIAL TREND

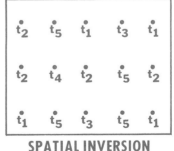

SPATIAL INVERSION

FIGURE 5-8. Spatial-trend and spatial-inversion patterns of diffusion (schematic). Times refer to times of adoption at specific locations.

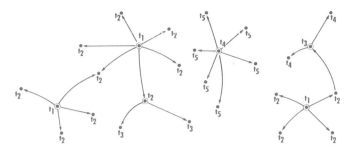

FIGURE 5-9.(*a*)   A large-scale inversion pattern of spatial diffusion with small-scale diverging trends.

Obviously the distinction between spatial-trend diffusion patterns and spatial-inversion diffusion patterns is a very arbitrary one, and most spatial diffusions seem to contain elements of both as can be seen in the maps above. What in general seems to occur, however, is that inversion elements dominate at one geographical scale while trend components dominate at another, smaller geographical scale. Thus in Figure 5-9*a* there is a small-scale diverging diffusion superimposed on an inversion pattern. This is the type of pattern which frequently results from plant colonization where the initial colonies are spread randomly across space and then diffusion of seedlings takes place from those locations. In still other patterns the diffusion is of the frontier-trend type with occasional small-scale inversion components (see Figure 5-9*b*). This is

rather like the pattern of ripples created by randomly throwing pebbles into a slowly moving stream.

What is striking about these patterns, however, is that in all of them apart from the pure spatial-inversion type of pattern there is a tendency for innovation to spread *from* a place *to* a place *close by*. This proximity or adjacency effect will be the major focus of our explanatory efforts in this section.

INNOVATION DIFFUSION PROCESSES

Two types of process appear to be responsible for such spatial patterns as those remarked on above: relocation and expansion. Figure 5-10 illustrates these two important ideas. In Figure 5-10*a* for t_1 there are six places; the ones colored black have the innovation in question while the empty places do not. For t_2 in

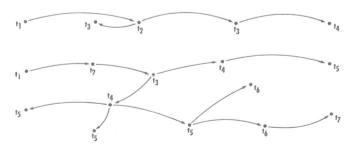

FIGURE 5-9.(*b*)   A large-scale frontier trend with small-scale inversion components.

Figure 5-10*a*, however, the situation is reversed—the places that did not have the innovation, now have it, while those that had it, have it no longer. The reason for this lies in the movement of the individuals who have the innovation at t_1 to new locations at t_2. An interesting case of such *relocation-type diffusion* is the spread of support for the Republican party into the larger cities of the Deep South in the United States. Though traditionally voting for the Democratic party, such places have since 1945 shown an increasing tendency to cast more votes for the Republican party. A number of observers have attributed this to the shift of a managerial Republican middle class from cities in northeastern United States to such metropolitan centers of the South as Atlanta, Dallas, and New Orleans. In Florida the displacement of the Democratic party has been more complete, owing to the large-scale immigration of a middle-class retired population from northeastern United States. Thus, in the context of Figure 5-10*a*, at t_1 the Northern cities are represented by the black cells and the Southern cities are represented by empty cells; in t_2 the Southern cities are black as a result of the relocation of some Republicans from Northern cities (empty cells).

More usually, however, relocation demonstrates a strong distance-decay characteristic so that the innovation spreads in a trendlike manner away from the place of origin. Examples of such distance-biased relocation processes include the spread of Negroes away from a ghetto.

Figure 5-10*b* illustrates the idea of *expansion-* or *contagion-type diffusion.* Diffusion because of expansion involves the adoption of the innovation at new places in time t_2 while the innovation is still found in places at which it was located in time t_1. It assumes some sort of functional or contagion type of link

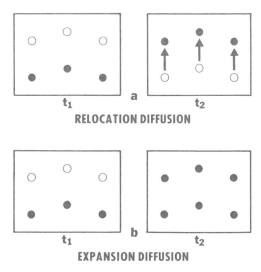

FIGURE 5-10. Expansion- (or contagion-) and relocation-type diffusion patterns.

between the innovators at time t_1 and innovators at time t_2. Most of the research in spatial diffusion has concentrated upon the expansion type of diffusion and so will our discussion here. The relocation type of diffusion is much more adequately explained by reference to migration theory.

The major source of ideas regarding the forces generating spatial diffusion patterns has been the Swedish geographer Hägerstrand. Hägerstrand has suggested a fairly simple theory based on lengthy observation of maps of actual diffusion patterns in Sweden. Hägerstrand chose as points of departure for the formulation of his theory two empirical regularities that had to be incorporated into the theory itself.

The two empirical regularities that Hägerstrand noted are: (1) *the S-shaped growth curve* and (2) *the neighborhood effect.* Hägerstrand noticed that when he plotted the cumulative number of adopters or the number adopting as a percentage of those who could adopt against time, the result was an *S-shaped*

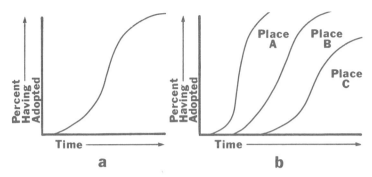

FIGURE 5-11. The S-shaped or logistic growth curve. Figure 5-11(*a*) indicates the characteristic time path of innovation diffusion; as Figure 5-11(*b*) shows, however, the *rate* of diffusion may differ appreciably from one location to another.

or *logistic growth curve* divisible into three stages (see Figure 5-11*a*): (1) an early period of slow but accelerating diffusion, (2) an intermediate period of rapid diffusion, and (3) a final period of slower decelerating diffusion. Hägerstrand also noticed that these S-shaped or logistic growth curves varied in slope from place to place and from one innovation to another (Figure 5-11*b*). Clearly an adequate explanation of spatial diffusion would have to explain or be consistent with the production of such S-shaped curves.

In addition to the S-shaped curve of diffusion over time, Hägerstrand recognized a regularity in the diffusion of items from one place to another. The likelihood of adoption of an innovation seemed to be higher in the neighborhood of an adopter and to decrease with increasing distance from an adopter. Hägerstrand has termed this the *neighborhood effect.* He found it operating at a variety of geographical scales ranging from the diffusion of innovations in small areas of Sweden to diffusion across the whole of western Europe. A process analogous to the spread of innovations is the spread of a contagious infection. Infections such as measles or influenza or mumps operate by a strong neighborhood effect so that

whole classes in schools may be infected as a result of local spread within the classroom. Think also of fads like stamp collecting, which might undergo a period of popularity in one school while in a school a few miles away the hobby languishes. Clearly, diffusion of items like microbes or hobbies is strongly constrained by distance.

In addition to these empirical regularities Hägerstrand also observed important characteristics of the diffusion process. Specifically, the relationship between distance and adoption seemed to be subject to certain random influences. Thus the nearest nonadopter to an adopter would not necessarily adopt before the next-nearest nonadopter. A host of very varied influences might interfere. All that Hägerstrand could say was that there was a higher *probability* of adoption the closer a nonadopter was to an adopter.

Equipped with these observations, Hägerstrand then proceeded to formulate a theory regarding the processes underlying the diffusion of innovations over space. Hägerstrand's theory represents the combination of two basic ideas. First, the neighborhood effect is mediated by social contact between people. In order for adoption of an innovation to occur, the individual must receive information about it just as migrants have to receive information about possible destinations. Such information, Hägerstrand claimed, is largely disseminated through private group conversation following a social contact, and social contact is more likely at a short distance. Contact is not inevitable, however, as it is subject to a variety of random influences.

Second, if the individual obtained information about the innovation (i.e., contact with an adopter occurred), adoption would be contingent upon the resistance of the adopter. For a variety of reasons individuals could be expected to be resistant to the innovation. Some of the sources of the resistance might be psychological in character, for example, the fear of novelty exhibited by some people; other sources, however, might be economic, deriving from the inability of the individual to buy the innovation, such as a tractor or a color TV set. The adoption of the innovation at a point in space, therefore, is contingent upon the nonresistance of the individual and his obtaining information. Obtaining information is, in turn, related to the individual's nearness to previous adopters. To be nonresistant but not to receive information, or to have received information but to be resistant, would not be followed by adoption. Only the combination of nonresistance and contact could result in adoption although contact would reduce the resistance of an individual so that after a number of contacts he would be nonresistant. The basic elements of Hägerstrand's theory are presented in diagrammatic form in Figure 5-12. Using this theory Hägerstrand has predicted the spatial diffusion of innovations in real world geographical situations and obtains spatial patterns remarkably similar to those found in the real world. Hägerstrand's predicted patterns, for example, exhibit the neighborhood effect which, when proceeding from a single point- or line-source, pro-

duces a spatial trend in a diffusion pattern. They also reveal the effects of geographical variations of resistance and the randomness of contact upon the degree to which spatial-trend patterns must coexist with spatial inversion components. And finally the S-shaped growth curves over time are evident.

SOME PROBLEMS

Despite the versatility of Hägerstrand's theory of the spatial diffusion of innovations, there are some serious shortcomings of his theory which require attention; specifically these are the problem of *removals;* the problem of explaining spatial-inversion patterns; and the reliance upon interpersonal-contact mechanisms.

The concept of *removals* stems from work on the spread of human diseases, but it does seem to have interesting implications for an understanding of the diffusion process. Epidemiologists, when considering the spread of a disease, divide the population into three groups: (1) the *susceptibles* who could get the disease; these are analogous to those who could adopt but have yet to adopt the innovation; (2) the *infectives* who have the disease and can pass it on to susceptibles; these are equivalent to the innovation adopters who tell the nonadopters about it; and (3) the *removals,* or those who have had the disease but for a variety of reasons such as immunity cannot communicate it to others; these are equivalent to those who have adopted the innovation but who are no longer instrumental in the adoption of the innovation by nonadopters. It seems that in some spatial-diffusion situations this classification is particularly relevant. Consider, for instance, the diffusion of the English language in Wales: the group of susceptibles is represented by those who speak Welsh only; the infectives are those who speak both languages and

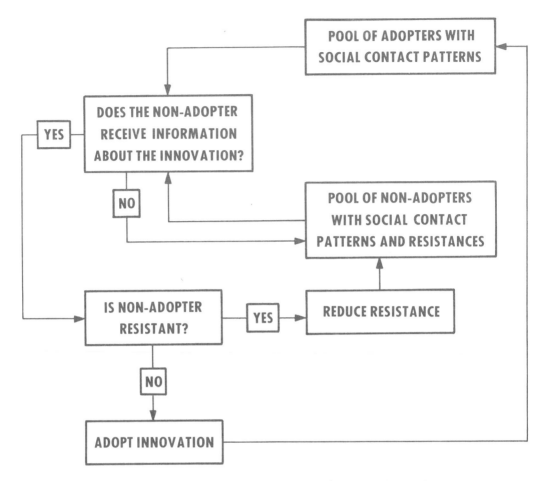

FIGURE 5-12. Flowchart for Hägerstrand's theory of the spatial diffusion of innovations.

who, by such agencies as marriage with those who speak only Welsh, are instrumental in spreading the English language; and the removals are represented by those Welsh people who speak only English and can no longer be effective in the spread of the English language. In this case, of course, the removals are easily identifiable. It is likely, however, that most diffusion processes are characterized by a removal phenomenon; for example, the novelty of the color TV set wears off for a family and they no longer invite others around to see it. Clearly the continuation of the diffusion in such a situation is likely to be highly contingent upon the presence of infectives: re-

movals cannot be the agents in further spread among the mass of susceptibles.

A second major problem is that of explaining the inversion elements in spatial-diffusion patterns. The mechanism which Hägerstrand relies on is a distance-biased communication mechanism subject to chance. Because of its chance element, this can produce an inversion pattern. But it seems that there are other mechanisms which could produce such inversion. One, for example, might be a connection bias present for a small proportion of the population randomly distributed across space such that they first hear of the innovation through the mass media and then tell individuals close by (i.e., the distance-biased communication mechanism). This is known as the *two-step-flow hypothesis of information dissemination* and could conceivably give rise to a diffusion pattern with a large-scale inversion component and a small-scale spatial trend component (see Figure 5-13).

Finally, there is the question of the appropriate means of communication. For the diffusion of many types of innovation it is unlikely that private contacts play the role which Hägerstrand ascribes to them. The spatial diffusion of color TV sets, for example, was almost certainly highly influenced by advertising in newspapers and other mass media. For the diffusion of the agricultural innovations which Hägerstrand studied, however, his emphasis upon private contact seems well-placed and does seem to produce the observed regularities.

THE DYNAMIC DIMENSION OF INFORMATION ACQUISITION: LEARNING AND LOCATIONAL PROBLEMS

We have reviewed some current ideas on the mechanisms producing migration patterns and spatial-diffusion patterns in an effort to identify the role which information about places and about different items has upon a diversity of locational patterns. Unfortunately, however, neither the migration topic treated nor the innovation-diffusion patterns which we have discussed lend themselves well to an illustration of the effects of the **progressive acquisition of information** about the environment upon man's decisions and their reflection in terms of some locational pattern. That is the aim of this section.

Many of the choice situations we face are repetitive: the choice of a grocery store at which to shop is made daily or weekly, for instance; we choose a vacation spot every year; we choose a restaurant every time we eat out; we choose a route to our place of employment or to our lecture hall every morning. In solving any repetitive problem of this nature, whether it is locational or not, we tend to acquire knowledge which allows us to solve the problem in a more *optimal* manner — either by allowing us to obtain some increased reward as a result of modifying our choice or by lowering the penalty imposed by choosing a particular alternative. Such knowledge may be acquired consciously or by trial and error.

Take, for example, our procedure for choosing a brand of sausage when faced

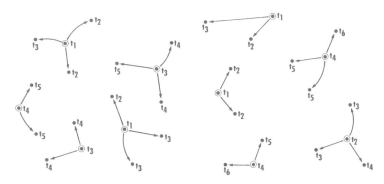

⊚ **INDIVIDUALS RECEIVING INFORMATION FROM MASS MEDIA**

• **INDIVIDUALS RECEIVING INFORMATION VIA FACE-TO-FACE CONVERSATION**

FIGURE 5-13. The two-step flow hypothesis and spatial-diffusion patterns.

with the problem of such a choice for the first time. We first choose one probably on the basis of price or packaging or the pinkness of the sausage. Consumption of the sausage allows us to acquire some further information about it and may lead to a modification of our brand choice the next time we buy sausage. By *trial-and-error information,* therefore, we eliminate those brands which we judge inadequate and ultimately reduce the range of choices to the more rewarding choices. An optimal choice in such a situation can be defined as one where the amount of satisfaction derived per dollars worth of sausage is maximized. In a situation of complete lack of information the probability that we will initially make an optimal choice is very low. Only as we acquire more information does the probability of making an optimal choice increase; thus the selection of a satisfactory brand of sausage reinforces our tendency to patronize that brand the next time we select a sausage. Indeed, experiments with learning situations have shown that the probability of making an optimal choice increases with time in a manner akin to the logistic or S-shaped growth curve discussed in the section on spatial diffusion.

Clearly this learning process has locational relevance. Many of the problems that we have to solve are locational problems—where to shop, where to live, where to go to a movie, etc. Consequently, much of what we learn involves the locational attributes of places. People's perceptions of the space surrounding them are based on the information they have. As they gather more and more information, it is reasonable to expect that their perceptions of relative location will become more accurate and they will adjust their movements over space so as to avoid those which are more costly than they need be and replace them with less costly, more optimal

movements. That is, people *learn* about the space around them and *learn* least-effort movements. We can illustrate these ideas with reference to shopping trip behavior. If you have ever moved to a new town or a city from your previous town it may be helpful to try and remember the procedures you or your family went through in establishing a cluster of shops to be repetitively patronized. It is probable that in the first week or so while you lived there, several stores offering the same good were patronized. By the act of patronage you obtained certain information about that store—especially how accessible it was to your home or to the routes which you regularly traveled. On the basis of this infor-

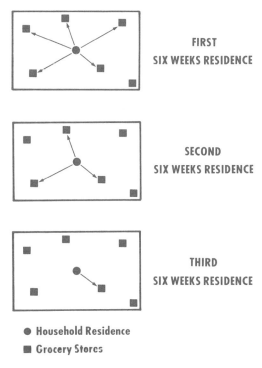

FIRST
SIX WEEKS RESIDENCE

SECOND
SIX WEEKS RESIDENCE

THIRD
SIX WEEKS RESIDENCE

● Household Residence
■ Grocery Stores

FIGURE 5-14. Hypothetical patterns of grocery trips at successive time periods for a new resident. Note how learning about the new environment and the location of grocery stores is reflected in an increasing tendency towards least-effort shopping trip behavior.

mation you or your family then narrowed down the set of stores you regularly patronized to those which involved less movement effort (all other things, such as service offered, being equal). This process conversely requires elimination of those stores involving relatively more movement effort. By such a trial-and-error process, therefore, of testing, information gain, and elimination of the more costly moves, the individual *learns* those shopping trip movements which are likely to incur less movement. Consequently, at any one time a map of movements consists not only of least-effort movements or movements approaching an optimal, least-effort solution characteristic of people who have *learned,* but also of relatively wasteful movements characteristic of people who have *yet to learn.* Figure 5-14 presents a hypothetical sequence of trips to grocery stores for a family moving into a new area.

Many other movements over space may be fruitfully viewed as learning processes: the marketing of livestock by a new farmer, for example, where possible markets exist in several neighboring towns. The actual movement itself, when holding the destination constant, is also subject to revision as a person finds routes which are more attractive in some way: prettier, faster, etc.

While decision makers learn about their places and adjust their behavior in accordance with what they have learned, however, what they learn is affected in itself by locational factors. We tend to learn first about those things closer to us in space and only later do we learn about more distant things. Consider, for instance, relationships between interurban and intra-urban migration: migration between cities is often followed by migration within the city. A businessman, when assigned to a new city, selects a residence on the basis of very limited information about the city. It is only when his family moves there that he might realize that his new residence leaves something to be desired in terms of accessibility to shopping, schools, or pleasant neighbors. Residence, however, allows the gathering of more information and learning about the city and is frequently followed by a second move within the city.

CONCLUSIONS AND SUMMARY

The material presented in this chapter suggests that spatial interaction is a considerably more complex phenomenon than we initially indicated in Chapter One. In Chapter One we made these assumptions about locational choice: men have perfect cognizance of the locational alternatives available to them and the movement costs associated with each alternative and they choose that alternative which minimizes effort. This chapter, however, suggests that this is a very partial view of the forces generating geographical patterns. There are many locational decisions which attest to man's selection of less-than-minimal-effort solutions. Most important, however, the variable amounts of information that men have about different places or about innovations affect their choices and resultant locational patterns.

We have illustrated these ideas of the impact of variable information upon decision making in a locational context and therefore upon locational patterns with two cases of this. The first concerned *migration patterns* resulting from decisions which are specifically locational in character—"Where to move to?" for example. The second focused upon *locational patterns of innovation adoption.* Innovation adoption is not a locational decision in the sense that migration decisions are, but it is affected by the locational context in which the individual finds himself and this is manifested in the resultant geography of adoption.

Migration fields, whether they are in-migration or out-migration fields, exhibit at least two components: a *distance-decay component* which can be explained in terms of least effort, and a *deviant component* which does not exhibit the same locational regularity. Some of these deviations can be explained by place utility considerations. In many cases, however, it has not been possible to explain deviations from the distance decay in this manner.

In order to account for such deviations we have expounded a theory of migration which is based on two mechanisms: *the occasionally random nature of the initial acquisition of information about a place* and *the role which friends and relatives play* in feeding back information from possible migration destinations, in subsidizing movement expenses, and in assisting adaptation by means of housing and job assistance. Considering mechanisms such as these, it is easy to envisage migrational bonds of increasing intensity over time between a given origin and a given destination. This seems particularly useful in explaining the deviant component in migration fields and we have termed such migration *chain migration.*

The second case study considered locational patterns of *innovation adoption.* A great many innovations can be seen to *spread* or *diffuse* over the landscape as individuals at successive locations adopt them. In terms of their locational patterns, innovation diffusions can be regarded in the purest terms as exhibiting either *spatial trend* or *spatial inversion.* In spatial-trend patterns, dates of adoption increase in a regular manner with distance from some point or line, whereas in spatial-inversion patterns no such regularity is apparent and the locational pattern of adoption dates is much more random.

The processes generating diffusion patterns are twofold: *relocation processes* and *expansion* or *contagion processes.* The first type of process results from the migration of the individuals who have already adopted the innovation. The second type of explanation depends on some functional link between a would-be adopter and an actual adopter producing the passage of some information about the innovation: hence the concept of *contagion.* This explanation is particularly apparent in Hägerstrand's theory of innovation diffusion. Hägerstrand was struck by what he termed the *neighborhood effect:* the tendency for earlier adoption to occur in places closer to those who had already adopted with a greater likelihood than in places more remotely located. Hägerstrand explained this in terms of *social relations* between would-be adopters and actual adopters which (a) allowed the transmission of information about the innovation, and (b) were more likely at a short distance than at a long distance. Where the would-be adopter was resistant, of course, the adoption did not take place until the *resistance* had been broken down by repeated contact.

In the context of both migration decisions and innovation-adoption decisions, however, information is dynamic rather than static. Man is continually gathering information and *learning to adjust* his movement patterns in the direction of a solution that is more economical in terms of movement to the items he requires like food and recreation. Many locational choices are repetitive, such as the patronization of a grocery store. Solving the problem repetitively, moreover, leads to the acquisition of increased amounts of information by trial and error or from external sources such as friends. Over time, therefore, one would expect the new resident to develop a more optimal pattern of movement which maximizes his rewards and/or minimizes his costs.

An assumption implicit in the discussion presented in this chapter is that although people's information about different places varies, at least it is accurate. The assumption is, of course, not completely justified because decisions, locational and otherwise, are made not in terms of objective reality as determined by accurate measuring instruments, but in terms of perceived reality. How this affects locational decisions we shall see in Chapter Six.

CHAPTER SIX

Space Perception and Locational Decisions

THE CONCEPT OF SPACE PERCEPTION

If we exercise a little introspection and ask ourselves about the nature of the knowledge that we have about the world around us it will be quickly apparent that that knowledge is (1) often inaccurate and (2) often tinged with value judgments. The inaccuracy of our knowledge may be revealed when we find out for example that what we thought were the nearest tennis courts are actually not. Our knowledge of locations is also often endowed with some value judgment of places: many of us see San Francisco as a hedonistic heaven, London as swinging, Paris as the city of light, New York City as threatening to our personal security, and Toledo, Ohio as just a dump.

Such knowledge of our environment cannot be regarded as knowledge in the scientific sense of the word. It is usually not knowledge that has been validated by some sort of experiment or objective measuring instrument applied by a scientist and subject to the canons of scientific accuracy. Rather it is our own individual reactions acquired through visual, auditory, tactile, and verbal contact with our environment and subject to all the distortions which can be imposed by the human mind. It is therefore more accurate to speak not of our knowledge of the environment but of our *perceptions of the environment*. These perceptions of reality may accord with an objectively measured reality but more usually they do not.

▶ *Perceptions are pieces of knowledge which are acquired by the individual as a result of his visual, tactile, verbal, and auditory contacts with the environment about him. They are not necessarily accurate by scientific standards; rather they are more or less accurate.*

Why are perceptions important to our understanding of locational patterns? Simply because it is their perceptions of reality that guide people in their decisions and in their movement behavior. In Chapter Five we related migration to such factors as economic opportunity as measured by median income or unemployment rate. This type of interpretation, however, implicitly assumes that the potential migrant goes to the United States Census, extracts data on state median incomes, ranks the states, and then makes his choice accordingly. This is clearly absurd. What actually occurs is that the individual migrant is guided by his perceptions of the relative attractiveness of different places, and these perceptions may deviate considerably from the reality of attractiveness as measured by such criteria as income and unemployment levels. An interesting demonstration of this occurred in a recent effort to measure the residential attractiveness of the 48 continental states by a group of undergraduates at The Ohio State University. Far down on the list in terms of preference was West Virginia, while above West Virginia were a number of Southern states and Great Plains states which in many *objective* respects are much less attractive residentially than West Virginia. Presumably, however, the economic plight of West Virginia has received such attention in the popular press of the United States that a great deal of popular attention has been focused on its unattractiveness as opposed to the more longstanding unattractiveness of such states as South Carolina, Alabama, Arkansas, Tennessee, North Dakota, or Montana. As a consequence of considerations such as these the predictions which geographers make of migratory movements are often inaccurate simply because they are making the assumption that perceptions of attractiveness can be measured by objective Census data such as measures of median income. While as we shall see there is not a little equivalence between perception and reality, there are occasional distortions of reality which exercise a great effect on movement patterns and make that assumption an erroneous one.

Beyond the general relevance of the concept of perception of environment to an understanding of locational patterns, there are two types of space perception which need to be recognized: *designative perceptions of locations* and *appraisive perceptions of locations.*

▶ *Designative perceptions are those perceptions that we have of the attributes of places and which are devoid of all evaluation of those attributes.*

Such and such a place is "a long way from here"; "Arizona has a warm climate"; "the Sahara Desert is arid and covered with sand dunes"; "Harlem is a Negro slum"; "Illinois is in the Corn Belt"; etc. These are perceptions of the attributes of places but they are not statements that we would get emotional about since, apart possibly from the Harlem reference, they contain very little connotation of evaluation — statements of nice or not nice, good or evil, etc. are not involved.

▶ *Appraisive perceptions, on the other hand, are those value judgments that we have of places.*

"Colorado is beautiful"; "New York City is unpleasant"; "Las Vegas is evil"; "South Lancashire is ugly"; "Paris is beautiful"; "It's nicer at Nice but cannier at Cannes"; etc. All these statements imply some *evaluation* of places. They are the evaluations which we use when we rank places in order of preference for some purpose such as residence or vacation. They are also statements that, because of their emotional content, people might quarrel over. While to some people Las Vegas is evil, to others it is an exciting, attractive place. Both types of perception — appraisive and designative — however, are significant for an understanding of locational problems and we will take each of them in turn, consider them at length, and show how these various perceptions of the world around us affect our locational decisions.

DESIGNATIVE ASPECTS OF SPACE PERCEPTION

We have argued elsewhere that the attributes of locations can be classified under two headings: site attributes and situation attributes. Here we think it would be useful to differentiate between the two considering first of all perceptions of the situation aspects of places and then considering perceptions of their site characteristics.

A number of years ago an American magazine published a map entitled "A New Yorker's Idea of the United States of America": some features of that map can be found in Figure 6-1. It was meant to depict in a humorous fashion the way in which an *average* New Yorker might *perceive* the relative locations of places in the United States and it reveals many of the *perceptual distortions* which we are all guilty of in varying degrees in our knowledge of places. Several features of the map may be remarked upon:

1. Distortion of distances between places: distances between some places are seen as shorter than they should be while other distances are seen as longer. Florida, for example, is seen as nearer to New York than say, Illinois; in fact, of course, quite the reverse is true. A more general feature of distance distortion is that places which are in reality closer to New York City seem to be conceived as further away than they actually are while places which are in reality further away are perceived as closer than in actuality. Thus, the state of Illinois is seen as over half as distant as the state of California whereas in reality Illinois is only approximately one-third the distance from New York to California.

2. Distortion of directions: Oregon is perceived as north of Washington whereas in fact the opposite is true.

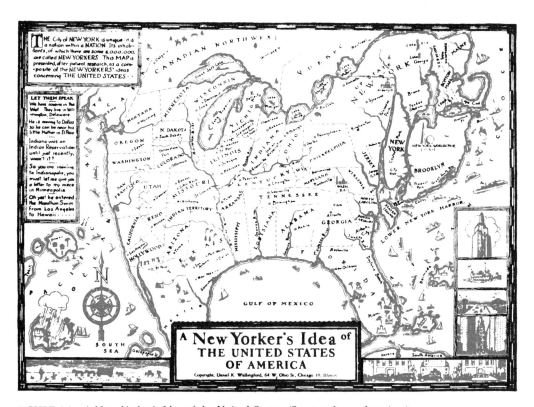

FIGURE 6-1. A New Yorker's Idea of the United States. (See text for explanation.)

Pittsburgh is seen as west of Dayton while in the real world Pittsburgh lies to the east.

3. Distortion of connections: the different connections of the states are also very much misunderstood; Missouri for example most certainly does not abut on Utah or Colorado.

4. Distortion of area: not only does the average New Yorker as seen by this cartoonist inflate Manhattan Island and Long Island way beyond the area of any state except possibly New York State but Florida is seen as the second largest state of the union! Likewise Hollywood is given the dimensions of a state as are San Francisco and Philadelphia while the states of Pennsylvania and Nevada shrink to points!

To the geographer such a map is a hopeless jumble but it is a surprisingly accurate image of the erroneous judgments which people do make. In particular it is clear that people tend to overestimate the distances to nearby places and underestimate distances to places further away. This was verified in an experiment with students at The Ohio State University where they were asked to take a piece of paper on which were plotted the positions of only two cities — Columbus and Cincinnati — and place the names of twenty other cities on the map. The resultant relationship identified between perceived distance and actual distance is shown in Figure 6-2.

This is consistent with the tendency for *areas* close to New York City to be exaggerated in size relative to areas further away. By exaggerating an adjacent area you are also overestimating the distance to its furthermost point; the northern boundary of New York State, therefore, is seen as considerably more distant than in reality.

The second interesting feature of the map is the way in which Florida is perceived as closer to New York City than it

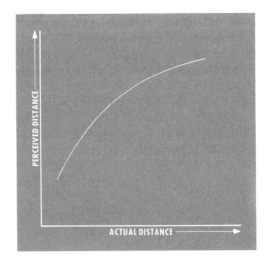

FIGURE 6-2. The relationship between actual distance and perceived distance; the graph is based on estimates made by a sample of Ohio State undergraduates of distances to a number of urban places in the United States. Note how distances to closer towns tend to be overestimated relative to the estimates of distances to more distant towns.

actually is. This is possibly associated with the greater attractiveness of Florida for New Yorkers due to its role as a vacationland and place for retirement. Certainly there is other evidence that more attractive places are seen as closer in space than they actually are. Thus, it seems that distances to larger cities with many amenities are underestimated compared with distances to smaller cities.

Clearly, in discussing the New Yorker's map of the United States we are discussing perceptions of a relatively large-scale environment. If we narrow down our focus a little and examine the perceptions which people have of different locations within a city we may get a rather different picture of the ways in which relative locations are perceptually distorted. Thus, travel time has been found to be an important factor in affecting perceptions of distance. In a study of such perceptions in the city of Columbus, Ohio it was found that distances towards the city center tended to be overestimated while those towards the suburban fringe were underestimated: a not surprising result when one considers that traffic congestion, traffic lights, and therefore travel time, increase as one goes toward the city center.

If there are regular distortions of reality in the perceptions which people have of locations this should affect their movement behavior in some predictable manner. If people, as they seem to do, underestimate longer distances then this should result in a greater tendency to move over longer distances than would be apparent if there were no perceptual distortion of reality. An interesting case of the way in which perception affects movement behavior is afforded by a tendency noted in at least two British towns for housewives to patronize grocery shops that are not their nearest ones but are in the general direction of the city center. It has been suggested that this is due to an underestimate of distances in the direction of the city center than in other directions. This, interestingly enough, conflicts with the evidence assembled on perceptions of distance in Columbus, Ohio but this discrepancy may be due to the greater reliance of the British housewife on bus and pedestrian movement rather than upon the automobile.

DESIGNATIVE PERCEPTIONS OF SITE CHARACTERISTICS

The environment around us consists of places which vary not only in terms of their situations but of places which vary in terms of both site and situation. Places differ in terms of their agricultural systems, for example: "the Corn Belt," "the Cotton Belt," "the Peach State," "America's Dairyland," etc.; they differ in terms of income and employment levels, racial composition, and a host of other nonsituational attributes.

In interacting with this environment of places we have to use the information we have acquired about them in as efficient and as economical a way as we possibly can. We receive a great many sensory, visual, and verbal impressions of places and in order to use that information we have to have some way of ordering it, eliminating redundancies in it, and occasionally extracting more knowledge from it than might at first seem possible. A scrap of information about a particular resort, for example, may offer us a clue as to other attributes of that place: the knowledge that many Spanish resorts are now hosts to Fish 'n Chip shops tells us a great deal about the type of patronage and the type of amusements likely to prevail in such resorts.

What devices do we use in order to maximize the utility of the information we acquire for the purposes of dealing with our environment? In brief, we tend to *classify* or *type* locations in terms of their similarities with each other. Consider our classification of places as suburbs, inner city, slum, etc. The fact that such and such a location is a suburb—or alternatively a slum—tells us a great deal about its income characteristics, property values, racial composition, quality of schools, housing stocks, and lot sizes. If the realtor tells us that the particular house is *not* in the suburbs it may save us a journey to check the place out for ourselves since the word suburb, like slum, is so rich in its connotations. Other classifications which we use in ordering information and in extracting the maximum possible information from a small clue come readily to mind: urban size, for example, with its two polar opposites of the quiet, amenity-less, provincial, but violence-free small town and the metropolitan center with its richness of cultural life, its crime, and its cosmopolitanism. We often tend to array nations on a developed–underdeveloped classification: or on a communist–noncommunist axis and this helps in extracting some information about, for example, Cuba or the Congo, even when all we have been given are two facts: (1) the place name and (2) the level of economic development of the place involved.

Not all classifications have such universal worldwide applicability as the underdeveloped–developed nation typology or the urban size dimension. A classification of the areas of London, for example, is applicable only to that segment of the world. Yet for the people in that area it may be an important classification assisting them in their locational behavior in that specific environment. Here we examine one specific locational classification system — that applicable to the states of the United States; and a more general classificatory system — that applicable to a *typical* American city.

THE CLASSIFICATION OF STATES IN THE UNITED STATES

If an American student were asked to take each of the states in turn and ask himself "Which three other states is this state most similar to?" it is likely that he would not find it difficult to come up with a list of similar places for each of the states. Of course some states would give more trouble than others; in many ways California and New York are unique, for example, and it would not be easy to decide which states are most similar to them. Other states, however, are much easier to deal with: for Mississippi, for instance, we are so used to seeing it lumped with certain other states such as Alabama and Louisiana that we would probably include these as similar places.

This little exercise was actually carried out with a class of about forty undergraduates at The Ohio State University and the results are so interesting and provide such good examples of place classifications as to be worthy of our attention here. What emerged in the study was that for each state there was a great

deal of consensus from student to student as to the three most similar states. This does not mean to say that every student chose the same three states: rather what seems to have happened is that they chose three out of a small number of the total possible states from which they could choose. Thus, for the state of Rhode Island they seemed to choose three of the following states: Vermont, New Hampshire, Maine, Connecticut, and Massachusetts; for the state of Alabama they seemed to choose three out of a small group of states including Mississippi, Georgia, Louisiana, South Carolina, and Arkansas; for the state of Vermont they seemed to choose from the same "pool" of states as they selected from for Rhode Island; and likewise for the states similar to, say, Georgia.

These pools or groups of states represent the *classes* to which states are allocated on the basis of similarity by the forty students. A plotting of these classes or pools of states about which there seemed to be a high degree of agreement revealed some rather interesting locational patterns. The major conclusion was that the classification of states in the United States took the form of a regional classification in which similar states were found located close to each other geographically. Figure 6-3 presents the outlines of the regions and names which seem to be appropriate.

The most striking feature of this map is the role which *situation* appears to have played coincidentally or purposely in the classification of states: states appear to have been seen as similar to nearby states. Of course, this could be coincidental in that many site characteristics such as income levels and urbanism are distributed geographically in such a way that a state is, in many site characteristics, most similar to adjacent states. It could, on the other hand, be purposeful; it may be, for instance, that the students interpreted similarity as

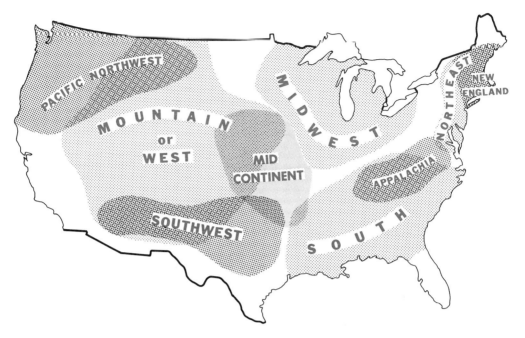

FIGURE 6-3. Perceived regions of the United States; note the tendency for the regions to overlap (i.e., they are blurred at the edges), the failure to perceive California as belonging to a regional grouping and the surprising emergence of a mid-continent region. These are the perceived regions of a group of beginning geography students at Ohio State University, Columbus, Ohio.

meaning similarity with respect to situation characteristics rather than with respect to site attributes. Most likely, however, it represents a mixture of the two forces—classifying by situation and classifying by site characteristics clustered in space—and symbolized in the awareness of the student of the classical regional divisions of the United States employed by the media and the layman and based on these two similarity criteria. Thus, all Americans carry around in their heads a classification of states into groups which has been implanted in them by the American educational system and by the media: they think in terms of the South, New England, and the Pacific Northwest, for example. It seems that the state name serves as a cue which evokes a regional grouping from which three similar states are chosen. For most states, for example, the pro-

cedure which the students probably went through was: (1) which regional grouping does that state belong to? (2) select three states from that regional grouping.

Another interesting facet of the locational classification is the emergence of Mid-Continent and Appalachian regions. This is surprising in that in most geography textbooks these areas have not been regarded as possessing a great deal of similarity across their constituent locations. The emergence of Appalachia can probably be attributed to its recent exposure in popular discussion in the mass media but the Mid-Continent region is more problematic. This region seems to overlap two of the regions commonly treated in textbooks of the geography of North America—the Great Plains on the west stretching from North Dakota in the north to northern Texas on the south; and on the east the western margins of the Midwest in the form of Iowa and Missouri. Certainly there is a great deal of difference between the classical Corn Belt farm economies of Missouri and Iowa and the dominantly Wheat Belt economies of the states immediately to the west.

THE CLASSIFICATION OF PLACES
WITHIN CITIES

The investigation above into the classifications which people make of their perceptions of the states applies to a specific context—the United States—and to a rather large geographical scale. Most of us live in cities and need to develop a classification of places within the city to guide us in our locational behavior. We move from one city to another and moreover we need some image of locational patterns within the city that is general enough to apply to a large number of other cities.

In an effort to obtain some insight into the locational images of cities that people use to classify and order their perceptual experiences within cities and to guide them in their locational behavior, an investigation was carried out into the images of about forty undergraduates. Investigation was confined to five elements of the geography of the city: racial distributions, the distribution of population, social-class patterns, the geography of land values, and the distribution of crime. Students were provided with five maps, each divided into 49 rectangular cells, and asked to fill in each cell according to whether it, for example, was likely to be dominantly Negro or white; dominantly middle class or lower class, etc., in a typical city. They were also told that the central cell in the map should be assumed to represent the central business district.

The picture which emerged of student images of urban geography was one dominated by *concentric patterns.* The major differentiation made was between: (1) a central city with relatively dense, Negro, lower-class populations with low land values and a high crime rate, and (2) a suburban ring with less dense populations, white, middle-class populations with relatively high land values and low crime rates. There was a high degree of agreement among the students about these images.

Two points need to be made about these classifications. Firstly, location relative to the central city seems to provide a potent cue to the students in ordering information on racial composition, social class, etc. Presumably the perceptions which they have of the city fitted into a concentric ring-type image of the city. It is perhaps for reasons such as this that proposals for the political unification of a city and surrounding independent suburbs are often opposed so vigorously by suburban populations.

The second interesting point is that even allowing for the fact that the maps are intendedly general, they are in important ways inaccurate classifications of urban geography. For one thing, the students perceived the central business district to be surrounded by the Negro ghetto: this in actuality and for a variety of reasons rarely happens. Generally the ghetto tends to be to one side of the business district.

Another, and possibly the most critical, discrepancy is in the perceived locational pattern of land values. According to the responses, land values per unit area are lower in the central city and higher in the suburbs. This is quite definitely the reverse of what occurs in reality for reasons which will be discussed at length in a later chapter. What we seem to be witnessing here, however, is an effort to deduce land-value patterns from other patterns about which the students have more information. In particular it must seem not very plausible that the housing of lower-class, largely Negro populations can stand on land of much higher value than that occupied by suburban housing. However, that indeed is the case.

And finally, the image of population distribution fails to catch an important nuance of the pattern. The image is one of a densely populated central city surrounded by a less densely populated suburban periphery. This does not deviate too severely from reality except that it does fail to recognize the relatively low population densities characteristic of the very center of the city where business buildings prevail over residential structures. This will be discussed at length later. The important points for us at this stage are that people do, on the basis of their perceptions, develop locational classifications of the world around them and use these to filter and order subsequent perceptions; and, also, in some important respects these perceptions of locational pattern do not square with reality.

THE LOCATIONAL IMPLICATIONS OF CLASSIFICATIONS OF PLACES

Given that we have these classifications of places, how specifically do they assist or affect us in *navigating* from place to place and in our locational behavior in general? An initial point is that knowledge of where a place fits in our system of pigeonholes or locational types allows us to formulate an appropriate locational policy with respect to that place. If we are planning a trip west, for example, we will tend to plan our overnight stops in the context of the urban size typology which we carry around with us. We know, for example, that larger places offer a greater variety of restaurants, motels, and entertainment in general. The knowledge which we can obtain from a road map

that such and such a place is very small will lead us to reject it as a possible overnight stop; the knowledge—also obtained from the map—that some other town has a population of 20,000 will lead us to plan that as a possible overnight stop on our trip even though we may never have heard of the town before looking at the road map.

Similarly, in looking for a new home in a strange city, the description "suburban location" applied by a realtor to a particular house allows us to place that particular house in our locational classification and develop a much more positive set of expectations about it than would the description "close to downtown." The terms "suburban location" and "close to downtown" are for most of us rich in their connotations. "Suburban," for example, provides the basis for deducing something about the social class and race of the people in the area, something about the quality of the local school system and the level of local property taxes, and something about the incidence of crime. The use of terms such as "suburban location" and "close to downtown," therefore, allows us to organize our search for a residence in a much more efficient manner than if we were told simply the street address of the house. This is because it allows us to eliminate houses that cannot be placed in those particular pigeonholes of our locational classification which correspond to more attractive residential sites.

The classifications which we use, moreover, often have a marked hierarchical nature. The perceived regions of the United States, which we discussed above, for example, are divisible into smaller locational classes which we call states; each state is likewise divisible into certain other still smaller classes such as "upstate New York," "the Texan Panhandle," "near to Kansas City," "central Ohio," "near to St. Louis," etc.

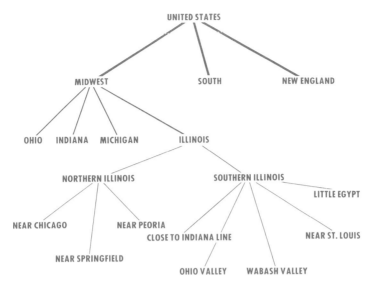

FIGURE 6-4. An example of a hierarchical classification of places.

(see Figure 6-4). *In ordering places in that hierarchical classification, however, the hierarchy tends to be much more finely developed for areas closer to us in space than for more distant areas.* Thus, if I live in southern Illinois and ask where the town of Herrin is, the fact that it is in Little Egypt will have some meaning to me; likewise the fact that it is near to Marion will be meaningful since "Little Egypt" and "near to Marion" will be classes in my hierarchy of locational classes. For someone living in New York City, however, it is very unlikely that "Little Egypt" or "near to Marion" will be meaningful. If he is told, however, that it is in southern Illinois he will be able to place it on his mental map of the United States.

Consider how this affects our navigational behavior, our problem of getting from one location to another. If I live in Columbus, Ohio and wish to visit someone in Circleville, Ohio my navigational problem will be very minor since Circleville, being only twenty miles from Columbus, will form a class in my locational classification. If I wish to visit someone

in Sweetwater, Texas, however, I will need a little more knowledge since, while Texas features on my locational classification, it is unlikely that Sweetwater does. In order to find it on a map, therefore, I will need additional information which is meaningful to me, that is, which places Sweetwater in a class of my locational classification. One such meaningful class, for example, might be "west of Dallas"; if I lived closer to Texas and therefore knew more about Texas the more specific "west of Abilene" or "between Abilene and El Paso" might have a place in my locational classification.

This type of hierarchical classification, which we each have and which is developed in finer detail for the area which is closer to us and therefore more familiar to us is implicit in the sign-posting policy of transportation and highway departments. The longer distances on sign posts, for example, refer to places that are more likely to be in our locational classification—specifically larger cities. The shorter distances, on the other hand, refer to not only the larger cities but also the smaller cities of which the shorter distance traveler is likely to have heard.

A second major locational implication of these classifications is that they may exercise an effect on our perceptions of the distances to various locations. It seems likely, for example, that if two places are placed in the same pigeonhole of our locational classification they may be perceived as closer together than two places that are placed in different pigeonholes. If the pigeonholes are defined by the individuals in terms of situation criteria or site criteria that cluster in space then this tendency for perceiving distances within classes as shorter than distances between classes may be particularly marked. It seems highly feasible, for example, that Iowa is seen as further away from Illinois than is Ohio, simply because Illinois and Ohio are both allocated to the Midwest whereas Iowa is allocated to the Mid-Continent region. The average Britisher may perceive a Welsh county such as Flint to be closer to another Welsh county such as Cardigan than to any English county that is objectively closer to Flint than Cardigan.

Clearly our navigational behavior and our estimates of movement costs are strongly affected by our designative perceptions of places and of their locations. What, however, of our appraisive perceptions—our preferences for one location or type of location relative to some other? It is to these that we now turn.

APPRAISIVE ASPECTS OF SPACE PERCEPTION

In any of the multitude of movement decisions that men are called upon to make—moving into a new home or new job, changing the site of the annual vacation, or choosing the university to attend—the information that one has about places must be evaluated or ap-

praised in terms of the goals of the individual: Which place is best for the annual holiday? Which place in the city is best as a place of residence for my particular family? Prior to choosing a place to move to, therefore, we can imagine the individual evaluating possible destinations and *ranking* them in terms of his needs or goals in order to derive a *space preference scale* at the top of which is the most preferred place and at the bottom of which is the least preferred place. A number of studies of space preferences have been made and their results provide interesting evidence on the rankings of places made by people. Here we will examine one particular bundle of studies associated with Dr. Peter Gould: studies of *mental maps of residential desirability.*

Imagine that you drew up a list of ten possible vacation places, gave it to ten of your friends, and asked them to rank the places in order of their preference from one to ten. The chances are that you would probably get ten different listings. If you inspect the listings more carefully, however, you would find that while each one was unique in some respect, they also have something in common: for example, while some would rank place A first, others rank it second, and still others rank it third, it is probable that no one would rank it less than third. Also, there might be places which would be ranked the same by everybody. It seems therefore that each listing would contain both a general component which it would share with other listings and a unique component which by definition would have no point of similarity with anyone else's unique component. In still other cases, there may be two general components or viewpoints in addition to a unique component or viewpoint.

For example, examine rankings in Table 6-1 made by five individuals of ten places. An initial survey of the listings

TABLE 6 1.

Individuals	I	II	III	IV	V
Places					
A	1	1	2	3	2
B	3	3	5	5	5
C	8	10	3	2	6
D	7	7	7	6	8
E	10	8	8	7	10
F	2	2	9	9	9
G	6	4	10	8	3
H	5	6	1	1	1
I	9	9	4	4	4
J	4	5	6	10	7

reveals that nobody's listing is exactly the same as anyone elses. A closer survey, however, indicates that there are similarities across all listings: for example, all individuals rank place A in the first three; all individuals accord place D a rank of sixth, seventh or eighth; all individuals rank B third or fifth. There seems to be support in this table, therefore, for the idea that while rankings are unique in some respects they are also similar in other respects, that is, the individuals do have a general viewpoint as well as specific viewpoints.

Still closer inspection suggests that there might be other general viewpoints shown by small groups of individuals. There are some grounds, for instance, for suspecting that individuals 1 and 2 have some common viewpoint which they do not share with individuals 3, 4, and 5. Both individuals 1 and 2 rank place B third, for example, while the remainder of the five individuals rank it fifth. Both 1 and 2 rank place I ninth while it received the ranking of fourth from the others.

Precisely why such general viewpoints should emerge is currently under investigation. A plausible suggestion, however, is that the rankings depend on (a) the information received by the individual, and (b) the goals of the individual. If the group members receive similar information and have very similar goals then we should have every reason to expect a strong general viewpoint to be present in their rankings. Thus, skiing afficionados in Missouri, Kansas, and Iowa are likely to favor Colorado as a place for vacations, while those in the northeast of the United States would probably opt for New Hampshire and Vermont. If we take the rankings of each individual and plot them on a map of the places ranked we obtain a mental map of residential desirability for each individual. Such maps may provide clues as to why individuals rank places in the way they do: do they, for example, tend to rank places *visited* higher than places never visited simply because they know more about such places?

If we can obtain measures of the general viewpoint rankings (one method might be to compute an average ranking for a place) we can map these to get an idea of which places are *generally* ranked higher than others. Does the group, for example, tend to rank places nearer to the group location higher than places further away on the grounds of greater familiarity?

Peter Gould of the Pennsylvania State University has carried out extensive investigations into these problems in the United States, Britain, Western Europe, and Africa and his results are so interesting as to merit a detailed consideration by us. Gould's strategy has been to give older school children in a specific school, or university students at a specific university, a list of places with which they are likely to be familiar—the states of the United States for Americans or the counties of Britain for the British, for example. The students are then asked to rank the places in order of their preference for them in terms of *residential desirability:* where would they like to live most, where least, etc. Clearly Gould would obtain different answers if he framed his question in terms of vacation desirability. Again, when interpreting the results which Gould obtained we must bear in mind that the groups who have been given the questionnaire are in some ways, elite groups. University students are better educated than most people and know more about different places simply because they read more and usually travel more. Also, the British school children sampled were largely the better-educated grammar school children. It would be interesting to compare the results obtained from such groups with the results obtained from groups who have less information about places further away — a group of factory workers or housewives, for example.

Given these rankings of places by a set of individuals, Gould has manipulated the rankings in such a way as to obtain one or more general viewpoints or sets of rankings which all individuals more or less accord to places. Gould has called these general rankings *percepts* and has constructed maps in which places having similar general rankings or percepts are joined by a line known as an *isopercept*. An example of such a map is provided by Figure 6-5. We now proceed to a discussion of the content of the mental maps of residential desirability which Gould has been able to construct in this way.

For each set of school children questioned in Britain and for each set of university students questioned in the U.S.A., Gould has been able to derive a general viewpoint or space preference which he has mapped. As an example, the general viewpoint of the school children in Liverpool, England is presented in Figure 6-5. When all the maps of general viewpoints for students in Britain are examined, a first striking aspect of their content is their *general similarity*. Similar places are ranked low by school children in Falmouth, England as by school children in Newcastle, England;

FIGURE 6-5. The mental map of residential desirability of the school children of leaving age of Liverpool, England. Note the *neighborhood effect* or tendency to give high levels of preference to the area immediately surrounding Liverpool; also, there is a general tendency for more southerly locations to be preferred to more northerly locations. Shaded areas are those where isopercepts are greater than 80; i.e. the most desirable areas.

similar places are ranked high by school children in those two places. Of course, there are exceptions which we will discuss shortly but nevertheless there are very striking similarities between the general viewpoints of schools at different places in Britain. On the basis of this observation, therefore, Gould and a collaborator, Rodney White, have proceeded to construct a map of rankings based on the general rankings of all schools ques-

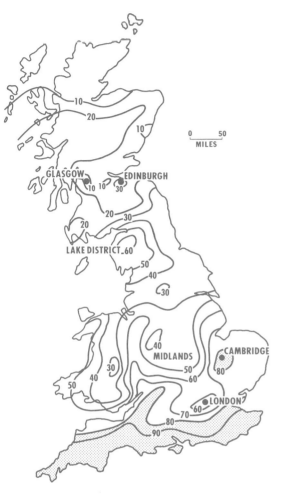

FIGURE 6-6. The mental map of residential desirability of the school leavers of Britain; this map is based on the residential preferences of school children of leaving age from a sample of schools distributed throughout Britain. Note the tendency for more southerly locations to be preferred to more northerly locations and the preference for areas of amenity value such as the Lake District, the west Wales coast and the Scottish Highlands. London does not appear to be all that attractive—Glasgow even less. The high preference for the Cambridge area in eastern England, however, is an interesting comment on the intellectual pretensions of the English school leaver! Shaded areas are those where isopercepts are greater than 80; i.e. the most desirable areas.

tioned in Britain as a whole: the map, which can be regarded as a general viewpoint of British school children independently of where their school is located, is presented in Figure 6-6.

The major features of this map are twofold: firstly there is a general decline in *perceived desirability* from the southern portion of Britain to the north of Scotland: the highest scores occur on the south coast; second, well-known tourist areas such as the English Lake District (see map), the west coast of Wales, the south coast of England, and Edinburgh received relatively high rankings compared with areas lacking such scenic attractiveness as in the case of the English Midlands, London, and Glasgow. We will return to these features shortly.

No such general map for the United States has been computed from the combined rankings of the different universities at which students have been questioned. However, for three out of the four universities sampled—California, Minnesota, and Pennsylvania State—striking correspondences are revealed: such a viewpoint is not shared, however, by the students of the University of Alabama—a legacy perhaps of old Civil War rivalries and resentments. The general picture revealed by the mental maps of the students of Minnesota, California, and Pennsylvania State, however, is of a United States the most desired portions of which are: (1) the vacation areas of the Pacific Coast, Colorado, Florida, and New England; and (2) the northeastern states bordering on the Great Lakes and the Atlantic Coast. The least preferred areas, on the other hand, include the South, the Great Plains, and the arid West centering on Utah (see Figure 6-7).

Precisely why these preferences take the form they do is open to question and all we can do here is offer some plausible suggestions. Gould has suggested that they may in fact reflect realistic perceptions by the students sampled of social welfare differences from one place to another. He has plotted the perceptual scores accorded the states by students at Pennsylvania State University against a social welfare score for each state, and

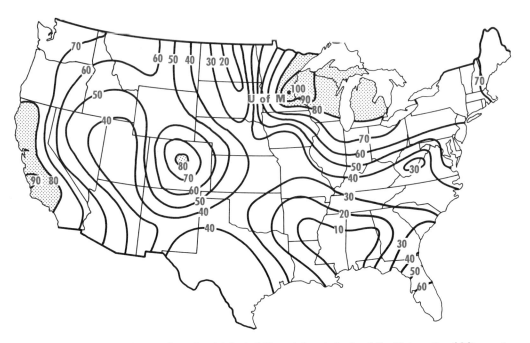

FIGURE 6-7. The mental map of residential desirability of the students of the University of Minnesota; note the preference for the Minnesota area (a *neighborhood effect*) together with amenity-rich areas such as Florida, California, and Colorado. The areas of economic opportunity in the Great Lakes area and the northeast also receive a high rating. The poorer areas of the nation, such as the South and the Great Plains, receive very low ratings. Shaded areas are those where isopercepts are greater than 80; i.e. the most desirable areas.

the results in terms of a linear array of points are very impressive (see Figure 6-8). Indeed the preferred states of New York, California, Washington, Connecticut, Massachusetts, Oregon, Wisconsin, Colorado, Michigan, Ohio, and Rhode Island do have high levels of social welfare while the least-preferred states of Mississippi, Alabama, South Carolina, Louisiana, Tennessee, West Virginia, Nebraska, and Oklahoma have relatively low levels of social welfare. There are exceptions of course: Nevada, Iowa, Utah, and North Dakota, for example, are less preferred than we would have anticipated on the basis of their social welfare levels, while the popular vacation areas of Maine, New Hampshire, Vermont, Florida, Virginia, New Mexico, and Kentucky are more preferred.

No similar analysis is available for Bri-

tain. However on the basis of a number of separate indices it is known that social welfare levels broadly decline with distance northwards from the London area: salary and wage levels decline, unemployment tends to increase in its incidence, and automobile ownership declines. Scotland and the north of England are also well known for their relatively poor housing conditions. The exceptions from these relationships with social welfare levels are of course analogues of the American cases; the tourist areas of southwestern England, the Lake District, Edinburgh, and West Wales, for example, are analogues of Maine, New Hampshire, Vermont, Florida, Virginia, and Kentucky; while the dull Midlands must be perceived in much the same way as dull Iowa and North Dakota as far as residential desirability is concerned.

These comments upon the broad geographical characteristics of the general viewpoint maps of residential desirability, however are far from exhaustive of the map content. A very important feature of nearly all *the general viewpoints* of the specific schools or universities has been the *neighborhood effect*. While the Minnesota students (see Figure 6-7) had a general viewpoint very similar to the California students, they preferred Minnesota before any other state: Califor-

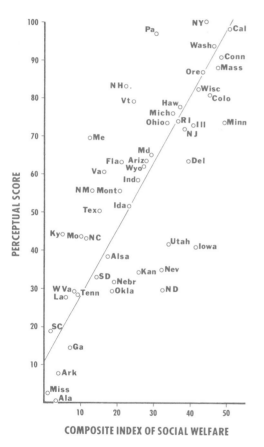

FIGURE 6-8. Residential desirability as perceived by students at the Pennsylvania State University and a social welfare index. In general, states with high levels of social welfare tend to be more preferred; note also that states with amenity advantages such as Maine, New Hampshire, and Florida tend to be *more* preferred than we would expect on the basis of social welfare differences, while amenity-poor states such as North Dakota and Iowa are less preferred than expected.

nians were also parochial in according their first ranks. In Britain the school children of Liverpool (see Figure 6-5) gave their county of Lancashire top ranking and saw neighboring counties in similarly glowing terms; the general viewpoint of the school children of Newcastle-upon-Tyne was very similar but for Lancashire they substituted their own county of Northumberland. Such a neighborhood effect is highly interesting since it lends support to the idea that mental maps are moulded by information flows and attachments to places. We would expect students to know most about and to feel most attached to those places of which they have most experience and knowledge.

A second important feature is what we shall call here the *spatial discrimination effect*. The general viewpoints obtained at the different schools and universities suggest that students differentiate and discriminate in terms of their rankings between nearby states more than they do for states further away. Thus, the Alabama students, while indulging themselves with a *neighborhood effect* and endowing nearby Florida, Georgia, North Carolina, and Texas with high rankings, accord the equally nearby states of Mississippi and South Carolina exceedingly low rankings; the students of distant Pennsylvania State, on the other hand, saw relatively little difference between North Carolina, South Carolina, Georgia, and Mississippi. In Britain, the isopercepts accorded Scotland by the school children of Liverpool range only from 10 to 40; while the school children of Kirkwall in the north of Scotland accorded rankings resulting in isopercepts which range from a low of 10 to a high of 90. Clearly, familiarity not only breeds desirability but it can also breed contempt!

The third feature of interest in the content of mental maps of residential desirability is the way in which they reveal space preferences which, while explainable in terms of certain geographical factors, are surprising in terms of the power one would have been inclined to allocate to such explanatory factors. For the British school children, for example, a surprisingly important feature appears to be the border between England and Scotland. The students of Liverpool (see Figure 6-5) preferred almost all counties of England to any county in Scotland. For the school children of Inverness in the north of Scotland, on the other hand, most of Scotland is preferred to all of England and Wales apart from the south coast. In view of the fact that the border has not been a barrier to movement since 1707 this residual patriotism is surprising.

In the case of the American university students a similar surprise is apparent when examining a second general viewpoint that has been obtained after the first general viewpoint. The isopercepts in this case tend to run north–south suggesting that on one of the general viewpoints the students tend to discriminate between places on an east–west axis. The only reason that can possibly explain such a space preference is that much of American movement is dominated by east–west tendencies: "go West young man" has been a theme in American history reflected not only in the movement of people but also in the routing of railroads, airlines, and subsequent commodity and passenger flows. Other factors such as time zones emphasize the possibility that Americans do think of their country in east–west terms.

We commenced this section by suggesting that the space preferences that people have would shed some light upon their movement behavior, particularly migration. As yet little evidence exists on this point so what follows is highly speculative. Relating space pref-

erence scores to migration is bound to encounter difficulties since: (1) students are not representative of the total migration population and the space preferences accorded by the general population might be very different from those accorded by students, and (2) while residential desirability must be an important factor in estimating the *place utilities* relevant to the migration decision, other desirabilities, such as type of job available, are also important.

Nevertheless, some broad relationships may be referred to. The north–south distinction in the mental maps of British school children, for example, does find a reflection in the "drift to the south," the southward migration which has been such a common feature of post-1900 British geography. In the United States, also, areas of highest in-migration agree with the generally high rankings given to the Pacific states while the negatively evaluated Great Plains and South have been areas of marked out-migration in recent years.

This is a question which needs to be pursued further, however, as it is of the utmost importance. If space preferences can be identified and shown to be related to migration they may prove a strong weapon in the kit-bag of tools currently being gathered by government planning agencies. By adding incentive payments for work in the least-desired areas (for example, for key management and technicians), governments may be able to manipulate the location of industry in an efficient manner which they have yet to approach. Gould is currently working on such a plan for the Tanzanian government. Its applicability to the governments of industrial nations, however, should be equally apparent. The British and French governments, among others, have spent vast sums of money on subsidizing the construction of new factories and highways in areas of high unemployment or relative poverty. What may be more important than this type of assistance, however, may be persuading the vital management and tech-nicians to live in the grime and drab isolation of least-preferred places. Such persuasion might be afforded by some scheme of incentive payments.

CONCLUSIONS AND SUMMARY

It should be clear from this chapter, therefore, that the knowledge which we have of the world around us is often inaccurate and/or tinged with value judgments. Indeed, the knowledge which we acquire by visual and tactile contact with the environment around us is often not amenable to scientific confirmation; we call such bits of infor-mation, therefore, *perceptions.* Perceptions of places, moreover, are broadly divisible into two classes: there are, firstly, *designative* perceptions that have no evaluative con-tent whatsoever, and there are also *appraisive* perceptions that contain an evaluation of the place concerned. Such perceptions are important for understanding locational pat-terns; man makes his locational decisions not in the world as it actually is but in the world as he perceives it.

We have designative perceptions of both the site and situation characteristics of places. A good example of designative perceptions of *situational characteristics* is provided by the "New Yorker's Idea of the United States." A marked feature of this map is the way in which areas closer to New York City are exaggerated in size relative to areas further away. This suggests that *we tend to overestimate shorter distances relative to longer distances* and, indeed, this does seem to be so. Within cities, however, percep-tions of distance seem strongly affected by travel time; the latter, of course, is in turn much affected by traffic congestion and controls.

In handling the vast quantities of information which he receives about the environ-ment around him, however, man must develop some sort of ordering system which will allow one piece of information to be related to another, permit the elimination of redundancies, and also function as a prediction device useful in searching the envi-ronment for various purposes. The ordering system which seems characteristic of man is one of *a set of locational pigeonholes* in which incoming bits of information can be placed.

Such *locational classifications* or *spatial images* have important locational implica-tions. If we can put a specific place in a locational classification, for example, it will as-sist us in evaluating its attractiveness; such evaluation is a *sine qua non in any efficiently organized search procedure,* whether it is for a new residence, a place of work, or a place of play.

Appraisive perceptions, on the other hand, are particularly in evidence in so-called *mental maps of residential desirability;* these maps provide us with some idea of the pref-erences which people have for different places and, therefore, whether they are nice or repellent, attractive or unattractive, etc. Such maps have been studied for the United

States and for the United Kingdom on the basis of student evaluations of places and there appear to be some very broad similarities between the two countries. In both countries, for example, the *general viewpoint* subscribed to by students independent of location appears strongly related to perceptions of differences in social welfare—in employment opportunity, physical amenity, etc.

In addition to this general viewpoint, however, there appear to be other effects. Specifically there is a *neighborhood effect* manifest in a strong preference for locations near to where the students are currently located. And there is also a *spatial discrimination effect;* the students appear to discriminate much more between locations closer to them in space than between locations which are more distant.

This chapter has been the second of two chapters dealing with the bases of locational decisions; such locational decisions can be related to the movements considered in the earlier chapters of this volume. Both locational decisions and resultant movements, however, need to be seen in the context of linear features—specifically, boundaries which separate and lines of communication which channel. Such linear patterns form the subject matter of the next three chapters.

CHAPTER SEVEN

Bounded Spaces: Locational Configurations and Locational Effects

INTRODUCTION

So far in this book we have considered movement over space and human decisions in a locational context insofar as they affect a variety of other locational patterns, such as the pattern of residential development within a city. Such decisions and movements, however, are executed in a locational context which is *bounded* either *conceptually* or *legally*. As we saw when discussing migration in Chapter Four, such boundedness can constrain movement (as with the White Australian immigration policy); it also affects the geographical coverage of the information that we have when we make locational decisions and therefore exercises a very important role in structuring geographical processes and resultant geographical patterns.

The locational significance of the boundaries which surround the spaces in which locational decisions are made is indicated very powerfully by the correlation of bounded spaces with other geographical patterns. Thus, as we shall show at greater length in this chapter, the geometry of national transportation networks tends to show a very close relationship to the surrounding national boundary, with, for example, railroad lines terminating near the boundary, running parallel to it, but rarely crossing it. Indeed, knowing whether a specific location is in one bounded space or another is a very useful predictor of the content of the space surrounded by the boundary. In general, *geographical variation within bounded spaces is reduced relative to the variation between bounded spaces.* In the bounded spaces that we call the nations of Europe, for example, average incomes vary much less across two areas of a given nation such as France or England (i.e., *within nations*) than they do *between nations* of the continent. The ideas of *between-area variation* and *within-area variation* are important concepts in discussions of bounded spaces and we will refer to them again below.

Such bounded spaces as nations or states or counties do not derive their sole geographical interest from their impact on other locational patterns, such as that of income, across the nations of Europe. Bounded spaces also have distinctive locational attributes of their own— specifically shape, area, and connectivity—and these bear important relationships to factors of an explanatory character both at a single point in time and at succeeding points in time. In particular, we shall find that the broad locational context of bounded spaces and the purposes which bounded spaces are intended to fulfill exercise an important effect on their geometries.

Finally bounded spaces are tools of the

urban and regional planner. He is concerned, for example, with delineating the boundaries of areas (such as depressed areas) that are to receive preferential treatment in the granting of governmental credits. He is also concerned with designing school districts—another example of a bounded space—in such a way as to provide for the efficiency of movement of school children to schools.

As can be seen, there are a whole range of geographical problems in which it is very useful to have a knowledge of the distinctive locational characteristics of bounded spaces, the forces affecting those distinctive locational characteristics and the manner in which they affect other locational patterns. In this chapter we begin by defining more specifically the concept of a bounded space and identifying the functions which they are intended to fulfill. Secondly, certain concepts of the geometry of bounded spaces are identified, and an attempt is made to identify some of the factors affecting these geometrical attributes. As a third problem, we take up the geographical evolution of bounded spaces, identifying some of the long-term changes in their geometry and some of the factors that affect the speed of change. What are the factors, for example, which impede the substitution of one large metropolitan bounded space for the many smaller bounded spaces into which most metropolitan areas are fragmented? Finally, we turn to an examination of the way in which bounded spaces structure movement patterns and hence other locational patterns such as those of communication networks and retailing. We have argued elsewhere that movement plays a decisive role in generating locational patterns. If boundaries separate and therefore impede movement we would expect them to have a very critical impact on a wide variety of locational distributions.

THE CONCEPT OF BOUNDED SPACES: DEFINITION AND FUNCTION

Bounded spaces are very simply spaces with a boundary surrounding them: nations, counties, school areas, farms, air fields, islands, etc., are all, therefore, bounded spaces. In addition, it is possible to recognize two types of bounded space according to the nature of the boundary.

▶ *Legally bounded spaces are those in which one's legally defined rights and obligations change when crossing the boundary.*

Legally bounded spaces are usually identified by landscape features signifying a boundary, "Trespassers will be Prosecuted" signs, tangible barriers in the form of hedges, fences, or even barbed wire. Legally bounded spaces include private properties, nations, counties, planning regions, and common markets. Crossing such a boundary changes a person's rights and obligations. For example, crossing a state line to reside in another state alters one's voting rights and one's taxation obligations from what they were in one's previous location.

In contradistinction to such *legally bounded spaces* one can also imagine a set of *conceptually bounded spaces.*

▶ *Conceptually bounded spaces involve no change in one's legally defined rights and obligations. The boundary surrounding such spaces is usually much more vague and ill-defined although the existence of such a bounded space will be subscribed to by a large number of people.*

Conceptually bounded spaces, therefore, are similar to the regions of the locational classifications identified by American university students that we described in

Chapter Six: Appalachia, New England, Midwest, and the South are all examples of conceptually bounded spaces. They consist of locations which for some reason people group together and set apart from other groups of locations. Similar bounded spaces are apparent elsewhere. Most notable are the *pays* or small regions into which the Frenchman has traditionally divided his nation: Aquitaine, Perigord, Normandy, Brie, etc. Nor are such conceptually bounded spaces limited to the larger geographical scale. We also tend to divide cities this way, for example: Harlem, the Gold Coast, the West End, the East End, etc. The ghetto is perhaps the clearest example we have of a conceptually bounded space.

Such conceptual boundaries which have no legal status whatsoever usually enclose a space consisting of locations which are similar to each other and different in some sense from surrounding areas. The Midwest, for example, probably gains its distinctiveness from the fields of corn, the rectangular pattern of land division, and the flatness of the landscape which distinguishes it from surrounding bounded spaces. Also, as we suggested in Chapter Six, there may be a tendency to group locations together simply because they are close together and accessible to each other.

Indeed, one often finds that such conceptually bounded spaces are also bounded in the sense of having restricted access to adjacent areas. Islands and peninsulas tend to be isolated, for example, and are often seen as bounded spaces by people. The Italian islands of Sicily and Sardinia are seen as distinctive; the Gaspé Peninsula of Canada, the Catawba Peninsula of Ohio, the Delmarva Peninsula of the U.S. east coast, Brittany in France, and Fife in Scotland are all regarded as possessing some type of unity distinguishing them from adjacent spaces.

In cities one sees similar associations between the conceptually bounded spaces to which people allocate locations within the city and the problems of accessibility created by such barriers to movement as lines of transportation. High-speed highways, railroads, etc. tend to create barriers to movement from one side of the line of movement to another. One frequently finds that such accessibility difficulties are strongly associated with differences in social composition on the two sides of a transportation route.

Both types of bounded space—the *conceptually bounded space* and the *legally bounded space*—function as crutches in organizing our knowledge of the space around us and in navigating from one location to another. As we saw in the last chapter, man needs a set of pigeonholes with which he can order the various bits of information he collects from the environment around him. Bounded spaces perform a function of organization by allowing the unambiguous location of any bit of information and by permitting inferences based on what we already know about a particular bounded space.

The *legally bounded space,* however, has rather more important functions which we must deal with at some length. Specifically, these functions concern the *organization of space for collective purposes.* To fulfill certain of their needs people must organize themselves collectively; public goods and services such as police, highways, education, sanitation, water, defense, pollution control, etc. must be provided; representation in government must also be obtained if the collectivity is to have control over its collective destiny. The fulfillment of such needs requires collective agencies and organizations to perform the necessary functions and taxation to support these functions. Usually we find that the *spatial organization of territory* which people adopt for such collective purposes is one which emphasizes the locational closeness of the people being served by these collective functions and the boundedness of the area being served. As a consequence, space is subdivided into a mosaic of administrative areas, Congressional Districts, states, school areas, sanitation districts, port authorities, etc. Why are these functions organized locationally in this manner? Why must we send our children to one school if we are on one side of a boundary and to another school if we are on a different side of a boundary? Strictly speaking, two problems of locational organization are involved here: firstly, that of the locational proximity of the people served by a function; secondly that of the boundedness of the spaces served by a function. Let us first consider the problem of locational proximity.

The principle of locational proximity in the provision of public goods and services derives from economic and political principles. Economically, for example, a service can be provided much more cheaply if the consumers of the service are located close together in space. Thus it is much cheaper to provide garbage collection services for one-thousand people in a single area of ten square miles than for one-thousand people in two areas of five square miles separated by a distance of ten miles.

Politically we have to recognize that many of the demands for public goods, services, and political representation have a highly *localized origin*. Intense air pollution is a relatively localized phenomenon, for example, and so demands for pollution control are likely to come from people located relatively close to one another. Also, many of the political issues over which people desire representation are localized in character: the location of a federal government investment or of an obnoxious land use in the

vicinity of the community involved provide examples of those *localized political issues* which form an incentive towards a territorial organization emphasizing geographic closeness.

Why, however, are the spaces supplied with goods and services *bounded* so that one receives services from, and pays taxes to, one authority on one side of a boundary and transacts with another authority if on a different side of the boundary? A major force producing such territorial fragmentation is the *spillover effect*. This concept will be treated at greater length in Chapter Thirteen when we discuss land-use problems, but it is also of importance in the current context. Briefly, spillover effects are classified as either *positive,* in which case they yield a *benefit* for someone; or they are *negative,* in which case they incur a *cost penalty* of some sort. In the present context consider a group (a collectivity) who decide to tax themselves and establish an organization to supply a collective good such as education or police protection. In such a case, the collectivity may not be the sole recipient of the benefits of their action nor of the costs of their action.

▶   *Positive spillover effects are unpriced benefits to individuals in areas outside the area commanded by the collectivity. Negative spillover effects are unpriced costs to individuals in areas outside the area commanded by the collectivity.*

Thus if a town institutes a system of river pollution control, points downstream will also benefit. This would be an example of a positive spillover effect. Similarly, investment in educational services will provide positive spillover effects to employers of skilled labor in the vicinity of the school or if the population shows a strong propensity to migrate to other more distant locations. In this sense, of course, Britain contributes many doctors to the United States and is therefore actually subsidizing the economic growth of the U.S.A. through the positive spillover effects which America obtains from such migration.

Negative spillover effects can be illustrated by the effect of the construction of a public housing project on property values in an adjacent wealthy suburb. The negative spillover effects from the public housing project will appear in the form of lowered property values in the wealthy suburb. Negative spillover effects are also the result of communities that export their troubles by migration; a community may refuse to invest in education for its citizens who then migrate to other communities and impose a burden as a result of their high demand for welfare services relative to their low skill and their inability to add significantly to the tax base. In this sense the poor Southern states which invest relatively meager amounts in education bestow negative spillover effects, because of migration, upon Northern cities.

What does all this have to do with boundaries? Briefly this: by placing a boundary around the area served by public goods and services the collectivity is able to control spillover effects to its benefit by *internalizing positive spillover effects* and *externalizing negative spillover effects*. What is meant by internalization? If a community decides to institute a pollution program on the basis of self-imposed taxes that pollution control program will provide benefits to all people within the community irrespective of whether they are paying taxes or not. Consequently, even though the benefits of pollution control are spread quite widely, the costs could be borne by a minority—a dwindling minority—as soon as householders realize that they could obtain the benefits without the costs. By placing a boundary around the area receiving benefits, however, and

obtaining authority to tax within the area, such spillover effects—in the form of higher and hitherto untaxed property values—can be incorporated into the tax base of the pollution program with advantages for the minority who have paid so far and a consequently more equitable distribution of costs and benefits.

Consider the problem of positive spillover effects resulting from migration. By investing in a high-quality educational program, a community may be merely subsidizing other communities that have not so invested. The benefits of a high school educational program in terms of the economic productivity of its students will therefore be lost to the community. By erecting a boundary around the community, however, and establishing laws regarding the crossing of that boundary, such a positive spillover effect can be *internalized.* Portugal has attempted to mitigate its "brain drain" problem by imposing on its skilled labor a time period during which they must work within Portugal. Of course, positive spillover effects can also be internalized by devolving the function to a larger area administrative unit. It is for this reason that communities probably find it more equitable to have the nation as a whole take charge of financing education. Positive spillover effects from the nation are much less likely than from the smaller individual community.

There is also the problem of *externalizing negative spillover effects.* Boundaries allow communities to control the entry of people and land uses that will adversely affect the tax base and the demand for public goods and services. Restrictions can be placed on the in-migration of workers' families much as Switzerland does on migration from Italy; or alternatively, zoning legislation applying within the boundaries can be developed in such a way as to externalize low-value properties that would detract from the tax base. Thus zoning can be for large one-acre lots; this effectively minimizes the probability of low-value housing being constructed.

Boundary lines, then, assist the community in obtaining a maximum return on the tax investment that each member of the community makes. They allow the incorporation into the tax base of all those who benefit from the service. They also provide a means of controlling those comings and goings that can detract or alternatively enhance the return on the individual taxpayer's investment. Clearly, spillover effects are never entirely eliminated; a community may construct parks for its citizens but that does not mean that the parks will not be used by those from other communities who pay nothing for the service they receive.

The end product of these considerations is a geographical organization of service areas that tends to maximize the internalization of positive spillover effects and the externalization of negative spillover effects. Economic and political factors provide the rationale for the localization of service areas. What of the more detailed geometry of such service areas?

THE GEOMETRICAL PROPERTIES OF BOUNDED SPACES

Three geometrical properties of bounded spaces are of interest at any one point in time: (1) area, (2) shape, and (3) connectivity. Each is examined in turn from both the descriptive and analytical viewpoint.

AREA

If we examine most maps of administrative units, such as the counties of England, one of the most striking features of such maps is the variety of areal size present. Furthermore, groups of small administrative areas tend to cluster

together just as groups of larger counties tend to cluster together, suggesting that territorial area varies systematically with certain other factors. What might such factors be?

A factor frequently associated with variations in areas of administrative units is that of population density —larger bounded spaces tend to have smaller population densities. Figure 7-1 plots the areas of the counties of Maine against their population densities to verify this point. Note that the relationship between population density and area is *negative exponential.*

▶   *Territorial areas decrease in size at a decreasing rate with increasing population density.*

A reason for such a relationship between area and population density can be found in the concept of threshold. Counties or communes or parishes per-

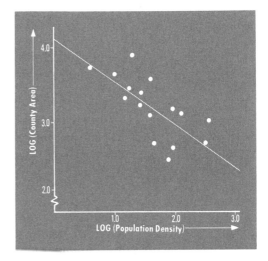

FIGURE 7-1.   County area and county population density in Maine, 1950. As population densities decline, county areas increase suggesting the operation of some threshold factor. Note, however, that both attributes of counties are expressed as logarithms on this scatter diagram; the relationship, therefore, is negative exponential.

form services for their populations. Such services are maintained, at least in part, and frequently wholly, by tax levies on the population being served. The tax revenue from a small population, however, probably cannot pay for a policeman much less a fire service, and in order to achieve that critical tax revenue level the people must group themselves into larger administrative units. We refer to that demand level at which it becomes economical to supply a good or service as the *threshold level.* Clearly, where the demand for a fire service is very small (as measured by tax receipts) some form of subsidy from outside would be required to pay for an adequate fire service or, alternatively, the fire service would operate at a loss.

SHAPE

A similar variety of locational pattern is apparent in the *shapes* of bounded spaces. Compare, for example, the elongation of Italy with the compactness of France or Spain (see Figure 7-2). Similarly, if one examines the counties of the United States there are striking differences between the rectangularity of counties in the Midwest and West and the irregularity of the shapes of counties on the East Coast.

A desired shape for many types of space would appear to be one that provides a high degree of compactness, and certainly many nation states seem to pursue the property with great zeal and much bloodletting. Germany's territorial acquisitions in the Second World War, for example, were aimed partly at eliminating indentations of its boundary in order to provide a more compact shape.

Compactness may be defined as:

▶ *That shape which maximizes the nearness of locations within the area to each other relative to their nearness to locations outside the area.*

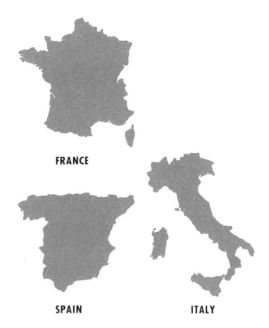

FIGURE 7-2. Shapes of some bounded spaces. National territories are bounded spaces and manifest a considerable diversity of shape; in the examples shown here France clearly has the most compact shape and Italy the least compact shape. Italy also has a serious problem of lack of connectivity.

The virtues of such a situation for bounded spaces, considering the rationale of bounded spaces discussed earlier, should be readily apparent. Compact shapes can maximize the closeness of group members to one another, allow them to share out their positive spillovers with one another and minimize the negative spillovers imposed by nonmembers. Compactness keeps the costs of public services low and permits less costly internalization of positive spillover effects and externalization of negative spillover effects by minimizing boundary length relative to area. It also minimizes the positive spillover effects that would ensue if, for example, territorial shapes were linear; the spillover benefits of, say, air pollution control would be very great in a linear state.

Assuming that compactness is a desired shape for bounded spaces, what are

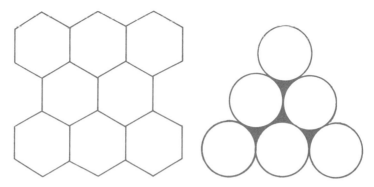

FIGURE 7-3.   The packing of bounded spaces of different shape: circles either overlap or are nonexhaustive; hexagons do not overlap and are exhaustive.

the properties of compactness that make it recognizable and measurable? Two criteria seem to be important for the compactness of an area to be maximized: (1) average access to the most central point of the cell should be maximized so that when travel distances from all places to the center are aggregated the sum is at a minimum, and (2) the length of the perimeter or boundary of the cell should be minimized. Hence, on this account a *circle is the most compact shape we know, while a square is less so, and a triangle even less compact.*

The circle, therefore, is that shape which maximizes the closeness of the people within the shape to each other relative to their degree of closeness to people outside the bounded space. The shapes of the territories of groups surrounded by relatively alien or hostile populations are interesting in this respect. Thus the Amish community of northern Indiana is apparently circular in shape. An interesting and plausible hypothesis would be that the edge of the Negro ghetto would tend to be smooth rather than indented in shape.

While a circle is the most compact shape we can have, however, a moment's thought will tell us that it is an impractical method of land subdivision. While circular fields would minimize the

hedging and fencing costs of the farmer, for instance, they would also leave bits of unused space (see Figure 7-3). What is frequently sought in divisions of space into cells, therefore, is a shape which maximizes compactness with the proviso that all the area being subdivided be exhausted; the shape which does this is the hexagon or six-sided polygon (see Figure 7-3).

Some effort has, therefore, been devoted to exploring the idea that legally bounded spaces tend to be hexagonal in form. Since shape is a difficult geometrical property to measure a number of these efforts have revolved around the counting of the sides of territorial subdivisions with the idea that six-sided bounded spaces will tend to have a hexagonal shape. Figure 7-4 demonstrates the numbers of French *départments* having different numbers of sides; as can be seen, the most frequently encountered geometrical figure characteristic of the French *départments* tends to be six-sided.

A glance at many maps of bounded spaces, however, will quickly convince the student that while some evidence may point in the direction of compact shapes, there are many exceptions to the compact territorial unit. In many cases deviation is guided by resource factors:

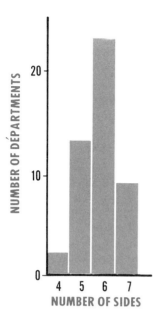

FIGURE 7-4. The frequency of French *départments* with a given number of sides; note that only *départments* removed from the national border or the coast have been considered and that the mean number of sides is 5.8. The prevalence of the six-sided shape provides some evidence for hexagonality though of course six-sided shapes are not necessarily hexagonal since, for example, the lengths of the different sides can vary a great deal.

the desire to obtain land that contains a large amount of high-value property, for example, that will enhance the local tax base. Resources, however, need not be economic alone; they can also be political. The alterations in the western boundary of the Soviet Union following the end of the Second World War are particularly instructive in this regard (see Figure 7-5). Two major changes in the western boundary are observable: (1) the westward extension resulted in increased Baltic Sea frontage for the Soviet Union, and (2) the contiguity of the Soviet Union with its western neighbors was increased. While before 1939 the Soviet Union was contiguous only with Poland and Rumania, after 1945 it was contiguous also with Hungary and Czechoslovakia. Such boundary alterations must be seen in the light of two

of Russia's historic political goals. First, successive rulers of Russia from Peter the Great onwards have invested a great deal of time and trouble in trying to ensure for Russia "warm water" ports. Because of Russia's northern location, much of her oceanic frontage is frozen for a large part of the winter. Such periodic immobilization has been not only a handicap to trade, but also a serious disadvantage in the use of naval power. A second

FIGURE 7-5. Changes in the boundary of Russia in eastern Europe, 1938–1946. The dotted line refers to the 1938 boundary between Czechoslovakia and Rumania on the one hand and Poland on the other hand. As a result of post-1945 boundary changes, Russia lost some of its compactness, replacing a relatively straight western boundary with a much more indented one. This change, however, allowed Russia greater access to certain locational resources, such as access to warmer oceanic water in the Baltic and access to the nations of eastern Europe which she wished to control. Note how in contrast to the 1938 situation, Russia is able in 1946 to make territorial contact—though limited—with Hungary and Czechoslovakia.

historic goal of Russian rulers has been to dominate the nations immediately adjoining Russia on the west in order to protect herself from invasion. The increased contiguity of Russia with the nations of eastern Europe has meant an increased military accessibility that has proven of great utility in the case of the Hungarian uprising in 1956 and the suppression of the liberal Czechoslovakian regime in the summer of 1968. It is significant that Yugoslavia and Albania, the only East European Communist nations that have managed to completely escape from Soviet domination, do not share a boundary with Russia.

A second factor affecting the shape of bounded spaces is the type of dividing line that is already present in the landscape and that does not interfere drastically with existing movements. Such lines are extremely useful as bases for political boundaries, not only because of their visual distinctiveness but also because of the fact that interactions are already constrained by them, and therefore, the use of the line as a political boundary is unlikely to impose any new impediment effect. Thus, rivers and mountain ranges are prominent quasilinear features that impede movement anyway and are, therefore, frequently employed as boundary lines.

CONNECTIVITY

A geometrical property of bounded spaces strongly related to the property of compactness is that of connectivity. Some bounded spaces consist of places that are enclosed by only one boundary line; the state of Switzerland is an example of this. Other bounded spaces consist of places enclosed by more than one boundary line; the United States is an instance of this as was the state of Pakistan. Spaces that are enclosed by one boundary line alone can be regarded as highly connected while spaces that are surrounded by more than one boundary line are less well connected and pose problems for movement and the efficient organization of space.

Note, however, that lack of connectivity in bounded spaces can take two forms: first, bounded spaces can exhibit lack of connectivity because they are *exclaves* relative to each other. This idea is illustrated in Figure 7-6. Examples of the exclave form of disconnectivity include Germany in the 1930s and the unconsolidated farm still common in parts of peasant Europe. In addition to the exclave form, however, there is also the *enclave form* of disconnectivity. South Africa suffers in this respect since Lesotho forms an enclave within its territory limiting the accessibility of one location in South Africa to another. This type of disconnectivity is relatively uncommon though there are numerous historical examples of it in the territorial growth of France and Germany and also in some contemporary American cities.

Disconnectivity in bounded spaces is a relatively uncommon phenomenon simply because of the costs and spillovers with which it is associated. In terms of costs, lack of connectivity increases the distance that must be traveled in order to service the populations within the

a   b

FIGURE 7-6. Lack of connectivity in bounded spaces. Type (*a*) occurs when the bounded space is broken up into two parts that are both exclaves relative to each other; type (*b*) occurs when a second bounded space forms an enclave within the bounded space. Both types of disconnectivity provide problems in the low cost distribution of public services and also in controlling spillover effects.

bounded spaces. Indeed the cost of movement between the different disconnected bounded spaces frequently leads to neglect of the less powerful of the exclaves: this has been the case in the disconnected state of Pakistan where a sizeable separatist movement developed in less powerful and neglected east Pakistan.

Disconnectivity also maximizes the spillover problem since it results in a *very high ratio of boundary length to area enclosed.* Disconnectivity tends to maximize contact with surrounding areas and any such contact is bound to create spillover problems. This is an especially critical problem for the farmer whose farm is disconnected: the probability of weeds or animal diseases spreading from adjacent properties onto his is increased by the large length of boundary with which he has to contend.

THE DYNAMICS OF BOUNDED SPACES

A general long-term feature of bounded spaces is for *their average area to grow.* Smaller school areas are merged and replaced with larger school areas; district-wide police organizations replace local municipal police forces; the nations of Germany, Italy, and France emerge from respective conglomerations of smaller duchies, margraves, counties, and kingdoms; the modern empires of the Soviet Union and the 19th-century empires of Britain and France exceed in geographical scale the empires of Rome and Byzantium.

This long-term tendency for bounded spaces to expand in area is as apparent in *conceptually bounded spaces* as it is in *legally bounded spaces.* Whereas the Englishman in the 18th century tended to think in terms of counties and small regions such as the Lake District, the Vale of York, Holderness, the Fylde, the

Home Counties, etc., as peoples' travel behavior and knowledge have increased in geographical scope so conceptually bounded spaces have come to be defined in terms of greater area and in terms of location relative to some central point in the nation as a whole. The modern Englishman thinks in terms of such spaces as the South, the Midlands, the Southwest, the North; from the past, only larger spaces with a high degree of cultural distinctiveness have tended to persist as elements in peoples' cognitive organization of the space around them. Wales and Yorkshire are cases in point, just as New England has persisted in the United States along with the South, the West, and the Midwest.

The expansion of *conceptually bounded spaces* can be linked to peoples' travel behavior and knowledge and the problem of developing a *small* set of pigeonholes to sort out an increasingly wide range of variation. The expansion of *legally bounded spaces* can be attributed to three major factors: (1) economies of scale, (2) improved communication, and (3) the increasing geographical range of positive spillover effects and the need to internalize them.

Economies of scale in the provision of public goods and services such as hospitals, police forces, fire services, and education provide incentives for enlarging the area served. The larger school, for example, allows the teaching of subjects with a minority appeal, such as classical Greek, at a smaller cost per pupil than in the small school where only two or three pupils in any one year may be interested.

The incentives for expansion, however, come not only from civil servants and the providers of public goods and services. Innovation in industry and resultant economies of scale provide the basis of a business lobby for common markets, free trade areas, or complete unions with neighboring states. A major force in the U.S. Civil War, for example, was the desire of New England industrialists for unrestricted access to Southern markets. Arguments for membership of the European Common Market also stress the tremendous market it offers for large-scale industry and the competition it provides as a stimulus to increased economies of scale and lower per capita production costs.

The ability to take advantage of such economies of scale, however, is very much dependent on *communication technology*. It is little use having a large hospital if patients cannot get to it; the large school with an enrollment of one thousand would be futile without an adequate school bus service—certainly such schools would have been an impossibility given the transportation technology of the 19th century. A great deal of expansion in legally bounded spaces, therefore, is dependent upon communication technology although the incentive may come from the desire to cut costs and increase the return on investment or on taxpayer money by taking advantage of economies of scale.

In other cases the incentives for expansion of legally bounded spaces have been more complex; this is particularly true of imperial expansion where a mixture of economic and nationalistic motives (e.g., the "Herrenvolk," "Manifest Destiny," and "the White Man's Burden") is often apparent. The geographical scope of imperial expansion, however, has also been dependent upon *communication technology*. Until the 16th century all large empires were established and held together by foot soldiers; foot soldiers could be marched on a six-day-a-week basis for only 20 miles per day which must have placed a considerable strain on maintaining control of empires. Courier services could bring news of provincial dissension to the capital at a rate of about 190 miles a day. In the 19th century, on the other hand, information became instantaneous as a result of the telegraph and telephone; and troops could be immediately and quickly dispatched by railroad and ocean-going vessel at a rate of 190 miles a day or more. In the 20th century, massive airlifts of troops have cut these times even more drastically. The effective range of control from some central point, therefore, has become much, much greater than it ever was in the classical world, thus allowing imperial boundaries to encompass ever larger areas.

A third and final incentive for the expansion of legally bounded spaces comes from the desire to *internalize positive spillover effects*. Comings and goings, as we have seen above, produce spillover effects: the educated leave the community that funded their education; the distant visit the city and use its parks without paying for them. One way of eliminating such spillover effects is to draw the boundary so that it includes as taxpayers most of the direct patrons (park visitors) and indirect patrons (the employers of the educated) of the community's public goods and services. As communication technology has improved, however, the comings and goings have become greater in their scope and the geographical size of the bounded space that would internalize the spillover benefits has increased vastly. In some cases this has resulted in actual mergers of territorial units; in still more cases it has resulted in the abdication of power to tax and provide public services on the part of the local community and the transference of such power to a larger political community such as the nation. The latter course of action seems to be occurring in the United States with increasing federal aid to local education and with the widely heard demands for making welfare a federal rather than a local responsibility.

There are, then, powerful forces promoting the expansion of legally bounded spaces; the technology of production and of communication play an important role in this. Nevertheless there is important evidence to suggest that such expansion is less rapid than is technically feasible and economically desirable. A major reason for such locational inertia is that while, on the one hand, the integration of several bounded spaces into one bounded space will produce consequent net benefits for the populations as a whole over and above what they would have obtained without integration, *the costs and benefits of political integration tend to be unequally distributed from one bounded space to another.* There will usually, therefore, be a variation in the support given to integration from one bounded space to another. Thus metropolitan integration will benefit the population of the city as a whole in terms of the services they will be able to afford and also in terms of the economies of scale to be reaped in the production of services, but certain of the constituent bounded spaces will suffer from the change more than others. For the independent suburb, for example, the right to zone will be vested in the city as a whole, opening the way for public housing projects in the suburban municipality which may lower property values there. Also, the wealthier citizenry of the suburb are likely to be taxed more heavily than before in order to redistribute income in a more egalitarian fashion.

The significance of economic costs and benefits suggests that union is most likely between bounded spaces with similar average levels of income. In such cases, the economic costs and benefits of integration are less likely to be distributed in an uneven manner from one bounded space to another and indeed there is actual evidence that this type of situation is more propitious for integra-

tion. In the Philadelphia metropolitan area, for example, intermunicipality cooperation in the provision of educational services is much more likely between adjacent municipalities of similar median income than between municipalities of dissimilar median income.

The costs and benefits involved, however, may not be simply economic in character involving questions of government revenue, expenditure, and economic growth. They may also be emotional in character. The inhabitants of administrative areas frequently develop strong loyalties to the bounded space in which they live, particularly if it has a colorful past or if it encompasses much of the life of its citizens. This was apparent in Britain some years ago when there were plans for merging the smallest English county—Rutland—with one of its larger neighbors in order to eliminate the costly supply of services to a small population. The result of these efforts was a local "Free Rutland" opposition surprising in its intensity.

Bounded spaces, therefore, are of geographical interest in their own right. They have distinctive geometries that can be related in a meaningful sense to various locational processes; they also change over time in a comprehendible fashion. In addition, however, they exercise important effects on other locational configurations. These are considered in the second half of this chapter.

BOUNDED SPACES AND OTHER LOCATIONAL PATTERNS

Since locational patterns are strongly affected by movement over space and by the accounting of movement costs by locational decision makers, it seems only reasonable to preface our remarks on the impact of bounded spaces on locational patterns with some remarks on how they affect movement patterns.

BOUNDED SPACES AND
MOVEMENT PATTERNS

Let us first recall that in Chapter Three we explained geographical patterns of movement in terms of three concepts: (a) attractiveness, (b) movement costs, and (c) the locational pattern of movement opportunities. All three factors affect the levels of movement across boundaries and hence illustrate the *barrier function* of boundaries.

At many boundaries, movement is subjected to a considerable *cost penalty*. This may be in the form of the cost resulting from a change of railroad gauge at the frontier or, alternatively, from the fact that the railroad freight rate taper is frequently returned to zero when crossing an international boundary.

In similar manner, bounded spaces alter the locational pattern of *movement opportunities:* immigration quotas alter the pattern of opportunities for migrants, for example, as do quotas or trade bans for the export of goods.

A frequently overlooked factor in accounting for variations in movement across boundaries, however, is that of *attractiveness.* Locations on either side of a boundary represent varying degrees of attractiveness according to the bounded space being considered. For French-speaking Belgians, for example, locations within northern France are much more attractive as places of employment than locations within Belgian Flanders simply because they speak French while the people of Flanders speak Flemish. This is reflected in studies of migration and commuting within Belgium. It has been found that even when the effects of intervening distance and economic opportunity components of place utility are taken into consideration, migration and commuting are still greater between places within the same linguistic space than between places in different linguistic spaces. The problems of adapting oneself to a linguistically alien social environment should be self-evident.

In many cases, locations within one's bounded space are much more attractive than locations beyond. In the United States, for instance, interstate migration is reduced and American economic growth probably impared as a result of certain restrictions which, while not necessarily designed to limit interstate movement, do have that as one of their effects. In professions such as law, dentistry, or teaching, the exercise of the profession in another state may involve costly and time consuming subjection to state accreditation procedures to redetermine the migrant's qualifications. Migration from one state to another can also involve loss of retirement benefits accumulated in state employment in the state that one is leaving—benefits which are not transferable. In addition, there are petty but costly considerations such as obtaining a new registration for one's car, a driver's permit for the state to which one has just relocated, establishing residency requirements for voting, etc.

A major assumption implicit in this discussion, however, is that people are equally well informed about all bounded spaces. Just as the perfect knowledge assumption was challenged in our discussions of migration in Chapters Four and Five, however, so it appears of dubious validity in the present discussion of movement. Obviously, we know much more about locations and their associated opportunities within our own bounded space then we do about those present in other bounded spaces. A number of reasons account for this but in particular we would like to emphasize the role of language and of segregation of interpersonal and mass media communication networks by bounded spaces.

Language is usually homogeneous within a bounded space of either the legal or conceptual variety and is an obvious control of communication between and consequently about locations. Striking evidence for this has been provided by a study of intercity telephone communication in Canada between cities in the French-speaking province of Quebec and the English-speaking province of Ontario. Of major significance in predicting levels of telephone communications between cities are: (1) intervening distance: more communication occurs between places closer together in space; and (2) the populations of the towns between which communication is taking place; where the populations are of such magnitude that their *product* is high, telephone communication levels also tend to be high; where the product is low, telephone communication also tends to be low — all other things being equal. This is a verbal statement of the gravity model frequently used by geographers. When applied to telephone communication, the gravity model usually provides very accurate predictions.

When applied to the intercity data for Canada, however, its predictive ability was reduced. Telephone communication from Montreal (Quebec) to a city of a given size at a given distance in Quebec tended to be significantly higher than telephone communication from Montreal to similar cities in Ontario.

A similar situation where intra-bounded space telephone communication is significantly greater than inter-bounded space communication, when holding such factors as population size and intervening distance constant, comes from Australia and the two bounded spaces formed by the states of Victoria and South Australia. As Figure 7-7 shows, telephone communication predicted on the basis of distance and

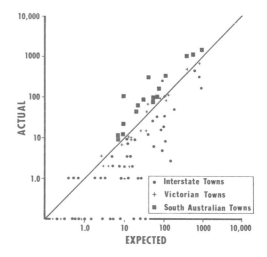

FIGURE 7-7. The relationship between actual telephone communication levels and expected telephone communication levels for pairs of towns in South Australia and Victoria; expected levels have been calculated on the basis of intervening distance and the product of populations; note that communication between towns in different states is *lower* than expected while communication between towns in the same state is generally *higher* than expected.

population size is less than actual communication between towns within the same state and greater than the actual level between towns in different states. Unfortunately, language differences cannot be held responsible in this case. One likely explanation in this case is the relationship between such boundaries and a host of other boundaries that structure opportunities for interpersonal contacts.

It is a truism that interpersonal contacts tend to be with those one knows, and opportunity for acquiring such knowledge is very dependent upon membership of various networks of association, such as the high school with its territorially defined catchment area for the high school pupil. Thus we tend to communicate with people at different locations because we had some initial opportunity for contact. Such opportunities tend to be partly structured by territorially based organizations which do not overlap state boundaries but which may overlap with those of other organizations *within* the state.

Given this geography of interpersonal contact, in which contact is more likely within bounded spaces than between spaces, the type of chain migration processes considered in Chapter Five are apt to increase the likelihood of migration within bounded spaces and decrease its likelihood between bounded spaces.

As we remarked in Chapter Five, however, interpersonal contacts are not the only source of information about locations and about the opportunities available at locations. The mass media are also critical. In the current context their importance derives from the fact that their circulation areas often show a strong coincidence with bounded spaces. This is most evident at the national level where, for example, the national press and TV and radio broadcasts are largely received within the bounded space represented by the nation. To some extent, however, it is also evident at the subnational level, particularly in the bounded spaces represented by the states of a federation. Thus in the Australian context considered above, there is strong segregation of state press readership by the boundary between Victoria and South Australia. On the Victoria side of the border at least 75% of the sale of newspapers consists of sales of the Victorian newspaper the *Melbourne Sun*. On the South Australia side of the boundary readership habits are reversed with the *Adelaide Advertiser*, emanating from the state capital of Adelaide, dominating newspaper sales. Only in one small area in South Australia does the *Melbourne Sun* attain sales in excess of 25% of total newspaper sales.

Such segregation of circulation areas by bounded spaces is reflected in the information carried by the mass medium involved. It will tend to be bounded-

space specific. More concretely, it will refer in its news content and, more importantly, in its advertising to employment, housing, and shopping opportunities within the bounded space, thus increasing the tendency for bounded spaces to structure a variety of movement behaviors.

Given that the boundaries of bounded spaces are often associated with impediments to movement either due to movement cost considerations, relative attractiveness considerations, restrictions on the locational pattern of movement opportunities, or the knowledge limitations just discussed, it should be reasonable to expect communication networks to exhibit some of this barrier effect. Routes of communication are constructed to satisfy a demand, and if the demand for communication across a boundary is limited, the incentive for constructing a line of communication across a boundary is also limited. This effect is particularly noticeable in the configuration of railroad networks in the vicinity of international boundaries. Figure 7-8, for example, presents the railroad network of Portugal; the effect of the boundary with Spain upon route alignment should be particularly evident.

Where such effects upon route network configuration are not in evidence at an international border the reason can often be found in radical boundary change consequent to the period of route construction. The Irish railroad network, for example, seems totally insensitive to the boundary between Eire and Ulster: a quite reasonable situation when one recalls that partition dates only from 1922.

LOCATIONAL EFFECTS

Bounded spaces, as a result of their effects on movement patterns, tend to be associated with two types of locational

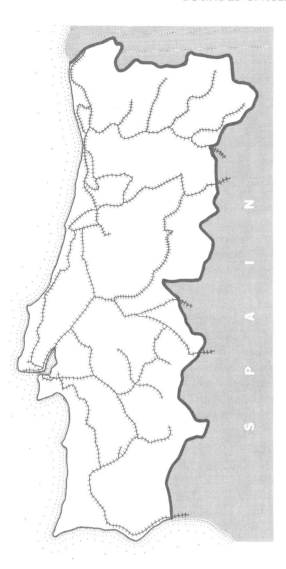

FIGURE 7-8. The railroad network of Portugal. Note the tendency of railroads to stop short of the boundary with Spain; this is especially apparent in northeast Portugal.

effect: there are *constant effects in which the effect is exercised on all locations within a bounded space to the same degree,* and there are also *variable effects in which the effect is dependent upon location relative to the boundary line.*

In many senses, locations within bounded spaces are much more similar in their attributes and activities than locations in *different* bounded spaces. Average income levels tend to be more similar, for example, as do ethnic and occupational composition, levels of agricultural mechanization, literacy, and a host of other attributes. In many, many ways geography *within* states tends to be homogeneous, while geography *between states* tends to be *heterogeneous.*

Much of this intrastate homogeneity and interstate heterogeneity can be attributed to the fact that *economic competition tends to be more perfect within nations than between nations.* That is not to say that it is perfect, as there are many rigorous assumptions that have to be satisfied before perfect competition can be inferred as taking place; but at least it is more perfect between locations *within* bounded spaces than between locations in different bounded spaces.

Perfect competition in the labor market, for example, tends in the long run to produce equality of wages from place to place. If wages are higher in one area than in another, migration of labor will take place bringing labor supply into congruence with demand in both the places of migrant origin and the places of migrant destination—thus raising the price of labor in places of origin and lowering it in places of destination. Also, if the price of wheat is higher in one area than in another, similar movements will be precipitated leading to a similar *equilibriation of prices across space.*

Among the assumptions required for the perfect equilibriating competition to take place two are of special interest. First, competitors should have perfect information, that is, the worker should have complete knowledge of the wages available to him at different locations and the wheat producer should have perfect knowledge of the prices available to him at different locations. Secondly, movement costs should be zero. If they are not, then movement of labor and wheat will be restricted and complete equilibriation of labor and wheat prices will not be attained.

These are rigorous assumptions indeed and they are never completely fulfilled. The important point, however, is that they are more nearly satisfied *within* bounded spaces than *between* bounded spaces. Information circulates more efficiently within bounded spaces as we have seen in our review of studies examining telephone communication and newspaper readership. Movement costs are also likely to be lower per unit distance within bounded spaces than between them due to such costs as those of changing railroad gauge and recommencing freight rate tapers on crossing an international boundary. Also, there are no cost restrictions on the movement of labor and goods within bounded spaces comparable to those between such spaces.

While the market mechanism tends to exercise a homogenizing influence, however, the perfect competition that would result in perfect homogeneity never exists. A major aim of government interference in the market economy, therefore, has been to rectify the heterogeneities resulting from imperfect competition so that people have similar access to employment in different areas of the national realm and the same chance of earning a high income as someone located elsewhere. The same ethic of *territorial justice* has also guided the supply of public goods and services by governments so that the quality and quantity of public goods and services varies very little from one location to another. In brief, governments exercise a homogenizing influence on intrastate geography by smoothing out those variations that would be apparent from the imperfect mechanics of the market and by supplying services in a territorially equitable manner.

In addition to such *constant* effects there are also effects which are variable in their incidence within a bounded space. When we consider a single bounded space we can often find evidence of geographical patterns related in their intensity to location vis-à-vis a boundary. At least two types of variable effect can be identified: (1) an *intervening opportunity effect,* in which places close to the border are highly attractive locations, and (2) a *halo effect,* in which places close to the border are relatively unattractive locations.

To exemplify the idea of intervening opportunity relative to boundaries, consider the case of two bounded spaces *A* and *B* located adjacent to one another. *A* has some desired attributes which *B* does not have: all locations in *A* can supply this attribute for the inhabitants of *B*. However, for the usual effort minimizing reasons, it is important for inhabitants of *B* to minimize the distance between themselves and the locations in *A* where they can obtain the attribute that *A* has. Under such circumstances, locations in space *A* close to the border have a competitive advantage over places further away, that is, they have an "intervening" location.

As an example, consider the situation existing between England (*A*) and Wales (*B*) on Sundays. The desired attribute which England has on Sundays and which Wales does not have is that of more liberal liquor legislation; in England taverns are open on Sunday while in Wales they are not. Yet for a Welshman crossing the border to obtain a drink on a Sunday it is important that he not travel too far. (The transferability of liquor is low!) Hence, places in England close to the border can gain additional patronage on Sundays from Welshmen; places further away cannot benefit from such additional sales due to the intervening opportunity closer to the Welsh border.

Clearly not all intervening opportunity locations are so close to the international boundary. Air communication has made airports into frontier posts even though they are remote from the historic frontiers of a nation and it is probably for this reason that London has become the abortion capital of Europe. Because of the pattern of intercity air links in Europe, it is the closest English city to other European cities such as Paris, Brussels, and Munich. Presumably, before aviation the white cliffs of Dover would have welcomed the desperate and bid farewell to the thankful!

However, for many types of activity, particularly economic activity, the zone of territory adjacent to the boundary is not a favored location. We shall call this situation, in which more attractive interior locations are surrounded by less attractive exterior locations adjacent to the boundary, the *halo effect.*

One index of relative prosperity, for example, is urban growth. Table 7-1 presents urban growth rates for the

larger cities of the Soviet Union over the period 1913–1939 and compares rates for cities within 150 miles of the western frontier with those cities beyond 150 miles of the western frontier. As can be observed, cities beyond 150 miles of the western frontier have experienced considerably more rapid growth rates.

The reasons for such halo effects are strategic, political, and economic. Strategically, border zones are frequently zones of military activity in time of warfare with all the disruption and destruction which war brings. The need for the protection of expensive capital investment in factories, houses, public utilities, and lines of communication from such destruction suggests that such locations should be avoided. The relative attraction of locations away from the boundary, therefore, increases. This certainly seems to have been the reasoning underlying differential investment in cities of the Soviet Union according to their location relative to the western boundary. Not only was the western boundary zone of Russia considerably devastated in the First World War, but the imminent holocaust of the Second World War was already apparent to the rulers of Russia by 1935. Consequently, economic planning stressed the development of new natural resources and the creation of new urban centers in Siberia and Central Asia far from the possibility of German military devastation. The invasion of Russia in 1941 by Germany not only seemed to justify the locational neglect of the western border zone, but it encouraged the shift of existing industrial plants from that area to places further east away from the war zone. Ironically enough, similar defensive considerations seem to have discouraged post-1945 West German investment in the boundary zone adjoining Russia's satellite, East Germany.

Politically one also observes an avoidance of boundary locations. State capi-

TABLE 7-1. Border zone location and urban growth in Russia, 1913–1939; note how cities further removed from the strategically vulnerable western border zone grew more rapidly than places in that zone; this was a result of deliberate locational policies carried out by the Soviet government.

Urban places within 150 miles of western frontier		Urban places beyond 150 miles of western frontier	
Leningrad	52%	Moscow	128%
Kiev	42%	Kharkov	236%
Odessa	decrease	Baku	260%
Nikolaiev	17%	Gorky	491%
Smolensk	46%	Tashkent	115%
Minsk	71%	Rostov	155%
Vitebsk	22%	Sverdlovsk	447%
		Stalingrad	288%
		Stalino	484%
		Novosibirsk	292%
		Khabarovsk	290%

tals, county seats, and a whole range of administrative centers tend to locate towards the center of the inhabited territory in order to minimize distance from the population being governed and administered. If government is to serve the people it is important that it should be *accessible* to the people. As Figure 7-9 shows, most English county towns tend to be located towards the centers of their counties.

Emphatically, however, it is *accessibility to the inhabited area* that is important for an administrative center and this has been reflected in the locational shifts of various administrative centers. The states of the U.S.A. in the 19th century, for example, underwent very rapid changes in their internal distribution of population prompting reevaluations of old state capital sites and shifts to new sites. In Iowa the eastern half of the state filled up first and this is reflected in the early choice of Iowa City as the state capital. As the rest of the state filled up, the most accessible point for the inhabited area shifted westward, so that today Des Moines is the state capital.

These centrality considerations affecting the location of administrative centers and tending to deter them from boundary locations are by no means of minor significance. Administrative labor forces provide very important additions to consumer demand that can stimulate the local economy and encourage consumer goods industries to locate there. Administration also requires improved transportation facilities from which businessmen can also benefit. Such reasoning was clearly in view some years ago when it was suggested that the capital of the United Kingdom should be moved north from London to York in an effort to stimulate the lagging economy of the area.

The punishments associated with boundary zone locations by govern-

FIGURE 7-9. County seat locations in England. The points represent the present sites of county administrations in England; note how they tend to be located fairly centrally relative to the county as a whole. There have, in fact, been some interesting recent shifts to bring locations more in accord with the inhabited areas of the different counties; in the case of Lancashire, for example, the county seat has been relocated from Lancaster, which is relatively remote from the densely populated areas of South Lancashire, to the more southerly location represented by Preston.

ments and entrepreneurs, however, are not only strategic and political in character; there are also purely economic motivations that need to be taken into account. Consider, for example, the case of a product for which demand is distributed evenly over the territory of a bounded space; let us also assume that surrounding bounded spaces impose heavy duties on that product when it crosses the international boundary. To all intents and purposes the market area for a firm producing this product can be assumed to lie within the bounded space. Now, if the firm producing this product wishes to distribute it to all areas of the space, locations near the boundary will impose disadvantages: thus location at such points will entail heavy distribution costs compared with location at a more central point. Such heavy distribution costs will eat into the profits and/or competitive position of firms located in the boundary zone. For many types of economic activity, therefore, the boundary zone seems to be avoided. It is possibly for reasons such as these that many of the seaside resorts of England and Wales have serious seasonal unemployment problems.

CONCLUSIONS AND SUMMARY

A major feature of the geography of an area as it is and also as we conceive it is the bounded space. *Legally* we divide space up into discrete packages which we call school areas, sanitary districts, states, and common markets. *Conceptually* we also tend to divide space up into discrete areas which we call *regions.*

Both *legally bounded spaces and conceptually bounded spaces* perform important functions in assisting us to order information about space. States, counties, and conceptually defined regions provide *a set of locational pigeonholes* which, as we saw in Chapter Six, assist in reducing our perceptions of the world around us to some sort of order and conceptual coherence.

Legally bounded spaces, however, perform a second and possibly more important function: that of providing a *territorial framework for the supply of public goods and services.* The supply of goods and services necessarily involves the *geographical proximity of the population being served* and the *boundedness of the space* occupied by that same population. Proximity is required by the economics of supplying public goods and services and also by the *localized nature of the demands* giving rise to them.

The property of boundedness derives largely from the problem of *the effects of spillover on the economics of supplying public goods and services.* Boundaries permit the easy externalization of negative spillover effects and the internalization of positive spillover effects.

When we turn and examine the *locational properties of these bounded spaces* we find a good deal of predictability which itself reflects on the economic, political, and spillover bases of *territorial organization.* The areas of bounded spaces often vary in such a way that they are smaller for more densely populated spaces and larger for less densely populated spaces. This suggests that there is some sort of *threshold factor at work such that a minimum population is required* before certain types of public good or service become worthwhile investments for taxpayers' money.

Shape emphasizes the virtue of *compactness* for bounded spaces. Compactness, by maximizing the nearness of locations within the area to each other relative to their nearness to locations outside the area facilitates the public service economic functions of bounded spaces. By maximizing the area of the space relative to the length of the enclosing boundary, it also permits less costly internalization of spillover benefits and externalization of spillover costs.

The third property is that of *connectivity*. Bounded spaces may consist of several discontinuous portions of territory or may alternatively be internally as well as externally bounded as a result of some enclave. Such disconnectivity is uncommon partly because of the costs of controlling spillovers under such conditions and partly because of the costs of providing public goods and services.

Over time, bounded spaces (both legal and conceptual) have shown a tendency to *expand geographically*. For conceptually bounded spaces such growth is associated with the effect of increasing travel distances on our knowledge of area and our inability to differentiate between more than a very few locational pigeonholes.

The *expansion of legally bounded spaces* such as school areas, on the other hand, is associated with economies of scale in providing public goods and services, a communication technology facilitating rapid movement over long distances and the need to control spillover effects which are increasingly wide in their geographical impact.

In turning to the effects of bounded spaces on other locational patterns we attempted to trace a sequence of events leading from the pattern of bounded spaces at one end, through *their effects on movement,* to the effects of such constrained movements on locational patterns at the other end. The constraining of movements by bounded spaces, moreover, is reflected in the resultant pattern of transportation networks, with railroads ending short of the boundary or running parallel to it. Such a structuring of transportation networks increases the strength of the forces limiting movement across boundaries.

Within this context, two types of locational effect were examined; there was first an *intervening opportunity effect* in which locations close to the boundary gained advantages and rewards not available to locations more remote from the boundary. There were also *halo* effects in which border locations for a variety of economic or strategic reasons were perceived in a largely negative light.

Bounded spaces, therefore, constrain movement by imposing barriers; as a result they have important effects on a range of other locational patterns. Other lines on the landscape, however, such as railroad lines and highways facilitate and channel movement. In so doing they too exercise important effects on other locational patterns. Such lines of communication, their locational configurations, and their effects on other locational patterns are considered in the next two chapters.

CHAPTER EIGHT

The Structure of Communication Networks

INTRODUCTION

The earlier chapters of this volume concentrated upon locational patterns of movement and the effect of movement upon other locational patterns such as those of ethnic groups or of population within a city. It is self-evident, however, that movements from one place to another are dependent upon the existence of routes: highways, railroads, telegraph and telephone lines, airline routes, etc. Sets of such routes joining up sets of places also form locational patterns that we call *networks*. Networks of communication and their characteristics provide the subject matter of this chapter.

There is a wide range of line patterns along which flow messages, goods, men, etc., and that can be thought of as networks. Transportation networks are obvious, but, in addition, there are communication networks consisting of telephone links between places; we can also think of social networks in which pairs of people are regarded as links if they communicate a great deal with each other. In addition, we should include such networks as those made up of the political interactions of nations: nations belong to diplomatic networks in which the links are forged by the exchange of ambassadors. All networks, however, have certain locational characteristics in common. Furthermore, the forces producing these locational patterns are very similar from one type of network to another type of network, and they have similar effects upon other locational patterns. The centralization of a telephone network, for example, has locational effects that are highly comparable with the locational effects of a centralized railroad network.

Network structure, however, can be approached from a diversity of viewpoints. One viewpoint is the *static viewpoint* which looks at networks at one point in time and asks the question: what structural patterns are present and what are the attributes of areas associated with these structural characteristics? The second viewpoint is more *dynamic* and asks the question: how have networks evolved over time and space and with what historical or geographically located events has this evolution been associated? Obviously neither viewpoint is complete: associations with other locational attributes at one point *in* time may give us a rather false impression of the factors that have been important *over* time. Both approaches are therefore taken in this chapter, starting with the more static viewpoint and concluding with the more dynamic, evolutionary approach.

NETWORKS AT ONE POINT IN TIME

Four spatial characteristics of networks are important to us in terms of their geographically differentiating properties at one point in time and in terms of their effects on movement and, hence, upon other locational patterns: (1) network deviousness, (2) network density, (3) network connectivity, and (4) the hierarchical organization of networks. Each of these concepts of locational pattern will be discussed in turn from the viewpoints of their measurement, their utility in explaining other locational patterns, and in terms of their correlates.

NETWORK DEVIOUSNESS

If one examines a route network, be it a highway network, a railroad network, or an airline network, and be it within a city or connecting cities one to another, a common geographical feature is that of the deviousness of the links in the network:

▶ *Network deviousness is the property whereby the lengths of the individual links in a communication network differ from the straight line distances between the places being linked up.*

The railroad network of the United States, for example, includes some links that are astonishingly deviant as far as crows' flight paths are concerned. Outstanding in this regard is the New York Central Railroad linking New York City to Cleveland and Chicago; this initially goes in a northerly direction for 150 miles before swinging westward towards the Great Lakes.

Most attempts to measure deviousness have based themselves upon the concept of the *route factor*. This is simply the ratio of the observed route distance to the straight line distance. Clearly the route factor has important implications for the cost of movement over a particular network, higher route factors signifying more devious and therefore costlier movements. It is also conceivable that it has some effect on perceptions of distance. One would certainly expect the perceived distances to bear a closer relationship to the actual distances experienced, that is, the distances over which movement actually takes place, than to straight line measures of distance from a map.

What factors affect the value of the route factor for particular networks? Of some importance is urban size: route factors tend to be lower, at least in Britain, for routes between larger cities than for routes between smaller cities. It may be, therefore, that an attractiveness factor is at work here: for some reason the route factors for routes connecting more attractive places are lower than for routes linking up less attractive places.

A second factor appears to be that of barriers. Where barriers to route construction exist, as in the case of ranges of mountains, one can expect the route factor to be higher as routes follow valleys rather than the direct paths over the mountain ranges. Route factors for hillier Wales, therefore, are considerably in excess of those for the flatter English Midlands.

A final consideration appears to be that of a route layout which bears little relationship to barriers or to the relative attractiveness of the places being joined but which stems from the manner of initial land division. Route factors in the American Midwest are often rather high due to the impediments imposed on diagonal movement by the rectangular highway system originating in the township and range land division process. The frequent gridiron pattern on which towns are laid out, not only in North America but also to a certain extent in Western Europe, may also account for another facet of findings on route factors:

route factors for trips across town tend to be higher than for trips directed towards the central business district. This is consistent with the fact that in a gridiron town most of the few diagonal routes that there are tend to focus on the downtown area.

NETWORK DENSITY

The density of route networks or *the length of the route network per unit area* (square mile, acre, etc.) is important because it is a rough guide to *mean accessibility* to a transportation route. Thus, the knowledge that the density of railroads per unit area is 4.47 in the United States and 7.23 in France is interesting, because it suggests that in France, on the average, a railroad, and probably, therefore, a railroad station, is nearer to a person than in the United States. Obviously, the density measure does not take into account the density of population or the distribution of that population: in the United States there are vast uninhabited areas in the West and Southwest so that the density per unit area gives an unfairly low estimate of accessibility to the transportation network. However, it does provide a crude guide.

A major factor associated with network density is the medium involved. In general, railroad network densities tend to be considerably smaller than highway network densities. The two densities for the United States, for example, are 4.47 and 58.7, respectively. A recent study of a wide range of national transportation networks in the world found the mean railroad density to be 0.95 and the mean highway density to be 10.3.

When we examine other factors which seem to be associated with variations in network density it is important to qualify our statements by referring to the *scale of our comparison*. If we compare national communication networks with each other, for example, a different set of factors are associated with variations in density than if we compare the different states of the United States with one another or the different parts of a metropolitan area with each other.

When nations are compared, the density of highway and railroad networks seems strongly related to level of economic development as measured by such items as gross national product per capita and the proportion of the labor force employed in manufacturing. Wealthy manufacturing nations such as the United States, Britain, France, and West Germany have relatively dense networks. Since economic development is accompanied by the need to assemble raw materials from diverse sources, distribute finished products to different markets, and generally to move people and commodities from one area to another, these relationships should not be too surprising. As the demand for movement increases, so one can expect an increasing length of route to be constructed to cater to that demand.

National route networks do not respond only to the forces of the economic market, however. There are a number of interesting cases where network density is rather higher than one would imagine on the basis of economic criteria alone. India, for example, has a very dense railroad network for such a poor country: Burma falls in a similar category. Both countries probably owe their relatively dense networks not to the demand for moving goods from place to place but to the demand of governments for control of colonial populations. Certainly in the case of India the British government played a significant role in the development of the network and saw it as an important means for moving armed forces from one part of the subcontinent to another in order to control subject populations.

A third factor associated with network density variations from country to country is area. In general, certain types of transportation network require longer distances in order to be competitive with other media. We saw in an earlier chapter, for example, that airlines have a competitive advantage over railroads in Europe only over distances in excess of 300 miles. This means that in a small nation like Belgium or Holland or Ireland or Israel, airline services are hardly likely to be an economically viable proposition so that densities will tend to be low. Even in nations such as Britain and France, densities are unlikely to be high because of the generally short distances over which the aircraft must operate. It is in the nations of continental proportions like those of the U.S., U.S.S.R., Canada, and Australia that the airline route density is likely to be relatively high—all other things being equal.

While route densities seem to vary from one nation to another as a function of level of economic development, we also find when examining networks closely that route density varies from one *region* of a country to another. In view of the fact, noted in Chapter Six, that levels of income and other measures of economic development vary relatively little across regions of a single nation compared with variations from one nation to another, it is unlikely that such variations are associated with economic development differences. Little attention has been given to this problem, but what is known is of great interest.

A study has been completed of transportation networks in West Africa. One of the foci of interest in this study was the road density variation within the nations of Ghana and Nigeria. What is clear from these studies is that both the population of an area and its geographical extent are related to road network density. Population size is clearly the most important factor such that the more populous areas of Ghana and Nigeria have the

densest road networks. This is in accord with what we know of the United States where the densest portions of the U.S. Interstate Highway System (see Figure 8-1) are in the more populous northeastern sections of the country. U.S. railroad densities follow the same sort of pattern.

Assuming that the more populous areas are joined up with one another by transportation links, one should also expect to find relatively high route densities in areas intervening between more populous sections of the country: the area of England lying in the triangle of which the apices are London, Birmingham, and Leicester, for example, has one of the highest railroad densities in Britain even though it has a relatively low population density. The reason lies in the fact that the railroads link up the largest city in Britain—London—with the populous manufacturing districts of the Midlands, Lancashire, Scotland, Yorkshire, and Northeastern England. The same route densities do not apply to the west of London even though the area has a similarly low population density.

Within cities the major factor controlling network density appears to be population density as in the case of density variations across the regions of a nation. This is probably associated causally not so much with population density itself but with the locational pattern of land values which impose severe constraints on maximum lot size close to the center of the city. In the central business district, land values are so high that lot sizes have to be small compared with lots in suburban districts. This means that if each lot is to have street frontage, streets will tend to be placed relatively close together in the downtown area. In suburban locations, on the other hand, lot sizes are usually much larger and streets are correspondingly further apart, producing a lower network density.

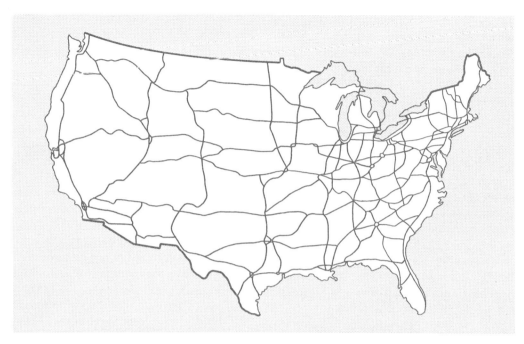

FIGURE 8-1. The network of interstate highways in the United States. Network density is particularly high in the more densely settled portions of the east.

CONNECTIVITY

Consider in Figure 8-2 the three transportation networks joining up four places *a*, *b*, *c*, and *d*. In all networks it is possible to get from one place to another in a finite series of steps. However, there are variations in the deviousness involved in traveling over a route in any of the three networks. Thus, in (i) travel from *a* to *d* must proceed by two intermediate places, *b* and *c*. In network (ii) there is some improvement in this situation in that there is now a direct route joining *a* to *d* as well as an indirect route. Network (ii), however, still contains indirect routes between pairs of places with no direct routes existing between those pairs of places: thus, *a* still is linked to *c* by only an indirect route as is *b* to *d*. Network (iii) eliminates one of these indirect routes (*b,d*) replacing it with a direct route. We refer to the degree to which direct movements are possible as opposed to indirect movements as *the*

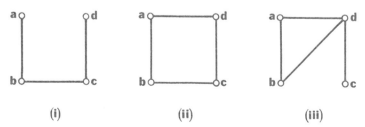

FIGURE 8-2. Three networks to illustrate the concept of connectivity. (See text for explanation.)

connectivity of the network: the networks which are most connected are those in which the directness of routes joining up pairs of places is maximized.

An interesting facet of more connected networks is that they tend to consist of *circuit networks* in which there is more than one path or route between at least two places. Less connected networks, on the other hand, tend to be dominated by *branching networks* or *trees* in which there is only one possible path between a pair of places (see Figure 8-3). Branching networks have the property that the number of links is equivalent to $n - 1$ where n refers to the number of places being linked up. Clearly, therefore, a single link joining up two places constitutes a branching network or a tree. Circuit networks, on the other hand, have the property that the number of links is equal to

or greater than the number of places being joined up. Conversion of a branching network into a circuit network therefore involves an increase in network connectivity.

> *In branching networks there is only one possible path between two places; in circuit networks there is more than one possible path between at least two places.*

The notion of connectivity can be easily generalized to other types of network. Figure 8-4 shows a portion of the world diplomatic network and is included not only to illustrate the idea of connectivity, but also some ideas regarding the structure of that particular network. Several features of this network are of interest from the connection standpoint. First, and obviously enough, this portion of the world diplomatic network is not completely connected: if Ethiopia wishes to communicate with Chile it must do so via the United States—possibly by a meeting of the Ethiopian and Chilean ambassadors in Washington. There are a number of such indirect linkages in the network. Secondly, and of more substantive interest, is the fact that Zambia and Ethiopia must communicate via their ambassadors in London or Washington; even though the two nations are located close together in space they do not have any diplomatic ties. The reasons for such lack of connectivity will become clearer shortly.

If networks can be regarded as being more or less connected, however, we do need some way of measuring that connectivity so that: (a) we can compare one network with another and ask the question, why are some networks more connected than others? and (b) we can relate connectivity to spatial properties of flow and hence to ensuing locational patterns. One way of measuring connectivity is to relate the actual number of links between

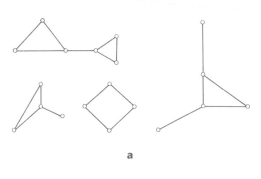

a

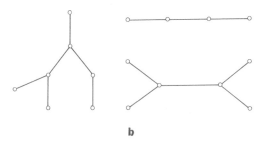

b

FIGURE 8-3. (*a*) Some examples of circuit networks. In every circuit network there is more than one possible path between at least one pair of places. (*b*) Some examples of branching networks. In every branching network there is only one possible path between each pair of places.

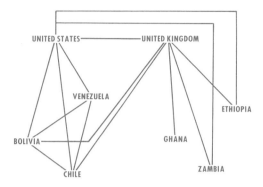

FIGURE 8-4.   A segment of the internation diplomatic network. The more developed nations — the United States and the United Kingdom — tend to be more connected; they are more attractive from the viewpoint of the trading and political interests of the underdeveloped nations and they also provide, by their large numbers of embassies, the possibility of communication between nations that do not formally exchange ambassadors: Chile and Ghana, therefore, communicate via London and Washington.

places or *nodes* in a network to the maximum possible for a network linking that number of places: Actual Number of Links/Maximum Possible Number of Links. Then, if the quotient is multiplied by 100 we have a measure of percentage connection. Where links are allowed to cross each other and are symmetric (as in an airline network) the maximum possible number of links is $n(n-1)/2$ where n refers to the number of places in a network. Where links are allowed to cross each other and are asymmetric, on the other hand, as in a friendship network in which a link represents a friendship choice, the maximum possible number of links is $n(n-1)$ where n is the number of persons in the network. Moreover, where links *cannot* cross each other without defining a new place in a network — as in a railroad network — the maximum possible number of links is provided by the expression $3(n-2)$ where n is the number of places linked up in the network. Figure 8-5 presents three different types of network along

with connectivities: z refers to the actual number of links present.

In addition to examining and defining the connectivity of the total network linking up a set of places, we can also define the connectivity of a place in terms of its linkage to the total network. Places which have many links are highly connected to the network while places

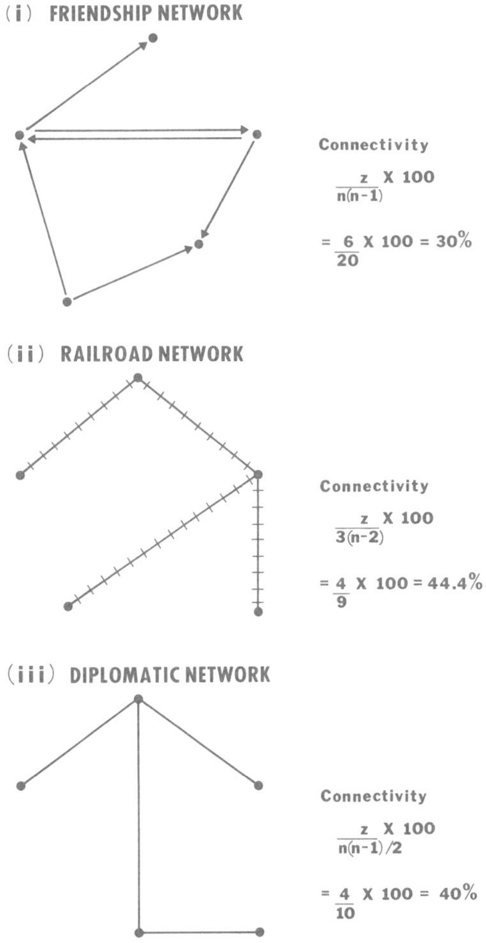

(i)   **FRIENDSHIP NETWORK**

Connectivity

$$\frac{z}{n(n-1)} \times 100$$

$$= \frac{6}{20} \times 100 = 30\%$$

(ii)   **RAILROAD NETWORK**

Connectivity

$$\frac{z}{3(n-2)} \times 100$$

$$= \frac{4}{9} \times 100 = 44.4\%$$

(iii)   **DIPLOMATIC NETWORK**

Connectivity

$$\frac{z}{n(n-1)/2} \times 100$$

$$= \frac{4}{10} \times 100 = 40\%$$

FIGURE 8-5.   The measurement of connectivity in three different types of network. The friendship network is an asymmetric network in which a link from x to y does not necessarily imply a link from y to x. The railroad network and the diplomatic network are both symmetric, but in the railroad case links cannot cross without creating a new node or vertex on the network. z and n refer to the actual numbers of links and nodes in the network respectively.

which have relatively few links are only weakly connected. In most networks there is variation in the connectivity of different places to the total network; clearly in the completely connected network, however, there will be no differences in the connectivity of different places.

If we take the nations in the diplomatic network defined above and rank them in terms of their connectivity to the network as a whole we obtain the following ranking:

Nation	Connectivity
United Kingdom	7
U.S.A.	7
Venezuela	4
Bolivia	4
Chile	4
Ghana	2
Ethiopia	2
Zambia	2

The two "North Atlantic" nations are the most connected, therefore, followed by the Latin American nations and then, finally, by the African nations.

Given that we can describe the property of connectivity for communication networks, however, with what other properties of places does it vary? If it can be shown that connectivity is high when some attribute is present and low where that attribute is not present we may be assisted in our effort to find an explanation for variations in connectivity from one network to another. Obviously, it helps if we have some theory about the sources of variations in connectivity to begin with. A theory would provide predictions about those attributes of places which would be associated with network connectivity. We could then examine some real world data to see if such predictions are valid.

Most of the research into the connectivity of the network as a whole has been directed towards finding associations between the connectivity of transportation networks and certain attributes of places which theory would predict as being associated with connectivity. One such attribute is the economic development of the nation in which the network is located. The more economically developed a nation is, the higher its gross national product per capita, the higher the proportion of the labor force employed in industry, and the higher the proportion of the population living in cities (i.e., in a situation of spatial concentration). In such economically developed nations not only is there capital available for investment in lengthy transportation networks, but there is a large demand for transportation from one place to another if factories are to obtain their raw materials and distribute their products and if people are to travel to the extent that they desire: the mileage traveled by a person in any given period of time, it might be added, seems to vary with his income and, hence, where incomes are higher, as in economically developed nations, we would expect travel to be higher. All these factors encourage the linkage of places into a connected transportation network, and indeed the more economically developed nations do tend to have the more connected railroad networks.

We also know something about the connectivity of different places to the total network in which they are involved; such place connectivities can also be related to other attributes of those places. Urban places, for example, exhibit differing connectivities with transportation networks. If we look at a map of a transportation network joining up towns we find that some towns are at the centers of stars in the network; a lot of routes radiate from them. Other urban places, on the other hand, are more peripheral to the network as a whole and may have only one link each. Studies of the connectivity of towns in Spain and Portugal with the international highway system have provided some interesting results in this context: these studies show that such town connectivities tend to be higher for larger cities and for cities with large traffic flows. Such relationships are quite reasonable. We would anticipate that larger towns would generate more highway traffic and hence be the targets of government highway investment to a greater extent than small towns.

What seems to be at issue here is some sort of relationship between the attractiveness of a place and its connectivity. This is brought out rather strikingly where the attractiveness of a place derives from something other than its population size: thus resort cities such as

Las Vegas and Miami in the United States and Nice in France are more highly connected to their respective national airline networks than their size would warrant.

Finally, there is the possibility of a two-way relationship: connectivity may not be simply an end product of traffic generation, but it may also stimulate traffic generation itself by providing an accessible location for factories and other generators of traffic. This will be explored further in Chapter Nine.

Instead of analyzing the connections of urban places to a transportation network we can examine the connectivity of nations to the diplomatic network. Figure 8-6 plots the number of nations to which

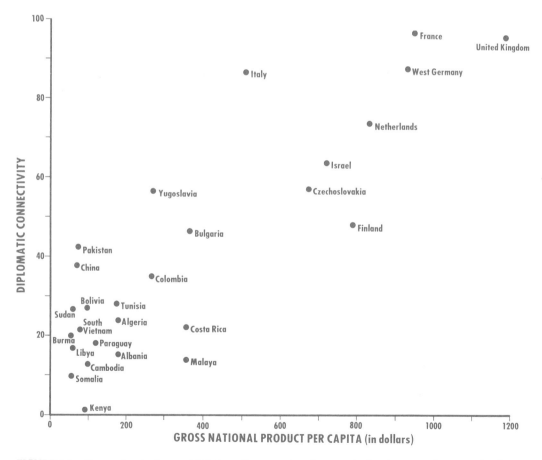

FIGURE 8-6.   Connection to the world diplomatic network and economic development (for a sample of nations): the more developed nations tend to be considerably more connected than the less developed nations.

diplomats are sent by given nations against economic development; as can be seen, the poorer nations are represented in far fewer capitals than are the wealthier nations such as Britain and West Germany. Such lack of connectivity by poorer nations is partly a result of lack of resources to support diplomatic missions throughout the globe. It is also, however, a reflection of the limited geographical scope of the areas of interest of poorer nations. Poorer nations tend to trade with a smaller range of nations and also lack the worldwide interests which imperial histories have bestowed on nations such as Britain, France, and Belgium.

On the other hand, the identities of the nations which do receive diplomats from the relatively underdeveloped nations is quite revealing. The U.S., Britain, France, and the Soviet Union are almost invariably represented among the chosen few. Such choice is not merely a reflection of limited resources and limited spheres of interest for the underdeveloped nations. It also represents what the geographer calls an *economy of agglomeration*. When people or activities cluster together at one particular place the costs of communication are drastically reduced; such reduction is particularly important for poorer nations. Hence, while a poorer Latin American country such as Paraguay does not exchange ambassadors with poorer African countries such as Kenya, representatives of the two countries can meet on neutral territory in the nations such as the United States and Britain to which they both send their ambassadors.

Much the same economy of agglomeration effect probably plays a part in the routing choices of U.S. airlines. Certainly the purely domestic airlines find unusually attractive the possibility of obtaining a service to one of the international airports of the United States, such

as San Francisco or Chicago, as a result of which they can obtain a share in the ferrying of passengers—within the United States—who are ultimately bound for an international destination.

THE HIERARCHICAL ORGANIZATION OF NETWORKS

The facts that the network links between more attractive places are likely to be less wandering and more direct, that more attractive places have higher degrees of place connectivity, and that there are gradations in the quality of links joining up places on the network (e.g., single-track or double-track railroads) suggests that *a communication network may have some hierarchical organization*. Such hierarchical organization in which some places and some links are *more important* than others is locationally interesting since: (1) the degree of hierarchization may differ from one network to another (e.g., France versus the United States) generating some pattern of locational variation from one network to another, and (2) the hierarchical organization may exhibit a certain geographical order within the particular network. Such hierarchization is reflected in the relative importance of both the links and the nodes (or places connected by the links).

Some nodes are more important in the communication network than others since they have a higher level of connectivity. A trip of a given length will more likely have to pass through such a place than through a place having lower connectivity. Also, some links are more important than others: they carry more traffic, often at a higher speed, and this is often reflected in the physical quality of the link. The Motorway or Turnpike, for instance, is straighter, more gently graded and has more lanes than the regular highway; the speed limit may also be somewhat higher. Similarly, there are variations in the quality of railroads summarized by such variables as the number of tracks and the frequency of service; while in the case of air transportation, one can differentiate between piston and jet aircraft services.

There is some relationship, moreover, between the importance of nodes, or places, and the importance of the links which intersect at them. The more important nodes usually have more important links radiating from them than the less important nodes. Thus, in the jet transportation network of the United States, New York City has a greater proportion of its links expedited by jet aircraft as opposed to piston engine aircraft than does, say, a less important node such as Peoria, Illinois, or Fort Wayne, Indiana. On railroad networks, the less important nodes are likely to be served only by the slow, stopping train, while the places with higher connectivity will be served by fast express links. Consequently, the greater the importance of a node, the more likely it is to have a direct link with the most important node (the most connected) in the system.

When we compare networks with each other we find great differences in the degree of hierarchization of both nodes and links. As far as nodal connectivities are concerned *some networks are more centralized than others,* that is, there is a greater inequality in the connectivities of places in some networks than in others. Likewise, some networks exhibit greater

inequalities of link quality than do others. Each of these concepts of hierarchization will be treated in turn, the first at greater length and the second more briefly. Consider the networks in Figure 8-7. In (i) no single place is more connected (i.e., more central) than any other place. In (ii), on the other hand, places *b* and *c* are more central than *a* and *d*, that is, they are the focus for more routes. In (iii) place *b* is clearly preeminent in its centrality for the network as a whole.

While it is easy to see that networks (i), (ii), and (iii) differ in their degree of centralization and that intuitively at least, network (iii) is more centralized than network (ii), which, in turn, is more centralized than network (i), how can we clarify the notion of centralization so that it can be measured? It would seem that what we are talking about when we discuss relative degrees of centralization in different networks is the *variation in connectivity from one place to another.* In Figure 8-7 (i) there is no variation—all places are connected to the same degree, while in (ii) and (iii) there is more variation.

A simple measure of variation across a set of places and one which has an infinity of applications in all sciences is the *variance.* Here we will go over the method of computing this simple measure, and the student is advised to follow the working closely as the concept will be referred to at other points in this book. Figure 8-8 represents a network of

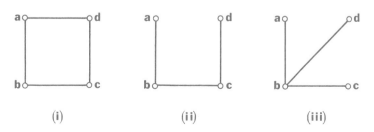

FIGURE 8-7. Three networks to illustrate the concept of network centralization. (See text for explanation.)

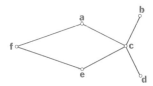

PLACE	CONNECTIVITY	(CONNECTIVITY-MEAN)	(CONNECTIVITY-MEAN)^2
a	2	0	0
b	1	-1	1
c	4	2	4
d	1	-1	1
e	2	0	0
f	2	0	0
Sum	12	$\sigma^2 = 6/6 = 1.0$	6

FIGURE 8-8. Computing the variance as an index of centralization for a sample network.

some sort and the places are connected to the network to variable degrees. For example, *c* is much more connected than *a* or *e*, which, in turn, are more connected than *b* or *d*. We can represent this information in tabular form as in Figure 8-8 and then compute the *average connectivity* of a place to the total network by summing its individual connectivities and dividing by the number of places; hence, the average or mean connectivity equals 12/6 which equals 2. We can now express the individual connectivities in terms of their deviations from their mean as in Column 3 of Figure 8-8. This merely represents the same information as is contained in Column 2 but in terms of deviations from a mean value. The variance is obtained by: (1) squaring each of the entries in Column 3 and placing the answers in Column 4; these entries are known as squared deviations; (2) summing the entries in Column 4: this is the sum of the squared deviations; and (3) dividing that sum by the total number of places. The sum of the squared deviations in this case is 6 and the number of places involved is 6 so the variance is 6/6 = 1.

Consider now what would happen to the variance if the network was as in Figure 8-9. The data for computing the variance are shown in the figure. The mean is the same as before—12/6 = 2—and the sum of the squared deviations is now only 4. Hence, the variance of the connectivities is smaller than in Figure 8-8, and this agrees with our intuitive notions of centralization; we would certainly expect the network in Figure 8-8 to be more centralized than that in Figure 8-9 simply because Figure 8-8 is so focused on a single place.

As yet little work has been done on the centralization of networks whether they are transportation networks, diplomatic networks, social networks, or any other form of communication network. All we can do here is make some preliminary comments on some of the factors which seem to be associated with centralization as opposed to decentralization. We will look first at transportation networks and then, finally, see if there are any generalizations emerging.

Table 8-1 presents some centralization indices (using the variance of place connectivities as a measure of centralization) for a set of railroad networks. Considerable variation in centralization can be observed with nations such as France and Austria appearing highly centralized and nations such as Algeria, Turkey, and Italy appearing much less centralized. An obvious distinction between the nations with more centralized networks and those with less centralized networks is that the former nations are characterized by a population distribution in which one city is very dominant in terms of its population size. In France, for example, the population of Paris accounts for 15% of the population of the nation as a whole; in Austria, Vienna accounts for approximately 22% of the population. In nations like Spain, or Italy, on the other hand, more than one city has been dominant: in Spain, Madrid and Barcelona account for 8% and 7.2%, respectively, of Spain's total population; while in Italy, Milan accounts for rather more population than does Rome (4.1% for Milan versus 3.7% for Rome).

Such a relationship between *centralization* and *the primacy of the largest urban center* can be given a rationale. Larger population centers generate more traffic

TABLE 8-1.   Centralization indices for a sample of railroad networks. Rather high levels of centralization are recorded for such nations as France, Austria, and the United Kingdom, where one city dominates the urban structure of the nation. Where such dominance is less in evidence as in Spain, Rumania, and Italy, network centralization is correspondingly reduced.

	Centralization (connectivity variance)	Population of capital as a % of total population
France	2.00	15.0%
United Kingdom	1.60	14.4%
Austria	1.56	22.0%
Italy	1.05	3.7%
Spain	0.94	8.0%
Turkey	0.94	2.7%
Rumania	0.88	7.1%
Algeria	0.87	7.7%

and also have larger demands for goods from the rest of the country. Railroad connections to or from the larger population center are, therefore, more profitable investments than railroad links to or from smaller population centers. Smaller

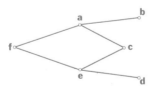

PLACE	CONNECTIVITY	(CONNECTIVITY-MEAN)	(CONNECTIVITY-MEAN)^2
a	3	1	1
b	1	−1	1
c	2	0	0
d	1	−1	1
e	3	1	1
f	2	0	0
Sum	12		4

$$\sigma^2 = 4/6 = .66$$

FIGURE 8-9.   Computing the variance as an index of centralization for another sample network.

cities trade more with larger cities than they do with smaller cities and, hence, connections between pairs of places in which one place is large and the other is relatively small are much more profitable than links between smaller places.

We are suggesting, therefore, a sequence of events in which the railroad companies perceived highly variable traffic demands, and, therefore, railroad profitabilities across a set of pairs of places. To the degree that such profitability was monopolized by linkages with one particular urban place, the network constructed was of a centralized nature; to the extent that such profitability was not monopolized by linkage with any one urban place, but was more evenly spread over linkages with several urban places, the resultant network was of a more decentralized character. This, at least, is one theory which might plausibly account for the centralization of networks. We will see shortly, however, that it is not the only one and that the issue is more debatable than we have immediately indicated here.

The concept of link hierarchization or inequality is more tentative and less subject to measurement since so many factors can be regarded as affecting the importance of a link. The idea has been little researched but it seems plausible that the degree to which there is inequality in the importance of links within the network should vary from one network to another. It seems likely, for example, that the differentiation of route quality is related to economic development for at least two reasons. Economic development brings with it a greater variety of vehicles with a greater range of track needs: in road transport, for example, one has the horse and cart at one end of the scale to the truck and trailer at the other end of the scale. While most highways are suitable for the horse and cart, this is not true for the truck and

trailer. Also, economic development brings with it a greater need for long-distance transportation and the creation of routes to satisfy that demand. Certainly a 200-mile trip through the winding lanes of England, for example, would be painfully slow and hence the need for more direct, high-speed routes. The same rationale helps to explain the superimposition of diagonal routes on the rectangular route pattern of the Midwest.

Apart from system variations in the level of hierarchization, however, there is also the question of a possible geographical order being present in the hierarchical structure of nodes and links in a network. It is apparent, for example, that if there are fewer places with high connectivity than with low connectivity, then it is likely that the places with higher connectivity will be located farther apart. This certainly seems to be so from map evidence. Also, if there is differentiation in route quality, are higher quality routes spaced farther apart than less important routes? This, in fact, seems to be the case for reasons which will appear clearer in the next chapter.

Quite apart from examining the geographical relationships of links at one particular level of quality or importance, one very interesting question concerns the geographical relationships existing between links not of the same importance but of differing importance. Specifically, consider the *angles* at which links of differing importance meet one another. Assuming for the moment that the more important routes are characterized by higher levels of movement (this seems in general to be so) there are some interesting theories of an analog nature which can be advanced on the basis of other hierarchically organized movement systems such as the system of veins and arteries conducting blood through the human body. A student of vascular

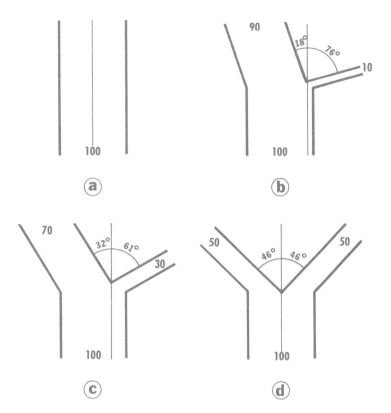

FIGURE 8-10. Average relations between mean branching angle and percentage of main stem flow for a sample of 243 highway junctions in Portugal. As the proportion of flow entering the main highway from a branch highway diminishes, the angle it makes with the main highway increases: thus in (b) above the branch highway contributes only 10% of the total flow and therefore its angle of entry is correspondingly large (76 degrees).

systems, Roux, for example, advanced the following hypothesis summarized by the biologist Darcy Thompson: " . . . (i) if an artery bifurcates into two equal branches, these branches come off at equal angles to the main stem. (ii) If one of the two branches be smaller than the other, then the main branch continuation of the original artery makes with the latter a smaller angle than does the smaller or 'lateral' branch. (iii) All branches which are so small that they scarcely seem to weaken or diminish the main stem come off from it at a large angle from about 70 to 90°." [Darcy W. Thompson, *On Growth and Form*

(Cambridge: Cambridge University Press, 1917)]. The geographer Haggett has taken this notion and applied it to the branching of a sample of highway junctions in Portugal. Figure 8-10 summarizes his results and shows that as the proportion of flow entering the main highway from the branch highway diminishes, the angle it makes with the main highway increases. This suggests that the less important the highway relative to the highway it is linking up with, the greater the angle of branching. This is intuitively reasonable when we consider the form of road junctions encountered in our own travels.

NETWORK DYNAMICS

An alternative viewpoint on the factors associated with the geometry of networks can be obtained by a study of their changing locational pattern over time. Examination of successive spatial patterns may reflect on the factors that entered into the locational decisions and priorities involved in such evolution and, hence, upon the factors which account for variation in densities, connectivities, and degrees of centralization observable across different networks.

In this treatment the focus is largely, though not entirely, upon the *locational evolution* of *railroad networks* with particular reference to European network evolution and the networks of contemporary underdeveloped areas. We proceed by two stages: first, a set of four successive network locational patterns against which actual railroad networks can be compared is suggested. Second, we examine the implications of this four-stage model for the factors affecting the generation of such railroad nets.

FOUR STAGES OF SPATIAL GROWTH

Four stages in the geographical growth of railroad networks are envisaged: an initial stage of localized linkage, a second stage of network integration, a third stage of intensification, and a final stage of selection in which unprofitable or less

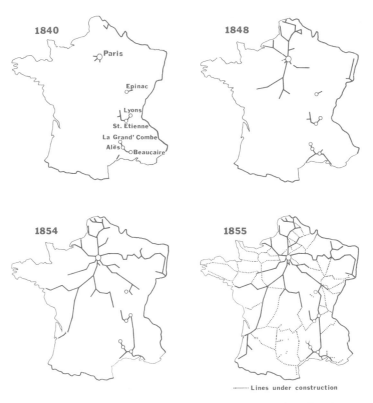

FIGURE 8-11. The geographical evolution of the French railroad network. Note the shortness of the earlier links and the isolation of the individual network segments from each other. The branching nature of early network development is also clearly in evidence.

profitable lines are closed down. Each of these stages is treated in turn from the point of view of its characteristic locational pattern and the factors that produce that pattern.

Localized Linkage.   The initial stages of network development in a national territory are characterized by a structure in which four components are outstanding: the prevalence of short links rather than longer links, the prevalence of isolated network segments, the prevalence of links which are complementary to the previous network of navigable waterways, and the prevalence of branching or treelike networks rather than circuit networks.

These points are illustrated by the maps of the railroad networks of France for 1840 and 1848 (see Figure 8-11). In these maps the isolation of network segments from one another is readily apparent as are the shortness of the lines relative to the length of possible linkages and the prevalence of branching as opposed to circuit structures. Complementarity to the waterway network is also present. In France, for example, the short railroad from Epinac linked up with the Canal de Bourgogne to expedite the shipment of coal from the LeCreusot area to Paris, while in the southeast the line to Beaucaire linked up the coal mines of la Grand' Combe and Alès with the navigable water of the river Rhône and the Mediterranean.

Such network features are particularly in evidence in underdeveloped areas of the globe. Figure 8-12, for example, presents the railroad network of the Congo (Leopoldville). Not only is the network broken up into separate subsystems consisting of treelike structures of rather short links, but its complementarity to the navigable stretches of the Congo River and its tributaries is particularly in evidence: railroads have frequently been built as a means of cir-

FIGURE 8-12.   The railroad network of the Congo. Note the complementarity to water transportation and the emphasis on branching structures characteristic of underdeveloped nations.

cumventing rapids and other unnavigable stretches of river, for example.

Why do such geometrical properties obtain? In the context of uncertainty that surrounds the construction of railroads in a new area, there is a desire on the part of entrepreneurs to minimize the capital: output ratio. In railroad construction this signifies a selection of links in which construction costs are minimized while movement is maximized, thus driving total costs and risk of failure to a low level and minimizing the debt burden on future expansion. Priority is therefore given to (a) the shortest desire lines in the spatial system of demands, and (b) those desire lines which reflect high levels of demand for movements capable of providing a high return per dollar invested. Particularly important historically were the short-distance lines connecting large cities with each other or with their hinterlands or with coal fields or connecting mineral exploitation sites with nearby water transportation. In France, for example, Paris was an early focus for a segment of the emerging national network while the coal fields of the North and of the St. Étienne area and of the Alès-Grand' Combe area also received railroads to link them with markets such as Lyons or to navigable waterways. It is interesting to note in this respect that the first steam railroad in the world was a railroad built to carry coal from the English town of Darlington to the neighboring market and navigable waterway town of Stockton. It was such lines as these that were most likely to provide a high initial return on capital invested and these were the lines sought out just as in Africa today many of the lines are built with the intention of extracting localized mineral wealth.

Integration. The dominant changes reflected in this phase of network evolution involve the linkage of isolated network segments into an integrated network and the circumventing of the once complementary waterways so that they become more competitive than complementary. Such linkage into an integrated net clearly connotes an increase in connectivity and density. Integration of this type is apparent in France in 1855 (see Figure 8-11) with Paris emerging as a very dominant focus in the network.

In a sense integration represents an extension of the first phase of railroad network development since it involves the construction of new routes on heavy desire lines replacing the bottlenecks of complementary systems of water transportation. Thus, the construction of a railroad from Paris to Marseilles eliminated the need for a complementary river transport route by way of such rivers as the Rhône and Saône and the Canal de Bourgogne. Similarly, the bridging of the North American continent in 1869 eliminated the complementarity of the route around Cape Horn.

The reason that it is possible to detect an earlier phase of isolated linkage before the emergence of an integrated network probably can be found in the element of learning. Early railroad ventures on routes of short length and very heavy demand provided important knowledge about the possible profitability of the "new-fangled" railroad. The localized linkage phase also provided the capital necessary for further expansion of the network. Thus, in the French case the ratio of railroad receipts to expenses rose to a very lofty 2.25 just prior to integration in 1851. The high profits yielded by many early railroad ventures must have provided a great source of temptation for further network construction.

Nor in the French case do the hopes of the entrepreneurs appear to have been futile. The highest receipts–expenses ratio ever achieved by the French

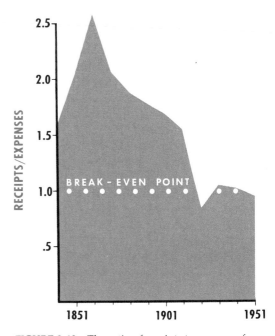

FIGURE 8-13. The ratio of receipts to expenses for the French railroad network. Early returns on investment were high and reached a peak in the phase of integration: extension of the network along less profitable routes led to a deterioration in the financial position of the railroads during the intensification phase after 1860. This became particularly critical after 1911 with competition from public motor transportation.

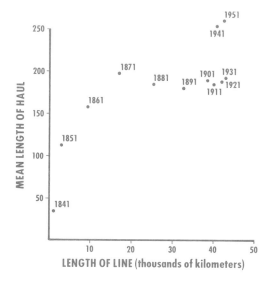

FIGURE 8-14. Network length and mean length of haul for goods traffic in France, 1841–1951.

gular structures. More specifically, this requires the construction of connecting links between places already linked in a more circuitous manner. This phase is represented in the map of lines in existence and under construction in France in 1855 (see Figure 8-11).

A secondary feature of the evolving network structure at this time is the emergence of feeder lines designed to tap the traffic of rural areas or small ports and usually ending in cul-de-sacs. Conceptually this may be represented as the addition of new branching treelike structures to a network now dominated by circuit structures. Though such feeder lines may be regarded as a further effort to increase railroad income by tapping new markets, their low profitability was clearly recognized by the utility of such low-cost construction methods as the building of single track lines.

It seems, however, that some of the optimism regarding the financial viability of new lines constructed during the in-

railroad system was obtained in 1861 immediately following integration (see Figure 8-13). Also, the mean length of goods haul rocketed to a maximum in 1871 (Figure 8-14) while goods and passenger traffic also increased (see Figure 8-15). The growth in passenger traffic was particularly dramatic suggesting that integration and the consequent elimination of waterway bottlenecks was much more important for this source of revenue than for goods traffic.

In these earlier stages of network growth, therefore, there is a gradual shift from a priority on short links connecting highly localized traffic generating points to longer links connecting up similar places of localized traffic characteristics or sub-networks in order to eliminate inefficient complementary systems of transportation.

Intensification. A major feature of this phase is the conversion of the branching structures that dominated the first two phases of railroad network evolution into circuit networks represented by triangular or delta shapes or by rectan-

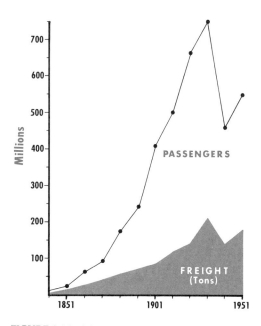

FIGURE 8-15. Movement of passengers and goods traffic in France, 1841–1951.

tensification stage may have been unjustified—at least in France. Thus, as Figure 8-13 shows, the receipts/expenses ratio underwent a dramatic decline in the six decades after 1861. It is very interesting in this respect to compare the routes constructed in France before 1855, after 1855, and traffic flows as they exist today. In general, flows, particularly of passengers, are much more considerable on the lines constructed by 1855 than on those completed after that date (compare Figure 8-11 with Figure 8-16), suggesting that many of the lines constructed after 1855 were relatively uneconomical. This view has received some support from work carried out on the development of the American railroad system. It has been shown that the gains in cheaper movement from development of the railroad system as compared with the

gains which could have been realized from development of the existing waterway and highway system were much smaller than it has been thought before, and that many of the lines constructed in the 19th century turned out to be uneconomic propositions.

Selection. The high-risk potential of such feeder lines and duplications is amply illustrated by the spatial patterns of the fourth and final period characteristic of railroad growth in Europe and North America. Generally the last links added to the network have been the first to be deleted. This final period, therefore, is one in which there is a conscious selection and discrimination between the more profitable and less profitable lines with the less profitable feeder lines and duplicate links being closed down. Geometrically it has involved the deletion of many of the branching components of a network, leaving behind a network more completely dominated by circuit structures than before.

Undoubtedly a major force resulting in closure of such short-distance lines as the feeder line has been the development over the past 50 to 60 years of motor transportation, the truck being a particularly cheap carrier over shorter distances and hence having an economic complementarity to the railroad. The development of rural bus services has had a similarly disastrous impact upon the passenger market for many short-distance railroad trips.

A second factor has been the emergence of economies of scale in the handling of large quantities of goods both at terminal points and in transit. Thus, during the late 19th century, feeder lines were frequently constructed to join up ports to major trunk lines as a means of capturing the trade of such ports in commodities like lumber and agricultural feeding stuffs. The massive increase in the size of ocean-going vessels, how-

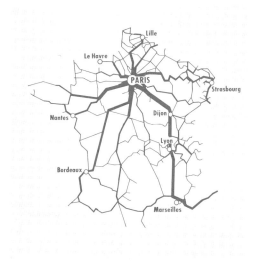

FIGURE 8-16.   Railroad passenger traffic in France, 1959. The thickness of the line is proportional to traffic flow. Compare this map with the map of the railroad network as it existed in 1855 (see Figure 8-11); in general the railroads carrying large numbers of passengers were built by 1855; railroads carrying relatively few passengers today tend to have been built later. Is this a tribute to the careful locational strategy of the French railroad builders? Or does it suggest that earlier links tend to channel flows to the detriment of later links?

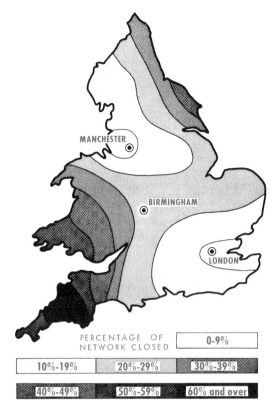

FIGURE 8-17. Railway closures in Britain 1962–1967. Note the high closure rates in such remote areas of low traffic generating capacity as Wales and southwest England.

line terminals and discouraged it between places which lack such facilities. Programs of route electrification have also been accompanied by concentration of traffic on one route in order to maximize the payoff of the heavy investment involved. Branch lines and small terminals or ports or lines generating only small amounts of traffic, therefore, have clearly been at a disadvantage. As a summary comment on the closure of feeder lines and lines in areas of dispersed traffic generation, Figure 8-17 is highly eloquent. The less densely settled west of England and Wales and the northeast coastal areas, for example, have been hit particularly severely.

Finally, the concentration of railroad ownership (as a result of falling profits) either in the hands of the government or in a small number of companies has led to a reassertion of monopolistic or oligopolistic conditions and a reduction in competition between railroads. This has permitted the closure of redundant lines. In France, for example, the state has undertaken a deliberate policy of concentrating traffic on the electrified route between Paris and Marseille via Lyons

ever, has made many such ports with their narrow channels and their meager capital investment hopelessly inadequate for maritime trade. Also, the development of high-powered locomotives capable of handling much larger loads at a much lower movement cost per ton mile than has ever been realized before has encouraged the concentration of goods traffic on only one of several approximately parallel routes in order to lift demand to that level where the use of such cheaper movement methods can be justified. The development of piggyback services as a cheaper method of handling goods traffic has also encouraged movement between places having such freight

FIGURE 8-18. The selective development of alternative Marseilles–Paris routes.

rather than the parallel route of less traffic-generating capacity which goes by Clermont-Ferrand (see Figure 8-18).

These ideas on the geographical evolution of communication networks are presented schematically in Figure 8-19. As can be seen, the phase of localized linkage is presented as one dominated by branching networks, short links, isolated network segments, and a complementarity to water transportation. The second phase sees the linkage of these segments into an integrated network while the third phase involves the conversion of the branching network into a set of circuit networks with new branches in the form of feeder lines. Finally, the phase of selection as shown in Figure 8-19 involves the pruning of the net-

work by the closing of many branch lines and duplicate lines. Clearly as more and more route is laid, so density increases, though it seems to reach its peak in the phase of intensification rather than in the more recent phase of selection. Undoubtedly the closure of many branch lines in such countries as Canada, the United States, Britain, and France has resulted in a diminution of track density compared with what it was, say, 50 years ago. The increase in connectivity has not been without its ups and downs, as the values for the schematic diagrams indicate; while connectivity is initially low and reaches a peak in the selection phase, it is lowest in the intensification phase as a result of the construction of feeder lines.

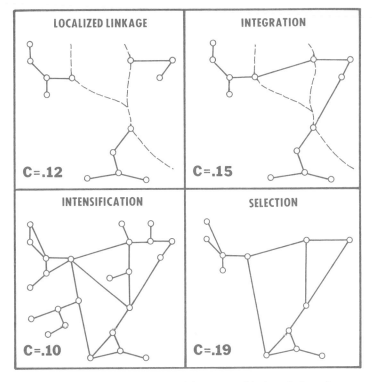

FIGURE 8-19. A schematic view of the geographical evolution of communication networks. Note the initial complementarity to other transport media and the emphasis upon branching network segments; circuit networks develop later. The dotted line indicates navigable waterway; c = the index of connectivity.

IMPLICATIONS

Much of this material on the dynamics of network evolution, therefore, confirms material we have discussed in our static approach in the first part of this chapter. The connectivity and density of networks in less developed countries, for example, is seen as particularly reduced in magnitude. We have also added some new ideas, especially with reference to the sequence of branching and circuit-type networks which networks seem to undergo as they change over time. Two implications of this review of network evolution, however, are particularly worthy of note: the idea of route location as a learning process and the significance of the perceived level of demand in locating routes.

We have argued that the early railroad entrepreneurs went through a phase of learning in which they acquired knowledge about the factors—such as town size and distance—affecting the profitability of projected railroad links. Their initial railroad building efforts were very cautious and they concentrated on the linkages which seemed to be most likely to yield a high profit, neglecting those which would (on the basis of what little knowledge they had) yield a lower return per dollar invested. Only as they acquired large profits from their initial investments and acquired more knowledge of the economics of railroads and of the geographical environment in which they were operating did they move from their more cautious phase into a more adventurous phase in which mistakes were likelier due to overoptimism on the basis of past financial successes.

The second implication is that the perceived level of demand for railroad services is a particularly critical factor in network construction. It is possibly for this reason that railroads spread from northwestern Europe very slowly into southern and eastern Europe: the direction of the diffusion corresponds to a socioeconomic gradient of considerable steepness. Railroads were first introduced in the more industrialized sections of Europe in Belgium and England. Only later in the 19th century did they spread to the less industrial areas of eastern and southern Europe as economic development occurred and raised the demand for railroad transportation to that level at which it was worth providing it.

CONCLUSIONS AND SUMMARY

This chapter has been primarily descriptive. We have examined the locational patterns of a variety of communication networks both as they exist at one specific point in time and as they change over time. Little has been offered regarding explanation of these patterns; only an occasional hint has been thrown out.

Major concepts of network geometry include *deviousness, density, connectivity, circuit networks* and *branching networks,* and *hierarchical organization.* These are associated with various factors: the level of economic development appears to be especially important since more developed nations have denser and more connected transportation networks. Within nations, the density of population seems to exercise a critical control over network density. All this suggests that demand factors may be important in *explaining* network geometries.

Network geometries, however, change over time and we have tried to conceptualize this evolution in the form of a four-stage sequence of geometries: consecutive stages of *localized linkage* in which isolated branching networks prevail, *integration* in which there is a transformation towards circuit networks, *intensification* involving line duplication and feeder development, and a final stage of *selection* or weeding out. Our treatment underlined the possible significance of behavioral factors in explaining this sequence of events: the *searching out* of profitable investment opportunities for network construction, the accumulation of knowledge regarding the conditions of profitability and the use of that knowledge in determining further investments. The technological environment in which these decisions are made also seems highly significant: the growing economies of scale in transportation seem to have adversely affected the future of routes and service points which cater to only relatively small levels of demand.

We have, however, only hinted at explanation; there is no profound, conclusive discussion of causes in this chapter. Neither is there any discussion of the impact of networks on a whole host of other locational patterns as a result of their alteration of accessibility relationships. The problems of looking back to the causes of network geometry and forward to their diverse locational effects are treated in the following chapter.

CHAPTER NINE

Communication Networks: Locational Forces and Locational Effects

THE PROBLEMS

Chapter Eight reviewed the various structural characteristics of communication networks and identified some of their more important correlates. We found, for example, that denser communication networks tended to be associated with more developed rather than less developed nations; and that the angle of branching for two links in a communication net tends to be greater for the link carrying the smaller volume of goods, passengers, or whatever. Why exactly do we find associations such as these? This is the first problem confronted in this chapter.

Networks, however, are not only effects; they are also causally linked to a variety of other locational patterns. Networks and the geographical evolution of networks revolutionize accessibility relationships and alter the movement costs according to which many locational decisions are made. Not only that, but the locational patterns produced by networks feed back to affect the further geographical development of the network. The problem of the locational effects of networks is discussed in the second half of this chapter.

Before considering the various forces affecting the location of railroads, of highways, of airline routes, etc., consider first the functions of a communications network. The network is developed presumably in response to some demand for movement between a variety of places: movements of commuters, tourists, goods, electricity, oil, etc. To move items or people over space requires a means of locomotion and, as a very frequent addition, a specialized track or terminal facility such as are represented by a railroad and an airport, respectively. Hence, given a set of places between which movement is required, two questions arise: first, what type of facility should be provided? Should it be a highway or a railroad, for example? Second, there is the question of where that facility should be located. The major factors affecting the solution of these two problems are economic and political. Each of these is considered below.

THE ECONOMICS OF ROUTE CONSTRUCTION

The design of a communication network is preceded by the identification of those places between which movement is required. Such requirements may be estimated by some sort of travel survey or they may be predicted by some sort of gravity model formulation. In the light of gravity model formulations and empirical findings, for example, it seems rea-

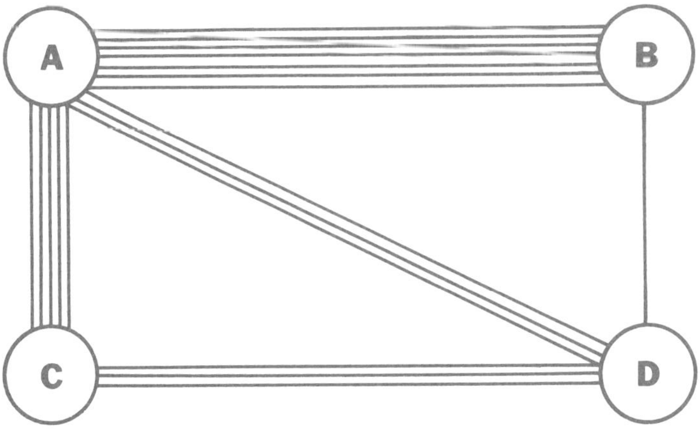

FIGURE 9-1. A desire-line diagram. The number of lines connecting two locations is an indication of the intensity of the demand for movement between the two locations.

sonable to expect the desire for movement facilities to be greater between large places separated by a short distance than between large places separated by a very long distance. Such demands can be conceptualized in the form of a *desire line* diagram, the number of lines connecting a pair of places indicating the intensity of the demand for movement between the two places (see Figure 9-1).

As Figures 9-2, 9-3*a*, and 9-3*b* indicate, a number of network configurations could be constructed to satisfy these demands. A number of these configurations, however, such as Figure 9-2, involve a principle which we shall explain in this chapter: the principle of *bundling or merging* of flows.

▶ *Bundling or merging of flows occurs when flows between different pairs of places are moved in part over a common transportation line.*

Thus in Figure 9-2 flows from *A* to *B* and from *C* to *D* are moved for part of their respective trips over the same network segment *E–F*. Obviously some economies can be realized in the construction of the network though at the expense of

higher costs for the movement itself. Such economic factors, however, are instrumental not only in deciding where to place the transportation facility but whether to place it at all. It is to the latter question that we address ourselves first.

THRESHOLD CONSIDERATIONS

Investment in a particular type of transportation facility to link up two places will only occur if the dollar return per dollar invested is regarded as "sufficiently high" by the transportation company whether it is a railroad, airline company, or trucking company. The term "sufficiently high" is deliberately vague but the evaluations of relative profitability will depend on such criteria as the availability of alternative, more profitable forms of investment, upon the perceived length of life of the facility before obsolescence, and upon the expectation of the company regarding the market for the facility.

For the dollar return per dollar invested to be "sufficiently high" there must be a certain level of demand for the facility. That critical level of demand below which the link will not be judged

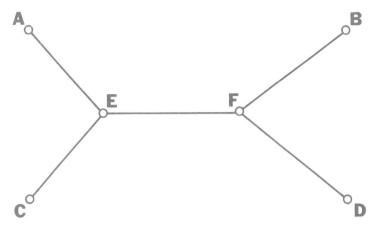

FIGURE 9-2. A possible network design. This design involves the princi-
ple of the *merging* or the *bundling* of flows; thus flows from A to B and from
C to D are merged for part of their route along the network segment E–F.
This type of design economizes on costs of network construction.

sufficiently profitable is known as the
threshold demand.

▶   *The threshold demand for a transportation facility is that level of demand below
which the expected profit would be judged
to be of insufficient magnitude.*

An obvious and important point is that
the threshold level for a link varies from
one transportation mode to another. It is,
for example, higher for a double track
railroad than for a single track railroad
and higher for a single track railroad
than for a Grade A highway. (Class 1
highways in Britain and U.S. highways
in the United States.)

While such threshold requirements are
of primary significance in explaining
why a certain type of link is constructed
rather than some other type of link, they
also have some interesting locational implications that help us in understanding
some of the correlations referred to in the
last chapter. Thus one of the points made
in the last chapter was that highway densities were considerably greater than
railroad densities; and that for highways,
lower-grade forms of highway such as
those represented by state highways in
the United States were somewhat denser
than the higher capacity, more expensive, higher-grade highways. This may
be clarified when we remember that not

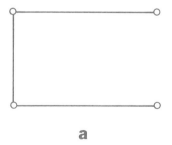
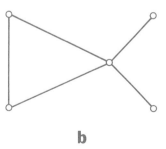

a   **b**

FIGURE 9-3 *a* and *b*.   Two alternative designs. Which network involves
merging of flows: one of them, both of them, or none at all?

only are the threshold requirements for a railroad greater than for a highway and greater for a U.S. highway than for a state highway, but more sets of desire lines satisfy low threshold requirements than satisfy high threshold requirements. If we were to take all possible pairs of towns in the United States and work out the demand for movement between them, most of the figures would be very low—too low for a railroad though almost certainly not too low for a highway of some sort. If the settlement pattern consisted of more large cities than small cities, instead of the reverse, then this might be different and we might have a situation in which the railroad density was not so different from the highway density.

This also helps to clarify the relationship between economic development and density of communication networks. As economic development proceeds and as, concurrently, the demand for the movement of goods and people to feed and man the factories increases, so the critical threshold for the construction of railroads between more and more places is achieved.

The threshold requirement, therefore, does help to clarify not only why certain links are built and certain others are not but also some of the aspects of network design discussed earlier. Its explanation of the locational features of communication, however, is far from exhaustive. What factors, for example, account for the deviousness of routes and why does deviousness tend to be greater for canals than for railroads? Why does connectivity tend to increase with increasing economic development and why are shorter routes substituted for more indirect routes at certain stages of network evolution? In order to explain these facets of network structure we have to examine the issue of the *specific route* of a

railroad or highway or airline linking up two places or, alternatively, three or four places.

SPECIFIC LOCATIONAL CONSIDERATIONS

In order to understand the specific locational patterns of routes it is useful to break down the total costs of providing a transportation service per unit carried into two components: a fixed-cost component and a running-cost component. The fixed costs consist largely of costs incurred at the time of track construction: the cost of buying the land for the canal or highway or railroad, the cost of constructing bridges, the cost of drainage and pavement or track, the cost of relocating displaced residents, the interest on money borrowed to construct the route, etc. Running costs, on the other hand, consist of items which vary in proportion to the amount of business carried out by the transportation company—fuel, labor, maintenance of the vehicles, etc.

For any given medium the cost structure can be summarized in terms of a ratio of fixed costs to running costs for a given time interval. This ratio is of rather critical importance in evaluating the different network configurations associated with different media. In general it tends to be higher for water transportation, of intermediate significance for railroads, and lowest of all for road transportation. Its implications for connectivity and route deviation will now be explored in some depth.

Consider two extreme cases of transportation cost structure. On the one hand, there is a medium in which the ratio of fixed costs to running costs is infinitely large, i.e., total costs are made up almost entirely of fixed costs. This will be called medium X. On the other hand, there is a medium in which the ratio of fixed costs to running costs is infinitely small, i.e., total costs consist almost entirely of running costs. Let this be medium *Y*.

Now consider the locational context. The route is to be constructed between two places *A* and *B*. Intervening between *A* and *B* is some barrier having an adverse effect on fixed costs; this might be a range of mountains requiring expensive tunneling costs or high land values incurring high land acquisition costs.

Two possible routes are indicated on Figure 9-4. The continuous line indicates the *deviant route*; on this route medium *X* incurs minimal fixed costs. The dashed line indicates the *direct route*; this imposes minimal running costs on medium *Y*. Recall that for medium *X* the fixed-cost–running-cost ratio is infinitely high. Given that the deviant route is the minimal fixed-cost route, the least *total-cost* route for medium *X* will be the deviant route. For medium *Y*, on the other hand, the obverse obtains: the least total-cost route will be the direct route; running costs account for almost all the total costs for medium *Y*, and the minimal running-cost route is the direct, minimal distance route.

Clearly we are considering polar types of transportation media in this hypothetical example. Nevertheless real world media can be assigned positions on a cost structure continuum, ranging from those for which running costs are a very high proportion of total costs to those for which fixed costs are a very high proportion of total costs. For the former, deviation from the straight line path is likely to involve an increase in total costs; for the latter, the direct path across a barrier imposing higher costs will also involve an increase in total costs.

▶ *More generally, media for which the fixed-cost–running-cost ratio is relatively high tend to be attracted to the least fixed-cost route; media for which the fixed-cost–running-cost ratio is relatively low tend to be attracted to the least running-cost route.*

For the single route between two places, several interesting locational implications can be deduced from these locational rules and matched up with some real world examples:

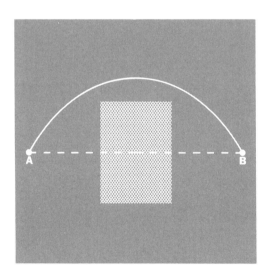

FIGURE 9-4. Transportation medium cost structures and minimal cost route alignments. The cross-hatched area represents a barrier resulting in increased fixed costs. The continuous line is the minimal cost route for a medium in which the ratio of fixed costs to running costs is infinitely high. The dashed line is the minimal cost route for a medium in which the ratio of fixed costs to running costs is infinitely small.

1.   Deviation for a barrier will be greater for those media where the ratio of fixed costs to running costs is higher rather than lower. Canal transportation, for instance, usually involves higher fixed costs relative to running costs than does railroad transportation.

   A striking example of the sensitivity of canal transportation to cost barriers and the lesser sensitivity of railroads can be found in the trans-

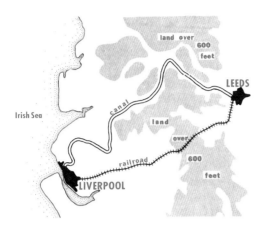

FIGURE 9-5. The relative deviousness of railroad and canal routes between Liverpool and Leeds. The canal deviates much more to avoid the topographic barrier than does the railroad. The ratio of fixed costs to running costs is much higher for canals, and deviations are important to economize on fixed costs.

portation links between Liverpool and Leeds in Northern England. The first bulk commodity route connecting Liverpool to Leeds was the Liverpool–Leeds Canal constructed in the second half of the 18th century. As can be seen from Figure 9-5 this canal deviates far to the north through a gap in the Pennine Mountains in order to avoid the high relief barrier in the crow's flight route from Leeds to Liverpool. The railroad, constructed about 60 years later, however, was far less sensitive to the cost barrier and tunneled under the mountains in order to link Liverpool and Leeds by a much more direct route.

2. Increasing volume of movement permits the locational substitution of more direct or speedier routes for more devious or time-consuming routes since running costs will increase relative to fixed costs. Over long periods of time, there is a tendency (since the advent of the automobile) for movement to increase

over many routes; this has been accompanied by "route straightening" as running costs increased relative to fixed costs and made the building of bridges or of shortcuts more economical. Thus, in the United States over the period 1935 to 1960 the shortest distance from Portland to Seattle has decreased by over 13%. In less dramatic cases it is accompanied by the construction of bypasses around cities and by the replacement of short bridges requiring right-angle turns by longer, more expensive bridges which eliminate this inconvenience.

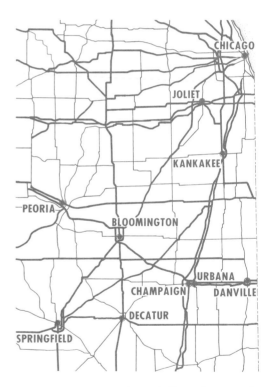

FIGURE 9-6 Rectangular and diagonal route patterns in Illinois: the initial road pattern of Illinois followed the lines of land division laid down by the township-and-range system. The demands for cheaper movement between the larger urban centers, however, has led to the laying out of diagonal routes joining up these cities more directly than they could have been linked by the rectangular system.

In the Midwest of the United States such route straightening has frequently taken the form of diagonal highways that cut across the predominantly rectangular road pattern to link those cities between which volumes of movement—and hence running costs—are relatively great. This is brought out very strongly in central Illinois (see Figure 9-6) where the diagonal route network linking the larger cities of Peoria, Bloomington, Springfield, Decatur, Champaign, and Chicago is superimposed upon the earlier rectangular pattern on which the larger majority of small towns continues to depend.

LINKING THREE PLACES

Similar arguments apply for locating routes among three places as apply to the question of locating a route between two places, but with some interesting and novel locational implications. Here we initially concentrate on three places at the apices of an equilateral triangle and we evaluate two possible network patterns: a pattern in which all sides of the triangle are linked up—this is the so called *Delta* pattern; and a pattern which produces the form of a letter Y—the so-called *Wye* pattern. The *Delta* shape, of course, is an important form of the circuit networks which we discussed in Chapter Eight while the *Wye* shape is the basic component of branching networks. If we are to understand the forces which lead to the emergence of circuit networks from branching networks, we should understand the relationships between Delta and Wye configurations. Some of the more interesting work which geographers have done in their exploration of networks involves specifying the conditions under which one shape is transformed into the other.

Assume that for both running costs and fixed costs the three external links of the triangle carry with them a cost penalty of 100 (see Figure 9-7); let us assume also that for the three possible links inside the triangle, running costs are 120 and fixed costs are 60. This is logical since while the Wye shape minimizes construction costs for the *producer* of transportation services, it maximizes the running costs for the *consumer* of trans-

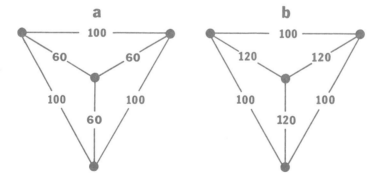

FIGURE 9-7. (*a*) Fixed costs and (*b*) running costs for delta and wye network configurations. In (*a*) the figure 100 signifies that fixed costs for any possible link in the delta network would be 100 monetary units; for the wye configuration fixed costs for any possible link in the network would be 60. Similar arguments apply to the running cost diagram. As the ratio of fixed costs to running costs increases, total costs favor the wye shape; as the ratio decreases due, for example, to increased demand for movement, the delta shape becomes the least total cost configuration.

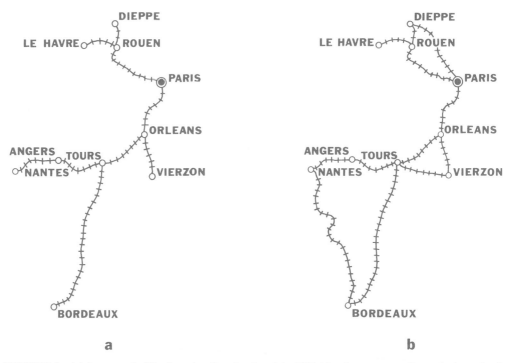

FIGURE 9-8. (*a*) A segment of the French railroad network in 1854. Note how wye configurations predominate; these patterns are typical of the early stages of railroad network evolution. (*b*) The same segment of the French railroad network some years later; note how deltas have been added to the wye shapes. As the volume of movement increases so the ratio of fixed costs to running costs declines and the delta shape attains *total* cost advantages over the wye shape.

portation services. The Delta shape, on the other hand, provides lower running costs for consumers but higher fixed costs for the transportation agency. Clearly as the ratio increases in value, the cost advantages from the transportation agency viewpoint shift in favor of the Wye shape. Conversely, as the ratio decreases, the total-cost advantages of the Delta configuration become increasingly apparent. This Delta–Wye relationship is rich in its geographical implications, some of which are explored below.

1. *Bundling of Flows.* The first and the most obvious implication is that this mechanism provides a rationale for the bundling of flows in the network in the manner described at the beginning of this chapter. Networks with reduced bundling of flows may be assumed to have much higher

running costs relative to their fixed costs.

2. *Connectivity Effects.* A second implication of these ideas is that increasing traffic volumes should be accompanied by the construction of Delta-like configurations superimposed upon the earlier Wye shapes characteristic of a period of lower volume movement. This is amply reflected in the geographical evolution of the French railroad network where earlier segments of the network took the form of Wyes with their roots at Paris (see Figure 9-8*a*). Later links often added a Delta shape or partial Delta shape (see Figure 9-8*b*). The railroad networks of many underdeveloped countries seem to expand in this Wye-type fashion from a limited number of nodes (e.g., Senegal,

Sudan) and it will be interesting to see if the Deltas are added later with increasing traffic volume.

The Wye–Delta transformation with increasing volume also provides a rationale for increasing network connectivity. As economic development proceeds, the volume of movement, particularly over longer distances, increases and one can expect the addition of Deltas to the existing Wyes. The gross effect is the addition of links and the increasing connectivity of the route network. This should apply especially to larger urban places between which the demand for movement should be greater than between smaller places. Recall that in Chapter Eight we pointed to the tendency for larger urban places to be more connected than smaller urban places.

3. *Branching Angles.* An additional facet of network geometry considered in Chapter Eight concerned the angles of branching of routes in the network. It was suggested that the mag-

nitude of the angle between a branch route and the main stem will be smaller the greater the proportion of total movement along that branch. Thus if a branch accounted for 90% of the flows along the two branches its angle with the main stem would be very small, while the angle of the smaller branch would be relatively great. An argument to elucidate this relationship can now be structured in terms of Wye configurations distorted by higher levels of movement between two of the three places on the network.

We have already noted that as the ratio of fixed costs to running costs declines, the Wye configuration is replaced or complemented by a Delta configuration. If the volume of movement is particularly high between two of the three then the ratio of fixed to running costs will tend to be low leading to a straightening of the route between that particular pair of places. Thus if Figure 9-9a represents the desire lines

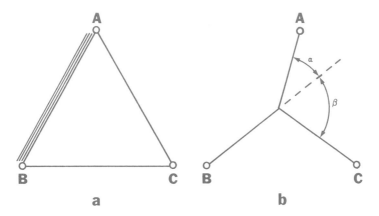

FIGURE 9-9. (*a*) Desire lines for movement among three places; note how the demand for movement is much greater between A and B than between any other pair of places. Consequently, we would expect that the fixed cost/running cost ratio would be much lower for the link A–B leading to a straighter route than on those links such as A–C and B–C where demand is much lower. This is reflected in the resultant network and angles of branching in (*b*). Note that angle alpha between the route carrying the largest amount of movement and the main stem is much smaller than angle beta.

between the two places, then we would expect the link *A–B* to be much straighter than either the links *A–C* or *B–C* (see Figure 9-9*b*). Also, angle alpha separating the higher volume branch from the main stem will be considerably smaller than angle beta separating the lower volume branch from the main stem.

THE POLITICS OF ROUTE CONSTRUCTION

While the foregoing material has emphasized the economic costs and benefits of particular route locations, there is no doubt that political factors have locational implications because of the political costs and benefits of particular routing policies. If a city planning commission permits the routing of a freeway through a Republican suburb, for example, it may challenge the very basis on which its own power rests in the Republican-dominated city; and similarly routes may be constructed long before they are economically feasible simply because of the political benefits that may flow from the railroad in addition to those economic benefits which per se would not justify the construction of the route at that time. It seems, therefore, that political factors can affect network location in two ways. First, political factors can alter the *threshold* for a particular form of route; this may take the form of subsidizing private contractors or of the government moving directly into transportation itself. Secondly, political costs of a particular route alignment may be so high as to lead to selection of a politically less sensitive route though possibly one which is economically more costly. Here political factors seem to affect the *fixed costs of construction*. Each of these types of political effect will be considered.

In discussing density variations of

transportation networks we remarked upon the relatively high density railroad networks prevailing in such nations as India, Burma, and Taiwan and we attributed this to political factors—specifically the construction of railroads which would not have been justified upon strictly economic grounds but which were justified from the viewpoint of political control and moving armies rapidly from one part of the territory to another. This is a case in which the economic threshold was insufficiently high for railroad development on the scale actually observed; the threshold was lowered, however, by either government construction of the railroad on the basis of taxes or private construction with government subsidy.

The question of political interference is particularly apropos in the context of current debates regarding the future of intra-urban transportation networks. If the economic forces of the market are allowed to prevail then it is clear that the bus line networks which have existed for a large number of years in cities will be forced into liquidation. However there seem good reasons of a public interest nature—as opposed to private interest—which suggest that it would be more socially efficient to maintain public transportation systems by some form of subsidy. Not only do large numbers of poorer and handicapped people rely on the public transport network but the private automobile creates certain costs which are experienced not only by the motorist himself but by the inhabitants of the city at large whether or not they drive an automobile: congestion, atmospheric pollution, and the cost of buying expensive central city land for automobile parking appear to be some of the more significant of these costs. If bus networks are to be allowed to assume a greater proportion of the demand for intra-urban movement, however, it seems likely that a small subsidy will have to be combined with some sort of penalty imposed on the private motorist. This might take the form, for instance, of some special decal purchased specifically for the purpose of driving within the central portions of the city and which has to be exhibited at all times.

While government agencies can alter the threshold conditions under which certain communication facilities are supplied, political factors may also be instrumental not simply in deciding whether or not a particular network will be provided but in deciding the specific location of that network. Political boundaries, for example, are often constructed in such a way as to cut across crows flight paths between two places within the same nation; the route, however, often betrays an extreme sensitivity to the political boundary by deviating in order not to cross it. This is reflected in the location of the railroad in the African nation of Mauretania where the deflection is particularly abrupt (see Figure 9-10). For a variety of reasons, constructing a railroad route or any transport link partly through another country is more expensive in terms of either political or economic costs. As far as economic costs are concerned, for example, there is a threat of interference with the operations of such a link by a government not susceptible to influence by the owner of the link itself in the same way that the home government would be. Thus, pipelines connecting Saudi Arabian oil fields to the Mediterranean coast undergo continual harassment from Syria through which the pipelines must pass.

Such route deviations as a function of the political costs involved on alternative economically cheaper routes are not confined to surface links such as railroads and oil pipelines; airlines are also susceptible. A current case in point is represented by the way in which South Afri-

FIGURE 9-10. A railroad deviation in Mauretania. Note how the railroad deviates to avoid crossing Spanish Sahara territory. Relationships have been tense between Spain and Mauretania since Spain considers the valuable iron-ore workings at Fort Gouraud to be part of the Spanish Sahara; the iron ore provides over 90% of the value of Mauretania's exports, however.

can Airline routes between South Africa and Western Europe must deviate far to the west (see Figure 9-11), in order to avoid the territories of the large majority of African states which have banned that airline from their air space.

THE LOCATIONAL IMPLICATIONS OF COMMUNICATION NETWORKS

For the geographer, networks are not simply phenomena the locational patterns of which have to be explained; they are also locational factors in their own right. We have tried to argue earlier in this book, for example, that the movement behavior of an individual is strongly affected by the cost of movement between different locations. This is also a vital concern to other locators such as industrialists who try to locate in such a way as to hold the various movement costs (assembling raw materials, distributing the finished product, etc.) down as far as possible. By means of

FIGURE 9-11. Airline route deviations and political boundaries. Links between South Africa and Western Europe deviate as a result of restrictions on the use of national airspace.

their effects on movement, therefore, networks of communication can exercise a decisive affect on the locational patterns of a whole host of other phenomena such as residential development, factories, agricultural development, stores and banks, etc. They exercise this effect because of their impact on the *accessibility* of places to one another.

THE CONCEPT OF ACCESSIBILITY

Accessibility contains two important notions: that of being able to reach a place — the *connection component* of accessibility; and that of being able to get there quickly and/or cheaply — the *movement cost component* of accessibility.

▶ *The accessibility of one place to another depends upon two factors: whether or not they are connected by a route and the magnitude of the movement cost involved in getting from the one place to the other.*

If movement cost is related to distance — and clearly it often is — then there will be a relationship between accessibility and distance relationships.

A number of measures have been proposed for the concept of accessibility; some of these are more adequate than others in terms of the definitions set forth above. We could, for example, employ place connectivity as a measure of accessibility. Here, however, we wish to focus on two concepts which will be involved in the ensuing discussion: (1) the concept of *network accessibility* and (2) the concept of *population potential*. These two concepts will be illustrated with reference to the data shown in Figure 9-12*a*.

The routes on the diagram signify the connection component of accessibility while the figures attached to the routes are a measure of movement cost; this could be measured in miles or time or cost of travel. The figures attached to the locations are a measure of the population, in thousands, at the respective locations. The network accessibility measure for a location is computed in the following manner: first the route distances or travel costs, etc., between all places are computed and placed in a table or matrix (see Figure 9-12*b*); each cell entry of the

	A	B	C	D	E
A	...	170	70	130	210
B	170	...	100	160	240
C	70	100	...	60	140
D	130	160	60	...	80
E	210	240	140	80	...
Sum	580	670	370	430	670

FIGURE 9-12*b*. The network distance matrix: cell entries indicate the distance in miles along the shortest route between a pair of towns; column totals provide an index of the network accessibility of a place, with the largest totals denoting the lowest levels of accessibility and the smallest totals indicating the highest degrees of accessibility. Thus place *C* has the highest degree of accessibility while places *B* and *E* share the honors for the most inaccessible place.

table gives the distance or movement cost between the place indicated at the end of the row and the place indicated at the top of the column in which the cell entry happens to fall. Summing the figures in each column then gives the network accessibility index for the place indicated at the top of the respective column; low indices indicate a high degree

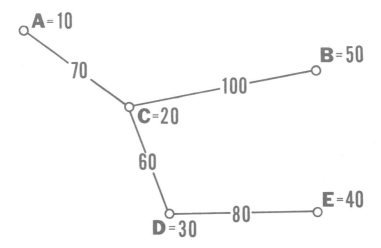

FIGURE 9-12*a*. Hypothetical data for computing accessibility measures. There are 5 towns, A, B, C, D, and E; the figures by each town give its population in thousands; connecting routes have intervening distances in miles attached.

of accessibility so that, for example, place C is the most accessible place on the network.

The concept of population potential, on the other hand, is a measure of accessibility not simply to locations but to the populations at locations. This measure of accessibility may therefore be important to someone evaluating locations from the viewpoint of, for example, access to a consumer market. It is computed by: (1) dividing each cell entry in the matrix in Figure 9-12b into the population size of the place indicated at the end of the respective row; where the movement cost is zero (i.e., to the town for which one is computing population potential) a constant of one is added to ensure a

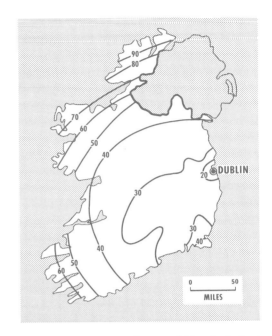

FIGURE 9-13. Network accessibility in Ireland based on the arterial road network: low values indicate high degrees of accessibility. Note the high degree of network accessibility enjoyed by the Dublin area.

Location

	A	B	C	D	E
A	10.00	0.06	0.14	0.08	0.05
B	0.29	50.00	0.50	0.31	0.21
C	0.29	0.20	20.00	0.33	0.14
D	0.23	0.19	0.50	30.00	0.37
E	0.19	0.17	0.29	0.50	40.00
Population potential =	11.00	50.62	21.43	31.22	40.77

FIGURE 9-12c. The computation of population potentials: the population potential for a column location is computed by dividing the populations of the places to which the respective rows in the table above refer, by the respective distances of those places from the column location. Thus for location (column A) population potential = 40/1 + 50/170 + 20/70 + 30/130 + 40/210 = 10.00 + 0.29 + 0.29 + 0.23 + 0.19. Distances are shown in Figure 9-12b. Note that although a location is zero miles from itself, we have to insert a positive number (in this case we have chosen 1.0) in order to obtain a quotient. While this is not illustrated very well by the present diagram due to the rather limited range of population sizes, small cities close to larger cities tend to have higher population potentials than small cities surrounded by other small cities. Thus the population potential of New Brunswick, N.J. between Philadelphia and New York City is much, much higher than that of Fargo, North Dakota even though they have very similar population sizes.

meaningful answer; (2) summing down columns (see Figure 9-12c).

Clearly this does not measure the same concept as the concept of network accessibility; indeed the rank order of network accessibility for the places in Figure 9-12b is not the same as the order of population potentials for those places shown in Figure 9-12c. Nevertheless where accessibility must be qualified by the further question, "How accessible to the population located at different places?," population potential seems an adequate measure. It is one to which we will refer again when we try to explain the reciprocal relationships existing between networks and the locational patterns of activities which are attracted to different places on networks.

Given a set of places such as those in the hypothetical example just discussed, it is possible to compute either network accessibility or population potential for all places and plot the values on a map. When this is done it is frequently found that places close to each other tend to have very similar values. This fact permits the drawing of isolines of equal accessibility on the map to produce something akin to isopercept maps discussed in Chapter Six and to the more familiar topographical contour map. Figure 9-13, for example, presents a network accessibility map for the arterial road network of Ireland. The effect of the centralization of the network on Dublin is clearly apparent in the map with places further away from Dublin having high values and therefore low degrees of network accessibility. Obviously if there was no such centralization in the arterial road network, network accessibility

would tend to be greater (i.e., lower values) in central Ireland. Figure 9-14 presents a map of population potential for England and Wales; the effect of the heavily populated areas of London, Birmingham, Lancashire, and Yorkshire is clearly evident on this map.

ACCESSIBILITY AND LOCATION

Accessibility reduces the costs of carrying out certain activities. Its significance for location, therefore, should be obvious. Dramatic examples of the effect which improved accessibility can have upon locational patterns are provided by the construction of bridges, tunnels, and bypasses which revolutionize man's spatial relationships and his consequent movement patterns. The implications for locational patterns however are not always simple; nor are they the same for different individuals.

The construction of new bridges across previously unbridged rivers or estuaries, for example, is usually rich in its locational effect. Most immediate are the changes in travel behavior with increased numbers crossing to the other side of the barrier over and above those who previously took a more devious route. The opening of the Philadelphia–Camden Bridge was accompanied by a 78% increase in traffic between the two destinations; the construction of the San Francisco–Oakland Bridge resulted in a 64% increase.

Not all of the locational changes induced by such accessibility-increasing improvements as bridges and bypasses are positive in the form of benefits accruing to people or communities, however. The decline of through traffic for a bypassed town, for example, may lead to loss of part of its retailing market; the construction of a bypass surrounding the city may hasten the decline of the city center as industries and retailers relocate

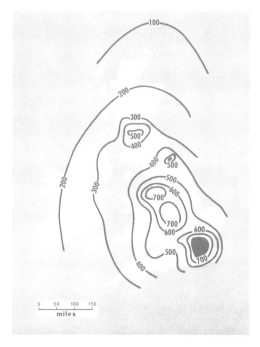

FIGURE 9-14. Population potential in the United Kingdom, 1961. Population potential at a place is a measure of the accessibility of that place to other populations. Note how population potential is especially high in southeast England and in an area extending northwest from there.

to where arterial roads transect the bypass; and the construction of a bridge will have negative repercussions upon the business of places on the older, more devious, route. Nevertheless for any one community affected by such accessibility changes the effects are often and surprisingly a mixture of both the beneficial and the penalizing. Thus in a study of a bypass around the Washington town of Marysville it was shown that while there had been some negative effects on the town's business the dramatic decrease of through traffic had made the place a quieter and more attractive place to live in, land values had increased, and a period of increased residential construction activity for commuters to local cities seemed imminent.

However, one can also imagine cases in which accessibility declines, placing certain locations at an absolute disadvantage; bridges are swept away, railroads and railroad stations are closed, airports are closed, etc. Clearly, in many cases this can be disastrous for the social and economic life of the community; it is also likely to be felt harder by some than by others. If a railroad station in a rural area is closed down, for example, and is not replaced by an adequate bus service the middle-class residents with their automobiles are unlikely to be affected as much as the more economically disadvantaged. In Los Angeles, the mobility problem for poorer ethnic minorities is severe; as a higher proportion of the population has obtained automobiles, bus services have contracted, effectively isolating many Negroes and Mexicans from the rest of the city around them. Many Negro women, for example, find it difficult to get to their place of work as domestics in the white areas of the city. This situation has fostered the development of all manner of private transportation companies who ferry Negro women around the city at extortionate prices.

Closure of a transportation facility, of course, frequently involves denial of access by closing down some terminal facility; a railroad station is closed down, or an airport or ocean port is closed for lack of business. Such denial of access to an increasingly large number of places seems inextricably intertwined with the evolution of the means of transportation.

▶ *Succeeding transportation innovations have increasingly emphasized limited access to the facility.*

The early highway was accessible to anyone living along it: it has been replaced by the limited access freeway. The canal permitted locators access anywhere along its banks, and canals were the foci of industry in the industrial areas of Britain in the late 18th century, giving rise to marked *linear* patterns in the location of industry within towns and of land values in rural areas. The canal, however, was succeeded by the railroad with its limited access and stations creating little nuclei of high land values and economic activity around the stations. Since then, many stations have been closed producing an even greater concentration of locational attractiveness in a still smaller number of places.

While the withdrawal of a transportation service is often disastrous for a community, however, it is not necessarily so. There are a number of cases in which the growth of a community has been originally dependent upon a given form of transportation route; that route has been withdrawn but the town has continued to prosper. A number of years ago, for example, great concern was expressed about the future of many small towns in the Canadian province of Saskatchewan. Such towns had originally developed as grain-shipment points and it was felt that their future was threatened by (1) the abandonment of uneconomical railroad branch lines involving about one-third of Saskatchewan's railroad mileage and (2) the consolidation of grain elevator facilities in a smaller number of towns. It has since been shown, however, that such concern was misplaced; while the original raison d'être of these towns was grain shipment they are no longer so dependent upon this function and the railroad route as they were formerly. Rather the initial nucleus of population around the grain elevator attracted to it all kinds of retail and service functions for the surrounding rural population who could move to it by highway thus providing the town with a completely new economic base. Consequently, today there is very little relationship between the population growth of towns in Saskatchewan and the rate of growth in grain shipments.

The effects of accessibility upon locational patterns, however, are far from only local. When we examine the configurations of a nation's economic and social geography we can frequently trace out some relationships to the underlying locational pattern of accessibility. More accessible locations allow economic activities to reduce their movement costs, for example, providing an incentive for industrial investment. Demand for the more accessible locations leads to a bidding up of the prices of local land and labor so that only the more productive economic activities—those producing greater dollar returns per dollar input—can compete and they have to compete with higher wages. Ireland is a case in point. We demonstrated earlier how network accessibility was greatest in the area around Dublin and declined in all directions away from Dublin; the relationships between these differences in accessibility and some facets of the economic and social geography of Ireland are shown in Table 9-1. Clearly there are strong differences and they are reasonable ones. It is reasonable to ex-

TABLE 9-1. Network accessibility and the economic and social geography of Ireland. Note how the more accessible areas of Ireland tend to be wealthier, more industrialized, more rapidly growing in population, and more commercial in their agriculture.

	More accessible locations	Less accessible locations
Income per capita	+	−
Percent of labor force employed in manufacturing and service industries	+	−
Agricultural incomes	+	−
Percent population growth	+	−
Commercial agriculture	+	−
Subsistence agriculture	−	+
Rates of in-migration	+	−
Percent speaking Irish	−	+
Government expenditure/ government revenue	−	+

pect a more commercial agriculture in more accessible locations, for example, since in those locations farmers can find a market for their surplus produce and have an incentive to invest in productivity-increasing technology. Where the farmers are isolated, subsistence agriculture dominates because of the inaccessibility of markets for any surplus agricultural products. The concentration of the Irish-speaking population in the more inaccessible west of Ireland (see Figure 9-15) can likewise be related to the network accessibility map; high degrees of network accessibility are related to nearness to Dublin and it is from Dublin that most English language influences have emanated. Also, it is possible to see plausible causal sequences relating accessibility to the various locational patterns identified in Table 9-1. If accessibility differences have attracted higher-paying industries to the more accessible locations, then one should expect to find relatively high industrial employment and relatively high incomes in those

FIGURE 9-15. The distribution of the Irish-speaking population in Ireland. Note how the Irish language is now dominant only in the most inaccessible western portions of Ireland. Areas closer to Dublin have been much more subject to the anglicization funneled through, and then based upon Dublin.

places. This is what we *do* tend to find. Such differences in income across the nation of Ireland are likely to prompt migratory movements from the less accessible, less industrialized, poorer areas to the wealthier, more accessible areas such as Dublin; this is reflected in the growth of population in the more accessible places, particularly Dublin, and their relatively high rates of in-migration. Such differential population growth and accessibility advantages have stimulated commercial agriculture in the area around Dublin, while the more accessible west of Ireland with its declining population and hence deteriorating market for agricultural products has

experienced little stimulus to pull itself out of its subsistence rut. Finally the income differentiation which we have related to network accessibility variations has produced variations in tax revenue relative to expenditure. These variations have been aggravated by political pres-

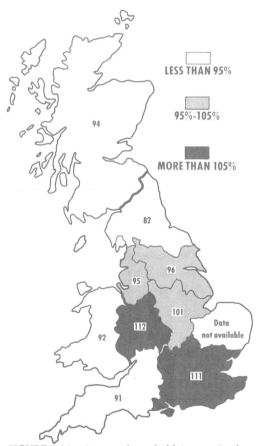

FIGURE 9-16. Average household income in the United Kingdom by region, 1964–65. The figures are percentages of the national average (=100). Note how southeastern areas again have advantages over the remainder of the nation. This figure (and Figure 9-17) depicts rather graphically certain important and related aspects of the contemporary human geography of the United Kingdom. The differences are possibly related to the variations in accessibility shown in Figure 9-14, the more accessible southeastern portions of the nation having advantages for the location of industries with their ability to generate high incomes and demand for labor.

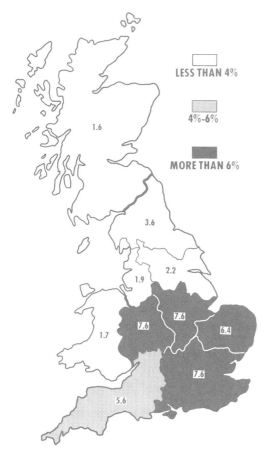

LESS THAN 4%

4%-6%

MORE THAN 6%

FIGURE 9-17. Percentage population increase in the United Kingdom, by region, 1951–1961; note how southeastern portions of the United Kingdom have grown at a much more rapid rate, largely due to inmigration.

France. Figure 9-14, for instance, presents a map of population potential for Britain; Figures 9-16 and 9-17 present the locational patterns of income per capita and population growth, respectively. The identities of the maps are quite striking.

THE MUTUAL RELATIONSHIPS OF ACCESSIBILITY AND LOCATION

Despite these strong relationships between accessibility and location and the fact that we can build plausible causal relationships between accessibility as a cause and a wide variety of other locational patterns as effects, it would be shortsighted to leave the issue at that. As Gauthier has pointed out elsewhere, we may be involved here with a very critical chicken and egg problem: "The provision of improved highway facilities might precede by some period of time an expansion of investment in manufacturing or a rapid increase in urban population. Conversely the provision of transportation investments might lag behind the demands for increased accessibility that are generated by increases in industrial or population growth in the urban centers. Both sequences provide incentives and pressures either to take advantage of the lower transportation costs provided by improved accessibility by expanding production, or to reduce certain costs of production by providing improved transport facilities."[1]

Thus, on the one hand, it is possible to recognize that accessibility advantages precede the increased economic activity and residential construction which emerge to take advantage of those accessibility advantages. On the other hand, it is also plausible that differential accessi-

sures leading to greater government expenditures in the more inaccessible areas of Ireland in order to even out the income inequalities which have resulted from relative network accessibility advantages.

Nor is Ireland unique in this respect. Similar relationships between accessibility and a whole host of other locational patterns of a social and economic character can be found in Britain and

---

[1] Howard L. Gauthier, "Transportation and the Growth of the São Paulo Economy," *Journal of Regional Science*, Vol. 8, No. 1 (1968), pp. 77–94.

bility only emerges *as a result of* differential demands from place to place resulting from variation in economic activity. Gauthier's own research into the situation in São Paulo province, Brazil, suggests that *changes in accessibility* play a *leading role* in the growth of population and of manufacturing in specific cities. It is interesting to note, however, that the significance of this lead factor is somewhat greater in the case of manufacturing production than in the case of population growth. It is possible, therefore, that there is a third solution to the problem; in the specific Brazilian case it is possible that increased accessibility is a response to increased population growth while manufacturing tends to follow the upgrading of accessibility. More generally we would like to suggest that accessibility and other locational patterns exercise strong mutual effects on each other: just as locational patterns such as population growth can affect those transportation investments leading to variations in accessibility, so accessibility changes can stimulate new locational patterns, as in the form of industrial activity. It is this third theory of mutual relationships which is explored in this section.

In order to demonstrate how such mutual relationships can occur and affect the changing map of accessibility let us consider a likely sequence of changes in accessibility and other locational patterns starting from the situation in which there are no variations in population size from one place to another, only variations in accessibility. We have a situation, therefore, in which there are some variations in network accessibility and in population potential; this is graphically depicted for a hypothetical set of towns in Figure 9-18a. Thus towns 3 and 4 have higher network accessibility and population potential than places 2 and 5; places 1 and 6 are the most inaccessible

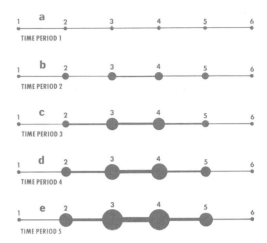

FIGURE 9-18. The mutual relationships of urban growth and accessibility. Initial differences in accessibility in time period 1 are translated into differential urban growth (*b*); this then creates a differential demand for improved accessibility (*c*) which then leads to further differential urban growth in time period 4, and so on. The thickness of a line indicates the quality of the route affecting, for example, traffic volume, speed, and travel cost. The size of a ball indicates urban size.

and have the lowest population potentials.

Now it is plausible to imagine that in this initial time period these variations in network accessibility and population potential present a map of varying attractiveness to the locator. The industrialist, for example, who wishes to minimize his distribution costs will find places 3 and 4 considerably more attractive than places 1 and 6. The retail outlet which needs to distribute to all places in order to stay in business is much more likely to attain that market level if it locates in 3 or 4 than if it locates in 1 or 6. In brief, locators have certain movement needs and minimization of movement costs is more likely to be achieved in places 3 and 4 than in 2 and 5; places 2 and 5, on the other hand, have advantages over 1 and 6.

This differential attractiveness of places should touch off differential population growth of cities according to network accessibility and population potential advantages (Figure 9-18*b*). As populations increase at either end of a transportation link we can expect the demand for movement along that link and for improved facilities to expedite that movement to increase. Where population growth at either end of the link is less, then the increased demand will be commensurately diminished.

As the demand for movement increases, therefore, existing facilities become congested, slowing down travel times and at the same time raising demand above that threshold level which certain improved types of transportation demand. Thus one can imagine such upgrading as the replacement of a single track railroad by a double track railroad; the construction of a motorway alongside the existing highway; the straightening of the highways; or the substitution of jet aircraft service for piston engine aircraft service.

Given a differential demand for the upgrading of transportation links and the differential attractiveness which links offer to new transportation media, such as aircraft, one can imagine a situation in time period 3 in which links are differentially upgraded, that is, we move away from the situation with which we started in which all links were of similar quality to one of differential quality. This differential quality of links affects travel effort and hence accessibility. Network accessibility in time period 3, therefore, is likely to be considerably more varied than it was in time period 1 (Figure 9-18*c*). Furthermore, as a result of this increased variability in network accessibility and as a result of the variable population growth in time period 2 we have increased variation in population potential from place to place.

These variations in network accessibility and population potential as a result of differential population growth and differential upgrading of links combine to produce a locational pattern of attractiveness to locators in time period 4 that is also considerably more varied than in time period 2. The result is further differential growth of urban economies and urban populations with an increased concentration on the most attractive places over and above that which existed in time period 2. Thus the attractiveness of places 3 and 4 is now much greater than that of places 2 and 5 than it was in time period 2. This will be reflected in growth rates; that is, the greater the population potential and network accessibility of the city, the greater its incremental growth in a succeeding period of time.

This differential growth of places and of population potential is also accompanied by an increased differential growth in their demand for movement over that which exists in time 2. Thus, whereas in time period 2 the demand for upgrading on link 3–4 was not much greater than on link 2–3, now it is much, much greater simply because places 3 and 4 have grown so much in population compared with place 2. The result will be further selective upgrading of links with particular attention being paid to link 3–4 (see Figure 9-18*e*) for time period 5.

Note that this tendency for the upgrading of links to become increasingly selective over time is a result not only of differential growth in demand for movement but also of the economics of transportation innovations. Even though there may be a demand for upgrading of a link, such upgrading may not take place because threshold conditions for upgrading and innovation may not be satisfied. This has been particularly common since transportation innovations have tended to emerge in such a way that: (1) Fixed costs have become a larger proportion of total costs; consequently flows have had to be bundled or merged in order to lift demand above the threshold level. Thus airline passengers from a wide area have to be concentrated upon one particular airport in order to justify an airline link to some other city close to the final destinations of those airline passengers. Airline services between more points to bring the services closer to the residences of the customers would not be economically justified. (2) Also tending to produce merging of flows and therefore the highly selective upgrading of routes between places has been the fact that the minimal capacity of new transportation media has increased more rapidly than the average traffic between places. Compare the jumbo jets with the 50-passenger planes common in the earlier '50s,

for example; it was possible to have air links using 50-passenger planes over far more routes than for the jumbo jet with its huge capacity. As a consequence of these economic factors, therefore, transportation innovation is only possible between a diminishing number of locations; and those locations tend to be the ones which were generating most traffic at the preceding time interval, and because of their transportation innovations will go on generating increased amounts of traffic in the next time interval.

The simple message inherent in this process and shown diagrammatically in Figure 9-18 is "To he who has, shall be given." Those places which initially occupied more accessible locations on the communications network were more attractive to locators and consequently attracted more population to them. De-

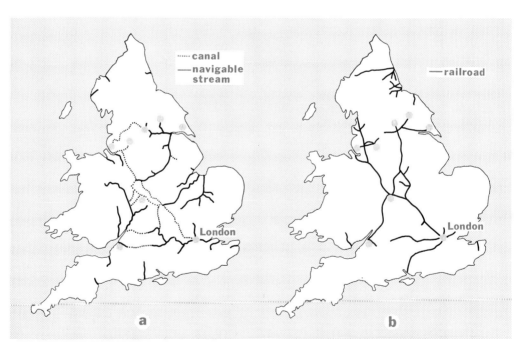

FIGURE 9-19. (a) Navigable waterways of late 18th-century England and Wales and (b) the pattern of early railroads. Note the striking similarity of the two configurations. Provision of a route tends to lead to location relative to that route which provides a demand for an improved means of transportation. The networks formed by successive transportation innovations, therefore, are often strikingly similar; Britain's motorway network, for instance, bears a striking resemblance to the map of early railroads in (b) above.

FIGURE 9-20. French railroad commodity flows, 1913. The thickness of the line indicates the amount of traffic.

mand for upgrading of links between these growth points, therefore, increased much more rapidly than elsewhere; demand levels on those links were also the first to attain the threshold levels required by transportation innovations with high fixed costs and/or high minimal capacity requirements. Several implications follow directly and indirectly from this analysis.

The first implication is that an initial network configuration tends to become more resistant to change over time and efforts to drastically alter the network configuration will involve construction of routes where demand is initially very low; the free market forces or taxpayer pressure are likely to oppose such diversionary efforts vigorously, thus guaranteeing the continued existence of the existing network geometry. Networks, therefore, have a very strong historical persistence. This is apparent in the communication networks of France and Britain both past and present. Thus the pattern of navigable waterways in England

in the period 1750–1800 bears a striking similarity to the pattern of the earliest railroads in Britain in 1825–1850 (see Figure 9-19).

Also if this theory is valid one should find that movement patterns are very similar from one time period to another with the more frequently used routes growing in importance. A comparison of French railroad flow data for 1913 and 1963 suggests that, for this restricted case at least, this is so (Figures 9-20 and 9-21).

Finally, the notions that the locational patterns of economic activity and of population, on the one hand, and accessibility, on the other hand, are mutually dependent and that accessibility differences tend to intensify over time suggests that the locational variations of economic activity and of population tend to intensify over time. We argued earlier that the centralization of the French railroad network resulted from the overwhelming dominance and locational at-

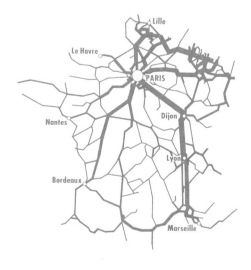

FIGURE 9-21. French railroad commodity flows, 1963. Note the striking resemblance to the map shown in Figure 9-20. If anything, the dominant features of the map in 1913 had become even more dominant by 1963.

tractiveness of Paris in the system of urban places in France. Our theory of mutual dependence and some hard facts, however, suggest that this may not be so. Indeed in 1830, on the eve of the railroad-building era, the population of Paris accounted for only 5% of France's population; by 1960 Paris accounted for over 15% of France's population. In the intervening period a railroad network cen-

tered on Paris was constructed making Paris considerably more attractive for economic activity and reinforcing the tendency towards centralization in future transportation networks. The result has been a situation of locational concentration of the French economy which has proven exceedingly resistant to alteration. We shall discuss this problem at a greater length later in the volume.

CONCLUSIONS AND SUMMARY

Communication networks provide patterns to be explained; they also provide a source of locational differentiation which exerts powerful effects on a wide variety of other locational patterns.

The major factors accounting for the geometry of transportation networks appear to be largely economic in character. Demand for a transport link has to attain a certain *threshold level* before the facility can be offered economically, and this threshold level varies from one medium to another producing variations in density not only according to demand conditions in an area but also according to the medium we are considering. The threshold phenomenon also helps to account for the *bundling* or *merging* of flows.

Also important are the *relative proportions of fixed costs and running costs* involved in the long-term conduct of a transportation operation. This helps to explain the greater deviousness of certain media, the substitution of more direct for less direct routes, and the transformation of Wye configurations into Deltas.

Communication networks are not merely a manifestation of economic forces, however. Political forces can also enter in to disturb the economic mechanism in a direction regarded as in the national interest.

For the locator, however, communications networks drastically change accessibility relationships usually, though not always, in a positive manner. In this way, communication networks exercise powerful effects on a wide diversity of locational patterns. This was demonstrated particularly urgently in the context of the Irish situation but many examples can be found in North America also and should be intuitively obvious.

The final thought offered was that locational patterns may not be merely dependent upon the variable accessibilities created by communication networks. Rather there may be a very strong mutual dependence between the two, with alterations in locational patterns stimulating alterations in the geometry of communication networks and vice versa.

Clearly communication networks and other locational patterns are strongly related to one another. Communication networks channel movement and exert a powerful effect on movement costs; the map of movement costs becomes a decisive influence on the locational decisions of the retailer, the farmer, the industrialist, the residential developer, etc. These decisions, in turn, create distinctive patterns. In this book we have decided to classify these patterns into two groups: the punctiform or point pattern, exemplified by the pattern of towns, and the area pattern, exemplified by patterns of agricultural land use. Broadly, two locational problems are involved: locating points and locating areas. Chapters Ten, Eleven, and Twelve treat the first problem, while Chapters Thirteen and Fourteen focus upon the problem of locating areas.

CHAPTER TEN

Locating Nodes: Some Basic Concepts

INTRODUCTION

Among other topics covered in this book we have considered both movement and the route networks along which diverse movements are channeled. Movements and routes, however, presuppose some origin and destination for the movement, some set of places to be connected by the routes that will facilitate the necessary movements demanded by society. What, therefore, of the places and their associated activities — hospitals, towns, factories, town-halls, plantations, etc. — that form the origins and destinations of movements?

Such discrete agglomerations of activity are known as nodes.

▶ *A node is a permanent or quasi-permanent cluster of social, economic, or political activity.*

Nodes include towns, industrial plants, administrative centers, schools, and periodic markets, among other things.

What aspects of nodes are we interested in from the geographical viewpoint, however? An initial problem is the geographical basis of the node: why do activities cluster in a few select locations rather than being scattered willy-nilly across space? A second problem is that of the locational patterns assumed

by nodes: is there any regularity in the geographical locations of such nodes as towns? Do towns cluster in a few select areas or do they try to keep as far away from each other as possible? Or is there a bit of both tendencies? A third problem is that of explaining such locational regularities as we find existing in the pattern of nodes. If there is clustering, why? Furthermore, why are larger towns spaced further apart than smaller towns? The answer to this question, of course, will allow us to understand much more completely some of the regularities identified in Chapter Two relating a town to its sphere of influence and the nesting of the spheres of influence of less dominant places in the spheres of influence of more dominant places.

The next three chapters are devoted to these problems both in more abstract and in more real world fashion. This present chapter presents a fairly abstract consideration of nodes from four viewpoints: the geographical basis of nodes, the locational pattern of nodes, the processes which generate this pattern, and the real world locational patterns of nodes, which can be compared with more abstract concepts of locational pattern. The next two chapters are devoted to applying these ideas to two case studies: towns as nodes and industrial plants as nodes.

THE GEOGRAPHICAL BASIS
OF NODES

In order to function at a level of efficiency adequate to the aspirations of its members, society must fulfill certain social goals; thus, society must be governed, laws must be applied, goods produced for society to consume, goods distributed to different households, etc. It is not difficult to see that certain economies of time and effort accrue to society from carrying out these activities at a limited number of discrete locations. Thus the scheduled market is a much more efficient means of distributing goods than the solitary unpredictable pedlar.

The geographical rationale for the node, therefore, is the *economy of agglomeration.* An obvious economy that comes from agglomeration is that of *movement.* People, factories, retailers, and hospitals cluster in towns because it reduces the costs of people moving to work, of people going to shop, of moving goods from one factory to another, of getting patients to the hospital, of the hospital consulting with the doctor, etc.

The agglomeration also realizes economies in terms of *specialization.* In an agglomeration of activities, for example, the factory can buy the services of the specialized transportation firm for its external movement needs, whereas if the factory is isolated in the countryside it will have to provide its own transportation services. This may be very costly for a small factory that does not have sufficient movement demand to realize the economies of scale which accrue to the specialized transportation company in an agglomeration.

Economies are also possible in the *provision of public services* such as piped water and sewage. The provision of wells is generally much more expensive per household than piped water; piped water, however, is only economically feasible in an agglomeration above a certain size, so there are additional cost advantages for locating residentially in such an agglomeration. Other services such as gas are more likely in such an environment due to the economies of movement which accrue to the service company when supplying the service in such an agglomeration. It is clearly much cheaper to service a town with gas than a rural population dispersed across the landscape.

There are very important arguments, therefore, for the concentration of activities at a few discrete locations on the earth's surface. For a variety of reasons, moreover, these arguments seem to be increasingly *more* powerful rather than less powerful: populations are increasingly concentrated in larger cities; larger power stations at fewer locations replace the smaller, more dispersed power stations of the past; small cottage hospitals in rural areas close down as health care is increasingly centralized in larger city hospitals; rural schools are deserted as education becomes concentrated at an increasingly small number of locations. Some of the reasons for these are technical: only larger hospitals, for example, can afford the expensive x-ray and therapeutic equipment now demanded by modern medicine; only a large comprehensive school can offer a wide array of subject choices to its pupils.

Other reasons, however, lie in the realm of transportation innovations. The cottage hospital can be closed down because it is now feasible for patients to get from the rural area to the large city hospital. Electricity generation can be concentrated at fewer and fewer power stations because of the economies of moving power realized by the high tension grid. The transportation innovation of the automobile also permits the concentration of retailing in larger agglomerations and the decline of the village store.

The growth of a few select nodes is accelerated still further by the economies of scale which transportation agencies can realize by concentrating their services on a few routes and at a limited number of nodes on those routes — arguments which we reviewed in Chapter Nine. Economies of agglomeration in railroad operation, for example, frequently encourage concentration of traffic on a limited number of lines and increasing concentration of activities at nodes on those lines at the expense of nodes on lines that are being closed down or downgraded.

A moot question is, is there a limit to such economies of agglomeration and the concentration of activities at a smaller and smaller number of locations on the earth's surface? A major policy issue in many Western countries, for example, is whether or not cities have become too large. Have they become so large, in other words, that economies of agglomeration are no longer being realized and *diseconomies of agglomeration* have set in? The assumption that indeed they have is based on such external nonmonetary costs of agglomeration as pollution, congestion, and crime and is used as a weapon in the armory of those who would wish to develop *New Towns.* The assumption may not be valid and it is a problem we shall have to discuss.

A further fact which we can deduce from our discussion of the geographical bases of nodes is the idea of a *hierarchy of dominance* which we also discussed in Chapter Two. Obviously if economies of agglomeration result in the increasing concentration of activities at fewer and fewer points, it is likely (though it is not inevitable) to signify an increasing differentiation of locations according to their importance and dominance as locations for social, political, and economic activities. Why *certain places* in *certain*

types of location become more dominant than others, however, is another important issue which we shall consider in this chapter and the next two chapters.

The carrying out of activities at nodes involves a constant to-and-fro of movement. Meeting places require the assembly and dispersal of members, schools require the assembly and return of school children, while churches require movements to and from the households of parishioners. No node can internalize all its related movements. In order to provide for the full range of social needs, each node must supply goods or services which can be exchanged with goods or services produced by other nodes. In this sense, therefore, the market is the prototypical node since it involves the buying of goods from a wide variety of sellers, their assembly at a discrete point in space, and their sale to consumers who have traveled to market to obtain the needed goods. The factory is also a node; it involves the assembly of labor, power, and raw materials and the distribution of the finished products to diverse other nodes. Hence, nodes are connected to each other by a continual flow of people, goods, raw material, and information, the state of flow through the system of nodes at any one time being dependent on the state of any single node. The impact of a strike at an auto components factory, for example, spreads slowly but inexorably through the system of nodes as the movement of the needed component evaporates and other linked factories curtail their output and, hence, incoming movements and outgoing movements.

The fact that nodes are dependent on interactions with other nodes, moreover, suggests that a search for pattern and order in their location may not be in vain. Movement over space, after all, exhibits some geographical regularity as in the *distance bias* phenomenon which we discussed in Chapter Two. If movement exhibits some geometrical regularity it is only logical that order ought also to be manifest in the locational arrangement of the nodes being tied together by these movements.

In summary, the geographical rationale for the node is the economy of agglomeration. Such economies seem to be increasing in scope, allowing a growing concentration of activities at a smaller and smaller number of locations and the emergence of a more sharply differentiated hierarchy of dominance-dependence. Despite their economies of agglomeration, however, nodes continue to be tied to each other with a dense mesh of movements and interactions. The significance of such movements for the continued health of nodes and the geometrical regularity exhibited by movement over space suggests that the locational patterns of nodes may contain some geographical order of their own. It is these locational patterns and components of locational patterns that we shall consider next.

THE LOCATIONAL ARRANGEMENT
OF NODES

Three concepts of the locational arrangement of nodes are discussed here. These concepts appear frequently in the geographical literature and they need to be carefully distinguished. There is a serious danger of confusing the concepts with one another, and we shall be careful to point out, with examples, the areas of overlap and the areas of differentiation which exist among these concepts. The three concepts are: (1) dispersion (2) spacing and (3) localization.

Dispersion.

▶   *Dispersion is the degree of spread of a set of points relative to some delimited area.*

The towns of Missouri, therefore, have a dispersion as do the creameries of Wisconsin and the banks of Ohio. Students of the dispersion of nodal patterns have suggested that *degrees of dispersion* can be placed on a continuum ranging from *clustered* dispersions at one end of the scale, through more *random* dispersions, to what is termed a *uniform* dispersion.

In a clustered dispersion the points tend to be concentrated in one or two small segments of the space involved (see Figure 10-1a): in a uniform dispersion, on the other hand, points tend to be arranged in such a manner that the distance from one point to any one of its six nearest neighbors is the same as the distance from any other point to any one of its six nearest neighbors (see Figure 10-1c). The most clustered dispersion that we can imagine is the single point and as the number of clusters in the area increases and the space between any two clusters increases, the dispersion is likely to become less clustered. The most uniform dispersion which is possible is the *triangular lattice* in which the points are located at the apices of equilateral triangles. The uniform dispersion represents the situation in which a given number of points in an area are trying to get as far away from each other as possible. Presumably something like this pattern would emerge in a locked room containing a group of people who are told that one of them (unspecified) is the carrier of a deadly disease! A less uniform

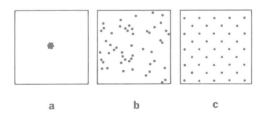

FIGURE 10-1.   Types of nodal dispersion: perfectly clustered (*a*), random (*b*), and perfectly regular or uniform (*c*). Note how in the perfectly regular dispersion the nodes are arranged as if at the apices of equilateral triangles; for this reason, such a dispersion is often referred to as a triangular lattice.

dispersion is one in which the points are located at the corners of squares. The random pattern, on the other hand, is one in which there is a clear case of neither clustering nor uniformity, though it is likely that a true random dispersion would reveal some evidence of local clustering. This idea of a continuum or continuous scale of point dispersions against which we can compare real world nodal or point dispersions is presented in Figure 10-1 where points have been allocated to the same geographical area, but in different patterns.

Spacing.

▶ *Spacing is the locational arrangement of objects with respect to one another, that is, not with respect to some delimited area, as in the case of dispersion.*

The concept is not an easy one to define. Two aspects of spacing, however, appear to have been the focus of the geographer's interest: the mean spacing of nodes, that is, the average distance they are apart from each other; and the uniformity of spacing, that is, the degree to which distances between nodes deviate from that average.

The distance between nodes is usually measured as the distance between a node and its *nearest neighboring node;* these distances are then summed and divided by the number of nodes in order to derive an average spacing. The deviation of these distances from the average is taken as a measure of uniformity of spacing. In order to illustrate these ideas, Figure 10-2 presents some hypothetical arrangements of points with different mean spacings but similar degrees of uniformity of spacing.

Several points emerge from a consideration of these diagrams. First, *spacing is independent of any area one might care to delimit around the points.* Thus the spacing is the same in diagrams 1A

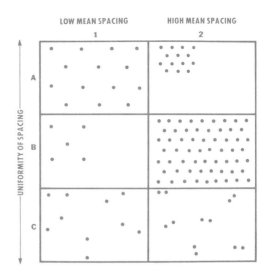

FIGURE 10-2. Spacing of nodes: mean spacing and the uniformity of spacing. Note that spacing is not affected by any line one might draw around the points; the spacing is the same in 1A and in 1B, therefore. Note also that uniformity of spacing does not imply necessarily a uniform dispersion; 2B has both a uniformity of spacing and a uniform dispersion; 1C and 2C, however, have only uniformity of spacing.

and 1B even though the points in B occupy a smaller area. The second major point is that *uniformity of spacing as measured on a nearest-neighbor basis does not necessarily imply a uniform dispersion:* thus the spacing has a high degree of uniformity in diagram 1C and 2C but the dispersions are far from uniform. This is important because, as we shall see, one might be misled into arguing for the existence of a uniform dispersion on the basis of a uniformity of spacing: the former does not necessarily follow from the latter, though the latter is obviously necessitated by the former.

Localization. A concept that has also been used in the study of nodes is that of *localization;* it has been particularly important in studies of the location of industry, and we shall discuss it here.

▶ *Localization is the variation in the relative frequency with which an event occurs across a set of subdivisions of some delimited area.*

Assume, for example, that there are 10 factories and 16 subdivisions; Figure 10-3 presents some sample distributions in increasing order of localization.

It is very important, however, to distinguish the concept of localization from that of the clustering aspect of dispersion. *It is perfectly conceivable, for example, to have a set of distributions each one with the same degree of localization but with differing degrees of clustering.* This is demonstrated in Figure 10-4.

With this body of concepts, it is possible to examine a point pattern—whether it is a pattern of towns, of churches, of factories, of farmhouses etc.—and attempt to evaluate that pattern. A major problem, however, is that of the *geographical scale* of the area for which we are evaluating locational arrangement. As far as dispersion is concerned, it should be clear that a particular spatial arrangement can be region-specific and that as we expand the area to include other types of locational arrangements, our determination of dispersion for the area as a whole may change. Thus, if we examine the South alone we find that Baptist churches are quite uniformly distributed; if we examine the United States as a whole, however, our conclusion as to the appropriate pattern would have to be in terms of a clustering

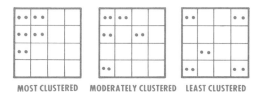

MOST CLUSTERED   MODERATELY CLUSTERED   LEAST CLUSTERED

FIGURE 10-4. Localization and clustering: patterns that exhibit clustering are not necessarily more localized than patterns that show less clustering. All the patterns in this figure have the same degree of localization but vary in their degree of clustering.

of Baptist churches (in the South). Indeed as a general rule we would expect the possibility of the uniform dispersion being converted into a clustered dispersion to increase as we increase the geographical scale of our study area since the increased scale increases the probability of some heterogeneity in the environment which would in its turn induce clustering in the dispersion of points.

What this discussion suggests very strongly is that *dispersion is scale-specific.* If we examine the pattern of nodes for a small area we may come to one conclusion, while if we examine it for a larger area we may come to a quite different conclusion regarding the locational nature of the pattern. In fact it is useful to arbitrarily set up two geographical scales and examine the mutations of dispersion which are logically possible. In Figure 10-5 we have related uniform and clustered dispersions to each other at two different scales: a relatively small scale and a relatively large scale. Furthermore, not only are these dispersions logically possible, but they also have real world analogues with which we can compare them. Each cell of the table defining a hybrid pattern type will be discussed in turn.

The first pattern in the top left-hand corner of the diagram is one which shows a tendency towards uniformity at whatever geographical scale it is viewed. This is the type of pattern often assumed

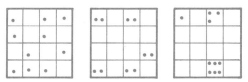

LEAST LOCALIZED   MODERATE LOCALIZATION   MOST LOCALIZED

FIGURE 10-3. The concept of localization: where nodes are concentrated in a few of all possible areas we say that the pattern is localized; where the nodes are not concentrated in a limited number of all possible areas, the pattern is said to be non-localized.

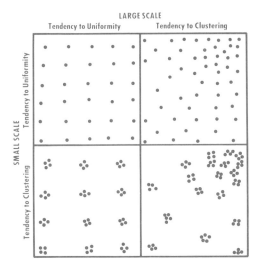

FIGURE 10-5. Scale, nodal dispersions, and hybrid pattern types. Nodal dispersions are scale-specific; therefore, that which appears clustered at the large scale may actually exhibit strong tendencies towards uniformity at the small scale. A number of mutations are possible and a few of them are presented in this figure.

by county seats in the American Midwest. Figure 10-6 shows the pattern for part of Iowa, for example. The cell in the top right-hand corner accepts the small-scale uniformity characteristic of the previous pattern but superimposes a large-scale clustering such that there are geographical variations in the density of nodes. This type of pattern is similar to that found in Nebraska: in eastern Nebraska and in western Nebraska there is a tendency towards uniformity but when the state as a whole is examined there is a tendency towards clustering due to differences in node density between the eastern and western portions of the state.

The second row of the 2 × 2 diagram compares large-scale uniformity and clustering superimposed on small-scale clustering. The intersection of small-scale clustering and large-scale uniformity, for example, produces a dispersion such as that associated with the location of banks or other urban functions; at the

small scale they tend to cluster in the places known as cities; when viewed at a larger scale, however, these clusters often seem to be distributed fairly uniformly across the landscape.

The final cell in the bottom right of the diagram exhausts the logical possibilities: clustering is present at both the small and large scale of observation and this type of pattern is perhaps exemplified by the pattern of larger cities in the United States (see Figure 10-7). At the scale of the United States as a whole, cities tend to cluster in the northeast sector. For smaller segments of the United States, however, there are smaller-scale clusters, such as those on the northeast coast or around the Great Lakes or in California.

It should be clear that the scale problem also applies to the evaluation of spacing and most importantly to the concept of uniformity of spacing. When we examine the settlement pattern of eastern Nebraska, the spacing seems fairly uniform, as it also does when we examine the spacing of settlements in western Nebraska. Examination of Nebraska as a

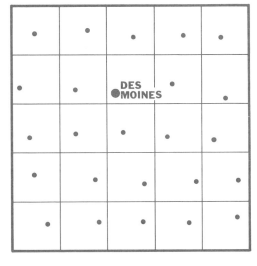

FIGURE 10-6. The uniform pattern of county seats in part of Iowa.

FIGURE 10-7. The locational pattern of metropolitan centers in the United States. This pattern combines large-scale clustering (i.e., in the east and particularly in the northeast) with small-scale clustering along the Pacific coast, the Atlantic seaboard, and in parts of the Midwest.

whole, however, suggests that settlements are not spaced uniformly since spacing is considerably greater in western Nebraska than in eastern Nebraska.

The abstract node dispersions and spacings that we have defined, therefore, can be related to real world patterns. This suggests that we might be able to identify the forces producing these patterns if a given pattern occurs in repetitive geographical circumstances. On an abstract level, therefore, prior to examining real world processes, what forces might generate such patterns and how might they generate them?

AN ABSTRACT VIEW OF PROCESS

Two major types of pattern-producing process will now be considered: *competitive processes and clustering processes.*

> *Competitive processes involve the competition of locationally mobile activities for some economically desirable items distributed over space.*

Such a process concerns the location of coal mines in an area underlain by coal:

if the coal mines are placed close together some mines will have insufficient coal to justify the heavy capital investment involved. In order to monopolize the resource to a greater extent, therefore, and assure future reserves, mines are spaced a considerable distance from one another. Some locations for coal mines are more competitive than others and will not lead to the premature elimination of the coal mine. This also applies to retail activities, where competition is for a market spread over space. Locations at a distance from other purveyors of the same retail goods or services are more competitive than those closer locations since the greater distance affords a protection from the competition of the other retailers. That is, in the competition for a scarce, geographically distributed resource such as land or purchasing power, location becomes a means of monopolizing a portion of the resource and reducing the level of competition. Some locations are more competitive for the individual locator than others since they permit some local monopoly.

In clustering processes, on the other hand, the objective of the locator is to maximize nearness rather than distance. Just as in a competitive process locators try to locate as far away as possible from their competitors, so:

▶ *in clustering processes the locators try to get as close as possible to some geographically restricted element.*

Thus, the attractive element may be a line as with the clustering of gas stations along major highways relative to minor highways or the clustering of medieval settlements along spring lines where an all-season supply of water was available. Alternatively, it may be a point around which locators cluster as with a desert oasis or capital city as in the case of Paris. Or again, it may be some restricted area around which locators cluster. As we shall see below the early masters of industry in the 18th and 19th centuries tended to locate their new textile and iron and steel industries on the coal fields where a ready supply of fuel and power was available. Particularly important in promoting clustering appear to be the economies of agglomeration discussed earlier in this chapter. In brief, the basis of the clustering process is a more positive evaluation of a restricted segment of the space by a large number of locators relative to other segments which tend to be devalued and indeed avoided.

In actuality, there is a mixture of the two types of process so that *while at one scale one process may be dominant, at another scale another process is important.* Thus, *between* towns a given retail function is viewed by retailers as competitive: for example, the addition of an extra shoestore at place X may possibly take business away from place Y if X is near enough to Y to lead to a wide zone of indifference in the shopping trip behavior of consumers located in that zone. *Within X*, however, the location of the

shoestore will be close to other shoestores due to a recognition of the importance of *comparison shopping*. Another case of the applicability of one type of process at one scale and another type of process at another scale concerns the location of coal mines: at one scale the decision must be one to cluster—to locate on the coal field—since location off the coal field would result in absurd capital expenditure on tunnels! On the coal field itself, however, the locational process is competitive since there are important reasons, as outlined above, for keeping the coal mine as far away from other coal mines as possible.

These locational processes of *competition* and *clustering,* moreover, take place in an environment that differs from place to place not only in the relative locations of places as measured by distance and direction relationships, but also in terms of accessibility as transformed by the connections of places and in terms of site characteristics—density of population, income, natural resources, etc.

▶ *If the environment is invariant from place to place in its site and accessibility characteristics we say that it is homogeneous; if it is variant, however, we say that it is inhomogeneous.*

Inhomogeneity of the environment is important because it is strongly associated with *clustering* processes: inhomogeneity is often associated with variations in the attractiveness of the environment for settlements or factories, for example. To the Anglo-Saxons who colonized Britain in the period between about 600 A.D. and 800 A.D., particularly attractive sites for settlement were represented by small patches of sand and gravel offering well-drained sites plus the possibility of well water at a fairly shallow depth. The surrounding clay lands offered neither of these advantages, so at the small scale the settlement dispersion of eastern and southern Britain today indicates a certain clustering though competition between settlements keeps the *spacing* of nearest neighbors — as we shall see shortly — fairly uniform.

In Nebraska the large-scale clustering of settlements in the eastern half of the state is a response to a large-scale inhomogeneity — the distribution of moisture, which is much more favorable to agriculture in the eastern half of the state than in the western half. Other inhomogeneities with effects on the locational arrangement of settlement derive from situational inhomogeneities rather than site attributes, such as climate or land drainage. The clustering of large cities along coast lines which we briefly alluded to in Chapter Two is a case in point.

Whether an inhomogeneity will be associated with a large-scale or small-scale clustering is clearly dependent on the *scale of the inhomogeneity.* Local variations, such as those of sand and gravel or clay in England, produce small-scale clustering; regional variations, on the other hand, such as those of moisture in Nebraska produce rather large-scale clustering in the pattern of nodes. The repercussions for uniformity of spacing and the scale at which it occurs should also be apparent.

Our discussion has focused on *inhomogeneity;* what about the concept of the *homogeneous environment?* This concept is a highly abstract one and it should be seen more as a *limiting case* than as something which actually occurs in the real world. *All environments are inhomogeneous to varying degrees:* the act of settlement itself, or of establishing factories, for example, creates inhomogeneities — advantages of being close to existing factories or settlements, etc. However, some environments are *less*

inhomogeneous and therefore *more* homogeneous than others. Iowa, for example, is a more homogeneous environment than say Pennsylvania. Environments which are *more* homogeneous, moreover, are less likely to be associated with clustering processes and more likely to be associated with purely competitive processes than the more inhomogeneous environments. The idea of a completely homogeneous area, invariant in site and accessibility variations, is like the physicist's vacuum — a useful analytical tool in that it allows one to deduce patterns that may never be produced in the real world but that may be increasingly approximated by environments of increasingly lesser degrees of inhomogeneity. In looking at the pattern of nodes, therefore, we should always say to ourselves, what is the effect of inhomogeneity on that pattern and attempt to take it into account. In examining the settlement pattern of Nebraska, for example, we should look at eastern Nebraska and western Nebraska in turn and not both together.

REAL WORLD LOCATIONAL PATTERNS OF NODES

Given the variety of environments of differing degrees of homogeneity in which people select locations and given the presence of both clustering and competitive processes, we should have extremely open minds in our expectations regarding the locational arrangement of nodes.

Dispersion. An extensive study of dispersions has been made by King who has examined such patterns for small areas spread across the United States. King has used a method known as *nearest-neighbor analysis:* the scale shown in Figure 10-8 presents the results for the different areas relative to the scale of

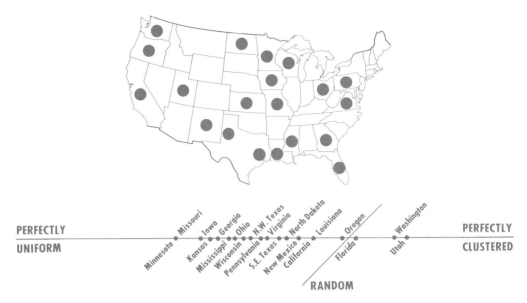

FIGURE 10-8. Settlement dispersions for the United States. Most dispersions shown here tend to be random; in areas where there are strong environmental inhomogeneities there are clear clustering tendencies, as in Utah and Washington; in some of the flatter, more homogeneous areas of the Midwest, such as Iowa and Missouri, there are tendencies towards uniformity.

clustering—uniformity that nearest-neighbor analysis employs. Several conclusions emerge from an examination of this scale: (1) there is a tendency for dispersions to be random rather than either clustered or uniform, but (2) there is a spread of values around this mean pattern such that some dispersions (e.g., Utah in Figure 10-9) show a tendency towards clustering while others show a tendency toward uniformity as in Minnesota, Iowa, or Missouri (Figure 10-9).

The patterns identified seem intuitively reasonable in light of what we know about the areas. In Utah, settlements tend to cluster around the oases at the foot of the north–south trending Wasatch Mountains. In areas like Missouri or Minnesota, on the other hand, such inhomogeneities are largely absent and there are no great variations of accessibility that would lead to a clustered dispersion. In states like Kansas, on the other hand, the dominant east–west bias of the railroads does impose an inho-

mogeneity in the area of accessibility and this is reflected in the linear clusters of settlements characteristic of the state (see Figure 10-9).

Spacing. A major finding on the spacing of nodes has been that *more dominant nodes tend to be spaced further apart than less dominant nodes.* This finding is documented from a very wide variety of areas. In Southern Germany, it has been found that, on the average, while villages were seven kilometers apart, and county seats were 21 kilometers apart, smaller provincial capitals were 108 kilometers distant from each other, and the five largest cities of Southern Germany were 178 kilometers apart. In Iowa and Wisconsin in the United States and in Somerset in England similar results have been found when relating *population size* as an indicator of dominance to mean spacing. If we plot on a scatter diagram the dominance of a town against its distance to the nearest town of similar dom-

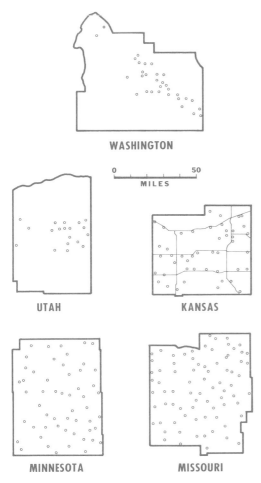

FIGURE 10-9. Settlement patterns in five selected areas of the United States. The areas in Washington and Utah show a tendency towards clustering. The sampled areas in Minnesota and Missouri demonstrate a tendency toward uniformity, while the area in Kansas shows the impact of railroad lines on settlement patterns.

inance, therefore, we should get a relationship something like that shown in Figure 10-10.

When we examine the spacing of settlements at a given level of dominance there appear to be strong tendencies towards uniformity in the pattern. Beresford and St. Joseph, for example, have remarked on this tendency in the case of parts of rural England and have related it to both a competitive process and a rela-

tively homogeneous environment: "In two sample areas the distance from each village church to the nearest adjacent church has been measured. The uniformity is remarkable. In the first place, that part of Northamptonshire which lies to the east of Banbury, there are 53 modern villages which were also recorded in Domesday Book. The average distance to the nearest village is 1.2 miles and 30 of the 53 villages have their nearest neighbor between 1.0 and 1.2 miles away. In the second area, that part of Huntingtonshire lying west of the Great North Road there are 53 villages which date from at least the time of Domesday Book: the average distance from each to the nearest neighbor is 0.95 miles and 14 of the 37 villages lie between 0.90 and 1.00 miles apart. . . . Such contiguity could hardly be expected in a countryside dissected by valleys with intervening uplands: the sample areas lie in undulating country without marked barriers to equal colonization in all directions. In an area such as the neighborhood of Salisbury where a number of valleys converge, the villages are necessarily confined to the valleys, and the distance over the plateau to the next valley may be considerable. . . . It is

FIGURE 10-10. City dominance and city spacing (schematic): more dominant, larger cities tend to be spaced further apart than less dominant, smaller cities.

obvious from these samples that where the physical conditions are uniform or nearly uniform, settlements have been tolerated at about the same distance from each other, with a strong preference . . . for having neighbors about a mile away."[1]

It is important to underline that this conclusion regarding the uniformity of spacing does not necessarily conflict with the conclusions regarding dispersion that we noted above. While dispersions seemed to be more random than uniform in the United States, uniformity of spacing is perfectly compatible with this. It is well within the bounds of probability that the areas of Britain discussed by Beresford and St. Joseph above combine a *random dispersion* of settlements (due to local clustering on sands and gravels) *together with a uniformity of spacing.*

It is probably most realistic, therefore, to see the geographical arrangement of towns, as we have tried to emphasize above, as a result of *both* competitive and clustering processes, each possibly operating at different geographical scales. Where competitive processes are strong and clustering is weak as in the relatively homogeneous areas of Missouri, Minnesota, and Iowa then greater *uniformity of dispersion and of spacing* will result. Where competitive processes are weaker and clustering is stronger as in Utah or Washington then uniformity of dispersion will be much weaker, though there may be uniformity of spacing *within a cluster* as a result of competitive processes on the attractive segments of the inhomogeneous environment.

Localization. The discussion so far has been almost entirely in terms of the locational patterns of those nodes that we call settlements. Another very large set of nodes, however, includes productive units such as factories, plantations, stores, and warehouses. Such nodal patterns have tended to be examined in terms of the concept of *localization,* and also in terms of the *localization of the employment that they generate across a set of subdivisions.* Towards these ends a number of measures have been proposed, and here we briefly describe one of them: the coefficient of localization.

The coefficient of localization is usually applied where it is required to measure the degree of localization of employment in some restricted sector of manufacturing (such as, e.g., the electronics industry or the baking industry). Localization of that particular sector moreover is usually measured as relative to some underlying distribution such as that of employment in manufacturing as a whole. Where the locational pattern of a particular sector differs greatly from that of manufacturing as a whole it is said to be *localized;* where the differences between the two patterns are neglible or nonexistent the locational pattern is said to be nonlocalized. Furthermore, the varying importance of a sector or of manufacturing as a whole, across the subdivisions of the area one is interested in, is measured as a percent of the sum total across all subdivisions.

As an example to clarify these ideas, consider the data in Table 10-1 for Australia's states, Northern Territory and Capital Territory. If one subtracts the entry in the second column from the entry in the same row in the first column, a set of positive and negative deviations are obtained. The sum of the positive deviations should equal the sum of the negative deviations (in this case, they do not because of a rounding error). The coefficient of localization is either the

---

[1] M. W. Beresford and J. K. S. St. Joseph, *Medieval England: an Aerial Survey* (Cambridge: Cambridge University Press, 1958).

TABLE 10-1.

	x % of Australia's manufacturing employment	y % of Australia's employment in chemicals	Deviation $(x - y)$
New South Wales	39.8%	33.8%	+5.0
Victoria	33.2%	51.4%	−18.2
Queensland	10.6%	3.8%	+6.8
South Australia	8.8%	4.9%	+3.9
Western Australia	4.8%	1.5%	+3.3
Tasmania	2.6%	4.7%	−2.1
Northern Territory	0.04%	0.007%	−0.33
Capital Territory	0.09%	0.0%	+0.09
	100.0%*	100.0%*	

* Subject to rounding errors.

sum of the positive deviations or the sum of the negative deviations. Maximum localization is indicated by 100% or 1.0, while minimal localization is indicated by a coefficient of 0% or 0.0. In this case, the coefficient is only 20.3 suggesting very little localization for the Australian chemical industry.

Coefficients of localization have been computed for Great Britain (1935 data) and the U.S.A. (1939 data) for a variety of industries. The values of the coefficients for different industries in Britain and the U.S.A. are presented graphically in Figure 10-11. At least two facets of the graph are significant for us. Firstly, there is a fair range of variation in the magnitudes of the coefficients from low coefficients for such industries as baking and printing to high coefficients for such industries as cotton weaving and cotton spinning. Clearly, to the extent that the geographer is interested in unearthing the reasons for locational pattern we should be interested in identifying the determinants of such variable degrees of localization.

The second facet is that the points form a reasonably linear array on the scatter diagram such that similar industries in the two countries tend to have similar degrees of localization. Hosiery,

for example, is localized to similar degrees in the two countries, as is the baking industry. This suggests, therefore, that there are some systematic factors operating independently of national contexts that can be used to explain such localizations.

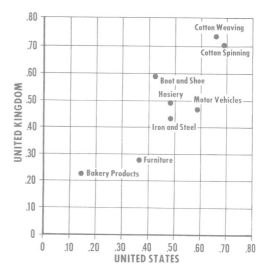

FIGURE 10-11. Coefficients of localization for industries in the United States and in the United Kingdom. Note how some industries (such as the textile industries) tend to be much more localized than others: why do you think bakery products are so nonlocalized? Also note how the coefficients of localization tend to be very similar in the two countries, suggesting that there are certain systematic locational factors at work in both nations.

CONCLUSIONS AND SUMMARY

Nodes can be simply defined as discrete clusters of social and/or economic and/or political activity. On a map we usually represent nodes as *points* and refer to their locational arrangement as a *point pattern.*

The geographical raison d'être of the node is the *economy of agglomeration.* Agglomeration of activities is cost reducing in a number of ways; movements, for example, are less costly. Agglomeration at an increasingly smaller number of nodes, moreover, seems to be *facilitated by the revolution in transportation* which has made smaller outlying nodes more accessible to—and increasingly dependent upon—larger nodes. Another factor aiding agglomeration at such dominant nodes has been the *increasing internal economies of scale* available to industry, retailing, etc. The realization of such economies of scale depends upon demand and, therefore, larger places where such demand is likely to be met are favored over smaller, dependent places, thus enhancing the growth of the larger places. The locational qualities of the point pattern can be evaluated from the standpoint of three concepts: *dispersion, spacing, and localization.* All measure different aspects of locational arrangement, however, and need to be carefully distinguished from one another.

An additional problem in evaluating the locational arrangement of nodes is that of *geographical scale.* At one geographical scale the locational arrangement may present one face; but at a larger scale it may present quite a different face. The idea of clustered dispersions and uniform dispersions at different geographical scales allows us to think in terms of certain *hybrid pattern types* combining, for example, a large-scale clustered distribution with a small-scale clustered distribution as in the locational arrangement of cities in the United States.

The major processes producing these various spatial arrangements of nodes can be called *competitive* or *clustering.* In a competitive process the activity is trying to get as close to the resource (e.g., a market for retail goods) as it can and as far away from its competitors as possible. In the clustering process, attraction to the localized resource seems to be the major locational criterion. Most locational decisions within an inhomogeneous environment, therefore, seem to involve *both competitive and clustering elements.*

In the real world it would seem that *settlement dispersions,* at least, tend to be more random than clustered or uniform. It is important to recognize, however, that the random dispersion does involve some *local clustering of nodes.* In spacing studies, on the other hand, the *uniformity of spacing* has been identified in several areas of England. This does not necessarily imply a *uniformity of dispersion:* most probably it indicates a random or clustered dispersion within the clusters of which settlements are spaced uniformly. An important fact to keep in mind in examining the spacing of nodes, on the other hand, is that the average spacing of nodes varies with nodal dominance: more dominant nodes tend to be spaced further apart than less dominant nodes.

Finally studies of *localization* have concentrated largely upon the geography of different branches of manufacturing industry. Bakery products, for example, seem relatively unlocalized compared with such branches as textiles. Different branches of industry also show different degrees of localization.

The next two chapters inquire more specifically into issues raised in this present chapter. Chapter Eleven examines the spacing regularities of urban places noted in this chapter, while Chapter Twelve focuses upon the varying degrees of localization of different industries.

~~~~~~

Case Study: Urban Places as Nodes

INTRODUCTION

As the discussion has emphasized so far, one of the most commonly encountered and indeed most studied of nodes is the town or urban settlement. The previous chapter presented some abstract ideas on locational processes and locational arrangement along with some statements regarding real world locational patterns. In particular we emphasized *spacing regularities,* the fact that larger, more dominant towns tend to be spaced further apart than smaller, more dependent towns. We also emphasized *uniformity of spacing,* suggesting the relevance of competitive locational processes, though we found that this does not necessarily indicate a uniform dispersion. And, in fact, we found that within a sample of areas in the United States at least, dispersions tend to be random rather than uniform or clustered, attesting to the probable role of local, small-scale inhomogeneities.

The major purpose of this chapter is to explain these aspects of locational arrangement by relating the locational processes of the latter chapter more to the real world. We intend to do this by introducing some new concepts, such as *threshold,* that have great explanatory power when dealing with locational arrangements of settlement. Finally at

the end of the chapter we attempt to relate regularities in the pattern of settlements of different size to other locational patterns, specifically locational regularities in the spatial diffusion of certain innovations.

THE LOCATION OF RETAILING

Geographical theories that have examined and attempted to explain the spacing regularities and uniformity of spacing exhibited by urban settlements have emphasized the explanatory role of the location of retailing. This is the strategy followed in this section where the location of retailing is explained as a function of locational competition. In the following section the locational characteristics—dispersion and spacing—of the hierarchy of retail centers, and therefore of the population generated by such retailing activity, will be explained as a function of such locational competition.

Simply stated, the retailer's economic problem is to sell sufficient goods in order to provide himself with a living. Various strategies are available to him in order to achieve this goal. Pricing, advertising, and personal service, for example, are some of the strategies that may increase his sales. Given what we know about consumer trip behavior, however, one of the most powerful strategies he has is locational. Certain locations will provide him with more sales than others.

The "most valued locations" for the retailer are those that are as close to the market as possible and as far away from competitors as possible. The locational problem of the retailer, therefore, is to minimize the distance from his market and maximize his distance from competitors. Only in this way can he monopolize a large enough market for his product and protect himself from competition. Now theoretically, *if* demand is spread uniformly over the area for the good being retailed, *if* there are no locational variations in accessibility to the market due to localized communication availability or to the location of movement foci such as post offices, *if* the retailer's sole goal is to maximize profits, *and if* people show least-effort shopping trip behavior, *then* the locational pattern of retailing resulting from retailers carrying out the optimal locational strategy outlined above is a *triangular lattice.* This tendency towards uniformity in the locational pattern can be argued both by

analogue and by deduction from a theoretical retailing situation. Working by analogy, Bunge has described an experiment in which small magnets were attached to corks and thrown into a tub of water. The magnets, of course, repelled each other just as retailers tend to repel each other by keeping as far away from each other as possible. The corks were repeatedly taken out of the tub and thrown back in, and the pattern they assumed was examined for regularity. The most common pattern was a "nearly perfect hexagon with a central point," that is, a triangular lattice.

We can also develop an argument which leads to a similar uniform nodal pattern on the basis of certain restrictive assumptions (see Figure 11-1). Assume that the territory in which retailers locate is a linear one and that each retailer requires four miles of line in order to stay in business; assume that demand is distributed evenly along the line and that consumers patronize the nearest retailer. Now, in Figure 11-1 retailers are located along the line at t_1 and their ser-

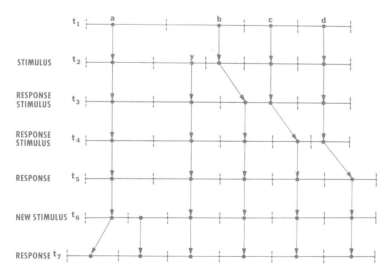

FIGURE 11-1.   Retail locations and service areas at a sequence of time intervals. Note the locational implications of competition for the geographically distributed demand.

vice areas are indicated by dashed vertical lines. Retailers *a* and *b* have very large market areas—six miles each—arranged in such a way as to suggest that another retailer could locate and survive between them. In t_2 a new retailer *y* has located between *a* and *b* but much closer to *b* than to *a*. This curtails *b*'s market area so that he has to relocate (t_3) in order to regain his former profit level. This relocation of *b* stimulates further relocations by retailers located near him (t_4, t_5) so that there is a situation in which the retailers of the same good are continually trying to get as far away from each other as possible—with a resultant tendency towards uniformity in the locational pattern. If, of course, the retailers are located too far from each other this presents an opportunity for another retailer to locate in between them (t_6) and touch off a new series of relocations as the alternative to bankruptcy. Such a situation is the antithesis of clustering, where the locators are trying to get as near to a small segment of the earth's surface or as near to each other as possible.

Precisely how far apart the retailers will have to locate, however, is dependent upon two factors: (1) *the density of demand for a particular product or service* and (2) *the market demands of a particular product or service*. As far as the first factor is concerned, it is obvious that if a grocery store requires a market of 2000 people in order to survive economically, grocery stores will have to be spaced further apart when the density of population is 10 per square mile than when it is 1000 per square mile.

The second factor is equally important and has far-reaching implications for the spatial structure of settlement patterns. Different retail goods and services require different market sizes in order for the retailer to make a profit distributing the good or service. A grocery or a dry-cleaning establishment, for example, can easily be supported by a market of 2000 households. A high-class furrier, on the other hand, needs a market of 100,000 simply because most people do not buy furs very often and of those who do buy furs many of them will only buy once in a lifetime. Similar arguments apply to other goods. A seller of phonograph records, for example, would never locate in a town of 2000 simply because there would not be sufficient business in that town and in the immediately surrounding area to provide him with a profit. A town of 20,000, however, could provide him with a large enough market. This minimum market is frequently referred to as the threshold market.

▶ *The threshold market for a retail good or service is the minimum size market, comprising the people who shop in a town, capable of supporting that retail good or service at a profit.*

Table 11-1 presents the order of threshold requirements for functions in towns in southwestern Iowa; as can be seen, a larger market is required for a florist or an electrical repair store than for a beauty parlor, an insurance agency, or a doctor. Moreover, the concept has important geographical implications; retailers selling goods and services with high threshold requirements must locate further apart than those purveying goods and services with low threshold needs. Groceries are therefore spaced closer together across the landscape than phonograph stores; and phonograph stores are thicker on the ground than high-class furriers!

Stemming from the threshold concept and the fact that different goods and services have different thresholds is the hierarchical component of the settlement pattern: that some places are more dominant than others in the marketing of

TABLE 11-1. Order of threshold requirements (small to large) for selected urban functions in southwestern Iowa.

Gas and Service Station	Lawyer	Radio TV Sales and Service
Restaurant	Doctor	Funeral
Bar	New Auto Sales	Shoes
Grocery	Real Estate	Motel
Barber	Newspaper	Florist
Hardware	Shoe Repair	Bakery
Post Office	Plumbing	Bus, Taxi Station
Bank, Savings and Loan	Movies	Telegraph Office
Appliances	Women's Clothing	Candy
Furniture	Supermarket	Music and Records
Beauty	Dentist	Children's Clothing
Insurance	Hotel	Electrical Repair
Drug	Jewelry	County Government
Indoor Amusements (Billiards, etc.)	Liquor	Mission
Self Service Laundry	Men's Clothing	Sporting Goods

goods and services and that all levels of the dominance hierarchy are subject to locational competition and the tendency towards uniformity of spacing and dispersion that it induces. The argument can be stated briefly and simply.

If a good or a service has a higher threshold requirement than another good this means it can be distributed from fewer places than a good or service with a smaller threshold. Those fewer places will be chosen on the basis of two criteria: (1) locational competition: the purveyors of the good or service will keep as far away from other distributors as possible and (2) accessibility: a selection of locations will be made from those places already distributing goods since they have a greater accessibility to the market than places that do not distribute goods or services. Further, the accessibility advantage increases with the number of goods sold since a larger market is needed to support the wider range of goods and services and some of the goods will have relatively high thresholds leading to patronization from a wider geographical area. Moreover, as we shall show later, the patronage for a clothing store in a city performing many retail functions tends to come from a

wider area than the patronage of a similar clothing store in a place distributing fewer different goods and services. The more goods and services a place distributes, therefore, the more it tends to act as a focus of consumer movements and to be an attractive place for a retailer desiring accessibility to a larger market.

Hence there is a hierarchy of goods and services. Places distributing goods and services with high threshold requirements tend also to distribute the full range of goods and services having smaller threshold needs; places distributing goods and services with small thresholds, on the other hand, tend to distribute in addition only those goods and services having even smaller threshold needs. Thus the place with a high-class furrier will also have a phonograph record shop and a grocery; a place with a phonograph record shop will have a grocery but may not have a high-class furrier. Similarly, working from Table 11-1, a town in southwestern Iowa with a candy store will also have a doctor, a lawyer, a newspaper, a hotel, and a dentist. If we know that the town has a variety store, we know that it will almost certainly have in addition a hardware store, a barber, a bar, and a grocery. However, we are not sure whether it will offer goods and services with higher threshold requirements such as a motel, a telegraph office, or a children's clothing store.

In summary, we are suggesting that whatever regularity there may be in the locational arrangement of urban places stems from the locational competition of retailers trying to get as close to their market of consumers as possible and as far away from their competitors as possible. The size of market the retailer has to be accessible to, however, varies with the retail good or service; some goods or services—or urban functions as they are sometimes called—have low threshold or minimum market requirements while others have higher threshold needs and have to be purveyed from fewer locations. But which locations will be chosen? Briefly, those which keep the retailer as far away from competitors as possible and as accessible to the consumer as possible. The latter implies a selection of a location from those already distributing goods or services because of their consumer-congregation function. The result is a hierarchy of urban functions. Places distributing a retail good or service at a given threshold level distribute all goods and services with lower threshold requirements. What are the locational implications of all this?

LOCATIONAL COMPETITION AND THE LOCATIONAL PATTERNS OF RETAIL CENTERS

Considering the arguments above regarding locational competition, several relationships logically follow and they are supported with a wealth of empirical verification: (1) *There is a direct relationship between the number of retail and service functions performed by an urban place and its population size.* As Figure 11-2 shows, larger places offer more re-

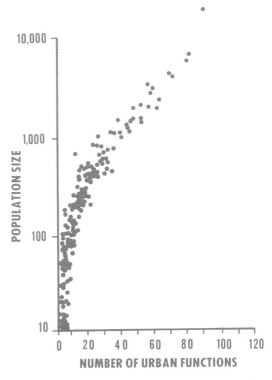

FIGURE 11-2. Population size and the number of urban functions performed in southwest Iowa, northeast South Dakota, and the Rapid City area.

tail goods and services or functions, as they are sometimes called, than smaller places. Presumably part of this relationship originates in the employment generated by the retail activity. Equally important, however, is the fact that larger places are more likely to satisfy the threshold requirements of a wider array of functions than smaller places.

(2) *There is a direct relationship between the number of retail and service functions performed by an urban place and the magnitude of its trade area.* Places distributing fewer goods and services distribute them to a smaller area than places distributing more types of goods and services. This is partly due to the fact that places distributing more goods and services have

to distribute some with higher threshold requirements than the place performing fewer functions. It is also due, however, to a fact which we remarked upon above and that will be expanded further below: that a place distributing more goods and services has a larger market area for, say, a clothing store than does a place with fewer functions for its clothing store. An important geographical implication of these ideas is that, as noted in Chapter Two, service areas for centers purveying a small range of goods and services tend to "nest" within the service areas of larger places offering a greater number of functions. Thus, while the population of a small town may patronize its own grocery store it travels to a neighboring larger town for lawyer services or for dental services, and indeed some people will even buy the occasional groceries there. It is easy to see, moreover, that a corollary of (1) and (2) is that larger urban places have larger trade areas than smaller urban places.

(3) *There is a direct relationship between the number of functions performed by an urban place and the population of its sales area.* This follows from what we have said regarding (a) the threshold requirements of goods and services and (b) the hierarchical manner in which they are offered by different places.

(4) *There is a direct relationship between the number of functions performed by an urban place and the distance to a place offering a similar number of functions.* This follows from the fact that places offering more functions offer some goods with higher thresholds and that goods with higher threshold requirements can only be distributed from places located further apart.

All of these empirical relationships suggest that it is quite realistic to think in terms of a hierarchy of settlements ranging from the hamlet with its small range of functions and its miniscule ser-

vice area nesting within the service area of a town offering more functions, and through larger towns, cities, and metropolitan centers with more functions and correspondingly large market areas, each nested within the market area of a place on the next rung of the hierarchy.

These relationships further clarify some of the ideas first presented in Chapter Two. The *sphere of influence,* for example, emerges as the trade area. *Dominance* is seen as associated with the number of *functions* which a place performs and therefore with its *urban size;* this also helps to explain why larger cities are more *attractive* as presented in Chapter Three. *More dominant centers* can now be seen to have *larger spheres of influence* because they attain the threshold level for goods and services requiring large market areas. This is also the reason why *more dominant centers are fewer and are located further apart* than the smaller, more dependent centers with their smaller number of functions requiring smaller threshold markets.

However a number of issues which we have been raising remain unanswered; a comment was made earlier, for example, regarding the possibility of finding settlements arranged in a *triangular lattice.* Such would be the geographical output under certain highly restrictive assumptions: (1) if purchasing power for the retail goods and services that settlements purvey were evenly spread over geographical area so that one square mile of surface would contain the same amount of purchasing power as any other; (2) if there were no variations in accessibility to the market due to highway locations or to the establishment of some *focus* of movement such as a post office or tavern or periodic market; (3) if the retailer had no needs other than to maximize his accessibility to the market relative to the accessibility of other retailers selling the same good; (4) and if shopping trip behavior was least effort, then the result would be a triangular lattice of settlements.

It would seem, therefore, that in order to obtain a fuller understanding of the locational arrangement of nodes we must examine the effects of these factors on that locational arrangement. Our arguments here are structured under two headings: (1) the role of homogeneity and inhomogeneity at a variety of geographical scales, and (2) the locational behavior of consumers.

THE ROLE OF HOMOGENEITY AND INHOMOGENEITY AT A VARIETY OF GEOGRAPHICAL SCALES

As far as inhomogeneities of purchasing power are concerned, variations of both income and population density over space result in variations in the *area* needed to support a given urban function. The impact of income variations has been little studied up to now, but more is known about the impact of population density on the spacing of settlements and it is worth retelling here. First, as population density declines the *area* needed to support a given function expands in order to satisfy the threshold requirement, and hence the trade area should expand even though the population patronizing the retail outlet remains the same. This is illustrated very graphically in Figure 11-3 where data from five areas of differing population density are presented ranging from the densely populated metropolitan area of Chicago through progressively less densely settled areas of suburbia, the Corn Belt, and the Wheat lands to the thinly settled Range lands. As the diagram shows, holding the total population served (a crude measure of threshold) constant the *area* served varies as a function of population density such that, for example, trade areas for a given size of population

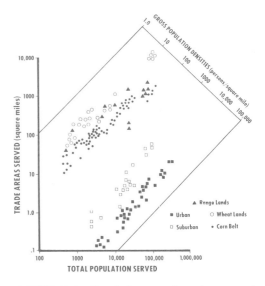

FIGURE 11-3. Population served, trade area and population density. In general urban places serving larger populations have larger trade areas. In areas of lower population density, however, a town serving a given population will have to have a larger trade area than a town serving that same population in an area of high population density. This has implications for spacing so that (e.g.) towns serving populations of 10,000 are closer together in the Corn Belt (e.g. Illinois) than in the Wheat lands (e.g. North Dakota).

served are much larger in the Wheat lands of the Dakotas than in the suburban areas of northeastern Illinois. It is largely for this reason that settlements of a given size are further apart in thinly settled Nebraska or Kansas than they are in more thickly peopled Ohio or Indiana. The same locational principle is largely responsible for the fact that cities of similar size are separated by shorter distances in England (more densely populated) than in the American Midwest (less densely populated).

Further inhomogeneities are induced in the arena of settlement, however, by variations in accessibility such that some places are more significant foci of movement, and hence, markets, than other places. Thus, the names of many towns in England betray their locational origin at points of slightly greater accessibility:

Ox*ford*, Cam*bridge*, Strat*ford*, Castle*ford*, *Bridge*water, Trow*bridge*, etc. Many other towns have historical advantages of accessibility not betrayed by their names: the early growth of urban settlements in southwestern Iowa, for instance, was oriented towards points of consumer assembly as at grist mills, post offices, county seats, and later railroad stations. However, despite the prevalence of such cases we should be careful not to exaggerate their significance. They do not account for the location of a settlement; rather they account for the deviation of a settlement from that point at which it would have been located with no local inhomogeneities of accessibility. Oxford would probably have still been close to where it is today without a ford.

Finally, in this discussion of inhomogeneities we need to recognize that the retailer's needs are not limited to accessibility to his market vis-à-vis the accessibility of his competitors for purposes of profit maximization. Other needs have historically included such things as a reliable supply of drinking water, defense, and a disease-free environment. We should therefore expect and indeed we can find, the deviation of settlements from uniform lattice locations by the attraction of defensive sites and sites with all-year water or protection from endemic diseases like malaria. In areas once subject to periodic war and attack such as the Welsh and Scottish borderlands or the Mediterranean areas of France once threatened by the Saracens, many of the settlements occupy sites clustering around a castle or on top of a good defensive position like a hill. The castle towns of the Scottish borders are well known, particularly those of Newcastle and Edinburgh; the Bastide towns built on hills in southern France as a defense against the Saracens represented a similar defensive response.

All these inhomogeneities produce deviations from the triangular lattice of settlements. Clearly, however, there are scale differences involved in these inhomogeneities; the variations in accessibility and site characteristics generate rather small-scale deviations from the triangular lattice. The density of demand distribution, however, is likely to give rise to more regional scale variations in the spatial form of the settlement hierarchy.

THE LOCATIONAL BEHAVIOR OF CONSUMERS

A prerequisite for a triangular lattice of urban places to emerge is *least-effort shopping trip behavior*, that is, trip behavior in which consumers patronize the *nearest* place offering the good or service. That this is a prerequisite for a triangular lattice of settlement logically follows from the assumptions of locational competitors; they try to locate as close to consumers as possible and as far away from competitors as possible. This assumes, however, that consumers in whose vicinity they have located will patronize them. This only follows, however, if shopping trip behavior is least effort.

In fact, of course, shopping trip behavior is not least effort. Not only are there deficiencies in the *knowledge* which consumers have about the availability of goods and services at different towns—especially critical for new arrivals within an area as we saw in Chapter Five—but there is also the phenomenon of the *multiple-purpose shopping trip*. The *major* purpose of a household traveling a long distance to a town may be to buy a new suit of clothes for the head of the household. The trip, however, also makes the consumer accessible to other goods and services such as groceries; purchase of such goods in the larger city is economical of the time and effort involved in returning home and going to the small town close by where groceries are also sold. As a result of the multiple-purpose shopping trip, therefore, the more distant but larger city is substituted for the closer, smaller city in the purchase of groceries.

In fact the bases of shopping trip behavior in a given locational structure of shopping opportunities, seem to be pretty much the factors we identified in Chapter Three—*attractiveness* and *movement costs*. *Attractiveness* from the shopper's viewpoint can be equated largely with the *number of functions purveyed* though there are some interesting cases in which superior quality goods make some places more attractive shopping centers. Attractiveness in the form of the number of functions offered promotes non-least-effort trip behavior in that it encourages the substitution of more distant multiple-purpose shopping trips for shorter distance single-purpose shopping trips for lower-order goods such as groceries.

Movement costs are of declining significance in shopping trip decisions; the convenience of the automobile has made an extra mile of travel much less critical than before and has altered the terms of the tradeoff between movement costs and attractiveness in the direction of attractiveness. The motorist is much more likely to substitute a more distant, though more attractive, shopping center for a nearer, less attractive shopping center. This has been illustrated rather strikingly with some data on the shopping trip behavior of those who have access to an automobile and those who do not in northeastern England. The study was particularly concerned with the shopping patronage of three types of retailing centers: closely spaced neighborhood centers, more distant high street centers of an intermediate attractiveness

and—spaced even further apart—regional centers. As can be seen from Figure 11-4 the patronage of the more distant regional centers is definitely related to car ownership. Nor is this simply the result of the fact that, in general, car owning households are wealthier and have more money to spend on the high threshold goods and services that the regional centers alone have to offer. Figure 11-4 also differentiates households according to their socioeconomic status with Grade 1 as the highest level and Grade 4 the lowest. Even when taking such income differences into account, the more mobile families were more likely to patronize the more distant regional centers.

Improved mobility and the decreasing overall significance of least-effort trip behavior have very important locational

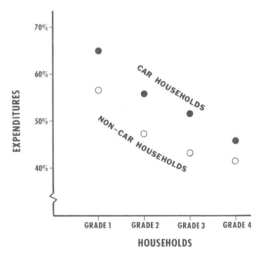

FIGURE 11-4. Percentage of total shopping goods expenditure spent in some regional centers of northeast England by socioeconomic status and automobile ownership. Both automobile ownership and socioeconomic status encourage substitution of more distant regional centers for closer small centers in shopping trip behavior. As more people obtain automobiles and as average socioeconomic status increases, it is likely that patronage of smaller centers will decline to the benefit of the larger, more distant centers.

TABLE 11-2. Changes in the average spacing of towns in Saskatchewan. Differential growth of retail centers has resulted in growth of larger centers and decline of smaller centers; as a consequence smaller places of a given size in 1961 are further apart than small places of the same size in 1941; larger places, however, are closer together.

| Classification | Number in 1961 | Average spacing (in miles) | |
		1941	1961
Hamlet	404	9.1	9.6
Village	150	10.3	13.5
Small Town	100	15.4	19.8
Town	85	25.9	22.5
City	29	40.4	39.5
Regional city	9	119.8	67.5
Regional capital	2	144.0	144.0

ment generators and as the larger towns wax with the attraction of new customers, certain changes are bound to occur in the spacing of settlements of different size. Smaller towns of, say, 1000 inhabitants become further apart while larger towns become more geographically frequent and therefore closer together. This is reflected in data for Saskatchewan in Table 11-2; in 1961 the larger regional centers were almost twice as close as they were in 1941 while smaller villages were about 30% further apart.

The tendency for the substitution of larger, more attractive, but more distant centers for smaller, less distant centers, moreover, has been geographically uneven. Those consumers located close to the larger city, for instance, have been much more likely to divert their patronage than have those shoppers located at greater distances. Areas surrounding the major cities, therefore, have shown a much greater depletion of their smaller retailing centers than have areas more remote from such larger, attractive centers. As Table 11-3 shows, in Saskatchewan the density of small retail centers close to large centers has declined much more precipitously than in areas further away. Clearly, moreover, these losses have not been completely compensated by the arrival of commuters from the nearby city and the bolstering of the local retail market. The creation of

consequences. The increasing substitution of the more attractive, more distant, larger center for the closer, smaller center results in the slow decline of the latter as its market of consumers increasingly patronizes the more distant shopping facilities. Not only that, but the increased patronage of the larger, more distant centers makes them still more attractive for new retailers since it permits them to achieve still higher threshold levels.

As smaller towns wane with the erosion of one of their important employ-

TABLE 11-3. Change in density of small trade centers in relation to distance from large centers, Saskatchewan 1941–61. Small towns closer to larger urban centers have been particularly susceptible to population decline and ultimate extinction due to the ease with which the location of the larger center permits substitution in shopping trips.

Distance zone	1941 No./1000 sq. mi.	1961 No./1000 sq. mi.	Percent change 1941–61
Within 10 miles	5.2	4.0	−23.1
10–15 miles	7.6	6.3	−17.1
15–20 miles	8.2	7.3	−11.0
Provincial Average All Small Centers	7.2	6.2	−16.7

such deserts of small town retailing activity around larger centers makes the emergence of a triangular lattice settlement most unlikely, to say the least.

GENERALITY OF THE CONCEPTS

The concept of threshold and of variable thresholds for different goods and services has been applied largely to retail goods and services in this chapter; it can also be applied to many other urban functions that are not usually regarded as retail goods and services; educational institutions, government services, hospitals, specialized banking and stock exchange facilities, and communication facilities such as jet transportation provide examples. Such services require large thresholds so that larger centers are favored. Also many of their threshold requirements seem to be increasing. Medical men seem increasingly dissatisfied with the inadequacy of the small hospital and demand a large hospital which can offer a complete range of health services but which at the same time needs the patronage of patients from a very large population. Railroads demand larger populations to justify stopping for passengers or even to take on freight; and jets serve only a minority of the airports served by piston aircraft.

Such large, increasing threshold requirements favor the larger more dominant cities at the expense of smaller more dependent cities and serve to make the latter even more dependent and the former more dominant. However it would be a mistake to imagine that such differential growth is a feature of the contemporary scene alone; it is probable that even in the 19th century urban places grew at different rates as, for instance, the construction of a railroad gave a larger place some advantage not enjoyed by a smaller town. Probably what makes the situation so noticeable

today is that smaller centers have ceased to grow at all.

These ideas regarding differential growth of cities as a result of their population size and resultant dominance have some interesting implications for the *historical geography of towns.* One would expect, for instance, cities which were founded *earlier* to have advantages over those established *later.* The earlier cities would have obtained a population size by natural growth and in-migration that newer cities would have to make up; they would also, because of the forces of locational competition, be further apart while later urban foundations would have to fill the space in between. The earlier and probably larger cities, therefore, would be more attractive for retailers purveying new functions demanding a larger threshold. In this way one can conceive of a differential growth process in which earlier cities would have advantages which later cities would not enjoy.

Table 11-4 suggests that there is some substance in these arguments. An examination of the dates of incorporation of different sized urban places in Indiana shows that larger towns do tend to have been established earlier than smaller towns. Seventy-four percent of the towns founded in or before 1850 are over 2500 in population size today. Less than 10% of the cities incorporated after 1900 enjoy that population size status today.

The ideas which we have been presenting in this chapter, therefore, seem to clarify not only the pattern of settlement as it exists today and as it is changing but also the locational arrangement of towns from which the present urban system evolved. Apart from an interest in the bases of the locational arrangement of towns, however, what light does that locational arrangement throw on other geographical patterns? Patterns of migration, commuting, and innovation

TABLE 11-4. Urban size and dates of foundation in Indiana. Earlier established towns tend to be larger today than those founded later; this may be due to the growth advantages which "an early start" bestows. Rows sum to 100%.

Date of incorporation*	Population in 1960					
	10,000 or more	2500–9999	1000–2499	500–999	250–499	0–249
1850 and before	39%	35%	16%	6%	3%	1%
1860	4%	26%	37%	17%	13%	2%
1870	7%	26%	24%	24%	13%	7%
1880	4%	15%	34%	20%	11%	17%
1890	7%	20%	13%	47%	13%	0%
1900	0%	2%	19%	12%	30%	12%
1910	1%	9%	14%	31%	33%	7%
1920	0%	5%	14%	24%	48%	10%
1930	0%	3%	16%	19%	29%	29%
1940	0%	0%	25%	0%	50%	25%
1950	0%	0%	17%	33%	33%	17%
1960	7%	7%	13%	33%	20%	20%

* The date of incorporation is given as the first year in which a town name appeared in the census.

diffusion, for instance? This is the final problem to be considered in this chapter.

SPATIAL STRUCTURAL IMPLICATIONS OF NODAL PATTERNS

This chapter has drawn attention to certain broad predictabilities in the geographical arrangement of towns of varying size. We have found, for example, that larger cities tend to be further apart than smaller cities; larger cities have larger market areas than small cities, and the distance between cities of a given size class is a function of population density.

The attribute of urban size that is central to these locational predictabilities, however, is correlated with certain other attributes of locational significance. Larger urban places, for example, are more attractive from the retailing viewpoint than smaller cities. It seems logical, therefore, that activities which are locationally sensitive to such attributes should reveal a similar locational pattern as that of the nodes of a given size class. If the activity is particularly attracted to

large urban markets it should present a much sparser locational pattern than an activity which can tolerate a smaller urban market. Thus TV stations in the United States are, on the average, further apart than radio stations. In this section we pursue this argument further by examining the impact of the urban hierarchy upon locational patterns of innovation adoption.

In the section dealing with the spatial diffusion of innovations above (see Chapter Five) one of the types of locational pattern which we referred to was that of *spatial inversion*, a pattern in which there is no relationship between the date of adoption and distance from some point or line. This was exemplified most clearly with the case of the spatial diffusion of postal agencies in Uganda, Africa. A possible reason for such inversion, however, is frequently suggested when dates of adoption are plotted on a scatter diagram against urban size; very often people in larger urban places are found to adopt before people in smaller urban places. This has been noted in the spread of ham radio operation in the United States and in the case of the diffusion of automobiles and radios in southern Sweden. This type of relationship is also evident for innovations which are adopted by communities rather than by individuals: Rotary Clubs, for example, or crematoria. As Figure 11-5 shows, such a diffusion through an urban hierarchy with larger places spaced further apart than smaller places could easily produce an inversion-type pattern. It is unlikely, however, that such an inversion would be perfect; most probably, there would be some localized neighborhood effect around the larger urban places to smaller urban places in their vicinity before spread to small towns not in the vicinity of larger cities.

Why, however, should such a relationship between the time of adoption of such items as radio, TV, and household appliances and urban size apply? What correlates of urban size are significant here? One student of this problem, Lawrence A. Brown, has stressed the role of the *availability of the innovation*. It will be recalled that in Chapter Five we stressed the role of information and individual resistance for the adoption of an innovation; it seems that we must now qualify this by isolating the importance of variations in availability. Clearly, for many innovations while the person may have information about an innovation

and be unresistant to it he may not adopt simply because the innovation is not available to him in a locational sense.

What does availability depend upon? Brown has stressed the role of two factors: (1) *the locational policy of the company distributing an innovation* — thus a TV company must decide which of its agencies will sell color TV initially, (2) *shopping trip behavior* — does the would-be adopter ever make shopping trips to a place where the innovation is purveyed? The first factor is related to urban size and in combination with short-distance shopping trip behavior produces the hierarchical diffusion effect.

Consider the viewpoint of the company distributing the innovation. Profitability is a prime criterion in the establishment of distribution agencies and such profitability is closely dependent on market size; market size for goods such as TV sets or automobiles or radios is very much a function of urban size. It seems likely, therefore, that the first places to receive distribution agencies would be the larger urban places due to their greater profitability. In such places the good would be *available* earlier than in smaller places and hence would be adopted earlier.

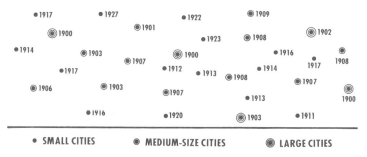

* SMALL CITIES   ◉ MEDIUM-SIZE CITIES   ◎ LARGE CITIES

FIGURE 11-5. Diffusion through the urban hierarchy and spatial inversion patterns of adoption (schematic): if large cities adopt an innovation first, medium-sized cities later, and small cities later still, the result will be a spatial-inversion pattern of innovation adoption. Dates refer to times of adoption.

Shopping trip behavior underlines the role of urban size. As most shopping trips are for necessity-type goods over short distances (e.g., groceries) inhabitants of larger cities will have a greater opportunity to purchase the innovation than will the inhabitant of smaller cities. For shopping trips less based on necessity, of course, larger cities still have an advantage due to the greater size of their sales areas, and therefore people in small towns in the vicinity of larger urban places are likely to adopt before those living in small places at some geographical remove from a larger urban place.

This theory has been tested for the diffusion of TV sets in part of southern Sweden and the results are consistent with the theory. Also important, however, is the fact that by drawing attention to marketing factors, Brown helps to explain the effect of the urban hierarchy upon the diffusion of such collective innovations as Rotary Clubs. Such collective innovations need a *pool* of potential members and such pools are initially to be found in larger urban centers; it is only with the passage of time and growth of interest in the collective innovation that a smaller town will have a pool sufficiently large to justify the adoption of the innovation.

CONCLUSIONS AND SUMMARY

Chapter Ten provided us with some regularities to explain — particularly the fact that *larger settlements are spaced further apart than smaller settlements* and that spacing tends to increase as population density declines. It also provided us with a theoretical pattern of settlements which would emerge under certain circumstances — *the triangular lattice of settlements.* We need to inquire into the factors which hinder the emergence of such symmetry. Such, very broadly, have been the aims of this chapter.

Explanation of the regularities in the geographical literature has been largely in terms of the location of retailing. This has been the course adopted in this book. What, therefore, influences the location of the retailing sector? Presumably the retailer tries to get as *close to his market of consumers as he can and as far away from his competitors as possible;* that is, he is involved in that competitive process which under certain restrictive conditions produces the triangular lattice of settlements. But how far away should he get? In order to purvey the given *urban function* — a retail good or service — he must be accessible to a consumer market which satisfies the *threshold requirements* for that urban function. Such a threshold requirement varies from one function to another; *purveyors of low threshold functions can therefore be spaced closer together than distributors of higher threshold urban functions.* Not only that, but if a place can achieve the threshold level for a function requiring a high threshold it can also satisfy the threshold needs of all goods requiring smaller thresholds.

Several consequences follow from these ideas: firstly, *the number of functions performed by an urban place increases as the population of the place increases;* secondly, *places distributing more urban functions require larger trade areas and trade area populations* in order to satisfy the threshold needs of the higher threshold goods or services that they

are distributing; and thirdly, if trade areas are to be larger for larger urban places performing a large number of urban functions then those *larger places will be spaced further
apart than smaller places.* These relationships are strongly supported by real world evidence.

The triangular lattice, however, is not, simply because the restrictive assumptions
under which it would emerge do not apply in the real world. There would have to be,
for example, an *environment homogeneous in the distribution of purchasing power.* In the
United States, however, *variations in population density* produce great variations in
purchasing power per square mile so that in less densely populated states *urban places
of a given size are spaced further apart* than urban places of the same size in more
densely populated states.

The second assumption is that there should be *least-effort shopping trip behavior.* If
the retailer is to compete by locating as close to his market of consumers as possible he
must assume that those customers will patronize him rather than someone further
away. In fact the multiple-purpose shopping trip encourages *substitution of more distant
larger shopping centers for closer smaller centers and the differential growth of those centers.*
This has been accelerated by the automobile, especially around large cities where
smaller places have declined leaving considerable gaps in the urban pattern.

Of course, we are not interested in the locational pattern of cities for its own sake
alone. That pattern also has important influences on many other geographical patterns,
such as those of migration and of the diffusion of innovation. As far as the latter is concerned, for example, we find that for many innovations residents of larger cities or
from the vicinity of larger cities are likely to be the earliest adopters. Larger cities not
only provide more profitable markets for distributors of the innovations; they are also
accessible to a wide surrounding area due to the long shopping trip movements with
which larger centers are associated.

Retailing, however, is not the only source of urban growth. Manufacturing has historically also been very important and many small retail centers in the shadow of larger
cities have grown to prominence on the basis of manufacturing, thus producing
striking discordances in the spacing of settlements of a given size. A complete understanding of the factors accounting for the locational arrangement of settlements of different size, therefore, requires that we examine the factors affecting the location of
manufacturing. That is the topic we shall treat in the next chapter.

CHAPTER TWELVE

Case Study: Industrial Plants as Nodes

INTRODUCTION

The second example of a node is the industrial plant. This is of interest to geographers for two reasons. First, industrial plants form distinctive geographical patterns which are interesting in their own right; in this chapter such locational patterns are treated largely from the viewpoint of the concept of localization discussed in Chapter Ten.

Second, the locational patterns of industrial plants are of assistance in explaining the locational patterns of urban places. While Chapter Eleven was very concerned with the role of the location of retailing in producing urban patterns, it is apparent that its explanatory power is not exhaustive. Towns fulfill industrial as well as retail functions, and the locational demands of industry will affect the locational patterns of the towns that develop around the industrial plants. Only in this way can one explain such clustering of urban places as is apparent in, for example, the Ruhr of West Germany or in eastern Pennsylvania.

In this chapter we accomplish four specific tasks: first, we develop a theoretical treatment of reasons for the localization of manufacturing and mining activities; second we consider the impact of different types of homogeneity—inhomogeneity on the localization of

such activities and hence upon the resultant locational patterns of industry; third, we review the problem of locational decision making and finally, we attempt to relate the findings of this chapter to those of the previous chapter in order to provide more generality about the locational patterns of nodes and their economic structures.

AN ABSTRACT VIEW OF LOCALIZATION

The problem of the industrialist or the mine owner is to locate in such a way as to minimize the cost of his product and to sell his product for as big a profit as possible over the long term; that is, to maximize the return on his investment. Assuming pure competition in an economic activity, however, the entrepreneur's latitude in maximizing the price for his product will be limited and by far the major attempt to maximize return on investment will come from minimizing his costs of production. The locational significance of production costs, therefore, forms the major thrust of the theoretical arguments presented here.

Production costs can be apportioned to two major sources: (1) *movement or transfer costs:* these include the costs of procuring the factors of production for processing at one site and the cost of distributing the finished product to the consumer, and (2) *process costs* or the actual costs of buying some raw materials and transforming them in order to produce a saleable item. Such process costs can be further broken down into a set of factor costs per unit of output: raw material costs, labor costs, capital costs, and land costs. As factor productivity alters (as a result of some technological change or as a result of changes in the supply of and demand for capital, labor, and land), factor costs per unit of output change and alter the total process costs per unit of output.

Given data on such costs for a given product across an array of places it is possible to imagine a *cost map* in which the isolines would join places having given production costs—movement plus process costs—for a particular item (see Figure 12-1). Certain points follow from this map: first, with such knowledge it would be a relatively easy matter to select a least-cost location, and second, there is likely to be considerable variation in costs from place to place. We shall return to the first point shortly when we discuss the vagaries of decision making in relationship to the cost pattern. The immediate problem, however, is to discuss the components of the cost pattern and how they might affect the loca-

tional choice of a highly rational, omniscient industrialist.

The hypothetical cost distribution presented in Figure 12-1 can be broken down into two components: that portion of the distribution attributable to geographical variations in process costs (i.e., to variations in process cost per unit of output), and second, that portion of the distribution attributable to geographical variations in movement costs per unit product (i.e., to procurement and distribution costs per unit product). Thus the factors of production for a particular product are spread in a highly uneven manner over the landscape. In some areas skilled labor is available, while in others it is not. Also, coal can be mined in some areas but not in most. In addition to considering the *locational availability* of a certain factor input, however, we also have to consider *variations in the cost* of a given factor per unit product. Wage rates per hour may vary, for instance, without any concomitant variation in labor quality; similarly, the cost of electrical power and of timber for the saw-milling industry may vary from one location to another.

Of course, locational disadvantages in the cost of factor inputs may be alleviated by moving in cheaper factor inputs from elsewhere. This, however, is not cost free because the raw materials must be transported and management often demands moving expenses, etc. The locator, therefore, is frequently involved in a trade-off between using the more expensive local factor inputs and moving in cheaper factor inputs from elsewhere. His decision will be strongly affected by a comparison of the difference in factor costs between locations, on the one hand, and the costs of movement between locations, on the other hand. Thus, the cheaper iron ore may not be so distant from the industrialist as to make the cost of the iron ore per unit

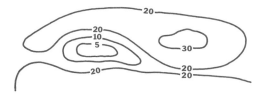

FIGURE 12-1. A hypothetical total production cost map. Total production costs per unit of output are a function of both movement costs (distribution of product and procurement of factor inputs) and processing costs; the latter is dependent on the costs of factor inputs such as labor, land, raw materials, and so on. On each *isoline* total production cost in monetary units is the same.

product and the procurement costs of the iron ore per unit product equal to or greater than the cost of the iron ore per unit product available in the industrialist's own backyard.

Additional trade-offs are involved when one remembers that location has to be made not only with reference to the locational patterns of factor inputs but also with reference to the locational pattern of markets. Just as factor inputs vary in their availability and cost from place to place, so, analogously, markets vary in their availability and density, the denser markets (in terms of population and disposable income) being clearly more attractive. Thus, not only must a trade-off often be made between cheaper factor inputs per unit product and higher factor movement costs per unit product but one must also frequently balance the advantages of greater access to markets and hence lower distribution costs against a higher bill for process costs.

The industrialist, therefore, is faced with a highly complex locational problem. Confronted with locational variability in the availability and cost of raw materials and in the availability and attractiveness of markets, the locator, in his efforts to minimize production costs, must be prepared to trade off the relative costs of factor inputs against their procurement costs, distribution costs to market against the process or procurement costs associated with varying distances from the market, etc. The whole problem is an extraordinarily difficult one with the determination of optimal location a highly elusive goal.

Nevertheless, in the general case it is possible to say that locational patterns of industry are dependent upon four general factors: (1) *the movement costs of factor inputs* as affected by such considerations as freight rate structures, (2) *the costs of moving the output* to the market as affected by similar considerations, (3) *the*

locational pattern of factor input sources for a given cost of factor input (some factor input costs vary over space and cluster in specific locations more than others — the locator is always involved in a trade-off between the cost of a factor input and movement costs for that factor input), and (4) *the locational pattern of markets;* again, markets vary in their incidence and density and the locator will often be involved in a trade-off between locating close to the attractive market and minimizing distribution costs per finished product, on the one hand, and incurring a higher process cost or a higher procurement cost, on the other hand.

The significance of these factors for the locational pattern of industry, however, varies according to two other conditional factors: the industry being considered and the scale of operation for that industry. First, industries differ in their factor inputs, and therefore factor cost structures vary a great deal from one industry to another. Labor, for example, is a much more significant cost item in textiles than in the iron and steel industry. Differences in factor inputs also affect movement costs since, for example, different freight rates apply to different commodities. Industries also differ in the markets for which their output is destined; a steel plant, for example, has engineering plants as its markets while a soda bottling plant will be oriented towards the general populace as its market. The different nature of final products is also reflected in the output movement costs.

In addition to the type of industry involved, however, a further conditional factor is that a given industry can operate at a variety of scales or sizes. In some industries, such as iron and steel or automobiles, efficiency as measured by production cost per unit output increases very rapidly as plant size increases. Such economies are termed *internal economies of scale:*

▶ *Internal economies of scale are cost economies resulting directly or indirectly from the large size of an industrial firm.*

Such *internal economies of scale* are also reflected in the structure of factor costs and movement costs. In general, a larger plant will be able to obtain cost concessions on the larger shipments of raw materials and finished product involved than a smaller plant. The larger plant may also be able to obtain cut-rate raw materials as a result of its bulk buying. It is possible therefore, that costs are less elevated the bigger the scale of plant operation, and a range of scales may well be feasible within any given industry.

In conclusion to this abstract consideration of industrial location in a geographical context it would appear that one could expect localization of industries where either: (1) a critical factor input is localized at its lowest production cost, and the critical factor input has a high procurement cost associated with it relative to the procurement cost of other factor inputs and relative to distribution costs; or (2) markets are localized in space and the finished product is not very transferable relative to the transferability of the factor inputs. In other words, the critical issue underlying the localizing process is the interaction of movement costs and inhomogeneities in factor input availabilities and costs and market distributions. It is to these inhomogeneities and to that interaction that we now turn.

THE SOURCES OF HOMOGENEITY–INHOMOGENEITY IN THE PRODUCTION COST MAP

THE LOCATIONAL PATTERNS OF FACTOR INPUTS AND OF FACTOR INPUT COSTS

Raw Materials.   A glance through an economic atlas would quickly convince the reader that the different raw materials required by industries either for processing or, in the case of extractive industries, as their raison d'être, exhibit varying degrees of localization. Copper ore, for example, is much more localized than iron ore; coal is more localized than sand and gravel; while sugar cane production is much more geographically restricted in its location than, for example, wheat or rice. It is possible, therefore, to think of a scale of localization of raw materials that has highly localized or sporadic raw materials such as some of the nonferrous ores at one end, and less localized and more ubiquitous raw materials such as sand, clay, air, and water at the other end.

The impact of this variable localization of raw materials of a given production cost on industrial location depends on a number of factors. The nature of the economic activity and raw material movement costs appear to be of major significance, however. Thus, for extractive industries, such as mining or lumbering, location anywhere else but at the raw material is illogical. Coal mines are found in areas underlain by coal; the lumber industry is located at the lumber source and migrates whenever that source is depleted as with the 19th-century shift of the American lumber industry from the Upper Great Lakes to the Pacific Northwest. The localization of extractive industries, therefore, is closely related to the localization of the material being extracted; sand and gravel pits are less localized than coal mines partly because sand and gravel is a more ubiquitous material.

With an activity—such as a manufacturing activity—that is not necessarily tied to its raw material source, however, the question arises as to the feasibility of transporting the raw material to some other point in space for fabrication there; that is, to what extent is the raw material transferable? A location theorist who addressed himself to just this problem was the German economist Alfred Weber. Weber's theory was a *minimum movement cost theory* based on the idea that a manufacturer will seek out that location which minimizes movement costs for procuring raw materials and distributing the finished products. Weber was particularly impressed with the idea that many manufacturing processes involved a change of weight over the weight of the original raw material inputs and that minimization of the transportation of added weight would assist in a highly substantial manner in the minimization of total movement costs.

Looking at the problem from the viewpoint of raw materials Weber classified them along two scales, one locational and one relating to weight change. On the locational scale some raw materials were *sporadic* while others were *ubiquitous.* On the other scale, raw materials were classified according to their weight loss in the manufacturing process. Weight was an important consideration for Weber because he assumed that the freight rate per unit distance for an item varied with its weight. The freight rate on a ton of pig iron, therefore, would be much lower than the sum of the freight rates on the iron ore, coal, and limestone that had been used to produce that ton of pig iron. Clearly, therefore, loss of weight in the manufacturing process would, according to Weber, have a powerful effect on total movement costs and hence upon the location of least-cost production.

Thus if the manufacturer wished to minimize his movement cost and was engaged in a manufacturing process involving a high degree of weight loss, then location at the source of the raw materials would be the most efficient. Obviously this idea of the locational relevance of weight loss applied only to *sporadic* raw materials since *ubiquitous* raw materials could, by definition, exert no localizing influence. As far as the weight loss characteristics of the sporadic raw materials were concerned, Weber defined materials that had a heavy weight loss as *gross* while those with no weight loss were termed *pure.* These two classifications are used in Table 12-1 to develop a 2×2 classification of raw materials.

Weber calculated the *weight loss* characteristics and hence localizing effect of a *sporadic gross material* by means of a Material Index. This was measured by the ratio:Weight of Sporadic Materials/Weight of Product. Indices greater than one were regarded as predicting a least movement cost location at the site of the raw materials. Indices with values less than one indicated a market location, since in that case the production process would result in a gain of weight over that of the sporadic raw materials as a consequence of the incorporation of ubiquitous raw materials into the product. The same logic that Weber applied to weight loss in manufacturing and its effect on the least movement cost location was also applied to weight gain.

TABLE 12-1. A Weberian classification of raw materials. Raw materials with no weight loss in consequent processing were termed pure by Weber while those with a heavy weight loss were termed gross; the terms "ubiquitous" and "sporadic" are self-explanatory.

		Weight change	
		Gross	Pure
Localization of raw material	Sporadic	e.g., coal iron ore	e.g., sand and gravel cotton
	Ubiquitous	e.g., water for cooling	e.g., water for beer and soft drinks

To what extent does Weber's emphasis upon the weight loss of sporadic raw materials during manufacturing provide a good predictor of the localization of industries at the sites of such raw materials? In some cases it appears to be a powerful tool. Thus, as Figure 12-2 shows, sugar beet refineries tend to be attracted towards areas of heavy sugar beet production. This relationship is clarified when we learn that the material index for the production of raw sugar is 8,8 cwt., largely of sugar beet, being required to produce 1 cwt. of raw sugar. In the case of the location of blast furnaces for the production of pig iron, the material index is relatively high: 3 to 4 given that the weight of the resultant pig iron is only $\frac{1}{4}$ to $\frac{1}{3}$ of the initial blast furnace charge. Blast furnaces, therefore, have *tended* to be attracted to iron-ore fields as in the case of Lorraine (France), Duluth (Minnesota), Northamptonshire (England), etc., or to the coal fields as in the case of Pittsburgh and eastern Ohio, the Ruhr coal field of Germany, and the Donbas coal field of the Russian Ukraine.

Moreover, according to Weber's theory one would expect blast furnaces to be more attracted to those ore fields where the iron ore loses more weight in the pig-iron producing process (so-called lean ore with a low iron content) than to those ore fields where the iron ore loses less weight (so-called rich iron ores). Indeed there is some evidence that this is so: blast furnaces have located on the lean iron-ore field of Lorraine (approximately 30% iron content) but not on the rich iron-ore fields of northern Sweden (60% iron content) from which the ore is transported for smelting either to southern Sweden or to Germany or Britain.

Several problems arise, however, in the further application of Weber's scheme. These problems revolve largely around Weber's ideas regarding movement costs. As we pointed out in Chapter Three, movement costs are not simply a function of the weight of the item being transported or of the distance over which it is being moved. Three factors are particularly important in estimating the movement costs and hence the transferability of raw materials entering into manufacturing processes: perishability of the raw material, value per unit weight of the raw material, and the structure of freight rates.

As far as perishability is concerned, there are a variety of raw materials the condition of which will deteriorate rapidly if transported over lengthy distances. Fruit, for example, must be canned soon after picking and so the

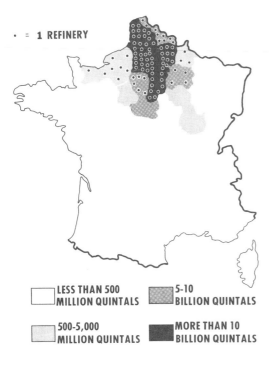

= **1 REFINERY**

☐ **LESS THAN 500 MILLION QUINTALS**

☐ **500-5,000 MILLION QUINTALS**

▨ **5-10 BILLION QUINTALS**

■ **MORE THAN 10 BILLION QUINTALS**

FIGURE 12-2. The location of sugar beet refineries and the production of sugar beet in France, 1963. Note that there are 11 other refineries elsewhere in France. There is a very striking correspondence between the two distributions due to the raw material orientation of sugar beet refining: the sugar beet undergoes a very substantial reduction in weight during the sugar extraction process.

fruit canning and preserving industry tends to be located in the areas where the fruit is produced. The production of milk products faces a similar problem unless expensive refrigeration is resorted to and therefore, in general, milk product factories are attracted to the sites of their raw materials.

In addition to this perishability factor raw materials of a higher value per unit weight tend to be more transferable than raw materials of low value per unit weight. Coal, therefore, can be shipped further than sand and gravel even though the weight loss of coal in the manufacturing process may be considerable. Similarly a ton of copper is more valuable than a ton of steel; consumers of copper, therefore, do not have to be located quite so close to the copper refinery as do consumers of steel with reference to steel mills.

Finally, there is the question of freight rate structures. As we demonstrated in Chapter Three, the freight rate on a heavier product is not necessarily more expensive than on a less weighty product, nor indeed does the cost of transportation increase in a linear manner with distance from the raw material source (another assumption of Weber). We have also alluded to the implications of such freight rate structures for the location of iron and steel blast furnaces with the effects of backhauling economies upon location at Duluth. Other important effects include the tendency for industries to gravitate to the terminal points of transportation routes because of the convex rather than linear form of the relationship between freight rate and distance. We also showed in Chapter Three that transportation cost per unit distance tends to decline with distance from the point of origin. Processing at a point midway between raw material and market where the material does *not* have to be transhipped anyway is therefore

likely to result in an additional movement cost. The location of manufacturing industries at such *break-of-bulk* points as ocean ports and regional metropolises from which an item will be distributed to a variety of small markets should be seen in this light. The location of industries processing imported raw materials such as sugar refining and nonferrous metals in port cities like San Francisco and Liverpool, respectively, are classic cases of break-of-bulk industries.

Labor. Just as for a given industry and scale of operation raw material availability and/or costs per unit of output vary from location to location so also do the availability of labor and labor costs per unit of output. Moreover, just as the unavailability or high cost of raw materials at some locations can be alleviated by transportation so the unavailability or high cost of labor per unit of output can be mitigated by labor mobility. Such movement of labor to places of demand may take the form of voluntary and individual migratory movements, or they may take the form of a collective migration resulting from localized recruitment by industrialists, or from a forced recruitment by slave traders.

An interesting facet of contemporary labor mobility is the marked reluctance of higher management to locate anywhere but in larger towns. Higher management echelons are usually of middle-class origin and of an educated background; they have instilled in them the desire for large-city amenities such as high-quality stores, theaters, restaurants, etc. Attracting such integral labor to a location outside of the major metropolis is often very expensive. When the Renault Automobile Company established a factory at Rennes in northwestern France, for example, they experienced great difficulty in recruiting qualified management from Paris where the main plant of the firm was based. A number of costly inducements had to be offered including that of ferrying the wives to and from Paris once a month by air for shopping trips! The costs of not meeting these demands of qualified management, however, may even be greater in the form of the mistakes made by the less-qualified personnel. Such labor cost factors provide an increasingly powerful force towards the localization of industry in larger urban centers particularly if the educational level of labor forces in many industries—such as electronics—continues to increase.

Below the echelons of higher management white-collar labor tends to be more highly unionized and therefore less likely to differ in its costs per unit of output. Blue-collar labor, on the other hand, is often localized in its cost per unit of output. Thus, unionization and union militancy exhibit sharp geographical variations as does the availability of the generally cheaper female labor.

Such blue-collar labor, however, is usually less mobile than its white-collar counterpart and hence certain industries with high blue-collar labor costs as a proportion of total process costs will tend to be attracted to areas offering cheap labor costs per unit of output. An outstanding example of just such a locational impact is the shift of the American cotton textile industry after 1900 from New England locations in Massachusetts, Rhode Island, and Connecticut to Piedmont locations in such towns as Roanoke, Virginia, Winston-Salem, North Carolina, Greenville, South Carolina, and Augusta, Georgia. All the evidence suggests that the high and increasing labor costs of a militantly unionized labor force in New England relative to that available in Georgia, the Carolinas, and Virginia prompted the shift.

In other cases concerning largely blue-collar labor, labor costs per unit of output may be even more localized. This is the case with some industries that require large amounts of skill and preliminary specialized training; watchmaking, pottery, and cutlery are prime examples. Such industries tend to be highly localized: pottery in Britain, for example, is concentrated in Arnold Bennett's Five Towns all within a ten-mile radius of each other; cutlery is concentrated in Sheffield, England; while watchmaking in Western Switzerland is another example of an industry requiring highly skilled labor. Such persistent localization seems to be a result of the localization of the necessary skilled labor in those places and the continual and gradual (and therefore relatively cheap) replenishment of that supply by training within the plant or within specialized community educational facilities. Industries requiring high degrees of blue-collar skill tend to be highly localized and very immobile.

Labor costs, however, must be seen in perspective. Not in all industries are labor costs a critical proportion of total production costs. Some indication of the relative significance of labor costs in a limited number of industrial sectors in the U.S.A. can be obtained from Table 12-2, which shows labor costs as a proportion of total value added by manufacturing in 1955. As can be seen, textiles tend to be sensitive to labor costs as are such industries as readymade clothing. An industry like chemicals, however, has a cost structure that is much more affected by other costs, for instance, capital costs.

Capital. Capital occurs in two forms: (1) *liquid assets* as represented by loans, checks, cash, etc., and (2) *fixed capital assets* as represented by buildings, machinery, etc. Liquid assets, of course, are fairly mobile within the nation: interest rates tend to be rather invariant within a nation at any one time. Capital equipment in the form of factories and machinery, however, is often much less transferable: a plant cannot be moved, and therefore shifts in the site of industrial operations may imply abandoning plants, the cost of which has not been completely written off by income. Such industries, therefore, exhibit a high propensity towards *locational inertia*. This is the case, for example, with iron and steel mills which have gradually lost former locational advantages in terms of access to markets and/or raw materials.

TABLE 12-2. Labor costs as a proportion of total value added by manufacture for selected industry groups in the United States, 1955. Industries such as cotton textiles, in which labor costs as a proportion of total value added tend to be high, are especially sensitive to regional variations in labor costs; industries such as electrical machinery and chemicals, on the other hand, are not.

	%
Apparel and related products	62
Leather industries	60
Textile-mill products	51
Fabricated metal products	43
Machinery (except electrical)	34
Electrical machinery	30
Chemicals	29

In other cases, the location of existing capital equipment may offer an attraction to new industries. Where the equipment is flexible as to its use—the shell of a building is a good example—it may offer a locational incentive to firms having a great deal of locational flexibility. Thus, in the South Lancashire area of England deserted cotton mills have provided premises for new firms manufacturing small household chemicals such as pharmaceutical products.

Again, as in the case of the labor factor, capital costs vary a great deal from one industry to another. Heavily capitalized industries such as iron and steel or

shipbuilding, therefore, have tended to exhibit a high degree of geographical inertia while industries such as cotton textiles, where capital costs per unit product are not nearly so critical, have shown high degrees of locational mobility.

FACTOR INPUTS AND THE SCALE OF PRODUCTION

Given that the locational patterns of factors of production may exert an impact upon the locational patterns of industries, the *scale of operations* envisaged does act as a filter through which the map of factor costs and availabilities is viewed, resources of inadequate size being passed over in favor of resources sufficiently large, cheap, and accessible enough to justify investment on the scale envisaged. It is for this reason that one frequently encounters the situation in which a resource exists at some location, but is regarded as not worth using since "commercial quantities are not available." Clearly, the idea of "commercial quantities" is defined in terms of the scale of operation envisaged. With the increase in the possible internal economies of scale available to industries one would expect to find an increasing stringency in locational choice so that, for example, only larger resources capable of supplying the needs of a large plant are of interest. This is partly reflected in the increasing localization of French iron-ore production (see Figure 12-3). In 1850 the production of iron ore was extremely widespread; by 1960 only the larger iron-ore bodies of Lorraine retained any significance.

Similarly, the large internal economies of scale accruing to many industries make locations in large labor markets (such as those provided by larger cities) particularly attractive. For the cotton textile industry, large internal economies of scale were not attainable, plants re-

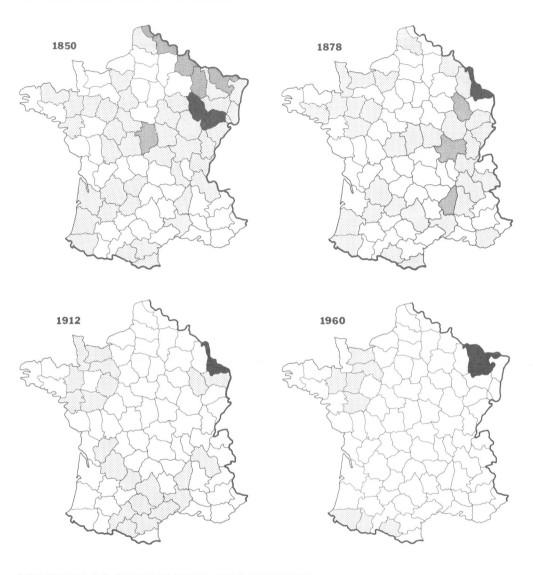

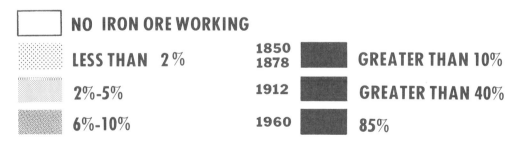

PERCENTAGE OF NATIONAL PRODUCTION

NO IRON ORE WORKING

LESS THAN 2%

2%–5%

6%–10%

1850
1878   GREATER THAN 10%

1912   GREATER THAN 40%

1960   85%

FIGURE 12-3. The historical geography of French iron-ore production. Note the increasing concentration in fewer and fewer areas. This was partly a result of the needs of internal economies of scale in iron and steel production and therefore the need for larger ore bodies only.

mained small and so were able to relocate from New England into small Piedmont towns. The cotton textile industry, however, is probably atypical in this respect: witness by contrast the recent decentralization of the American auto assembly industry to such large labor market locations as Atlanta, Dallas, Kansas City, San Jose, and Los Angeles.

Over and above the selection of the localized resources upon which to cluster, however, scale has other implications both for location at any one time and for the dynamics of locational patterns. At any one time, for example, scale dictates the rules of the competitive game between different plants for the same localized resource. Just as the size of coal mine operation determines the distance between mines—allowing for geographical variations in the thickness of coal seams—so the distance between sugar beet refineries tends to be constant within an area characterized by a similar intensity of sugar beet production. Thus, as the intensity of sugar beet production declines, we would expect the sugar beet refineries to be further apart. Figure 12-2 for France is *consistent* with this idea in that the number of refineries seems to vary directly with the magnitude of sugar beet production per *département*.

Dynamically the presence of several scales of operation in an industry frequently contains within it the seeds of locational change since the larger-scale plants will be able to undercut the price of the product from smaller-scale plants and extend their markets at the expense of those smaller-scale plants. Such a locational change has been accomplished in the state-owned British coal industry where the stimulus to the closing down of small-scale pits has not been intra-industrial competition but rather interindustrial competition resulting from the impact of oil and natural gas on British

fuel consumption patterns. Large numbers of small pits in sections of coal fields with a long history of mining have therefore been closed down (the small pits of west Durham, west Yorkshire, and south Lancashire are cases in point); while the larger pits characteristic of such areas as east Durham and Nottinghamshire can compete more effectively with natural gas and imported oil.

MARKETS: LOCATIONAL PATTERN
AND DISTRIBUTION COSTS

With many manufacturing industries markets are almost as localized as sources of raw materials. The markets for iron and steel producers, for example, are the metal-using industries primarily concentrated, in the case of the United States, in the Manufacturing Belt; the markets for textile machinery producers in New England are the cotton textile producing areas of the Piedmont and the much diminished producing areas in Massachusetts, Connecticut, and Rhode Island.

As with factor inputs, it is possible to offset the problem of localization of markets by locating relatively close to them. For some industries such accessibility is highly important while for other industries it appears to be much less critical. The problem seems to revolve largely around the transferability of the finished products to markets relative to the transferability of the factor inputs. Several factors appear to decrease the transferability of the products relative to that of the factor inputs.

First, following from Weber's theory of weight loss and weight gain, many industries undergo a weight gain during the fabricating process because of the incorporation of ubiquitous raw materials. Pop bottling is a classic example of such an industry, as is the fixing of nitrates from atmospheric nitrogen. Such an addition of weight may add greatly to the movement cost of the finished product over and above that of the input raw materials. Consequently industries like pop bottling tend to be found in more sizeable urban centers with large consuming populations.

A second factor decreasing the transferability of the finished product is that of perishability. A number of products such as bakery products are considerably more perishable than the raw materials used in their manufacture (see Figure 12-4). This is the inverse of the situation in which the raw materials are perishable and the finished products are not, leading to a raw material orientation as in the case of the vegetable canning industry.

A third factor is that of the value per unit weight or bulk of the finished product. Usually the higher the value per unit of weight or bulk of a product, the more transferable it is due to its ability to absorb freight costs without absorbing all the profit. Hence less valuable products tend to show greater market orientation

in their locational patterns than more valuable products. An interesting example of this concerns the relative market orientations of different mineral workings such as coal, copper, sand and gravel, etc. Such minerals can be ranked in terms of the value of the refined product per unit of weight. Those minerals with a high value per refined unit of weight can be produced economically at greater distances from the market than minerals with a lower value per refined unit of weight. Thus, sand and gravel and coal are usually produced close to the market while the production of such minerals as copper and tin is *not* contingent upon location close to final markets. Figure 12-5 presents a graph relating value per unit of weight to the market orientation of different types of mineral workings. Clearly it is for this reason that the major worked coal fields of the United States are found in Pennsylvania, West Virginia, and east Kentucky in the populous Manufacturing Belt despite the existence of large coal *reserves* in the Great Plains and Rocky Mountain regions. A similar situation prevails in Russia where vast coal reserves are known to exist in northeastern Siberia at a long distance from major Russian markets which are served by the closer coal producing regions of the Donbas, Urals, and Karaganda coal fields.

Fourthly, the fragility of, or bulkiness of, the product seems to affect its transferability to market. This factor seems to account for the recent decentralization of some final auto assembly capacity in the United States. The transportation cost on an assembled automobile is appreciably greater than that on the "knocked down" vehicle transported in a compact form in a crate. Increased automobile demand in such distant markets (from Detroit) as California and the South has encouraged the establishment of final automobile assembling plants at such locations as

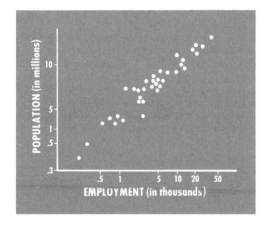

FIGURE 12-4. Employment in the bakery industry and population by state. The relationship is a close one due to the market orientation of the baking industry: this market orientation is due to the perishability of bakery products. Note, however, that the relationship is exponential.

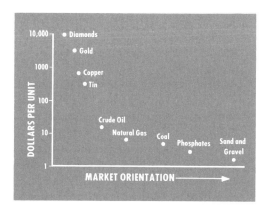

FIGURE 12-5. Mineral exploitation and market orientation. Minerals with a low value per unit of weight or bulk cannot be transferred very far before all the profit attached to the mineral is absorbed by freight charges; they tend to be worked close to the market, therefore. Sand and gravel is a good example. Minerals with a high value per unit of weight or bulk can be transferred much further and hence can be exploited much further from the market if necessary.

San Jose, California, Arlington, Texas (a Dallas suburb), Atlanta, and Los Angeles. Until recently auto demand in such areas was *not* of such a magnitude as to permit final assembly on the *scale* required for profitable operation.

Finally, as with raw material location orientations, freight rate structure seems to play a significant role in the location of various industries vis-à-vis the market. An outstanding example of the influence of freight rate structures on the market orientations of industries concerns the continued dominance of iron and steel production by the Pittsburgh area *despite* an industrial cost structure promoting increased market orientation and increasing locational disadvantage for Pittsburgh relative to the national market. A major factor at work here appears to have been the operation of a freight rate structure for steel working in favor of the Pittsburgh producer. For the first quarter of this century a *single basing point* freight rate known as *Pittsburgh Plus* was in operation. According to this

structure steel had to be sold in a given market at the same basic price as Pittsburgh steel plus the freight rate on Pittsburgh steel to that given market irrespective of the location of the steel plant in the United States. Hence Pittsburgh producers were able to quote the same price in a given market as a producer located closer to that market. This system restricted the market orientation of iron and steel production and even though the *single* basing point system was replaced by a *multiple* basing point system Pittsburgh retained advantages that were not entirely limited until legal fiat intervened in 1948. The fact that U.S. iron and steel production is not more market oriented than it is is partly attributable to such freight rate manipulation.

MARKET FACTORS AND
THE SCALE OF PRODUCTION

Just as factor input sources must be large enough and accessible enough to justify expenditure on the *scale* envisaged, so the market must be large and accessible enough. Industrial plants operate at different scales and accordingly their output is oriented to different scale markets. A soda bottling plant, for example, usually operates on a scale sufficient only to satisfy the demand in a metropolitan market. Such a market scale might be termed *local*. Other plants, on the other hand, produce on a scale which necessitates sale to a wider or *regional scale* market; breweries are an example of this, as are steel plants. And finally, there are some industries in which a single plant operates on a scale that, in a brand-competitive context, necessitates that sale be to a *national market*. Automobile production is a major example of this, as is the production of agricultural machinery.

Clearly there should be some sort of relationship between the scale of an industry, the magnitude of a market in an area, and the resultant locational decision. All the evidence we have at present suggests that this is indeed so. Thus considerable discussion has centered around the possibility of constructing an integrated iron and steel mill in New England; projections of regional consumption, however, suggest that the New England market is just not large enough to consume the full range of products of such a mill and as yet no such mill has been built.

FACTOR INPUTS AND MARKETS:
ECONOMIES OF AGGLOMERATION

So far we have tried to relate spatial clustering of plants in a specific manufacturing industry to inhomogeneities of factor input sources and markets. However, while the localization of many economic activities can be explained by an inhomogeneity or localization in a critical factor or market in combination with a severe cost constraint on the movement of the factor input or the finished product, respectively, there are a number of cases in which such an explanation would be inapplicable. At least three types of situation can be envisaged and each is described and exemplified.

1. One frequently finds a localization of industry where there is no reason based on inhomogeneities and transferability at the time of original location to account for such clustering. An example is the American typewriter industry which is geographically concentrated in upstate New York between Buffalo and Schnectady–Troy.

2. A second common locational pattern is one in which there is a relationship between localization and inhomogeneity but the localization of industry is greater than the localization of the critical factor input or

market to which it is related. Thus, cotton textile production in the United States is now concentrated in the Piedmont zone largely as a result of the labor costs prevailing there. However, similar low labor costs prevail throughout much of the South; why, therefore, did the industry cluster in Piedmont Carolinas, Georgia, and Alabama instead of also spreading into Mississippi, Louisiana, Arkansas, and beyond? Similarly in Britain pottery manufacture is concentrated in a ten-mile radius of the town of Stoke on Trent in an area known literally as "the Potteries." However, there are many locations in England and Wales which have similar factor endowments of clay and coal, but no pottery industry.

3. Finally, there is the case of localization in which location is related to an inhomogeneity that was relevant at an earlier date, but for reasons such as resource exhaustion is no longer relevant or has been replaced by another inhomogeneity with a different locational pattern. An outstanding case of this type of situation is the continued localization of iron and steel production in the Pittsburgh–Youngstown area even though one of the basic factors leading to original location there—iron ore—has been exhausted for a long time.

The reasons for such localizations unrelated or only partially related to critical factor input or market inhomogeneities can frequently be linked in part to so called *economies of agglomeration* or economies of operation that result from the clustering of similar enterprises and/or of related enterprises. Thus, the localization of a type of industrial plant in a particular area may be because the firms can gain economies from cooperation with each other or from the exploitation of jointly required services or because they are all related to some other type of plant located in that area—a plant consuming one of their products or supplying them with one of their raw materials, for instance.

Thus, economies of agglomeration provide the larger group of plants with certain cost economies not available to smaller clusters of plants. It is for this reason that textile plants cluster in the Piedmont area rather than spreading themselves throughout the South, that porcelain firms cluster in the Potteries district of England, that typewriter manufacture is concentrated in upstate New York, and that iron and steel is still produced in Pittsburgh. What processes, however, create the initial nuclei of industrial plants which permit economies of agglomeration to be obtained? At least two can be recognized: *random nucleation* and *historical inertia.*

In *random nucleation* processes it is possible to conceive of a set of locators locating their plants at random relative to an area which is either homogeneous or inhomogeneous with respect to relevant factor inputs and markets. In a true random node dispersion there is always *some* local clustering of points and so one can imagine a situation in which the clusters are able to obtain economies of agglomeration and reduced operation costs that are not available to the non-agglomerated locator. In some cases, moreover, these economies may outweigh the diseconomies to the locator of not being located on the critical and localized factor input or market or of not spreading out over the localized factor or market. Such agglomeration advantages provide the cluster with a competitive advantage which forces other, nonclustered locators either to abandon or scale down operations or relocate to an agglomeration producing the localizations that we observe today. Thus, according to this random nucleus argument, there

is no reason for the concentration of typewriter manufacture in upstate New York other than that of the existence of the agglomeration itself. Similarly, localization of cotton textile production in the Piedmont area would be ascribable to economies of agglomeration that outweigh the economies to be obtained from spreading throughout the Southern area of lower labor costs. By the economy of agglomeration mechanism, therefore, an initial random pattern is transformed into a highly localized pattern. This type of process is most applicable to the Type (1) and Type (2) situations defined above.

In the *historical inertia* case, there is no shift from one type of node pattern to another. Rather, the industry remains localized in areas where it once gained an economy due to a situation close to a localized factor input or market. The initial reason for the localization of iron and steel production in the Pittsburgh–Youngstown area, for example, was the presence of coal and iron ore there along with access to national metal-consuming markets. There is no longer any iron ore and markets have tended to shift westwards further away from the Pittsburgh area—yet there is still a concentration of iron and steel production in that area that cannot be explained by transportation costs to market and factor input prices alone. Rather the clustering of iron and steel plants around Pittsburgh seems to have led to the emergence of economies of agglomeration that have *replaced* the old locational cost advantages generated by access to iron ore and to metal markets.

LOCATIONAL DECISION MAKING AND THE COST MAP

Hypothetically, therefore, it is possible to imagine a location cost map resulting from the impact of such forces as factor input inhomogeneity, factor input movement costs, distribution costs, and savings resulting from economies of agglomeration. We have also indicated that the locations of industries bear some relationship to that cost surface such that the pattern is not a random one with respect to the magnitude of these forces.

However, we should not expect a complete relationship between a location cost pattern and actual industrial locations such that the locations of minimal cost are ultimately selected. Just as we saw how the assumption of least effort was not completely valid as an explanation of migratory movements, so in the case of the location of industrial plants we can expect deviations from a least-cost solution for several important reasons.

Firstly, and most importantly, the locator usually does not have available to him the location cost map that we have defined above. He probably has some knowledge of the configuration of the location cost pattern, but his knowledge will err on the side of inaccuracy. Few firms have the resources available to them to make a conscious inventory of location cost factors and only the bigger firms will be able to engage in a detailed evaluation of alternative locations, usually by seeking out the advice of a firm of location consultants. Not only that, but it is likely that more is known about certain locations than about others. Almost certainly, for example, there is much less uncertainty about the cost variations across a set of larger cities than across a set of smaller cities. Almost certainly, again, more will be known about the cost structures of locations that already have industry than about those that do not. Will the local council be friendly or hostile to industry for instance? There is no way of telling unless some industry is already located there. These problems are especially acute in underdeveloped nations that are defi-

cient in industrial employment; such industrial employment as exists tends to be concentrated in larger urban places.

Even if it were possible to obtain knowledge of all possible locations and costs at the time of location, however, the dynamics of the location cost situation would probably be beyond the grasp of the locator. The location cost pattern is dynamic: new production technologies or the discovery of new raw material sources, for example, can alter it in a matter of months and such events may be difficult for the locator to predict. The geographical cost configuration is also dependent upon the locational strategies of competitors in the sense that unforeseen competition can force up prices in an area. Also, as we emphasized earlier, the scale of operations operates as an important qualifying factor upon the determination of least-cost locations; yet when the locational choice is made the information one has about the future scale of operations may be only sketchy at best. As a consequence of such knowledge limitations, therefore, locational errors are frequently made and if the locational error is severe then the plant will go out of operation. Alternatively, knowledge may be inadequate, but by chance the locational error is minimal so that the plant may survive. Clearly, the locational pattern of industry at any one time represents decisions made with varying degrees of information and therefore with varying locational error.

The second reason for deviation from the least-cost location is that there are frequently forces of an external or environmental character leading to deviation; that is, a goal of the firm is not only maximization of profit, but also adherence to externally imposed laws or pressures. The most frequent type of pressure resulting in such locational deviation is political in character and it is to such political forces that we now turn.

The reasons for government interference in the locational choice process are twofold: strategic and social. In the first case, the strategic costs of certain locations in a situation of military conflict can offset the advantages of their low location costs. The concentration of population in large metropolitan centers such as Paris or London, for example, was of great concern to pre-war governments viewing the increasing possibility of aerial bombardment. The eastward shift of industry and population away from Russia's western boundary can be traced to the military threat posed by Hitler's Germany—a threat perceived to be of such a magnitude in the years immediately preceding 1939 as to offset the low locational costs for that area with its relatively rapid access to the major urban markets of Leningrad, Moscow, and the Ukraine. The resultant location of industry in Siberia and other parts of Asiatic Russia represented a not inconsiderable locational cost.

Interference on grounds of high social costs relative to low locational costs, on the other hand, takes two forms, though the two forms are frequently found together. There is first the *depressed region* case in which certain areas of high unemployment or underemployment and/or relatively low living standards are repeatedly avoided by industries thus producing a high degree of social inequality from place to place. Appalachia is a case of this nature with its relatively low incomes from an inadequately capitalized agriculture and localized unemployment in the contracting coal mining areas of West Virginia and eastern Kentucky. Further examples are common in Western Europe. Certain areas of Britain, for example, experienced unusually high rates of unemployment in the nineteen-thirties as a result of their reliance upon a narrow spectrum of contracting industries—coal, ship-

building, and steel. The British coal field areas were particularly hard hit and still have higher than average unemployment rates.

The second case of social cost is that resulting from *centralization* of industrial activity in a very small number of all possible locations. In some cases such centralization has attained a very high level. Thus, to take a very extreme case, in the Paris region there is 70% of France's employment in the pharmaceutical industry, 58% of the aircraft industry, 54% of the electrical goods industry, and 51% of the automobile industry. In Eire, 20% of the population and 90% of the nation's manufacturing employment are found within 10 miles of the capital city of Dublin. Such centralization is a social cost because industries in such locations are subsidized by society as a whole. Congestion, pollution, and lack of recreational space resulting from excessive concentration of industry must be combatted by publicly financed capital improvements and services that are *not* paid for by the industries concerned to the extent that they produce such problems. Rather they are paid by public monies drawn from *all* areas of the nation and aid people in the *centralized* industrial zone in a disproportionate manner.

Some of the solutions that governments can adopt in such a situation are relatively easy to effect. Where the government is the owner of the industry, as in the case of Russia or in the case of the British steel industry, locational policy is easily enforced. In Italy, also, the government is in a position to influence the locational policies of those firms in which it has a controlling interest; indeed semistate corporations are legally required to allocate 60% of their new investments and 40% of their total investments to the depressed area of southern Italy. Even in the more competitive

American economy such direct state interference is not unknown in times of national stress. Thus, during the Second World War the government established new iron and steel plants in western locations at Provo, Utah, and Fontana near Los Angeles in order to supply the naval shipyards of the West coast and to decrease the cost of transporting the large quantities of steel required from the East Coast to the West Coast.

In other cases the government is a provider of educational and social services that may provide important external economies for industries and act as an inducement to locators. Such institutions have been prime fodder for decentralization policies aimed at locating industry in more peripheral areas. Thus in France the government has shifted two industrially oriented educational institutions from Paris to locations where they can fruitfully interact with manufacturing industries: the Marine Engineering School has been moved to the naval shipyard town of Brest while the Aeronautical School has moved to Toulouse, the site of the Sud Aviation Company charged with the French share of developing the Concord Supersonic transport.

In cases where the government does not have control over the industrial or service facility, however, other locational strategies must be resorted to, and these have taken the form of both the carrot and the stick. Carrot-type policies have included the offering of financial inducements to industries, such as tax-free loans if the firms locate in certain specified areas or factory buildings at unusually low rentals. The latter has been one of the strategies adopted by the British government since 1945 for dealing with its depressed areas or so called Development Areas outlined in Figure 12-6. Similar policies have been employed in France in an effort to move industry away from the Paris region.

DEVELOPMENT AREAS

• TOWNS INCLUDED
○ TOWNS EXCLUDED

FIGURE 12-6. The development areas of the United Kingdom, 1960. Towns and areas indicated are those qualifying for government assistance under the 1960 Local Employment Act. Many of these areas, such as south Wales, central Scotland, and northeast England, suffered from heavy unemployment in the 1930's; today they suffer from an overrepresentation of contracting employment sectors such as coal and shipbuilding and an underrepresentation of such growth sectors as automobiles and aircraft.

However, experience suggests that the simple carrot policy has not proved effective alone and a more restrictive approach in combination with carrot-like inducements has been introduced in some countries. In Britain, for example, any projected industrial or office building with floor space in excess of 5000 square feet must obtain government approval before it can begin unless the project happens to be located in a Development Area. A similar government sanction has been applied in France to all new industrial and office construction of a certain size within a 40- to 50-mile radius of Paris.

To what extent have such locational policies been effective in inducing firms to deviate from the least-cost location predicted by the location cost map? There are a number of outstanding cases which suggest that these policies have achieved a certain degree of success. In France, for example, automobile factories have established branch plants in such locations as Rennes in depressed Britanny and in LeMans. In Britain the Development Areas have been the beneficiaries of investment programs of the major automobile firms so that since 1955 Liverpool has become a major center of the automobile industry while central Scotland (Paisley and Bathgate) and South Wales (Swansea) have also received important injections of such investment with its massive repercussions upon the location of ancillary automobile component firms. More general quantitative evidence supports this detailed picture. Thus in France within two years of the passage of a law restricting development in the Paris region the share of that region in total new national factory construction declined from 37% to just under 20%.

Nevertheless such evidence might be misleading. There is a tendency, for instance, for industrialists to be highly selective in their choice of a depressed area in which to locate. In France while new development has been banned within a 40- to 50-mile radius of Paris, it has tended to cluster just outside that radius leaving locations at a long distance from Paris almost as deprived of

industry as they were before (see Figure 12-7). Presumably firms are loathe to relocate too far from Paris for fear of losing access to the economies of agglomeration available in that metropolitan center. Such selectivity also seems apparent in the British case: depressed areas closer to the London–Midlands area of relatively rapid industrial and population growth seem to have benefited much more than those located further away in Scotland, Cumberland, Durham, or Southwest England. Liverpool's attraction for the automobile industry is a case in point, accessible as it is to the British automobile producing centers of the Midlands and London.

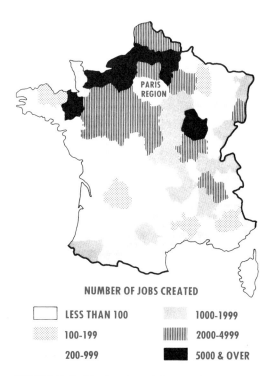

NUMBER OF JOBS CREATED

	LESS THAN 100		1000-1999
	100-199		2000-4999
	200-999		5000 & OVER

FIGURE 12-7. The location of decentralized industries in France, 1950–1958. A ban on new industrial development within 40 to 50 miles of Paris has led to some relocation from Paris of firms seeking to expand. Note, however, that locations just beyond this limit have proven much more attractive than those more peripheral westerly locations in France most in need of industrial development.

ECONOMIC STRUCTURE AND THE LOCATIONAL PATTERN OF URBAN SETTLEMENTS

In the last chapter we developed the thesis that much of the regularity and symmetry which exists in the locational arrangement of cities of different size can be traced to the forces structuring the location of retailing. In particular, we found that retailers try to get as close to their market as possible and as far away from competitors as possible. This, along with the fact of variable threshold requirements for different urban functions and a modicum of least-effort shopping behavior produced a settlement pattern in which larger places with more retail functions were spaced further apart and had larger trade areas than smaller places with fewer functions.

In explaining the relationship between retail functions and urban size it will be recalled that we emphasized the effect of the labor needs of retailing upon city size: the more functions that are purveyed the greater the labor required to purvey them and therefore the greater the population size. It should now be clear, however, that *retailing functions and associated needs for labor are not the sole generators of urban growth.* Manufacturing employment is also an important stimulator of urban growth and the locational relationship between retail employment and manufacturing employment, therefore, becomes of major importance in explaining locational patterns of cities of different size. In brief, to the extent that manufacturing employment is not subject to either the same locational rules as retailing or alternately to rules that produce similar locational patterns of population as retailing then the locational arrangement of urban places will lose whatever symmetry it has.

Particularly important in this context is the fact that the location of much manufacturing and therefore of manufacturing employment has been dependent upon *localized resources:* this has been especially true of the extractive industries which are tied to coal fields or to bodies of ferrous and nonferrous ore. Other processing industries are also attracted to localized natural resources and raw materials: iron and steel works to coal fields, sugar beet refineries to sugar beet growing areas, jam factories to fruit growing areas, etc. In still other cases, the localized resource has actually been other firms in an area and the labor force and allied services that they have generated: the English Black Country around Birmingham, for example, provides a low-cost environment for engineering concerns due to the localized economies of agglomeration that it can provide. And there are also dependencies on localized accessibility as with the importance of break-of-bulk points on coastlines.

The impact of manufacturing employment oriented to localized resources on the locational arrangement of the urban hierarchy can be clarified in a hypothetical manner by taking a linear distribution of towns of similar size (see Figure 12-8*a*). Assume that each town requires a trade area of the same size: these trade areas are indicated by dotted lines. Now assume that coal is discovered in the vicinity of town *D* and two new centers *G* and *H* develop in order to house miners and industrial workers (see Figure 12-8*b*); these towns will be of the same population size as *A, B, C, D, E,* and *F.* As a result two types of town will be represented in the area: the specialist mining-manufacturing towns and the preexisting specialist retailing towns. Specialization by *G* and *H* in mining and manufacturing, moreover, will be increased by the fact that they will have much smaller retail trade areas than the cities *A, B, C, E,* and *F* and will therefore

INITIAL URBAN PLACES AND TRADE AREAS

EMERGENCE OF SPECIALIST MINING-INDUSTRIAL CENTERS

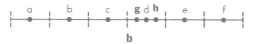

EMERGENCE OF NEW TRADE AREAS

FIGURE 12-8. The impact of specialist mining–industrial centers on the locational arrangement of urban places and their trade areas: trade area boundaries are indicated by dotted lines. (See text for explanation.)

not be able to attain the higher threshold levels for retail goods and services that *A*, *B*, *C*, *E*, and *F* can attain (see Figure 12-8*c*). *C*, *D*, and *E* will also undergo some contraction of retail business as their trade areas contract.

Several consequences for the urban hierarchy as a whole can be predicted from this simple hypothetical example. *For towns of a given population size:* (1) specialist mining-manufacturing towns will have fewer urban functions than specialist retailing centers, (2) specialist mining-manufacturing towns will have smaller trade areas than specialist retailing centers, and (3) specialist mining-manufacturing towns will have shorter distances to their nearest neighbor of a similar size than specialist retailing towns.

The evidence of such distortion is readily apparent in the world around us. Large localized resources such as those represented by coal fields are associated with large numbers of specialist mining-manufacturing towns that distort the regularity of the urban hierarchy existing prior to the Industrial Revolution. The large agglomerations of towns found in

the Ruhr area of West Germany, in Lancashire, West Yorkshire, and the Black Country in the vicinity of Birmingham, England are of this genre. In the U.S.A. the clustering of mining-manufacturing towns in eastern Pennsylvania and around Pittsburgh on the borders of Ohio, West Virginia, and Pennsylvania represent the spatial products of similar processes. Nevertheless it would appear that such urban agglomerations are less prevalent in North American than in Western Europe. In much of the Midwest and beyond, for instance, much manufacturing came after the invention of electricity had liberated manufacturing from a dependence on coal field-bound steam engines.

More generally we need to consider those countervailing forces allocating manufacturing employment proportional to urban population size. It is apparent that if the pre-Industrial Revolution urban places attract manufacturing proportional to their population sizes, there will be no specialist manufacturing-mining towns to distort the spacing of urban settlements. Indeed there have always been forces promoting such proportional attraction and thus limiting the degree to which the urban hierarchy is distorted. For many industries, for example, the urban market is the major attractive force; employment in such industries as baking, pop bottling, and newspaper manufacture, therefore, tends to show a strong relationship to urban size.

More important still, a variety of economies of agglomeration are associated with urban size: the larger a city, for example, the larger the labor reserve is likely to be, the more likely there will be necessary technical training institutes and the more likely a city will be providing public utilities of the necessary quality. It is probably for reasons such as these that larger cities tend to be much more diversified in their industrial employment structure: they are more attractive to a wider range of industries which in turn attract other industries.

It is likely that these forces are increasing in importance. Localized resources, particularly natural resources, are losing their locational attractiveness as transportation cheapens and resource extraction technology improves. Markets are increasingly centralized in a few urban centers, and the larger cities attract labor because of the amenities they have to offer. These are things that we shall explore at greater length in Chapter Sixteen. Their immediate implication for us, however, is that they are probably having a correcting influence on the distortions from symmetry exhibited by urban settlement patterns.

CONCLUSIONS AND SUMMARY

Like the town, the industrial plant can be regarded as a node. Locational patterns of industrial plants are not only interesting for their own sake, however; as a result of their association with employment generation and resultant residential expansion they can also tell us a great deal about the forces that produce real world patterns of towns.

In an abstract sense the locational problem of the industrialist or mine owner in a market characterized by perfect competition is to locate his operations in such a way as to minimize his costs and sell his product for as big a profit as possible. Furthermore, the costs which are to be minimized can be divided into two major categories: *movement costs* and *process costs.*

Theoretically it would be possible for an industrialist or mine developer to collect information on these costs for a variety of locations and plot the resultant *total costs* on a map to produce a *cost map.* Such a map would almost certainly present a picture of considerable *cost variation* over space: *factor inputs tend to be localized in their availability,* for example, as do markets. Such *localization of markets and of factor input sources* can be mitigated somewhat by *movement of final product and factor inputs,* respectively; there are, however, cost limitations on such movement which need to be traded off against possible lower process costs.

In brief, the variable *localization of industries* can be explained in terms of *environmental inhomogeneities in factor input sources and markets* and in terms of the *costs of movement* of factor inputs and finished product, respectively.

A major source of environmental inhomogeneity is represented by variation in the availability of raw materials. Some raw materials tend to be *sporadic* while others are *ubiquitous.* For the sporadic raw materials the movement cost question is important and this forms the kernel of *Weber's theory of industrial location.*

Other inhomogeneities in factor input sources include those involving *labor and labor costs.* These can be offset by labor mobility, though labor may be reluctant to move to a certain area due to its lack of amenity. Immobility is particularly apparent however in the availability of another factor input, that of *fixed capital* in the form of factory buildings and some types of machinery. While changes in the total cost map may encourage a relocational strategy, the heavy investment represented by such buildings and machinery acts as a brake on such relocation and introduces an element of *inertia* into the locational pattern.

A critical determinant of the locational relevance of certain environmental inhomogeneities, however, is the scale of production at which the industrialist operates. Small pockets of cheap labor, for instance, are of no significance to the automobile producer since his scale of operations is so large; for the textile factory, however, such small pockets may be highly relevant.

Moreover, markets also form an important aspect of environmental inhomogeneity and for some types of industry *access to market* is very important. Scale considerations are again significant, however. There should be some congruence, for instance, between the scale of a market and the most efficient size of an industry designed to serve that market: some markets just are not big enough to support an industrial plant at its most efficient size.

A final set of environmental inhomogeneities result from *economies of agglomeration.* Localization of industries frequently cannot be explained very adequately by inhomogeneities of labor cost or of raw material availability, for example. In such cases, one often finds that the cost reductions resulting from economies of agglomeration have been critical in localization, the origin of the original nucleus being quite random or a result of another environmental inhomogeneity that was once relevant but is no longer so.

If our hypothetical industrialist had such a cost map in front of him, an optimal locational choice would be relatively easy. In fact, however, for a variety of reasons locational choices often show considerable deviation from the locations predicted by the cost map. In terms of *information,* for instance, the industrialist may know more about total costs at some locations than at others; he also has to cope with the problem of predicting future changes in those costs. In addition, there are *political constraints on decisions* flowing from the government's need to guide location for *strategic* and *social* reasons.

The location of manufacturing and mining activity, however, is also of interest because of its effects on urban growth. Factories and mines need labor; this labor must be housed and serviced. The locational patterns of cities, therefore, should partly reflect the distribution of industry and of mining activity. Where the factors affecting the location of industry and mining are different from those affecting the location of retailing *or* where they produce a pattern of cities different from that created by retailing activity there is a lack of proportionality between retailing labor forces, on the one hand, and manufacturing-mining labor forces, on the other hand—a lack of proportionality manifest in the specialist manufacturing-mining town. This has locational implications in that it superimposes, in a nonuniform manner, new towns on the regular spacing of the urban hierarchy associated with pre-Industrial Revolution times.

In review, the last three chapters have concerned themselves largely with phenomena that can be treated conceptually as points—cities and industrial plants in particular. Landscapes, however, cannot be adequately described and summarized only in terms of such points as cities and industrial plants. What of the spaces between the points? What occupies such space, what are the locational patterns of such occupation, and what are the forces structuring such *space filling?* These considerations concern the next two chapters.

CHAPTER THIRTEEN

Space Filling

INTRODUCTION

To satisfy his diverse needs for food, shelter, recreation, lumber, etc., man must utilize the space around him in some way. In short, he must *fill* that space with his fields, highways, homes, parks, woodlands, and highways. It is in this *land-use* sense that we discuss *space filling* in this chapter.

That there is something here of analytical interest to the geographer can be grasped very quickly from a brief review of the recurrent geographical patterns of land use that we encounter in the real world. There are symmetries in the structuring of land use on the individual farm, for example, that involve the *allocation* of land close to the farm house to dairy pasture and the allocation of more distant fields to other uses such as arable cultivation. There are the metropolitan parks that surround most of the large American cities and the zone of nursery gardens and truck farming which is also frequently found on the metropolitan periphery.

Apart from such *concentric* patterns of land use there are also *linear* patterns. The linear patterns of industrial land use that lined the canals in the towns and cities of 19th-century England and the stores and retail services that provide so much *ribbon development* in contemporary cities are examples.

And finally, on a grander geographical scale there are *land-use regions;* large areas of a nation in which the land is or was devoted predominantly, in a readily apparent manner, to one particular type of use. In America, for example, we are familiar with the Dairy Belt of the Upper Great Lakes, the Corn Belt of the Midwest, the Wheat Belt of the Great Plains, and the Cotton Belt of the South. Such zones are also found elsewhere in the world: the French Dairy Belt is found in Normandy and is noted for its butter and Camembert, while to the southwest of Paris, in Beauce, is France's Wheat Belt.

Such *zones* of relatively homogeneous land use divide nations into a patchwork quilt of land uses that demands explanation. Within the city, residential land-use *zones* provide a similar challenge; why, for example, are certain parts of the city dominantly white middle class and why are some parts of the city just as stubbornly Negro slums?

In addition to the analytical interest of the space-filling problem, the human interest side of the coin should also be evident. In the management of his environment, man is perpetually faced with the problem of conflict between different land uses. It may be a conflict between an airport with its attendant noise and smell and a nearby residential area, or it may involve the need to mediate between conflicting demands for the use of the same piece of land. In countries like the United States and Britain, for instance, the flat, well-drained areas which form excellent sites for schools and residential housing also provide some of the most fertile farm land. In a country lacking sufficient land to feed itself, as with Britain, such a conflict may pose great problems of equitable arbitration in the public interest. Nor is this problem one that affects only Britain; the whole world faces a growing food crisis as its population increases at a much more rapid rate than does the ability of the world to feed itself. A clear set of priorities for land use are necessary, therefore, not only on the national scale but on a worldwide scale. That such priorities are likely to be established is a utopian dream in the present state of citizen awareness; a knowledge of the land allocation problem faced by each of us as citizens, residents, producers, farmers, etc. is a prerequisite for increased awareness.

This chapter attempts to offer a general explanation for the allocation of space to diverse uses; it emphasizes the economic and political factors that underlie the decision to locate a particular land use in a particular area. It also draws attention, however, to some of the factors that lead to deviations in the real world from any predictions we might care to make on the basis of the explanation; questions of awareness of all the available land-use alternatives for instance. This general exposition is followed in Chapter Fourteen by a more substantive treatment involving a case study—the allocation of space to agricultural land-use purposes. In that chapter we shall attempt to apply some of the principles derived in the present chapter.

SPACE ALLOCATION

In explaining the *allocations* that man makes of space to diverse possible uses, it is useful at the outset to distinguish between four sets of phenomena involved in this process.

1.   There is, first of all, the *set of locations* or *segments of space* that can be used by people for fields, parks, woodlands, housing estates, etc. These segments of space vary in terms of their situations—how near they are to other types of land use, to highways, to markets, to public services such as water mains, etc; they also differ in their site characteristics, such attributes as flatness, soil fertility, swampiness, depth of soil, etc. These qualities of site and situation are what make tracts of land more or less valuable for particular purposes. Thus, flat, well-drained lands are particularly valuable for large housing developments or schools, flatness and good drainage facilitating cheaper construction and obviating the need for expensive drainage works.

2.   Secondly, there is the *set of land users,* the people who want to use land for homes, for their farm crops, for their factories, parks, highways, etc. The land users may or may not be different from the landowners.

3.   *The set of landowners,* thirdly, are people who own the land but may or may not use it; rather they may rent the land to someone else. The landowner can be an important element in the pattern of space allocation; consider the problem of urban sprawl, for example, where residential development around the city takes place in a discontinuous "spotty" manner as a result of the variable reluctance or eagerness of

landowners to sell land to builders and forego the possibility of larger speculative gains at some future date.

4. Finally, there is the *set of land uses* to be assigned to different locations in space: agricultural uses, recreational uses, residential uses, etc. This is the focus of the problem: which land uses will be located where? What will be their locational patterns? The answer is provided by the interaction of land users, landowners, land uses, and locations in an *allocative* mechanism. It is to that allocative mechanism that we now turn.

A *land user* can put a *location* or segment of space that he owns or rents to a great variety of *land uses;* he can build apartments on it, grow crops, keep pigs and poultry, lay out a parking lot, or even build a zoo. From each use he can expect some *reward* or benefit, usually, though not necessarily, measurable in monetary terms. This may take the form of the price he receives for the agricultural produce he has grown on his land, of the rents he receives from his apartment tenants, or of the price he receives from visitors to his zoo, etc. Clearly, items differ in their monetary yield per acre and in maximizing his rewards the land user will have to differentiate between high-yielding and low-yielding land uses. Given two crops with the same sale price per ton, for example, the advantage will probably be with that crop having the highest yield per acre. In the same way, if the individual land user is constructing apartments on this land he can probably increase the revenue yield of his land up to a point by crowding more apartments on to it.

Each possible use to which the land could be devoted also involves some *cost.* If it is a farming operation, for example, one has to consider the cost of getting the produce to market or the cost of farm labor. The land user must also make allowances for a *normal profit;* while he will be probably looking towards some *excess profit* he will also have in mind some normal profit level below which he is not prepared to go. He must also consider such costs as that of initially draining the swamp on his land before he can use it or sinking a well if the land is outside the city limit and he wants to build a house on it. Some of the costs involved may not be immediately obvious; they may only become apparent after the land has been allocated to a specific use as, for example, the cost of contesting lawsuits brought by irate local residents who object to the establishment of a zoo in their neighborhood.

However, the costs and rewards involved in devoting a *particular* plot of land to a specific land use depend upon the intensity of land use. In order to make his land productive the land user must apply labor and capital. The more labor and capital applied to the land, the more productive that land is likely to become. The larger capital investment represented by a larger skyscraper, for instance, produces more revenue than that represented by the smaller skyscraper. The greater the amount of fertilizer and seed (capital) applied to the cropland, the greater its yield. And the more labor one applies to pruning fruit trees, spraying insecticides on the maturing fruit, and keeping the surrounding ground clear of competing vegetation, the greater the yield in terms of fruit.

A critical question, however, is what is the form of the relationship between the increasing application of labor and capital and yields in the form of revenue?

▶ *Successive amounts of productive effort in the form of labor and capital tend to yield decreasing increments of production so that a given addition of productive effort where productive effort is already high yields a lower additional return than when productive effort is at a relatively low level. Otherwise stated, production increases at a decreasing rate as productive effort increases. This is the so-called law of diminishing returns.*

Thus, if one builds an additional floor on a skyscraper the cost will be greater than the cost of the floor below but will not yield more revenue than the floor below—except possibly that chargeable for the view. As the skyscraper is built higher and higher so the cost for each additional floor increases. Similarly, in cultivation the initial day of labor has a higher revenue yield than successive applications of labor.

For each plot of land, therefore, it should be possible, theoretically at least, to work out the rewards and costs for each of all possible land uses at all possible intensities of production. Subtraction of costs from the reward produces a net reward or what is known as *location rent* or *land rent* or *economic rent*.

▶ *Location rent for a given land use at a given intensity in a specific location is the difference between the rewards flowing from that land use minus the costs involved in that use of the land, where costs include a normal profit. Location rent is not the same as rental payment.*

Location rent is divided between the land user and landowner. Ordinarily, as we shall see in a moment, in a perfectly competitive land market we would expect the landowner to convert the location rent to his own use in the form of rental payment. Usually, however, the market is less than perfectly competitive and the land user obtains a share of the location rent in the form of an *excess profit*. Where the land user is the same as the landowner then the totality of the location rent or net reward becomes *excess profit*.

We can now summarize and conclude this argument in the form of some hypothetical tables or *matrices* (see Tables 13-1 to 13-4 and Figure 13-1). The first matrix (Table 13-1) has three possible land uses as rows—urban residential, agricultural, and commercial woodland—to be allocated in some way to three locations: #1, #2, and #3; we shall call this the *land-use–location matrix*. Because rewards and costs are partly a function of the intensity of land use, we should also imagine one separate land-use–location matrix for each possible level of the intensity with which labor and capital are applied to the land.

The matrix in Table 13-2 attempts to provide some hypothetical monetary reward per acre at each location under each of the different land uses; the third matrix (Table 13-3) does the same for costs per acre. It is very important to note again, however, that costs and rewards will differ with the intensity with which labor and capital are applied. Conceptually, therefore, we should imagine a whole collection of cost and accompanying reward matrices corresponding

TABLE 13-1. The land-use location matrix.

	Locations:		
	#1	#2	#3
Urban residential			
Agricultural			
Commercial woodland			

TABLE 13-2. The reward matrix.

	Locations:		
	#1	#2	#3
Urban residential	7200	4000	2980
Agricultural	700	700	500
Commercial woodland	400	420	500

TABLE 13-3.   The cost matrix.

	Locations:		
	#1	#2	#3
Urban residential	2000	3750	3000
Agricultural	200	300	150
Commercial woodland	120	140	100

TABLE 13-4.   The net reward or location rent matrix.

	Locations:		
	#1	#2	#3
Urban residential	5200	250	−20
Agricultural	500	400	350
Commercial woodland	280	280	400

to different intensities of land use. The entries in the cells of the appropriate cost matrix are then subtracted from the entries in the respective cells of the relevant reward matrix to yield the *location rent matrix* or *net reward matrix* shown in Table 13-4.

Assuming that land users are rational economic beings who desire to maximize their net reward (their location rent) and also that they are aware of the entries in these matrices for the particular location that is relevant to them, *we can expect them to select that land use that maximizes location rent at their location at their chosen level of land-use intensity.* Thus, we would expect location #1 to be devoted to urban residential uses, location #2 to agricultural purposes, and location #3 to commercial woodland. With a map of these locations as shown in Figure 13-1 we can then draw a hypothetical land-use map indicating the land uses that our explanation—or model as social scientists call it—predicts (see Figure 13-1).

Having summarized the argument thus far, two outstanding questions may be apparent. The first, superficially at least, concerns terminology: why do we talk about *location rent?* The term seems to imply a landowner distinct—or possibly conceptually distinct—from the land user. The second question is: what factors, very broadly, affect the rewards and costs and, therefore, the location rent of a specific land use at a specific location?

To clarify the first problem, assume that there are two tracts of land owned

by two different landlords who rent them to tenants. Further assume that the rent for each tract is $5.00 per acre per week but that the highest possible location rents for the two tracts differ: $30.00 and $10.00 per acre, respectively, for Tract 1 and Tract 2. Under these conditions a tenant in Tract 1 is appropriating an excess profit after his normal profit of $25.00 ($30.00 − $5.00) per week per acre. The tenant in Tract 2, however, is only obtaining an excess profit of $5.00 ($10.00 − $5.00).

Under these unequal circumstances it is likely that a tenant in Tract 2 would obtain a higher net reward if he could rent land in Tract 1. He may therefore bid a higher rent, say $10.00 an acre for land in Tract 1, thus providing him with a possible excess profit of $20.00 ($30.00 − $10.00).

Consider this problem now from the viewpoint of the tenant in Tract 1. With an excess profit of $25.00 he knows that he is on to a very good thing. We would expect him to be prepared to offer a still higher rent of say $15.00 an acre to retain the land in Tract 1 and obtain an excess profit of $15.00 ($30.00 − $15.00)—which is still quite good. In this situation, however, it is worthwhile for the tenant in Tract 2 to outbid the tenant in Tract 1 for his land again All the time, of course, in this bidding process excess profit in the form of location rent is being increasingly transferred to the landlord in the form of rental payments.

The *ultimate* effect of such competition in the bidding of rent for land is to take

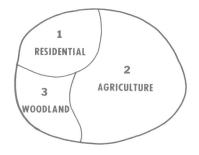

<table>
<tr><td></td><td colspan="3" align="center">LOCATIONS</td></tr>
<tr><td></td><td>1</td><td>2</td><td>3</td></tr>
<tr><td>Urban Residential</td><td>5200</td><td>250</td><td>-20</td></tr>
<tr><td>Agricultural</td><td>500</td><td>400</td><td>350</td></tr>
<tr><td>Commercial Woodland</td><td>280</td><td>280</td><td>400</td></tr>
</table>

FIGURE 13-1. The allocation of location rent-maximizing land uses to locations. Optimal land uses for the different locations can be derived from the location rent matrix above the map.

away all the land user's excess profit and to transfer it to the landowner. If excess profits are still obtainable in Tract 2, competition for the land will again eliminate that excess profit to the advantage of the landowner.

For a variety of reasons, however, this rarely happens in the extreme form discussed above, so that rental payments are seldom equal to the location rent. The land user under these circumstances will obtain some of the location rent in the form of excess profit—and farmers who are lucky enough to hold land capable of yielding a high location rent will be blessed. This is not to say that there will be *no* relationship between location rent and rental payments. In general, where land is let to tenants, actual rental payment tends to be higher where the highest possible net reward is high and lower where for reasons of, for example, infertility or inaccessibility, the highest net reward is rather low. Consequently, in the city the land close to the central business district with its advantages of accessibility tends to carry a very high

rental. Such high rental payments will also be reflected in higher land values for the outright purchase of land.

Such relationships among rental payments, land values, and the highest possible location rent at a location offer an *efficiency check* on the allocation of land uses to locations. They ensure, in a perfect land market, that only those land uses that can offer a high enough location rent will be allocated to locations with high land values and/or high rental payments. Central city land therefore, is not appropriate for half-acre residential lots; nor, on the other hand, is attractive land in the middle of an exclusive residential neighborhood likely to be offered at a sufficiently low rent or price for the developer of cheap public housing. Even where the owner of the land is also the land user the same concepts apply; the only difference is that if the user does not devote the land to that use or intensity of use which provides the highest location rent, he is only robbing himself.

The second problem which we raised above was that of the sources of variable costs and rewards. What specifically are the factors affecting the costs and rewards associated with the allocation of a piece of land to a particular type of use? Elsewhere we emphasized site and situation factors in geographical explanation. Each plot of land has certain site and situation characteristics and these both affect in a very decisive manner the *productivity* of a piece of land relative to the *costs* of managing it in a particular manner.

Site conditions exercise a very strong control over the level of yield produced by a given land use in a specific location. Certain parts of the United States, for example, are much more conducive to the cultivation of cotton than other areas. The best conditions are found in areas where there are more than 200 frost-free days per year, more than 20 inches of precipitation per year but no more than 10 inches of rain in the fall. As one deviates from these limits, yields tend to decline but, of course, where irrigation water is available, as in California and Arizona, this may not be so and, in fact, yields are higher there than in the classic cotton-growing areas of the American South.

Site conditions, however, also exercise cost controls. Thin topsoil and hard bedrock may impose severe cost restraints on development of land for housing, particularly where basements are required, thus necessitating heavier capital investment than on, say, clay land. Also, topography may affect construction costs, particularly for such land uses as factories or shopping centers which require large level areas. In agricultural land use, also, topography is often an important cost consideration, flatter areas permitting the substitution of machine cultivation for more expensive labor and horses.

Situational factors also exert an important effect upon the reward and cost levels one can expect from using a piece of land in a particular manner. An important concept here is that of the *spillover effect.* Spillover effects, as observed in Chapter Seven, can be positive or negative in character.

▶   *A positive spillover effect is an unpriced benefit to individuals in areas outside the area of the land-use decision maker; a negative spillover effect is an unpriced cost to individuals in areas outside the area of the land-use decision maker.*

An example of a *positive spillover effect* is the appreciation of residential property values consequent to the establishment of a park across the street. Housing developers attempt to obtain positive spillover effects by locating new developments close to the already urbanized area. In this way connection to water mains and sewage is feasible and the need for constructing costly wells and septic tanks is eliminated. The housing may also sell at a higher price as a result of its location relative to schools, shopping facilities, places of work, and entertainment.

The reverse side of the coin is the negative spillover effect. The deterioration in property values incurred as a result of the location of the municipal incinerator down the block is an example; air pollution drifting across the city from an industrial site inducing bronchial disorder in the population would be another such case. In the agricultural land-use context, location of cropland in the Great Plains prior to the invention of barbed wire was costly because of the proximity of the range lands and the periodic invasions of cropland by herds of cattle.

Note, however, that spillover effects are: (1) unpriced, and (2) not necessarily only local in their effect. As far as (1) is concerned the pollutor of the atmosphere does not pay compensation to the people adversely affected by his smoke and dust; likewise, though the city council can obtain some reward in the form of increased tax on the citizen whose property value has increased, the city obtains nothing in exchange for the increased resale value of the house. Nor are spillover effects necessarily only local in their effects. While urban renewal has some local positive spillover effects because it benefits the local tax base, its spillover effects are also more widely felt because the city will be less reliant on federal subsidies as a result of its new-found income.

Concepts akin to that of the spillover effect are those of *economies* and *diseconomies of agglomeration.* The *economy of agglomeration is an external benefit to individuals in the local area of the decision maker and one which is priced.*

Thus, if several housing developers develop adjacent tracts of territory they may be able to obtain an extension of gaspipes at a cheaper price than if they each developed more isolated tracts. In the same way, the cooperative dairy may produce a cost benefit to the farmer's participating by eliminating some of the middlemen involved.

The *diseconomy of agglomeration is the reverse; an external cost to individuals in the local area of the decision maker and one which is priced.* If farmers in an area specialize in a product requiring highly skilled labor, competition for this labor may force the price up with repercussions on the production costs for the product and its location rent.

Situation, however, exerts its effects on the location rent of a piece of land for a specific land use not only through negative and positive spillover effects and economies of agglomeration. The use of land in a certain manner frequently requires costly *movements* connecting that piece of land to other locations. The use of land for residential housing, for example, implies a commuting cost and the higher that commuting cost the lower the location rent is likely to be for housing. This is demonstrated rather graphically in the case of land values around London. In the period 1960–1964 residential building land per acre cost 32,000 pounds within 10 miles of the city center, 17,000 pounds between 10 and 20 miles, 8500 pounds between 20 and 30 miles and about 3000 pounds per acre at a distance of 65 to 70 miles from the capital. We shall find that similar problems are encountered in the evaluation of land for agricultural purposes where the resultant product incurs a heavy transportation cost to market.

Of course, the land-use decision maker is faced with a wide variety of intensities with which he can apply labor and capital to his land. Should he irrigate or dry farm? Should a ten-story or five-story house be built? These are questions of the *intensity* of land use and will be strongly affected by the cost of labor and capital available. In poor agricultural societies, labor is often cheap and capital is expensive so that intensification takes the form of applying large amounts of labor to, for example, the construction of terraces for irrigated rice and to transplanting the rice and growing another crop the same season. Under such circumstances of intense application of labor, yields per acre are very high. In more industrial, wealthier nations, on the other hand, labor is much more expensive relative to capital and so intensification takes the form of labor-extensive land use with high yields per employee but lower yields per acre.

The problem of intensification needs to be seen, however, in the context of *prices* received for an acre's product and in terms of the *law of diminishing returns.* Increasing intensification results in a lower additional increment of output per acre per additional increment of labor and capital, and the critical question is: are prices sufficiently high to justify intensification? If prices are high then intensification will be worthwhile, but if they are low then the converse will apply. A critical control of prices is demand for the product. In Britain in the 1930s the price for an acre's wheat was so low compared to the price that could be obtained from building houses on the land that the urbanized area expanded relative to the agricultural area of the country—and at a pace that has not been equalled in the more affluent post-1945 years. High demands convert into high prices which convert into more intensive land uses; witness the relationship in the United States between urban size and the extent of skyscraper development (an indicator of intensive urban land use)—a relationship, moreover, that is mediated by the high demands for land associated with larger cities.

Location rent as a function of the rewards and costs associated with a particular land use, moreover, is dynamic. Increases in urban population result in changes in the demand for urban land and hence higher prices for devoting land to that purpose. Changing accessibility relationships also alter location rents for different uses. Consider, for instance, the rapid appreciation in land values that takes place around projected intersections on a city bypass months before the bypass is constructed. Access to such knowledge, is clearly vital; moreover, it frequently hinges on the relationship that a land user enjoys with the local political system making decisions on such matters as the location of bypasses. It is to *information factors* and *political factors* of this kind that we turn next.

DEVIATIONS FROM THE ALLOCATIVE MECHANISM

The type of allocative mechanism that we outlined above is a highly simplified model of reality. In the real world there are a number of factors that lead to systematic deviations from the land-use allocations predicted by the theory outlined here; the availability of information and political factors both need to be taken into account. Each of these sources of deviation will be discussed in turn.

INFORMATION FACTORS

An initial consideration in evaluating the allocative mechanism that we have developed above is that it contains within it *the assumption that land users — and landowners — are aware of all the possible uses to which their land could be devoted and in particular of the use that would yield the highest location rent.* This assumption, of course, is not valid. That there are lags in the acquisition of knowledge regarding land-use possibilities is borne out by the conclusions of spatial diffusion studies. The spatial diffusion of a number of agricultural innovations in Sweden such as pasture subsidies, new seed types, and measures against bovine tuberculosis have been examined and it is readily apparent that some land users are more aware of the innovation and the possible land-use changes implicit in it than others.

Knowledge of land-use possibilities and of the location rent attached, however, implies some knowledge of future events, such as the state of the market or the weather. A particularly interesting aspect of this uncertainty problem concerns the behavior of landowners on the edge of an expanding city. Should a specific landowner sell his land for building or keep it in agriculture? If one sells, many others may also be selling land at the same time, lowering the price below that location rent obtainable from retaining the land in agricultural use and selling it at a later date. The unpredictability of the situation leads to a random element in the pattern of land sales as the more confident landowners sell and the more cautious keep their land in agriculture. The result is the spotty urban sprawl pattern so characteristic of the fringes of many cities.

The same problem is inherent in agricultural land-use planning. If the prices for wheat look promising and one decides to allocate a large proportion of one's land to wheat, what are the chances of large numbers of other farmers doing the same, a resultant glut and precipitous decline in prices? One effect of this is for the farmer to spread his risks over several land uses; the farm specializing in one land use and one alone is therefore a relative rarity, though in an area such as the Great Plains it took a number of years to *learn* the dangers of overconcentration on wheat and to revert to a more mixed system of agricultural land use.

POLITICAL FACTORS

A frequent finding associated with the close examination of geographical land-use patterns is that while the land-use allocations of the competitive market are economically efficient (location rent maximizing) they may not be so efficient from the *social* or *public* viewpoint. It has been pointed out that in Colorado, for instance, the irrigated land, which is so valuable for the cultivation of sugar beet, is rapidly being encroached upon by residential developers and public highway departments who find the flat stretches of terrain exceedingly attractive for houses and highways. The result is a net contraction of the area under sugar beet—hardly a reassuring thought considering the continuing growth of world population and of the demand for food and for the land upon which to grow it.

Such conflicts of private and public interest are frequently used to justify political interference in the allocation of land uses to locations, and such interference may be manifest in both formal and informal ways. A highly common method of regulating land use in the public interest is the *zoning restriction*. One form that such zoning restrictions take is that of the British *Green Belt*. Land around cities is always highly valued by private developers and by the householders for whom they build houses. Given the free operation of a private land market, such land would assuredly be developed in the face of sufficient demand for new housing. Such development, however, conflicts with the public

interest. It removes the citizen even further from the aesthetic and recreational pleasantries of the surrounding countryside. An effort to safeguard the public interest in this context in Britain has been Green Belt legislation. Green Belts are zones surrounding major cities in which new building is subject to very rigorous restrictions—usually it is only permitted within the boundaries of existing villages. Geographically the implications are very interesting; developers "jump" the Green Belt and locate just beyond the outermost edge where restrictions are relaxed and where home buyers will still be within commuting distance of the city.

The United States has no comparable Green Belt legislation, and the geographical forms of growing cities in the two countries are correspondingly rather different with residential development going on at a greater distance from city centers in Britain than in the United States (see Figure 13-2). That is not to say that the American scene is devoid of such legislation; every municipality has zoning legislation covering its own restricted geographical area and manipulated in the context of a conception—albeit a frequently myopic one—of the public interest and of the spillover effects that must be manipulated to sustain that interest. Thus, wealthy municipalities are attractive for a variety of housing developers since they frequently offer quality school systems for the children of home purchasers. While it is in the individual interest of every home purchaser with children to locate in such a community the arrival of lower-income families may not be in the "public" interest since while they will contribute very little to that tax base which keeps the school system a quality one, they may burden the school system with their children. By zoning residential land only for low-den-

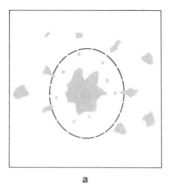 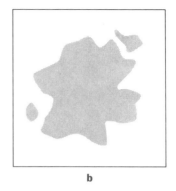

a   b

FIGURE 13-2. Alternative urban forms in the United Kingdom (*a*) and in the United States (*b*). In the United Kingdom the delimitation of a Green Belt around the city (within the dotted line) within which new building is strictly controlled has encouraged urban development at some distance from the city. In the United States, where there is no comparable legislation, new urban development takes place more on the periphery of the already built-up area of the city.

sity housing (large half-acre to one-acre lots, say) the wealthy community can safeguard its interests by ensuring that the newcomers will be of an adequately middle-class character.

Such zoning regulations are relatively passive factors within the context in which locators must operate. They do not *force* locators into particular areas; the locators are always left with the option of the locational status quo. Land-use planning, however, has also obtained more sharp and positive tools for controlling and channeling land use allocation into publically desirable ends. *Compulsory purchase for urban renewal* is one such case where although renewal is probably opposed by the homeowners in the area, renewal may benefit the city as a whole through the appreciation of property values and hence of the city tax base following from the construction of some desirable residential or commercial property on the cleared area. Whether the public interest is accurately conceived in such cases is highly debatable. While it is difficult to put accurate assessments on the public benefits (in the form of a higher tax base) and on the private costs

(in the form of displaced neighborhoods and business) urban renewal proponents usually have much more articulate and influential protagonists to argue their case than the quasi-slum dwellers about to be "renewed." Therefore, in land-use planning also, the lot of the poor and the underprivileged is not a happy one.

A major problem in such political interference, of course, is the fact that different groups have different conceptions of the public interest that is to be served by controlling the locational pattern of land uses. A common conflict in Britain occurs between *economic- and leisure-oriented* views of the public interest. Cities such as Birmingham, Liverpool, and Manchester which provide a large part of the stimulus for Britain's continuing economic growth have to rely on distant highland areas of Britain for the satisfaction of their increasing water demands. Birmingham and Liverpool, for example, obtain water from reservoirs in Wales while Manchester obtains much of its water from reservoirs in the picturesque Lake District. Demands for increased reservoir construction and the flooding of more land for this purpose are usually met by a flurry of opposition from Britain's well-organized nature lovers on the grounds that such development represents a further assault of Mammon on some of the few remaining attractive areas of the country. The argument is clearly a good one because not only do reservoirs obscure once beautiful country but they also impose ugly concrete structures and have (in the past at least) restricted the access of tourists to the water for fear of pollution. In Wales, the Welsh nationalist conception of the public interest ("Wales as a servile colony supplying its water to a rapacious imperial master") represents another source of conflict.

In such conflict situations it is exceedingly difficult to establish land-use allocation priorities "in the public interest" simply because it is so difficult to determine what exactly that public interest is! More often than not it represents the conception held by the planners of what is good for the public. Planners, being largely middle class in origin and being more accessible to middle-class pressures, have a built-in bias towards that viewpoint. In the United States this biased viewpoint is apparent in the construction of urban freeways which aid the suburban middle-class whites but do very little for the lower class and blacks in the inner city who need public trans-

port rather than freeways. One wonders if the violence of recent American urban history would have been very different if municipal resources had been devoted to restricting the use of the private automobile within cities and establishing viable, unsubsidized public transit authorities. This is a theme to which we shall return at some length when we consider the city in greater detail in Chapter Fifteen.

Political interference in the land-use allocation mechanism, however, need not necessarily be formal in manner involving legally established councils, planning commissions, etc. It is also possible to envisage more informal but no less powerful pressures on land-use decisions. It is not uncommon, for example, for private residential developments to establish housing committees to oversee the architectural plans of people planning to buy lots in the development. Such overseeing and control forestalls the possibility of negative spillover effects on local property values that might flow from establishing a one-room shack or piggery in what is a select residential neighborhood. Whether the influence is formal or informal, however, it is clear that the allocation of land does not operate completely in the unfettered way that we outlined earlier in this chapter.

CONCLUSIONS AND SUMMARY

To satisfy his diverse needs, man needs space on the earth's surface; space on which to grow his crops, build his homes, his roads, his schools, and his factories and space to set aside for recreation. In devoting space to various uses we find that certain *geographical patterns of land use* emerge suggesting the operation of certain systematic factors producing such order as seems to exist. Not only that but land use is also closely related to the problem of *locational conflict;* some land uses are incompatible with one another and their close proximity is likely to result in costly litigation and general human wear and tear. The general problem of locating airports is critical in this respect.

In the allocation of land to various uses four sets of items are involved: the *set of locations* to which uses are to be assigned, *the set of landowners*, the *set of possible land uses*, and *the land users themselves*. In the *allocation* process the critical concept is that of the *location rent* yielded by a particular land-use type at a particular level of *intensity*. *Location rent* is the *net reward* involved in a particular land use: the reward per acre minus the costs involved in producing that reward with the land users normal profit appearing on the debit side of the account ledger. The rewards per acre from a particular land use are highly sensitive to such factors as the yield per acre and the price of a given unit of the commodity, whether it is a ton of potatoes, a bushel of wheat, a ticket to the zoo, or a parking fee.

The cost of production, on the other hand, is sensitive to both *site* factors (such as topography, land drainage, and climatic hazard in the form of, for example, severe winters upon factory heating bills or hail) and to *situation factors*. The situation of a plot of land dictates the production costs associated with a particular land use through *spillover effects* and *economies of agglomeration* and also by the costs of moving (moving to market or commuting) associated with a particular type of land use. Of course, the yield and, therefore, the reward can be increased by intensifying the application of labor and capital as in irrigation or fertilizer-intensive agriculture. However, there are limits to such intensification; not only is it costly in the form of labor and capital but there is also the *law of diminishing returns*, that is, successive applications of units of labor and capital produce successively smaller increments of product.

Theoretically the land user should be able to establish the *location rents* for different land uses at different intensities of land use and then select the maximum one. If he owns the land, he will appropriate the location rent for his own purposes; if he is a tenant then the landowner will share the location rent with him, the landowner taking his *rental payment* and the tenant taking his *excess profit*. Under conditions of perfect competition the landowner would take all the location rent leaving no excess profit to the farmer. In practice this rarely happens; the more usual situation is one in which tenant and owner divide the location rent. Where maximum location rents are high, both rental payments and *land user incomes* tend to be high. *Land values* follow the same general pattern.

The allocational mechanism outlined above, however, is a simplification. It depends on certain assumptions—such as perfect competition for land—that do not exist in reality. Major interfering factors include differences in the *information held by land users and landowners* regarding prices, land-use alternatives, and so on, and also interference in the land market by government institutions in order to protect various conceptions of the *public interest* as opposed to the *private interest* of the individual landowner or land user. The *zoning ordinance* is an outstanding case of such interference.

The view of land-use allocation presented in this chapter is a very broad one. We have drawn our examples from both urban land development and the development of land for agricultural land use. The picture lacks some of the clarification that often comes from a more detailed substantive canvas. The next chapter attempts to paint such a canvas in the form of a discussion of agricultural land-use patterns. It is against the backdrop of this, more general chapter, however, that the contents of the next chapter must be viewed.

CHAPTER FOURTEEN

Land Use Patterns: The Case of Agricultural Land Use

INTRODUCTION

The last chapter elaborated a general explanation of land-use allocation in an attempt to shed some light on the diverse geographical patterns of land use in the world around us. This chapter illustrates those ideas a little more concretely by developing a case study—locational patterns of agricultural land use.

Maps of agricultural land use are classic assignments for geographic field studies. They have also been a common object of governments seeking some assessment of the uses to which the national domain is put. Britain, for example, organized a very large Land Use Survey in the 1930s producing a field-by-field inventory of land use that is staggering in its detail. One of the major features of the maps produced by such surveys is their complexity. Not only do actual land uses vary over space but they also vary a great deal over time: the patterns revealed by the British Land Use Survey of the 1930s revealed patterns very different in their outline from those manifested by 19th-century tithe maps for the same areas—and indeed from maps which have been produced since 1945. Not only that but the intensity of agriculture is seen to vary—and from one scale to another: from field to field, from county to county, from state to state, and so on.

The aim of this case study is to try and reduce all of this complexity to some sort of order while applying our land-use allocation model (along with its qualifications) to land-use patterns in diverse areas of the globe. The first step is to refine the allocative mechanism discussed above and to redefine its concepts to apply more accurately to the agricultural case. The second step will be to apply it to our explanatory purpose; and in the third step we shall examine deviations in actual land-use patterns from the predictions of the allocative mechanism.

THE ALLOCATIVE MECHANISM APPLIED TO THE CASE OF AGRICULTURAL LAND USE

In the last chapter we identified *location rent* as the critical determinant of land use: land in the presence of perfect knowledge and the desire to optimize the return on one's investment is assigned to that use characterized by the highest location rent. Location rent was defined as the difference between the rewards from using the land in a certain way and the costs of such utilization, a normal profit being considered as one of the costs of utilization.

In the agricultural land-use case the *reward* from the land use is a function of two factors: (1) the *price* of a unit of a particular agricultural commodity; for example, the price of a bushel of wheat or of a gallon of milk. The price should, in the absence of political interference, be an expression of supply and demand with prices rising as demand increases and/or as supply decreases. (2) the *yield* of the land in, for example, bushels of wheat per acre, gallons of milk per acre, or eggs per acre. The major determinants of yield are site characteristics of fertility, climate, and so on, and the intensity with which capital and labor are applied to the land. In summary, the reward per acre received by the farmer for his efforts is equal to the product of the yield per acre in units such as tons, or bushels, and the price of one of the same units on the market.

Costs, on the other hand, are more complex in their determinants. There are first the *production costs* involved in carrying out a particular land use at a particular level of intensity. Such costs are partly a function of the physical environment—they are likely to be higher on swampy land than on well-drained land, for instance. It is also important to note once more the intimate tie between costs of production per acre and the yield per acre; according to the *law of diminishing returns,* as costs per acre increase so yields increase at a decreasing rate.

The second major component of costs is *movement costs.* A great deal of movement is required in agricultural operations: for example, livestock and crops must be moved to market, seed must be transported from the seed agency, and labor must get to the fields. The most significant movement costs, however, are the *marketing costs* and the *input movement costs.* The marketing cost is the cost of getting the product to market; the market may be a distant consuming city or it may, alternatively, be a local processing plant that absorbs the ultimate costs of the movement of the processed product to the consumer. Here we define the marketing cost as the cost of moving one acre of farm produce to market. This cost varies rather critically from one agricultural product to another.

The second type of movement cost is that represented by the cost of moving inputs such as food, supplies, and labor. Here it is conceptually useful to distinguish between the cost of moving labor from farmstead to field, and the cost of moving inputs from their sources to the farm. The cost of moving the labor per acre is largely implicit in the relationship between the wage received by the labor and time actually spent in productive effort. We can establish an analogous term for moving the other inputs required by one acre. Hence, in summary:

Location rent per acre
= Market price received per acre
− Production cost per acre
− Movement cost of an acre's product
− Movement cost of an acre's labor
− Movement cost of an acre's inputs

Of course, the expression above does *not* make allowance for agglomeration and spillover effects. These will be merely reflected in the production and movement cost components of the expression. One reason for not taking a separate accounting is that the effects of spillover are very difficult to give a precise monetary value to; the same applies to some though not all economies and diseconomies of agglomeration. It is our intention to take a separate accounting of such effects in our discussion below.

In our more detailed treatment we commence by considering cost factors and their effects on location rent and ultimate land-use patterns and then proceed to a consideration of the effect of the reward or benefit factors. We then discuss the light that the land-use allocation mechanism sheds on *changing* land-use patterns over time, and we conclude by examining the sources of deviation from land-use predictions that we would make on the basis of the allocation mechanism.

THE COST FACTORS

(1) Marketing Costs. The clustering of land uses and land-use intensities around larger urban markets or along lines of transportation leading to those urban markets suggests some relationship to the marketing costs for agricultural commodities. In terms of intensity of farming there are a number of interesting cases to which we can refer. Farming in the vicinity of urbanized areas (i.e., major markets for agricultural products) often appears to be more highly capitalized, technically sophisticated, and associated with higher median incomes than farming at a distance from such areas.

As Figure 14-1 shows, taking the case of California the highest values of

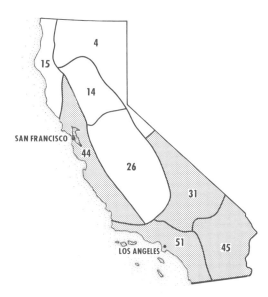

FIGURE 14-2. Expenditures in dollars per cropland acre in California, 1954. Note the intensity of the agriculture around the urbanized areas of Los Angeles and San Francisco. The irrigated agriculture of the southeast is also highly capital intensive.

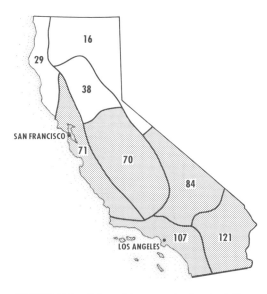

FIGURE 14-1. Value of farm production in dollars per cropland acre in California, 1954. Stippled areas have above average values; note relatively high values in the vicinity of the urbanized areas of Los Angeles and San Francisco and also the high values in the desert areas of the southeast of the state. Cropland there is of very small acreage, but it is almost all irrigated producing very high yields per acre.

farm produce per cropland acre apart from these in the irrigated southeast are found in heavily urbanized southern California which includes the cities of Los Angeles and San Diego. Market-oriented locational patterns are even more evident for another indicator of agricultural land-use intensity—farm expenditures per cropland acre (see Figure 14-2). Two of the most intensively farmed areas include southern California and the central coastal region on either side of San Francisco. The less urbanized central valley and northern sections of California are considerably less intensively farmed.

Likewise, when we turn to the spatial "sorting" of specific land-use types around markets or lines of transportation there is some interesting evidence available. Thus in the contemporary United States the more densely settled northeast with its large urban markets specializes in the production of perishable or bulky products such as milk and truck-farm products (as in New Jersey and Connecticut) and poultry products. In fact, for the United States as a whole every urban center seems to be surrounded by a *ring* of dairy farms supplying liquid milk for the consumer—even in such environments as those of Phoenix, Arizona, Salt Lake City, and Albuquerque, New Mexico. As one gets further away from larger urban markets, more of the milk seems to be devoted to local butter production; such is the case with Minnesota and Iowa, for instance.

Elsewhere, analogous *linearities* along the lines of communication leading to market have been noted. Consider the settlement of the North American Prairies in the late 19th century, for example. Two modes of transportation were available: the railroad and the horse and cart. Farms near the railroad found it profitable to produce wheat for shipment by rail as grain. Farmers further away from the railroad, however, who would have found themselves involved in repetitive, lengthy horse-and-cart trips, developed a more diversified farming economy with the wheat providing feed for cattle; the cattle then provided their own locomotive power to the nearest railroad depot for shipment east.

In brief, there seem to be a variety of agricultural land-use patterns that *suggest* some sort of relationship to access to market. Precisely what, however, is that relationship connecting intensity of land use and land-use type, on the one hand, and market access considerations on the other hand? Consider the source of the farmer's location rent as specified above. If agricultural products are being transported to a city for consumption, then the profit that the farmer obtains is clearly related to the cost of transportation to market (i.e., the movement cost of an acre's product). If transportation costs decline with distance from the city (however irregularly) then, *all other things being equal,* for a given

land use a farmer closer to the city will make a larger profit than a farmer further away. That is, if we have one land use and one land use alone in an area; and market price, production costs, and the movement costs for labor and other inputs do not differ at all from place to place; but movement cost varies such that farmers for which distance to market is greater incur greater movement costs: then one can expect a lower location rent the further one is away from the market. This idea is illustrated for a hypothetical case in Table 14-1.

In view of this situation, in which excess profits are squeezed by increasing transportation costs with distance from market, how can the distant farmer maintain his profits despite his locational disadvantage? An important area of flexibility for the farmer lies in the manipulation of his *production costs.* According to the law of diminishing returns a given decrease of input should be

TABLE 14-1. Marketing costs and location rent. Yp = market price; k = distance from market in miles; f = freight rate per mile; Yfk = movement cost; PC = production cost; LR = location rent = $Y_p - (Yfk + PC)$; with increasing distance from market more and more of the profit, and therefore location rent, is consumed.

Yp	k	f	Yfk	PC	LR
80	1	1	1	66	13
80	2	1	2	66	12
80	3	1	3	66	11
80	4	1	4	66	10
80	5	1	5	66	9
80	6	1	6	66	8
80	7	1	7	66	7
80	8	1	8	66	6
80	9	1	9	66	5
80	10	1	10	66	4
80	11	1	11	66	3
80	12	1	12	66	2
80	13	1	13	66	1
80	14	1	14	66	0
80	15	1	15	66	0

associated with a less than proportional decrease of output; that is, the farmer, by decreasing the intensiveness of his farming practice, reduces the cost of producing a given unit of wool, or wheat, or whatever. He can therefore curtail the amount of labor he applies to his land or the amount of fertilizer in order to maintain his profits at a level similar to that experienced by farmers closer to the market. The logical consequence of this, all other things being equal, is a decline in the intensity of agricultural production with increasing distance from the market.

Some products cost more to transport a given distance than others: products like milk, for example, are perishable and require specialized transportation equipment. Other products, such as wheat, are much cheaper to transport over a given distance. Hence, for some products the profit is eaten up by transportation costs with distance from market at a faster rate than for other products. Therefore, at certain locations, the production of some items is just not profitable because they are too expensive to transport to market; at other locations, on the other hand, there is a choice of products which, if farmers are trying to maximize their incomes, will be decided by the relative profit margins of the crops. Thus, Figure 14-3 presents schematically the probable relationships between profit for different agricultural products and the distance from London in the early 19th century. At point *x*, milk would no longer be profitable since it is beyond the range of economical transportation to market; farmers at *x* would have a choice between hay and wheat, a choice that on the basis of greater profitability would probably be decided in favor of wheat.

Several implications follow from this analysis. The first is that if an agricultural commodity can be processed in

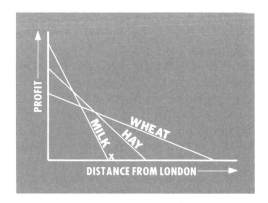

FIGURE 14-3. Probable relationships among profit, land use, and distance from London in the 19th century. The relationship between profit or location rent, on the one hand, and distance, on the other hand, tends to vary from one land use to another. The result is that different land uses are more profitable than other land uses at different locations. Thus dairying is more profitable than hay or wheat closer to London and wheat is more profitable than either hay or dairying further away from London.

such a way as to become *more cheaply transportable,* then it may be possible to carry on that land use a long distance from market. The transportation cost per mile on an acre's production of butter, for example, is much, much lower than the transportation cost per mile on an acre's production of milk and so butter tends to be produced at a greater distance from urban markets than liquid milk. In the same way canning and freezing of vegetables and fruit allow highly profitable truck farming and fruit farming in Texas, Florida, and California at a considerable distance from the large urban markets of the northeast and allow these areas to compete vigorously with the truck farmers of, say, New Jersey.

The second implication is that decreasing intensity of production is not the only method of trying to sustain location rent and the excess profits that flow from location rent in the face of increasing marketing costs. The farmer can also choose to farm more land. Consequently around many of the larger cities there does seem to be some relationship between distance from the city and farm size, with smaller farms being found largely in the vicinity of the city and larger farms being found further away. Another factor producing this locational pattern, of course, is the problem of land costs. As location rents tend to increase with decreasing distance to major urban markets so farm land becomes more expensive to buy or rent imposing a constraint on farm expansion.

Finally, the arguments developed above help us in understanding the locational patterns of commercial and subsistence agriculture in the world today. For most of the worlds' farmers farming is a matter of producing food for oneself and for one's family. Over most of Asia, Africa, and Latin America one farms to subsist and not to sell. One reason for this should now be clear: the major world demands for foodstuff imports and trade in foods are found in North America and Western Europe and most surplus foodstuffs must move over oceanic trade routes to these areas. This requires adequate railroad links for getting foodstuffs from continental interiors to the coast—a facility that, as we saw in Chapter Eight, most of the underdeveloped countries of Asia, Africa, and Latin America do not have. Commercial agriculture on these continents, therefore, is usually confined either to areas that have adequate railroad transportation (such as the Pampas of Argentina), or to the areas surrounding the growing cities, or to the coastal lands where cheap water transportation is possible. It is not accidental that plantation agriculture in the tropical zones of Africa, Asia, and Latin America and oriented towards large-scale production of such tropical foodstuffs and raw materials as sugar, rubber, cacao, and palm oil for Western

markets has been carried on largely along the coasts of such zones. The inland areas with their extreme problems of access have remained devoted to subsistence farming.

(2) Input Movement Costs. Other than marketing costs, the farmer incurs other movement costs. The most outstanding are the costs of getting labor to fields and of moving such inputs as fertilizers from their source to the farm. Both these movement considerations exercise constraints upon the land-use type and land-use intensity decisions of the farmer. The labor movement problem appears to be especially critical for explaining land-use variations on the individual farm; the movement of other inputs seems to be more important for explaining variations from one farm to another. Each of these problems is treated in turn.

When we examine the use that a farmer makes of fields on his individual farm, two types of locational predictability are apparent, both involving the distance from farmstead to field and both resulting from similar considerations.

First, one often notes striking differences between the use to which a field close to the farmstead is put and the use made of land further from the farmstead. In the United Kingdom this is most usually evident in the reservation of the fields closest to the farmhouse for dairy cattle pasture. The locational patterns involved, however, can be more complex than this. In Sicily, for example, farmsteads are located in the villages and a concentric pattern of land use around the village testifies to the farmers' discrimination between fields closer to the farmsteads and fields further away. First comes a zone dominated by the vine and other tree crops; this is followed by a zone in which olives replace the preponderance of vines. The second zone then gives way to an outer zone in which unirrigated land is preeminent.

A second set of examples of locational predictability refer to variations in yield with distance from the farmstead; such variations in yield appear to reflect variations in the intensity with which the land is farmed. Studies in Finland, for example, have focused upon variations in the gross and net output (in monetary terms) per acre with increasing distance from the farmstead. As Table 14-2 shows, both gross and ·net output have a clear tendency to decline with distance in a fairly regular manner.

How can such concentricities in type and intensity of land use be accounted for? An explanation that is both simple and logically appealing can be derived by considering the productivity of the unit period of labor at different distances from the farmstead. Let us assume that we are considering a farm in which all fields have the same productive capacity: that is, the application of a given amount of labor to a given field will produce the same yield as the application of that same labor to another field. The fields, however, differ in their distance from the farmstead: some are close to the farmstead while some may be at a considerable distance particularly if the farm is fragmented. These variable distances affect the time it takes to get to a given field. Let us further assume that an hour's labor is made up of two components: (1) movement effort as measured by the time it takes to get to a field, and (2) productive effort as measured by the time spent in productive effort; this will decline with distance from the farmstead while the proportion of time spent in movement will increase. Now labor is being paid whether that labor is involved in movement effort or productive effort; the amount of productive effort per dollar expended, therefore, declines with distance from the farmstead. Consequently if the farmer allocates as many days to the cultivation of the furthermost fields as he does to the nearest fields on his farm, there will be strong differentials in the productive effort applied to the two sets of fields, and this should be reflected in a decline of yields with distance from the farmstead.

This is not the whole story, however. A moment's reflection will show you that the farmer can manipulate the situation in order to increase the productivity and hence production of his whole farm. In order to do this he must increase his productive effort and reduce his movement effort. This can be achieved if he consciously applies less labor to his more

TABLE 14-2. Gross output per hectare, net output per hectare, and distance from farmstead for 3 sample areas in Finland; 0-0.1 kilometers = 100. Note the decline in both gross and net output with increasing distance from the farmstead. To what might this be attributed?

| Distance in kms. | WIIALA | | VIRRI | | SUOMELA |
	Gross output	Net output	Gross output	Net output	Net output
0-0.1	100	100	100	100	100
0.5	92	78	89	67	83
1.0	84	56	80	50	68
1.5	77	34	73	40	56
2.0	69	13	67	33	46
3.0	· · ·	· · ·	57	25	32
4.0	· · ·	· · ·	50	20	· · ·
5.0	· · ·	· · ·	44	17	· · ·

distant fields; this will cut down movement effort and permit the application of the labor time released to movements to, and productive effort upon, the nearest fields. By investing less productive effort in more distant fields and minimizing movement effort the farmer is increasing the total amount of time devoted to productive effort and hence to raising yields on his farm in an efficient manner.

If production increased in an amount proportional to successive applications of labor the farmer could withdraw labor from his furthest fields and apply it to his nearest fields ad infinitum. Unfortunately, according to the law of diminishing returns, successive amounts of productive effort tend to yield decreasing increments of production so that a given addition of productive effort where productive effort is already high yields a lower additional return than when productive effort is at a relatively low level. This clearly imposes a limit on the degree to which the farmer can farm the more peripheral areas less productively than the nonperipheral areas. The farmer is involved in a trade-off: up to a certain point he can increase production relative to costs by reducing movement effort relative to productive effort; beyond a certain level of productive effort on the nearest fields, however, production costs (the cost of producing a given amount of output) will increase to such an extent that the economies obtained by reducing movement effort will be eliminated.

The resultant distance decay in application of labor to fields on the farm is shown in Table 14-3 where the actual man hours per year worked on a given hectare of land at different distances from the farmstead in Holland are presented. There is also evidence that the application of fertilizer to fields tends to decline with distance from the farmstead. These variations have been re-

TABLE 14-3. Applications of labor per hectare per year (in man hours) for the Netherlands; the data apply to plots in excess of 15 hectares in area. Can you see any reason why applications of labor should decline with distance in this manner?

Distance from farmstead in kms.	Grassland plots	Arable plots
0.5	220	400
1.0	210	360
2.0	180	300
3.0	160	240
4.0	130	190
5.0	110	150

flected in declines in the mineral status of the soil with increasing distance from the farmstead.

Variations in the intensity of land use with distance from the farmstead, however, are not the only solution to the problem of the increasing cost of productive effort with distance. Land uses differ in the productive effort they require—dairy cattle require a great deal of attention, for example, while unirrigated arable cultivation requires much less. As a consequence one can select those land uses that are more demanding in terms of labor for fields close to the farmstead and place less demanding crops on fields further away. Assume, for example, that a farmer produces four items A, B, C, and D, each needing a certain number of man days of productive effort per year. Let $A = 50$, $B = 65$, $C = 100$, $D = 150$. Also, assume that the farmer has four fields at varying distances from the farmstead: travel times might be 10, 20, 30, and 40 minutes, respectively (see Figure 14-4. Clearly, the land-use pattern shown in the first section of Figure 14-4 would be a relatively inefficient solution because the land use requiring most productive effort has been placed in the furthermost field, thus increasing movement effort. The locational solution presented in the second row, on the other hand, is much more efficient because the land use that is most demanding in terms of productive effort is closest to the farmhouse while the least-demanding land use is placed in the most distant field.

To present a more substantive justification for this argument, reconsider the land-use concentricities reported for farms in Sicily. In Sicily, it will be recalled, vines and other tree crops were cultivated closest to the farmhouse; then came the zone in which the olive replaced the vine; and finally a zone of unirrigated arable. Of these four types of land use it is interesting to note that it is the vine which requires the highest number of man days per unit area (90) and the unirrigated arable which requires the least (35). Olives and other tree crops require intermediate amounts of productive effort (45 and 40 man days per unit area, respectively).

Labor is not the only item which needs to be brought to the fields in order to make them productive, however. One

must also take into consideration other inputs, such as fertilizers. There is excellent evidence that prior to the emergence of public sanitation systems, farmers close to the city benefited a great deal in terms of increased productivity from their access to a source of cheap fertilizer. This not only involved human excrement transported to the fields but also the excrement of animals that were to be found in large numbers in cities prior to about 1850. Not only were horses a prerequisite for intra-urban mobility but the population also maintained large numbers of pigs and poultry. The reports on the agriculture of British counties prepared by Arthur Young in the late 18th century are replete with references to the beneficial effect of such an accessible source of fertilizer upon the productivity of surrounding cropland.

(3) Production Costs. Decisions as to the type of farming to engage in and the intensity with which to apply labor and capital are also affected by the costs of producing an acre of a given land use at a given intensity. Especially significant in this are the costs of labor, land, and capital in a particular location and the nature of the physical environment to which one has to apply that labor and capital in order to make it productive. All other things being equal, hilly land is costlier to cultivate than flat land; swampy land prone to flooding imposes higher capital costs in the form of tile drain than does well-drained land, and so on.

The costs of labor, land, and capital do not exhibit a geographically random pattern. Superimposed on broad *regional* variations in these costs are certain more *local* variations that seem to be dependent on location relative to cities. Farms closer to cities encounter a different production cost structure than farms further away. In general, farms closer to cities

INEFFICIENT

Distance from Farmhouse ⟶

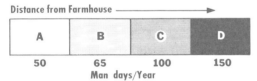

EFFICIENT

Distance from Farmhouse ⟶

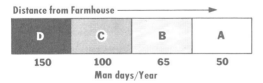

FIGURE 14-4. Land-use labor needs and the geographical efficiency of land-use patterns. Efficient patterns minimize the sum total of travel involved from farmstead to field; inefficient patterns do not.

incur higher labor costs because of competition from higher paying nonagricultural employment opportunities. They also have higher land costs due to competition for land for nonagricultural purposes: farmland on the margins of an urban area is usually very expensive. The availability and price of capital, however, is likely to be a little more favorable; farmers close to the city may hold a part-time nonagricultural job providing them with a source of capital to finance their farming operations. Bank deposits per head are likely to be very much greater in the urbanized area and the terms of loans a little more favorable. Farmland surrounding a city is also a prime target for urban capital investments; city businessmen may buy land close to the city to finance an agricultural operation either to diversify their business interests or to provide an activity (e.g., raising dairy cattle) complementary to their urban activity (e.g., selling milk).

These cost considerations related to location vis-à-vis cities put a premium on highly capitalized agriculture, using small amounts of labor on smaller plots of the expensive land found close to cities: an agriculture, however, that produces high yields for the nearby urban markets. The agriculture of the southern California area is of this type with dairying carried out on small feed lots to which all feed is imported, and egg production being concentrated in battery houses—both examples of an agriculture that economizes on labor and land by employing large amounts of capital per acre. The same phenomenon can be observed around many Western cities in the form of greenhouse cultivation; the capital represented by the glass and concomitant heating permits a year-round growing season to extract more from the expensive land per time period and to allow economies on labor costs by geo-graphically concentrating farming activities.

In the contemporary context, however, it seems apparent that these arguments do not apply to land too close to a growing city. While such locations will also be expensive in land and labor costs, capital intensive agriculture is unlikely to be the result simply because of the increasingly costly nature of the environment for farming operations and because of the anticipated development of the land for urban uses. Land on the margins of residential development is very costly to farm: wells lower the water table making the land drier; the large mass of concrete and man-made topography plays havoc with land drainage producing localized swamps; children leave gates open or steal fruits; picnickers throw careless matches and leave their garbage. For agricultural investments requiring a longer period to yield an adequate return, moreover, the anticipated conversion of the land to urban purposes may also provide a constraint on the possibility of using the land for high yielding agricultural purposes. This is particularly true for fruit farmers whose fruit trees may take at least five years of growth before they begin to bear fruit. If the orchards are on the edge of urbanized areas, the landowner may be reluctant to grant a long-term lease that would permit such investments to show yields; or the farmer himself, if he is a landowner, may see the imminent sale of land for urban uses as providing a more enticing financial prospect than investment in fruit trees to show a yield five years hence. Such reasons have been adduced to explain the contraction of the fruit-growing area in the rapidly urbanizing Niagara-Hamilton area of Ontario.

While location close to a city can impose high labor costs and provide a stimulus toward a labor economizing, highly capitalized land use, areas close to a national boundary may find it cheaper to concentrate on land uses that economize more on capital than on labor simply because of their access to a pool of low-cost, unorganized labor across the boundary. Undoubtedly a major factor permitting the fruit and vegetable producers of California and Texas to compete with the producers of similar products in the urbanized northeastern United States has been their access to a source of cheap, nonunionized labor across the boundary in Mexico.

An analogous case concerns the production of sugar beet and potatoes in northeastern Germany prior to the First World War. Such forms of agriculture had a high demand for seasonal cheap labor that was made good from Polish underemployed rural populations just across the boundary to the east — workers who were willing to work for a cheaper wage than the native Germans.

Of course situational factors are not the only determinants of agricultural production costs. Equally and possibly more important at larger scales are *regional* variations in labor, land, and capital costs, in the quality of labor and in the nature of the physical environment to which labor and capital are applied. Farm labor in the South, for example, is considerably cheaper than elsewhere in the United States; this has reduced the incentive for the considerably greater mechanization of cotton production that has taken place in California and Arizona where labor is substantially more expensive. Comparing nations with one another, it is also possible to see differential land costs as one of the reasons why North American wheat producers could undercut British wheat farmers in the 19th century. Low land prices in North America not only kept

the price of wheat per acre down but they also permitted the cultivation of wheat on much larger farms than in England; this allowed the early use of machinery and economies on labor that were not possible on the smaller English wheat farms.

The physical environment itself is an important cost factor as it presents controls on the cheapness with which land can be farmed for a particular purpose. An excessively dry climate, for example, may impose the costs of well drilling on the farmer as in the western Great Plains of the United States; a relatively cold climate may impose the occasional costs of the late frost that nips the developing plants in the bud.

One of the more interesting manifestations of environmental costs upon the pattern of land use concerns the role of flat land upon the development of cash grain farming in the American Midwest. The cultivation of wheat and corn for cash in the United States is dependent upon mechanization; the use of hand labor would be ridiculously expensive. On hilly land, however, mechanization is a relatively costly operation; not only are farming operations slowed down by the gradient but the problem of the tractor overturning necessitates the ploughing of a furrow aligned with the gradient; this presents a considerable soil erosion problem that will be ultimately reflected in lower yields and the need for expensive soil conservation techniques. As a consequence, one would expect cost considerations to confine the production of grain for cash to flatter lands and this is precisely what one finds. The percentage of all farms gaining over half their income from the sale of grain for cash is particularly high in east-central Illinois, Kansas, and North Dakota. North Nebraska, eastern Minnesota, and the Ozark area of south

Missouri tend to have relatively low percentages of farms classified as cash grain. Proportions of land classified as flat are very high in precisely the areas concentrating on cash grain production—east-central Illinois, North Dakota, and Kansas, and low in such areas as the Ozarks and northern Nebraska.

(4) *The Role of Economies of Agglomeration.* Up to now we have considered the production costs and movement costs on a farm virtually as if they were not affected by events on the surrounding farms. In many cases, however, this is untrue because farming, like industrial activity, is subject to *economies of agglomeration.*

Such economies and diseconomies may result from farmers in an area concentrating on the same type of land use (e.g., market gardening). Or they may result from farmers in the same area concentrating on complementary land uses: sugar beet cultivation, for example, can complement livestock fattening—the feeding of beet pulp and associated plant trimmings to cattle in small area feeding lots occurs in places like Colorado. Such economies of agglomeration assume a number of different manifestations.

In terms of production costs, agglomeration of farmers specializing in similar lines of agricultural activity frequently facilitates a lowering of a variety of costs. Cooperation on a formal or informal basis, for instance, can facilitate the buying of feedstuffs in bulk at a lower price than if smaller amounts of the same feedstuffs were bought by each farmer. Production costs may also be lowered by the spreading of costs of large, necessary investments over several farms. In the earlier days of farm mechanization, for instance, the threshing of grain was often a special function carried out by a team who would travel from farm to farm simply because no single farmer could afford the requisite invest-

ment. The provision of such a service, however, was dependent upon there being a sufficient number of grain farms to be serviced in the area.

One of the major purposes for which farmers specializing in the same type of activity have cooperated in the past has been that of processing their goods. Eggs and fruit are marketable at a higher price if they are first graded and packed and such cooperative packing stations are common features of the fruit and vegetable growing areas of California, Texas, and Florida. In many cases this cooperation has been carried out to eliminate the profits of a middleman and to hold down the ultimate price of the product on the consumer market. One of the major reasons for the competitiveness of the Danish pork, bacon, and dairy industries has been low prices; these result from high levels of cooperative activity in the form of cooperative dairies, creameries, and meat packing plants.

Over and above these obvious economic factors the agglomeration facilitates the spread of information relevant to the agricultural specialization of an area, thus allowing the area to keep ahead of its competitors by continual technological innovation. If a potato grower has a pesticide problem, for example, he is much more likely to get advice if he is next to the farm of another potato grower than if his potato farm is set in the middle of a cattle pasture area. County fairs and state fairs also usually manifest the agricultural biases of the region and facilitate the movement of agronomic information.

The agglomeration of similar farmers also receives benefits from the activities of third parties in the form of supply, processing, and marketing agencies. Such economies of agglomeration are less intended by the farmers involved, but result from perceptions of economy by external agencies. Groups of farmers concentrating on the same products, for example, tend to be the first adopting a new and profitable innovation; this is partly because the agency marketing the innovation locates its outlets with reference to clusters of farmers who will be interested in the innovation. Alternatively, the innovation may be developed with the large clusters (i.e., markets) of farmers in mind. Hybrid corn is a case in point. Providing the farmer with high corn yields, a different hybrid corn had to be developed for different areas of the United States: hybrid corn developed for Ohio, therefore, would have rather limited effectiveness in Georgia. Clearly, the greatest profits for the seed producers would be made in those areas producing the most corn, and it was for those areas that a hybrid was first developed. Consequently, the spatial diffusion of hybrid corn in America tended to be closely related to the proportion of the arable area under corn.

The agglomeration is also attractive to processing industries that eliminate the need for a costly and possibly prohibitively costly haul of the agricultural produce to a processing center at a distance. In Colorado, for example, one sugar beet refinery is supported by the sugar beet produced on an average of just over 300 farms. Clearly the isolated sugar beet producer would be at a considerable disadvantage because he would not be at all attractive in the locational planning of sugar refining companies. Similar arguments apply to the locations of condensed milk factories, jam factories, and abattoirs: their need for a large supply area greater than that of two or three solitary producers militates against the unagglomerated producer and makes his costs of production and movement so high that they are probably prohibitive.

Finally, economies of agglomeration in agriculture are also frequently observ-

able in terms of an increase in price allowing the farmer increased profit. Such increased prices are a result of the development of reputation that most certainly could not develop around a single farmer producing a product. Everyone in the United States has heard of Idaho potatoes and Maine potatoes, but whoever heard of the solitary Ohio or Virginia potato grower? The possibility of making increased profits as a result of higher prices, moreover, tends to encourage other farmers to produce that particular agricultural line.

(5) Spillover Effects. In addition to economies of agglomeration one must also take into consideration, on the cost side of the account ledger, the factor of spillover effects. These can have beneficial or deleterious effects over a wide area and they tend to be difficult to price. Negative spillover effects are particularly critical in agricultural land use. A stark example was recently provided by the death of large numbers of sheep in Utah as a result of the drift of nerve gas from the U.S. Federal Government's Biological Warfare Proving grounds located in that state. In Britain, a common negative spillover effect is that experienced by farmers as a result of the activities of fox hunters whose horses trample down crops, batter down gates allowing livestock to escape, and so on. When England was more feudal this type of position was tolerated by the tenant farmer much more than today when there is a rising tide of resentment against such costly antics.

Farmers also create negative spillover effects for each other. A poorly managed farm may become so overgrown with scrub and vegetation as to harbor pests and weeds which spread to adjacent properties. This problem is likely to be particularly severe where land holdings are fragmented and in need of consolidation. Possibly more critical than this, however, is the problem of soil erosion encountered in either subarid climates or in climates characterized by intense precipitation of the thunderstorm variety. A farmer who ignores principles of soil conservation creates problems not only for himself but also for adjacent farm families. Deforestation of hillsides and overcropping of land without adequate replenishment of soil nutrients in the Tennessee river basin up until the 1930s not only facilitated the erosion of the fertile topsoil for the particular farmer who had deforested and overcropped: water ran off the slopes more rapidly carrying with it a large burden of detritus to flood the lands of possibly innocent farmers further downstream, destroy buildings, and clog drainage ditches with eroded topsoil. On the subarid fringes of the Great Plains as in western Oklahoma the problem was wind erosion rather than water erosion; here the problem for the innocent was not to be located downwind of the eroded area.

Positive spillover effects for farmers include access to public services installed not merely for the use of the farmer but for the surrounding rural population at large. The introduction of piped water into rural areas of Britain, for example, has greatly facilitated the development of irrigation in that country. The idea of irrigation in a country so notoriously wet as Britain may appear a little odd until one remembers that dry spells do occur and exercise a detrimental effect on agricultural productivity. Piped water can be used to even out such deficiencies in the supply of moisture particularly for such crops as potatoes and grass. The irrigation of potatoes in climates like that of southeastern England, for example (approximately 25 inches of rainfall per year), increases potato yields by two tons per acre. This type of intensification of agricultural production is a positive spillover effect of the diffusion of public ser-

vices to rural areas. Rural electrification has had analogous effects on such things as the provision of heat for calves and piglets and the provision of power for mechanical milking machines. It is clear, however, that the availability of such spillover benefits has been rather unequally distributed over the landscape. Farmers close to the towns from which water and electricity have emanated have been the first to benefit and therefore are provided with further possibilities for the application of capital and the intensification of agricultural production. In more remote areas such as Appalachia, Wales, southwestern England, and much of Scotland such positive spillover effects have yet to appear.

REWARD FACTORS

(1) The Role of Price. With the advent of the railroad, price variations in agricultural products within nations are now relatively small and are not important differentiators of agricultural land-use decisions. When we compare one nation with another, however, there are some differences stemming from demand conditions within those nations and from differences in agricultural policies. Of greater significance in differentiating land use and its intensity both between and within nations are the yields per acre that, when multiplied by the price per unit product, provide the farmer with his rewards per acre.

(2) Yields. The yields obtained from one acre of a given land use are strongly affected by natural environmental factors: soil fertility, temperature and precipitation conditions, and slope all play an important role in the magnitude of the harvest. Particularly critical in this regard is the *net photosynthesis* or *potential photosynthesis* as it is sometimes called. This is a measure of net organic matter production in the plant, after losses due to

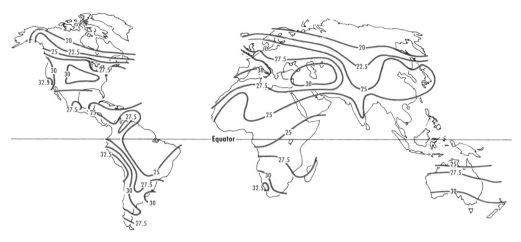

FIGURE 14-5. Potential photosynthesis for the 8 months from March through October in the northern hemisphere and from September through April in the southern hemisphere. In the northern hemisphere the best environment for plant growth—assuming adequate water—is found in southern California.

respiration are subtracted and assuming adequate water supply and soil nutrients. Figure 14-5 presents the geographical distribution of potential photosynthesis in the world for the average eight-month growing season. In the United States, therefore, the area offering the best environment for plant growth—assuming adequate water—is found in southern California. Also highly favorable, however, is a large area along the West Coast and in the central United States stretching from Kentucky in the east to Wyoming in the northwest and Arizona in the southwest. As one goes north towards the pole, potential photosynthesis rapidly declines; there is also some decline as one gets nearer the equator suggesting that the new tropical nations of Africa and Asia are not necessarily in a happy position as far as their future agricultural productivity is concerned.

That potential photosynthesis is an important determinant of crop productivity is demonstrated in Figure 14-6, which plots *rice yields per hectare* against *potential photosynthesis* for a four-month period (the four-month period is due to the relatively short growing period for rice). It is immediately obvious from the diagram that there is a fairly close relationship between rice yields and potential photosynthesis. It is also interesting to note that it is those Oriental countries relying heavily on rice (Japan excepted) that have the lowest yields while nations in which rice is not the staple foodstuff

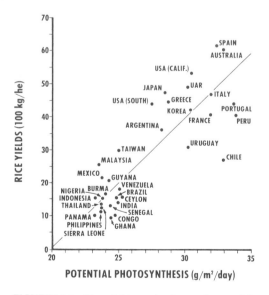

FIGURE 14-6. Rice yields per hectare and potential photosynthesis. The line is a "least squares" line.

report higher yields. Note also that there are differentials in the United States: the higher potential photosynthesis of California is associated with higher rice yields than the lower potential photosynthesis of the South—largely Louisiana.

Yields are also a function of the intensity of agricultural production. Most of the areas of the globe with high potential photosynthesis, for example, could not realize their immense agricultural potential without investment of large amounts of capital in irrigation works. Peru, the United Arab Republic, and the Soviet Union report some of the highest cotton yields in the world but their cotton is grown almost entirely under irrigation conditions. Indeed intensive cultivation as represented by irrigation produces very large yield increases in such climates. Irrigated land in some areas of California, for instance, produces nine to ten times as much as the same area dry farmed.

In other types of environment, fertilizers, the application of new seed types, and the selective breeding of livestock can also raise yields per acre in an otherwise unpromising environment. Given the fact of diminishing returns, however, the utility of such intensity of production is dependent upon such factors as access to markets and the cheapness of the labor and/or capital required to intensify production. Certainly the incentives to intensification, are, as we saw above, greater where the excess profit incurred is likely to be higher.

These points regarding the dependence of yields upon technology and natural environmental factors are illustrated rather nicely with some data from the *départments* of France on the relationship between *milk produced per cow* and the *percent of the population which is urban.* The latter is intended to indicate incentives to intensification caused by the excess profits likely to accrue to dairying

as a result of access to urban markets. Milk yield per cow, however, is slightly unsatisfactory from our point of view because we are really interested in yields per acre. We are therefore making the possibly unwarranted assumption here that the number of dairy cows per acre of pasture does not vary in France from one area to another.

As Figure 14-7 shows there is a relationship between milk per cow and access to urban markets with areas having larger urban populations reporting higher milk yields. A line has been drawn in to indicate the average position of the points on the graph. As can be seen from this graph there are a number of points—each point representing a French *départment*—a considerable distance above or below the line. The dotted lines enclose a band in which milk per cow is fairly closely related to percent of the population, urban. The *départments* outside that band, however, represent just as clearly places where the

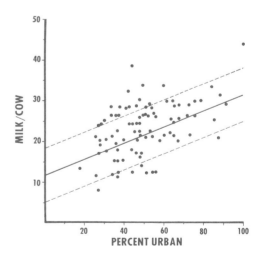

FIGURE 14-7. Urbanization and milk per cow in France; the line is a "least squares" line and represents the average position of the points. *Départments* with higher productivity than expected on the basis of urbanization are above the upper dashed line; *départments* with lower productivity than expected on the basis of urbanization are below the lower dashed line.

relationship is not so close: places above the *upper* dotted line have higher milk yields per cow than we would expect and places below the *lower* dotted line have lower milk yields per cow than we would expect. We call these *départments deviant cases.*

These deviant cases from Figure 14-7 have been plotted on a map of France (see Figure 14-8) with those above the upper dotted line shaded in black and those below the lower dotted line left blank. One thing is immediately evident from this map: the black *départments* are found largely in northern France and the blank *départments* are confined almost wholly to southern France. The significance of this is probably climatic: southern France is much drier, particularly in the summer, than northern France and the growth of grass, except where irrigated, is considerably less lush. Normandy in northern France, for example, is famous not only for its dairy cows but also for the luxuriance of its pasture.

In summary, milk yields per cow in France seem to respond to two major factors: the lushness of the pasture as a function of climatic conditions and intensity of production which seems to respond largely to access factors. Presumably for farms close to towns there are incentives to invest in higher yielding cows and in the purchase of manufactured feedstuffs.

Yields and prices, however, are not unchanging over time; nor, in fact, is the structure of costs within which the farmer must make his land-use decisions. Land-use patterns change, often quite suddenly, in response to these developments. It is to the dynamics of land-use patterns that we turn next.

THE DYNAMICS OF PATTERN

Changing prices in response to the changing demands for and supplies of

FIGURE 14-8. Urbanization and milk per cow in France — the deviant cases. Areas that are shaded black have yields that are higher than we would expect on the basis of urbanization; areas that are blank have lower yields than expected. Note the north–south difference in the pattern of deviant cases. Can you suggest why?

different foodstuffs, changing transportation costs on various agricultural commodities, changing production costs and technology, and so on all lead to continual reevaluations by farmers of the use to which their agricultural land is allocated. The lower cotton yield resulting from destruction by the boll weevil in the American South, for example, has made cotton a more rewarding land use farther to the west in the dry lands of Arizona and California: the boll weevil has difficulty surviving there. Likewise, the decline of world wheat prices in the 1870s had severe repercussions on the land-use decisions of the British farmer who found that his wheat was too expensive compared to that being imported from the cheap virgin lands of North America. Large acreages were taken out of wheat cultivation and were put down to grass.

A dramatic and large-scale example of the effects of the changing cost and price environment on the agricultural land-use decision has been provided by Richard Peet.[1] His work on the geographical expansion of commercial agriculture in the 19th century is so interesting that it merits an extended consideration at this point. Peet is mostly concerned with the effect of changes in prices and movement costs upon location rent and upon consequent land-use decisions.

Assume initially a situation in which movement costs to market exercise the major differentiating effect on location rent and assume that movement costs increase in a regular manner with distance from the market. For cultivated land therefore one can imagine a location-rent–distance relationship something like that shown in Figure 14-9. Now if the demand for foodstuffs increases, the location rent for cultivated land will also increase and to the same extent at all distances from the market. Two locational consequences follow from this. One is that the external margin of cultivated land will be pushed outwards since prices have been brought up *above* that level at which land at the geographical margin of cultivation is not worth cultivating (i.e., cultivation is now profitable at the geographical margin as a

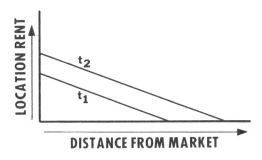

FIGURE 14-9. Market price, location rent, and distance from market. As the market price for a product increases between time t_1 and time t_2, the location rent increases by the same amount at all distances from the market, thus allowing the profitable allocation of land to that use at greater distances from the market than at time t_1.

result of the general increase in location rent). This is represented, for example, by the extension of colonized agricultural lands around a village as the population of the village grows. Anglo-Saxon settlements in Britain tended to expand in this way colonizing the frontier as the demand for food increased.

A second consequence is that cultivation will be intensified in order to pay higher rental payments resulting from the increase in location rent or, if the owner is also the occupier, because the increased price has increased the value of the output of an additional unit of labor and capital at all points. This is reflected in the extreme intensity of Oriental agriculture under conditions of high population density and demand for foodstuffs. The terracing of steep hillsides providing small areas of flat land for irrigated rice cultivation is an excellent example of this.

Changes in transportation costs have analogous consequences. If the cost of transporting a given commodity a given distance declines then location rents increase, as shown in Figure 14-10, allowing extension of the cultivated area and intensification of cultivation as a result of increased location rents (Figure 14-10a). If, however, demand is not increased, the extension of the cultivated zone resulting from the decline in transportation costs would lead to a glut of production, a drop in price, and a geographical contraction of the margin towards the position it occupied before the decline in transportation rates (Figure 14-10b). Obviously an expansion of the cultivated zone and an intensification of farming within that zone will only be maximized if decreases in transportation costs per unit distance are accompanied by rising prices resulting from increasing foodstuff demands.

Also, if prices increase as a result of an increasing demand for foodstuffs

[1] J. Richard Peet, "The Spatial Expansion of Commercial Agriculture in the Nineteenth Century: A Von Thünen Interpretation," *Economic Geography,* Vol. 45, No. 4 (October, 1969), pp. 283–301.

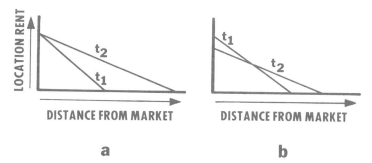

FIGURE 14-10. Location rent and transportation innovation. Reduction in movement costs per unit distance should permit higher location rents at greater distances from the market [t_2 in (a)], thus permitting a geographical extension of the area devoted to the particular land use; however, such extension could result, in the absence of increased demand, in a glut of the market resulting in a decline of location rents and a contraction of the t_2 line [see (b)] from the position it occupied in (a).

without being accompanied by a decline in transportation charges the price of foodstuffs will become prohibitively high as foodstuffs are transported over increasing distances from the geographical margin of cultivation to satisfy the demand. Eventually food prices will become so high that urban growth will be curtailed.

The major conclusion from this brief analysis, therefore, is that expansion of cultivated land in the absence of changing production costs is greatly facilitated by a concurrent decline of transportation costs and an increase of foodstuff prices. We will now apply this analysis to the case of the expansion of the cultivated area supplying Britain's growing food needs in the 19th century.

Britain underwent a steady growth in population from about the middle of the 18th century on, with the rate of growth becoming very high in the 19th century. From about 1750 onwards Britain found herself in a position where domestic food supplies were insufficient to satisfy domestic demand. The resultant rise in prices stimulated the extension and intensification of commercial wheat production in areas close to Britain: Ireland

and the Baltic countries of Prussia, Poland, Sweden, and Russia were particularly affected in this regard.

About the middle of the 19th century Britain's food imports underwent a dramatic increase resulting in an extension of the area in the world supplying foodstuffs to Britain. The progressively increasing distances over which foodstuffs were being shipped to Britain throughout the 19th century are shown in Table 14-4. Undoubtedly a major facilitating factor in the expansion of these foodstuff zones was the revolution of transportation in the 19th century including the railroad and the transoceanic steamship. Indeed, oceanic freight rates for American exports underwent an almost continuous decline during that period. It is interesting to note from Table 14-4, however, that some zones seemed to expand more rapidly than others. The supply zones for wool and hides expanded very rapidly, for example, to the periphery of Britain's supply area. This is a function of the relatively low transportation cost on the product compared with its price; similar arguments apply to wheat. A further factor permitting their earlier expansion

TABLE 14-4. *Average distances over which some British agricultural imports were moved, 1830–1913. Note the gradually expanding area of foodstuff supply throughout the 19th century; note also the slower expansion for such perishables as butter, cheese, and eggs prior to refrigeration at the latter end of the 19th century compared with the earlier expansion for high value–low transport cost products such as wheat and hides.*

Import type	Average distance from London to regions from which each import type derived (miles)				
	1831–1835	1856–1860	1871–1875	1891–1895	1909–1913
Fruit and vegetables	0	324	535	1150	1880
Live animals	0	630	870	3530	4500
Butter, cheese, eggs, etc.	262	530	1340	1610	3120
Feed grains	860	2030	2430	3240	4830
Flax and seeds	1520	3250	2770	4080	3900
Meat and tallow	2000	2900	3740	5050	6250
Wheat and flour	2430	2170	4200	5150	5950
Wool and hides	2330	8830	10,000	11,010	10,900
Weighted average all above imports	1820	3650	4300	5050	5880

was their nonperishability: fruit and vegetables, butter, cheese, and eggs, for example, had to be allocated to land closer to market (in or close to Britain) as a result of their perishability and the lack of refrigeration. Only with the advent of refrigeration in the late 19th century did the supply zones of these products markedly expand. Other crops that were less valuable in price terms relative to their transportation costs—such as feed grains—were also imported over shorter distances.

In an important sense the advance of the agricultural frontier in the United States was a response to conditions of high food prices in Britain and the revolution in transportation that allowed the Atlantic to be bridged relatively cheaply. The expanding wheat frontier, however, did not leave behind it a golden field of wheat stretching along the East Coast of the United States and in Britain itself. As the frontier expanded into the flat fertile lands of the Midwest and as mechanization was introduced into these propitious environmental conditions, the production costs fell rather dramatically and the wheat farmers of Iowa, Minnesota,

Illinois, and beyond were able not only to undercut the British wheat farmer but also the wheat farmer on the East Coast of the United States and in the hillier portions of the eastern Midwest.

Not only that, but in the eastern United States expanding cities were providing demands for other foodstuffs that had to be produced closer at hand. Wheat fields in New York and New England were converted to dairy farms to supply milk to Boston, New York City, Philadelphia, and other growing East Coast cities. Land in the eastern Midwest was gradually converted to more of a livestock–feed grain economy to supply the demand for meat from the cities. Both land uses carried a higher location rent in those areas than wheat cultivation and so wheat was increasingly assigned to the more western regions of the cultivated areas in the United States. Part of this shift in the area of American wheat production is shown in Figure 14-11.

In brief, land-use patterns present a continually changing kaleidoscope as changing movement costs, production costs, prices, and yields lead to reevalua-

FIGURE 14-11. The westward shift of wheat production in the Midwest, 1839–1859. Wheat production shifted westwards as land to the east was converted to uses that catered to the growing demands of the urban population of the Northeast for milk and meat.

tions of existing land uses by farmers. While the allocative mechanism that we outlined in the previous chapter seems to have a good deal of explanatory power, there are nevertheless some facets of land use that it does not explain. Why, for example, has the British farmer reconverted much of his land back to wheat despite much lower cost production of wheat in Canada, Australia, and Argentina? For an answer to such questions we must examine some of the deviations from the allocative mechanism.

DEVIATIONS FROM THE ALLOCATIVE MECHANISM

Deviations from the allocative mechanism outlined above stem from two forces or sets of forces. There are: (1) information factors—the knowledge and variations in knowledge that farmers have about the land-use alternatives open to them, the prices associated with

different agricultural commodities, the land use policies of other farmers, and so on, and (2) the fact that governments play a role in land-use decisions either actively by telling the farmer what to do or passively by providing an environment of controls in which the farmer has to make his land-use decisions. We shall examine the information factors first and then look briefly at the role of political factors.

INFORMATION FACTORS

Historically man has often been grossly misinformed about the agricultural potential of areas and this has been reflected in his agricultural policy towards such areas. For some areas, pessimism regarding agricultural productivity has served to restrain agricultural colonization. This is true of the American Great Plains which were dubbed "the American Desert" by early 19th-century explorers of the area—an image which helped to deter colonization till very late in the 19th century. In still other cases, the image has been an overly optimistic one. Agriculturists and governments in Western Europe and North America, for example, have traditionally had a very rosy image of the agricultural potential of tropical lands. The Australian government has for years promulgated ambitious plans regarding the agricultural development of its northern tropical fringe. Britain thought that it could solve its post-1945 animal fat deficiency by large-scale groundnut (peanut) production in what was then Tanganyika (now Tanzania). The tropical forest girdling the globe is literally strewn with the wreckage of ambitious Western land development programs ("ambitious" because the tropical forest suggests fertility and optimal conditions for plant growth, but "wreckage" because the reality does not correspond to this perception of fertility).

The farmer, however, is not only interested in the land-use alternatives and their location rents at a specific place at a specific time. He is also interested in knowing the *future* behavior of crop markets, of the weather, and of government policies towards him. Obviously such contingencies are not easy to foresee and the farmer is faced with a great deal of *uncertainty* about future location rents. Under such circumstances he is likely to *spread his risks* by concentrating on several land uses on the basis of the argument that all agricultural commodities are rarely affected by the same unpredictable events.

The problem of uncertainty is likely to be particularly severe when moving into a new environment as the North American colonists did. Production costs on various land uses are unknown quantities as are movement costs and the vagaries of the climatic environment. The spreading of risks over a variety of land uses in that situation allows the farmer to acquire knowledge and *learn* about the environment in which he must make his land-use decisions. Future land-use decisions can then be altered in the light of what has been learned — in the same way as the learning decision makers in a locational context described in Chapter Five.

This does not mean to say, however, that the ultimate land-use pattern resulting from such trial and error will be the *optimal* one in the sense of *maximizing location rent*. More likely it will be a highly satisfactory one that reduces the incentive for further costly search for a land-use system that provides only a slightly higher return on the farmer's investment. It is only when external events make the land-use system unsatisfactory that farmers are likely to see renewed search for a more satisfactory land-use system as worthwhile. It has been argued, for instance, that change in land-use patterns in Britain has probably been much more rapid in times of agricultural depression than in times of agricultural boom.

The notion of learning about the environment and adjusting the land-use pattern in the direction of the more satisfactory land use indicated by what one has learned can be partly illustrated by some of the forces promoting the corn-hog-cattle farming system which developed in the American Midwest in the 19th century. Early cropping efforts, for example, were directed towards corn *and* wheat. Wheat, however, was found to be much less reliable in the Midwest environment due to periodic plagues of the wheat disease known as *rust*. Corn was early discovered to be a much more reliable crop. Not only that but it was soon discovered that corn had marketing advantages over wheat. Before railroads reached the Midwest in the period between about 1850 and 1860 transportation of bulk commodities such as corn and wheat was excessively expensive. Converting corn into a more transportable and valuable product, such as hogs or cattle, proved to be one answer and it was soon discovered that prices for corn-fed livestock were much higher than livestock fed in any other way. From the point of view of both reliability and movement costs, therefore, corn in combination with livestock proved to be a more satisfactory farming system than one based on wheat or having wheat as a component.

Learning about the environment and about land-use possibilities in that environment, however, is carried out in a locational context. Some farmers learn before others as a result of locational factors. In learning about the environment one relies partly on one's neighbors facing similar problems, and the learning process is to a very large extent a collective one resulting from the exchange of information between people who farm in close proximity to one another. The effect of location upon learning about new land uses and new technologies that have implications for production costs and hence for land-use decisions is brought out very effectively by the spatial diffusion of innovation phenomenon that we discussed in Chapter Five. In such cases the likelihood of a person adopting an innovation often seems to be greater the closer he is to someone who has already adopted. Innovations, moreover, include new land uses and also techniques that affect the level of intensity of land use. Furthermore, there is more than enough evidence to show that such agricultural innovations often do spread by a *neighborhood effect*. Two of the innovations originally discussed by Hägerstrand in his work on spatial diffusion were aimed at increasing the intensity of farming: the adoption of measures to combat bovine tuberculosis and the acceptance of agricultural subsidies. The spatial diffusions of both innovations were shown to be structured by a neighborhood effect. It seems more than likely, therefore, that completely new land uses could spread by a similar process or that farmers could dramatically increase their investment in certain lines of production as a result of communication with a neighbor.

These ideas on information spread and learning about the environment in which land-use decisions have to be made allow us to offer an explanation for certain geographical localizations of land use that do not have such a ready explanation as the Corn Belt does. Often localization of similar land uses and intensities is related to such factors as similarity of production costs or of access to an urban market. Thus, as we noted above, neighboring farms in the Corn Belt tend to concentrate on corn with stock feeding. Experimentation by farmers with the agricultural potentialities of the physical environment of the Corn Belt led to the finding that corn fed to stock was the most profitable agricultural specialization over a wide geographical area. In other cases of localization, however, such explanations are insufficient. Clusters of farms concentrate on the same product even though the physical environment and location relative to the market are not optimal. In still other cases, the production of some agricultural products is clustered in space even though the area in which they could be grown at a profit is much more extensive. Potatoes could be grown in the United States at far more locations than the ones shown in Figure 14-12 might suggest. Furthermore, many of these locations would be closer to the major metropolitan areas of consumption—an important consideration one would think for such a cheap yet bulky product.

What other processes, therefore, other than physical location relative to a required physical environment and/or urban markets might give rise to such clusters of farms concentrating on similar products and at similar levels of intensity?

One process that comes to mind combines notions of *random origin, spatial diffusion of innovation*, and *economies of agglomeration*. We have already seen that innovations spread over short distances. Also, in Chapter Five we showed that individuals who have not yet adopted are characterized by varying levels of resistance to the innovations; such resistance may stem from the low level of economic return anticipated from an innovation. Thus, if a farmer notes that the adoption of a new seed by his neighbors has increased production so dramatically that prices have been depressed, he is hardly likely to adopt a new seed type.

We have suggested above, that in

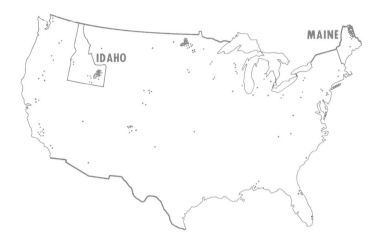

FIGURE 14-12. The geography of white potato production in the United States. Each dot represents 20,000 acres. Note the concentration in Idaho and Maine and lesser degrees of concentration in North Dakota and Colorado. The pattern is not related to any obvious natural environmental or market accessibility factors usual in such cases. How, therefore, can the distribution be explained?

many cases of clustering there is either no apparent cost advantage or there is an apparent cost disadvantage resulting from environmental and/or relative locational factors. What other factors, therefore, would lower costs and/or increase market prices in an area and thus increase the profits from an agricultural innovation in such a way as to break down resistance to the further spread of that innovation? One important factor is that of *economies of agglomeration.*

Assuming that the availability of economies of agglomeration lowers resistance to the land-use innovation, however, what situation allows economies of agglomeration to occur? How is it that a small group of farmers find themselves producing the same crop at the same time in an area even though the area has no special merit for that particular line of production? One possibility is that the original nucleus was a purely random occurrence. Each farmer had quite different and unrelated reasons for adopting the land use when he did.

Whatever those unrelated reasons might be, random events can produce a distribution of adopters which exhibits some *local* clustering.

It seems, therefore, that clusters of farmers producing the same item *could* result from a process of local spread around a small random nucleus of farmers, the spread being encouraged by the low costs resulting from economies of agglomeration. A ceiling on local spread would result from saturation of the market for the product thus making further adoption of the land use unattractive. This provides one possible explanation for such puzzling land-use localizations as potatoes in Maine, broiler chickens in northern Alabama, northern Georgia, and central Mississippi, and rhubarb at Leeds, England.

POLITICAL FACTORS

In the last chapter we discussed the role that conflicts between public and private interests in land-use allocation play in providing a justification for political interference in the land-use allocation mechanism. In agricultural land use this frequently takes the form of some sort of price support or subsidy. Britain's current land-use map, for example, is very much a function of government crop subsidies. Without such subsidies the British wheat farmer would be unable to compete with cheaper wheat imported from abroad.

The American agricultural landscape also bears the traces of government interference in prices. In this particular case, however, guaranteed prices for agricultural commodities such as wheat and cotton have been tied to acreage quotas; that is, for the farmer to be eligible for price supports he must limit his acreage to a specified amount. The farmer's response to this new *decision environment* has been an intriguing one. He has cooperated with the government in the sense of limiting his acreage in exchange for fixed prices. The acreage limitation, however, has taken place in a way, that maximizes the farmer's return from the fixed price regime; that is, acreage has been restricted to more fertile, better yielding areas of the farm. While this type of behavior is within the letter of the American agricultural policy it is hardly within the spirit of it.

Political interference, however, is not confined to safeguarding the public interest by means of price supports and subsidies. It also extends to the creation of an infrastructure for farmers—an infrastructure for which individual farmers would obviously not have had the necessary resources. In this context governments have attached particular interest to *integrated drainage basin development*. By the spread of information about soil conservation techniques by government agents in a drainage basin and by the planting of forests on government land, it is possible to reduce the severity

of flooding in the lower levels of a drainage basin as well as raise agricultural yields throughout. Dam construction also helps to control flooding and provide electricity to increase farm productivity. The electricity may also be used to attract industries to employ poorer farmers who might otherwise be driven to poor land management practices and resultant soil erosion in an effort to eke out an existence. This is the philosophy behind such schemes as the Tennessee Valley Authority in the United States involving government financing of dams, power generation, and a highly active Soil Conservation Service contacting, informing, and persuading farmers in the area to adopt good soil conservation practices. It is also the basic idea behind the much discussed but little realized Missouri Basin Scheme.

For many underdeveloped countries that suffer from low levels of precipitation, reliance on irrigation and the need to industrialize make such *integrated drainage basin projects* particularly attractive. The United Arab Republic is a case in point. The aim of the Aswan dam built on the Nile with the assistance of the Soviet Union is not only to provide electricity for the country's growing energy needs; it is also to provide a more even spread of irrigation water throughout the year thus allowing multiple harvests and the irrigation of larger areas of the Nile Valley to sustain a population that is growing rather rapidly. Flood control is another by-product.

If government policies are to have a modicum of success in the drainage basis context, however, it is clear that the government should have control of all parts of the drainage basin. Thus, if the upper part of a basin lies outside control, flood control policies in the lower part of the river basin are likely to have only limited success if it is not possible to effect improved land conservation techniques in the upper portions of the basin. A major reason for a new political unit like the Tennessee Valley Authority was the fact that several states shared the basin. Such problems of political division also explain the interest which Egypt has traditionally shown in the Sudan astride the middle basin of the Nile.

CONCLUSIONS AND SUMMARY

We have now applied the land-use allocation mechanism first outlined in Chapter Thirteen to the case of agricultural land-use patterns. *Location rent,* it will be recalled, is (theoretically at least) the critical determinant of land use in that land in the presence of perfect knowledge and a desire to maximize returns on the part of land users will be devoted to that use characterized by the highest location rent.

Location rent, however, is a function of the rewards and costs attached to a particular land use. In the case of agricultural land use, *movement costs* are particularly important involving not only the costs of *marketing,* or getting the goods to market, but also the cost of *transferring factor inputs* such as labor to the fields. Marketing costs seem especially related to concentricities in land-use intensity and land-use types around major urban markets. Thus the cost of movement to market erodes the farmer's excess profit. Such erosion can be limited, however, by reducing inputs of capital and labor and therefore cultivating less intensely. *The law of diminishing returns* in association with less intense production results in lower costs per unit of production and, therefore, increased excess profits over and above what would have resulted at previous levels of intensity.

Different movement costs on the products of different land uses and different market prices help to create *concentricities in land-use type.* Land uses with higher market prices and higher movement costs per unit distance tend to be cultivable only close to the market; at greater distances from the market land uses with products that incur lower movement costs come into their own.

A crucial problem in the *spatial organization of the individual farm* involves the transfer of labor from the farmstead to the individual field. Locational strategies designed to maximize the return on labor costs include concentrating labor on fields closer to the farm rather than on those further away. Alternatively the farmer can allocate those land uses that are most consuming of labor time to the fields closer to the farm.

In addition to movement costs, however, the farmer must also consider *production costs,* such as costs of land, labor, and capital. These production costs exhibit *broad regional variations* that are apparent in resultant land-use patterns. Superimposed on these regional variations are some *smaller-scale geographical regularities.* These include regularities in production costs *surrounding cities* — higher labor and land costs tend to prevail though capital may be cheaper. One consequence of this is that land use around larger cities is often capital intensive economizing on labor and land.

Also on the cost side of the account ledger one must take into consideration cost variations resulting from *economies of agglomeration* and *spillover effects.* The costs that the farmer faces, however, have to be balanced against the rewards he can gain from different land uses. Such rewards are a function of *price,* which is a function of *supply and demand conditions,* and of *yields.* The latter responds to natural environmental factors and also to the intensity with which labor and capital are applied to the land. Intensification of cultivation is more likely, however, where the resultant excess profit is likely to be higher.

Just as in the industrial location case, however, one finds *deviations* from the land-use pattern predicted by the allocative mechanism outlined above. Again, as in the industrial location case, these deviations can be traced to *information factors* and *political factors.* Over space, inadequate information is reflected in relatively unsuccessful land-use policies. Over time, the *environment of uncertainty* that the farmer faces is reflected in a tendency to spread risks across several different land-use types. The role of information factors is also strongly apparent in the learning of optimal land-use strategies over a period of time; it is by such a learning process that we can *ultimately* explain the emergence of regions of agricultural specialization such as the Corn Belt or the potato-growing area of Maine.

Finally, deviations are induced by political factors. Western farmers, due to their productivity in a context of only slowly increasing domestic food demands are a political problem and are therefore the beneficiaries of all sorts of assistance such as subsidies and price support programs. Also the government is often a provider of the infrastructure that is important for the individual farmer who could not possibly afford it on his own.

The interest of the government in the problems of the farmer provides a useful springboard for the three last chapters of this book. Governments are faced with an increasing range of problems in which a major component is locational in character. The urban crisis provides an example. In view of the locational content of these problems, the geographer should be able to shed some light on them and suggest mitigating policies. Such is the task of the last three chapters, examining, from a locational viewpoint, the problems of the city, of economic development, and of environmental quality.

CHAPTER FIFTEEN

The Urban Crisis in a Locational Context

INTRODUCTION

That the city has become the prime focus of most of the social and domestic political concerns of the Western world is a truism that does not need extensive justification. Racial tensions and riots, the virtual bankruptcy of many municipalities, inequalities of wealth, and the increasing role of the government in the urban economy have brought the city into the social conscience and into the political forum to a much greater extent than at any time in the past. This is obviously reflected in the increasing emphasis of the mass media on urban problems and in the platforms of political parties where issues of urban housing, welfare, and pollution assume a growing prominence.

For the geographer, the major interesting fact is that many of these social and political problems have a very strong locational component. The fact that *cities vary* in their tax bases and in their abilities to supply the needs of their citizens is a striking denial of that egalitarian philosophy in the context of which Western governments operate. Such contrasts are expressed very strongly in conflicts between localities as in the fervent desire of poor inner cities for political integration with their less-than-enthusiastic suburban municipalities.

The locational element in urban social and political problems has not gone unnoticed by politicians and it is reflected in the policies that they propose. School bussing policies, for example, are conceived not only from an ideological stance but also in an effort to correct the inequality of educational opportunity present in even a small metropolitan area.

With this as a point of departure, this chapter attempts to place the social and political problems of the city in a locational perspective. To do this, however, assumes that we know something of the geography of the modern city and of the processes that underlie it. A consideration of the basic dimensions of that geography from both static and dynamic viewpoints constitutes the first half of this chapter. In the second half of the chapter we relate these locational patterns—as they are and as they are changing—to the social, economic, and consequently political problems of the contemporary city. We conclude with some ideas on locational policies designed to mitigate these problems.

THE LOCATIONAL CONTEXT OF URBAN PROBLEMS

Cities in North America and Western Europe exhibit at any one point in time a great deal of similarity in their internal locational patterns and in the processes underlying those patterns. This makes it possible to present some generalizations regarding the locational structure of the city from a static viewpoint, that is, at a given point in time.

The city, however, is not unchanging; in fact it is the rapidity of the change and the failure or inability of large numbers of people to adjust to that change that produces so many of our current urban problems. Not only that but the fact of change is interesting and important from another viewpoint: change has proceeded further in some cities than in others. In many respects, for example, the North American city passes through phases of locational development which are not reached by Western European cities until 10 or 20 years later. This has important implications for urban policy since it allows the planners of the laggard cities to *learn* something about the environment with which they will have to deal and also about the efficiency and the pitfalls of different policies capable of dealing with it.

Change, however, has to be appreciated in the context of a base line — the city as it is at a given point in time. Our more dynamic considerations, therefore, will follow a consideration of the city from a more static viewpoint.

THE CITY FROM A STATIC VIEWPOINT

Three types of locational pattern observable within cities have been studied and are useful as background for studying urban problems: (1) the *locational pattern of population densities* within the city, (2) the *geography of land values* in the city (this gives us some idea of which locations are more valued than others), and (3) the *geography of social composition* — the geographical incidence of social, occupational, racial, educational, and income attributes. Each is discussed below.

Population Density. If we were to take population densities for, say, the census tracts of Detroit and plot them on a scatter diagram against distance from the central business district, we would obtain a configuration much like that shown in Figure 15-1. Three features of this figure are important: (1) the manner in which population densities, in general, decline with distance from the central business district, that is, there is a distance decay, (2) the way that the rate at which decline takes place itself declines with distance, that is, it is a *negative exponential curve,* and (3) the way in which the population densities at the center of the city are somewhat lower than the densities at a short distance from the center. If, on a map, we were to join up places with similar population densities just as we join up places with similar altitude to obtain a topographic surface, the contours for our population density surface would take the form of a volcano, steep sides representing the exponential distance decay and a hollow or

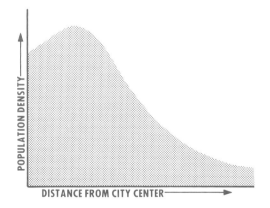

FIGURE 15-1. The relationship between population density and distance from the city center. Note (1) the general decline in population densities with increasing distance; (2) the "crater"; (3) the negative exponential rate of decline with distance.

crater in the middle representing the relatively lower population densities associated with the central business district.

Land Values. These variations in population density can be understood in a slightly greater depth when we examine the geography of land values in cities. A map of land values tells us a great deal about the locations that men value the most. It is, therefore, an extremely important guide to other types of distribution in the city and also to the criteria by which locations are evaluated.

The map of land values for Topeka, Kansas (see Figure 15-2) suggests that one of the most important criteria by which locations are evaluated is accessibility. Specifically two types of accessibility appear to be stressed: (1) *accessibility to the downtown area*—the negative exponential curve is shown in

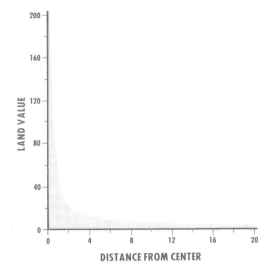

FIGURE 15-3. Land values and distance from city center in Topeka, Kansas. Note the negative exponential form of the curve.

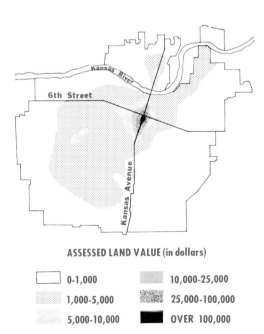

ASSESSED LAND VALUE (in dollars)

☐ 0-1,000	▨ 10,000-25,000
▨ 1,000-5,000	▨ 25,000-100,000
▨ 5,000-10,000	■ OVER 100,000

FIGURE 15-2. The distribution of land values in Topeka, Kansas. In the Western city, land values tend to be highest at the center of the city and lowest towards the edge; major traffic arteries, such as Kansas Avenue in this map, tend also to be associated with higher land values.

Figure 15-3, and (2) *accessibility to major business thoroughfares,* Kansas Avenue being a prime example for the case of Topeka. These generalizations have been confirmed in a number of other studies of the geography of land values.

In a number of respects, therefore, the spatial arrangement of land values is strikingly similar to that of population density: particularly important is the similar distance decay from the central business district (though with no crater). The source of this locational pattern and of the pattern of population densities with which it appears to be associated can be readily grasped from an understanding of some basic principles of *urban land rent theory.* This theory is concerned with the allocation of urban land to different uses and is merely an extension to the *within-city case* of the ideas which we presented in Chapter Thirteen on space filling.

An initial question that the locational pattern of land values prompts is "Why should locations near the city center have higher values attached to them?" Presumably, because there are a lot of peo-ple bidding for such pieces of land, and hence, the market value of the land rises. All types of economic activity used to regard locations close to the city center as more valuable than locations on the urban periphery. For the retailer the downtown area has historically been the focus of the mass transit system, and, therefore, the most accessible point in the city for his market; location of his shop elsewhere would have entailed considerable reductions in profit. For the manufacturer and office employer, the downtown area was for similar reasons at the most accessible point of the labor market, while, in addition, for the manu-facturer, railroads focusing on the town frequently had their loading and un-loading facilities close to the downtown area. For all these activities, but particu-larly for retailing, downtown locations were extremely important.

Presumably, even though retailing, residential, and manufacturing activities all value land at the center of the city more than land anywhere else, not all activities are equally susceptible to dif-ferences in accessibility. For each activity we can draw a rent curve describing the relationship between rent offered and accessibility for different activities (see Figure 15-4). Those activities that have steep curves, such as *A*, are highly sensi-tive to accessibility: they place a very high value on downtown locations rela-tive to suburban locations. Those activi-ties that have relatively gentle curves, such as *C*, are much less sensitive to accessibility.

In reality it has been retailing, that, up until quite recently, has had the steepest bid rent curve (*A*), while residential uses have had the gentlest curves (*C*). Indus-trial activities have had bid rent curves of intermediate slope (*B*). The effect of these curves of varying steepness is that at point *K* on the horizontal axis the

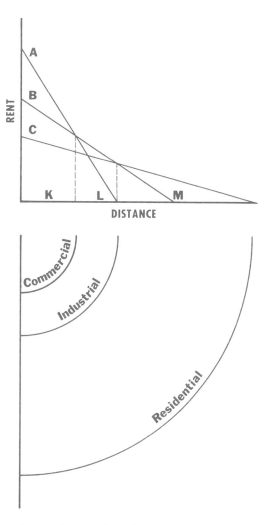

FIGURE 15-4. Hypothetical bid rent–distance rela-tionships within a city. Historically, line A corre-sponded to the relationship for commercial land uses, line B to industrial land uses, and line C to residential land uses. Assuming that land was allo-cated to that use bidding the highest rent at a given distance the resultant pattern of land use was a con-centric one. Note also how rents offered decline with distance from the central business district.

activity bidding the highest rent is re-tailing. At point *L*, however, the highest bidder is industrial use, while at point *M*, residential developers are bidding more than their retailing and industrial competitors. The result is an allocation of land uses according to zones arranged in such a way that the zones closest to the point of maximum attraction (in this case the central business district) receive the activities prepared to pay the highest rents (see Figure 15-4). Also of interest, relative to the spatial arrangement of urban land values identified earlier, is the concave upwards character of the combined rent-accessibility curve (see Figure 15-5) further suggesting that our theory is at least on the right track.

Although we have developed a theory of urban land value distributions for the case in which accessibility to the total urban area declines at the same rate in all directions at a given distance from the central business district, it is quite easy to make allowances for such factors as the increased accessibility associated with major thoroughfares. Such a revision would allow us to explain such facets of urban land values as the importance of distance from Kansas Avenue in the case of Topeka. Thus, locations by major thoroughfares have highly superior access to the rest of the city and will be associated with a family of rent–distance relationships similar to those which we postulated for the central city though of greater steepness.

These ideas are also of great utility in explaining the locational pattern of population density within the city. Recall that two of the empirical regularities identified were: (1) the distance decay in population density, and (2) the craterlike form of the population density surface in the center of the city.

The reason for the *crater* should now be evident: *land uses near the center of the city are less likely to be residential in function* simply because residential developers (considering what people today are prepared to pay for housing and what they want in terms of space) cannot compete with retailing firms and, to a lesser extent, office developers. This does not mean that downtown areas are devoid of residential activity; indeed, one of the more interesting trends of recent years has been the construction of high-rise apartment buildings in downtown areas in conjunction with urban renewal projects. But, at the center of the city competition for space is much more intense and residential purposes are frequently subjugated to those retailing and office functions that are prepared to pay more per square foot of real estate.

As one leaves the center of a large city, the crater is superseded by high population densities that then decline to the low population densities characteristic of the spacious suburb. In explaining this facet of the population density pattern we need to consider the amount of space consumed by a household. Closer to the center of the city, lots are smaller simply because land values increase and the lot sizes characteristic of suburban locations would be astronomical in price. The implication of smaller lot sizes is that more people can be squeezed into a given space. If you do away with yards or build multistory apartment blocks population densities can rise to high levels. In the

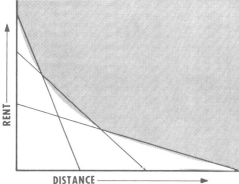

FIGURE 15-5. Bid rent–distance relationships and the combined negative exponential bid rent–distance curve. When we draw a curved line to approximate the highest rents offered at given distances, the result is a negative concave upward curve similar in form to the relationship between land values and distance from the central business district.

suburbs, on the other hand, land is valued less highly due to its low access relative to the downtown area and the individual can indulge himself in a larger lot size. The implication of the larger lot is a lowering of population densities.

Social Composition. Population density and land value differences across different areas of the city are not likely to impinge sharply on our consciousness even though they are likely to exercise considerable effect on our behavior, locational and otherwise. With social differences, however, it is somewhat different. Thus, we are all aware of variations in population composition within cities. Every Englishman, for example, has heard of the East End and the West End of London: for many years the West End of London centering on Chelsea, Kensington, and Mayfair, has been the residential area for the English aristocracy, while the East End has been a predominantly working-class area. Likewise, we are aware of New York City's Harlem with its predominantly working-class Negro population, Brooklyn with its lower middle-class Jewish population, and Westchester and Scarsdale with their affluent middle-class and professional families. However small the town, there is likely to be some neighborhood difference in social composition, even if it is only between the right side and the wrong side of the tracks! The important question for the geographer is: Is there any locational predictability in the geography of such population attributes as income, race, and occupation? The answer is an emphatic yes.

In the larger cities of Western industrialized nations two and often three locational patterns are evident in population composition patterns: (1) there is a concentric zonation of family structure: there are considerable differences in family structure between central-city areas and suburb and there is a fairly

regular gradient in-between. At one end of the gradient in the suburbs are relatively large families, living in single-family dwelling units, in which the mother is a professional homemaker and generally does not go out to work. At the other end of the gradient, closer to the city center are smaller families, often associated with older people whose children have left home or younger people who have yet to marry or have children, multiple-family dwellings, as in apartment developments, and a relatively large proportion of the women are employed.

(2) A second broad locational pattern superimposed upon this concentric zonation according to family structure and

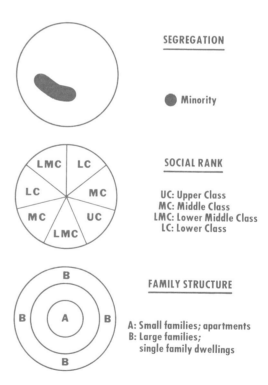

SEGREGATION

● Minority

SOCIAL RANK

UC: Upper Class
MC: Middle Class
LMC: Lower Middle Class
LC: Lower Class

FAMILY STRUCTURE

A: Small families; apartments
B: Large families;
    single family dwellings

FIGURE 15-6. A schematic view of the locational patterns of social composition in the Western city. Three locational patterns tend to be present: a concentric one differentiating larger suburban families from smaller central-city families; a sectoral one differentiating areas of different social rank; and an ethnic segregation pattern confining a minority to a limited area close to the center of the city.

position in the life cycle consists of a sectoral pattern in which the sectors radiate like wedges in a pie from the city's center and are differentiated from each other in the social status or rank of their population (see Figure 15-6). Some of the wedges consist of populations that in general are relatively wealthy, well-educated, and living in valuable homes. Other of the wedges consist of relatively poorer, less well-educated populations. This type of sectoral arrangement is contrary to many of the ideas we have regarding a city center slum of poorer people and a homogeneous, affluent suburbia. But a moment's reflection will show that it does match up with some aspects of reality. Suburbs are not homogeneous, for instance: in London, to take an example, the upper- and the upper middle-class suburbs of South London contrast very markedly with the working-class suburbs of East London (see Figure 15-7). In fact, we can take the distance decay of family structure and the directional orientations of social rank and arrange them into four ideal-type communities (see Table 15-1). An interesting exercise would be to try to match up the cells of the table with real world neighborhoods with which you are familiar.

(3) In addition to these concentric and sectoral components of the geography of population composition, cities with ethnic or racial minorities are likely to have a segregation factor in which the minority group occupies a small compact area—frequently known as a *ghetto*—of the city. The best-known contemporary examples of ghettoes are the Negro ghettoes of North America, though ghettoes of recent Indian and West Indian migrants appear to be emerging in Britain, while in France it is the Algerians who are the object of such residential exclusion. In cities where religious passions run high as between the Protes-

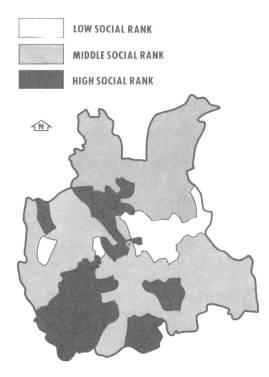

LOW SOCIAL RANK

MIDDLE SOCIAL RANK

HIGH SOCIAL RANK

FIGURE 15-7.   The geography of social rank in London. The asterisk indicates the approximate center of the metropolitan area. Note the generally sectoral arrangement of social rank with southwestern and northwestern sectors of higher social rank and an eastern sector of lower social rank especially in evidence.

tants and Catholics of Belfast (Northern Ireland) segregation may have a religious basis. Usually also the ghetto is associated with relatively dilapidated, overcrowded housing along with a low-income population, although in a number of American cities there are affluent neighborhoods that are so dominantly Jewish that they are also regarded as ghettoes.

In terms of the sources of this patterning, the *concentricity of family structure* seems particularly associated with *differential preferences for land consumption* in an urban context in which land values decline markedly with distance from the downtown area. It seems reasonable, for example, that the space

TABLE 15-1. Four ideal-type urban communities. Based on the concentric and sectoral components of urban social composition it is possible to think in terms of lower-class suburbs, middle-class suburbs, lower-class inner city areas and middle-class inner-city areas. Can you match up these ideal types with areas in a city with which you are well acquainted?

			Family Structure	
			Urban	Suburban
S	R	Sector 1	Small, middle-income families living in apartments or other multiple-family dwellings	Large, middle-income families living in single-family houses
o c i a l	a n k	Sector 2	Small, lower-income families living in apartments or other multiple-family dwellings	Large, lower-income families living in single-family houses

needs of a large family with small children should be greater than those of a small family. Play space is needed in the form of a large yard, as well as a relatively big home, and it is in the suburb with its lower land values that these needs can be met. Close to the city, available housing is more likely to take the form of a high-rise apartment building without yards or a townhouse development with a veto on children above a certain age. To this extent the allocation of larger families to the suburbs and smaller families to locations closer to the central city has an explanation.

Preferences for different amounts of space, however, are not the only factors that differentiate people's residential location behavior within an urban area. Equally and possibly more important are *preferences based on perceptions of negative and positive spillover effects.* For a given person specific groups residing close by are seen as bestowing negative spillover effects that impose certain penalties and that may be reflected in the value of his property. Other social groups, on the other hand, are more acceptable since they can provide positive spillover effects for him and his property value. This is obviously an important basis for the desire to keep Negroes out of white neighborhoods. It also forms the basis for opposition by private

householders to subsidies to enable poorer families to live in their midst. It is feared that such poorer families will lower the tone of the neighborhood, fail to maintain their property adequately, and hence exercise a deleterious effect on property values in the neighborhood. Or the perception of a negative spillover may have a more indirect stimulus as in the case when the location of poorer people close by is seen as having a detrimental effect on the quality of local schools and therefore on local property values.

Other types of spillover effects are represented by preferences for contact with certain types of people rather than with others. The middle-class person probably avoids lower-class people not because of an innate snobbery but because he really does not have anything to say to them; culturally, middle-class people and lower-class people live in quite different worlds and contact is often painful and embarrassing for both. Other preferences are based more on prejudice as in the desire to minimize contact with blacks.

In order to eliminate such negative spillover effects one often finds the emergence of neighborhood organizations to oppose the development of nearby land for, say, public housing, or to residentially stabilize an area threatened with racial invasion. Such groups may, depending on their power, be able to exercise an effect on zoning decisions that reduce the probability of the negative spillover effects inherent in contact with undesirable social groups.

In brief, residential segregation is based on an attempt by groups that are relatively homogeneous in income, racial, or ethnic terms, to share the positive spillover effects that members of a group can create for each other and protect members of the group from the negative spillover effects created by another group. Such protection on the part of groups already in an area often requires resort to informal and sometimes formal political means. The capability to be successful in such an endeavor is clearly dependent on the economic and political power of the groups involved. In such a conflict the less powerful groups—the disadvantaged ethnic minorities and the lower class—are bound to lose out. This can be illustrated with a review of the cases of the Negro ghetto and of social class segregation, respectively.

(a) The Negro Ghetto Case. Undoubtedly, many whites perceive the potential residential location of Negroes in their midst as something to be avoided both socially and economically. Social prejudice stems partly from historical causes such as the idea that Negro and white must have slave–master relationships or that white women must be protected from sexual contact with Negro males. Economically, it is expressed in the fear that Negro residential incursion will lower property values in the neighborhood: a thesis, incidentally, that is far from proven. So strong are these forces that whites may go to extreme lengths (such as violence to or boycotting of Negroes who do move into their neighborhood) in order to keep the area white.

As the object of prejudice and of the behavioral expression of prejudice in the form of threats to life and property, the Negro is naturally fearful of whites; in choosing a home in the city he will exercise care not to place himself in a position where such threats will be elicited and/or where other Negroes are not present to protect him from the social isolation resulting from boycotting.

Such forces of intergroup alienation would in and of themselves be sufficient to maintain a segregated residential pattern by race. In actuality, however, because the ghetto is constantly expanding in population as a result of the arrival of more Negroes from the depressed rural Southern areas and also because the ghetto is surrounded by white areas, white areas see themselves threatened with Negro incursion. In an effort to limit such incursion and the perceived negative spillover effects associated with it, therefore, a number of institutional mechanisms have developed, foremost of which are real estate practices, bank loan practices, and, until a few years ago, government legislation of residential zoning. A student of the spatial evolution of the Negro ghetto, Richard Morrill, has commented on this problem, and it is worth quoting him at some length: "Segregation is maintained by refusal of real estate brokers even to show, let alone sell, houses to Negroes in a white area. Countless devices are used: quoting excessive prices, saying the house is already sold, demanding unfair down-payments, removing 'For Sale' signs, not keeping appointments, and so on. Even if the Negro finds someone willing to sell him a house in a white area, financing may remain a barrier. Although his income may be sufficient, the bank or savings institution often refuses to provide financing from a fear of Negro income instability and of retaliatory withdrawal of deposits by whites."[1]

Such segregation, is clearly not confined to the Negro nor is it confined to the United States. East European groups who migrated to America at the end of the 19th century and at the beginning of the 20th century for a long time maintained an existence segregated from the host population. Little Italys, Greek areas, small Slovak enclaves, and so on with their own ethnic institutions such as ethnic food stores and churches developed in the larger American cities. The residential segregation of such groups, however, has tended to decline as they have learned the English language and lost their identity with their native land. White acceptance of anglicized white populations has never been difficult, except possibly in the case of Jews where there has always been an element of prejudice reflected in country club membership rules and occasionally in real estate practices. What is perturbing about the Negro–White segregation is the extent of the prejudice that it reveals and the resistance of that prejudice to mollification. Other ghettoes have come and gone, but the Negro ghetto still persists.

(b) Social Rank. Ethnic group membership, however, is not necessarily the only basis for those perceptions of negative and positive spillover effects that underlie residential segregation: social class or social rank also seems to be important.

People can be classified according to their incomes or according to the prestige of their occupations or education and such criteria seem to be very important in the social relationships people have with each other. People tend to marry within and confine their friendships to their own social class. Different social classes seem to patronize different churches, schools, and other services. It is not surprising, therefore, that people of similar social class should choose to live close to each other and prefer to limit the number of people of dissimilar social class in their midst.

The significance of negative and positive spillover effects is probably less immediately apparent than in the black segregation case. In the latter case, blacks and whites are often competing for the same housing. With lower-class and middle-class people, however, competition is much reduced since they are competing in different markets, the lower class for lower-priced housing and the middle class for upper-price-range housing. Where lower-class housing is constructed close to middle-class housing, however, there has often been a strong reaction by the middle-class neighborhood in order to protect its property values. In a number of British cases this has taken the extreme form of constructing a wall across a connecting street in order to preserve the tone — and hence the property values — of the middle-class neighborhood.

Assuming that we can explain social rank segregation in cities, how can we continue the argument to explain the sectoral arrangement of population by social rank that seems to be common in a large number of cities? This is difficult, but one explanation can be presented in terms of the intergroup relationships we have discussed above and in terms of population growth.

Consider a city at time t_1 with three residential areas distinguishable in terms of social rank (see Figure 15-8). To each of these residential areas we can imagine population of similar social rank being added by in-migration from outside. As in the case of the Negro reviewed above, such in-migration exerts pressure upon available housing and leads to a demand for additional housing. For a given residential area where

---

[1] Richard L. Morrill, "The Negro Ghetto: Problems and Alternatives," *Geographical Review* Vol. LV, No. 3 (July, 1965), p. 346.

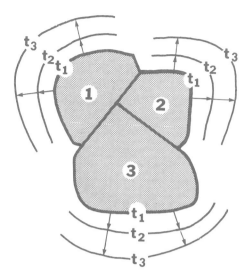

FIGURE 15-8. Development of social rank sectors by outward expansion. Sectors probably form as a result of expansion on the outermost edge of class-segregated residential districts. Such expansion of a similar social rank on the edge of a district minimizes contact with other social ranks and preserves positive spillover benefits.

should expansion of housing take place? Clearly, if proximity to one's social class is an important criterion of residential selection, then expansion of housing of a given quality should take place *on the edge of an area of similar housing quality*. If the argument is followed through, as in Figure 15-8, it will be seen that it leads to a sectoral arrangement of residential areas by social rank. An additional mediating force in the process is the real estate market because land in proximity to an area of high social rank is likely to be more expensive per square foot than land elsewhere.

In summary, and very broadly, the contemporary city at a given point in time can be characterized geographically in terms of two types of pattern: (a) *distance decay phenomena* that derive ultimately from differential demands for accessibility to the central business district and their expression in terms of land value differences, and (b) *residential segregation phenomena* that derive from the

different perceptions that groups of people hold of the negative and positive spillover effects of having members of other groups reside in close proximity. The most telling manifestations of these residential preferences are the opposite poles of the Negro ghetto at one end and the exclusive silk-stocking neighborhood at the other end.

Such is the picture at a given point in time. The urban scene, however, is dynamic: the distance decays alter in their gradient in response to new technological, social, and economic forces. Residential neighborhoods expand and others contract in response to the changing balance of power within the city. It is such changes and the forces that produce them that we shall discuss next.

THE CITY FROM A DYNAMIC VIEWPOINT

The distance decays relating population density and land values to distance from the central business district have both undergone a *flattening* in the recent past. In the case of population density, Figure 15-9 for Chicago shows that for

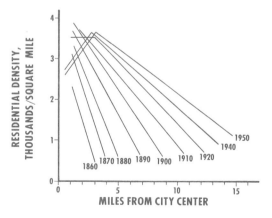

FIGURE 15-9. The changing relationship between population density and distance from city center for Chicago: 1860–1950. Population densities are expressed in natural logarithms. Note the emergence of a "crater" after 1910 and the flattening of the slope indicating suburbanization of population.

the past 80 years or so there has been a continual *suburbanization of population* resulting in a decline in the gradient of the distance decay. These changes in the locational pattern of population density, moreover, do not seem confined to Chicago: they have been confirmed for other large metropolises in Western industrial societies.

In view of the relationship between population density and land values, moreover, it would be surprising if we could not observe similar changes in the locational pattern of land values over time as we observe for population density. Indeed this does seem to be so because the decay of land values with distance from the central business district has become much less steep largely due to an appreciation of suburban land values. The latter is a product of the increasing suburbanization of population in Western cities.

In the geography of social composition the most important change in the American city has been the *great expansion in the size of Negro ghettoes* that has taken place at an increasing pace in the larger cities of the country since 1945. The ghettoes, with their nuclei close to the downtown areas of major cities, have swollen immensely producing an increasingly dominant geographical pattern of a black city surrounded by lily-white suburbs. In the 10 years from 1950 to 1960 for instance, the percentage of the population which is nonwhite in Washington, D.C. increased from 32% to 55%, in Chicago from 14% to 24%. Projections of nonwhite population suggest that in 1980 Washington D.C. will be 95% nonwhite while Cleveland will be 55% nonwhite and Chicago will fall just short of a nonwhite majority. The increasing polarization in the composition of city and suburb is already evident in the recent emergence of Negro mayors in such dominantly Negro cities as Cleve-

land, Ohio and Newark, New Jersey. Such trends in locational patterns seem bound to continue for reasons that we shall explore below.

These changes in the locational patterns of population density, land values, and social composition are attributable to a variety of factors, some endogenous to the city and some exogenous. Within the city, however, everything is related to everything else and it is not an easy task to distinguish between cause and effect — simply because the relationships are often mutual rather than one-way. In the interests of conceptual clarity, however, we shall try to treat two topics separately — suburbanization and ghetto expansion — and then show how they are also intimately related to each other.

The *suburbanization of population* and its consequent effects on the locational pattern of land values and of population density can be explained ultimately in terms of two factors: (a) *transportation innovation* and (b) *increasing population. Both* are required for suburbanization to occur; *neither* could produce suburbanization on its own. Transportation innovation has revolutionized accessibility relationships within the city over the past 60 or 70 years, as we reviewed in Chapter One. The increasing relative accessibility of more peripheral locations and the decreasing relative and absolute access of downtown locations in the metropolitan area have provided the necessary preconditions for the massive relocations of people, stores, and employment. It is necessary to emphasize the word *preconditions*. Transportation innovation has to a large extent been a *permissive* factor. There is no point in increasing the supply of accessible locations unless there is a *demand* to use them; and demand for residential land is strongly related to the growth of population and of income. As the population of a town grows, the demand for residential development grows. Before the automobile era, population growth led to the development of the city upward and the confinement of residences to very small lots. Improved accessibility from the periphery of the city *permitted* suburban expansion. Demand is also affected by income: the demand for the high-quality low-density residential development so characteristic of suburbs, for example, has a very high income elasticity so that as incomes have risen so has the demand for such suburban-type housing. On the basis of this analysis, therefore, it should come as little surprise that the rate of suburbanization for six American cities studied—Baltimore, Denver, Milwaukee, Philadelphia, Rochester, and Toledo—has been largely a function of changes in income and population.[2] As the population of a city and/or its median family income have increased so the population density gradient has flattened over time.

However, suburbanization has not been confined to residential population and it is doubtful that we can understand the intensity of the residential component of suburbanization without considering also the *suburbanization of employment*—manufacturing, retailing, office employment, and so on. For these, the preconditions for suburbanization have been the same: demand and accessibility improvements. As far as demand is concerned, the suburbanization of employment in the six cities referred to above has shown a strong relationship to the overall growth of employment in a given economic sector in a specific city. Where a city has undergone a large growth in its number of manufacturing employees so suburbanization of industry has proceeded apace; where retail employment increased, so has the suburbanization of retailing.

Accessibility changes have also been important in increasing the supply of feasible locations. *Truck transportation* has released the factory from dependency on downtown railroad goods yards; the *automobile* has released the factory from the most accessible point of the early 20th-century *labor market*—the downtown area with its mass transit focus. Retailing has also benefited from such changing accessibility relationships: with the consumer moving to shop by private automobile the focus of the public transportation system has lost much of its significance.

Other factors have been important, however—for example, *land costs*. As we demonstrated in Chapter One, factories, offices, and shops consume more space today than they did sixty or seventy years ago, thus increasing the attractiveness of suburban locations with their relatively low land values.

Not that these ideas apply to manufacturing and retailing alone. Even offices have tended to relocate from the downtown area. They are attracted by lower land costs but also frequently by access to the city airport. Air has replaced rail as the major transportation medium for executives and so the attractiveness of sites close to the airport—almost always in the suburbs due to lower land costs—increases.

Another facet of the suburbanization phenomenon involves the relationships between the suburbanization of population and the suburbanization of employment. This, of course, is another chicken-and-egg problem since there could conceivably be causal connections in both directions. On the one hand, for example, factories could have moved to the suburbs to be closer to their labor force; but on the other hand, the labor force could have moved to the suburbs in order to be closer to the factories. In actual fact there is strong evidence that

---

[2] Edwin S. Mills, "Urban Density Functions," *Urban Studies*, Vol. 7, No. 1 (February, 1970), pp. 5–20.

population suburbanized *earlier*, which suggests—but does not prove—that suburbanized labor forces and markets provided important reasons for the suburbanization of manufacturing and retailing, respectively. Figure 15-10 plots average gradients over time and the earlier flattening of the population gradient is clearly evident. Interestingly enough, the gradients have not only flattened, they have also tended to become more similar over time.

No matter what the exact causal relationships are, the changes in locational pattern have been little short of revolutionary. Thus, in 1948 the central cities contained 64% of metropolitan-area population; by 1960 that proportion had shrunk to 52%. In terms of manufacturing employment in 1929, 74% of the manufacturing employees in 18 selected American metropolitan areas were located in the central city; this proportion had declined to 60% in 1958. The stories of *relative* growth in the suburbs and *relative* decline in the central city are repeated for other activities such as wholesaling and retailing. Let us emphasize, however, that we are talking about *relative* growth and decline and not necessarily *absolute* growth and decline; the suburbs could have increased their share of total manufacturing employment in the metropolitan area without any absolute change in the central city at all and in some cases this presumably has happened. Likewise, in other cases, there could have been absolute growth of population in the central city and suburbs, but suburban populations could have grown at a faster rate, and undoubtedly this has happened. It may be incorrect, therefore, to take the respective percentage shares of suburb and central city and infer from them a vast exodus of people and jobs from central city to suburb. Indubitably, this has been part of the story in many cities, but there are other aspects, too, such as the location of completely

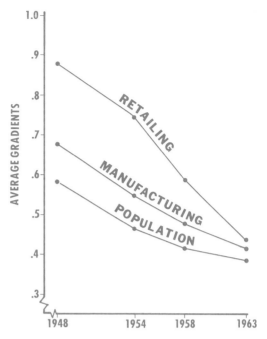

FIGURE 15-10. Average gradients for population densities, retailing employment densities and manufacturing employment densities for 18 American cities 1948–1963. The gradients relate density to distance from the CBD: where the gradient is steeper, population or employment is more *centralized;* where the gradient is less steep, population or employment is more *suburbanized.* Note the way in which population was suburbanized earlier than employment suggesting that employment and retailing relocated in the suburbs in order to be closer to their labor markets and consumer markets, respectively.

new and rapidly growing industries, such as electronics, in suburban areas.

In view of these changes in population location within the metropolitan areas, the historically declining distance-decay rates in population density can be seen in a clearer perspective. Population has become more evenly distributed within metropolitan areas, and less concentrated in the central-city area. The dispersion of population and manufacturing, retailing, and office facilities, moreover, has increased the demand for land in suburban locations. This has raised land values relative to central-city land values, thus producing a declining distance-decay rate in land values over time. The pressure on land has been particularly intense at certain highly accessible locations in the suburbs, particularly where freeways from the downtown area cross bypasses around the city. Such points have been extremely attractive to suburban shopping centers, cinemas, hotels and motels, auto distributors, and physician and dental services. In many cities, therefore, what seems to be emerging is a situation in which the downtown area is one attractive node among several with other nodes at the intersection of freeways in the suburbs emerging as competing locations. It is likely, therefore, that the land value distribution will eventually be transformed from a concentric arrangement with high land values at the center and relatively low land values at the periphery to a situation in which there are several concentric arrangements coexisting side by side.

Within this context of suburbanizing population and employment the *Negro ghetto slowly expands,* driven by the external forces of in-migration and the internal forces of racial prejudice and fear. The ghetto, particularly in the larger metropolitan centers, has undergone a steady accretion in numbers not only due to high birth rates but also to migration from rural areas of the South and from smaller cities. Within the city the geographical expansion is dictated by similar forces to those that we identified when discussing segregation. As we might anticipate, *expansion tends to take place at the edge of the ghetto* rather like the expansion of frontier settlement in North America in the 19th century. Figure 15-11 demonstrates very clearly the way in which the ghetto tends to expand at its edge: houses close to the ghetto—say, a block away—are much more likely to be bought by Negroes than houses two blocks away.

Locations along the edge of the ghetto are ones in which whites see their property values and themselves most threatened. They will have to mix with Negroes in stores, they risk the white man's fear of interracial marriage more than whites elsewhere in the city and their children go to school with Negro children. Furthermore, the advance of the ghetto in their direction accentuates the notion that things are unlikely to get better in the future; rather, they will get worse. Such white families, therefore, are more likely to move out than families further away from the ghetto.

For the Negro family, however, the formerly white house on the edge of the ghetto offers a relatively optimal location. For although it may be surrounded by whites, Negroes are sufficiently close by to insulate the Negro family from any white boycott and to offer support in case of threat; furthermore, the whites are thinking of moving anyway.

The wheels of this relocation mechanism are assiduously oiled by the real estate man. The real estate brokers instill panic among white sellers in order to obtain the property at low prices and sell to the Negro at inflated prices. For most real estate men, moreover, expansion of the ghetto into adjacent areas signifies that pressure in other white areas will be reduced.

Given that the ghetto expands from an initial nucleus close to the downtown area it is easy to detect another force promoting suburbanization of the white segment of the population. Suburbs are increasingly seen as havens of security fortified by a variety of informal mechanisms, such as the rigged real estate market, against black infiltration. The suburbs allow whites to obtain those positive spillover effects that they do not think are possible if they live adjacent to the ghetto.

An important implication of these

• NEW STREET FRONTS WITH SALES TO NEGROES, 1955

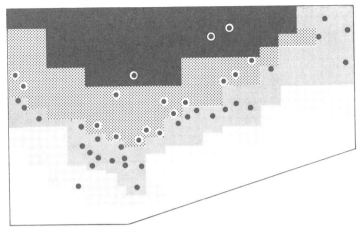

	NUMBER OF WHITE PURCHASES	PERCENT OF TOTAL PURCHASES	PERCENT OF AREA NEGRO
AREA 1	8	3.9	32
AREA 2	26	4.3	16
AREA 3	65	40.6	5
AREA 4	72	96.7	1
AREA 5	112	100.0	<1

FIGURE 15-11. The expansion of the Negro ghetto. Note how the ghetto expands at its edge; Negro home purchases are much more likely closer to the area with a high proportion of its population Negro than further away. Such locations minimize interracial contact and maximize intraracial contact.

ideas is that the image of the city's geography held by the layman is an increasingly concentric one. This *concentric image* was strongly apparent in the results of the survey of student images of the city discussed in Chapter Six. There it was shown that a sample of undergraduate students saw the city as divided into (1) a central core area, largely black, low income, with a high population density and high crime rates, and (2) a white, middle-class, low-density, low-crime, suburban periphery. Nor, in terms of what has been happening and

what *is* happening in the city does this seem to be totally unjustified. The dynamics of urban locational patterns have a strong concentric component. Also, the ever larger Negro ghettoes close to the downtown area increase the racial and income components of concentricity; the sectors of social rank are now much less clear at the level of the city as a whole than they were, say, before 1939.

Nevertheless, one should be careful not to overestimate the overall geographical significance of this concentricity. Such *concentricity seems to be most appar-*

TABLE 15-2.   City-suburban differences in some measures of social rank. Note that the dichotomy of a middle-class suburb and a lower class inner city tends to be more frequently encountered in larger cities than in smaller cities.

Size of urbanized area	Percentage of urbanized areas in which suburbs rank higher			Number of areas
	Median family income	Percent completing high school	Percent white collar	
1,000,000 and over	100.0	100.0	87.5	16
500,000–1,000,000	100.0	100.0	86.4	22
250,000–500,000	79.3	75.9	55.2	29
150,000–250,000	72.1	62.8	48.8	43
100,000–150,000	70.3	64.9	40.5	37
50,000–100,000	56.6	49.1	30.2	53

ent in larger urban centers. As Table 15-2 shows, it is in the larger cities that the image of concentric income differences between a poorer central city and a wealthier suburb seems most accurate. In addition, the larger cities have shown greater increases in black populations and have also shown the greatest degrees of suburbanization of residences and employment. In smaller cities, these changes in urban locational patterns have been much less apparent, largely because such cities just have not grown so rapidly.

It is in the larger cities, moreover, that the social problems of the city have been most in evidence. The great black riots of the 1960s took place in larger cities such as Los Angeles, Detroit, Washington, and Newark. Given this backcloth of an increasingly concentric metropolis, what is the nature of its relationship to the social problems of such metropolitan centers? It is to those problems that we now turn.

THE PROBLEMS OF THE CITY

We have now delineated one important basis of the contemporary urban crisis: the locational context in which that crisis is being played out. Before proceeding to the effects of that locational arrangement on contemporary problems, however, we also need to consider a more generalized concept of "social problem."

Social problems are problems of social welfare, that is, of the happiness of people in society. If some people are unhappy with their lot then their discontent will emerge as a social problem. Moreover, for both moral and political reasons governments have attempted to mitigate such social problems by a variety of means but largely by *income redistribution.* Since a large number of social problems result from some people having inadequate access to resources while others have more than adequate access, this approach seems a reasonable one. In North America and Western Europe it has given rise to a whole host of redistribution policies among which progressive taxation is most prominent; in different nations such devices as old-age pensions, family allowances, unemployment benefits, and subsidized public housing for lower-income groups are also important.

However, such social welfare policies are based on the idea of a rather close relationship between social welfare and income before redistribution. In fact there is growing evidence that such may not be the case: a person who earns 20,000 dollars per year may be *more* than twice as wealthy as a person who earns 10,000 dollars a year because of the incidence of certain additional benefits and the absence of certain costs that the lower-income person incurs. Certain benefits and costs remain unequally distributed and are not affected by income redistribution policy. A major example of this is the expense account, which gives the higher-income executive certain benefits—a free car, dining in good restaurants, etc.—that the lower-income person does not get.

What we are arguing for here is an enlarged concept of income to take into account benefits and costs that are not reflected in the taxable pay packet, that may or may not have a price attached to them, but that exercise a very potent effect on social welfare. We can term such nonpay-packet items of income *invisible income*. What is most interesting *from the viewpoint of the geography of the city* is that this *invisible income is distributed in a highly uneven manner.* In particular it tends to be distributed in such a way that it *confers greater net benefits on suburban locations than on inner-city locations.* This is reflected in such phenomena as fresher meats in suburban supermarkets than in a city markets. Most supermarket chains in the United States operate on the principle of allocating the fresher foods to their branches in the more discriminating suburban consumer market and then, if it does not sell there, transferring it to their inner-city branches. Similarly central-city populations are more subject to the hazards of pollution. The Welcome Wagon does not call downtown either—it is strictly a suburban institution!

Assuming this broadened concept of income and its geographical applicability within the city, we need to ask about the geographical arrangement of the invisible portion of income within the city. What is the pattern of costs and benefits and why? This is the first question we tackle. We then try to relate these costs and benefits to the geography of poverty within the city and show how the urban political system has tended to intensify these related problems of poverty and of the inequitable distribution of costs and benefits. We conclude by looking at some possible solutions to the urban problems of the Western world, but particularly of the United States.

THE GEOGRAPHY OF INVISIBLE INCOME IN THE CITY

People's receipts of invisible income depend very much on their *accessibility* to various beneficial locations and upon their *proximity* to certain nonbeneficial locations. To be *accessible* means that one does not incur more than a very modest movement cost on the needed good or service and the advantage of accessibility may be reflected in increased property values: to be *proximate* to an obnoxious location means that one must suffer it and incur the cost of decreased property values and/or the costs of moving away from the area. Let us review some of the costs and benefits and proximities and accessibilities associated with differing locations in the city.

Accessibility to Places of Employment. People within a metropolitan area vary in their accessibility to employment. Most important has been the increasing suburbanization of employment in manufacturing and retailing which has brought the already advantaged suburban population closer to their places of work and imposed an increased movement cost on inner-city populations. There is also some evidence that the low-skilled jobs for which inner-city residents are most likely to qualify have been suburbanizing fastest of all. Among the slowest to suburbanize has been office employment which usually requires levels of education not typical of the inner-city dweller.

The most obvious effect of such suburbanization of employment opportunities is the increasing distances over which ghetto dwellers must travel to work. In Chicago, for example, the average length of travel-to-work for blacks is 30% greater than for whites. Such relative and increasing inaccessibility also presents handicaps to actually searching for jobs and obtaining information about job vacancies. Job information seems to be primarily disseminated by word of mouth through friends and relatives — such communication is much more persuasive and interest arousing than the newspaper advertisement. But as long as inner-city residents are so poorly represented in the new suburban centers of employment then other inner-city residents will also have trouble finding work.

These problems of accessibility are exacerbated by the low availability of transportation to inner-city dwellers. In Chicago only 15% of Negro householders own cars. In the United States as a whole 47% of family units with before-tax incomes of between $2000 and $2999 did not own an automobile in 1967, and most poor urban residents are concentrated in the inner city.

Public transportation is also deficient. Not only has the widespread use of the automobile led to an increasing lack of profitability in mass transit systems and hence deterioration in the service that they offer; there is also the problem of the dispersion of employment opportunities among many suburbs. A profitable transit service depends on demand for a large flow between pairs of places; if employment is dispersed this situation is less likely to be realized than in the days when employment opportunities were concentrated in the central business district. In some cities where the automobile ownership rate is especially high and where employment opportunities are dispersed over a wide suburban area, the problem is particularly critical. Such is the case in Los Angeles as the McCone Commission remarked in its report on the Watts riots: "Our investigation has brought into clear focus the fact that the inadequate and costly public transportation currently existing throughout the Los Angeles area seriously restricts the residents of the disadvantaged areas such as South Central Los Angeles. This lack of adequate transportation handicaps them in seeking and holding jobs, attending schools, shopping and fulfilling other needs."

For whites and more middle-class elements of the population relocation to the suburbs has been the obvious solution to adjusting to the problem of accessibility to places of employment. For blacks and lower-income whites this is rarely a viable alternative. Blacks face a problem of housing segregation and the informal mechanisms that keep them out of the suburbs; both white and black face the problem that lower-price housing has been extraordinarily deficient in its supply. This is partly caused by the lack of subsidized housing projects such as those common in Western Europe; it is also caused by restrictive zoning practices to be discussed shortly.

The relationship between urban poverty and accessibility to employment seems to be a close one and plays a large part in explaining the very high rates of unemployment that exist among blacks in the contemporary United States. This is probably the most important of the inaccessibilities and proximities that the inner city suffers from; it is not the only one, however.

Other Accessibilities and Some Proximities. Consider recreation: the city attempts to provide parks and other recreational facilities for its population in a reasonably equitable manner across the city as a whole. It is faced with a problem, however. Land values are very high towards the center of the city and so, therefore, is the cost of buying land on the scale required to set out a park or a golf course. One of the major consequences of this is that the city has to buy land on the edge (where it is cheaper) for its golf courses and parks. Such recreational facilities are much closer to suburban populations than to inner-city residents and in a large city this will be reflected in relative frequency of patronage by the two residential groups. Ironically the suburbs are frequently independent municipalities and have not contributed one penny towards the cost of the recreational facilities.

In terms of access to shopping facilities, the inner city is also disadvantaged. The violence of recent urban riots and high crime rates have led to high insurance rates for retailers and have caused many businesses to close down. Poor transportation available to the consumer assists the remaining retailers in carving out a monopolistic situation for themselves. The result is higher prices for lower-quality goods. In the suburbs, on the other hand, a higher density of retailers and the ability of the automobile-driving consumer to shop around helps keep prices lower.

In still other cases, the problem is one of *proximity* to obnoxious land uses or just plain bad scenes rather than *accessibility* to some desired opportunity. Many of the industries that have left the central city have been of a cleaner, less polluting variety, while remaining behind in the city have been the dirtier, noisier, more 19th-century industries. Other obnoxious land uses are much more incident towards the center of the city: freeways with their noise and attendant air pollution, for example, achieve a much higher density towards the center of the city than in suburban locations.

A final consideration is crime. The general pattern of crime shows that crime rates are particularly high in the center of the city and decline to relatively low levels in the surrounding suburbs. Crime, moreover, is a strongly localized phenomenon within cities: it occurs close to where criminals live so that there is only a limited chance of it spilling over into adjacent suburbs. In a study of homicides in the city of Houston, for example, it was found that about 75% of the offenders and 87% of the victims lived less than two miles from the homicidal confrontation.

In brief the geography of invisible income in the city is one in which the already wealthier suburbs gain far more than the disinherited ethnic minorities and poor whites of the inner city. Not only that but the situation seems to have deteriorated in relative terms: the shift of employment opportunities to the suburbs has been matched by a residential shift of the young, the employed, the wealthy, and the white, leaving behind the older, the poorer, the unemployed, and the black.

Not only has there been relative deterioration in social welfare (income plus invisible income) differences between suburb and city but there is some alarming evidence that the situation in the ghetto may have undergone an *absolute* deterioration. Special Census surveys of black slums carried out in the mid-1960s after the riots in such cities as Los Angeles and Cleveland are indicative in this regard. Thus the survey of the south Los Angeles area showed that median family income *dropped* by 8% from $5122 in 1959 to $4736 in 1965, while a typical nonwhite family income in the United States as a whole rose 24%. That such a deterioration can occur in the wealthiest nation on the globe suggests that something is seriously amiss. It may well be that part of the explanation lies in the operation of the metropolitan political system.

THE POLITICAL SYSTEM AND
THE GEOGRAPHY OF POVERTY

For a variety of reasons the functioning of the metropolitan political system tends to reinforce suburb–central city inequality in invisible income. Most important is the *political fragmentation of metropolitan areas.* Nearly all larger metropolitan areas of the United States with populations in excess of 100,000 tend to be subdivided into several municipalities with taxing powers and with a power to provide certain public goods and services such as education, police, water, sewage, highway construction, and garbage collection. The usual geographic pattern is for the older and numerically more populous part of the city to be under one government and to be surrounded by a number of smaller suburban municipalities like leeches on a sore. As we shall see, the simile is not altogether inappropriate since this system of fragmentation of political power is a major reason for the current urban crisis in America.

An initial effect of fragmentation is the *lack of congruence between tax bases and needs for public services* across the municipalities of a metropolitan area. In general the central city has a relatively high demand for poverty-linked services, such as health and welfare, in addition to demands for such services as education and fire protection which it shares with the suburban municipalities. This is reflected in municipal expenditure patterns. In 1957 average expenditure per capita in central-city municipalities was $185.49 while in surrounding suburbs the average was $159.83—a difference of $25.66.

The distribution of need for services, however, bears no equitable relationship

to the ability to satisfy those needs by property taxes. Suburban assessed valuations per capita, and therefore tax bases, are considerably higher. The irony is that in order to meet their heavier demands the city must tax at a correspondingly higher rate. In 1957, central cities taxed at a per capita average of $109.07 compared with $85.78 in surrounding suburbs —and this on a considerably poorer population. A person occupying residential property of a given value in the central city, therefore, is likely to be taxed considerably heavier than a person occupying property of similar value in the suburban municipality. Consequently there is very little income redistribution between central-city and suburban municipalities other than that achieved by federal taxation and federal subsidies to central-city governments.

This inequity has been aggravated by the *flight of industry and other employment generators* to the suburbs. Relocation has robbed the central city of a very important element of its tax base and transferred it to the already wealthier suburbs. In some situations there has been a temptation to tax remaining industry even more but this has only aggravated the situation by stimulating relocation at a still faster rate. This seems to have been the case in New York City, for instance. The usual municipal response to such a situation has been a cutting back on taxes and consequent reduction in services rendered to the needy.

The third problem flowing from the political fragmentation of metropolitan areas is that of *zoning regulations.* The independent municipalities have the power to zone land within their boundaries for different purposes. It is possible, for example, to zone-in clean industry and zone-out dirty, polluting industry. Many suburbs have done this, taking employment away from the downtown area and leaving the dirtier polluting industry behind. The insidious effects of municipal zoning on the distribution of income (including invisible income) in the urban area, however, derives largely from its use to regulate the type of residential development in a municipality and therefore the health of the suburb's tax base. By zoning for half-acre or whole-acre residential lots, for instance, lower-income groups can be kept out and the tax base of the community conserved. By keeping lower-income people out, of course, the suburb is merely aggravating the tremendous fiscal burden which the central city must handle.

A fourth major manifestation of the inequitable effects of municipal fragmentation is the *suburban exploitation of the central city.* For a variety of reasons the central city provides or subsidizes services that the whole metropolitan area benefits from. Park facilities, golf courses, and swimming pools, for example, are accessible to the suburban municipality as well as to the central-city dweller—but it is the city dweller who supports these services in the form of taxes while the suburbanite contributes no part of that tax support. In the same way, many cities subsidize mass transit systems which serve suburban populations as well as the central city without any fiscal contribution from the suburb. Subsidies to symphony orchestras, art galleries, and municipal zoos fall in the same category.

It is easy to see, moreover, that the inequities caused by metropolitan fragmentation have a self-perpetuating character about them thus making the situation still more critical for the central city and still more comfortable for the suburban municipalities. Relatively high tax rates deter wealthier people who can improve the tax base from residing in the central city; the same effect accelerates the suburbanization of industry and other nonresidential land uses yielding

juicy property taxes to the municipality to which they relocate. The flight of industry is further encouraged by the low levels of skill of the population remaining in the central city.

These problems are particularly associated with municipal fragmentation and with the American city in which such fragmentation of power is so intense. In the European city not only is such fragmentation greatly reduced but the power of the individual municipality is also considerably reduced compared with that of the American municipality. This does not mean that a unified metropolitan area would be all sweetness and light and that the mechanisms that channel the benefits toward the upper-income areas and many of the costs toward the lower-income areas would be eliminated. Even in the nonfragmented city the poorer inner-city elements will tend to lose out because of the economic and political power of the wealthier sections of the city.

Upper- and middle-income groups, for example, are much more effective than lower-income groups at organizing themselves to combat the location of harmful or obnoxious land uses in their vicinity and have the power to pull the invisible strings that will produce zoning in their favor and locate noisy freeways and airports away from their doors. They also have the ability to organize and obtain the beneficial aspects of the city.

The poorer people of the inner-city lack such organizing ability and usually feel powerless in the face of some external locational threat such as a new municipal stadium or incinerator. The conflict between middle-class suburb and lower-class inner city is frequently one in which the winner takes all. Urban renewal is a case in point: it involves the displacement of inner-city populations and increasing pressures on housing prices for them; it also involves the provision of higher value property such as universities—as in the case of Chicago Circle—and prestige office blocks to provide benefits largely to the suburban populations. In all such locational contests the poor of the inner city usually lose out. What then is to be done?

SOME POSSIBLE SOLUTIONS

Social problems such as those which the contemporary city faces, give rise to a veritable plethora of proposed solutions, some of them more or less viable but most of them requiring large concessions by those who have economic and political power to those who do not. Broadly, two types of solution have been proposed: locational solutions designed to alter locational patterns within cities in order to reduce the present inequitable distribution of invisible income between central city and suburb, and national solutions with locational effects of an indirect character. It is likely that only some pragmatic mixture of the two will suffice.

Locational Solutions. It is widely recognized by students of the problem that a major factor producing suburban–central-city inequality is the municipal fragmentation of metropolitan areas. A widely mooted solution, therefore, is that of eliminating such fragmentation and replacing it with a *city-wide government responsible for taxation and expenditure and zoning throughout the metropolitan area.* Undoubtedly this would introduce a welcome redistribution of income between suburb and central city; the integration of zoning responsibility would make zoning suburban land for lower-income housing more likely— though not inevitable—and the problem of the suburban exploitation of the central city would be eliminated.

Unfortunately the prospects for such integration on a widespread level are not good. In 1957, for instance, there were 17,984 governmental units in the 212 Standard Metropolitan Statistical Areas of the United States; in 1962 there were 18,442 units or an increase of 3%. Instead of integration, therefore, there has been disintegration.

Metropolitan integration, however, would only be part of the answer because it would still leave the central-city dweller remote from places of work in the suburbs. A major and much publicized proposal to combat this problem has been the notion of *bringing industry into the ghettoes* by means of favorable government credits and tax concessions. This was a much featured aspect of the Republican party program in the 1968 elections but one that has not received wide publicity since then. The reason is clear: such a program of job creation would be exceedingly expensive in terms of subsidies. Not only that but it would also probably reduce the political pressure to open up the suburbs to blacks and thereby assist in perpetuating the ghetto. Alternatively, the growth of employment in ghettoes might only accelerate in-migration of Negroes from rural areas of the South thus reducing the ghetto once more to its former level of poverty. It is unlikely, therefore, that such a policy would be very effective in solving current urban problems over the long term.

Proponents of such schemes, however, have seen another advantage which ghetto industry would bestow: an addition to the nonresidential property tax base of the central city that would be very useful in lieu of that metropolitan integration which seems so unlikely. Another locational policy with a similar aim is that of *urban renewal.* A major aim of urban renewal has been to clear large areas of land of old, slum property with low property values in order to replace it with higher-value industrial, office, and residential properties that would boost the city's tax base. Unfortunately, clearance has often involved the demolition of some not-so-old properties; it has also involved the problem of relocating the poorer families who cannot afford the newer, higher-value housing property that has gone up on many urban renewal sites in order to attract wealthier residents back to the central city. In short, urban renewal has often been brutal to the very people it hopes ultimately to help. In a number of instances this short-term aggravation of the urban problem has probably led to severe conflicts. News reports of the Newark riots of 1967, for example, claimed that the riots were partly stimulated by resentment over the relocation program resulting from the urban renewal plans for the New Jersey School of Medicine and Dentistry. Although urban renewal may be a useful policy weapon if metropolitan integration is not feasible, it needs to be managed much more carefully from the viewpoint of protecting the interests of the lower-class inhabitants most directly involved.

The fourth proposal or set of proposals aimed at breaking the link between poverty and transportation has suggested a *greatly increased emphasis on public transportation relative to private transportation.* Such proposals have ranged from much increased subsidies at one end of the scale, to banning automobiles from downtown areas so that people would have to use public transportation. The problem should be obvious: a subsidy to public transportation and possible elaborate mass transit systems such as BART, being presently completed in the San Francisco Bay area, are politically acceptable; restrictions on the automobile to make such systems viable economic propositions and to make the city a pleasanter place to live in almost certainly are not. By differentiating between the central city and the suburbs such a policy of automobile restriction would only hasten suburbanization of employment and residences, thus leaving the central city even more deprived of a tax base than it is already.

Granting the problems of these locational policies, what type of mitigating policy is possible at the national level?

Nonlocational Policies. One way of correcting the present inequities of tax base and expenditure needs between the central city and the surrounding suburbs is by a *vastly increased program of income redistribution in the nation as a whole.* To a certain extent it has already alleviated the urban problem in the form of subsidies to inner-city education. The question is: Is enough redistribution at the national level being carried out in order to reverse the increasing disparity of central-city and suburban social welfare levels? One authority who thinks not is Daniel Moynihan who has drawn attention to the persistence of slums in America compared with their virtual extinction in other Western democracies which by means of vastly more severe income redistribution, full employment, and welfare policies in the form of, for example, national health services have almost eradicated the problem: ". . . The teeming disorganized life of impoverished slums has all but disappeared among the North Atlantic democracies—save only the United States. It requires some intrepidness to *declare* this to be a fact as no systematic inquiry has been made that will provide completely dependable comparisons but it can be said with fair assurance that mass poverty and squalor of a kind that may be encountered in almost any large American city simply cannot be found in comparable cities in Europe or Canada or Japan."[3]

The effects of effective full employment policies are illustrated by the much less severe problems of the British city. Many of the larger British cities have undergone an influx of colored population since 1945 but there has been far less of the ghettoization characteristic of the American situation. This has been partly attributed to the full employment that has made home ownership a reality for many of the immigrants. Indeed in many areas of London, property ownership is much more common among the black immigrants than among the native whites. Likewise, in British and other West European cities large allocations of public funds to subsidized low-cost public housing have allowed the clearance of slum areas with carefully programmed relocation into low-rent homes.

There are already signs in the United States of a growing realization that past federal interference in redistribution has been deficient in both intensity and scope. The notion of a *negative income tax* seems to be gaining popularity as does that of *family allowances* and a *national health scheme*. Perhaps, therefore, we can conclude on a note of optimism, because a greatly increased program of redistribution would have positive implications for other components of the urban problem. By reducing the need for the central city to be responsible for welfare payments, for example, and by improving the quality of central-city schools, it could reduce the current resistance of suburban municipalities to metropolitan integration schemes. That this will be accomplished is more likely than not; the United States confronted previous crises of income redistribution in the 1930s and passed them reasonably adequately. Now another backlog of needs and problems has been brought up in the context of the city and governments are showing an increasing willingness to confront them.

---

[3] Daniel P. Moynihan, "Poverty in Cities," in James Q. Wilson (ed.), *The Metropolitan Enigma* (Harvard University Press: Cambridge, Mass., 1968).

CONCLUSIONS AND SUMMARY

What light can a geographer shed on the source of contemporary problems of the city, particularly of the American city—problems of poverty, conflict, housing, etc.? This is the fundamental question with which this chapter has dealt.

Urban problems have to be viewed within a locational context. Certain things, for example, are arranged *concentrically* within the city, such as *population density, family structure,* and *land values.* Such concentricities can be largely traced to the functioning of the *urban land market.* In addition to such concentric patterns, however, there are also segregation patterns. Specifically we tend to find that *social rank is arranged in wedgelike sectors* while *ethnic minorities tend to cluster in ghettoes close to the downtown area.* Such residential segregation tends to be a function of the desire of households to *maximize positive spillover benefits* and to *minimize negative spillover effects.*

The city, however, is changing: (1) *residential populations and employment have been suburbanizing* and (2) *the ghetto has been expanding in area.* The result is a *popular image of the city,* which as we saw in Chapter Six is increasingly *concentric in form:* a *poor black inner city surrounded by a ring of white and relatively wealthy suburbs.* This image, however, corresponds increasingly to the reality of the situation particularly in larger cities.

What does all this have to do with social problems (i.e., problems of social welfare)? Critical differences in social welfare are usually attributable to differences in access to resources. Governments have seen this as largely soluble by income redistribution policies. This, however, fails to touch the problem of the *fringe benefits or costs which form invisible income and which are partly a function of location within a city.* These tend to aggravate rather than mitigate the maldistribution of monetary income.

Particularly critical is access to employment which affects both wages and unemployment rates in different parts of the city. *With the increasing suburbanization of employment the suburbs have gained where the inner city has lost.* This problem is sorely aggravated by *housing segregation,* by lack of *private transport* for poor inner-city families, and by the *sad state of most urban public mass transit systems.* This differential accessibility problem is duplicated in *shopping facility* and *recreation* accessibilities; it is aggravated by *proximities* that favor suburb over inner city—the *crime* and *pollution* that the inner city suffers are cases in point.

Nor is the situation ameliorated by the prevailing *political fragmentation* of most large American cities. Needs for public services are usually higher where tax bases are lower—in the inner city—and inner-city populations consequently tend to lose out from either higher tax rates, lower-quality services, or both. The *flight of taxable business property* from the central city has only depleted the tax base still further while the demands on central-city services are inflated by those services that the central city provides for independent suburbs as well as for the city itself—a symphony orchestra or a zoo, for instance. Independent *zoning policies* add to the list of negative effects of political fragmentation.

To solve these social problems a variety of *policies* have been suggested, some of them *locational* in character and some of them *nonlocational. Industry-to-the-ghettoes, urban renewal, subsidized public transportation,* and *metropolitan integration* fall into the first category. Any one of these on its own, however, would likely have only partial success: metropolitan integration, for instance, would not prevent—though it might slow down—the suburbanization of employment; metropolitan integration policies, therefore, would probably have to be combined with an industry-to-the-ghettoes policy.

Most promising are nonlocational policies particularly those that aim at *a vastly more extensive redistribution of income* than has taken place up to now. This would have important effects not only directly upon the poverty of inner-city dwellers but also indirectly upon those accessibilities and proximities that determine fringe costs and benefits. It would, for example, make the inner city a more attractive partner for suburban municipalities in metropolitan integration plans; it would also alleviate the link between transportation and poverty by allowing poorer inner-city families to purchase automobiles.

The urban problem is currently in the public eye; it is by no means the only human problem that can be clarified by a geographical viewpoint however. Important for the differences in social welfare that exist between nations and between regions of a nation are *geographical differences in economic development.* If the problem of the city is an "inside" versus "outside" problem, where the suburban ring has a surfeit of resources compared with the inner city, in the geography of economic development the situation is usually reversed: a small section of the nation or of the globe has advantages that surrounding areas or nations do not enjoy. Such patterns and the processes that generate them are the concern of the next chapter.

CHAPTER SIXTEEN

The Geography of Economic Development

INTRODUCTION

A major world problem that has come to the attention of the educated public since the end of the Second World War is that of *economic development.* Just as the division of the economic pie within nations is reflected in a distribution between "haves" and "have-nots" so there are "have" nations like the United States and Sweden and "have-not" nations like India, China, and Indonesia. Similarly, within countries such as the United States, Sweden, or Indonesia, there are "have" regions and "have-not" regions.

The intent of this chapter is to take a look at locational patterns of economic development and attempt to explain them. In the first part of the chapter we are predominantly concerned with the idea of economic development and how we can measure it. Of what does economic development consist? Is it possible to rank countries in terms of their economic development in a precise manner? Second, we examine those elements of locational pattern or spatial predictability that seem to characterize economic development patterns. Are there neighborhood effects in economic development? Do economically developed areas tend to be clustered in space or be scattered widely across the land-

scape? These are the questions we ask in this section. Third, we ask the question, why should there be geographical predictability in economic development patterns anyway? What are the forces that produce whatever spatial regularity—localization, clustering, and so on—we are able to identify in economic development patterns? This problem of explanation is explored not only from the viewpoint of the geography of development *within nations* but also from the point of view of the geography of development *between nations.* Finally, we examine the geography of economic development as a political problem and explore some of the locational policies likely to resolve the problem. Before examining economic development from the geographical viewpoint, describing and explaining any spatial predictabilities inherent in its distribution over the earth's surface, however, it is necessary to ask "Of what does economic development consist? And how can we measure it?"

THE CONCEPT OF ECONOMIC DEVELOPMENT

We all have an image of underdeveloped countries acquired from newspapers, TV, and radio, and we have gained some idea about the types of distinctions existing between economically developed and economically underdeveloped nations. We know, for example, that the more developed nations such as the United States, France, and West Germany tend to be much richer than less developed countries such as India and China. This greater wealth is reflected in higher levels of personal welfare: medical care, diet, longevity, and so on. It is also associated with certain residential and occupational characteristics. The image of India is a rural one with the rice farmer working in his paddy field unaided by a machine, though possibly using a water buffalo. The image of the United States or of West Germany, on the other hand, is of large cities and machine civilizations in which large numbers of people earn their living at foundry, lathe, assembly line, or office.

These *images,* or what the scientist would call primitive unformalized *concepts,* allow us to think of some indicators of economic development or *variables* to which we can assign numerical values. We can think of certain indicators of national wealth, for example, such as the *gross national product per capita.* There are some problems associated with measuring this variable particularly in countries in which the cash economy has not penetrated the whole society, but in general this is a fair indicator of relative wealth across citizens of different countries. We measure it by dividing the monetary value (expressed in dollar terms) of all goods and services produced in a country by the number of people in that country.

In addition to such measures of national wealth, there are also certain measures of social welfare that will provide useful *indicators* of economic development across the nations of the world. *Death rates* and *infant mortality rates,* for example, are good indicators of nutrition, health, and medical care. Alterna-

tively, one may employ a measure such as the *number of physicians per capita* if data on mortality rates are unavailable. Measures of educational achievement also provide indications of the social welfare attributes that we associate with economic development: the *proportion of the population that is literate,* for example. And, in addition, access to urban amenity as measured by *the proportion of the population that is urban* provides an index of social welfare, being high in the more developed nations and low in the less developed nations.

There are also certain communication attributes associated with the concept of economic development that we need to take into consideration. We have already seen that the geometry of transportation networks as measured by the *density and connectivity* of railroad nets and highway nets varies with economic development levels. Other communication nets more concerned with the transfer of information are also denser in more developed societies: *newspaper circulation per population unit* and *telephones per population unit,* for example.

Different communication geometries connote differences in the circulation of goods between underdeveloped and more developed societies. In general the more developed society is thoroughly permeated with an exchange economy using cash as the medium of exchange; the less developed society, on the other hand, has a large subsistence sector to its economy so that trade is limited, and what trade there is often takes place by clumsy and inefficient barter. Such different levels of exchange are reflected in the values of such variables as the *tonnage of freight moved by railroads per population unit;* or the *foreign trade per capita.* In general, the more developed nations not only have higher levels of internal exchange but they also trade more with other nations.

TABLE 16-1. Selected indicators of economic development

	More developed nations	Less developed nations
Gross national product per capita	+	−
Birth rate	−	+
Death rate	−	+
Infant mortality rate	−	+
Proportion of the population, urban	+	−
Physicians per capita	+	−
Proportion of the population, literate	+	−
Railroad density	+	−
Highway density	+	−
Railroad connectivity	+	−
Newspaper circulation per population unit	+	−
Telephones per population unit	+	−
Tons/kilometers of freight per population unit	+	−
Motor vehicles per population unit	+	−
Foreign trade per capita	+	−
Proportion of the labor force employed in manufacturing	+	−
Proportion of the labor force employed in agriculture	−	+
Electricity consumption per capita	+	−
Capital per acre of agricultural land	+	−
Agricultural yields per farm worker	+	−

Finally, there are certain occupational differences that connote varying levels of economic development. The developed countries of the world have highly distinctive occupational structures: they tend to have relatively high proportions of their labor forces engaged in manufacturing and services with relatively low proportions in agricultural employment. These occupational differences involve differences in the demand for goods. The developed societies, for example, have much higher *electricity consumption per capita.*

These ideas reviewed above on the types of measure that discriminate between less developed and more developed countries are summarized in Table 16-1. Plus signs indicate that the variable is high in magnitude while minus signs indicate relatively low magnitudes. Other variables have been added to fill out our picture of economic development indicators.

In summary, it is possible to develop a list of *variables* or *indicators* indexing the *concept* of economic development across the nations of the world. Despite their variety—ranging from physicians per capita to trade per capita—these variables are highly *intercorrelated* so that, for example, nations that are high on physicians per capita also tend to be high on trade per capita, while nations that are low in levels of medical provision also tend to be low in trading levels. Table 16-1 gives some indication of the direction of the correlations between the different indicators: the correlation between birth-rate levels and gross national product per capita, for example, is negative: nations with high birth rates tend to be poor nations while richer nations tend to have lower birth rates. The correlation between the proportion of the population that is urban and the proportion of the population that is literate, on the other hand, tends to be positive: urban national societies are literate societies, while rural national societies have low degrees of educational provision.

Assuming these high correlations between the different variables, it ought to be possible to use any one of them as an *indicator* of economic development, plot its distribution across the nations of the world, and use that distribution as an indicator of the geography of economic development. Better still, however, would be some sort of average value across all indicators for a given nation. Since the correlations between the variables are not perfect, if we were to use any one particular variable as a measure of economic development we would be tempted to explain deviations between our expectation regarding development level in a country and the indicated level in terms of factors peculiar to the variable. Railroad connectivity and density, for example, are higher for India than our expectation would suggest, and we would be tempted to explain such discrepancies in terms of factors peculiar to railroad construction in India (i.e., the impact of British rule).

Just as we were able to develop general space preference viewpoints from the rankings of places by individuals in our discussion of mental maps, however, so it is possible to develop general economic development viewpoints or components from the rankings of nations by indicators such as gross national product per capita and infant mortality rate. Let us reconsider our treatment of the space preference case replacing the word "individual" with the word "variable" and the word "place" with the word "nation" but relating these to the original wordings by means of parentheses: "An initial survey of the listings reveals that no variable's (nobody's) listing is exactly

the same as any other variable's (anyone else's). A closer survey, however, indicates that there are similarities across all listings. For example, all variables (individuals) rank nation (place) *A* in the first three; all variables (individuals) accord nation (place) *D* a rank of sixth, seventh, or eighth; all variables (individuals) rank nation (place) *B* third or fourth. There seems to be support in this table, therefore, for the idea that while rankings are unique in some respects (i.e., the rank correlations between the variables would not be perfect), they are also similar in other respects [i.e., the variables (individuals) do have a general component (viewpoint) as well as specific components (viewpoints)]."

If the rankings of nations by the variables are highly similar, therefore, we can expect one very general component accounting for most of the variation of the original variables. This seems to be the case in economic development levels across nations of the world where a general component accounted for over 82% of the variation of the original 43 variables. According to the geographer, Brian J. L. Berry, who carried out this analysis: "The highest ranking countries are, of course, those which trade extensively and have many international contacts and well-developed internal systems of communications, including dense and intensively used transportation networks. They produce and consume much energy, have high national products, are highly urbanized and are well provided with such facilities as medical services."[1] Moreover, just as we can map scores for places to develop a mental map of residential desirability, so we can derive scores on the general economic development component for na-

---

[1] Brian J. L. Berry, "An Inductive Approach to the Regionalization of Economic Development" in Norton Ginsburg (ed.), *Essays on Geography and Economic Development*, Department of Geography, University of Chicago, Research Paper, No. 62, 1960.

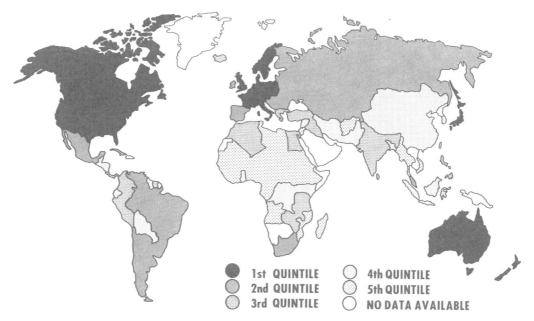

1st QUINTILE 4th QUINTILE
2nd QUINTILE 5th QUINTILE
3rd QUINTILE NO DATA AVAILABLE

FIGURE 16-1. The geography of world economic development. Economic development scores for nations have been calculated and ranked; nations were then classifed by quintile. Nations in the first quintile are the most developed; notice how they tend to cluster around the North Atlantic basin, though Japan and Australasia provide exceptions to this. Most of Southeast Asia, Africa, and parts of Latin America remain very underdeveloped. Original data refer to the 1950s.

tions of the world. This mapping is presented in Figure 16-1 and will be discussed shortly when we consider locational predictability. Certain elements of locational predictability are already clear from this map, however. Levels of development tend to cluster in space, for example, so that most of Africa is relatively underdeveloped as is South and Southeast Asia. The clustering of the most developed nations around the shores of the North Atlantic Ocean should also be evident though a new trading block seems to be emerging in the Pacific with strong ties among the developed nations of Japan, Australia, New Zealand, and the United States.

The idea of economic development variations also seems applicable to geographical scales other than those of the nation. If we consider subareas within a nation, for example, sharp variations in

economic development are frequently observable. For example, the Southern states of the United States have appreciably lower per capita incomes than elsewhere in America. Other instances of such regional inequality in levels of development within the same nation come readily to mind: in Southern Italy per capita incomes are less than 65% of the national per capita income, while per capita incomes in Northern Italy are over 150% of the national level.

For each country it is usually possible to obtain for subareas such as provinces, departments, or states a set of indicators of economic development. Such indicators frequently vary from one country to another, but the associations with well-tried indicators of economic development are usually high, attesting to the power of such nation-specific indicators. Consider the case of Peru, for

TABLE 16-2.　Variables indexing economic development in Peru. Each of these variables is strongly associated with levels of urbanization across subareas of Peru and can be regarded as an index of economic development in its own right. Thus, the less developed areas of Peru have very few industrial establishments per 1000 of the population, low proportions of households with electric light, radio, or piped water, low levels of fertilizer application, and relatively low proportions of school-age children actually attending school.

Percent of the population, urban
Number of industrial establishments per 1000 population
Percent of households with electric light
Percent of farm units given fertilizer
Percent of children over 4 at school
Percent of households with radio
Percent of households with piped water

---

example: data on at least 7 variables are available for 24 provinces; computation of *rank correlation coefficients* measuring the degree of association between the percent of the population that is urban and each of the variables resulted in high correlation coefficients, all in excess of 0.8. The variables, all of which were positively correlated with percent urban, are presented in Table 16-2. The distribution of the percent of the population that is urban in Peru is shown in Figure 16-2; as can be seen, the distribution is hardly geographically random and we shall comment on its locational predictability below.

It is clear, then, that the concept of economic development can be measured by a set of indicators organizing themselves into one component of economic development. It is also clear that there is considerable predictability in the patterns that can be described in terms of differences in economic development across nations of the world and across the subareas of any one nation.

LOCATIONAL PATTERNS OF ECONOMIC DEVELOPMENT

To what extent is the location of economic development predictable? If we know something about the economic development of a particular nation or subarea within a nation, does this tell us anything about levels in adjacent nations or subareas? Furthermore does it allow us to say anything about levels of economic development in adjacent locations at future points in time? In order to discuss locational predictability we need some descriptive and operational concepts of the locational pattern of economic development. In this treatment we draw upon some of the concepts discussed in Chapter Ten, specifically those of *localization* and of *clustering*. Though discussed in Chapter Ten largely as descriptors of point patterns they also seem useful as descriptors of density patterns.

Consider the concept of *localization* of economic development from the viewpoint of gross product per capita as an index of economic development. By calculating the localization of gross product relative to that of the population, we are implicitly deriving the localization of gross product per capita with reference to a set of locations. For example, Table 16-3 lists populations (Column 1) and gross regional product (Column 2) for five regions. These data have been used to derive regional shares as proportions of total national population (Column 3) and of gross national product (Column 4). Subtraction of Column 4 from Column 3, addition ignoring signs and dividing by 2 reveals that the coefficient of

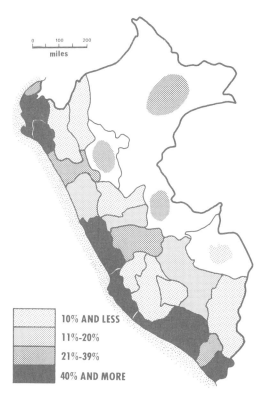

FIGURE 16-2. The percentage of the population in each department of Peru living in towns of over 5000 population, 1961. This is a measure of geographical differences in levels of urbanization, and since urbanization is so closely associated with economic development we can treat it as an index of economic development. Note the concentration of economic development along Peru's coastal strip and the relative backwardness of the interior.

localization in this hypothetical case is equal to 30% or 0.30.

Consideration of the mechanisms of computation will indicate that if the differences between the entries in columns 3 and 4, respectively, had all been zeroes then gross regional products per capita would have been equivalent and consequently there would have been no localization of gross product relative to the distribution of population.

Two points should be made. First, the index of localization of economic development could be applied to other indices of economic development. Column 2 in Table 16-3, for example, could have listed regional urban populations or, alternatively, regional manufacturing labor forces or any other index of economic development.

Second, as the localization of economic development increases, the variance of economic development across locations also increases. We shall find that the variance has been used to measure regional income inequality and this will be useful in evaluating evidence on the locational predictability of economic development.

A second concept useful in the description of the geography of economic development is that of *clustering* discussed previously in our consideration of point pattern dispersions. Economically developed locations can be characterized as more or less clustered, and as we pointed out in Chapter Ten this concept is quite independent of localization. Thus a given degree of localization of economic development can be associated with greater or lesser degrees of clustering.

In the literature on the geography of economic development particular interest has been attached to the most clustered form that a clustered distribution can assume: that of a single point. In the economic development literature this most clustered form is referred to as *primacy* and indicates in substantive terms a very intense localization of economic development where the locations are defined as urban centers.

In summary, the geography of economic development can be described in terms of its *localization*. Localized patterns are more or less *clustered*, and clustered patterns range from the extreme of primacy to the less extreme form represented by nonprimacy. Given such descriptive tools locational predictability can now be evaluated. It needs to be considered, however, from both static (i.e.,

TABLE 16-3.   Hypothetical data for computing the localization of economic development.

Region	Column 1 Population*	Column 2 Gross regional product**	Column 3 Share of national population	Column 4 Share of gross nat'l prod.	Column 5 Col. 3 − Col. 4
1	2	1	20%	10%	+10
2	2	2	20%	20%	0
3	1	4	10%	40%	−30
4	2	2	20%	20%	0
5	3	1	30%	10%	+20

* In hundreds of thousands.
** In billions of dollars.

single points in time) and dynamic (i.e., successive points in time) viewpoints. We need to consider not only subareas within nations but also the form of the economic development pattern in which individual nations are differentiated from one another.

SUBAREAS AT A SINGLE
POINT IN TIME

The most outstanding element of locational predictability in the geography of economic development across subareas of a nation is the localization of economic development. Thus we are intuitively cognizant of the sharp variation in gross regional product per capita that exists within the United States from the relatively poor South and not-so-wealthy Great Plains' states at one extreme to the wealthier Northeast and West Coast at the other extreme. In Canada similar localizations prevail with Ontario and British Columbia at one end of the development continuum and the Maritime provinces and Newfoundland at the less favored extreme.

In addition to localization, however, economic development tends to be more or less clustered. Clustering is particularly evident in the geography of economic development in nations that were at one time colonies of European nations:

the African and Latin American nations are prototypical in this respect. In Peru, for instance, the coastal strip is much more developed economically than the more landward sections of the country. As Figure 16-2 shows, the coastal regions are clearly the most urbanized sections of Peru. They also account for 91% of the value added in Peruvian manufacturing and are the source of more than 70% of Peruvian exports (fish products, fruit, and minerals). A similar clustering of the more developed locations occurs in Italy where the population of Northern Italy has much more than an equal share of national income, hospitals, automobiles, factories, and so on than does the remainder of the nation.

In other cases, clustering is so extreme that it is more aptly described by the *primacy* concept. Thus in Greece, the greater Athens area (although including only 22% of Greece's population) has 42% of the nation's manufacturing employment and a gross regional product per capita almost twice as large as that of the region with the next highest; in addition the ports of Athens unloaded 87% of Greece's imports in 1965. Elsewhere we have referred to the localization of Irish economic development in Dublin indicating similar levels of primacy.

Clustering is not apparent in all na-

ABOVE NATIONAL AVERAGE   BELOW NATIONAL AVERAGE

FIGURE 16-3.   Per capita incomes across the provinces of Spain, 1957. Note how income and therefore economic development tends to be higher in three distinct areas: Catalonia, centering on Barcelona, and the northern coast, centering on Bilbao and Madrid. Spain has several development nuclei rather than one alone, therefore. Tourism has been important in Catalonia and in the Balearic Islands.

tions, however. In Spain, for instance, economic development has been concentrated in three distinct areas: Madrid, Catalonia in the vicinity of Bacelona, and the Basque country of the northern Spanish coast. This is demonstrated in Figure 16-3. Such a spotty pattern was also true of the geography of economic development in 19th-century Britain as we shall demonstrate shortly.

NATIONS AT A SINGLE POINT IN TIME

Localization and clustering in levels of economic development also seem to be present in the economic development pattern describing differences from one nation to another. Thus, most of the nations of Latin America and of Africa tend to be relatively underdeveloped while the nations of North America and Western Europe tend to be more developed. Such clustering is particularly evident in the European context. Figure 16-4

presents a mapping of gross national product per capita for the nations of Europe. As can be seen, there is a considerable decay in levels of gross national product per capita with distance from a location somewhere in the neighborhood of Belgium. Indeed, as the distance from Belgium increases a whole variety of indicators of economic development tend to vary concomitantly: for instance, urbanization levels decrease, the proportion employed in agriculture increases, and levels of medical and educational provision deteriorate.

THE LOCATIONAL DYNAMICS OF ECONOMIC DEVELOPMENT PATTERNS

The fact that we have been able to isolate elements of locational predictability in economic development patterns, however, does not mean that such locational patterns are unchanging over time. In fact, there is a great deal of evidence accumulating to the effect that these locational patterns are not static: rather they change in a highly predictable manner that needs to be explained by a comprehensive theory of the locational pattern of economic development.

Localization of economic development describes, among other things, a regional inequality in levels of income per capita or of gross regional product per capita. Economists have been very interested in regional income inequality and have been concerned with the way it changes over time. The evidence that they have collected suggests that the more developed societies, such as the United States and France, are characterized by declining regional income inequalities, while more backward nations, such as Ghana or Nigeria or India, are characterized by increasing regional inequalities. It is probable, therefore, that for any one country undergoing economic development, regional income inequality at first

FIGURE 16-4. Economic development in the nations of Europe. The figures refer to gross national products per capita in dollars for 1957. The Soviet Union figure is probably exaggerated; the more developed nations cluster in northwest Europe with eastern and southern Europe lagging. Note how gross national products per capita *tend* to decline with increasing distance from Belgium. Do you think that this would also be true if we broke the nations down into subareas and obtained income estimates for those subareas?

increases and then decreases much as is shown in Figure 16-5.

Such a relationship applies to inequality or localization across regions within a nation. What happens to localization across nations as the world develops economically? There is a great deal of evidence to the effect that the richer nations are getting richer at a faster rate than the poorer nations, thus increasing the localization of economic development. Whether this increasing internation inequality can ever be reversed can only

be resolved at the present time by theoretical considerations.

THE PROCESS AND PATTERNS OF ECONOMIC DEVELOPMENT

Locational patterns of economic development are the result of the locational decisions of those who, by their investments in manufacturing and service industries, increase the level of economic development of the nation. Such locational decisions are a result of preferences for particular types of locations; a knowledge of the forces shaping such preferences and of the spatial arrangement of the preferred locations should shed light on the resultant pattern of economic development.

Locational preferences seem to be structured by two major forces: (1) the composition of demand for goods and services at any particular time, and (2) the locational constraints imposed by the available physical and social technology. With respect to the first factor, a demand composition that is, for example, biased toward iron and steel and heavy engineering products will be associated with a different set of locational requirements than a demand composition biased toward personal and financial services. With reference to the second factor, a resource conversion technology that is wasteful in its use of resources will involve a higher movement cost bill than a technology that is more economical in its use of resources.

Locational preferences provide the basis for evaluating different locations in terms of their utility and for selecting those with the greatest utility. The resultant locational pattern, therefore, partly depends upon the *locational structure* of

locations of different utility. If the more valued locations are clustered together, then the resultant pattern will also be a clustered one. In brief, activities on the stage are constrained by the structure of that stage. Locational preferences and the locational structure of development opportunities are treated below in greater detail.

LOCATIONAL PREFERENCES

The locational preferences of entrepreneurs are strongly affected by the type of goods and services demanded by the market, each good or service having a particular concatenation of locational requirements. With respect to this, economic development is characterized by a progressive shift in the composition of demand. Demand in earlier stages of economic development is dominated by an emphasis on *low value added manufacturing goods in which labor and capital form a low proportion of the total cost.* The cost of the raw materials and the costs of moving the raw materials and distributing the finished product to market form a commensurately large proportion of total cost. Examples of such low value added manufactures include the production of textiles and the processing of foodstuffs, timber, mineral fuels such as coal, and mineral ores.

In later phases of economic development, on the other hand, demand broadens to include *manufactured goods and services in which a much higher proportion of the ultimate value results from the application of labor and capital* while the costs of raw materials and of moving raw materials and the finished product represent a lower proportion of total cost. This is reflected in the importance of such manufacturing industries as aircraft. It is also reflected in the increased demands for services in which almost the entire value is represented by the costs of labor and capital. Administration, whether it is public or private, research, retailing,

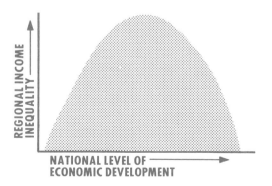

FIGURE 16-5. Regional income inequality and national levels of economic development. As a nation develops economically, its constituent regions first *diverge* in their different levels of economic development and then *converge.*

entertainment, cultural services, education, leisure and retirement industries, and personal transportation all expand greatly in terms of their markets.

With respect to technology four changes take place with economic development: (1) an increase in average plant size, (2) increased vertical integration, (3) increasingly economical resource extraction techniques lowering the ratio of the weight of raw material inputs to the output of the finished product, and (4) a decrease in the real cost of movement per ton-mile. All four changes have important locational implications. Thus, the increasing size of productive unit imposes a limitation on the minimal size of the city that can be considered as a possible location, so that preferences shift in the direction of larger cities. Increased vertical integration, on the other hand, increases the range of locational indifference by making the individual firm less reliant upon independent sellers of raw materials and buyers of its finished products.

Changes in resource technology and improvements in the input weight/ output weight ratio may be due to either the substitution of new raw materials for old ones or to improvements in resource extraction technology applied to the old raw material. Improved resource extraction techniques, for instance, have reduced the amount of movement necessary to produce a ton of pig iron (assuming unchanged locational patterns of coal and iron-ore supplies). Thus in 1829 in Britain, 8 tons of coal were needed to produce one ton of iron; by 1830 only $5\frac{1}{2}$ tons of coal were required; and by 1833 this had been halved. The effect of such changes on location within the Weberian system are easy to imagine. The recycling of finished products as raw materials—that is, scrap as an input for the production of iron and steel—has had similar effects

and locationally liberating implications.

With respect to movement costs per ton-mile it is apparent that economic development is characterized by the introduction of successively cheaper modes of transportation. The giant oil tanker, for example, has made it cheaper to transport oil around the Cape of Good Hope than through the Suez Canal. The development of unimodal transportation via the container revolution has reduced movement costs where several media are involved by drastically curtailing transshipment costs. All such innovations as these by reducing the movement cost per unit product have profoundly liberating implications for locational choices.

These changing demand and technology conditions combine to produce changing locational preferences on the part of economic developers. In general, early phases of economic development are characterized by a preference for locations at the sites of raw material sources, of markets, of break-of-bulk locations, and of other industries. Critical for the preference shown for raw material and market sites is the demand for low value added goods in which raw materials and movement costs comprise a very high proportion of the total costs. The weakly developed resource extraction technology also tends to increase the attraction of raw material sites as minimal movement cost locations.

Agglomeration of industries is also characteristic of this phase. This is partly caused by the technical limitations of industry in the earlier stages of economic development. As noted above, firms tend to be small, producing a single product or service and therefore have to rely on other firms for components or services such as transportation. There are consequently very large advantages in clustering, with other firms providing these components and services.

Later stages are characterized by a

preference for locations with (1) large amounts of localized resources (this is especially true of localized labor resources because of the large size of the firm during these later phases) and (2) maximum accessibility in terms of time to other locations with large manufacturing and service industries. In many industries characteristic of later phases of economic development, labor costs represent a high proportion of total costs; minimization of the time spent traveling by executives, educators, administrators, salesmen, and so on, therefore becomes important.

THE LOCATIONAL STRUCTURE OF DEVELOPMENT OPPORTUNITIES

Applying these locational preferences to the locational structure of development opportunities should permit one to predict the pattern of economic development. Generally over time with economic development, opportunities become: (a) less localized, and (b) concentrated in and around metropolitan centers in the different regions.

Decreasing Localization. In earlier phases of economic development locators confront a small set of development opportunities that are more preferable than those at other locations. In later phases of economic development however, development opportunities are locationally more widespread and locators are much more indifferent with respect to the total set of locations. Such decreasing localization of development opportunity can be ascribed to six major causes. All these reasons are strongly related to one another, however, and it is difficult to order them in any hierarchy of importance.

First, within many nations the set of locations to be developed to varying degrees is more completely known at later stages of economic development than at earlier stages; that is, *the geographical*

coverage of information is much more complete. This is particularly true in the case of areas that underwent an extension of the settled area during earlier phases of economic development. North and South America provide excellent cases in point: as settlement proceeded, more was discovered about locations that had not been considered at earlier stages of economic development. Earlier developed areas tend to be those with resources that were more completely known at an earlier date, for example, the coastal fringe of Latin America and the eastern seaboard of North America.

Second, within the expanding set of *known* locations, some locations become increasingly attractive for development due to their association with resources the demand for which increases at later stages of economic development. In brief, economic development is accompanied by a widening of the spectrum of resources demanded. Two types of resource are involved. On the one hand, there are resources catering to needs untypical of earlier phases of economic development: physical amenity resources for tourist and retirement industries, dust-free air for electronics industries, bauxite for the expanding aluminum industry, and so on. Second, there are new resources that can substitute for resources that dominate the demand spectrum at earlier phases of economic development. Scrap metal is substituted for iron ore in the production of iron and steel, and the attractiveness of areas producing large amounts of scrap metal for iron and steel mills increases commensurately. Similarly, electric power produced from the burning of coal or from falling water can substitute for the mechanical power of the steam engine with locationally liberating results. The availability of such resources is unlikely to have the same locational pattern as that of the much smaller range of resources employed in earlier phases of economic development. The net effect is a much reduced localization of development opportunity.

Third, economic development is accompanied by reduced localization of markets for goods and services. This is partly a function of the greater spread of economic development following from the more widespread availability of required resources at later stages of economic development. Employment in manufacturing and service industries creates an agglomeration of population which then provides a market for other industries, by so-called *multiplier effects*. Possibly of equal importance, however, are government redistribution policies characteristic of later phases of economic development. Thus the institution of progressive income taxes and public services, such as education and unemployment benefits, not only redistributes income from the wealthy individual to the poorer individual; it also redistributes income from the wealthier region to the poorer region thus increasing the relative market attractiveness of the poorer region for a variety of consumer goods industries.

Fourth, economic development is associated with a diffusion of the infrastructure required for profitable investment in manufacturing and service industries at different locations. We have already seen that increasing levels of economic development are associated with increasingly dense and connected railroad networks so that the mean accessibility of locations to low-cost transportation is increased. In addition, however, public utilities essential to industry also spread geographically; more towns acquire piped water, gas plants, and modern sewage facilities, for instance. All these considerations widen the range of locational choice for the production of a given good or service.

This increased infrastructural availability is partly a response to expansion in the number of locations known to have resources in demand. It is also, however, a response to supply factors: that is, to the increased supply of capital. Infrastructure is capital-hungry and earlier phases of development are capital-scarce. Not only are underdeveloped societies poor but they also lack institutions, such as savings banks, to mobilize what little surplus is available for investment. Societies at later phases of economic development do not encounter such problems so that interest rates tend to be appreciably lower and increased levels of infrastructural investment are feasible. The learning processes that tended to locationally restrict railroad development in the early 19th century are also significant in this context; uncertainty will tend to confine initial investments to those locations where capital-output ratios can be minimized.

A fifth factor altering the distribution of development opportunities so as to include locations not included at earlier periods is governmental in character. As we shall see shortly, localization of economic development and therefore of personal wealth tends to provoke demands from less developed areas for an increased accessibility to the manufacturing and service industries generating such wealth. As a result, most governments in more developed economies have programs of assistance to lagging regions; the net effect of these is to increase the attractiveness of locations in those regions for economic development. Such programs have already been referred to in Chapter Twelve.

A sixth and final consideration is the internal dynamics of the locational structure of development opportunities. Over the short term, development of some subset of the total set of development opportunities reduces the attractiveness of the remaining development opportunities. Development uses up relatively large proportions of that capital that is scarce at early stages of development. Such capital cannot be applied to assist locations that might, for example, wish to convert from a handicraft technology to a steam-power technology in order to compete with the locations that are being developed. The result is what has been called *backwash effects*. The relative attractiveness of the locations with the obsolescent technology deteriorates and capital and labor relocate to those locations that, because of the application of capital, have been able to switch to the more competitive steam-power technology. Furthermore, development of some subset of the development opportunities increases their attractiveness for the small firm, so characteristic of earlier stages of economic development and so dependent upon the services and outlets provided by other small industries. In brief, development of a small subset of the total set of development opportunities tends to restrict locational choice over the short run.

Over the long run the effect is rather different. Investment in a subset of development opportunities tends ultimately to drive up the prices of resources at such locations and increase the attractiveness of locations elsewhere. Agglomeration of industry in that subset increases the demand for labor and therefore increases wage levels relative to those elsewhere. The price of raw materials may also increase as, for example, mineral reserves are progressively depleted. The net effect is a set of *diseconomies of agglomeration* increasing the attractiveness of locations elsewhere where the prices of labor and/or raw materials are lower.

Increasing Metropolitanization. The decreasing localization of economic development opportunities, however, is not the only change that takes place over time in the locational structure of such opportunities. A second major feature of the changing locational pattern is the increasing metropolitanization of economic development opportunities. Economic development is strongly associated with the differential growth of cities: larger cities tend to show greater absolute growth than smaller cities, irrespective of region. The larger metropolitan centers (spaced relatively far apart) and their immediate vicinities become highly favored locations for reasons already discussed. Thus the large firms, characteristic of later phases of development, require the large labor forces that are to be found in major metropolitan centers. They also require markets for the high value added service industries also characteristic of later phases of economic development—markets that are concentrated in the larger metropolitan centers. And finally the larger metropolitan centers are minimal movement time locations: an important consideration considering the high opportunity cost of travel in such economies. The major metropolitan centers form the nodes of freeway systems both in the United States and Western Europe; they also form the nodes of high-speed railroad transportation networks.

LOCATIONAL PATTERNS OF ECONOMIC DEVELOPMENT

Considering the locational preferences outlined earlier and the changing locational structure of development opportunities described above what can we predict about the changing locational pattern of economic development?

Most generally we would expect early economic development to be highly localized at those locations where raw materials or markets are readily available or where other industries are already located. Choice is restricted to those few locations that have the raw materials required by low value added industries or that can absorb large amounts of the finished product. This is because of the high proportion of total costs represented by movement; this is a function of concentration on low value added industries, wasteful resource extraction technologies, and the relatively high cost of movement per ton-mile. The small scale of factory industry in this phase tends to encourage further agglomeration at such points while the localization of expensive infrastructure increases the attraction of those few agglomerations.

Later phases of economic development should be accompanied by an increasing *spread* of development *across regions.* The set of development opportunities widens and the larger size of firm makes locators more indifferent to location at such a geographical scale. At smaller geographical scales, however, it is clear that the larger cities have considerable advantages. These advantages deteriorate with distance from major cities, but where large cities are close enough the interstices may prove sufficiently attractive to provide an impetus towards *megalapolitan* urban growth.

In summary, we envisage earlier phases of economic development being characterized by *localization* of that development. Later phases are characterized by a locational dynamics in which there is: (1) *spread across regions* and (2) *concentration in and around large metropolitan centers.* Thus far, however, we have worked in the realm of conjecture. How applicable is this simplified model of locational patterns of economic development to patterns observed within nations?

APPLICABILITY AT THE NATIONAL LEVEL

LOCALIZATION

As noted above, earlier phases of economic development are characterized by an emphasis upon low value added manufacture thus increasing the attraction of minimal movement cost locations. Raw material sites that minimize the high cost of moving raw materials to the fabrication point are especially important. The degree to which industry clustered on the coal fields of Britain in the late 19th century is very striking in this respect. In 1800, 50% of Britain's 50 largest towns were on coal fields; by 1900 that figure was 65%. The coal fields were attractive to locators not only as a source of power to drive factory steam engines, but they were also highly important as a source of fuel for the iron and steel industry. By 1820, for example, 90% of Britain's pig-iron production was located on coal fields—a link that was strengthened by the fact that for the first half of the 19th century, at least, most of Britain's iron-ore needs came from the coal measures. The iron and steel industries, of course, attracted other metal-using industries such as ship building and the manufacture of items like locks and anchors.

The high degree of localization of British industry on the coal fields during the Industrial Revolution is brought out by a comparison of maps of population density for 1700 and 1851 (see Figures 16-6 and 16-7). In 1700 densities were highest in southeastern and eastern England with the London area being especially prominent. By 1851 the densest areas included West Yorkshire, Staffordshire, Warwickshire, Lancashire, central Scotland, Northumberland, and Durham— areas underlain by coal seams with a profusion of industries gaining their

FIGURE 16-6. The geography of population density in England and Wales, 1700. At this time densities were higher in southeast England particularly in the London area; this reflected the distribution of more fertile land in an essentially preindustrial, agricultural society.

Points of break-in-bulk at ocean ports and at other junctions on the transportation network are also favored with lower movement costs and tend to have attractions for industrialists that other places do not have because of the relative cheapness with which raw materials can be assembled and finished goods distributed. This is reflected in early patterns of urban growth in the industrial phase. In the United States, for example, in 1850 over 90% of the 50 largest cities were located on navigable waters; the early supremacy of New York City, Phil-

FIGURE 16-7. The geography of population density in England and Wales, 1851. By the middle of the 19th century, the pattern of population density had altered a great deal with the major concentrations of population clustering not only in the London area but also in the mining and manufacturing areas of the Midlands: Lancashire and West Yorkshire. All three areas had coal, an indispensable raw material for the steam engine—almost the sole source of industrial power—and for the production of iron and steel.

sustenance from them. Without it locators were lost unless (like London) they had cheap water transportation accessibility to a coal field such as that of Northumberland and Durham in northeastern England.

Similar relationships apply in the United States with the coal fields of Pennsylvania being an early attraction for industry and supplying coal by means of a network of water transportation to the New England textile mills and down the Ohio River to Cincinnati, Louisville, and beyond. But most importantly the coal of Pennsylvania and associated iron ores provided the basis for the growth of the iron and steel industry of the United States in such cities as Pittsburgh and Bethlehem.

adelphia, and Boston derived much from the advantages of cheap oceanic communication.

Also attractive in earlier phases of economic development were those localized clusters of population that had emerged as a result of some predevelopment political or commercial function. Thus the locational attractiveness of capital cities such as London and Paris and of commercial centers such as Amsterdam and Glasgow derived greatly from the market that they were able to offer for a variety of consumer goods at a time when the cost of transporting goods to market was often a very sizeable proportion of total product costs.

These initial choices, however, were obviously made with respect to the *known* environment and such information availability constraints will be apparent in the resultant pattern of economic development. This is particularly evident in nations that have a history of recent colonization. Where colonization has manifested a spatially sequential character as in the case of the American frontier or of the frontier in Latin American countries such as Brazil and Uruguay, so has the acquisition of knowledge about the possibilities of economic development. The areas that are colonized earlier tend to be known better in terms of geological, agricultural, and water resources; more distant peripheral lands are known only later with the arrival of the geological survey and the agricultural pioneer. It is probably for this reason that nations that have been colonized inland from restricted coastal footholds tend to demonstrate a high degree of clustering of economic development. This is true for instance, with the United States, Canada, Peru, Venezuela, Brazil, Uruguay, Ghana, and Nigeria. Nations like Britain, Germany, and Spain that did not experience such recent sequential colonization

have been known in a geographically much less biased manner. Whereas Americans knew only of the Pennsylvanian coal fields in the 1820s and had yet to discover the large coal resources in the Midwest and the Rocky Mountains, the British knew the location of almost all their coal resources. As one consequence, British economic development, though highly localized, was much less clustered than in the United States.

For a variety of reasons deriving from the preferences of locators and the development opportunities available to them, increased localization of economic development takes place around these initial locations. Thus, the characteristically small size of industrial firms with their low level of vertical integration imposes penalties upon location away from other firms producing required components and services. *Economies of agglomeration,* therefore, tend to be strong in this stage of economic development. Also providing an impetus to such economies of agglomeration is the importance of personal contacts in a situation where telephone communication may be inadequate or where mail may be erratic in its arrival.

Second, the localization of economic development and consequent localization in the growth of markets provides incentives for localized multiplier effects. Industrial development in an area produces an addition to the payroll and hence a net addition to the money circulating for consumption purposes. Such money provides the basis for an increased demand for other goods and services in the area: housing, retail services, and consumer goods industries, to mention a few. Putting money in the hands of the industrial workers, therefore, has a whole range of other favorable effects on the local economy. Such multiplier effects, moreover, tend to be highly localized in their scope and are consequently often referred to as *regional multiplier effects.*

Interestingly enough some types of economic development have stronger *multiplier effects* than others. Capital intensive industries such as petrol refining, for example, tend to be particularly bad in this respect because they have small labor forces per unit of capital employed and therefore add little to the consumer market. Labor-intensive industries, such as tourism, tend to be much more effective. Perhaps this explains why Florida has experienced much stronger multiplier effects than such oil-refining states as Oklahoma, Kansas, and Louisiana.

Third, initial locational choices in earlier phases of economic development tend over the short term to reduce the attractiveness of development opportunities not so chosen. This is partly caused by the consumption of scarce capital resources involved in providing infrastructure for a small number of development opportunities. Such localized infrastructure provides localized advantages that other development opportunities do not have. An interesting effect of such infrastructural bias is the *backwash effect* referred to above. Such backwash effects were particularly important in the concentration of textile industries and of iron and steel industries during the Industrial Revolution. In the preindustrial stage both industries tended to be locationally widespread (see Figure 16-8 for the French pig-iron case). The development of a machine textile industry and of a coal-based pig-iron technology in locations with infrastructural advantages made these more dispersed locations obsolete resulting in considerable transfers of labor and capital towards the new growth areas.

Also increasing the attractiveness of

the initially developed opportunities is the factor of *information availability.* While the locator may have in mind a mental map of attractiveness from which he will select his location, more *uncertainty* will be attached to some locations than to others. One will tend to know more, for example, about the availability of raw materials and services in or near areas that have already experienced economic development and far less about the less developed areas. Because of the tendency to minimize uncertainty, locators will tend to choose from areas about which more is known: this increases the existing localization of economic development.

In review, initial localization of economic development takes place at raw material sites, markets, or break-of-bulk points. An emphasis on low value added goods places a premium on such minimal movement cost locations. Choice of such locations, moreover, tends to be from the known environment, so that where the known environment has expanded dramatically since early development the pattern of economic development tends to be highly clustered as well as localized with respect to the total set of locations.

Such localized development tends to be intensified for a variety of reasons. First, there are *regional multiplier* effects resulting from the increased localization of consumer markets. Second, the development of an initial subset of the total set of development opportunities tends to increase their relative attractiveness. Thus less uncertainty will be attached to such developed locations and they will have a monopoly of scarce infrastructural investments. This monopoly increases their competitive advantage relative to other development opportunities having an adverse effect on the latter via *backwash effects.* The tendency towards

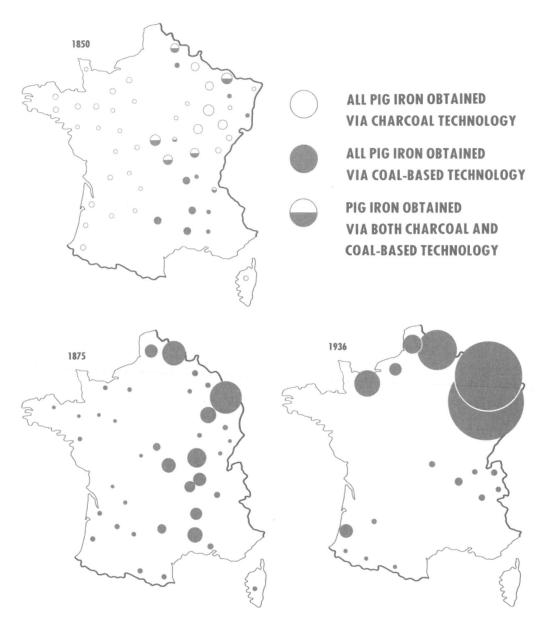

FIGURE 16-8. The geographical concentration of pig iron production in France, 1850–1936. Surface area of each circle is proportional to the volume of production. Note the gradual elimination of areas using the charcoal technology by the areas using coal in the smelting process. Such interregional competition on the basis of variation in the efficiency of technology is a typical feature resulting in backwash effects during the industrial stage.

agglomeration at the initial points of localized development is also increased by the particularly small size of firms and their desire for access to raw material supplies and outlets for their finished product.

SPREAD ACROSS REGIONS

The intense localization of economic development characteristic of earlier stages of economic development is transitory. Typically, spread to less developed regions has taken place while within regions there has been an increasing metropolitanization of economic development from which areas adjacent to metropolitan centers also have benefited. Initially we shall examine the evidence for interregional spread and then review the case for metropolitanization.

That interregional convergence has taken place is apparent from both American and French data. With respect to the French case, for example, we have already referred in Chapter Twelve to the

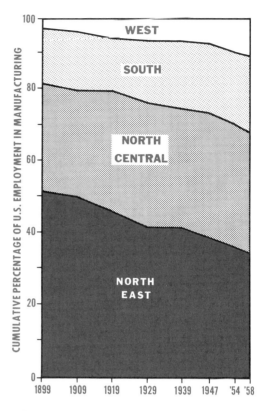

FIGURE 16-10. Changes in the regional distribution of employment in manufacturing in the United States, 1899–1958. The general pattern is very similar to that shown in Figure 16-9.

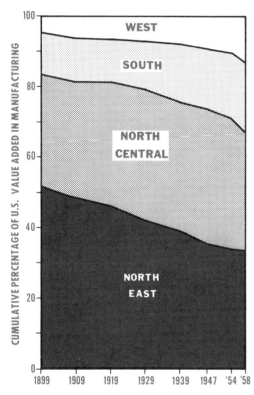

FIGURE 16-9. Changes in the regional distribution of value added by manufacturing in the United States, 1899–1958. The general tendency has been for the Northeast to lose at the expense of the South and West who have both claimed increasing shares of American manufacturing; the share of the North Central or Midwestern region has remained more stable. Note how these interregional convergences in shares of manufacturing have been going on at least since 1899.

relocation of industry from Paris. Figures 16-9 and 16-10 present graphically the changing shares of four large regions of the United States of national manufacturing in terms of value added and employment. Several features are apparent in these graphs: (1) in 1899 the Northeast was clearly the most significant region in terms of manufacturing followed by the North Central region (see Figure 16-11 for the geographical locations of the regions); the South and the West accounted for very little in manufacturing; (2) since 1899 the Northeast has undergone a steady decline in its domination of American manufacturing while the South and West have increased their shares very considerably; and (3) since

FIGURE 16-11. The four census regions of the United States.

1954 the North Central share has also started to decline.

Such changes can partly be attributed to changes in the composition of demand. Increased demand for high value added manufactured goods has reduced the attractiveness of raw material and market sites for industrial development. In the United States, this is apparent in the location of the aircraft industry in such areas as California, Texas, Washington, and Kansas: all locations that are removed from the classical sites of early American economic development in the Manufacturing Belt of the Northeast. In the production of aircraft, movement costs on raw materials and finished product are of very minor importance in relationship to the costs of labor and capital.

Changes in corporate structures have also tended to make manufacturing industries more locationally indifferent. Of particular importance has been the *emergence of the large firm with branch plants* supplying geographically extensive markets and capable of internalizing needs by vertical integration. Such large firms have been particularly mobile. In the United States, for example, the geo-

graphically most mobile industries have been those showing a high degree of ownership concentration; in Britain and France the large automobile firms have shown the way in the geographical decentralization of operations.

Also, changes in physical technology have altered the locational preferences of industrialists and reduced their dependence on locations favored at earlier phases of economic development. The substitution of electricity for steam power, for example, liberated British industry from dependence on coal-field locations and permitted spread to other locations. In the United States the use of scrap instead of iron ore as a blast furnace charge has permitted the development of iron and steel industries in locations distant from the classical Great Lakes source of iron ore. Steel plants established in such locations as southern California and Houston, Texas provide cases in point.

Superimposed upon these changes affecting the locational preferences of entrepreneurs has been the general downward trend of per-ton-mile movement costs reducing the movement cost per unit product and increasing the range of locational indifference. It seems unlikely, for instance, that coastal sites for steelworks as at Fos (Marseilles), Dunkirk, and Taranto in southern Italy would ever have become economical without the giant ore carrier which has permitted the transportation of iron ore over very long distances.

At the same time, the set of development opportunities from which locational choice is made has also expanded greatly. This is partly due to the *increasing geographical coverage of information.* As economic development has proceeded and—particularly in the case of North America and Latin American nations—as colonization has proceeded, more and more has been discovered about the natural resources of the less developed areas relative to those of the earlier discovered, more developed areas, setting in train reevaluation of the locational configuration of total production costs. The discovery and exploitation of oil and natural gas in the less developed states of Texas, Oklahoma, and Louisiana not only stimulated the growth of the chemical industry in those areas; it also led to a deterioration in the competitive position of fuel resources in the more developed states having particularly adverse effects on the coal-field states of West Virginia and Pennsylvania.

Of course, as techniques of gathering information improve, the long-settled lands of northwest Europe are discovering frontiers of colonization that they did not previously know existed. The discovery of natural gas resources in the North Sea off Britain's east coast, for instance, has led to plans for chemical plants along that relatively unindustrialized shoreline.

It is also due, however, to the expanded spectrum of resources required to fulfill the demand for higher value added goods and services. This is es-

pecially apparent in the relationship of recent increases in manufacturing employment in the United States to physical amenity. Figure 16-12 presents comparative gains and losses across the states in manufacturing employment over the period 1929–1954. The significance of the "Sun Belt" stretching from California in the southwest through Arizona, New Mexico, and Texas to Florida in the southeast is very apparent and is partly related to the attractions of the area for tourists and for scientific workers who are avid consumers of leisure industry services in their spare time.

The growth of tourism and leisure industries in such amenity-rich areas has also led to a change in the locational pattern of markets for a diversity of manufacturing and service industries touching off an array of *regional multiplier* effects. An additional factor promoting the geographical dispersal of consumer markets, moreover, has been redistribution of income policies. In the American context such policies have tended to transfer purchasing power from the more developed areas to such lagging regions as the South. This has undoubtedly been a stimulus to the location of a variety of consumer goods industries in the South.

In addition to the geographical dispersal of consumer markets and of needed resources, government activity has also been effective in widening the locational range of developmental opportunities. Governments have at their disposal a variety of methods for stimulating the economic development of backward regions. Also, the sharp interregional disparities of economic development and income associated with earlier phases of economic development often touch off a "poor neighbor complex" on the part of the laggard regions and pressures for political action aimed at rectifying the imbalance. An outstanding case of government attempts to stim-

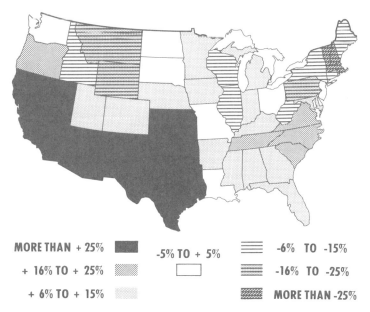

MORE THAN + 25%	▓	-5% TO + 5%	▢	☰	-6% TO -15%
+ 16% TO + 25%	▒			▤	-16% TO -25%
+ 6% TO + 15%	░			▨	MORE THAN -25%

FIGURE 16-12. Comparative gains and losses (percent) in manufacturing employment by state, 1929–54. The comparative gain of a state is the actual percentage growth in manufacturing employment for that state minus what that growth would have been if state manufacturing employment had grown at the same rate as in the nation as a whole. Thus, in the "Sun Belt," stretching from California through to Texas and Oklahoma, growth has tended to be more rapid than in the nation as a whole; in the Northeast, on the other hand, growth has been less rapid. Note how the "cold" states of Montana, Wyoming, and the Dakotas have also failed to record comparative gains of substance or have actually showed comparative losses.

ulate a laggard region concerns the efforts of successive Italian governments to introduce industry into the southern portions of the peninsula and into the islands of Sardinia and Sicily with their high rates of unemployment and low standards of living. Efforts to mitigate low standards of living in Southern Italy have taken the form of industrialization policies; specifically this has involved a program of long-term, low-interest loans to new industries in the south and recently some direct grants for equipment. The results have been mixed. There have been some outstanding successes, such as the establishment of a branch plant of the Alfa-Romeo automobile company at Naples and an iron and steel plant in

Taranto in the boot heel of Italy. Yet the rate of growth in manufacturing employment over the 1951–1966 period was only 20% compared with 28% in Northern Italy. Possibly, however, this represents the growing pains of industrialization in a laggard region: one of the effects of introducing modern low-cost industries into Southern Italy, for example, has been to throw industrial handicraft workers out of business in the manner classically described by the concept of *backwash effects*.

In other cases, of course, government action is less directed towards laggard regions but does have notable effects on economic development. Consider, for example, the large sums added to payrolls in California and Florida as a result of orders for military aircraft and of NASA activity, respectively. It is interesting also to consider the data on decentralization of American industry presented in Figures 16-9, 16-10 and 16-11 alongside data on the geographical incidence of Federal government and Federal payrolls (military and civilian). In the South in 1954 these payrolls constituted 10.7% of total personal income while in the West the figure was 8.3%. Corresponding figures for the more developed North Central and Northeast regions were only 3.1% and 3.8%, respectively. The implications of such injections of Federal money for regional multiplier effects can well be imagined.

Finally the initial localization of development in earlier phases of economic development has certain long-term effects that increase the attractiveness of the development opportunity not selected at earlier times. This is apparent in the phenomenon of rising raw material and labor prices in the earlier developed locations, increasing the attractiveness of locations characterized by lower prices for such resources. Extension of infrastructure, which comes with the increasing availability of capital in later phases of economic development, permits investment in such development opportunities.

Thus in the United States industrial development in the Northeast and North Central regions has tended to raise wages relative to those prevailing in the South. Not only that, but labor in the factories of the Northeast has been much more militant and organized than elsewhere in the nation. For industries in which labor costs form a high proportion of total costs this has been a very important consideration and has led to considerable relocation of industry from the Northeast and North Central regions (Midwest) into the South. The most no-

table of these relocations has been that of cotton textiles from New England to the Piedmont states. Also affected, however, has been New York's apparel industry and the ready-made clothing and furniture industries of the Midwest that have shown a tendency to relocate to the South.

Other relocations have been associated with depletion in the Northeast and North Central areas. Outstanding in this regard is the westward and southward movement of the lumber industry and associated pulp and paper industries. As timber was depleted in New England, the forests in Michigan and Wisconsin were exploited producing the now notorious Cutover Region. Depletion of timber resources there has led to a shift of lumbering and associated industries to southern states such as Mississippi, Alabama, and Georgia and to the Pacific Northwest. It is interesting to note that New England has also suffered from these changes as a result of relocation of the once important pulp and paper industry.

Thus, spread from more developed regions to less developed regions is partly a reflection of increasing locational indifference on the part of locators. Increasing corporate size, decreased per-ton-mile movement costs, and technical versatility assist in this direction as does the change in the composition of demand in the direction of goods and services in which movement costs are a low proportion of total costs. At the same time the set of known development opportunities increases partly as a result of increased information, increased range of resources demanded in later phases of economic development, regional multiplier effects in newly developing areas, government activity on behalf of lagging regions, and diseconomies of agglomeration in the more developed areas.

CONCENTRATION IN AND AROUND LARGE METROPOLITAN CENTERS

Spread of economic development across regions, however, is accompanied by another phenomenon at a smaller geographical scale: that of the increasing metropolitanization of economic development. Entrepreneurial preferences at later stages of economic development shift in the direction of locations with large labor forces, large markets for high value added service industries, and rapid access to other locations. On the side of the locational pattern of development opportunities, economic development is associated with increasing urban differentiation producing a small set of very large urban centers able to provide the large labor forces, the large markets for high value added service industries, and the demand thresholds for high-speed transportation services. Larger cities and their immediate vicinities, therefore, are endowed with considerable locational advantages in later stages of economic development.

Table 16-4 provides some evidence consistent with such metropolitanization. Metropolitan areas with over 1 million inhabitants have accounted for increasing proportions of the American metropolitan population over the 20-year period between 1940 and 1960. While in 1940 they accounted for 44.9% of metropolitan population with the remaining 55.1% being accounted for by metropolitan areas with less than 1 million inhabitants, by 1960 the proportions were almost completely reversed.

Consistent with the suggestions of this tabulation are some findings on the changing relationship between value added in manufacturing and population size for a sample of 81 standard metropolitan statistical areas. All the evidence here suggests an increasing concentration of value added in manufacturing in larger metropolitan areas.

TABLE 16-4. The concentration of population in larger urban agglomerations in the United States: 1940–1960. Percentages in a given year add up to 100% (apart from rounding errors) and refer to the percent of the American population in Standard Metropolitan Statistical Areas (SMSAs) of a given size. Note how larger SMSAs tend to be obtaining larger shares of total SMSA population than the smaller SMSAs.

	1940	1950	1960
3,000,000 or more	22.6%	28.9%	28.1%
1,000,000–3,000,000	22.3%	18.6%	26.4%
500,000–1,000,000	15.2%	16.2%	17.0%
250,000–500,000	16.5%	17.0%	14.0%
100,000–250,000	16.6%	15.7%	12.8%
Under 100,000	6.9%	3.6%	1.6%

There is no doubt, for example, that there are increasing disparities in value added in manufacture between larger and smaller cities. Thus, whereas in 1950 on the average a city of 3 million people had a value added by manufacture per capita that was $5 greater than for a city of 1 million people, by 1963 the disparity was about $63. In grosser terms, whereas in 1950 a city of 3 million had a value added by manufacture that was on the average greater than that for a city of 1 million by $130 billion, by 1963 the disparity amounted to $282 billion.

Closer scrutiny of Table 16-4, however, suggests something else. Over the decade from 1950 to 1960 the largest metropolitan areas with populations in excess of 3 million actually declined slightly in their share of American metropolitan population, while it was the metropolitan areas with populations between 1 and 3 million that registered the largest increase in their share of that population. This suggests some limited diffusion of economic development from larger metropolitan centers, and consistent with this are some preliminary findings from the 1970 census. Thus the twelve largest metropolitan areas with populations in excess of 2 million—including such cities as New York, Chicago, and Los Angeles—registered an increase in population of 12%; for the 21 metropolitan areas with populations between 1 and 2 million—cities such as Atlanta, Houston, San Jose, and Kansas City—the growth rate was a very high 27%; while the 32 metropolitan areas with populations between half-a-million and 1 million—Phoenix and Salt Lake City, for example—registered a growth rate of 18%.

This does not mean, however, that, for example, metropolitan areas with between $\frac{1}{2}$ million and 1 million inhabitants increased their share of the American population at the expense of the very largest metropolitan areas. Percentage growth rates are notoriously subject to misinterpretation for they are highly dependent upon the base figure upon which they are computed. Thus an 18% increase for a city of 1 million inhabitants would add an absolute number of 180,000 inhabitants; a 12% increase for a city of 2 million inhabitants, however, would add an absolute number of 240,000 inhabitants! But despite these caveats the growth of metropolitan areas of the 1-million–3-million class is impressive and needs some consideration.

Possibly, for example, it represents a spread from larger cities as an alternative to localized spread around those larger cities. There is no doubt, for example, that larger cities do tend to fulfill a growth pole effect for surrounding areas. Evidence for such an effect comes from southern Ontario where it has been found that much of the variation in population change is related to distance from a point in the vicinity of the large metropolitan center of Toronto. Thus, places close to Toronto have experienced rather rapid rates of population growth. Places further away from Toronto, however, have shown a marked tendency either to

grow only slowly or not at all. We shall need to consider our explanation of such growth pole effects from the viewpoint of its ability to also explain the growth of cities between 1 and 3 million in population.

With respect to the metropolitanization phenomenon itself, there is some evidence consistent with our explanation of it. Larger cities, for instance, do tend to have workers employed in larger plants than do smaller cities, suggesting that one of the advantages of the larger city for the industrialist is the access that it affords to a large labor market. Similarly, our evidence on the concentration of high value added manufacturing in larger cities is consistent with our contention that such cities provide important markets and communication advantages to industries of this nature.

In addition to the metropolitanization phenomenon, however, we have also remarked upon two diffusion phenomena: the growth pole effect around larger cities and the limited diffusion of economic development down the upper levels of the urban hierarchy that seems to be implicit in recent data on population growth. Initially we shall consider the growth pole effect and then attempt to apply our findings to the urban hierarchy case.

First, consider certain disadvantages of the large city in comparison with places outside the metropole. At least two disadvantages for some activities are associated with the city. First, there is the *noxiousness of the physical environment:* air pollution, congestion, and crime make for an unpleasant environment, and suburbanization is a reaction to this. As suburbs become less suburban, the resident looks further afield either for a permanent residence or for a weekend cottage from which he can occasionally escape the rigors of the city.

Second, there is the issue of *land costs.* As we saw earlier, land costs reach a peak at the city center and decline outwards. As land costs rise over time, however, certain activities can no longer afford the high rents demanded. Office users, for example, seem able to pay higher rents for land than factories, so the factories leave the city either for the suburb or for some small town close by. It has been suggested that the government-imposed migration of industry from Paris into the surrounding provinces has only made way for new office construction and service industries within the city. A further factor aggravating the land cost situation for industries and for certain retail services is the high consumption of land, not only because the operations of industries and stores are facilitated on one story, but also because of the needs for employee and customer parking, respectively.

Nevertheless, even though the metropolitan environment is noxious or costly from some points of view, there are also important reasons for remaining close to the city. First, while low land costs are attractive to industries, access to the *economies of agglomeration* provided by the city is also important—access to suppliers and buyers, for example, and access to the specialized services of the metropolis such as its airline links or its freeway links.

Second, as far as the environmental problem is concerned, while a small rural haven 15 miles from the center of the city may provide a buccolic charm impossible in the city, *access to metropolitan amenities and job opportunities* are also important. The further one is from the city the less one can take advantage of them.

Hence, while places outside the metropolitan area, but close to it, can have the best of both worlds—for example, low land costs and access to economies of agglomeration or a pleasant living environment and access to metropolitan amenities—the net advantages decline as distance from the city increases. Certainly there do not seem to be compensating advantages for the disadvantages of being further and further away from the metropolitan center. It seems possible, therefore, to imagine the metropolitan center as a *growth pole* with the rate of economic development as measured by such variables as population increase declining with distance from the city.

Similar forces appear at work in producing the spread of economic development down the upper levels of the urban hierarchy. The larger cities do have a strongly repellent effect in the sense that they have very high land costs and very noxious environments as measured by such objective indicators as crime rates. Smaller cities do not have the same cost factors but do have much the same benefits in terms of access to a high-speed communications network and ancillary service industries. Particularly relevant in this context is the relocation of office employment from New York City to other less large American cities: Houston has been a notable beneficiary in this instance.

APPLICABILITY TO INTERNATION DIFFERENCES IN ECONOMIC DEVELOPMENT

The ideas enunciated above relating processes of economic development to geographical patterns of development have been fashioned with the problem of *intranational differences* particularly in mind. It is clear, however, that similar arguments apply at the *internation* level to explain both concentration of economic development in a few favored areas of the globe and the tendencies for some limited spread of economic development to the lagging remainder.

Thus the *small size of firms* in earlier stages of economic development limits the spread of foreign investment into less developed areas. Not only are small firms less able to finance the heavy costs of such investment in an initially costly environment, but also their small size minimizes the power they can exercise on their own government. Such powers are important because their own government will be their sole savior if the government of the nation in which they have invested should arbitrarily seize, nationalize, or otherwise undertake policies harmful to their enterprise.

Also significant is the phenomenon of *backwash effects.* The early factory cotton textile industry of Lancashire, for example, thrived on an Indian market that had formerly been supplied by domestic cottage industries; the handicraft textile industries of China underwent a similar fate.

Spread effects from the more developed nations of the globe to the less developed are also apparent. Consider, for example, the *decreased transportation costs per ton-mile* achieved by the ocean-going giant ore carrier. This has permitted Japan (as we saw in Chapter Four) to stretch her overseas links, import ore from Latin American nations, and consequently provide investment capital to those nations. It has also allowed the forging of similar beneficial links between, on the one hand, West Africa and Latin America and, on the other hand, northwestern Europe. The giant oil tanker has had similar effects in spreading income more widely throughout the globe.

A second major spread factor has been *diseconomies of agglomeration in developed nations.* This has been particularly apparent in the effect of rising labor costs upon the locational patterns of labor intensive industries. The cotton textile industry, for instance, is highly dependent upon

cheap, not necessarily skilled, labor. Underdeveloped nations have exactly the pool of cheap unskilled labor required by such industries, while the more developed nations have experienced rising labor costs. The result has been a competitive situation that has favored the development of cotton textile industries in underdeveloped nations (i.e., *spread*); India, Pakistan, South Korea, and Hong Kong, for instance, now supply world markets for textiles once supplied by textile mills in northwestern Europe and North America.

A second effect of agglomeration of industry in developed nations has been rising raw material prices. This has encouraged commodity importation from less developed nations with important developmental effects. Britain, for instance, began importing iron-ore from northern Spain in the 19th century; the development of the iron-ore reserves in the Bilbao area encouraged the establishment of an iron and steel industry based on local coal reserves. More recently, the United States has started importing large quantities of iron-ore from underdeveloped Venezuela; the return of the empty iron-ore carriers from the United States allowed the Venezuelans to obtain backhaul economies on the transportation of coal from Pennsylvania to aid in the establishment of an iron and steel works. Venezuela now has a large iron and steel complex at the new city of Ciudad Bolivar in eastern Venezuela.

Third, there is *spread of economic development induced by the development of amenity resources for the tourist industries.* Poorer nations adjacent to wealthier nations have especially benefited in this regard: Mexico and the West Indies, for example, have very large receipts from the tourist trade with the United States; in Europe, Spain, Italy, Ireland, and Austria have benefited in the same manner. The cheapening of long-distance air transportation expressed in the form of special charter rates is increasing the geographical scope of this spread: Germans who once went to Yugoslavia and Greece are now going to the beaches of Rumania and Bulgaria; the French and English are beginning to substitute the North African countries of Morocco and Tunisia for Spain and Italy.

A further factor aiding spread which we identified at the intranational level was *firm size*. This also seems important at the internation level because it is the larger firms that have shown the greatest propensity to invest in manufacturing facilities overseas in general, and in underdeveloped areas in particular. Consider the overseas investments of large oil companies, for example; or the automobile assembly plants established by the American auto companies in Latin America. Large firms not only have the financial resources to cover the risks involved in such ventures but they also have "political pull" with their own government which allows them some degree of protection in their new location. Industries such as textiles, which have been characterized by small firms, have shown a much lesser tendency for foreign investment. The outcome, of course, has been demands for protection from foreign competition from the textile factories of the United States and northwestern Europe.

These factors facilitating *spread* gain most of their efficacy from their ability to transfer money and foreign exchange from wealthier nations to poorer nations. Such money has at least two effects: (1) regional multiplier effects in the form of the additions to consumer demand for locally produced consumer goods which it generates, and (2) additions to the savings available in the form of bank accounts *or* to forced savings in the form of taxation—both for investment in productive enterprise. Such foreign ex-

change can, for example, be used to purchase machinery from the more developed nations. This is by no means an exhaustive list of the effects of the spread factors, however. The extraction of raw materials, for instance, not only provides foreign exchange but it also necessitates the development of an infrastructure of railroad and/or port facilities useful in further economic developments. In some cases, exportation of raw materials may permit backhaul economies in the importation of the raw materials necessary for economic development.

Nevertheless, despite this abundance of examples of economic development diffusing from more developed to less developed nations, there is absolutely no doubt that because of the politically fragmented context in which the spread processes are operating they do tend to operate inefficiently. The spread of economic development over the earth's surface, therefore, occurs at a much slower pace than it would in the absence of that mosaic of legally defined bounded spaces that we call nations. In such a context the formal governmental mechanisms that redistribute economic development tend to be hampered or to not operate at all; and in addition the less developed nations provide a variety of positive spillover effects from which the more developed nations can benefit and increase their margin of economic advantage.

Within nations the formal mechanisms by which economic development is induced to spread from its localized phase to all sections of the nation are strong and effective. Redistribution of income through progressive income taxes, for instance, increases the relative attractiveness for economic development of the regions with poorer markets and at the same time detracts from the market advantages of those regions that are already more developed economically, thus increasing the entrepreneur's locational indifference and the probability of spread. Working in the same direction are those infrastructural and educational policies of governments that tend to treat regions in an egalitarian fashion. Thus, provision for public education will affect not only the more developed regions but also the less developed regions increasing the attractiveness of the latter for those industries that place a premium on skilled labor. Similarly, government grants for infrastructural development in the form of waterworks, improved highways, sewage facilities, and so on are usually made available to all sections of the nation, thus further increasing the locational options of the industrialist. Indeed, as we saw earlier, there may be attempts to favor the less developed regions in the form of investment grants, special labor training programs, and related activities.

Such formal mechanisms of redistribution, which are so important for the spread of economic development within nations, operate in a crippled condition or hardly at all between nations. Possibly the nearest global equivalent to a national redistribution of income policy is the system of foreign aid by which grants and loans are made available from the more developed nations to the poorer nations. Such aid in the past, however, has assumed very puny proportions: in 1962, for example, French foreign aid commitments represented 1.32% of gross national product, while at its most flattering evaluation American foreign aid represented only 0.66% of gross national product. Not only are these proportions of insignificant consequence but it is immediately apparent that the wealthiest nation in the world does not pull its weight. The fact that France, a nation with a gross national product per capita half that of the United States is prepared to provide twice the amount of foreign aid in proportion to its gross national product is a staggering indictment of the myth of American generosity. Considering the absolute magnitude of the American gross national product, for instance, an additional 0.66% contributed to the global aid flow would represent a handsome addition to those efforts designed to achieve greater internation equity.

Even with increased aid allocations on the part of the more developed nations, however, it is far from obvious that such aid could be employed effectively in the economic development of those nations. Especially important here are policies exercised by the more developed nations of the globe and designed explicitly to hinder such development. The tariff policies of Western Europe and North America for instance, have played a very important role in minimizing the spread of the cotton textile industry to such underdeveloped nations as India and Pakistan. Cotton textiles, because of its small demands on capital markets and its intensiveness in unskilled labor, represents an ideal industry for many underdeveloped nations. Yet tariff policies have worked to the short-term advantage of the cotton textile factories of Britain's Lancashire and the American Piedmont region and to the long-term detriment of the less developed nations.

Similar restrictive policies are apparent in the degree to which the more developed nations permit the less developed to obtain the benefits of those regional multiplier effects that would ordinarily follow from exploitation of natural resources in the less developed nations. While the more developed nations have had to look outside their boundaries for new sources of copper ore, iron ore, and so on, the refining processes have remained in the more developed nations—often as a result of protectionist policies designed to retain such high value added manufacture in the more developed nations. Indeed, in many senses foreign aid represents a soft option for the more developed nations since it provides them with a good public relations boost and a false sense of altruism without imposing the costs that would result from a more liberal trade policy.

This is not to say that such inefficiencies in the spread processes are entirely attributable to the more developed nations. The less developed nations themselves have often adopted policies that slowed down the spread of foreign capital into their territories for development purposes. Foreign-owned oil refineries, for example, have been a common target of the nationalization policies of many underdeveloped nations and by increasing the risks for foreign investors have tended to work against the long-term economic development of those nations. One wonders, for example, how many more oil refineries would have been consigned to the Middle East if the threat to those costly investments had been more limited in scope.

A final factor limiting the effectiveness of the spread forces discussed in this chapter are the positive spillovers which the less developed nations provide for the more developed. Particularly critical here are movements of skilled labor dramatized by the term "brain drain." Thus over the eighteen-year period between 1949 and 1967 the United States absorbed, and to some degree purposely recruited, 100,000 engineers, doctors, and scientists from developed and less developed nations of the globe. For the United States this represented a saving of about $4000 million in costs of education—a cost, moreover, imposed on the nations from which the migrants came; ironically enough, this represents more than American aid to other nations over the same period. Furthermore, such

movements are contagious. While the United States imports skilled medical manpower from Britain and less developed nations, Britain must recoup its losses by importing similar manpower from India and Pakistan.

Certainly the problem of the spread of economic development from one nation to another raises issues that create conflicts between nations. It is the conflicts created by differing rates of economic development and the locational policies propounded to resolve these conflicts that we shall consider next.

ECONOMIC DEVELOPMENT AS A POLITICAL PROBLEM: CONFLICT AND POLICIES

CONFLICT

Much political conflict between nations in the world today is between less developed and more developed nations and involves issues that are at least partly related to economic development. There is the conflict between more developed Russia, on the one hand, and poorer China, on the other hand. The conflict between Israel and the Arab states can also be viewed in this light, as can the periodic conflicts between the United States and Latin American nations such as Peru. Anticolonial movements such as those in Portuguese Angola and Mozambique are of the same genre.

What is the source of this political conflict? Undoubtedly a major bone of contention is *the ability of the more powerful, developed nations to impose their will on the less powerful, poorer nations in both an economic and a political sense* The more developed nations have greater material resources at their disposal and have their manpower better organized; this allows them to intervene much more directly in internation disputes than is possible for the less developed nations, and they can design the world according to their own requirements. The more developed nations can make arms sales to protect their interests in a manner that must strike the poorer, often excolonial nations as reminiscent of British 19th-century gunboat policy.

The conflicts are also bread-and-butter conflicts. Conflicts over *resources* provide major issues. A major problem for the underdeveloped nation is obtaining higher prices for its exports of raw materials. Such raw material prices often undergo wild fluctuations presenting serious problems for long-term economic planning. Also, prices are often low to begin with: this is partly due to gluts but the underdeveloped nations often see it as a result of collusion by the so-called imperialist nations to keep prices low by minimizing competition among each other. The conflicts between oil-producing underdeveloped nations and the oil-consuming nations of North America and Western Europe should be seen in the same light.

These conflicts are particularly intense where *foreign investments* are involved and where the underdeveloped nation, as a consequence, is likely to see an appropriation of its resources without proper compensation as resulting from such direct involvement by the developed nation. It is in this context that one should evaluate the harassments and insecurity to which foreign investments are subjected.

These conflicts of a fundamentally economic character are exacerbated by certain other cleavages that tend to coincide with the economic. The developed nations, apart from Japan, are dominantly white while most of the underdeveloped nations are black or yellow. There are also religious cleavages pitting, for example, the vast numbers of Moslems of the underdeveloped nations against the

Infidel. There are also historical cleavages between the once imperial nations of northwest Europe and the formerly colonial nations of Asia and Africa.

When we turn to the *intranational* scene, analogous conflicts and bases of conflict appear. Poor, laggard regions oppose themselves to wealthier regions, either one desiring independence from the other. For example, the poorer region may see its poverty as partially residing in its inability to control its own economic destiny. It may feel neglected by the national government or exploited: such has been the basis for separatist demands in the outer islands of Indonesia and in the case of the ultimate disintegration of the union that wealthier Senegal and poorer Mali once formed in West Africa.

However, a wealthier region may also feel itself oppressed by union with the poorer region; it may feel (e.g.) that its wealth is being taxed away to support wasteful investments in the less developed areas of the nation and that *national* policies that squelch its own *regional* economic growth are being promulgated. The parochial desire to conserve regional wealth, for example, was an important basis for the *Katanga separatist movement* in the Congo where it was feared that wealth from copper exports would be dispersed to poorer parts of the nation.

Furthermore, as in the internation case, the economic development cleavage frequently coincides with other cleavages of an historical, religious, linguistic, or ethnic character. In Peru, for instance, the poorer backland corresponds to the area of Indian settlement; in the Sudan the wealthier north with its Moslem and Arab population is pitted against the Negro Christian and pagan populations of the poorer south. In Belgium the linguistic differences between Flanders and Wallonia have aggravated tensions caused by the one time economically laggard status of Flanders.

Much conflict, therefore, can be traced either directly or indirectly to *geographical differences in levels of economic development*. For political reasons it is important that such conflicts be eliminated by eliminating differences in economic development. Morally the imperatives are in the same direction. What policy alternatives are available?

POLICIES

How should governments respond to these domestic and international issues? The problem is usually discussed in terms of two alternative policies or means: *dispersion of economic development* and *continued localization*. The major end is *equity* or a more equitable distribution of the fruits of economic development across space. For a variety of important reasons this goal has become convoluted with another related goal: that of *efficiency* as measured by the rate of national economic growth. A number of commentators, for example, have made the assumption that policies with equity as a goal also produce higher rates of economic growth. It may be important, however, to distinguish between immediate and long-term ends of policy. *Short-term efficiency*, for example, may allow *later equity* with much higher incomes than a policy of *equity now;* "equity now" may have a depressing effect on national efficiency and produce an equitable distribution of poverty rather than of wealth. In discussing policy, therefore, we should keep the two conceptually distinct goals of equity and efficiency clearly in mind as well as the long-term implications of policies that have either end as their goal.

A final prefatory comment that we need to make in this section is that the policy arguments are somewhat better articulated at the intranational level than at the internation level, and it is there that we shall begin our discussion, critically examining (1) alternative locational policies, their vices and virtues, and (2) means of implementing dispersion policies. We shall then examine the implications of this for international policy.

Policies aimed at promoting the economic development of a less developed region are usually presented not only in terms of an *equity* or humanitarian argument; frequently the foremost idea is that these policies also serve the goal of *national efficiency*. It is often claimed that in the larger industrial cities (or city) of the more developed region, for instance, per capita costs of production are much higher than in the less developed regions because of such problems as traffic congestion, high public utility prices, and well-organized and militant labor. Although the argument recognizes that urban size brings with it certain advantages in the form of economies of agglomeration and the achievement of threshold levels for important urban services, many argue that cities *can* and in many cases *have* become too big. On the other hand, so the argument goes, the laggard regions with their unorganized labor and unexploited resources would provide much higher returns on investments thus promoting the goal of efficiency as well as that of equity. These arguments have been accepted by a very large number of nations including France, Britain, Chile, the Soviet Union, Poland, Venezuela, Ghana, India, and Egypt.

However, there are often critical flaws in the argument. First, *it is by no means clear that dispersion serves the end of equity*—at least not initially. Industrial development of the less developed regions frequently involves the immigration and employment of a skilled labor force from the more developed areas rather than the employment of the local populace. Similarly, the resultant increase in the demand for food, raw materials, and so on, may raise their price above the level that the local population can afford.

Second, there are serious flaws in the efficiency arguments urging dispersion. If per capita production costs in the larger cities do increase above a certain size at what point is that critical level reached? Nobody really knows the answer. Most importantly, the argument ignores the fact that even though per capita costs *may* increase with increasing size, the goal of national efficiency will still be served if productivity per capita can increase at a more rapid rate. There is indeed some evidence for the latter case. In the United States, for instance, per capita incomes clearly rise with increasing population size; government expenditures per capita (a measure of the cost of congestion, public utilities, etc.) also tend to rise, though at a much slower rate.

It seems very likely, therefore, that dispersion policies in underdeveloped nations with their strong interregional disparities in economic development and their often strong primacy effects may be ill-conceived from both equity and efficiency viewpoints. Dispersion is not so humanitarian as it might appear; it may also hinder that national economic growth that would allow a more equitable spread of wealth rather than of poverty.

Nevertheless, setting aside these arguments on the broad goals of policy, it seems clear that most nations do have a commitment to an "equity-with-efficiency" policy, the idea being that dispersion serves both ends. The critical policy question for the planner then becomes, what are the most effective policies for obtaining equity along with a modicum of efficiency? Appropriate pol-

icies here have to be discussed at two levels: (a) the specific types of assistance or legal fiat to be instituted, and (b) the geographical scale of dispersion: should assistance be concentrated at a few selected locations in the laggard regions or more spread out?

With respect to the first issue, there are a variety of possibilities. *Efforts to attract industrialists to laggard regions* can take the form of loans, grants, payroll subsidies or government investments in the public utilities required by industry, for example. On the other hand, governments can *repel industry from the more developed regions* by outright bans on development or by restrictions on such items as floor space. In fact, as we pointed out in Chapter Twelve, it is probable that both attracting and repelling measures are necessary.

Which types of attracting and repelling measures best serve the ends of equity and efficiency? It is likely that loans and grants attract the wrong type of industry, that is, those that consume large amounts of capital (such as oil refineries) relative to the labor they employ. In order to maximize multiplier effects within the laggard regions it is important that development produce large returns to local labor. Labor intensive industries are much more effective in this regard, which suggests that the optimal attracting policy is likely to be one that emphasizes payroll subsidies or subsidizing the costs of training labor.

On the repelling side, the aims of efficiency and equity would be served by a floor-space restriction that would encourage larger firms to relocate. Such larger firms are less likely to founder in bankruptcy or uneconomic operations in the laggard region because of their internalization of such allied services as transportation and labor training. The dispersion of smaller firms should probably be discouraged, and this suggests that outright bans on all development in the more developed regions do not serve well the goal of national efficiency.

But what about the locational focus of policy? Should assistance be concentrated in a few locations in the laggard region or should it be more widely dispersed? Initial interest on the part of development planners has tended to focus on area-wide policies, delineating large areas in which assistance will be granted. This has been the basis of Italian governmental efforts to stimulate economic development in Southern Italy. Currently, however, there is a tendency to favor policies of locational concentration.

Locational concentration policies have employed the concept of identifying *growth centers* or *growth poles* within which government assistance in the form of loans to industrialists and funds for the development of public utilities should be concentrated. Such growth centers are usually the larger cities of the laggard region, and this choice is based on two assumptions: (1) that industrial firms obtain large cost reductions from economies of agglomeration and from the range of urban services that a large agglomeration of industry and associated population can support, and (2) there is the assumption that economic growth in the designated growth center will stimulate economic development in the surrounding area: it will increase the demand for agricultural products and raw materials from the hinterland, for instance, and provide employment to workers commuting from nearby towns.

These arguments seem plausible, and there is some evidence for beneficial growth center effects both within the larger center and in the surrounding area. A number of dispersion policies, moreover, have adopted these arguments. Possibly most noteworthy is the effort of the Brazilian government to stimulate the economic growth of the nation's periphery by relocating the capital city from Rio to an interior location at Brasilia. The French have also been prominent in incorporating the idea into their planning: eight large cities spaced widely apart have been designated as growth centers to offset locational concentration in Paris. Government investment in utilities and assistance to relocating industry will be concentrated in these eight selected centers. Indeed it seems likely that a dispersion policy combining equity with national efficiency is most likely to be successfully met by a growth center policy, but emphatically one that concentrates on attracting labor intensive industries that will maximize regional multiplier effects and consequent local spread of economic development.

At the international level, however, the arguments of equity versus efficiency seem irrelevant largely because of the strength of the political pressures for development *now*. In this context, what are the effective means of obtaining a measure of *global equity* along with a measure of *global efficiency?* Two major points can be made, one regarding the type of assistance to be provided by the more developed to the less developed nations and the second regarding the locational concentration of that assistance.

As far as assistance is concerned, capital movements in the form of intergovernmental loans and grants have been widely acclaimed as one means of lifting underdeveloped nations into the industrial stage. Ostensibly the case for such generosity might seem unimpeachable. A closer scrutiny of the situation, however, reveals that this may not be the most effective form of assistance in maximizing the rate of economic development. The first problem has already been reviewed: foreign aid is of little use to underdeveloped nations unless the trade policies of the more developed nations are so altered that the aid can be invested in the production of goods and services that will have *unimpeded access to the markets of those same more developed nations.*

The second problem is that the governments and civil services of most underdeveloped nations are notoriously corrupt. Except in a few cases, many grants and loans find their way by various chicaneries into the pockets of legislators and government officials. *Aid must be channeled in such a way as to bypass governments.*

Third, aid must be provided in such a way as to *stimulate those industries that will provide maximum multiplier effects* within the underdeveloped nations. Textile mills are more effective than oil refineries—and they are cheaper per man employed. Likewise, improved seed varieties are much more effective than tractors.

Considering these problems, some tentative suggestions can be made: (1) there should be less emphasis on financial aid and more on trade; (2) means should be found of transferring capital to underdeveloped lands by bypassing the government: this might be done by, for example, tax concessions to corporations undertaking foreign investment or by trade concessions giving a higher return to entrepreneurs in underdeveloped nations; and (3) these policies should show a preference towards those producers or foreign investors whose investments have local multiplier effects.

Such policies for developed nations would not necessarily be any more costly than present aid programs and they would probably be more effective. They would, however, *impose a cost on the developed nation that would be more localized in its incidence.*

It is very important, for example, that developed nations lift quotas and protective tariffs on imports of cotton textiles from underdeveloped nations; however, this imposes a burden on the cotton-textile-producing areas of Piedmont and Lancashire, for example. Clearly, a more effective dispersion policy at the international level requires careful articulation with locational policies at the intranational level with aid given to those areas likely to suffer from trading concessions to underdeveloped nations.

To which nations, however, should these preferential treatments be granted? How should assistance be allocated in locational terms? There seem to be strong arguments for concentrating assistance in the larger and more populous of the underdeveloped nations, such as India, Brazil, and Nigeria. Such nations have the size to obtain economies of scale important in the efficient low-cost operation of such technologies as steel plants, atomic energy reactors, and large chemical plants. Larger nations are also likely to have lower production costs due to their ability to bargain on favorable terms with other nations. The same logic suggests that the more developed nations should encourage the emergence of customs unions among underdeveloped nations, such as those recently established in Latin America, and strongly oppose separatist movements, such as that of Biafra. Development of such larger political groupings would then have favorable effects on adjacent underdeveloped nations in much the same way as growth centers on their hinterlands.

CONCLUSIONS AND SUMMARY

An idea which has been much bandied around by politicians and the news media is that of *economic development*. It is, however, an idea that can be given a rigorous definition in terms of a set of *indicators* that we intuitively associate with economic development: economically developed countries, for example, tend to have higher *gross national products per capita;* lower *infant mortality rates;* higher levels of *social provision* in terms of such things as the *availability of medical service;* a greater proportion of the *population living in cities;* a greater proportion of the labor force employed in *manufacturing;* and higher *transportation network densities.*

These indicators tend to be highly correlated such that, for example, a nation high on gross national product per capita will also be predictably high on percent urban. These high associations or correlations allow one to define a *composite index of economic development* to describe nations and subareas within nations in terms of their differing levels of economic development.

The geographical pattern defined by such distributions of economic development reveals considerable locational predictability in terms of *localization, clustering,* and *primacy*. Within nations localization is particularly evident though in some excolonial or recently settled nations a marked clustering is also often apparent. Comparing one nation with another, there is also evidence of considerable localization as well as a clustering pattern in which the underdeveloped nations of Latin America, Africa, and South and Southeast Asia are contrasted with the more developed nations on either side of the North Atlantic.

Over time, however, such patterns of economic development undergo some interesting changes. Generally in early phases of economic development the localization of economic development across the regions of a nation tends to increase. In later stages of economic development localization declines suggesting *a diffusion of economic development from the more developed to the less developed regions.*

These patterns of economic development are the result of the *decisions of entrepreneurs*, and these decisions are a result of *preferences for particular types of location* and the *geographical pattern of such locations.*

Locational preferences are affected by two major considerations: (1) the composition of demand for goods and services at any particular time, and (2) the available social and physical technology. Both change as economic development proceeds. Thus the composition of demand tends to shift in the direction of goods and services in which a higher proportion of the value of the product or service represents the value of the capital and labor required in the production process. This tends to reduce the locational significance of movement costs for both raw materials and finished product. Changes in technology also have locationally liberating effects. Thus resource technology becomes increasingly efficient reducing raw material inputs per finished product while increasing firm size reduces the importance of economies of agglomeration. Increasing firm size also increases the attractiveness of locations with large labor forces, while concentration upon high value added products and services increases preferences for locations with minimal movement time.

Changing locational preferences are reflected in a changing locational structure of development opportunities. With economic development, opportunities become less localized across regions. Information coverage is more even and a greater number of resources are required. Also, the spread of economic development and government income redistribution policies reduce the localization of consumer markets; industrial infrastructure is more widely available; central governments intervene in the locational process to the advantage of the backward regions; and diseconomies of agglomeration increase the attractiveness of relatively low labor and raw material prices in those same regions.

Simultaneously and within regions, there is an increasing metropolitanization of development opportunities. Major metropolitan centers have advantages of large labor forces, the markets for service industries, and centrality in the national high-speed transportation network; all become very important at later stages of economic development.

The locational implications of these changing preferences and opportunity patterns are threefold. In *earlier* stages there is a *high degree of localization* of economic development *around points of minimum movement cost.* In *later* stages of economic development there is (1) a *spread across regions,* and (2) a *concentration in and around metropolitan centers* within regions.

While this conceptual schema is broadly applicable at the national level and while the notions of sequential localization and spread find a reflection at the internation level, at the same *internation* level the *spread effects* are extremely *inefficient.* This is partly due to highly protectionist policies pursued by the more developed nations; it is also due to policies of the less developed nations that tend to deter foreign investment and also to bestow positive spillovers of the "brain drain" variety from which the more developed nations benefit.

Differences in economic development, however, connote differences in social welfare and therefore *conflict* both between nations and between regions within a nation. Geographical differences in economic development, therefore, are policy issues. Also, at the intranational level a body of ideas regarding the geographical bias of development policy has emerged. A major idea in this literature is that a policy of *dispersing* economic development aids both the causes of *equity* or equality between regions and *national efficiency* in terms of economic growth. Though the argument is far from proven, there seems a widespread commitment on the part of governments to dispersion policies. A major question for the geographer, therefore, is what locational policies of dispersion will best serve both the equity and the efficiency goals?

In review, why is economic development important? Presumably because it increases the happiness of the individual both by widening the range of private goods and services that he can purchase and by providing a more pleasant environment: purified water, housing that is resistant to the hazards of fire and weather, and social amenities in the form of education and health care. Economic development, however, is a double-edged sword. Although in some respects it makes the environment a more pleasant place to live in, it can also make it highly unpleasant: the crime associated with its cities, and the atmospheric pollution of its industries are cases in point. Solving the economic problem, therefore, seems to contain within it another problem: *the environmental quality problem.* Looking at this from the geographical viewpoint is the concern of our final chapter.

CHAPTER SEVENTEEN

The Geography of Environmental Quality

INTRODUCTION

The concept of economic development dominated the rhetoric of the publicists, politicians, and mass media in the 1950s and 1960s in both North America and Western Europe. All indications are that the new and domestically oriented concept of *environmental quality* will make a strong bid for prominence in the issues of the 1970s. This concern for environmental quality, moreover, is already apparent in the pronouncements and programs of politicians and in the greatly increased attention and allocation of funds to environmental planning.

There are good reasons why this should be so. The economic problem in the North Atlantic democracies is no longer as pressing as it once was; rising income levels and income redistribution policies have lifted most households above the minimal subsistence level. In addition, increasing urbanization has set in motion a range of nuisances that to many are increasingly intolerable: for example, atmospheric pollution, traffic congestion, and crime.

Whatever the reasons for it, however, there is no doubting the widespread and quite intense interest in environmental quality. To define the concept of environmental quality, however, is more difficult. All that we can do here is list a set

of *connotations* with which people frequently associate the concept and employ these connotations as a set of guideposts for channeling our discussion of the *geography of environmental quality*.

Of what, therefore, does the *good environment* consist? We can list at least eight criteria by which one would probably judge whether an environment is good, bad, or merely tolerable.

(1) The good environment is a nuisance-free environment. Many environments create, or are associated with, events that we regard as irritating in some sense, that is, time consuming, nerve racking, or dangerous to our personal security. Some environments are exceptionally smelly or noisy—pity the person who lives near a large airport, for example. Other environments impose subtle costs; thus air pollution imposes additional cleaning bills that are rather staggering when assessed in accurate dollar terms. The small town of Steubenville, Ohio, for example, in 1970 had the dubious distinction of being the most atmospherically polluted city in the United States. The average resident of that city pays eighty-five dollars a year more in resultant cleaning bills and home repairs than someone living some seventy miles away in Uniontown, Pennsylvania. Crime and traffic congestion are other nuisances

that detract from the quality of an environment.

(2) *The good environment is a healthful environment.* Environments with high levels of air pollution are not only costly; they are also unhealthy and are consequently characterized by relatively high rates of mortality from respiratory diseases such as bronchitis and lung cancer. Other health problems arise from the quality of drinking water. Thus in the coal-mining valleys of Wales unusually high rates of mortality from heart disease are found. This puzzled epidemiologists until recently when an association was found with the water in the area. It was discovered to be unusually and excessively soft. Finally, in addition to water, there are sometimes health problems related to food. One theory advanced to explain the high rates of stomach cancer in Iceland, for example, has focused upon the possible role of certain chemicals in the soil that are absorbed by vegetable and animal alike and that might prove ultimately irritating to the human digestive tract.

(3) *The good environment is an employment-opportunity environment.* In some areas employment is available for almost all who want it. Employment is diversified so that periodic downturns in one sector of the local economy may be accompanied by stability or upturns in another sector of the local economy. Employment is also generally available for both men and women. In other environments, one employer may dominate the local employment structure so that a decline in the market for his product may be followed by unemployment. Alternatively, industry may be largely heavy, placing severe constraints on employment opportunities for women and thus limiting household income. Employment structures that rely on one heavy economic sector are especially characteristic of coal-mining areas.

(4) *The good environment is a recreational-opportunity environment.* Parks should be available for organized sport and for evening walks. Large open spaces of natural beauty should be available for walking, climbing, and just "getting away from it all." The recreational environment is intimately linked with the healthful environment because healthy people tend also to be those who engage actively in some sort of physical exercise.

Recreation, however, also encompasses the intellectual as well as the physical. Listening to a symphony orchestra or watching a drama production are just as much matters of recreation and the replenishing of one's energies by a diverting, relaxing, but stimulating activity as swimming, hiking, or playing basketball are.

(5) *The good environment is a housing-opportunity environment.* The housing stock available to home seekers varies from area to area. In some areas rental housing may be in short supply: this is a severe handicap for those having insufficient money to qualify for a mortgage. Housing also varies in cost and rental and this imposes a geographically variable hardship on people: housing tends to be much cheaper in the Southern states of the United States, for example, than in the Northeast.

Quite apart from availability and cost, however, housing stock also varies very significantly in its quality. In some areas, such as Scotland and northeast England, houses may be very small in terms of the number of rooms that are characteristic; this is frequently a precursor of overcrowding that may foster such diseases as tuberculosis. The smallness of rooms may aggravate this problem. In addition, houses may lack modern amenities such as a separate bathroom or indoor toilet, or, alternatively, they may simply be in a bad state of repair and classified as *dilapidated* or *slum* by government agencies.

In general, housing that is dilapidated also tends to have smaller and fewer rooms per household unit and to lack modern household amenities. It also tends to be structurally older than higher-quality housing—a fact that is often betrayed by its Victorian architecture. The massive tenement buildings of the Gorbals district of Glasgow are prototypical in this respect as are the cores of many large cities of North America and Western Europe.

(6) *The good environment is an educational-opportunity environment.* Locally within a city there are often perceptible differences in the quality of schools: the repute of the teachers, the money invested in teaching aids, the physical plant, the playing fields, and so on. When viewed on a national canvas, however, the variations in environment are quite staggering. Most southern states of the United States spend barely 60% of the educational expenditures characteristic of Midwestern, Western, and Northeastern states. This is apparent in the low proportions of pupils who graduate from high school in the South, the low proportions who go to college, and the relatively high rates of illiteracy—still alarmingly high by West European standards.

(7) *The good environment is a modern amenity environment.* We all regard electricity, gas, piped water, and a flush toilet as necessary amenities of modern civilization—facilities that reduce the drudgery of mere existence and open up new realms to us. Certainly, for example, a household without electricity is intellectually much poorer—even if many embryonic geniuses were nurtured on candlelight and homemade entertainment. Yet in many rural areas such as Appalachia or parts of Wales and Scotland these amenities still do not exist. This lack is particularly hard to tolerate when one has been exposed to an alternative as a result of staying with a relative in a nearby town, for example.

(8) *The good environment is a health-opportunity environment.* Health is dependent not only on clean air, pure water, and nutritious nontoxic food: it also depends on the availability of health facilities such as doctors and hospitals. We shall see, for instance, that there are very large geographic disparities in the availability of health facilities in the United States as measured by the population per doctor. In terms of this measure, health care is particularly deficient in the South, a factor which must be held partly responsible for the high rates of infant mortality in that region.

The above listing of eight criteria is by no means definitive; undoubtedly there are a number of criteria that we have omitted. The good environment, for instance, is also the beautiful, aesthetically appealing environment. This is a rather vague and wide concept not usually given to definition; where it has been possible to define this below, however, we have not hesitated to employ it.

It is clear from this discussion that *environmental quality is something that varies over space:* some areas have high-quality environments while others have low-quality and unattractive environments. This focuses upon the importance of location relative to environments of varying attractiveness: specifically *proximity to unattractive environments* and *accessibility to attractive environments.* One does not have to live in a factory town in order to suffer from air or water pollution, for instance. Winds can scatter noxious fumes over wide areas while running water spreads industrial effluents downstream killing fish and making swimming a health hazard for a long distance from the pollution source.

Similarly, there is accessibility to an employment-opportunity environment as a result of the possibility of daily commuting. Health-care facilities also will be more readily accessible for the rural dweller with an automobile than for the rural dweller without one. Discussions of the quality of the environment and policies designed to provide greater geographical equity in quality are therefore inextricably bound up with discussions of the general availability to the public of transportation facilities.

A final introductory consideration, apart from those of defining the concept of environmental quality and pointing out geographical variation in the incidence of that quality, is that such differences raise policy questions. Both moral and political imperatives have led to a political context of locational egalitarianism in terms of opportunity and treatment. Unspoken but nevertheless real tenets of contemporary politics are that in the long term, at least, *no geographical area should be favored or handicapped over any other geographical area; the same opportunities should be available to all regardless of location.* Considering the policy interest of the subject matter, therefore, we need to ask what policies should be adopted to eliminate differences in and to improve environmental quality. What is the possible role, for example, of new towns?

Within this context, the remainder of this chapter is divided into three sections. The first and longest section attempts to identify three components or dimensions in the geography of environmental quality along which environmental quality can be seen to vary: urban size, urban–rural differences, and regional differences. The second section shows how various mechanisms resulting from initial geographical differences in environmental quality tend to aggravate such differences. Outmigration that is selective and the image that an area presents to prospective locators are of special significance here.

Finally, we examine the geography of environmental quality as a policy issue: what locational policies can be adopted to mitigate geographical differences in environmental quality? What are the problems and drawbacks associated with such policies?

COMPONENTS OF THE GEOGRAPHY OF ENVIRONMENTAL QUALITY

(1) THE URBAN SIZE COMPONENT

Urban size tends to be very strongly associated with certain important aspects of environmental quality. As urban size increases so in some ways the quality of the environment improves; in other ways, however, it tends to deteriorate — a modern-day jungle replacing the pristine innocence of the small town.

On the credit side of the ledger larger cities, as we mentioned in Chapter Twelve, *tend to have more diversified employment structures.* Larger cities such as Detroit and Birmingham (England) are noted for their automobile production; but, in fact, they are much less reliant on automobile employment than smaller cities such as Flint (Michigan) and Dagenham. Such diversification of employment tends to insulate the larger city from the hazards of the trade cycle while the smaller city often has to weather the storm. The result is that, in Britain at least, larger cities tend to have lower unemployment rates. This is not so in the United States where larger cities have higher unemployment rates. This has very little to do with diversity in employment structures, however, since the unemployment of the large American city derives largely from the problems of digesting into its occupational structure large numbers of unskilled and often barely literate migrants from backward agricultural areas such as Appalachia and the South. This is not a problem with which the British city has to contend.

A second major plus for the quality of the environment in the larger cities is their *greater access to health services.* Large cities can provide the thresholds required by large hospitals with their specialized medical services. In a context of limited long-distance transportation this advantage was almost entirely confined to larger cities though the spread of the automobile has done a good deal to spread the advantages of accessibility to health facilities through a greater range of urban sizes. This also applies to the greater accessibility of large city populations to cultural amenities such as museums, art galleries, symphony orchestras, zoos, and voluntary societies catering to esoteric interests.

Finally, and most importantly, larger cities are usually characterized by *better-quality housing stock* than smaller cities. Larger cities have shown a propensity for long-term growth not exhibited by smaller cities and this has stimulated the housing market in them leading to the erection of newer, larger structures either alongside or in place of older structures.

TABLE 17-1. Urban size and median income for males, 14 years and over with income, 1960. Note the regularity of the decline in income with declining urban size.

Urbanized areas	
3,000,000 or more	$3078
1,000,000–3,000,000	3026
250,000–1,000,000	2779
Under 250,000	2692
Places outside urbanized areas	
25,000 or more	2554
10,000–25,000	2484
2500–10,000	2354
1000–2500	2268
Under 1000	1935

Also stimulating improvement in the housing stock of larger cities has been the higher income prevailing in such cities; as Table 17-1 shows, larger cities tend to be characterized by appreciably higher median incomes than smaller cities and this is reflected in a keener demand for better-quality housing.

While living in larger cities provides certain unmistakable advantages over living in smaller cities, however, it also provides quite distinct penalties. Possibly most severe in this respect is *crime.* As Table 17-2 shows there is an unmistakable decline in crime rates in the United States with decreasing urban size for a wide variety of crimes from murder and non-negligent manslaughter at one end of the scale to auto theft at the other end. The relationships with urban size are quite staggering in their clarity, though quite why they should occur is not readily apparent.

Secondly, larger cities tend to be characterized by much more *severe air pollution* than smaller cities (see Table 17-3). As the destination for trips from a wide surrounding area and as a locally dispersed phenomenon itself, the larger city is associated with high levels of auto traffic producing under certain climatically propitious circumstances, as in Los Angeles, a virtual blanket of smog over the city. The association of larger cities with jet airports does little to relieve the concentration of suspended particles in the atmosphere. In addition, larger cities, particularly the older ones, are the seats of manufacturing industry based on solid and liquid fuels, which also produce a great deal of atmospheric effluvium. As Figure 17-1 shows, the five largest cities in Britain—London, Glasgow, Leeds, Manchester, and Birmingham—form the nuclei of the zones of excessively high air pollution in the United Kingdom. The fact that the incidence of death from certain respiratory

TABLE 17-2.   Crime rates* per 100,000 by urban size class, United States, 1965.

City size	Murder and non-negligent manslaughter	Forcible rape	Robbery	Assault	Burglary breaking or entering	Auto theft
Over 250,000	9.2	21.4	178.8	200.2	982.6	573.0
100,000–250,000	6.4	11.2	73.1	151.0	871.2	353.1
50,000–100,000	3.5	8.3	48.5	85.1	674.6	297.1
25,000–50,000	3.1	6.3	32.9	70.7	561.7	212.4
10,000–25,000	2.3	5.6	18.6	66.7	461.8	140.5
Below 10,000	2.0	5.0	11.8	62.0	368.9	98.6

* Offenses known to police.

diseases increases with urban size, in Britain at least, is probably far from coincidental (see Table 17-4).

A third negative feature often attributed to larger cities is that of *traffic congestion*. Longer journey-to-work trips and the attractiveness of the larger city to people from a wide surrounding area promote a readily apparent situation.

In summary, a lower probability of unemployment, better quality housing stock, and access to health and cultural amenities provide definite advantages for the larger city. However, high crime rates, high pollution levels, and traffic congestion emphasize the advantages of small-town living. That in the minds of the inhabitants the disadvantages outweigh the advantages is suggested

by opinion poll evidence from France. Thus a survey of people distributed throughout France and carried out in 1959–60 showed that given a choice of region in which to live and work those who would most willingly leave their present region were residents of greater Paris. In the light of the arguments presented in Chapter Sixteen regarding locational policies of equity versus national efficiency, this is quite interesting. While we argued there that concentration in larger cities probably aided the end of national economic efficiency, it seems likely that it does not aid the goal of social happiness—at least as far as the inhabitants of the larger cities are concerned.

(2) THE URBAN-RURAL COMPONENT

With respect to most facets of environmental quality, rural areas are at the lower end of the urban size hierarchy; most of the ideas presented above therefore apply. Rural areas are characterized by insignificant levels of crime and of atmospheric pollution, for example, with, as a result of the latter, lowered levels of mortality from respiratory diseases.

Nevertheless, certain debits characteristic of living in rural areas need to be underlined, since their significance is probably underestimated. The most critical concerns the low levels of *household*

TABLE 17-3.   Urban size and air pollution, United States, 1957–65. Air pollution is measured here in terms of the particulate matter level: suspended particles consist of smoke, dust, fumes, and droplets of viscous liquid.

City size group	Average particulate matter level
1,000,000 and over	170
700,000–1,000,000	127
400,000–700,000	126
100,000–400,000	113
50,000–100,000	113
2500–50,000	85

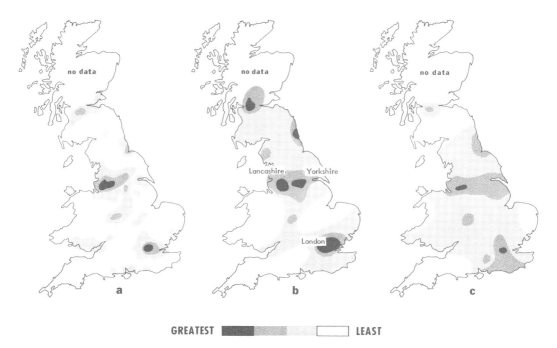

GREATEST ▬▬▬▬▭ LEAST

FIGURE 17-1.   The geography of atmospheric pollution in Great Britain. (*a*) is an index of coal burnt and therefore provides an estimate of the magnitude of the pollution producing agent; (*b*) is the distribution of atmospheric pollution measured at rural locations: note how intense it is around the industrial areas of London, northeast England, southeast Lancashire, and West Yorkshire; (*c*) shows the distribution of the average yearly number of hazy days.

amenity provision in rural areas; in North American and Western European nations rural households are still less likely to have piped water, sewer lines, and electricity. This not only imposes an

TABLE 17-4.   Mortality rates per 10,000 for respiratory diseases by city size class in England and Wales. Mortality rates from respiratory diseases seem to decline with population size; this may be due to pollution being greater in larger cities. Data are for 1968.

City size	Lung cancer	Bronchitis
Conurbations*	5.64	6.80
Over 100,000	5.26	6.24
50,000–100,000	5.06	5.70
Below 50,000	4.28	5.40
Rural areas	3.56	4.09

* These are large urban agglomerations generally in excess of 1 million people; Greater London is a conurbation.

inconvenience; it can also, in the case of the lack of piped water, pose a health hazard since certain diseases are associated with impure drinking water. Consider, for example, mortality rates from stomach cancer in England and Wales. As Figure 17-2 shows there is a very high concentration of high mortality rates in north and in west Wales. This localization has puzzled epidemiologists for a long time, but one of the more plausible theories has related it to chemical impurities in drinking water. It is known that the ions of many heavy metals can be fatal to fish, animals, and men and that they may well have cancer-inducing properties. North and west Wales contains a large number of spoil heaps from past mining activity for copper, lead, and zinc, and the streams and lakes in the vicinity of such heaps are almost inevitably polluted by water moving off the spoil heaps and containing residual amounts of these in solution. Water of this untreated nature may well be responsible for the high stomach cancer mortality rates in these areas. The provision of water by a large water company would almost certainly expose the purity of the water to more careful scrutiny and control, and therefore probably would lower the mortality rate.

Obviously such negative features of the rural environment are rather subtle and are probably underestimated or not estimated at all by individuals already living or planning to live in rural areas. Certainly the image of the rural area is largely one of "the good environment" as evidenced by the desire of people to get closer to the countryside by suburbanization and residential location in small villages near to larger cities. In such locations one can have many of the advantages of both the rural and urban environment.

(3) REGIONAL COMPONENTS

Independent of the urban size and the urban–rural dimensions one finds regional variations that cut across these regularities. On these regional dimensions several low-quality environments posing problems for national policy can be identified. Two in particular are worthy of extended consideration: (1) the 19th-century industrial region, and (2) the stagnant, agricultural, low-income region.

The 19th-Century Industrial Region. In a number of areas in North America and Northwestern Europe one encounters large clusters of towns and cities constituting dense agglomerations of population. A range of city sizes will ordinarily be present though usually the cities are smaller rather than larger. In North America such an agglomeration occurs in the upper Ohio Valley on the borders of Ohio, West Virginia, and Pennsylvania. Surrounding the city of Pittsburgh is a whole host of manufacturing and mining towns such as Youngstown, East Liverpool, McKeesport, Johnstown, Washington (Pennsylvania), Steubenville, and Wheeling. A similar agglomeration of manufacturing and mining towns occurs in east Pennsylvania in the Scranton–Wilkes-Barre–Bethlehem area. In Western Europe the same sort of phenomenon is found in West Yorkshire around Leeds, Bradford, Sheffield, and Halifax; in northeastern England, between New-

GREATER THAN THE NATIONAL AVERAGE

40% AND MORE THAN THE NATIONAL AVERAGE

FIGURE 17-2. The geography of male stomach cancer mortality in England and Wales. Note the very high death rates in north and west Wales; it has been suggested that it has something to do with pollution of water supplies from water running off the spoil heaps of old lead, zinc, and copper mines that are widespread in the area. Note also that for some reason the more urban areas of the nation (West Yorkshire, southeast Lancashire, Durham and Northumberland, and the Birmingham area have rates higher than the national average. Data are for 1954–58.

castle on the north and Middlesborough on the south; in Lancashire, in the triangle Manchester–Liverpool–Blackburn; and also in the Ruhr area of West Germany and in northern France around Lille.

All these densely populated industrial and mining areas grew up in the early stages of the Industrial Revolution and their contemporary occupational mix reveals this fact: coal mining and heavy industry such as iron and steel and shipbuilding are particularly important, as are the cotton and woolen textile industries in their gaunt brick mills originally driven by steam power.

Most important for us, however, is the fact that these environmental creations of 19th-century industrialism provide a contemporary ambience that is far from satisfactory by present-day criteria — and for a number of reasons. First, they are areas of *constrained employment opportunity*. Occupationally these areas still tend to rely on a very narrow spectrum of industry. These industries, moreover, are usually ones that, while growing rapidly in the 19th century, are no longer the growth industries of the economy. The growth industries of electronics, aircraft, household appliances, and automobiles are poorly represented in these areas. In addition, their basic industries are often facing severe competition from other areas: the market for coal, for example, has been severely curtailed by competition from natural gas and fuel oil. These problems of an essentially economic character combine to produce a situation of *relatively high unemployment levels* and *relatively low industrial wages*. This is an important basis for understanding much of the low environmental quality of these areas.

A second negative feature of these environments (but one that is difficult to rigorously measure) is that they are *aesthetically drab and repellent*. Housing is frequently of the terrace variety with houses joined together in a row — and standing behind the row are a set of outdoor privies. The brick is often soot stained, and a dismal view is relieved only by the chimneys of the factories or the spoil heaps of the mining activity. A great deal of land lies derelict: old spoil heaps of mining and metallurgical enterprise, land effectively sterilized by chemical fumes, and so on. Some idea of the localization of such derelict land in these areas of 19th-century industrialism can be gained from Figure 17-3 which

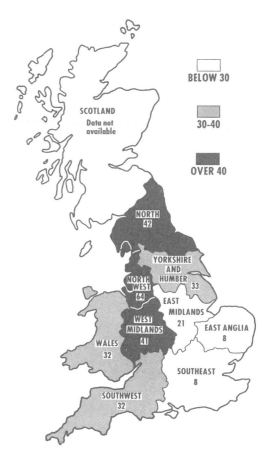

FIGURE 17-3. The geography of derelict land in the United Kingdom, 1965. Rates are in acres of derelict land per 10,000 acres. Note the concentration in areas that were the hearths of the Industrial Revolution: the North, the Northwest and the West Midlands.

plots the proportion of total area in regions of England and Wales consisting of derelict land. The low percentages are found in those regions barely touched by the 19th-century industrialism that we have outlined: the East Midlands, East Anglia, and the Southeast.

These environments are not only aesthetically repellent however; they also have poisonous air and water. Coal mining and heavy iron and steel and chemical industries are associated with high degrees of both *atmospheric and water pollution*. On the maps of atmospheric pollution of Britain in Figure 17-1, the 19th-century industrial areas stand out quite clearly: central Scotland, Lancashire, West Yorkshire, and the Birmingham area, in particular. In the United States, also, in terms of dirty air three of the ten dirtiest cities are found in the western Pennsylvania–eastern Ohio area: Steubenville, Washington (Pennsylvania), and Pittsburgh. Possibly as a result of such poisonous air, death rates from respiratory disease such as bronchitis tend to be particularly high in these areas as shown for England and Wales in Figure 17-4.

Unfortunately control of such pollution often poses problems of expense that the economic structure of the area cannot absorb easily. The coal mining, iron and steel, and textile industries of these areas are frequently engaged in severe competition in markets which are growing only slowly, if at all, and they can ill afford to improve the environment for people who may ultimately be thrown out of work as a result of the expense. In northeastern England, for example, fine sandy beaches along the coast are strewn with filth from local coal mines which dump their spoil into the sea. No control is exercised for fear that the expense of alternative waste disposal arrangements would be too much for the economically pinched coal industry on

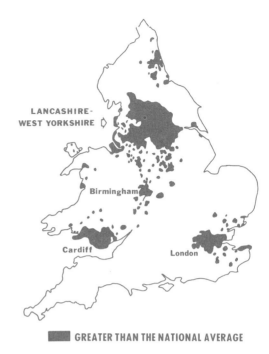

GREATER THAN THE NATIONAL AVERAGE

FIGURE 17-4. The geography of male bronchitis mortality in England and Wales. A comparison of this map with the atmospheric pollution distributions shown in Figure 17-1 is very instructive: bronchitis death rates are especially high in smoky industrial-mining areas such as northeast England, West Yorkshire, South Wales, London, and the Birmingham area. Data are for 1954–58.

which northeast England depends so much.

In terms of *housing,* also, these areas leave much to be desired. Relatively low incomes and slow population growth have cramped the demand for newer, more modern housing so that many of the structures are the original ones built when the coal mines were originally sunk or when the blast furnaces were fired for the first time. Houses are often very small in terms of the number of rooms they provide for their occupants and lack such basic amenities as a bathroom or indoor water closet.

The environment created by 19th-century industrialism (and in many areas not eliminated by later development) is an unattractive and repellent one that often contrasts with the buccolic charm of surrounding rural areas. Rural areas, however, may also have their disadvantages, as we shall now see.

The Low-Income, Stagnating, Agricultural Region. Within the economically advanced nations of North America and Northwestern Europe the 19th-century industrial region is not the only low-quality, unattractive environment with which society has to contend. The second major type of low-quality region is the low-income, economically stagnating agricultural region. The prototypical example of this is provided by two large areas of southeastern United States: the area classically known as the South, and the upland area of Appalachia, stretching from Alabama and Georgia in the south, northeast to Pennsylvania. In Western Europe such areas are generally absent

for reasons that will become clear shortly.

Such regions are *depressed agricultural regions.* In some cases they were previously much more prosperous on the basis of some crop exported for cash; in the case of the South, this crop was cotton. The development of this cash crop in California and Arizona and the emergence of synthetics such as nylon has bitten deep into the markets for the region's original major export. In other cases, poverty stems from an imbalance between regional resources and the population depending upon those regional resources. There has been no decline in demand for the staple crop of Appalachia—tobacco—but there has been little rationalization of the subsistence sector of the economy to cater for rising populations. The decline of export markets for a major cash crop and/or an insufficiently productive agriculture must be held

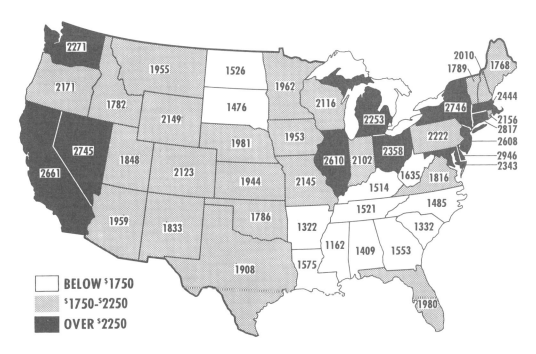

FIGURE 17-5. The geography of incomes per capita in the United States, 1961. Note the generally low income levels in the South and Appalachia though income levels in the Dakotas and upper New England are not much higher.

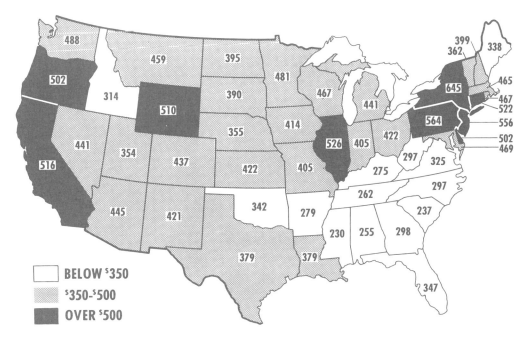

FIGURE 17-6.   The geography of public school expenditures per pupil in the United States, 1963. This map gives a useful impression of the geography of educational expenditure in the United States: note the low expenditures in the South and Appalachia; also compare this map with Figure 17-5; can you see any identities between the two maps?

largely responsible for the poverty of these areas. The relationship of the areas commonly known as the South and Appalachia to the other areas of low income in the United States is illuminated very clearly by Figure 17-5.

The poverty of the economic environment is matched by a poverty of the social environment. Access to educational facilities in the South and in Appalachia, for example, is appallingly low when compared with the rest of the nation. As Figure 17-6 shows, educational expenditures per pupil in the area are considerably below those elsewhere in the United States. Such relative lack of provision is also characteristic of the availability of health care to the region (see Figure 17-7).

The lower levels of educational provision are matched by correspondingly low levels of educational experience. As Table 17-5 shows, the proportions of

persons 25 years and over completing less than 5 years of school in the Deep South and Appalachia is much in excess of the national figure. The discrepancies between Negro and white experiences in the South are also strikingly large—a result in part of segregated schooling.

This not only creates a bad environment for the inhabitant of the South or of Appalachia; the migration of undereducated people and their children creates problems for the areas to which they migrate. Thus Northern cities have to cope with the problems of training individuals who are unusually weak in verbal and mechanical skills; the schools of those same cities have to cater to the unusual needs of the migrants' children imposing a burden on systems already strained by the forces that we outlined in Chapter Fifteen. This is a theme to which we shall return shortly.

The second feature of such environ-

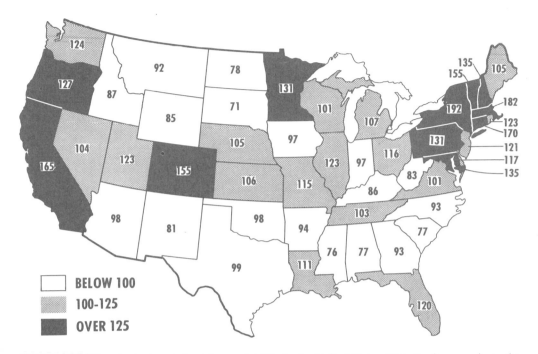

FIGURE 17-7. The geography of physician availability in the United States, 1961: the figures refer to the numbers of physicians per 10,000 people. The pattern is very similar to those shown in Figures 17-5 and 17-6. The South again emerges as an area of deprivation though the Dakotas, Montana, Idaho, and Wyoming are almost as badly deprived. In some states, such as Minnesota, California, Maryland, and Louisiana, the figure is somewhat inflated due to the presence of large medical schools.

ments in general and of the South and Appalachia in particular is the *low quality of their housing environment.* As Figure 17-8 shows, the proportion of housing that is dilapidated reaches very high levels in the two areas. Indeed in the Deep South (South Carolina, Alabama, Georgia, Arkansas, Mississippi, and Louisiana), only Louisiana has less than 35% of its housing dilapidated. The growing cities, such as New Orleans and Atlanta, stand out as islands in the generally unrelieved landscape of low housing standards.

A third and final feature of the Southern environment that is rather more problematic and not necessarily typical of stagnating low-income agricultural regions is the violence that seems so rampant. This is apparent not only in newspaper accounts of the pleasantries of Southern living; it is apparent in hard statistics. As Figure 17-9 shows, the homicide rate is considerably higher in the South than elsewhere in the United States, though exactly why this should be is not immediately apparent. Certainly much of the violence is interracial; but then there also seems to be appreciably more intraracial violence than elsewhere in the United States.

Unlike the 19th-century industrial region, therefore, the South does not have atmospheric pollution; what it does have, however, is a far more crushing poverty and also housing stock and educational services that are considerably more deficient. These problems, because of the way in which they are communicated by migration, pose a far more

TABLE 17-5. Educational experience in regions of the United States. Percent of persons 25 years and over completing less than 5 years of school by region and race: 1960. Note how the populations of the Core South and Appalachia have particularly unfavorable rates of schooling; the differential between non-whites and whites is also much greater than in the United States as a whole. Core South = Georgia, South Carolina, Alabama, Mississippi, Arkansas, and Louisiana; Appalachia = Tennessee, Kentucky, North Carolina, West Virginia, and Virginia; Borderland = Texas, Oklahoma, Florida, Maryland, Delaware, and District of Columbia.

Region	White	Non-white	All
United States	6.7	23.5	8.3
Northeast	6.6	12.9	7.0
North Central	4.8	14.0	5.4
West	4.8	16.0	5.6
South:	10.0	31.8	14.0
Core	10.6	39.2	18.3
Appalachia	11.6	29.3	14.2
Borderland	8.5	23.1	10.6

serious problem for regional planning than do the contemporary difficulties of the 19th-century industrial regions.

It would be erroneous, however, to assume that the problems of rural poverty in the United States are confined to the contiguous areas of the South and Appalachia. While these areas do include the poorest states of the union and are publicly prominent to a degree guaranteed by the size of the area they cover, there are also smaller areas of the United States that suffer from similar problems that, while not of the same degree, are certainly of the same kind. Thus a feature of the geographical distributions of educational expenditures, dilapidated housing, and so on, which we have examined so far, is that on a number of occasions some of the states in the Northern Plains and in upper New England are grouped with the South. In terms of housing, for example, the Dakotas and Maine are not much better off than the South. Also, the educational expenditures of Maine and Idaho are little in excess of those characteristic of the South; and in health care, also, the Dakotas, Idaho, Wyoming, and Montana are very similar to the South.

A glance at Figure 17-5, however, will demonstrate the reason for this situation: there really is not that much difference in income levels between the states of the Northern Plains, Wyoming, Idaho, and Maine and the states that we classically associate with the South. They are wealthier, it is true, but not by much. These, moreover, are also areas that have suffered from concentration on a single primary product. In the case of the Dakotas, for instance, a glut of world wheat markets has contributed to rural poverty.

At least two points emerge from this. First, it would be sad indeed if national concern with the South were to lead to a neglect of populations that are only slightly less needy than those of the South. They do not contribute large streams of migrants to Northern cities simply because they are now so sparsely inhabited; but it would be inhumane to ignore their problems on the grounds that they are of less practical concern to the nation as a whole.

The second point to emerge from this is the strong relationship between a number of facets of environmental quality and income levels. Particularly with regard to levels of social provision, wealthier areas tend to provide a much more favorable environment. Tax bases are larger and this is reflected in greater allocations of funds to education; the larger incomes also provide a demand for greater cultural amenity. The differences in environmental quality between poorer and wealthier areas, moreover, are not unchanging; there are important

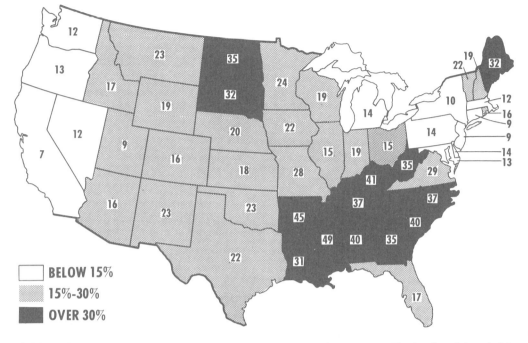

FIGURE 17-8. The geography of dilapidated housing in the United States, 1961. The South and Appalachia are outstanding for their deprivation though the Dakotas and Maine are about as bad; wealthier states such as New York and California tend to have lower rates of dilapidated housing. Figures refer to the percentage of the housing stock that is dilapidated.

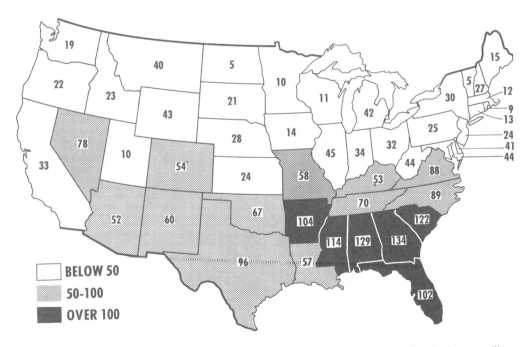

FIGURE 17-9. The geography of homicide in the United States, 1961. Figures are in homicides per million inhabitants; the South has unusually high homicide rates though quite why this is, is unknown.

mechanisms that tend to accentuate interregional differences—particularly in the context of a territorially fragmented political system such as that of the United States—and it is those mechanisms that we shall consider next.

FEEDBACK EFFECTS

The presence of a low-quality environment in an area often sets in motion certain changes that aggravate the low quality of that environment and make it less likely that it will be upgraded. Thus if modern, nonpolluting industry were to come into an area, the additions to regional income that it would create would be reflected in improvements in the housing stock, in the cultural amenities available to people, and also in the money available for investment in education. For a variety of reasons, the free market rarely operates in such a way as to encourage such favorable change. Indeed two factors in particular—*regional images* and *selective migration*—operate in such a way as to sink the low-quality environment areas further into the mire.

Problem areas such as the regions of 19th-century industrialism and the low-income, stagnating agricultural areas tend to have *very unfavorable images* from the residential desirability viewpoint. Recalling Chapter Six, for example, it is evident that on the mental maps of residential desirability of the United States the South was a generally very unattractive area. Similarly, in the maps of residential desirability of British school leavers the areas of 19th-century industrialism in Lancashire, Scotland, West Yorkshire, and northeastern England were generally repellent. These are important examples since the attraction of new industry to these areas is highly dependent upon being able to persuade certain management and skilled personnel to move to them. Clearly if the critical key personnel are reluctant to move into an area, then there is little possibility of introducing that employment necessary to diversify the occupational structure and to inject money that will find its way ultimately into better-quality housing and education.

A second feature of these low-quality environments is that migration from them tends to be highly selective in terms of the skills, ages, and education represented. In general, the younger, the better educated, and the more highly skilled are more likely to migrate elsewhere, leaving behind the older, the less educated, and the less skilled (see Table 17-6). If the losses of the more educated and younger elements are not replaced by in-migrants from elsewhere—and the generally unattractive image of these areas suggests that they will not be—then the result will be a population composition generally unfavorable to social and economic regeneration.

The reasons for this are several. First, the loss of skilled and educated labor reduces the attractiveness of the area for industrialists who might be contemplating locating plants in that area. This is particularly important given the high demand for skilled labor of those high value added industries that provide large additions to regional income and low additions to regional pollution.

Second, the loss of the most productive elements in the region imposes burdens on those remaining (who are less able to afford the burdens than those who have left). A greater proportion of the population will be older, calling for larger proportional amounts of spending on social welfare for the aged. Also, the burden of paying for education will be that much greater owing to the out-migration of those people who have benefited most from the educational system and who are most able to contribute to its continued maintenance. These considerations are especially important in the United States where the individual state is responsible

TABLE 17-6. Occupational differences in the rate of out-migration from Northeast Scotland. Out-migration tends to be occupationally selective with more skilled occupational groups showing higher rates of out-migration than the less skilled. This is particularly critical for lagging and depressed regions since it makes them even less attractive for manufacturing industries with high value added products.

Occupational group	Total cases in group	Percent of out-migrants in group	Occupational group	Total cases in group	Percent of out-migrants in group
		%			%
University students	20	85	Railway workers	48	19
Professional	72	54	Other non-manual	94	18
Armed forces	70	49	Other skilled	254	13
Managerial	63	25	Road transport	173	12
Clerical workers	95	25	Other skilled engineers	60	10
Fitters and electricians	193	25	Fishing and fish handling	63	8
Shop assistants	54	19	Other semiskilled and unskilled	246	1
				1505	

for much of its educational and welfare budget: it is not so true of centralized systems such as in the United Kingdom where the central government assures greater equity in local government spending. Indeed, as we shall see below, the elimination of political fragmentation in the raising and spending of taxes is a *sine qua non* for reducing geographical differences in the quality of the environment and reversing the tendency for better-quality environments to get better and for poorer-quality environments to get worse.

THE GEOGRAPHY OF ENVIRONMENTAL QUALITY AND POLICY

Certainly there are important reasons for instituting measures designed to eliminate inequity in environmental quality. These are not only moral—the right of a person to have a decent ambience no matter where he lives—but also political: witness the expression of Negro Southern poverty in political pressure groups demanding desegregation of schooling and the allocation of larger public spending to education in the South.

Apart from moral and political imperatives, however, there are also important economic reasons why all regions of a nation should be concerned with any inequity that exists in the opportunities accessible to people in different areas. It seems clear that to some extent the problems of the low-quality environment areas can spill over into the high-quality environment areas. Consider the current problems of Northern cities in the United States for example; as a result of large scale in-migration of poorly educated Negroes from the South these cities face the problem of growing unemployment with its expression in higher welfare rolls and social discontent. They also face a problem of housing a group notoriously discriminated against and therefore difficult to house. It seems very much in the interests of Northern cities, therefore, to stem this net migratory flow of low-skilled, uneducated labor as much as possible by, for example, supporting policies of greater investment in education in the South and also policies of economic development aimed at bringing higher incomes and therefore greater al locations of money to education and health in the South. The degree to which the urban crisis of the North is perpetuated by the rural crisis of the South is difficult to overestimate.

Policy proposals for rectifying such inequity in the quality of the environment between regions have taken two forms: there are, first, regional level policies designed to upgrade the quality of the environment for people living in a whole region; and there are also subregional policies that aim to achieve the former goal by relying on geographical concentration of government aid and investment in, and migration to, a few favored points within the depressed area. Regional policies have been especially apparent in programs designed to upgrade incomes and the availability of a diversity of employment opportunity in depressed areas. Such policies are apparent in the British programs, which we reviewed earlier, that are aimed at introducing new industry into the declining areas of 19th-century industrialism now overly dependent on a narrow range of mining and heavy industries and with relatively high unemployment rates. In the United States, efforts to introduce industry into, for example, Appalachia have taken the form of improving the infrastructure of the area, particularly its communication network, in order to make it more attractive to private industry. Thus the Appalachia Regional Development Act of 1965 was primarily a supplementary highway appropriation; of the total appropriation of funds approximately 70% was for the construction of highways. There has been in the United States, however, little effort to restrict industrial development in other growing areas of the country in an attempt to divert investment to depressed areas of the South and Appalachia and to the declining heavy-industry

mining areas of western Pennsylvania–eastern Ohio and of eastern Pennsylvania. As pointed out in Chapter Twelve, policies that do not combine a stick with a carrot are probably critically flawed in terms of their ultimate effectiveness.

The American problem makes it clear that economic development programs are not likely to be effective policy instruments for mitigating regional inequity, unless they are combined with policies of *social development* designed to make the backward areas more attractive to industrialists and to the people of the area. Especially critical here is the need for investment in education in order to provide those higher levels of skill attractive to industrialists. Also significant, however, are steps designed to upgrade the public image of the area and to make it more aesthetically attractive by policies of, for example, waste heap removal, pollution control, and upgrading of the housing stock by public housing projects.

Social development programs, however, call for the spending of public money, and in a situation where the local political unit doing the spending is also the major tax levier, this can exercise a decisive impact on the overall levels of equity in social services. For a variety of reasons, for example, the funding of education has remained largely a state responsibility in the United States producing a large range in educational investment which we reviewed earlier in this chapter. The poorer states invest relatively less per pupil than the wealthier states so that instead of providing the basis for escaping the vicious circle of poverty, dangerously low levels of investment merely lock areas still further into the poverty groove.

The relationship between income and social inequity across regions is also apparent in levels of welfare payments. Low-income states such as those of the

South and Appalachia pay much lower welfare benefits than the wealthier states thus stimulating migration to the cities of the North and West and adding to the unemployment rolls there. In early 1968 aid for dependent children averaged $8.45 per recipient per month in Mississippi, $15.30 per recipient per month in Alabama, $24.00 per month in Louisiana, and $18.65 per month in South Carolina; but, $44.70 per recipient per month in Illinois, $44.75 in California, $57.30 in New Jersey, and $60.00 per month in New York—all Northern or Western states that have experienced large influxes of in-migrants from the South. This clearly underlines the role that political fragmentation of government income and expenditure can play in jeopardizing policies aimed at reducing interregional inequity in the quality of the environment. It seems only fair to comment that if current efforts towards the regeneration of depressed areas in the United States are to have a modicum of success, federal expenditures aimed at eliminating differences in state expenditures will have to be greatly increased.

Within the depressed areas there is also the question of where public investment and assistance aimed at attracting industrialists should be concentrated. In the last chapter, we placed emphasis upon the benefits likely to flow from a policy of concentrating assistance in a few larger cities or *growth centers* that could provide economies of agglomeration for incoming industrialists. Similar arguments seem to apply to upgrading the quality of the environment with the *New Town* as conceptually analogous to the growth center. In some West European countries such as Sweden and Britain a number of completely new towns have been constructed, partly with a view to decentralizing employment and residences from already large cities such as Stockholm and London but also with a view to upgrading the environment in depressed areas of 19th-century industrialism. Such towns provide modern housing and large clusters of population capable of providing the thresholds necessary for a wide variety of retailing service and entertainment functions usually unattainable in the small towns characteristic of mining areas. Such new towns not only upgrade the image of areas and make them more attractive for both industrialists and migrants, but they can also be combined with the growth center notion outlined in the last chapter providing the basis of economies of agglomeration for self-perpetuating economic growth.

CONCLUSIONS AND SUMMARY

A problem of increasing interest is that of *environmental quality*. Precisely what environmental quality means is something of an enigma though it is possible to identify certain connotations associated with the concept. As our point of departure we have used eight such connotations, defining the good environment as one that is *nuisance free; healthful* in diet, water and air; and endowed with *modern amenities* and *economic, recreational, health care, housing,* and *educational opportunities.*

A major component of the *geography of environmental quality* is an *urban size compo-*

nent, larger cities having distinct advantages and disadvantages compared with smaller cities. Larger cities tend to have *more diversified employment structures* insulating them from depressions in the trade cycle; they have easier access to a wider range of *better-quality health services;* and their *housing* tends to be of a better average quality because of a sustained demand for new housing associated with newcomers to the cities and with the higher incomes typical of larger cities. Larger cities do suffer, however, from high *crime rates, air pollution,* and *traffic congestion.*

At the lower end of the urban hierarchy there are the *rural* areas which are in a number of ways quite distinct from *urban areas.* In particular, they tend to have much more *inadequate provision of modern amenities* such as electricity and piped water. The use of local stream water may be associated with toxic elements in suspension or in solution inducing unusually high levels of mortality from certain diseases.

Such *urban size* and *urban–rural* differentiations of environmental quality are super-imposed upon certain broad *regional variations* that may create "problem environments." Particularly notable here are areas of 19th-century industrialism with their *contracting employment opportunities* and generally *low industrial incomes.* The *landscape* of such areas is distinctive only for its *ugliness.* High levels of *atmospheric pollution* are associated with high mortality rates from *respiratory diseases* such as bronchitis, and the *housing stock* leaves a great deal to be desired.

In addition to such industrial problem areas there are also *agricultural problem areas:* regions of *low income* and *economic stagnation* where either a population has expanded faster than local resources or the cash crop basis of the economy has been eroded by contracting markets or by glut. The poverty of such areas is underlined by their *poverty of social provision* in terms of expenditures on education and health care. *Housing* is often dilapidated and lacking in urban amenities such as electric power, piped water, and sewage. Such problem areas underline the role that regional income levels play in sustaining a good environment and also the importance of bringing industry into such areas in order to create more wealth.

Unfortunately the possibilities of *regional regeneration* are often hindered by certain feedback mechanisms that make the area unattractive both to industry and to the skilled in-migrants who could lead the regeneration process. Particularly critical here are *negative regional images,* which deter both industrialist and migrant, and *selective migration,* which deprives the area of its most productive and educated elements.

For moral, political, and economic reasons, however, improvement of environmental quality in such areas is of critical significance and an indispensible tool in limiting the *spillover of problems* into areas of relatively high-quality environment. Toward these ends both *regional and subregional policies* have been introduced, the former aiming at economic development over wide areas and the latter aiming at concentrations of economic development and high-quality environments at select locations within those wide areas. Particularly important here is the concept of the *New Town* that can not only serve as a growth center but can also provide modern amenities to its inhabitants and upgrade the image of the area for those living outside it.

Epilogue

This book has covered a great deal of territory, probably virgin territory for many of the readers. Hopefully we have shed a rather new and different light on some old problems of man and the space he occupies. In retrospect, and also in prospect, it seems that three tasks remain. First, I would like to briefly review my objectives in writing this book in the particular manner I have chosen. Second, I would like to underline some of the dominant philosophical themes in this book regarding the approach to discovery in geography. And finally, we need to say something on "taking it further." If the book has fulfilled its aim in stimulating your curiosity about locational problems, what courses of action can you adopt to lead yourself into that cycle of alternate question posing and answering which is the basis of all rational approaches—geographical or otherwise—to the world around us? Let us now consider these problems.

PURPOSES

We have tried in this book to develop some basic geographical concepts of *locational pattern* and *locational process*. Concepts of locational pattern include those of *localization, distance bias, centralization, geographical trend, connectivity,* and *circuit networks*. The locational processes relevant to explaining many of these varieties of geographical arrangement and organization include *least-effort movement behavior, migration, locational competition,* and *spatial contagion.*

Thus, much of the locational pattern of economic development in Ireland can be related to least-effort movement behavior in the context of a centralized transportation network. The processes of locational competition shed a great deal of light on the spacing of urban settlements of different sizes. And the contagionlike spread of information has been employed to explain patterns of spatial diffusion of innovation.

Locational patterns, locational processes, and their mutual interrelationships are not only of interest for their own sake, however. They can also be related to certain current world problems and can provide the basis for ameliorating policies. Processes of suburbanization of employment and residences provide some clarification of the economic plight of the Negro in many cities; manipulating the factors that encourage such suburbanization (such as political fragmentation which encourages high inner-city tax rates) provides the basis for some mitigating policies. A Green Belt restriction on American suburban development such as that which prevails in Britain could provide some rather interesting locational results and probably a more equitable distribution of resources between the races.

Briefly, we have tried in this book to provide a *viewpoint for looking at the world around us* and for devising strategies for dealing with that environment. Furthermore, it is a viewpoint that is not identical to that offered by the economist or sociologist or psychologist; it has something quite novel to say, not just concerning the problematic but also in regard to the commonplace. It is also *a timely viewpoint:* problems of policy are becoming very much locational problems not only in the eyes of the geographer but also in the eyes of the politician and publicist. Whereas income redistribution, womens' suffrage, right-to-work, and the welfare state have provided the issues of the past, today's concerns revolve around such specifically geographical issues as *segregation,* the *location of industry in ghettoes, suburban exploitation of the central city, Appalachia, depressed areas,* and *underdeveloped countries.* In the past geography was considered a relatively unimportant part of the education of the informed layman; however, today it is increasingly important. Hopefully this book has contributed to the fulfillment of a growing need.

GENERAL PHILOSOPHY OF THE BOOK

Setting aside, for the moment, the locational concepts that have formed the core of this book, it is apparent that we have presented here certain philosophical convictions that do not stand or fall by virtue of their association with these specifically locational concepts. Rather they are philosophical convictions concerning *method* and *explanation* and they provide a very general basis for developing social science concepts in general and articulating their relationships to one another. Further, it is my belief that much of this book's validity stems from an adherence to these assumptions regarding *method* and *explanation.* Each, therefore, merits some words of clarification.

In terms of *method,* I have adopted the *model approach* to geography. At various points in the text I have referred to different models, leaving the exact meaning of the term "model" implicit rather than explicit. The perceptive student, therefore, will probably not be surprised by the general definition of the term model as it has been used in this book.

▶ *Models are verbal or mathematical abstractions from reality emphasizing certain characteristics of that reality and discarding others. The development of models generally involves a discarding of the unique or irrelevant characteristics of phenomena and a focus on the characteristics which phenomena share.*

Thus, models of nodal patterns emphasize the characteristics that nodal patterns have in common and ignore whatever is unique or appears irrelevant from the point of view of the concept being developed. The concept of *dispersion,* therefore, can be regarded as *a model of nodal patterns.* It focuses only on certain aspects of nodal pattern discarding such irrelevancies as nodal density or mean spacing. Dispersion, moreover, is something that all nodal patterns have—it is not unique to any one nodal pattern. All nodal patterns can be placed on the *dispersion scale* ranging from *perfectly clustered* at one end to *perfectly uniform* at the other end. In the same way, the concept of *connectivity* provides a model of *network geometry.* All networks have a given degree of connectivity; yet the concept of connectivity is a *simplification* of network geometry. What about network density, for instance, or, for a railroad network, the capacity of different links in the network? Such simplification, however, has great virtues as we shall see shortly.

The model approach in geography is not limited in its applicability to the descriptive alone; we can also develop *models of locational process* emphasizing those characteristics that movements share and discarding those that they do not. Thus, in Chapter Three we developed a *model of movement* based on the three factors of movement cost, attractiveness, and the locational pattern of movement opportunities. Such a model involves an abstraction of those characteristics that movements have in common from the sum total of all their characteristics. The fact that some movements are made by car, some by air, some at night, and some by day, for instance, is irrelevant to the task of developing a model of movement capable of explaining a large variety of types of movement. The fact that we use the concept of *place utility* in explaining migration patterns and the concept of *complementarity* in explaining commodity flow patterns is also irrelevant since both can be subsumed by the more general and therefore more abstract concept of *attractiveness.*

Why should we use the model approach in geography, however? How does it assist us in developing our knowledge of locational patterns and of the processes that produce them? Briefly, we use it because the model approach is the scientist's approach, and I have assumed throughout that our aims are congruent with those of the scientist: to develop laws, and specifically, in our case, *laws of location* that are applicable to increasingly broad segments of reality. Laws of shopping trip behavior applicable to Britain are interesting, but what we would really like are laws of shopping trip behavior that can be shown to

be valid in any national context. In order to develop laws, however, we need to develop theories and hypotheses that can be compared for their validity with the world around us. *The model provides a vehicle for developing those theories and hypotheses* that are likely to have a wide range of applicability.

Testing hypotheses, for example, demands that the locational events we are comparing have something in common. If we are interested in developing hypotheses regarding the geography of economic development across nations, for instance, it is important that we have a model of that geography which is applicable to all nations. A model stressing the economic development characteristics of the Western hemisphere, for example, while emphasizing characteristics shared by Western hemisphere nations may not be applicable to the world as a whole, since other nations may not share these characteristics. Similarly, hypotheses of network geometry require the development of concepts applicable to all networks: the concept of connectivity can be measured for all networks and compared with other characteristics of those networks to test hypotheses relating those characteristics to network geometry. The concept of centralization on Paris, however, is clearly one that is only applicable to French transportation networks. Models, therefore, facilitate comparison and hence the testing of hypotheses and the ultimate development of laws.

Models also facilitate *economy of explanation.* For example, they can often be transferred from the subject matter for which they were developed originally and applied in a fruitful and illuminating manner to other subjects. Thus, a model of *the geographical expansion of food supply areas* can help to explain *the geographical expansion of migration fields.* The model of the geographical expansion of

Britain's food supply area that we developed in Chapter Fourteen, for instance, was based on the two concepts of market price and movement cost. If we translate the concept of market price into that of place utility the model can also be applied to the expansion of the migration fields of growing cities.

Briefly, therefore, we are interested in developing the scientific aspects of geography: geography as a science of location. The model approach, with its ability to abstract from, simplify, and generalize reality is an indispensable aid in this task.

What, however, of the general philosophical assumptions that have guided our approach to *explanation?* What general assumptions have we made about the relationships between different phenomena at different locations? A major assumption, again implicit rather than explicit, is that locations are interdependent in such a way that they can be conceived of as belonging to *systems of interdependent entities.* What happens at one location affects another, which then affects another, which then, in a succeeding time interval, may affect the location at which the stimulus first originated. Some *systems of interdependent locations* are relatively easy to recognize: the city and the locations that form its sphere of influence form such a system so that we can legitimately talk about *urban systems.* Locations within nations tend to form systems to the extent that, as we pointed out in Chapter Seven, interdependence of locations is much greater *within bounded spaces* than *between bounded spaces.*

The fact that locations tend to be interdependent is one of the factors that makes urban and regional planning so difficult. Altering the employment structure at one location can reverberate throughout the whole system of places to which that location is connected and

have effects that, given the current state of knowledge, are not easy to predict. Such interdependence in a system of locations has to be constantly borne in mind by the planner. As discussed in Chapter Fifteen, for instance, a policy of "industry to Northern ghettoes" could possibly make no dent at all in the ghetto problem simply because it might only encourage additional migration from the South; one planning implication of this was that the problems of the Northern cities could best be tackled at their locational source—in the South. Similar interdependencies are at work in the aggravation of other problems; thus, one of the best things the United States could do for the impoverished millions of Indians would probably be to restrict the migration of British scientists to North America since it is this that creates the demand in Britain for Indian scientists—a demand which is only too readily satisfied.

The systems in which locations are embedded, however, also have a significant *time dimension* as well as a *space dimension.* The locational pattern at time t_2 can be seen as a function of the locational process at time t_1. The locational process at time t_3, however, is guided and constrained by the locational pattern already in existence at time t_2. Thus the demand for movement leads to the location (process) of a communication network (pattern) but the communication network then affects the location of other activities leading to the location (process) of additional capacity on that network—rather than to the construction of an entirely new network. We explored similar interdependencies of pattern and process in Chapter Nine, relating in a sequential manner the pattern of urban growth to the pattern of accessibility improvement to the pattern of urban growth ad infinitum.

One interesting aspect of such *feedback*

processes is that they tend to exaggerate geographical differences existing at a previous point in time. Thus, as we again saw in the last chapter, initial differences in environmental quality promote selective migrations that tend to make the low-quality areas even more unattractive for those economic activities that could regenerate them. The planner needs to recognize such feedback cycles, and in this detection a viewpoint emphasizing *systems of locations* is indispensable.

A second broad philosophical theme apparent in this book refers to small-scale events and consists of the idea that *ultimately locational patterns can be traced to human decisions:* decisions about whether and where to migrate; decisions regarding the location of a factory; decisions regarding the allocation of land for different uses, for instance. A knowledge of the factors affecting such decisions, therefore, is an indispensable tool in interpreting the resulting locational arrangements. It is for this reason that we have tended to emphasize the decision maker's viewpoint and the way it is structured by the locational context in which he finds himself. The information available to him, for instance, and the environment as the decision maker perceives it, rather than as it objectively exists, have been particularly stressed. Such an approach seems of increasing importance in geography simply because it can shed light on old problems that have previously resisted satisfactory explanation—consider the information-flow explanation of deviant migration patterns in Chapter Five, for instance.

All this emphasis on locational interdependence and the factors affecting decision making in a locational context, however, suggests that locational patterns are the resultant of extremely orderly, predictable processes. Such, obviously, is not entirely the case. In our explanations we must also leave room for a *random component*. There are many events that cannot be readily explained in an economical manner but can be treated as *random events:* we may not know what causes them, and even if we do, it cannot be readily incorporated into our explanation. Such random events have a powerful ability to constrain locational processes and resultant locational patterns. The discovery of North America from Europe rather than from Japan, for instance, can be treated as a random event: a random event, moreover, that, as we showed in Chapter Sixteen, resulted in the emergence of clustered economic development in the Northeast rather than on the West Coast. We have also called attention to the role of random events in creating areas of agricultural specialization such as the potato-growing area of Maine.

Such randomness of behavior, however, is not an insuperable obstacle to developing theories and laws of locational process and locational pattern. There are a variety of strategies for allowing for such randomness (try to predict *average* behavior rather than *individual* behavior, for instance) and these enable us to explore reality in a theoretically meaningful manner with the general emphasis on *systems* and *decision making* that we have stressed in this section.

TAKING IT FURTHER

With all this information, and hopefully some intellectual stimulation, where do you go from here? Academically the paths can be charted quite easily and they will not concern us here. Rather we are more concerned at this point with instilling the geographical viewpoint in the layman. How, therefore, can you consolidate your insights into locational problems and locational processes in the interests of being an informed citizen?

The first requisite is to be aware of locational patterns and problems. Much of our present awareness stems from the mass media, and undoubtedly many items of a locational nature can be gained from a critical study of newspapers and magazine reports, both directly and indirectly. Much of the material in newspapers, for example, concerns *locational conflict.* The conflicts of nations are disagreements between groups that are defined locationally and these conflicts involve locational issues. All conflicts over power, for example, have locational effects in the sense of altering the locational pattern of power. Local newspapers also find their prime interest in the locational issues of school district annexation, reevaluation of residential property for tax purposes as a result of a recently acquired proximity to some offensive land use, zoning and urban planning regulations, and conflicts regarding the location of new highways, parks, and housing developments.

It is important, however, that we place these problems in a broader *locational context* noting the locational configuration of events and land uses within which the problem is embedded. The better newspapers such as *The New York Times* and the *London Times,* and also magazines such as the *Economist,* are generally much more ready to fill this need by supplying maps relating the conflict to different and salient locations; the excellent maps of geographical differentiation across the states which *The New York Times* publishes to accompany articles such as those dealing with American educational expenditures come readily to mind in this context.

Similar remarks apply to the role of travel as a means of acquiring and developing an awareness of locational patterns, process, and problems. It is an ex-

cellent method of acquiring knowledge of, for example, land-use patterns and the locational arrangement of towns of different size. It needs to be accompanied, however, by an accurate and large-scale map such as those represented by the 1" to the mile Ordnance Survey maps of Great Britain.

Indirectly, however, the mass media can tell us other things of locational interest. Local newspapers, for example, such as those published in American small towns, often contain news reports from correspondents in surrounding villages regarding local events. The list of such villages alone is an excellent guide to the small town's sphere of influence. The locational pattern of advertisers is also instructive in this regard.

There are a number of opportunities for obtaining raw material about locational patterns and problems, therefore. However, what about the processes that give rise to these patterns and problems? Undoubtedly a rich source of insight can be provided by *introspection.* Locational patterns are a result of some form of locational behavior: shopping trip behavior, migration behavior, and so on. Examining our own motives and our reasons for selecting a particular destination can be a fruitful though not necessarily reliable way of shedding some light on the factors that affect our locational decisions.

In the same way, examination of the motives and assumptions of others when talking with them is a good guide to the factors structuring locational decisions. Why does the Englishman at your cocktail party say he is from England rather than from Sleaford, Lincolnshire, for example? Presumably because of that hierarchical structure in his locational classification of places that is better developed for areas closer to his place of origin and that he projects on to the people—presumably Americans—with whom he is communicating. He assumes that they have a similar hierarchical structure more finely developed for the United States.

Finally, there are possibilities of inferring locational process from simple armchair speculation involving the working out of *logical consequences of a situation.* What, for example, are the consequences of locating a large factory in your town? Presumably it would mean an increased number of residents, an addition to consumer demand reflected in a greater variety of retailing facilities, and ultimately an extension of the town's sphere of influence as a result of its increased attractiveness.

These are some suggestions for further developing the viewpoint of the world that has been presented in this book. Pursuing this matter further will be well worth the effort.

SUGGESTIONS FOR FURTHER READING

In any discipline undergoing rapid and revolutionary change the identification of supplemental reading at the beginning college level is particularly difficult. Geography is no exception to this. To a large degree the literature which reflects these changes is too difficult for beginning students to comprehend. Alternatively advances have taken place more rapidly in some sectors of the discipline than in others so that the filtering down of ideas into the college-level literature has likewise occurred more speedily.

A careful scrutiny of the available literature, however, suggests the following as reflecting or expanding on ideas presented in this book with the requisite simplicity. Where references are somewhat more difficult they have been indicated by an asterisk. The references are organized by chapter, however, and some chapters have more references than others. This is a consequence of the variable rates of progress in different sectors of the field which we referred to above.

CHAPTER 1   THE CONTENT OF HUMAN GEOGRAPHY

Abler, R. F., "Distance, Intercommunications and Geography," *Proceedings of the Association of American Geographers,* Vol. 3 (1971), pp. 1–4.

Gould, P. R., "The New Geography," *Harpers Magazine* (March, 1969), pp. 91–100.

* Nystuen, J. D., "Identification of Some Fundamental Spatial Concepts," *Papers of the Michigan Academy of Science, Arts, and Letters,* Vol. 48 (1963), pp. 373–384. Also in B. J. L. Berry and D. F. Marble (eds.), *Spatial Analysis* (Englewood Cliffs, N.J.: Prentice-Hall, 1968).

Watson, J. W., "Geography — A Discipline in Distance," *The Scottish Geographical Magazine,* Vol. 71, No. 1 (April, 1955), pp. 1–13.

CHAPTER 2   PATTERNS OF MOVEMENT

Bracey, H. E. "Towns as Rural Service Centers," *Transactions of the Institute of British Geographers,* Vol. 19 (1953), pp. 95–105.

Brown, R. W., "Upsala Community: A Case Study in Rural Dynamics," *Annals of the Association of American Geographers,* Vol. 57 (1967), pp. 277–300.

Dahl, S. "The Contacts of Västeras with the Rest of Sweden," in David Hannerberg, Torsten Hägerstrand and Bruno Odeving (eds.) *Migration in Sweden,* Lund Studies in Geography, Series B. Human Geography, No. 13 (1957), pp. 206–243.

Fleming, J. B. and F. H. W. Green, "Some Relations Between Country and Town in Scotland," *Scottish Geographical Magazine,* Vol. 68, No. 1 (April, 1952), pp. 2–12.

Green, F. H. W., "Community of Interest Areas in Western Europe," *Economic Geography,* Vol. 29 (1953), pp. 283–298.

Green, F. H. W., "Urban Hinterlands in England and Wales: An Analysis of Bus Services," *Geographical Journal,* Vol. 96 (1950), pp. 64–81.

Green, F. H. W., "Motor-Bus Centres in South-West England Considered in Relation to Population and Shopping Facilities," *Transactions of the Institute of British Geographers,* Vol. 14 (1948), pp. 59–68.

Johnsson, B. "Utilizing Telegrams for Describing Contact Patterns and Spatial Interaction," *Geografiska Annaler,* Vol. 50B (1968), pp. 38–51.

Lewis, G. J., "Commuting and the Village in Mid-Wales: A Study in Social Geography," *Geography,* Vol. 52, Part 3 (July, 1967), pp. 294–304.

Smailes, A. E., "The Analysis and Delimitation of Urban Fields," *Geography,* Vol. 32 (1947), pp. 151–161.

CHAPTER 3   THE BASES OF MOVEMENT

Alexander, J. W., E. S. Brown, and R. E. Dahlberg, "Freight Rates: Selected Aspects of Uniform and Nodal Regions," *Economic Geography,* Vol. 34 (1958), pp. 1–18.

Chinitz, B., *Freight and the Metropolis* (Cambridge, Mass.: Harvard University Press, 1960).

Deasy, G. F. and P. R. Griess, "Impact of a Tourist Facility on its Hinterland," *Annals of the Association of American Geographers,* Vol. 56 (1966), pp. 290–306.

Hoover, E. M. *The Location of Economic Activity* (New York: McGraw-Hill, 1948). Chapter 2.

CHAPTER 4   TWO CASE STUDIES OF MOVEMENT:
COMMODITY FLOW AND MIGRATION

Dayal, E., "Changing Patterns of India's International Trade," *Economic Geography,* Vol. 44 (1968), pp. 240–261.

Kant, E., "Umland Studies and Sector Analysis," in *Studies in Rural-Urban Interaction,* Lund Studies in Geography, Series B. Human Geography, No. 3 (1951), pp. 3–13.

Kosa, J., "Hungarian Immigrants in North America: Their Residential Mobility and Ecology," *Canadian Journal of Economics and Political Science,* Vol. 12 (1956), pp. 358–370.

Lee, F. S., "A Theory of Migration," *Demography,* Vol. 3, No. 1 (1966), pp. 47–57.

McDonald, J. R., "Labor Immigration in France, 1946–1965," *Annals of the Association of American Geographers,* Vol. 59 (1969), pp. 116–134.

Manners, G., "Transport Costs, Freight Rates and the Changing Economic Geography of Iron Ore," *Geography,* Vol. 52, Part 3 (July, 1967), pp. 260–279.

Manners, G., "The Pipline Revolution," *Geography,* Vol. 47, Part 2 (April, 1962), pp. 154–163.

Peach, G. C. K., "Factors Affecting the Distribution of West Indians in Great Britain," *Transactions of the Institute of British Geographers,* Publication No. 38 (1966), pp. 151–163.

Ullman, E. L., *American Commodity Flows* (Seattle: University of Washington Press, 1957).

Webber, M., "Culture, Territoriality and the Elastic Mile," *Papers and Proceedings of the Regional Science Association,* Vol. 13 (1964), pp. 59–70.

CHAPTER 5   INFORMATION AND DECISIONS
IN A LOCATIONAL CONTEXT

* Gould, P. R., *Spatial Diffusion* (Washington, D.C.: Association of American Geographers Commission on College Geography, 1969), Resource Paper No. 4.

* Hägerstrand, T., "Aspects of the Spatial Structure of Social Communication and the Diffusion of Information," *Papers and Proceedings of the Regional Science Association,* Vol. 16 (1965).

* _____, "Quantitative Techniques for Analysis of the Spread of Information and Technology," in C. A. Anderson and M. J. Bowman (eds.), *Education and Economic Development* (Chicago: Aldine, 1965).

Harrison, R. S., "Migrants in the City of Tripoli, Libya," *Geographical Review,* Vol. 57, No. 3 (July, 1967), pp. 397–423.

* Mabogunje, A. L., "Systems Approach to a Theory of Rural-Urban Migration," *Geographical Analysis,* Vol. 2 (1970), pp. 1–18.

Mead, W. R., "Britain in Scandanavia," *Geography,* Vol. 54, Part 3 (July, 1969), pp. 271–283.

Pemberton, H. E., "Spatial Order of Cultural Diffusion," *Sociology and Social Research,* Vol. 22 (1938), pp. 246–251.

Roseman, C. C., "Channelization of Migration Flows from the Rural South to the Industrial Midwest," *Proceedings of the Association of American Geographers,* Vol. 3 (1971), pp. 140–146.

CHAPTER 6   SPACE PERCEPTION AND LOCATIONAL DECISIONS

* Gould, P. R., "On Mental Maps," *Michigan Inter-University Community of Mathematical Geographers,* Discussion Paper 9, 1966. Reprinted in Paul English and Robert Mayfield (eds.), *Man, Space and Environment* (New York: Oxford University Press, 1972).

Haddon, J., "A View of Foreign Lands," *Geography,* Vol. 45, Part 4, No. 209 (November, 1960), pp. 286–289.

* Saarinen, T. F., *Perception of Environment* (Washington, D.C.: Association of American Geographers Commission on College Geography, 1969), Resource Paper No. 5.

Stea, D., "Space, Terrotoriality and Human Movements," *Landscape,* Vol. 15 (1965), pp. 13–16.

CHAPTER 7   BOUNDED SPACES:
LOCATIONAL CONFIGURATION AND LOCATIONAL EFFECTS

Dillman, C. D., "Commuter Workers and Free Zone Industry Along the Mexico-U.S. Border," *Proceedings of the Association of American Geographers,* Vol. 2 (1970), pp. 48–51.

Gottmann, J., "The Political Partitioning of Our World," *World Politics,* Vol. 4 (1951–52), pp. 512–519.

* Mackay, J. R., "The Interactance Hypothesis and Boundaries in Canada," *Canadian Geographer,* Vol. 11 (1958), pp. 1–8.

Mayer, H. M., "Politics and Land Use: The Indiana Shoreline of Lake Michigan," *Annals of the Association of American Geographers,* Vol. 54 (1964), pp. 508–523.

Stephenson, G. V., "Pakistan: Discontiguity and the Majority Problem," *Geographical Review,* Vol. 58, No. 2 (April, 1968), pp. 195–213.

Wolfe, R. I., *Transportation and Politics* (Princeton: Van Nostrand, 1963).

CHAPTER 8   THE STRUCTURE OF COMMUNICATION NETWORKS

Appleton, J. H., "Some Geographical Aspects of the Modernization of British Railways," *Geography,* Vol. 52, Part 4 (November, 1967), pp. 357–373.

Davies, W. K. D. and C. R. Lewis, "Regional Structures in Wales: Two Studies of Connectivity," in H. Carter and W. K. D. Davies (eds.), *Urban Essays: Studies in the Geography of Wales* (London: Longman, 1970).

* Garrison, W. L., "Connectivity of the Inter-State Highway System," *Papers and Proceedings of the Regional Science Association,* Vol. 6 (1960), pp. 121–137.

Meinig, D., "A Comparative Historical Geography of Two Railnets: Columbia Basin and Southern Australia," *Annals of the Association of American Geographers,* Vol. 52 (1962), pp. 394–413.

Pitts, F. R., "A Graph Theoretic Approach to Historical Geography," *Professional Geographer,* Vol. 17 (1965), pp. 15–20.

Siddall, W., "Railroad Gauges and Spatial Interaction," *Geographical Review,* Vol. 59 (1969), pp. 29–57.

Taaffe, E. J., R. L. Morrill, and P. R. Gould, "Transport Expansion in Underdeveloped Countries: A Comparative Analysis," *Geographical Review,* Vol. 53 (1963), pp. 502–529.

CHAPTER 9   COMMUNICATION NETWORKS:
LOCATIONAL FORCES AND LOCATIONAL EFFECTS

Christensen, D., "The Auto in America's Landscape and Way of Life" *Geography,* Vol. 51, Part 4 (November, 1966), pp. 339–348.

* Harris, C. D., "The Market as a Factor in the Localization of Industry in the United States," *Annals of the Association of American Geographers,* Vol. 44 (1954), pp. 315–348.

* Huff, D. L. and D. F. Marble, "Economic Impact of Highway Improvements," *University of Washington Business Review,* Vol. 19 (1959), pp. 3–20.

* Janelle, D. G., "Spatial Reorganization: A Model and Concept," *Annals of the Association of American Geographers,* Vol. 59 (1969), pp. 348–364.

Jefferson, M., "The Civilizing Rails" *Economic Geography* (1928), pp. 217–231.

* Kolars, J. and H. J. Malin, "Population and Accessibility: An Analysis of Turkish Railroads," *Geographical Review,* Vol. 60, No. 2 (April, 1970), pp. 229–246.

Sewell, W. R. D., "The Role of Regional Interties in Post-War Energy Resource Development," *Annals of the Association of American Geographers,* Vol. 54 (1964), pp. 566–581.

* Taaffe, E. J., "The Urban Hierarchy: An Airline Passenger Definition," *Economic Geography,* Vol. 38 (1962), pp. 1–14.

Wise, M. J., "The Impact of a Channel Tunnel on Planning of Southeast England," *Geographical Journal,* Vol. 131 (1965), pp. 167–185.

Wise, M. J., "The Common Market and the Changing Geography of Europe," *Geography,* Vol. 48, Part 2 (April, 1963), pp. 129–138.

CHAPTER 10   LOCATING NODES: SOME BASIC CONCEPTS

Chinitz, B., "New York: A Metropolitan Region," *Scientific American,* Vol. 213 (1965), pp. 134–148.

Chinitz, B., *Freight and the Metropolis* (Cambridge, Mass.: Harvard University Press, 1960).

Clark, C., "Transport—Maker and Breaker of Cities," *Town Planning Review,* Vol. 28 (1957–58), pp. 237–250.

Dacey, M. F., "The Spacing of River Towns," *Annals of the Association of American Geographers,* Vol. 50 (March, 1960), pp. 59–61.

Hoover, E. M. and R. Vernon, *Anatomy of a Metropolis* (Cambridge: Harvard University Press, 1959).

Vernon, R., "Production and Distribution in the Large Metropolis," *Annals of the American Academy of Political and Social Science,* Vol. 314 (1957), pp. 15–29.

CHAPTER 11   CASE STUDY: URBAN PLACES AS NODES

* Berry, B. J. L., *Theories of Urban Location* (Washington, D.C.: Association of American Geographers Commission on College Geography, 1968), Resource Paper No. 1.

Blouet, B. W., "Rural Settlement in Malta," *Geography,* Vol. 56, Part 2 (April, 1971), pp. 112–118.

Brush, J. E., "The Hierarchy of Central Places in Southwestern Wisconsin," *Geographical Review,* Vol. 43 (1953), pp. 380–402.

Burton, I., "A Restatement of the Dispersed City Hypothesis," *Annals of the Association of American Geographers,* Vol. 53 (1963), pp. 285–289.

Fleming, J. B., "An Analysis of Shops and Service Trades in Scottish Towns," *Scottish Geographical Magazine,* Vol. 70, No. 3 (December, 1954), pp. 97–106.

Getis, A. and J. Getis, "Christaller's Central Place Theory," *Journal of Geography,* Vol. 65 (May, 1966), pp. 220–226.

Gottman, J., *Megalopolis: The Urbanized Northeastern Seaboard of the United States,* (New York: Twentieth Century Fund, 1961).

Hart, J. F., N. E. Salisbury and E. Smith, Jr., "The Dying Village and Some Notions About Urban Growth," *Economic Geography,* Vol. 44 (October, 1968), pp. 343–349.

* Murdie, R., "Cultural Differences in Consumer Travel," *Economic Geography,* Vol. 41 (1965), pp. 211–233.

Ullman, E. L., "A Theory of Location for Cities," *American Journal of Sociology,* Vol. 19 (1946), pp. 853–864.

CHAPTER 12   CASE STUDY: INDUSTRIAL PLANTS AS NODES

Alexandersson, G., *Geography of Manufacturing* (Englewood Cliffs, N.J.: Prentice-Hall, 1967).

Alexandersson, G., "Changes in the Location Pattern of the Anglo-American Steel Industry, 1948–1959, " *Economic Geography,* Vol. 37 (1961), pp. 95–114.

Boas, C. W., "Locational Patterns of American Automobile Assembly Plants, 1895–1958," *Economic Geography,* Vol. 37 (1961), pp. 218–230.

Clout, H. D., "Industrial Relocation in France," *Geography,* Vol. 55, Part 1 (January, 1970), pp. 48–63.

Conkling, E. C., "South Wales: A Study in Industrial Diversification," *Economic Geography,* Vol. 39 (1963), pp. 258–272.

Craig, P. G., "Location Factors in the Development of Steel Centers," *Papers and Proceedings of the Regional Science Association,* Vol. 3 (1957), pp. 249–265.

Estall, R. C. and R. O. Buchanan, *Industrial Activity and Economic Geography,* (London: Hutchinsons University Library, 1966).

Estall, R. C., "Changing Industrial Patterns of New England," *Geography*, Vol. 46, Part 2 (April, 1961), pp. 120–138.

Fleming, D. K., "Coastal Steelworks in the Common Market Countries," *Geographical Review*, Vol. 57, No. 1 (January, 1967), pp. 48–72.

Fulton, M. and L. C. Hoch, "Transportation Factors Affecting Locational Decisions," *Economic Geography*, Vol. 35 (1959), pp. 51–59.

* Harris, C. D., "The Market as a Factor in the Localization of Industry in the United States," *Annals of the Association of American Geographers*, Vol. 44 (1954), pp. 315–348.

Isard, W., "Some Locational Factors in the Iron and Steel Industry Since the Early Nineteenth Century," *Journal of Political Economy*, Vol. 56 (1948), pp. 203–217.

Isard, W. and J. H. Comberland, "New England as a Possible Location for an Integrated Iron and Steel Works," *Economic Geography*, Vol. 26 (1950), pp. 245–259.

Kerr, D., "The Geography of the Canadian Iron and Steel Industry," *Economic Geography*, Vol. 35 (1959), pp. 151–163.

Lonsdale, R. E., "Barriers to Rural Industrialization in the South," *Proceedings of the Association of American Geographers*, Vol. 1 (1969), pp. 84–88.

Manners, G., "Regional Protection: A Factor in Economic Geography," *Economic Geography*, Vol. 38 (1962), pp. 122–129.

Pred, A., "Industrialization, Initial Advantage, and American Metropolitan Growth," *Geographical Review*, Vol. 55 (1965), pp. 158–189.

Pred, A., "The Concentration of High Value-Added Manufacturing," *Economic Geography*, Vol. 41 (1965), pp. 108–132.

Rodgers, A., "Industrial Inertia—A Major Factor in the Location of the Steel Industry in the United States," *Geographical Review*, Vol. 42, No. 1 (January, 1952), pp. 56–66.

Smith, W., "The Location of Industry," *Transactions of the Institute of British Geographers*, Vol. 21 (1955), pp. 1–18.

CHAPTER 13   SPACE FILLING

* Chisholm, M. *Rural Settlement and Land Use* (New York: Wiley, 1967).

Gottman, J., "Why the Skyscraper?" *Geographical Review*, Vol. 56, No. 2 (April, 1966), pp. 190–212.

Hansen, W. G., "How Accessibility Shapes Land Use," *Journal of the American Institute of Planners*, Vol. 15 (1959), pp. 73–76.

Harvey, R. C. and W. A. V. Clark, "The Nature and Economics of Urban Sprawl," *Land Economics*, Vol. 41 (1965), pp. 1–10.

Loeffler, M. J., "Beet Sugar Production in the Colorado Piedmont," *Annals of the Association of American Geographers*, Vol. 53 (1963), pp. 364–390.

Mayer, H. M., *The Spatial Expression of Urban Growth* (Washington, D.C.: Association of American Geographers Commission on College Geography, 1969), Resource Paper No. 7.

Mayer, H. M., "Politics and Land Use: The Indiana Shoreline of Lake Michigan," *Annals of the Association of American Geographers,* Vol. 54 (1964), pp. 508–523.

Sinclair, R., "Von Thünen and Urban Sprawl," *Annals of the Association of American Geographers,* Vol. 57 (1967), pp. 72–87.

CHAPTER 14   LAND USE PATTERNS:
THE CASE OF AGRICULTURAL LAND USE

* Chisholm, M. *Rural Settlement and Land Use* (New York: Wiley, 1967).

Chisholm, M., "Tendencies in Agricultural Specialization and Regional Concentration of Industry," *Papers and Proceedings of the Regional Science Association,* Vol. 10 (1963), pp. 157–162.

Dunlop, J. S., "Changes in the Canadian Wheat Belt, 1931–69," *Geography,* Vol. 55, Part 2 (April, 1970), pp. 156–168.

Gregor, H. F., "Regional Hierarchies in California Agricultural Production," *Annals of the Association of American Geographers,* Vol. 53 (1963), pp. 27–37.

Griffin, P. F. and R. Chatham, "Urban Impact on Agriculture in Santa Clara County, California," *Annals of the Association of American Geographers,* Vol. 48 (1958), pp. 195–208.

Grotewold, A., "Von Thünen in Retrospect," *Economic Geography,* Vol. 35 (1959), pp. 346–355.

Hidore, J. J., "The Relations Between Cash-Grain Farming and Landforms," *Economic Geography,* Vol. 39 (1963), pp. 84–89.

Horvath, R., "Von Thünen's Isolated State and the Area Around Addis Ababa, Ethiopia," *Annals of the Association of American Geographers,* Vol. 59 (1969), pp. 308–323.

* Jensen, R., "Regionalization and Price Zonation in Soviet Agricultural Planning," *Annals of the Association of American Geographers,* Vol. 59 (1969), pp. 324–347.

Kollmorgen, W. M. and G. F. Jenks, "Suitcase Farming in Sully County, South Dakota," *Annals of the Association of American Geographers,* Vol. 48 (1958), pp. 27–40.

* Nicholls, W. H., "Industrialization, Factor Markets and Agricultural Development," *Journal of Political Economy,* Vol. 69 (August, 1961), pp. 319–340.

Peet, R. C., "The Spatial Expansion of Commercial Agriculture in the Nineteenth Century: A Von Thünen Interpretation," *Economic Geography,* Vol. 45 (October, 1969), pp. 283–301.

Spencer, J. E. and R. J. Horvath, "How Does an Agricultural Region Originate?" *Annals of the Association of American Geographers,* Vol. 53 (1963), pp. 74–92.

CHAPTER 15   THE URBAN CRISIS IN A LOCATIONAL CONTEXT

* Alonso, W., "A Theory of the Urban Land Market," *Papers and Proceedings of the Regional Science Association,* Vol. 6 (1960), pp. 149–158.

Anderson, T., "Social and Economic Factors Affecting the Location of Residential Neighborhoods," *Papers and Proceedings of the Regional Science Association,* Vol. 9 (1962).

Boyce, R. R., "Changing Patterns of Urban Land Consumption," *Professional Geographer,* Vol. 15, No. 1 (January, 1963), pp. 19–24.

Brown, W. H., "Access to Housing: The Role of the Real Estate Industry," *Economic Geography,* Vol. 48, No. 1 (January, 1972), pp. 66–78.

* Chinitz, B., *City and Suburb* (Englewood Cliffs, N.J.: Prentice-Hall, 1965).

Colby, C. C., "Centrifugal and Centripetal Forces in Urban Geography," *Annals of the Association of American Geographers,* Vol. 23 (1933), pp. 1–20.

deVise, P., "Chicago, 1971: Ready for Another Fire?" in R. C. Peet (ed.), *Geographical Perspectives on American Poverty,* Antipode Monographs in Social Geography No. 1, 1972.

Davies, S. and M. Albaum, "Mobility Problems of the Poor in Indianapolis," in R. C. Peet (ed.) *Geographical Perspectives on American Poverty,* Antipode Monographs in Social Geography, No. 1 (1972).

Davies, S. and G. L. Fowler, "The Disadvantaged Urban Migrant in Indianapolis," *Economic Geography,* Vol. 48 (April, 1972), pp. 153–167.

Hoover, E. M. and R. Vernon, *Anatomy of a Metropolis* (Cambridge, Mass.: Harvard University Press, 1959).

Kain, J. F. and J. Persky, "Alternatives to the Gilded Ghetto," *The Public Interest* No. 14 (Winter, 1969), pp. 74–87.

Kersten, E. and D. Ross, "Clayton: A New Metropolitan Focus in the St. Louis Area," *Annals of the Association of American Geographers,* Vol. 58 (1968), pp. 637–649.

Manners, G., "Decentralization in Metropolitan Boston," *Geography,* Vol. 45, Part 4, (November, 1960), pp. 276–285.

Meyer, J. and J. F. Kain, "Transportation and Poverty," *The Public Interest,* No. 18 (Winter, 1970).

Morrill, R. L., "The Negro Ghetto: Problems and Alternatives," *Geographical Review,* Vol. 55 (1965), pp. 339–361.

* Rees, P. H., "Concepts of Social Space," Chapter 10 in B. J. L. Berry and F. E. Horton (eds.), *Geographic Perspectives on Urban Systems* (Englewood Cliffs, N.J.: Prentice Hall, 1970).

Rose, H. M., "The Spatial Development of Black Residential Subsystems," *Economic Geography,* Vol. 48 (January, 1972), pp. 43–65.

Rose, H. M., *Social Processes in the City: Race and Urban Residential Choice* (Washington, D.C.: Association of American Geographers, Commission on College Geography, 1969), Resource Paper No. 6.

* Simmons, J. W., "Changing Residence in the City: A Review of Intra-Urban Mobility," *Geographical Review,* Vol. 58 (1968), pp. 622–651.

Ullman, E. L., "The Nature of Cities Reconsidered," *Papers and Proceedings of the Regional Science Association,* Vol. 9 (1962), pp. 1–23.

Wheeler, J. O., "Work-Trip Length and the Ghetto," *Land Economics,* Vol. 44 (1968), pp. 107–111.

* Yeates, M., "Some Factors Affecting the Spatial Distribution of Chicago Land Values," *Economic Geography,* Vol. 41 (January, 1965), pp. 57–70.

CHAPTER 16   THE GEOGRAPHY OF ECONOMIC DEVELOPMENT

* Bauer, P. T. and B. S. Yamey, *The Economics of Under-Developed Countries* (Cambridge: Cambridge University Press, 1959).

Friedman, J., "Poor Regions and Poor Nations," *Southern Economic Journal,* Vol. 32 (1966), pp. 465–473.

Fryer, D. W., "World Income and Types of Economies," *Economic Geography,* Vol. 34 (1958), pp. 282–303.

Garwood, J. D., "An Analysis of Post-War Industrial Migration to Utah and Colorado," *Economic Geography,* Vol. 29 (1953), pp. 79–88.

Ginsburg, N. (ed.), *Atlas of Economic Development,* (Chicago: University of Chicago Press, 1961).

Ginsburg, N., "Natural Resources and Economic Development," *Annals of the Association of American Geographers,* Vol. 47 (1957), pp. 196–212.

Gottman, J., *Megalopolis* (New York: Twentieth Century Fund, 1961).

Gottman, J., "Megalopolis or the Urbanization of the Northeastern Seaboard," *Economic Geography,* Vol. 33 (1957), pp. 189–200.

Linsky, A. S., "Some Generalizations Concerning Primate Cities," *Annals of the Association of American Geographers,* Vol. 55 (September, 1965), pp. 506–513.

Mountjoy, A. B., *Industrialization and Underdeveloped Countries* (Chicago: Aldine, 1967).

Myrdal, G., *Economic Theory and Under-Developed Regions,* (London: Duckworth, 1957).

Naylon, J., "Tourism—Spain's Most Important Industry," *Geography,* Vol. 52, Part 1 (January, 1967), pp. 23–40.

Rodgers, A., "Migration and Industrial Development: The Southern Italian Experience," *Economic Geography,* Vol. 46 (April, 1970), pp. 111–135.

Smith, C. T., "Problems of Regional Development in Peru," *Geography,* Vol. 53, Part 3, (July, 1968), pp. 260–281.

Ullman, E. L., "Regional Development and the Geography of Concentration," *Papers and Proceedings of the Regional Science Association,* Vol. 4 (1958), pp. 179–200.

Ullman, E. L., "Amenities as a Factor in Regional Growth," *Geographical Review,* Vol. 44 (1954), pp. 119–132.

CHAPTER 17   THE GEOGRAPHY OF ENVIRONMENTAL QUALITY

Chisholm, M., "Must We All Live in Southeast England?" *Geography,* Vol. 49, Part 1 (January, 1964), pp. 1–14.

Coates, B. E. and E. M. Rawstron, "Regional Incomes and Planning, 1964–1965," *Geography,* Vol. 52, Part 4 (November, 1967), pp. 393–402.

Coates, B. E. and E. M. Rawstron, "Regional Variations in Incomes," *Westminster Bank Review* (February, 1966), pp. 1–19.

Edwards, K. C., "The New Towns of Britain," *Geography,* Vol. 69 (1964), pp. 279–285.

Estall, R. C., "Appalachian State: West Virginia as a Case Study in the Appalachian Regional Development Problem," *Geography,* Vol. 53, Part 1 (January, 1968), pp. 1–24.

Hansen, N. M., "Regional Development and the Rural Poor," *The Journal of Human Resources,* Vol. 4, No. 2 (Spring, 1969), pp. 205–214.

Hansen, N. M., "Some Neglected Factors in American Regional Development Policy," *Land Economics,* Vol. 42 (1966), pp. 1–10.

Howe, G. M., *National Atlas of Disease Mortality in the United Kingdom* (London: Thomas Nelson, 1963).

Leighton, P. A., "Geographical Aspects of Air Pollution," *Geographical Review,* Vol. 56 (1966), pp. 151–174.

Lewis, G. M., "Levels of Living in the Northeastern United States c. 1960: A New Approach to Regional Geography," *Transactions of the Institute of British Geographers,* Vol. 45 (1969), pp. 11–37.

Morrill, R. L. and E. H. Wohlenberg, *The Geography of Poverty* (New York: McGraw-Hill, 1971).

Morrill, R. L., "Geographical Aspects of Poverty in the United States," *Proceedings of the Association of American Geographers,* Vol. 1 (1969), pp. 117–121.

Murray, M. A., "Geography of Death in the U.S. and the U.K.," *Annals of the Association of American Geographers,* Vol. 57 (1967), pp. 301–314.

Parr, J. B., "Outmigration and the Depressed Area Problem," *Land Economics,* Vol. 42 (1966), pp. 149–160.

Rawstron, E. M. and B. E. Coates, "Opportunity and Affluence," *Geography,* Vol. 51 (January, 1966), pp. 1–15.

Rodgers, A., "Some Aspects of Industrial Diversification in the United States," *Economic Geography,* Vol. 33 (1957), pp. 16–30.

ACKNOWLEDGMENTS

The following figures and tables are adapted from copyrighted works. The author and publisher express their thanks for permission to use this material.

Figure 1–2: Association of American Geographers for Figure 1 from Russell B. Adams, "U.S. Metropolitan Migration: Dimensions and Predictability," *Proceedings of the Association of American Geographers,* Vol. 1 (1969).

Figure 2–5: Adapted from Catton, "The Concept of 'Mass' in the Sociological Version of Gravitation," in Massarik and Ratoosh, *Mathematical Explorations in Behavioral Science* (Homewood, Ill.: Richard D. Irwin, Inc.), c. 1965, p. 295.

Figure 2–8: Institute of British Geographers for Figure 2 from P. R. Odell, "The Hinterlands of Melton Mowbray and Coalville, *"Transactions of the Institute of British Geographers,* No. 23 (1957).

Figure 2–10: Geografiske Selskab (Copenhagen) for Figures 1–4 from Sven Illeris and Paul O. Pedersen, "Central Places and Functional Regions in Denmark: Factor Analysis of Telephone Traffic," *Geografisk Tidsskrift,* 67 Bind.

Figure 3–9: McGraw-Hill Book Company for Figure 2.2 from Edgar M. Hoover, *The Location of Economic Activity* (New York: McGraw-Hill, 1948), p. 21.

Figure 3–10: Paul Claval for Figure 10 from Claval, *Géographie Générale des Marchés* (Cahiers de Géographie de Besançon, No. 10), Annales littéraires de l'Université de Besançon, Volume 58, Chapter 6.

Figure 3–12: McGraw-Hill Book Company for Figure 2.1 from Edgar M. Hoover, *The Location of Economic Activity* (New York: McGraw-Hill, 1948), p. 20.

Table 3–2: The Brookings Institution for Table 8 (Appendix) from Wilfred Owen, *The Metropolitan Transportation Problem* (Washington, D.C.: The Brookings Institution, c. 1956, 1966), p. 235.

Figures 4–1 and 4–2: Gerald Manners and The Geographical Association for Figures 2 and 3 respectively from Manners, "Transport Costs, Freight Rates and the Changing Economic Geography of Iron Ore," *Geography,* Vol. 52, Part 3 (July, 1967).

Table 4–1: Anthony Fielding and Urban Studies for Table 1 from Fielding, "Internal Migration and Regional Economic Growth — A Case Study of France," *Urban Studies,* Vol. 3, No. 3 (November, 1966).

Figures 4–5 and 4–6: Institute of British Geographers for Figures 1A and 2A respectively, from G. C. K. Peach, "Factors Affecting the Distribution of West Indians in Britain," *Transactions of the Institute of British Geographers,* No. 38 (1966).

Figures 4–9 and 4–10: C. W. K. Gleerup for Figures 9 and 10 respectively from Edgar Kant, "Umland Studies and Sector Analysis," in *Studies in Rural-Urban Interaction,* Lund Studies in Geography, Series B Human Geography, No. 3.

Figure 4–13: Ronald Johnson and Urban Studies for Table 5 and Figure 5 from Johnson, "Some Tests of a Model of Intra-Urban Population Mobility: Melbourne, Australia," *Urban Studies,* Vol. 6, No. 1 (1969).

Table 5–2: C. W. K. Gleerup for a Table from Sven Dahl, "The Contacts of Västeras with the Rest of Sweden," in Hannenberg et al. (eds.), *Migration in Sweden,* Lund Studies in Geography, Series B Human Geography, No. 13, p. 214.

Figure 5–5: Agricultural Economics Society for Figure 5 from Gwyn E. Jones, "The Diffusion of Agricultural Innovations," *Journal of Agricultural Economics,* Vol. 15, No. 3 (June, 1963).

Figure 5–6: Northwestern University Press for Figure 1B from Törsten Hägerstrand, "On Monte Carlo Simulation of Diffusion," in W. L. Garrison and D. F. Marble (eds.), *Quantitative Geography Part 1,* Studies in Geography, No. 13 (Evanston: Northwestern University Press, 1967).

Figure 5–7: The Editor of the East Lakes Geographer for Figures 2 and 3 from Burton O. Witthuhn, "The Spatial Integration of Uganda as shown by the Diffusion of Postal Agencies, 1900–1965," *East Lakes Geographer,* Vol. 4 (December, 1968).

Figure 6–1: F. V. Thierfeldt Co., Milwaukee.

Figures 6–5 and 6–6: Peter R. Gould and Rodney R. White and the Editor of Regional Studies for Figures 7 and 11 respectively from Gould and White, "The Mental Maps of British School Leavers," *Regional Studies,* Vol. 2 (1968), pp. 161–182.

Figure 6–7: The Editor of the Discussion Papers of the Michigan Inter-University Community of Mathematical Geographers for Figure 3 from Peter R. Gould, "On Mental Maps," Discussion Paper No. 9 (1966).

Figure 6–8: Peter R. Gould and the Managing Editor of Geographical Analysis for Figure 6 from Gould, "Problems of Space Preference Measures and Relationships," *Geographical Analysis,* Vol. 1, No. 1 (January, 1969).

Figure 7–7: The Association of American Geographers for Figure 6 from W. S. Logan, "The Changing Landscape Significance of the Victoria-South Australia Boundary," *Annals of the Association of American Geographers,* Vol. 58, No. 1 (March, 1968).

Figure 8–10: Regional Science Research Institute for Figure 3 from Peter Haggett, "An Extension of the Horton Combinatorial Model to Regional Highway Networks," *Journal of Regional Science,* Vol. 7, No. 2 [Supplement], (Winter, 1967).

Figure 8–11: Librairie Armand Colin for cartes numéros 131 and 134 from *Atlas Historique de la France Contemporaine, 1800–1965* (Paris, 1966).

Figure 8–17: The Editor for Figure 7 from K. A. Bassett and G. B. Norcliffe, "Filter Theory and Filter Methods in Geographical Research," Seminar Paper Series, Series A, Number 20, Department of Geography, University of Bristol.

Figure 9–11: Penguin Books for Figure 55 from John P. Cole, *Geography of World Affairs* (London: Penguin Books, 1966).

Figure 9–13: The Editor for Figure 1 from Patrick M. O'Sullivan, "Accessibility and the Spatial Structure of the Irish Economy," *Regional Studies,* Vol. 2 (1968), pp. 195–206.

Figure 9–14: Regional Science Research Institute for Figure 2 from John Q. Stewart and William Warntz, "Physics of Population Distribution," *Journal of Regional Science,* Vol. 1 (1958), pp. 99–123.

Figure 9–15: The Editor for Figure 8 from Patrick O'Sullivan, "Accessibility and the Spatial Structure of the Irish Economy," *Regional Studies,* Vol. 2 (1968), pp. 95–206.

Quotation on p. 183: Regional Science Research Institute for textual material on p. 92 from Howard L. Gauthier, "Transportation and the Growth of the Sao Paulo Economy," *Journal of Regional Science,* Vol. 8, No. 1 (1968).

Figures 9–20 and 9–21: Librairie Armand Colin for cartes numéros 136 and 137 respectively from *Atlas Historique de la France Contemporaine, 1800–1965* (Paris, 1966).

Figure 10–8 and 10–9: Kon. Institut voor de Tropen for Figure 2 and Table 1 and Figures 3, 4, and 5 respectively from Leslie J. King, "A Quantitative Expression of the Pattern of Urban Settlements in Selected Areas of the United States," *Tijdschrift voor Economische en Sociaale Geografie,* Vol. 53 (1962), pp. 1–7.

Figure 10–1: Pion Publishing Company (London) for Figure 1.2 (p. 51) from Andrei Rogers, "Quadrat Analysis of Urban Dispersion: 1. Theoretical Techniques," *Environment and Planning,* Vol. 1 (1969), pp. 47–80.

Figure 10–11: Routledge and Kegan Paul (English-language rights excluding U.S.A., U.S. dependencies and the Philippines) and University of North Carolina Press (U.S. rights) for data from Tables 1D and 1E from P. Sargent Florence, *The Logic of British and American Industry* (1953), pp. 24–25.

Table 11–1: Regional Science Association for Table 3 from Brian J. L. Berry, H. Gardiner Barnum and Robert J. Tennant, "Retail Location and Consumer Behavior," *Papers and Proceedings of the Regional Science Association,* Vol. 9 (1962), pp. 65–106.

Figures 11–2 and 11–3: Prentice-Hall, Inc. for Figures 2–11 and 2–8 respectively from Brian J. L. Berry, *Geography of Market Centers and Retail Distribution* (Englewood Cliffs, 1967).

Figure 11–4: G. A. Nader and Urban Studies for Figure 4 from Nader, "Socio-Economic Status and Consumer Behavior," *Urban Studies,* Vol. 6, No. 2 (June, 1969), pp. 235–245.

Tables 11–2 and 11–3: Regional Science Association for Tables 6 and 4 respectively from Gerald Hodge, "The Prediction of Trade Center Viability in the Great Plains," *Papers and Proceedings of the Regional Science Association,* Vol. 15 (1965), pp. 87–118.

Table 11–4: John Fraser Hart, Neil E. Salisbury, and Everett G. Smith, Jr. and the Editor of Economic Geography for Table 1 from Hart, Salisbury and Smith, "The Dying Village and Some Notions About Urban Growth," *Economic Geography,* Vol. 44, No. 4 (October, 1968).

Table 12–2: Hutchinson University Library for Table 5 from R. C. Estall and R. O. Buchanan, *Industrial Activity and Economic Geography* (London, 1963), p. 83.

Figure 12–3: Librairie Armand Colin for cartes numéros 171–174 from *Atlas Historique de la France Contemporaine, 1800–1965* (Paris, 1966).

Figure 12–4: Prentice-Hall, Inc. for Figure 17–2 from John W. Alexander, *Economic Geography* (Englewood Cliffs, 1963).

Figure 12–5: Prentice-Hall, Inc. for Figure 12–1 from Harold H. McCarty and James B. Lindberg, *A Preface to Economic Geography* (Englewood Cliffs, 1966).

Figures 14–1 and 14–2: Association of American Geographers for material from Tables 3 and 7 respectively from Howard F. Gregor, "Regional Hierarchies in California Agricultural Production: 1939–1954," *Annals of the Association of American Geographers,* Vol. 53, No. 1 (March, 1963).

Tables 14–2 and 14–3: Hutchinson University Library for Tables 2 (p. 55) and 4 (p. 59) from Michael Chisholm, *Rural Settlement and Land Use* (London, 1962).

Figures 14–5 and 14–6: Association of American Geographers for Figures 3 and 6 respectively from Jen-Hu Chang, "Potential Photosynthesis and Crop Productivity," *Annals of the Association of American Geographers,* Vol. 60, No. 1 (March, 1970), pp. 92–101.

Table 14–4: Richard Peet and the Editor of Economic Geography for Table 1 from Peet, "The Spatial Expansion of Commercial Agriculture in the Nineteenth Century: A Von Thünen Interpretation," *Economic Geography,* Vol. 45, No. 4 (October, 1969).

Figure 14–11: John Wiley, Inc. for Figure 192 from Allen K. Philbrick, *This Human World* (New York, 1963).

Figure 14–12: Adapted from Norton S. Ginsburg, editor, *Aldine University Atlas* (Chicago: Aldine Publishing Company, 1969), copyright © 1969 by Aldine Publishing Company. Reprinted by permission of the author and Aldine-Atherton, Inc.

Figures 15–2 and 15–3: Duane S. Knos for Figure 1 and 3 respectively from Knos, *The Distribution of Land Values in Topeka, Kansas* (Bureau of Business and Economic Research, University of Kansas).

Figure 15–9: Prentice-Hall, Inc. for Figure 6–5 from Brian J. L. Berry, *Geography of Market Centers and Retail Distribution* (Englewood Cliffs, 1967).

Figure 15–10: Edwin S. Mills and Urban Studies for material in Table 2 from Mills, "Urban Density Functions," *Urban Studies,* Vol. 7, No. 1 (February, 1970).

Figure 15–11: American Geographical Society of New York for Figure 2 from Richard L. Morrill, "The Negro Ghetto: Problems and Alternatives," *Geographical Review,* Vol. 55, No. 3 (July, 1965).

Table 15–2: Leo F. Schnore and the American Sociological Association for Table 1 from Schnore, "The Socio-Economic Status of Cities and Suburbs," *American Sociological Review,* Vol. 28 (February, 1963).

Figure 16–1: University of Chicago Department of Geography Research Paper Series for Figure VI-1 from Brian J. L. Berry, "An Inductive Approach to the Regionalization of Economic Development," in Norton Ginsburg (ed.) *Essays in Geography and Economic Development,* Research Paper No. 62.

Figure 16–2: C. T. Smith and the Geographical Association for Figure 2 from Smith, "Problems of Regional Development in Peru," *Geography,* Vol. 53, Part 3 (July, 1968).

Figure 16–8: Librairie Armand Colin for cartes numéros 176–178 from *Atlas Historique de la France Contemporaine, 1800–1965* (Paris, 1966).

Figure 16–12: Yale University Press for Figure 3.3 (p. 53) from Victor R. Fuchs, *Changes in the Location of Manufacturing in the United States Since 1929* (New Haven, 1962).

Figure 17–1: National Society for Clean Air (United Kingdom) for Figures 17A, B, and C (p. 81), from H. H. Lamb, *The English Climate* (London: English Universities Press, 1964).

Figure 17–2 and 17–4: Cornell University Press (rights in the U.S. and Philippines) and William Collins (rights in the British Commonwealth) for Figures 25 (p. 118) and 26 (p. 123) respectively from L. Dudley Stamp, *The Geography of Life and Death* (1964).

Table 17–6: Milbank Memorial Fund for Table 4 from R. Illsley, A. Finlayson and B. Thompson, "The Motivation and Characteristics of Internal Migrants," *Milbank Memorial Fund Quarterly,* Vol. 41, No. 3 (July, 1963).

Index